P9-DEA-804

Top 100

CAREERS

Without a Four-Year Degree™

Your Complete Guidebook to Good Jobs
in Many Fields

TENTH EDITION

Laurence Shatkin, Ph.D., and
Michael Farr

JIST Works
America's Career Publisher®

Top 100 Careers Without a Four-Year Degree, Tenth Edition
Your Complete Guidebook to Good Jobs in Many Fields

© 2012 by JIST Publishing

Published by JIST Works, an imprint of JIST Publishing
7321 Shadeland Station, Suite 200
Indianapolis, IN 46256-3923
Phone: 800-648-JIST   Fax: 877-454-7839
E-mail: info@jist.com   Website: www.jist.com

Some books by Michael Farr:
Best Jobs for the 21st Century
Overnight Career Choice
Same-Day Resume
Next-Day Job Interview
The Quick Resume & Cover Letter Book
The Very Quick Job Search

JIST's Top Careers™ Series:
Top 300 Careers
Top 100 Health-Care Careers
100 Fastest-Growing Careers
Top 100 Careers Without a Four-Year Degree
Top 100 Careers for College Graduates

Quantity discounts are available for JIST products. Please call 800-648-JIST or visit www.jist.com for a free catalog and more information.

Visit www.jist.com for information on JIST, free job search information, tables of contents, sample pages, and ordering information on our many products.

Acquisitions Editor: Susan Pines
Development Editor: Stephanie Koutek
Database Work: Laurence Shatkin
Cover Photo: IStock
Cover Layout: Alan Evans
Interior Design and Layout: Marie Kristine Parial-Leonardo, Toi Davis
Proofreaders: Chuck Hutchinson, Jeanne Clark

Printed in the United States of America

16 15 14 13 12 11   9 8 7 6 5 4 3 2

ISBN 978-1-59357-784-1

Relax. You Don't Have to Read This Whole Book!

You don't need to read this entire book. We've organized it into easy-to-use sections so you can get just the information you want. You will find everything you need to

★ Learn about the 100 top careers that don't require a four-year college degree, including their daily tasks, pay, outlook, and required education and skills.

★ Match your personal skills to the careers.

★ Take seven steps to land a good job in less time.

To get started, simply scan the table of contents to learn more about these sections and to see a list of the jobs described in this book. Really, this book is easy to use, and we hope it helps you.

Who Should Use This Book?

This is more than a book of job descriptions. We've spent quite a bit of time thinking about how to make its contents useful for a variety of situations, including

★ **Exploring career options.** The job descriptions in Part II give a wealth of information on many of the most desirable jobs in the labor market. The assessment in Part I can help you focus your career options.

★ **Considering more education or training.** The information helps you avoid costly mistakes in choosing a career or deciding on additional training or education—and it increases your chances of planning a bright future.

★ **Job seeking.** This book helps you identify new job targets, prepare for interviews, and write targeted resumes. The advice in Part III has been proven to cut job search time in half.

★ **Career planning.** The job descriptions help you explore your options, and Parts III and IV provide career planning advice and other useful information.

Source of Information

The job descriptions come from the good people at the U.S. Department of Labor, as published in the most recent edition of the *Occupational Outlook Handbook*. The *OOH* is the best source of career information available, and the descriptions include the most current, accurate data on jobs. The figures on earnings have been updated with data from the Occupational Employment Statistics survey. Thank you to all the people at the Department of Labor who gather, compile, analyze, and make sense of this information. It's good stuff, and we hope you can make good use of it.

Contents

Summary of Major Sections

Introduction. Provides an explanation of the job descriptions, how best to use the book, and other details. *Begins on page 1.*

Part I: Using the Job-Match Grid to Choose a Career. Match your skills and preferences to the jobs in this book. *Begins on page 15.*

Part II: Descriptions of the Top 100 Careers Without a Four-Year Degree. Presents thorough descriptions of the top 100 careers that don't require a four-year degree. Education and training requirements for these jobs vary from on-the-job training to a two-year associate degree. Each description gives information on the nature of the work, working conditions, employment, training, other qualifications, advancement, job outlook, earnings, related occupations, and sources of additional information. The jobs are presented in alphabetical order. The page numbers where specific descriptions begin are listed in the detailed contents. *Begins on page 31.*

Part III: *Quick Job Search—Seven Steps to Getting a Good Job in Less Time.* This relatively brief but important section offers results-oriented career planning and job search techniques. It includes tips on identifying your key skills, defining your ideal job, using effective job search methods, writing resumes, organizing your time, improving your interviewing skills, and following up on leads. The last part of this section features professionally written and designed resumes for some of the top jobs that don't require a four-year degree. *Begins on page 295.*

Part IV: Important Trends in Jobs and Industries. This section includes three well-written articles on labor market trends. The articles are worth your time. Titles of the articles are "Overview of the 2008–2018 Projections," "Employment Trends in Major Industries," and "Job Outlook for People Who Don't Have a Bachelor's Degree." *Begins on page 367.*

Detailed Contents

Introduction

This book is about improving your life, not just about selecting a job. The career you choose will have an enormous impact on how you live your life.

A huge amount of information is available on occupations, but most people don't know where to find accurate, reliable facts to help them make good career decisions—or they don't take the time to look. Important choices such as what to do with your career or whether to get additional training or education deserve your time.

If you are considering more training or education—whether additional coursework, an apprenticeship, or a two-year degree—this book will help with solid information. Training or education beyond high school is now typically required to get better jobs, and the education and training needed for the jobs in this book vary enormously. This book is designed to give you facts to help you explore your options.

A certain type of work or workplace may interest you as much as a certain type of job. If your interests and values lead you to work in health care, for example, you can do this in a variety of work environments, in a variety of industries, and in a variety of jobs. For this reason, we suggest you begin exploring alternatives by following your interests and finding a career path that allows you to use your talents doing something you enjoy.

Also, remember that money is not everything. The time you spend in career planning can pay off in higher earnings, but being satisfied with your work—and your life—is often more important than how much you earn. This book can help you find the work that suits you best.

Keep in Mind That Your Situation Is *Not* "Average"

Projected employment growth and earnings trends are quite positive for many occupations and industries. Keep in mind, however, that the averages in this book will not be true for many individuals. Within any field, many people earn more and many earn less than the average.

Our point is that *your* situation is probably not average. Some people do better than others, and some are willing to accept less pay for a more desirable work environment. Earnings vary enormously in different parts of the country, in different occupations, and in different industries. But this book's solid information is a great place to start. Good information will give you a strong foundation for good decisions.

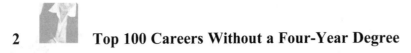
Four Important Labor Market Trends That Will Affect Your Career

Our economy has changed in dramatic ways over the past 10 years, with profound effects on how we work and live. Part IV of this book provides more information on labor market trends, but in case you don't read it, here are four trends that you simply *must* consider.

1. Education Pays

We're sure you won't be surprised to learn that people with higher levels of education and training have higher average earnings. The data that follows comes from the U.S. Department of Labor. We've selected data to show you the median earnings for people with various levels of education. (The median is the point where half earn more and half earn less.) Based on this information, we computed the earnings advantage of people at various education levels over those who did not graduate from high school. We've also included information showing the average percentage of people at that educational level who are unemployed.

Earnings for Year-Round, Full-Time Workers Age 25 and Over, by Educational Attainment

Level of Education	Median Annual Earnings	Premium Over High School Dropouts	Unemployment Rate
Professional degree	$79,508	$59,900	2.3%
Doctoral degree	$79,664	$56,056	2.5%
Master's degree	$65,364	$41,156	3.9%
Bachelor's degree	$53,300	$26,692	5.2%
Associate degree	$39,572	$15,964	6.8%
Some college, no degree	$36,348	$12,740	8.6%
High-school graduate	$32,552	$8,944	9.7%
High school dropout	$23,608	—	14.6%

Source: Bureau of Labor Statistics

As you can see in the table, the earnings difference between someone who holds an associate degree and someone with a high school education is $7,020 a year, money that could be used toward a car, a down payment on a house, or even a vacation. You can understand that this earnings difference, over a lifetime, will make an enormous difference in lifestyle.

The table makes it very clear that those with more training and education earn more than those with less and experience lower levels of unemployment. Jobs that require education and training beyond high school are projected to grow significantly faster than jobs that do not. People with higher levels of education and training are less likely to be unemployed, and when they are, they remain unemployed for shorter periods of time. There are always exceptions, but it is quite clear that more education results in higher earnings and lower rates of unemployment.

2. Knowledge of Computer and Other Technologies Is Increasingly Important

As you look over the list of jobs in the table of contents, you may notice that many require computer or technical skills. Even jobs that do not appear to be technical often call for computer literacy. Agricultural managers, for example, are often expected to understand and use scheduling and estimating software.

In all fields, those without job-related technical and computer skills will have a more difficult time finding good opportunities because they are competing with those who have these skills. Older workers, by the way, often do not have the computer skills that younger workers do. Employers tend to hire people who have the skills they need, and people without these abilities won't get the best jobs. So, whatever your age, consider upgrading your job-related computer and technology skills if they are not up to date—and plan to keep them current on your present and future jobs.

3. Ongoing Education and Training Are Essential

School and work once were separate activities, and most people did not go back to school after they began working. But with rapid changes in technology, most people are now required to learn throughout their work lives. Jobs are constantly upgraded, and today's jobs often cannot be handled by people who have only the knowledge and skills that were adequate for workers a few years ago.

To remain competitive, you will need to constantly upgrade your technology and other job-related skills. This may include taking formal courses, reading work-related magazines at home, signing up for on-the-job training, or participating in other forms of education. Upgrading your work-related skills on an ongoing basis is no longer optional for most jobs, and you ignore doing so at your peril.

4. Good Career Planning Is More Important Than Ever

Most people spend more time watching TV in a week than they spend on career planning during an entire year. Yet most people will change their jobs many times and make major career changes five to seven times. For this reason, it is important for you to spend time considering your career options and preparing to advance.

While you probably picked up this book for its information on jobs, it also provides a great deal of information on career planning. For example, Part III gives good career and job search advice, and Part IV has useful information on labor market trends. We urge you to read these and related materials because career-planning and job-seeking skills are the keys to surviving in this new economy.

Tips on Using This Book

This book is based on information from a variety of government sources and includes the most up-to-date and accurate data available. The entries are well written and pack a lot of information into short descriptions. *Top 100 Careers Without a Four-Year Degree* can be used in many ways, and we've provided tips for these four major uses:

- ★ For people exploring career, education, or training alternatives
- ★ For job seekers
- ★ For employers and business people
- ★ For counselors, instructors, and other career specialists

Tips for People Exploring Career, Education, or Training Alternatives

Top 100 Careers Without a Four-Year Degree is an excellent resource for anyone exploring career, education, or training alternatives. Many people do not have a good idea of what they want to do in their careers. They may be considering additional training or education but may not know what sort they should get. If you are one of these people, this book can help in several ways. Here are a few pointers.

Review the list of jobs. Trust yourself. Research studies indicate that most people have a good sense of their interests. Your interests can be used to guide you to career options you should consider in more detail.

Begin by looking over the occupations listed in the table of contents. Look at all the jobs, because you may identify previously overlooked possibilities. If other people will be using this book, please don't mark in it. Instead, on a separate sheet of paper, list the jobs that interest you. Or make a photocopy of the table of contents and use it to mark the jobs that interest you.

Next, look up and carefully read the descriptions of the jobs that most interest you in Part II. A quick review will often eliminate one or more of these jobs based on pay, working conditions, education required, or other considerations. After you have identified the three or four jobs that seem most interesting, research each one more thoroughly before making any important decisions.

Match your skills to the jobs in this book using the Job-Match Grid. Another way to identify possible job options is to answer questions about your skills and job preferences in Part I, "Using the Job-Match Grid to Choose a Career." This section will help you focus your job options and concentrate your research on a handful of job descriptions.

Study the jobs and their training and education requirements. Too many people decide to obtain additional training or education without knowing much about the jobs the training will lead to. Reviewing the descriptions in this book is one way to learn more about an occupation before you enroll in an education or training program. If you are currently a student, the job descriptions in this book can also help you decide on a major course of study or learn more about the jobs for which your studies are preparing you.

Do not be too quick to eliminate a job that interests you. If a job requires more education or training than you currently have, you can obtain this training in many ways.

Don't abandon your past experience and education too quickly. If you have significant work experience, training, or education, you should not abandon them too quickly. Many times, after people carefully consider what they want to do, they change careers and find that the skills and knowledge they have can still be used.

Top 100 Careers Without a Four-Year Degree can help you explore career options in several ways. First, carefully review descriptions for jobs you have held in the past. On a separate sheet of paper, list the skills needed in those jobs. Then do the same for jobs that interest you now. By comparing the lists, you will be able to identify skills you used in previous jobs that you could also use in jobs that interest you for the future. These "transferable" skills form the basis for moving to a new career.

You can also identify skills you have developed or used in nonwork activities, such as hobbies, family responsibilities, volunteer work, school, military, and extracurricular interests. If you want to stay with your current employer, the job descriptions can also help. For example, you may identify jobs within your organization that offer more rewarding work, higher pay, or other advantages over your present job. Read the descriptions related to these jobs, as you may be able to transfer into another job rather than leave the organization.

Tips for Job Seekers

You can use the job descriptions in this book to give you an edge in finding job openings and in getting job offers—even when you are competing with people who have better credentials. Here are some ways *Top 100 Careers Without a Four-Year Degree* can help you in the job search.

Identify related job targets. You may be limiting your job search to a small number of jobs for which you feel qualified, but by doing so you eliminate many jobs you could do and would enjoy. Your search for a new job should be broadened to include more possibilities.

Go through the entire list of jobs in the table of contents and check any that require skills similar to those you have. Look at all the jobs, as doing so sometimes helps you identify targets you would otherwise overlook.

You may want to answer questions about your skills and job preferences in Part I, "Using the Job-Match Grid to Choose a Career." Your results can help you identify career options that may suit you.

Many people are not aware of the many specialized jobs related to their training or experience. The descriptions in *Top 100 Careers Without a Four-Year Degree* are for major job titles, but a variety of more-specialized jobs may require similar skills. The "Other Major Career Information Sources" section later in this introduction lists sources you can use to find out about more-specialized jobs.

The descriptions can also point out jobs that interest you but that have higher responsibility or compensation levels. While you may not consider yourself qualified for such jobs now, you should think about seeking jobs that are above your previous levels but within your ability to handle.

Prepare for interviews. This book's job descriptions are an essential source of information to help you prepare for interviews. If you carefully review the description of a job before an interview, you will be much better prepared to emphasize your key skills. You should also review descriptions for past jobs and identify skills needed in the new job.

Negotiate pay. The job descriptions in this book will help you know what pay range to expect. Note that local pay and other details can differ substantially from the national averages in the descriptions.

Tips for Employers and Business People

Employers, human resource professionals, and other business users can use this book's information to write job descriptions, study pay ranges, and set criteria for new employees. The information can also help you conduct more-effective interviews by providing a list of key skills needed by new hires.

Tips for Counselors, Instructors, and Other Career Specialists

Counselors, instructors, and other career specialists will find this book helpful for their clients or students exploring career options or job targets. Our best suggestion to professionals is to get this book off the shelf and into the hands of the people who need it. Leave it on a table or desk and show people how the information can help them. Wear this book out—its real value is as a tool used often and well.

Additional Information About the Projections

For more information about employment change, job openings, earnings, unemployment rates, and training requirements by occupation, consult the Department of Labor's Career OneStop website at www.careeronestop.org. For information about industries, including some references to occupations and career paths that *Top 100 Careers Without a Four-Year Degree* does not cover, consult the *Career Guide to Industries,* a publication of the Bureau of Labor Statistics, now available only on the Web at www.bls.gov/oco/cg.

Information on the Major Parts of This Book

This book was designed to be easy to use. The table of contents provides brief comments on each section, and that may be all you need. If not, here are some additional details you may find useful in getting the most out of this book.

Part I: Using the Job-Match Grid to Choose a Career

Part I features an assessment with checklists and questions to match your skills and preferences to the jobs in this book. The seven skills covered in the assessment are artistic, communication, interpersonal, managerial, mathematics, mechanical, and science. The five job characteristics covered in the assessment are economically sensitive, geographically concentrated, hazardous conditions, outdoor work, and physically demanding.

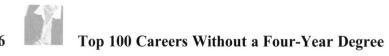

Part II: Descriptions of the 100 Top Careers Without a Four-Year Degree

Part II is the main part of the book and probably the reason you picked it up. It contains brief, well-written descriptions for 100 major jobs typically held by people without a four-year degree. A list of the jobs is provided in the table of contents. The content for each of these job descriptions comes from the U.S. Department of Labor and is considered by many to be the most accurate and up-to-date information available. These jobs are presented in alphabetical order.

Together, the jobs in Part II provide enormous variety at all levels of earnings and interest. One way to explore career options is to go to the table of contents and identify those jobs that seem interesting. If you are interested in medical jobs, for example, you can quickly spot those you will want to learn more about. You may also see other jobs that look interesting, and you should consider these as well.

Next, read the descriptions for the jobs that interest you and, based on what you learn, identify those that *most* interest you. These are the jobs you should consider, and Parts III and IV will give you additional information on how you might best do so.

How the 100 Jobs Were Selected

The jobs included in this book are selected from the 251 jobs covered in detail by the *Occupational Outlook Handbook,* published by the U.S. Department of Labor. They are jobs that normally require less education than a bachelor's degree (at a *minimum*) and that had a workforce of more than 200,000 people in 2008. (The largest had a workforce of over 10 million.) Any job that employs at least one-fifth of a million people is going to account for a lot of job openings and therefore is worth your consideration. Even if overall employment in the job is shrinking, you can expect many job opportunities because of retirements and turnover.

Details on Each Section of the Job Descriptions

Each occupational description in this book follows a standard format, making it easier for you to compare jobs. The following overview describes the kinds of information found in each part of a description and offers tips on how to interpret the information.

Job Title

This is the title used for the job in the *Occupational Outlook Handbook.*

O*NET Codes

The numbers that appear just below the title of every job description are from the Occupational Information Network (O*NET), a major occupational information system created by the U.S. Department of Labor and used by state employment service offices to classify applicants and job openings and by some career information centers and libraries to file occupational information.

At the O*NET site at www.online.onetcenter.org, you can search for occupations that match your skills, or you may search by keyword or O*NET code. For each occupation, O*NET reports information about tasks performed, knowledge, skills, abilities, and work activities. It also lists interests; work styles, such as independence; and work values, such as achievement, that are well suited to the occupation. The O*NET is also available as a book titled the *O*NET Dictionary of Occupational Titles* (JIST).

Significant Points

The bullet points in this part of a description highlight key characteristics for each job, such as recent trends or education and training requirements.

Nature of the Work

What workers do on the job, what tools and equipment they use, and how closely they are supervised are discussed in this section. Some descriptions mention alternative job titles or occupational specialties.

Work environment. This subsection discusses the workplace, physical activities, and typical hours of workers in the occupation. It describes opportunities for part-time work, the extent of travel required, special equipment that is used, and the risk of injury that workers may face.

Information on various worker characteristics, such as the average number of hours worked per week, is obtained from the Current Population Survey (CPS), a survey of households conducted by the U.S. Census Bureau for the Bureau of Labor Statistics (BLS). Other sources include articles as well as the websites of professional associations, unions, and trade groups. Information found on the Internet or in periodicals is verified through interviews with workers; professional associations; unions; and others with occupational knowledge, such as university professors and career counselors.

Training, Other Qualifications, and Advancement

After gathering your initial impressions of what a job is all about, you need to understand how to prepare for it. The "Training, Other Qualifications, and Advancement" section explains the steps necessary to enter and advance in an occupation.

Education and training. This subsection describes the most significant sources of education and training, the type of education or training preferred by employers, and the typical length of training. Note that for a few occupations, especially those in which skill requirements are advancing rapidly (such as Registered Nurses), this subsection may point out the advantages of getting a four-year degree to prepare for career entry. However, none of the occupations in this book requires a four-year degree for entry.

Licensure. The kinds of mandatory licenses or certifications associated with an occupation are described in this subsection. To be certified or licensed, a worker usually is required to complete one or more training courses and pass one or more examinations. Most occupations do not have mandatory licensure or certification requirements. Some occupations have professional credentials granted by different organizations, in which case the most widely recognized organizations are listed.

Other qualifications. Additional qualifications that are not included in the previous subsections, such as the desirable skills, aptitudes, and personal characteristics that employers look for, are discussed in this section.

Advancement. This subsection details advancement opportunities that may be available after you gain experience in an occupation. Advancement can come in several forms, including advancement within the occupation, such as promotion to a management position, advancement into other occupations, and advancement to self-employment. Certain types of certification can serve as a form of advancement. Voluntary certification often demonstrates a level of competency to employers and can result in more responsibility, higher pay, or a new job.

Information in the "Training, Other Qualifications, and Advancement" section comes from interviews with workers; websites; training materials; and interviews with the organizations that grant degrees, certifications, or licenses or are otherwise associated with the occupation.

Employment

This section reports the number of jobs the occupation recently provided, the key industries where these jobs are found, and the number or proportion of self-employed workers in the occupation, if significant. Information in this section comes from various surveys by the BLS.

When significant, the geographic distribution of jobs is mentioned.

Job Outlook

In planning for the future, you need to consider potential job opportunities. This section describes the factors that will result in employment growth or decline.

Employment change. This subsection reflects the occupational projections in the National Employment Matrix. Each occupation is assigned a descriptive phrase based on its projected percent change in employment over the 2008–2018 period. This phrase describes the occupation's projected employment change relative to the projected average employment change for all occupations combined.

Many factors are examined in projecting the employment change for each occupation. One such factor is changes in technology. New technology can either create new job opportunities or eliminate jobs by making workers obsolete. Another factor that influences employment trends is demographic change. By affecting the services demanded, demographic change can influence occupational growth or decline.

Another factor affecting job growth or decline is changes in business practices, such as restructuring businesses or outsourcing (contracting out) work. Corporate restructuring has made many organizations "flatter," resulting in fewer middle management positions. Also, in the past few years, jobs in some occupations have been "off-shored"—moved to low-wage foreign countries. The substitution of one product or service for another can also affect employment projections. Competition from foreign trade usually has a negative effect on employment. Often, foreign manufacturers can produce goods more cheaply than they can be produced in the United States, and the cost savings can be passed on in the form of lower prices with which U.S. manufacturers cannot compete. Another factor is job growth or decline in key industries. If an occupation is concentrated in an industry that is growing rapidly, it is likely that that occupation will grow rapidly as well.

Job prospects. In some cases, this book mentions that an occupation is likely to provide numerous or relatively few job openings. This information reflects the projected change in employment, as well as replacement needs. Large occupations in which workers frequently enter and leave generally provide the most job openings—reflecting the need to replace workers who transfer to other occupations or who stop working.

Key Phrases Used in the Job Descriptions

This table explains how to interpret the key phrases that describe projected changes in employment. It also explains the terms for the relationship between the number of job openings and the number of job seekers.

Changing Employment Between 2008 and 2018

If the statement reads	Employment is projected to
Grow much faster than average	Increase 20 percent or more
Grow faster than average	Increase 14 to 19 percent
Grow about as fast as average	Increase 7 to 13 percent
Grow more slowly than average	Increase 3 to 6 percent
Little or no change	Decrease 2 percent to increase 2 percent
Decline slowly or moderately	Decrease 3 to 9 percent
Decline rapidly	Decrease 10 percent or more

Opportunities and Competition for Jobs

If the statement reads	Job openings compared to job seekers may be
Very good to excellent opportunities	More numerous
Good or favorable opportunities	In rough balance
May face or can expect keen competition	Fewer

Projections Data

The employment projections table lists employment statistics from the National Employment Matrix. It includes 2008 employment, projected 2018 employment, and the 2008–2018 change in employment in both numerical and percentage terms. Numbers below 10,000 are rounded to the nearest hundred, numbers above 10,000 are rounded to the nearest thousand, and percentages are rounded to the nearest whole number. Numerical and percentage changes are calculated using nonrounded 2008 and 2018 employment figures and then are rounded for presentation in the employment projections table.

Earnings

This section discusses typical earnings and how workers are compensated—by means of annual salaries, hourly wages, commissions, piece rates, tips, or bonuses. Within every occupation, earnings vary by experience, responsibility, performance, tenure, and geographic area. Information may be given on earnings in the major industries in which the occupation is employed. Some statements contain additional earnings data from non-BLS sources. Starting and average salaries of federal workers are based on 2009 data from the U.S. Office of Personnel Management. The National Association of Colleges and Employers supplies information on average salary offers in 2009 for students graduating with a bachelor's, master's, or Ph.D. degree in certain fields. A few statements contain additional earnings information from other sources, such as unions, professional associations, and private companies. These data sources are cited in the text.

Benefits account for a significant portion of total compensation costs to employers. Benefits such as paid vacation, health insurance, and sick leave may not be mentioned because they are so widespread. Although not as common as traditional benefits, flexible hours and profit-sharing plans may be offered to attract and retain highly qualified workers. Less-common benefits also include child care, tuition for dependents, housing assistance, summers off,

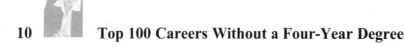

and free or discounted merchandise or services. For certain occupations, the percentage of workers affiliated with a union is listed.

Related Occupations

Occupations involving similar duties, skills, interests, education, and training are listed here. This allows you to look up these jobs if they also interest you.

Sources of Additional Information

No single publication can describe all aspects of an occupation. Thus, this section lists the mailing addresses of associations, government agencies, unions, and other organizations that can provide occupational information. In some cases, toll-free telephone numbers and Internet addresses also are listed. Free or relatively inexpensive publications offering more information may be mentioned; some of these publications also may be available in libraries, in school career centers, in guidance offices, or on the Internet.

Part III: *Quick Job Search—Seven Steps to Getting a Good Job in Less Time*

If you have ever experienced unemployment, you know it is not pleasant. Unemployment is something most people want to get over quickly—in fact, the quicker the better. Part III will give you some techniques to help.

We know that most of you who read this book want to improve yourselves. You want to consider career and training options that lead to a better job and life in whatever way you define this—better pay, more flexibility, work that is more enjoyable or more meaningful, proving to your mom that you really can do anything you set your mind to, and other reasons. That is why we include advice on career planning and job search in Part III. It's a short section, but it includes the basics that are most important in planning your career and in reducing the time it takes to get a job. We hope it will make you think about what is important to you in the long run.

The second section of Part III showcases professionally written resumes for some of America's top jobs for people without a four-year degree. Use these as examples when creating your own resume.

We know you will resist completing the activities in Part III, but consider this: It is often not the best person who gets the job, but the best job seeker. People who do their career planning and job search homework often get jobs over those with better credentials, because they have these distinct advantages:

1. **They get more interviews,** including many for jobs that will never be advertised.

2. **They do better in interviews.**

People who understand what they want and what they have to offer employers present their skills more convincingly and are much better at answering problem questions. And, because they have learned more about job search techniques, they are likely to get more interviews with employers who need the skills they have.

Doing better in interviews often makes the difference between getting a job offer and sitting at home. And spending time planning your career can make an enormous difference to your happiness and lifestyle over time. So please consider reading Part III and completing its activities. We suggest you schedule a time right now to at least read Part III. An hour or so spent there can help you do just enough better in your career planning, job seeking, and interviewing to make the difference.

Part IV: Important Trends in Jobs and Industries

This section is made up of three very good articles on labor market trends. These articles come directly from U.S. Department of Labor sources and are interesting, well written, and short. One is on overall trends, with an emphasis on occupational groups; another is on trends in major industry groups; and the third discusses the job outlook for people without a bachelor's degree. We know they sound boring, but the articles are quick reads and will give you a good idea of factors that will impact your career in the years to come.

The first article is titled "Overview of the 2008–2018 Projections." It highlights many important trends in employment and includes information on the fastest-growing jobs, jobs with high pay at various levels of education, and other details.

The second article is titled "Employment Trends in Major Industries." We included this information because you may find that you can use your skills or training in industries you have not considered. The article provides a good review of major trends with an emphasis on helping you make good employment decisions. This information can help you seek jobs in industries that offer higher pay or that are more likely to interest you. Many people overlook one important fact—the industry you work in is as important as the occupation you choose.

The third article is called "Job Outlook for People Who Don't Have a Bachelor's Degree." It identifies high-paying and high-growth career options for people who don't complete four years of college. It includes tables with facts about specific careers, including the typical entry route—which may be as quick as short-term on-the-job training or as long as an associate degree program.

Some Additional Jobs to Consider

Here is a list of additional jobs that may not require a four-year degree that you may want to consider. Their descriptions are not included in this book, but you can find them in the *Occupational Outlook Handbook*, *Top 300 Careers*, the *Enhanced Occupational Outlook Handbook*, or online at www.bls.gov.

- ★ Agricultural Workers
- ★ Air Traffic Controllers
- ★ Aircraft Pilots and Flight Engineers
- ★ Announcers
- ★ Barbers, Cosmetologists, and Other Personal Appearance Workers
- ★ Boilermakers
- ★ Bookbinders and Bindery Workers
- ★ Broadcast and Sound Engineering Technicians and Radio Operators
- ★ Brokerage Clerks
- ★ Bus Drivers
- ★ Cardiovascular Technologists and Technicians
- ★ Cargo and Freight Agents

- ★ Cashiers
- ★ Coin, Vending, and Amusement Machine Servicers and Repairers
- ★ Communications Equipment Operators
- ★ Computer Operators
- ★ Computer, Automated Teller, and Office Machine Repairers
- ★ Construction and Building Inspectors
- ★ Counter and Rental Clerks
- ★ Couriers and Messengers
- ★ Court Reporters
- ★ Credit Authorizers, Checkers, and Clerks
- ★ Dancers and Choreographers
- ★ Data Entry and Information Processing Workers

- ★ Demonstrators, Product Promoters, and Models
- ★ Desktop Publishers
- ★ Diagnostic Medical Sonographers
- ★ Dispatchers
- ★ Electrical and Electronics Installers and Repairers
- ★ Electronic Home Entertainment Equipment Installers and Repairers
- ★ Elevator Installers and Repairers
- ★ Fashion Designers
- ★ File Clerks
- ★ Fire Fighting Occupations
- ★ Fishers and Fishing Vessel Operators
- ★ Flight Attendants
- ★ Floral Designers
- ★ Forest, Conservation, and Logging Workers
- ★ Funeral Directors
- ★ Gaming Cage Workers
- ★ Gaming Services Occupations
- ★ Glaziers
- ★ Hazardous Materials Removal Workers
- ★ Home Appliance Repairers
- ★ Hotel, Motel, and Resort Desk Clerks
- ★ Human Resources Assistants, Except Payroll and Timekeeping
- ★ Insulation Workers
- ★ Interior Designers
- ★ Interpreters and Translators
- ★ Interviewers

- ★ Jewelers and Precious Stone and Metal Workers
- ★ Lodging Managers
- ★ Machine Setters, Operators, and Tenders—Metal and Plastic
- ★ Massage Therapists
- ★ Material Moving Occupations
- ★ Medical Transcriptionists
- ★ Medical, Dental, and Ophthalmic Laboratory Technicians
- ★ Meter Readers, Utilities
- ★ Nuclear Medicine Technologists
- ★ Occupational Therapist Assistants and Aides
- ★ Office and Administrative Support Worker Supervisors and Managers
- ★ Opticians, Dispensing
- ★ Order Clerks
- ★ Payroll and Timekeeping Clerks
- ★ Pest Control Workers
- ★ Photographic Process Workers and Processing Machine Operators
- ★ Physical Therapist Assistants and Aides
- ★ Postal Service Workers
- ★ Power Plant Operators, Distributors, and Dispatchers
- ★ Precision Instrument and Equipment Repairers
- ★ Prepress Technicians and Workers
- ★ Private Detectives and Investigators
- ★ Procurement Clerks
- ★ Production, Planning, and Expediting Clerks

★ Radiation Therapists

★ Rail Transportation Occupations

★ Reservation and Transportation Ticket Agents and Travel Clerks

★ Respiratory Therapists

★ Science Technicians

★ Semiconductor Processors

★ Small Engine Mechanics

★ Stationary Engineers and Boiler Operators

★ Stock Clerks and Order Fillers

★ Structural and Reinforcing Iron and Metal Workers

★ Surgical Technologists

★ Taxi Drivers and Chauffeurs

★ Teachers—Preschool, Kindergarten, Elementary, Middle, and Secondary

★ Teachers—Self-Enrichment Education

★ Television, Video, and Motion Picture Camera Operators and Editors

★ Tellers

★ Textile, Apparel, and Furnishings Occupations

★ Tool and Die Makers

★ Travel Agents

★ Truck Drivers and Driver/Sales Workers

★ Veterinary Technologists and Technicians

★ Water and Liquid Waste Treatment Plant and System Operators

★ Water Transportation Occupations

★ Weighers, Measurers, Checkers, and Samplers, Recordkeeping

Other Major Career Information Sources

The information in this book will be very useful, but you may want or need additional information. Keep in mind that the job descriptions here cover major jobs and not the many more-specialized jobs that are often related to them. Each job description in this book provides some sources of information related to that job, but here are additional resources to consider.

Occupational Outlook Handbook (or the *OOH*): Updated every two years by the U.S. Department of Labor, this book provides descriptions for 289 major jobs covering more than 85 percent of the workforce. The *OOH* is the source of the job descriptions used in this book, and the book *Top 300 Careers* includes all the *OOH* content plus additional information.

The *Enhanced Occupational Outlook Handbook:* Includes all descriptions in the *OOH* plus descriptions of more than 5,800 more-specialized jobs that are related to them.

The *O*NET Dictionary of Occupational Titles:* The only printed source of the more than 900 jobs described in the U.S. Department of Labor's Occupational Information Network database (O*NET).

Best Jobs for the 21st Century: Includes descriptions for the jobs with the best combination of earnings, growth, and number of openings. Useful lists make jobs easy to explore (examples: highest-paying jobs by level of education or training; best jobs overall; and best jobs for different ages, personality types, interests, and many more).

Using the Job-Match Grid to Choose a Career

By the Editors at JIST

This book describes so many occupations—how can you choose the best job for you? This section is your answer! It can help you to identify the jobs where your abilities will be valued, and you can rule out jobs that have certain characteristics you would rather avoid. You will respond to a series of statements and use the Job-Match Grid to match your skills and preferences to the most appropriate jobs in this book.

So grab a pencil and get ready to mark up the following sections. Or, if someone else will be using this book, find a sheet of paper and get ready to take notes.

Thinking About Your Skills

Everybody knows that skills are important for getting and keeping a job. Employers expect you to list relevant skills on your resume. They ask about your skills in interviews. And they expect you to develop skills on the job so that you will remain productive as new technologies and new work situations emerge.

But maybe you haven't thought about how closely skills are related to job satisfaction. For example, let's say you have enough communication skills to hold a certain job where these skills are used heavily, but you wouldn't really *enjoy* using them. In that case, this job probably would be a bad choice for you. You need to identify a job that will use the skills that you *do* enjoy using.

That's why you need to take a few minutes to think about your skills: the ones you're good at and the ones you like using. The checklists that follow can help you do this. On each of the seven skills checklists that follow, use numbers to indicate how much you agree with each statement:

3 = I strongly agree

2 = I agree

1 = There's some truth to this

0 = This doesn't apply to me

Artistic Skills

_____ I am an amateur artist.

_____ I have musical talent.

(continued)

(continued)

_____ I enjoy planning home makeovers.

_____ I am good at performing onstage.

_____ I enjoy taking photos or shooting videos.

_____ I am good at writing stories, poems, articles, or essays.

_____ I have enjoyed taking ballet or other dance lessons.

_____ I like to cook and plan meals.

_____ I can sketch a good likeness of something or somebody.

_____ Playing music or singing is a hobby of mine.

_____ I have a good sense of visual style.

_____ I have participated in amateur theater.

_____ I like to express myself through writing.

_____ I can prepare tasty meals better than most people.

_____ I have a flair for creating attractive designs.

_____ I learn new dance steps or routines easily.

_____ **Total for Artistic Skills**

A note for those determined to work in the arts: Before you move on to the next skill, take a moment to decide whether working in some form of art is essential to you. Some people have exceptional talent and interest in a certain art form and are unhappy unless they are working in that art form—or until they have given their best shot at trying to break into it. If you are that kind of person, the total score shown above doesn't really matter. In fact, you may have given a 3 to just *one* of the statements in this section, but if you care passionately about your art form, you should toss out ordinary arithmetic and change the total to 100.

Communication Skills

_____ I am good at explaining complicated things to people.

_____ I like to take notes and write up minutes for meetings.

_____ I have a flair for public speaking.

_____ I am good at writing directions for using a computer or machine.

_____ I enjoy investigating facts and showing other people what they indicate.

_____ People consider me a good listener.

_____ I like to write letters to newspaper editors or political representatives.

_____ I have been an effective debater.

_____ I like developing publicity fliers for a school or community event.

_____ I am good at making diagrams that break down complex processes.

_____ I like teaching people how to drive a car or play a sport.

_____ I have been successful as the secretary of a club.

_____ I enjoy speaking at group meetings or worship services.

_____ I have a knack for choosing the most effective word.

_____ I enjoy tutoring young people.

_____ Technical manuals are not hard for me to understand.

_____ **Total for Communication Skills**

Interpersonal Skills

_____ I am able to make people feel that I understand their point of view.

_____ I enjoy working collaboratively.

_____ I often can make suggestions to people without sounding critical of them.

_____ I enjoy soliciting clothes, food, and other supplies for needy people.

_____ I am good at "reading" people to tell what's on their minds.

_____ I have a lot of patience with people who are doing something for the first time.

_____ People consider me outgoing.

_____ I enjoy taking care of sick relatives, friends, or neighbors.

_____ I am good at working out conflicts between friends or family members.

_____ I enjoy serving as a host or hostess for houseguests.

_____ People consider me a team player.

_____ I enjoy meeting new people and finding common interests.

_____ I am good at fundraising for school groups, teams, or community organizations.

_____ I like to train or care for animals.

_____ I often know what to say to defuse a tense situation.

_____ I have enjoyed being an officer or advisor for a youth group.

_____ **Total for Interpersonal Skills**

Managerial Skills

_____ I am good at inspiring people to work together toward a goal.

_____ I tend to use time wisely and not procrastinate.

_____ I usually know when I have enough information to make a decision.

_____ I enjoy planning and arranging programs for school or a community organization.

_____ I am not reluctant to take responsibility when things turn out wrong.

_____ I have enjoyed being a leader of a scout troop or other such group.

_____ I often can figure out what motivates somebody.

_____ People trust me to speak on their behalf and represent them fairly.

_____ I like to help organize things at home, such as shopping lists and budgets.

(continued)

(continued)

_____ I have been successful at recruiting members for a club or other organization.

_____ I have enjoyed helping run a school or community fair or carnival.

_____ People find me persuasive.

_____ I enjoy buying large quantities of food or other products for an organization.

_____ I have a knack for identifying abilities in other people.

_____ I am able to get past details and look at the big picture.

_____ I am good at delegating authority rather than trying to do everything myself.

_____ **Total for Managerial Skills**

Mathematics Skills

_____ I have always done well in math classes.

_____ I enjoy balancing checkbooks for family members.

_____ I can make mental calculations quickly.

_____ I enjoy calculating sports statistics or keeping score.

_____ Preparing family income tax returns is not hard for me.

_____ I like to tutor young people in math.

_____ I have taken or plan to take courses in statistics or calculus.

_____ I enjoy budgeting the family expenditures.

_____ **Subtotal for Mathematics Skills**

x 2   **Multiply by 2**

_____ **Total for Mathematics Skills**

Mechanical Skills

_____ I have a good sense of how mechanical devices work.

_____ I like to tinker with my car or motorcycle.

_____ I can understand diagrams of machinery or electrical wiring.

_____ I enjoy installing and repairing home stereo or computer equipment.

_____ I like looking at the merchandise in a building-supply warehouse store.

_____ I can sometimes fix household appliances when they break down.

_____ I have enjoyed building model airplanes, automobiles, or boats.

_____ I can do minor plumbing and electrical installations in the home.

_____ **Subtotal for Mechanical Skills**

x 2   **Multiply by 2**

_____ **Total for Mechanical Skills**

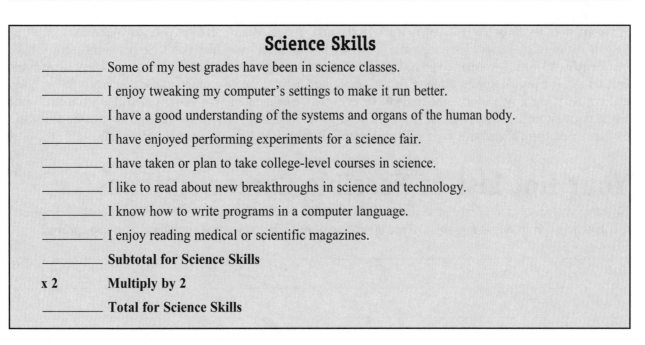

Science Skills

_____ Some of my best grades have been in science classes.

_____ I enjoy tweaking my computer's settings to make it run better.

_____ I have a good understanding of the systems and organs of the human body.

_____ I have enjoyed performing experiments for a science fair.

_____ I have taken or plan to take college-level courses in science.

_____ I like to read about new breakthroughs in science and technology.

_____ I know how to write programs in a computer language.

_____ I enjoy reading medical or scientific magazines.

_____ **Subtotal for Science Skills**

x 2 **Multiply by 2**

_____ **Total for Science Skills**

Finding Your Skills on the Job-Match Grid

Okay, you've made a lot of progress so far. Now it's time to review what you've said about skills so you can use these insights to sort through the jobs listed on the Job-Match Grid.

Look at your totals for the seven skills listed previously. Enter your totals in the left column on this scorecard:

Total	Skill	Rank
_____	Artistic	_____
_____	Communication	_____
_____	Interpersonal	_____
_____	Managerial	_____
_____	Mathematics	_____
_____	Mechanical	_____
_____	Science	_____

Next, enter the rank of each skill in the right column—that is, the highest-scored skill gets ranked 1, the next-highest 2, and so forth. **Important:** Keep in mind that _the numbers in the Total column are only a rough guideline_. If you feel that a skill should be ranked higher or lower than its numerical total would suggest, _go by your impressions rather than just by the numbers_.

Now turn to the Job-Match Grid and find the columns for your #1-ranked and #2-ranked skills. Move down through the grid, going from page to page, and notice what symbols appear in those columns. If a row of the grid has a black circle (●) in _both_ columns, circle the occupation name—or, if someone else will be using this book, jot down the name on a piece of paper. These occupations use a high level of both skills, or the skills are essential to these jobs.

Go through the Job-Match Grid a second time, looking at the column for your #3-ranked skill. If a _job you have already circled_ has a black circle (●) or a bull's-eye (◉) in the column for your #3-ranked skill, put a check mark next to the occupation name. If none of your selected jobs has a black circle or a bull's-eye in this column, look for a white circle (○) and mark these jobs with check marks.

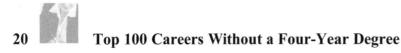

A second note for those determined to work in the arts: If a *particular* art form is essential for you to work in, you almost certainly know which occupations involve that art form and which don't. So not every job that has a black circle (●) in the "Artistic" column is going to interest you. Circle only the jobs that have a black circle in this column that *are* related to your art form (if you're not sure, look at the description of the occupation in this book) and that also have a symbol of some kind (●, ◐, or ○) in the column for your #2-ranked skill. As you circle each job, also give it a check mark, because there will be so few of them that you won't need to go through the Job-Match Grid a second time. If you have a more general interest in the arts, follow the general instructions.

Your Hot List of Possible Career Matches

Now that you have made a first and second cut of the jobs on the Job-Match Grid, you can focus on the occupations that look most promising at this point. Write the names of the occupations that are both *circled* and *checked:*

_____ _____

_____ _____

_____ _____

_____ _____

_____ _____

_____ _____

This is your Hot List of occupations that you are going to explore in detail *if* they are not eliminated by certain important job-related factors that you'll consider next.

Thinking About Other Job-Related Factors

Next, you need to consider four other job-related factors:

- ★ Economic sensitivity
- ★ Outdoor work
- ★ Physically demanding work
- ★ Hazardous conditions

Economic Sensitivity

You've read about how our nation's economy has gone up and down over the years. When the economy is on an upswing, there are more job openings, but when it veers downward toward recession, jobs are harder to find.

Are you aware that these trends affect some occupations more than others? For example, during an economic upswing, people do more vacation traveling and businesses send more workers on business trips. This keeps travel agencies very busy, so they need to hire more travel agents. When the economy is going down, people cut back on their vacation travel, businesses tell their workers to use teleconferencing instead of business trips, and travel agents are not in demand. Some may be laid off, and people who want to enter this field may find very few openings. By contrast, most jobs in the health-care field are not sensitive to the economy, and automotive mechanics are just as busy as ever during economic slowdowns because people want to keep their old cars running.

So this issue of economic sensitivity (and its opposite, job security) is one that may affect which occupation you choose. Some people want to avoid economically sensitive occupations because they don't want to risk losing their job (or having difficulty finding a job) during times of recession. Other people are willing to risk being in an economically sensitive occupation because they want to profit from the periods when both the economy and the occupation are booming.

> How important is it to you to be in an occupation that *doesn't* go through periods of boom and bust along with the nation's economy? Check one:
>
> _____ It doesn't matter to me.
>
> _____ It's not important, but I'd consider it.
>
> _____ It's somewhat important to me.
>
> _____ It's very important to me.

If you answered "It doesn't matter to me," skip to the next section, "Outdoor Work." Otherwise, turn back to the Job-Match Grid and find the column for "Economically Sensitive."

If you answered "It's not important, but I'd consider it," see whether any of the jobs on your Hot List have a black circle (●) in this column. If so, cross them off and write an "E" next to them.

If you answered "It's somewhat important to me," see whether any of the jobs on your Hot List have a black circle (●) or a bull's-eye (◉) in this column. If so, cross them off and write an "E" next to them.

If you answered "It's very important to me," see whether any of the jobs on your Hot List have *any* symbol (●, ◉, or ○) in this column. If so, cross them off and write an "E" next to them.

Outdoor Work

Some people prefer to work indoors in a climate-controlled setting, such as an office, a classroom, a factory floor, a laboratory, or a hospital room. Other people would rather work primarily in an outdoor setting, such as a forest, an athletic field, or a city street. And some would enjoy a job that alternates between indoor and outdoor activities.

> What is *your* preference for working indoors or outdoors? Check one:
>
> _____ It's very important to me to work **indoors.**
>
> _____ I'd prefer to work mostly **indoors.**
>
> _____ Either indoors or outdoors is okay with me.
>
> _____ I'd prefer to work mostly **outdoors.**
>
> _____ It's very important to me to work **outdoors.**

If you answered "Either indoors or outdoors is okay with me," skip to the next section, "Physically Demanding Work." Otherwise, turn to the Job-Match Grid and find the column for "Outdoor Work."

If you answered "It's very important to me to work **indoors,**" see whether any of the jobs on your Hot List have *any* symbol (●, ◉, or ○) in this column. If so, cross them off and write an "O" next to them.

If you answered "I'd prefer to work mostly **indoors,**" see whether any of the jobs on your Hot List have a black circle (●) in this column. If so, cross them off and write an "O" next to them.

If you answered "I'd prefer to work mostly **outdoors,**" see whether any of the jobs on your Hot List have *no* symbol—just a blank—in this column. If so, cross them off and write an "O" next to them. All the jobs remaining on your Hot List should have some kind of symbol (●, ◉, or ○) in this column.

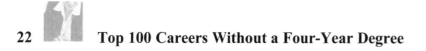

If you answered "It's very important to me to work **outdoors**," see whether any of the jobs on your Hot List have either *no* symbol or just a white circle (○) in this column. If so, cross them off and write an "O" next to them. All the jobs remaining on your Hot List should have either a black circle (●) or a bull's-eye (◉) in this column.

Physically Demanding Work

Jobs vary by how much muscle power they require you to use. Some jobs require a lot of lifting heavy loads, standing for long times, climbing, or stooping. On other jobs, the heaviest thing you lift is a notebook or telephone handset, and most of the time you are sitting. Still other jobs require only a moderate amount of physical exertion.

What is *your* preference for the physical demands of work? Check one:

_____ I don't care whether my work requires heavy or light physical exertion.

_____ I want my work to require only light physical exertion.

_____ I want my work to require no more than occasional moderate physical exertion.

_____ I want my work to require moderate physical exertion, with occasional heavy exertion.

_____ I want my work to require a lot of heavy physical exertion.

If you answered "I don't care whether my work requires heavy or light physical exertion," skip to the next section, "Hazardous Conditions." Otherwise, turn to the Job-Match Grid and find the column for "Physically Demanding Work."

If you answered "I want my work to require only light physical exertion," see whether any of the jobs on your Hot List have *any* symbol (●, ◉, or ○) in this column. If so, cross them off and write a "P" next to them.

If you answered "I want my work to require no more than occasional moderate physical exertion," see whether any of the jobs on your Hot List have either a black circle (●) or a bull's-eye (◉) in this column. If so, cross them off and write a "P" next to them.

If you answered "I want my work to require moderate physical exertion, with occasional heavy exertion," see whether any of the jobs on your Hot List have either a black circle (●), a white circle (○), or *no* symbol in this column. If so, cross them off and write a "P" next to them. All the jobs remaining on your Hot List should have a bull's-eye (◉) in this column.

If you answered "I want my work to require a lot of heavy physical exertion," see whether any of the jobs on your Hot List have either *no* symbol or just a white circle (○) or a bull's-eye (◉) in this column. If so, cross them off and write a "P" next to them. All the jobs remaining on your Hot List should have a black circle (●) in this column.

Hazardous Conditions

Every day about 9,000 Americans sustain a disabling injury on the job. Many workers have jobs that require them to deal with hazardous conditions, such as heat, noise, radiation, germs, toxins, or dangerous machinery. These workers need to wear protective clothing or follow safety procedures to avoid injury.

What is *your* preference regarding hazardous conditions on the job? Check one:

_____ I want hazardous workplace conditions to be very unlikely.

_____ I want hazardous conditions to be unlikely or minor.

_____ I am willing to accept some major workplace hazards.

If you answered "I am willing to accept some major workplace hazards," skip to the section "Geographically Concentrated Jobs." Otherwise, turn to the Job-Match Grid and find the column for "Hazardous Conditions."

If you answered "I want hazardous workplace conditions to be very unlikely," see whether any of the jobs on your Hot List have *any* symbol (●, ◐, or ○) in this column. If so, cross them off and write an "H" next to them.

If you answered "I want hazardous conditions to be unlikely or minor," see whether any of the jobs on your Hot List have a black circle (●) in this column. If so, cross them off and write an "H" next to them.

If Every Job on Your Hot List Is Now Crossed Off

It's possible that you have crossed off *all* the occupations on your Hot List. If so, consider these two options:

★ You may want to relax some of your requirements. Maybe you were too hasty in crossing off some of the jobs. Take another look at the four job-related factors and decide whether you could accept work that doesn't meet the requirements you set previously—for example, work that is not as much indoors or outdoors as you specified. If you change your mind now, you can tell by the letters in the margin which jobs you crossed off for which reasons.

★ You may want to add to your Hot List by considering additional skills. So far you have considered only occupations that involve your top three skills. You may want to add jobs that have a black circle (●) or a bull's-eye (◐) in the column for your #4-ranked skill and possibly for your #5-ranked skill. If you do add any jobs, be sure to repeat your review of the four job-related factors.

Evaluating Occupations Described in This Book

You are now ready to make the jump from the checklists to the detailed information about jobs in this book. The first detailed issue you need to consider is whether you will be able to find work in your area or have to relocate.

Geographically Concentrated Jobs

Turn to the Job-Match Grid one more time and find the column for "Geographically Concentrated." Look at all the occupations on your Hot List that haven't been crossed off. If there is a symbol in this column, especially a bull's-eye (◐) or a black circle (●), it means that employment for this occupation tends to be concentrated in certain geographic areas. For example, most acting jobs are found in big cities because that's where you'll find most theaters, TV studios, and movie studios. Most water transportation jobs are found on the coasts and beside major lakes and rivers.

If a symbol shows that a Hot List occupation *is* geographically concentrated, the location of the jobs may be obvious, as in the examples of acting and water transportation. If it's not clear to you where the jobs may be found, find the occupation in "The Job Descriptions" section and look for the facts under the heading "Employment" in the description. Once you understand where most of the jobs are, you have to make some decisions:

★ **Are most of the job openings in a geographic location where I am now or would enjoy living?**
If you answered "yes" to this question, repeat this exercise for all the other occupations still on your Hot List. Then jump to the next heading, "Nature of the Work." If you answered "no," proceed to the next bulleted question.

★ **If most of the job openings are in a distant place where I don't want to relocate, am I willing to take a chance and hope to be one of the few workers who get hired in an *uncommon* location?**
If you answered "yes," take a good look at the Job Outlook information in the job description. If the outlook for the occupation is very good and if you expect to have some of the advantages mentioned

there (such as the right degree, in some cases), taking a chance on being hired in an unusual location may be a reasonable decision. On the other hand, if the outlook is only so-so or not good and if you have no special qualifications, you probably are setting yourself up for disappointment. You should seriously consider changing your mind about this decision. At least speak to people in your area who are knowledgeable about the occupation to determine whether you have any chance of success. If you answered "no"—you are not willing to take a chance—cross off this occupation and write a "G" next to it. (If you now have no jobs left on your Hot List, see the previous section titled "If Every Job on Your Hot List Is Now Crossed Off.")

Nature of the Work

When you read the job description for an occupation on your Hot List, you will see that the "Nature of the Work" section discusses what workers do on the job, what tools and equipment they use, and how closely they are supervised. Keep in mind that this is an overview of a diverse collection of workers, and in fact few workers perform the full set of tasks itemized here. In fact, in many cases the workforce covered by the job description is so diverse that it actually divides into several occupational specialties, which are italicized.

Here are some things to think about as you read this section:

★ Note the kinds of problems, materials, and tools you will encounter on the job. Are these a good match for your interests?

★ Also note the work activities mentioned here. Do you think they will be rewarding? Are there many that stand out as unpleasant or boring?

The "Work Environment" section identifies the typical hours worked, the workplace environment (both physical and psychological), physical activities and susceptibility to injury, special equipment, and the extent of travel required. If conditions vary between the occupational specialties, that is mentioned here. Here are some things to look for in the "Work Environment" section:

★ If you have a disability, note the physical requirements that are mentioned here and consider whether you can meet these requirements with or without suitable accommodations.

★ If you're bothered by conditions such as heights, stress, or a cramped workspace, see whether this section mentions any conditions that would discourage you.

★ Note what this section says about the work schedule and the need for travel, if any. This information may be good to know if you have pressing family responsibilities or, on the other hand, a desire for unusual hours or travel.

★ If you find a working condition that bothers you, be sure to check the wording to see whether it *always* applies to the occupation or whether it only *may* apply. Even if it seems to be a condition that you cannot avoid, find out for sure by talking to people in the occupation or educators who teach related courses. Maybe you can carve out a niche that avoids the unappealing working condition.

Training, Other Qualifications, and Advancement

In the "Training, Other Qualifications, and Advancement" section, you can see how to prepare for the occupation and how to advance in it. It identifies the significant entry routes—those that are most popular and that are preferred by employers. It mentions any licensure or certification that may be necessary for entry or advancement. It also identifies the particular skills, aptitudes, and work habits that employers value. Look for these topics in this section:

★ Compare the entry requirements to your background and to the educational and training opportunities that are available to you. Be sure to consider nontraditional and informal entry routes, if any are possible, as well as the formal routes. Ask yourself, Am I willing to get the additional education or training that will be necessary? Do I have the time, money, ability, interest, and commitment?

★ Maybe you're already partway down the road to job entry. In general, you should try to use your previous education, training, and work experience rather than abandon it. Look for specifics that are already on your resume—educational accomplishments, skills, work habits—that will meet employers' expectations. If you have some of these qualifications already, this occupation may be a better career choice than some others.

Employment

The "Employment" section in the job description reports how many jobs the occupation currently provides, the industries that provide the most jobs, and the number or proportion of self-employed or part-time workers in the occupation, if significant. In this section, you'll want to pay attention to these facts:

★ Note the industries that provide most of the employment for the occupation. This knowledge can help you identify contacts who can tell you more about the work, and later it can help in your job hunting.

★ If you're interested in self-employment or part-time work, see whether these work arrangements are mentioned here.

Job Outlook

The "Job Outlook" section describes the economic forces that will affect future employment in the occupation. Here are some things to look for in this section:

★ The information here can help you identify occupations with a good job outlook so that you will have a better-than-average chance of finding work. Be alert for any mention of an advantage that you may have over other job seekers (for example, a college degree) or any other factor that might make your chances better or worse.

★ If you are highly motivated and highly qualified for a particular occupation, don't be discouraged by a bad employment outlook. Job openings occur even in shrinking or overcrowded occupations, and with exceptional talent or good personal connections, you may go on to great success.

★ These projections are the most definitive ones available, but they are not foolproof and apply only to a 10-year time span. No matter what occupation you choose, you will need to adapt to changes.

Projections Data

This section of the job description shows a table with projected figures for employment growth. Here are some things to think about when you read this table:

★ Notice that the columns headed "Change 2008–2018" show both the number of workers (gained or lost) and a percentage figure. You need to consider both figures. For example, an occupation with a very small workforce will not create many job openings even though it may be growing fast.

★ For many occupations, this table features two or more rows showing the projections data for various career specializations. By comparing the figures on different rows, you may identify which specializations are expected to grow fastest and create the most job openings.

Earnings

The "Earnings" section discusses the wages for the occupation. Here are some things to keep in mind:

★ The wage figures are national averages. Actual wages in your geographic region may be considerably higher or lower. Also, an average figure means that half of the workers earn more and half earn less, and the actual salary any one worker earns can vary greatly from that average.

★ Remember to consider *all* the pluses and minuses of the job. Not every day of the work week is pay-day, so make your choice based on the whole occupation, not just the paycheck.

Related Occupations

The "Related Occupations" section identifies occupations that are similar to the one featured in the job description in terms of tasks, interests, skills, education, or training. You may find this section interesting for these reasons:

★ If you're interested in an occupation but not strongly committed to pursuing it, this section may suggest another occupation with similar rewards that may turn out to be a better fit. Try to research these related occupations, but keep in mind that they may not all be included in this book.

★ You may want to choose one of these occupations as your Plan B goal if your original goal should not work out. In that case, it helps to identify an occupation that involves similar kinds of problems and work settings but requires *less* education or training.

Sources of Additional Information

This section in each job description lists several sources and resources you can turn to for more information about the occupation. Try to consult at least some of these sources. This book should be only the beginning of your career decision-making process. You need more detailed information from several viewpoints to make an informed decision.

Don't rely entirely on the websites listed here. You especially need to talk to and observe individual workers to learn what their workdays are like, what the workers enjoy and dislike about the job, how they got hired, and what effects the job has had on other aspects of their lives. Maybe you can make contact with local workers through the local chapter of an organization listed here.

Narrowing Down Your Choices

The information in the job descriptions should help you cross more jobs off your Hot List. And what you learn by turning to other resources should help you narrow down your Hot List jobs to a few promising choices and maybe one best bet. Here are some final considerations: Have I talked to people who are actually doing this work? Am I fully aware of the pluses and minuses of this job? If there are aspects of the job that I don't like, how do I expect to avoid them or overcome them? If the odds of finding a job opening are not good, why do I expect to beat the odds? What is my Plan B goal if I lose interest in my original goal or don't succeed at it?

The Job-Match Grid

The grid on the following pages provides information about the personal skills and job characteristics for occupations covered in this book. Use the directions and questions that start at the beginning of this section to help you get the most from this grid.

The following is what the symbols on the grid represent. If a job has no symbol in a column, it means that the skill or job characteristic is not important or relevant to the job.

Personal Skills

- ● Essential or high-skill level
- ◐ Somewhat essential or moderate-skill level
- ○ Basic-skill level

Job Characteristics

- ● Highly likely
- ◐ Somewhat likely
- ○ A little likely

Job-Match Grid

	Artistic	Communication	Interpersonal	Managerial	Mathematics	Mechanical	Science	Economically Sensitive	Outdoor Work	Physically Demanding	Hazardous Conditions	Geographically Concentrated
Actors, Producers, and Directors	●	●	●	●		○	○	○	◐	○	○	●
Advertising Sales Agents	●	◐	●	◐	◐	○	○	●	◐	○		
Aircraft and Avionics Equipment Mechanics and Service Technicians	○	◐		○	◐	●	○	◐	◐	●	●	◐
Animal Care and Service Workers		○	○	◐	○	◐	◐	◐	●	◐	○	
Artists and Related Workers	●	●	◐	◐	◐	◐	◐	◐	○	○	○	
Assemblers and Fabricators			○	○	◐	○		○	○	◐	◐	
Athletes, Coaches, Umpires, and Related Workers	◐	◐	●	●	○	◐	◐		◐	●	○	
Automotive Body and Related Repairers	○			○	○	●	◐		◐	●	●	
Automotive Service Technicians and Mechanics		○	○	○	◐	●	◐		●	●	●	
Barbers, Cosmetologists, and Other Personal Appearance Workers	●		○	◐		○	●	◐			○	●
Bill and Account Collectors		◐	◐	●	◐	◐	○	◐				
Bookkeeping, Accounting, and Auditing Clerks		○	○	◐	◐	○	○	○				
Brickmasons, Blockmasons, and Stonemasons	◐		○	○	●	◐	◐	●	●	●	◐	
Building Cleaning Workers						◐	●	○	◐	◐	◐	
Carpenters	◐	○	○	●	●	●	◐	●	●	●	◐	
Carpet, Floor, and Tile Installers and Finishers	◐		○	◐	●	●	○	●	◐	●	◐	
Cashiers	○				○			◐		◐		
Cement Masons, Concrete Finishers, Segmental Pavers, and Terrazzo Workers	○		○		●	◐	○	●	●	●	◐	
Chefs, Head Cooks, and Food Preparation and Serving Supervisors	◐	○	○	◐	○	◐	◐	●	○	○	◐	
Child Care Workers	●	○	◐	○		○	○		◐	◐	○	
Claims Adjusters, Appraisers, Examiners, and Investigators		●	●	◐	◐		○		◐		○	
Clinical Laboratory Technologists and Technicians	◐	◐	○	○	◐	●	●			◐	●	
Computer Control Programmers and Operators			○	●	●	◐	◐	○	◐	●	◐	
Computer Network, Systems, and Database Administrators	◐	◐	◐	●	◐	●	◐	○	○		○	

(continued)

Personal Skills: ●—Essential or high-skill level; ◐—Somewhat essential or moderate-skill level; ○—Basic-skill level
Job Characteristics: ●—Highly likely; ◐—Somewhat likely; ○—A little likely

(continued)

	Personal Skills							Job Characteristics				
	Artistic	Communication	Interpersonal	Managerial	Mathematics	Mechanical	Science	Economically Sensitive	Outdoor Work	Physically Demanding Work	Hazardous Conditions	Geographically Concentrated
Computer Support Specialists	○	○	○			◐		○	○	○	○	
Computer, Automated Teller, and Office Machine Repairers	○	◐	◐	◐	◐	●	●		◐	○	◐	
Construction Equipment Operators				◐	◐	●	◐	●	●	◐	◐	
Construction Laborers					○	◐	○	●	●	●	◐	
Cooks and Food Preparation Workers	○			○		◐	○	●	○	◐	○	
Correctional Officers			◐							◐	●	◐
Customer Service Representatives	○	◐	◐	○	○	◐		○				
Dental Assistants	○	◐	◐	◐		●	◐			◐	●	
Dental Hygienists		●	◐			●	●			◐	●	
Desktop Publishers		◐			○	○		○	○		○	
Diesel Service Technicians and Mechanics			○	○		●	◐	◐	●	●	●	
Drafters	●	◐	◐	○	●	○	◐	◐	◐		○	
Drywall and Ceiling Tile Installers, Tapers, Plasterers, and Stucco Masons	◐	○	◐	●	●	●	●	●	◐	●	◐	
Electrical and Electronics Installers and Repairers	◐	○	○	○	●	●	●		●	●	●	
Electricians	○		○	◐	◐	●		●	●	●	●	
Emergency Medical Technicians and Paramedics	○		○	○					●	●	●	
Engineering Technicians	◐	◐	○	○	●	●	◐	○	◐	○	◐	
Farmers, Ranchers, and Agricultural Managers	○	○	◐	●	●	●	●	○	●	●	◐	●
Fire Fighters		◐	●	●	◐	●	◐		●	●	●	
Fitness Workers	◐	◐	◐	○		◐	●	◐	○	●		
Food and Beverage Serving and Related Workers	◐					○		●	○	◐	○	
Food Processing Occupations	○			○		◐	○		○	◐	◐	
Food Service Managers	○		◐	●		○		◐	◐	◐	◐	
Grounds Maintenance Workers	◐			○		●	○	○	●	●	●	
Heating, Air-conditioning, and Refrigeration Mechanics and Installers	○	◐	◐	◐	●	●	◐	◐	●	●	●	
Heavy Vehicle and Mobile Equipment Service Technicians and Mechanics			○	○	○	●	◐	●	●	●	●	
Home Health Aides and Personal and Home Care Aides	◐	○	◐			○	○			◐	●	
Industrial Machinery Mechanics and Millwrights	○		○	○	●	●	●	◐	●	●	●	○
Industrial Production Managers	○	○	◐	●	○			○	◐	○	●	
Inspectors, Testers, Sorters, Samplers, and Weighers		○			◐	◐	◐		◐	○	◐	
Insurance Sales Agents	○	●	●	●	●	○		◐	◐			
Library Technicians and Library Assistants	○	○				○			○	○	◐	
Licensed Practical and Licensed Vocational Nurses	○		○				◐			●	●	
Line Installers and Repairers	○	○	○	◐	◐	●	◐	○	●	●	●	

Personal Skills: ●—Essential or high-skill level; ◐—Somewhat essential or moderate-skill level; ○—Basic-skill level
Job Characteristics: ●—Highly likely; ◐—Somewhat likely; ○—A little likely

	Personal Skills							Job Characteristics				
	Artistic	Communication	Interpersonal	Managerial	Mathematics	Mechanical	Science	Economically Sensitive	Outdoor Work	Physically Demanding Work	Hazardous Conditions	Geographically Concentrated
Loan Officers		◐	●	○	○			◐	◐			
Machine Setters, Operators, and Tenders—Metal and Plastic					○	●	◐	○	○	●	●	
Machinists	◐				○	●		○	◐	●	◐	
Maintenance and Repair Workers, General	○		○	○	○	●	◐			●	●	●
Material Moving Occupations						◐	○	●	●	●	●	
Medical Assistants	○	○	○							◐	◐	
Medical Records and Health Information Technicians										◐	○	
Musicians, Singers, and Related Workers	●	○	◐	○		◐	○		○	○	○	○
Nursing and Psychiatric Aides	○									●	◐	
Office Clerks, General		○			○			◐		○		
Painters and Paperhangers	◐			◐	◐	●	○	●	●	●	●	
Painting and Coating Workers, except Construction and Maintenance	◐			○	○	●	◐	○	●	●	●	
Paralegals and Legal Assistants	○	◐		○	○			○	○			
Pharmacy Technicians and Aides		◐			◐	○	◐			◐	◐	
Photographers	●	○	◐	◐	○	○	●	◐	◐	○		
Plumbers, Pipelayers, Pipefitters, and Steamfitters	○		○	○	○	●	○	○	●	●	●	
Police and Detectives		◐	●	○	○	○	○		●	●	●	
Postal Service Mail Carriers										●	◐	○
Printing Machine Operators	○				◐	●	◐	◐	○	●	●	
Purchasing Managers, Buyers, and Purchasing Agents		◐	◐	●	◐	◐	○	○	◐	○		
Radio and Telecommunications Equipment Installers and Repairers	○	○	◐	◐	◐	●	◐	○	●	●	●	◐
Radiologic Technologists and Technicians	○	◐	○		○		◐			●	◐	
Real Estate Brokers and Sales Agents	○	◐	●	◐			○	●	●	○	○	
Receptionists and Information Clerks		◐	○	○	○	○	○	○		○		
Recreation Workers	●	●	●	●	○	○	◐	◐	●		◐	
Registered Nurses	◐	○	◐	◐	○		◐			●	●	
Retail Salespersons	○	○			○			●	●	●	○	
Roofers			◐	◐	●	●	◐	○	●	●	●	
Sales Representatives, Wholesale and Manufacturing		◐	●	●	◐	○	◐	●	●	○	○	
Sales Worker Supervisors	○	◐	◐	●	◐	◐	○	◐	◐	◐	○	
Science Technicians	○	◐	○	◐	●	●	●	◐	◐	◐	●	
Secretaries and Administrative Assistants		◐	○	○	○			○	○		○	
Security Guards and Gaming Surveillance Officers	○							○	●	●	●	◐
Sheet Metal Workers	○	○	○			●	●	●	●	●	◐	
Shipping, Receiving, and Traffic Clerks		◐	○	◐	●	○	◐	○	●	●	○	
Social and Human Service Assistants	○	○	◐	○						◐	◐	

(continued)

Personal Skills: ●—Essential or high-skill level; ◐—Somewhat essential or moderate-skill level; ○—Basic-skill level
Job Characteristics: ●—Highly likely; ◐—Somewhat likely; ○—A little likely

© JIST Works

(continued)

	Personal Skills							Job Characteristics				
	Artistic	Communication	Interpersonal	Managerial	Mathematics	Mechanical	Science	Economically Sensitive	Outdoor Work	Physically Demanding Work	Hazardous Conditions	Geographically Concentrated
Surveyors, Cartographers, Photogrammetrists, and Surveying and Mapping Technicians	◉	○		○	◉	◉	○	◉	●	◉	○	
Teacher Assistants	◉	◉	◉		◉		◉		○	○		
Teachers—Preschool, Except Special Education	●	○	◉	○		○	◉		◉	◉		
Teachers—Self-Enrichment Education	●	◉	◉	○		○	○		○	◉		
Welding, Soldering, and Brazing Workers					○	◉	◉	○	○	◉	◉	
Woodworkers	◉				○	◉		●	◉	●	◉	

Descriptions of the Top 100 Careers Without a Four-Year Degree

This is the book's main section. It contains helpful descriptions of the 100 major occupations that don't require a four-year college degree.

The jobs are arranged in alphabetical order. Refer to the table of contents for a list of the jobs and the page numbers where their descriptions begin. Review the table of contents to discover occupations that interest you and then find out more about them in this section. If you are interested in medical careers, for example, you can go through the list and quickly pinpoint those you want to learn more about. Or use the assessment in Part I to identify several possible career matches.

While the job descriptions in this part are easy to understand, the introduction provides additional information for interpreting them. Keep in mind that the descriptions present information that is average for the country. Conditions in your area and with specific employers may be quite different.

Also, you may come across jobs that sound interesting but require more education and training than you have or are considering. Don't eliminate them too soon. There are many ways to obtain education and training, and most people change careers many times. You probably have more skills than you realize that can transfer to new jobs. People often have more opportunities than barriers. Use the descriptions to learn more about possible jobs and look into the suggested resources to help you take the next step.

Actors, Producers, and Directors

(O*NET 27-2011.00, 27-2012.00, 27-2012.01, 27-2012.02, 27-2012.03, 27-2012.04, and 27-2012.05)

Significant Points

■ Actors endure long periods of unemployment, intense competition for roles, and frequent rejections in auditions.

■ Formal training through a university or acting conservatory is typical; however, many actors, producers, and directors find work on the basis of their experience and talent alone.

■ Because earnings may be erratic, many actors, producers, and directors supplement their incomes by holding jobs in other fields.

Nature of the Work

Actors, producers, and directors express ideas and create images in theater, film, radio, television, and other performing arts media. They interpret a writer's script to entertain, inform, or instruct an audience. Although many actors, producers, and directors work in New York or Los Angeles, far more work in other places. They perform, direct, and produce in local or regional television studios, theaters, or film production companies, often creating advertising or training films or small-scale independent movies.

Actors perform in stage, radio, television, video, or motion picture productions. They also work in cabarets, nightclubs, and theme parks. Actors portray characters, and, for more complex roles, they research their character's traits and circumstances so that they can better understand a script.

Most actors struggle to find steady work and only a few achieve recognition as stars. Others work as "*extras*," with no lines to deliver. Some actors do voiceover and narration work for advertisements, animated features, books on tape, and other electronic media. They also teach in high school or university drama departments, acting conservatories, or public programs.

Producers are entrepreneurs who make the business and financial decisions involving a motion picture, television show, or stage production. They select scripts, approve the development of ideas, arrange financing, and determine the size and cost of the endeavor. Producers hire or approve directors, principal cast members, and key production staff members.

Large productions often have associate, assistant, or line producers who share responsibilities. The number of producers and their specific job duties vary with the size and budget of each production; however, all work is done under the overall direction of an executive producer. Together the producers coordinate the activities of writers, directors, managers, and agents to ensure that each project stays on schedule and within budget.

Directors are responsible for the overall creative decisions of a production. They interpret scripts, audition and select cast members, conduct rehearsals, and direct the work of cast and crew. They approve the design elements of a production, including the sets, costumes, choreography, and music. As with producers, large productions often have many levels of directors working on them. Assistant directors cue the performers and technicians, telling them when to make entrances or light, sound, or set changes. All directors must ultimately answer to the executive producer, who has the final say on all factors related to the production.

Work environment. Actors, producers, and directors work under constant pressure. Many face stress from the continual need to find their next job. To succeed, actors, producers, and directors need patience and commitment to their craft. Actors strive to deliver flawless performances, often while working under undesirable and unpleasant conditions. Producers and directors organize rehearsals and meet with writers, designers, financial backers, and production technicians. They experience stress not only from these activities, but also from the need to adhere to budgets, union work rules, and production schedules.

Work assignments typically are short term—ranging from one day to a few months—which means that workers frequently experience long periods of unemployment between jobs. The uncertain nature of the work results in unpredictable earnings and intense competition for jobs. Often, actors, producers, and directors must hold other jobs in order to sustain a living.

Work hours are often long and irregular—evening and weekend work is a regular part of life in the performing arts. Actors, producers, and directors who work in theater may travel with a touring show across the country, whereas those who work in film may work on location, sometimes under adverse weather conditions. Actors who perform in a television series often appear on camera with little preparation time, because scripts tend to be revised frequently or even written moments before taping. Those who appear live or before a studio audience must be able to handle impromptu situations and calmly ad lib, or substitute, lines when necessary.

Actors should be in good physical condition and have the necessary stamina and coordination to move about theater stages and large movie and television studio lots. They also need to maneuver about complex technical sets while staying in character and projecting their voices audibly. Actors must be fit to endure heat from stage or studio lights and the weight of heavy costumes. Producers and directors ensure the safety of actors by conducting extra rehearsals on the set so that the actors can learn the layout of set pieces and props, by allowing time for warm-ups and stretching exercises to guard against physical and vocal injuries, and by providing an adequate number of breaks to prevent heat exhaustion and dehydration.

Training, Other Qualifications, and Advancement

People who become actors, producers, and directors follow many paths to employment. The most important qualities employers look for are creative instincts, innate talent, and the intellectual capacity to perform. The best way to prepare for a career as an actor, especially in the theater, is through formal dramatic training, preferably obtained as part of a bachelor's degree program. Producers and especially directors need experience in the field, either as actors or in other related jobs.

Education and training. Formal dramatic training, either through an acting conservatory or a university program, generally is necessary for these jobs, but some people successfully enter the field without it. Most people studying for a bachelor's degree take courses in radio and television broadcasting, communications, film, theater, drama, or dramatic literature. Many stage actors continue their academic training and receive a Master of Fine Arts (MFA) degree. Advanced curricula may include courses in stage speech and movement, directing, playwriting, and design, as well as intensive acting workshops. The National Association of Schools of Theatre accredits more than 150 programs in theater arts.

Most aspiring actors participate in high school and college plays, work at college radio or television stations, or perform with local community theater groups. Local and regional theater experience may also help many young actors hone their skills. In television and film, actors and directors typically start in smaller roles or independent movie production companies and then work their way up to larger productions. Actors, regardless of their level of experience, may pursue workshop training through acting conservatories or mentoring by a drama coach.

There are no specific training requirements for producers. They come from many different backgrounds. Actors, writers, film editors, and business managers commonly enter the field. Producers often start in a theatrical management office, working for a press agent, managing director, or business manager. Some start in a performing arts union or service organization. Others work behind the scenes with successful directors, serve on the boards of art companies, or promote their own projects. Although there are no formal training programs for producers, a number of colleges and universities offer degree programs in arts management and in managing nonprofit organizations.

Some directors have experience as actors or writers, while others gain experience in the field by assisting established directors. Many also have formal training in directing.

Other qualifications. Actors need talent and creativity that will enable them to portray different characters. Because competition for parts is fierce, versatility and a wide range of related performance skills, such as singing, dancing, skating, juggling, acrobatics, or miming, are especially useful. Actors must have poise, stage presence, the ability to affect an audience, and the ability to follow direction. Modeling experience also may be helpful. Physical appearance, such as having certain features and being the specified size and weight, often is a deciding factor in who gets a particular role.

Some actors begin as movie extras. To become an extra, one usually must be listed by casting agencies that supply extras to the major movie studios in Hollywood. Applicants are accepted only when the number of people of a particular type on the list—for example, athletic young women, old men, or small children—falls below what is needed. In recent years, only a very small proportion of applicants have succeeded in being listed.

Like actors, directors and producers need talent and creativity. Directors need management ability because they are often in charge of a large number of people in a production. Producers need business acumen.

Advancement. As the reputations and box-office draw of actors, producers, and directors grow, some of them work on bigger-budget productions, on network or syndicated broadcasts, in more prestigious theaters, or in larger markets. Actors may advance to lead roles and receive star billing. A few actors move into acting-related jobs, becoming drama coaches, directors, or producers. Some actors teach drama privately or in colleges and universities.

Employment

In 2008, actors, producers, and directors held about 155,100 jobs, primarily in the motion picture and video, performing arts, and broadcast industries. This statistic does not capture a large number of actors, producers, and directors who were available for work but were between jobs during the month in which data were collected. About 21 percent of actors, producers, and directors were self-employed.

Employment in motion pictures and in films for television is centered in New York and Los Angeles. However, small studios exist throughout the country. Many films are shot on location and may employ local professional and nonprofessional actors. In television, opportunities are concentrated in the network centers of New York and Los Angeles, but cable television services and local television stations around the country also employ many actors, producers, and directors.

Employment in the theater, and in other performing arts companies, is cyclical—higher in the fall and spring seasons—and concentrated in New York and other major cities with large commercial houses for musicals and touring productions. Also, many cities support established professional regional theaters that operate on a seasonal or year-round basis.

Actors, producers, and directors may find work in summer festivals, on cruise lines, and in theme parks. Many smaller, nonprofit professional companies, such as repertory companies, dinner theaters, and theaters affiliated with drama schools, acting conservatories, and universities, provide employment opportunities for local amateur talent and professional entertainers. Auditions typically are held in New York for many productions across the country and for shows that go on the road.

Job Outlook

Employment is expected to grow as fast as the average for all occupations. Competition for jobs will be keen. Although a growing number of people aspire to enter these professions, many will leave the field early because the work—when it is available—is hard, the hours are long, and the pay is often low.

Employment change. Employment in these occupations is expected to grow 11 percent during the 2008–2018 decade, about as fast as the average for all occupations. Expanding cable and satellite television operations and increasing box-office receipts of major studio and independent films will increase the need for workers. Additionally, a rising demand for U.S. films in other countries should create more employment opportunities for actors, producers, and directors. Also fueling job growth is the continued development of interactive media, online movies, and mobile content produced for cell phones or other portable electronic devices. Attendance at live theater performances should continue to be steady and drive employment of stage actors, producers, and directors. However, station consolidation may restrict employment opportunities in the broadcasting industry for producers and directors.

Job prospects. Competition for acting jobs is intense, as the number of actors auditioning for roles greatly exceeds the number of parts that become available. Only performers with the most stamina and talent will find regular employment.

Venues for live entertainment, such as theaters, touring productions, and repertory theaters in many major metropolitan areas, as well as theme parks and resorts, are expected to offer many job opportunities. However, prospects in these venues are variable because they fluctuate with economic conditions.

Projections Data from the National Employment Matrix

Occupational title	SOC Code	Employment, 2008	Projected employment, 2018	Change, 2008–2018	
				Number	Percent
Actors, producers, and directors............................27-2010		155,100	172,000	16,900	11
Actors..27-2011		56,500	63,700	7,200	13
Producers and directors 27-2012		98,600	108,300	9,700	10

NOTE: Data in this table are rounded.

Earnings

Many of the most successful actors, producers, and directors have extraordinarily high earnings, but many more of these professionals, faced with erratic earnings, supplement their income by holding jobs in other fields.

Median hourly wages of actors were $16.20 in May 2009. The middle 50 percent earned between $10.18 and $29.33. Median hourly wages were $14.05 in performing arts companies and $27.17 in the motion picture and video industry. Annual wage data for actors were not available because of the wide variation in the number of hours worked by actors and the short-term nature of many jobs, which may last for one day or one week; it is extremely rare for actors to have guaranteed employment that exceeds three to six months.

Median annual wages of producers and directors were $66,720 in 2009. The middle 50 percent earned between $42,890 and $111,250. Median annual wages were $93,630 in the motion picture and video industry and $55,810 in radio and television broadcasting.

Minimum salaries, hours of work, and other conditions of employment are often covered in collective bargaining agreements between the producers and the unions representing workers. While these unions generally determine minimum salaries, any actor or director may negotiate for a salary higher than the minimum.

A joint agreement between the Screen Actors Guild (SAG) and the American Federation of Television and Radio Artists (AFTRA) guarantees all unionized motion picture and television actors with speaking parts a minimum daily rate of $782 or $2,713 for a five-day week as of June 2009. Actors also receive contributions to their health and pension plans and additional compensation for reruns and foreign telecasts of the productions in which they appear.

Some well-known actors earn well above the minimum; their salaries are many times the figures cited here, creating the false impression that all actors are highly paid. For example, of the nearly 100,000 SAG members, only about 50 might fall into this category. The average income that SAG members earn from acting is low because employment is sporadic and most actors must supplement their incomes by holding jobs in other occupations.

Actors Equity Association (AEA), which represents stage actors, has negotiated minimum weekly salary requirements for their members. Salaries vary depending on the theater or venue the actor is employed in. Many stage directors belong to the Society of Stage Directors and Choreographers (SSDC), and most film and television directors belong to the Directors Guild of America. Earnings of stage directors vary greatly. The SSDC usually negotiates salary contracts, which include royalties (additional income based on the number of performances), with smaller theaters. Regional theaters may hire directors for longer periods, increasing compensation accordingly. The highest-paid directors work on Broadway; in addition to their contract fee, they also receive payment in the form of royalties—a negotiated percentage of gross box-office receipts—that can exceed the contract fee for long-running box-office successes.

Stage producers seldom receive a set fee; instead, they get a percentage of a show's earnings or ticket sales.

Related Occupations

Other performing artists who may need acting skills include announcers; dancers and choreographers; and musicians, singers, and related workers.

Others whose jobs are related to film and theater include fashion designers; makeup artists, theatrical and performance; and set and exhibit designers.

Producers share many responsibilities with top executives.

Sources of Additional Information

For general information about theater arts and a list of accredited college-level programs, contact

▸ National Association of Schools of Theater, 11250 Roger Bacon Dr., Suite 21, Reston, VA 20190. Internet: http://nast.arts-accredit.org

For general information on actors, producers, and directors, contact the following organizations:

▸ Actors' Equity Association, 165 W. 46th St., New York, NY 10036. Internet: www.actorsequity.org

▸ Screen Actors Guild, 5757 Wilshire Blvd., 7th Floor, Los Angeles, CA 90036-3600. Internet: www.sag.org

▸ Producers Guild of America. Internet: www.producersguild.org

Advertising Sales Agents

(O*NET 41-3011.00)

Significant Points

■ Applicants who have sales experience and a college degree should have the best opportunities, but keen competition for jobs is expected during downturns in spending on advertising.

■ Educational requirements vary; the ability to communicate effectively and persuasively is important for entry-level candidates.

■ Performance-based pay, including bonuses and commissions, can make up a large portion of an advertising sales agent's earnings.

■ Pressure to meet monthly sales quotas can be stressful.

Nature of the Work

Advertising sales agents—often referred to as *account executives* or *advertising sales representatives*—sell or solicit advertising primarily for newspapers and periodicals, television and radio, websites, telephone directories, and direct mail and outdoor advertisers. Because such a large share of revenue for many of these media outlets is generated from advertising, advertising sales agents play an important role in their success.

More than half of all advertising sales agents work in the information sector, mostly for media firms, including television and radio broadcasters, print and Internet publishers, and cable program distributors. Firms that are regionally based often need the help of two types of advertising sales agents, one to handle local clients and one to solicit advertising from national advertisers. Print publications and radio and television stations employ local sales agents, who are responsible for sales in an immediate territory, while separate companies known as media representative firms sell advertising space or time for media owners at the national level. Sales agents employed in media representation work exclusively through executives at advertising agencies, called media buyers, who purchase advertising space for their clients who want to initiate national advertising campaigns. When a local television broadcaster, radio station, newspaper, or online publisher is working with a media representative firm, the media company normally employs a national sales manager to coordinate efforts with the media representative.

Most advertising sales agents work outside the office occasionally, calling on clients and prospective clients at their places of business. These agents may have an appointment, or they may practice cold calling—arriving without an appointment. Obtaining new accounts is an important part of the job, and they may spend much of their time traveling to and visiting prospective advertisers and current clients. Sales agents also may work on their employer's premises and handle sales for customers who walk in or telephone the firm to inquire about advertising. Some may make telephone sales calls as well—calling prospects, attempting to sell the media firm's advertising space or time, and arranging follow-up appointments between interested prospects and sales agents.

A critical part of building relationships with clients is learning about their needs. Before the first meeting with a client, a sales agent gathers background information on the client's products, current customers, prospective customers, and the geographic area of the target market. The sales agent then meets with the client to explain how specific types of advertising will help promote the client's products or services most effectively. If a client wishes to proceed, the advertising sales agent prepares an advertising proposal to present to the client. Preparation of the proposal entails determining the advertising medium to be used, preparing sample advertisements, and providing the client with cost estimates for the project. Because consolidation among media industries has brought the sales of different types of advertising under one roof, advertising sales increasingly are in the form of integrated packages. This means that advertising sales agents may sell packages that include print and online ad space and time slots with a broadcast subsidiary. Technological innovations also have created more products to sell, meaning that a local television sales agent might sell ad space on a station's website and mobile service in addition to selling commercials.

After a contract has been established, advertising sales agents serve as the main contact between the advertiser or ad agency and the media firm. They handle communication between the parties and

assist in developing sample artwork or radio and television spots if needed. For radio and television advertisements, they also may arrange for commercial taping sessions and accompany clients to the sessions.

In addition to maintaining sales and overseeing clients' accounts, advertising sales agents' other duties include analyzing sales statistics and audience demographics, preparing reports on clients' accounts, and scheduling and keeping appointments and work hours. They read about new and existing products and monitor the sales, prices, and products of their competitors. In many firms, the advertising sales agent handles the drafting of contracts specifying the advertising work to be performed and its cost and may undertake customer service responsibilities such as answering questions or addressing any problems the client may have with the proposal. Sales agents also are responsible for developing sales tools, promotional plans, and media kits, which they use to help make a sale.

Work environment. Selling can be stressful because income and job security depend directly on the agent's ability to maintain and expand his or her clientele. Companies generally set monthly sales quotas and place considerable pressure on advertising sales agents to meet those quotas. The added stress of rejection places more pressure on the agent.

Although most agents work long and often irregular hours, some have the freedom to determine their own schedules. The Internet and other electronic tools allow agents to do more work from home or while on the road, enabling them to send messages and documents to clients and coworkers, keep up with industry news, and access databases that help them target potential customers. Advertising sales agents use e-mail to conduct much of the business with their clients.

Many advertising sales agents work more than 40 hours per week, frequently involving irregular hours and work on weekends and holidays. However, many advertising sales agents are able to set their own schedules. Ten percent of advertising sales agents were employed part time in 2008.

Training, Other Qualifications, and Advancement

For sales positions that require meeting clients, large employers prefer applicants with a college degree. Smaller companies generally are more willing to hire individuals with a high school degree. Successful sales experience and the ability to communicate effectively become more important than educational attainment once the candidate is hired. Most training for advertising sales agents takes place informally on the job.

Education and training. Although a high school diploma may be sufficient for an entry-level advertising sales position, some employers prefer applicants with a college degree, particularly for sales positions that require meeting clients. Courses in marketing, leadership, communication, business, and advertising are helpful. For those who have a proven record of successfully selling other products, educational requirements are not likely to be strict.

Most training, however, takes place on the job and can be formal or informal in nature. In most cases, an experienced sales manager instructs a newly hired advertising sales agent who lacks sales experience. In this one-on-one environment, supervisors typically coach new hires and observe them as they make sales calls and contact clients. Supervisors then advise the new hires on ways to improve their interaction with clients. Employers may bring in consultants to lead formal training sessions when agents sell to a specialized market segment, such as automotive dealers or real estate professionals.

Other qualifications. Employers look for applicants who are honest and who possess a pleasant personality and neat professional appearance. After gaining entry into the occupation, the advertising sales agent will find that successful sales experience and the ability to communicate effectively become more important than educational attainment. In fact, when the agent is selling or soliciting ad space, personality traits are equally, if not more, important than one's academic background. In general, smaller companies are more willing to hire unproven individuals.

Because they represent their employers to the executives of client organizations, advertising sales agents must have excellent interpersonal and written communication skills. Being multilingual, particularly in English and Spanish, is another skill that will benefit prospective advertising agents as media increasingly seek to market to Hispanics and foreign-born persons. Self-motivation, organization, persistence, independence, and the ability to multitask are required because advertising sales agents set their own schedules and perform their duties without much supervision. Creativity also is an invaluable trait for advertising sales agents, who must come up with new ways to attract clients and to serve existing ones.

Advancement. Advancement in the occupation means taking on bigger, more lucrative clients. Agents with proven leadership ability and a strong sales record may advance to supervisory and managerial positions, such as sales supervisor, sales manager, or vice president of sales. Frequent contact with managers of other departments and people in other firms provides sales agents with leads about job openings, enhancing their advancement opportunities. Successful advertising sales agents also may advance to positions in other industries, such as corporate sales. In small firms, where the number of supervisory and management positions is limited, advancement may come slowly. Promotion may occur more quickly in larger media firms and in media representative firms.

Employment

Advertising sales agents held about 166,800 jobs in 2008. Workers were concentrated in three industries: 33 percent were in advertising, public relations, and related services; about 32 percent were employed in newspaper, periodical, book, and directory publishers; and 17 percent were in radio and television broadcasting. Media representative firms are in the advertising and related services industry. A relatively small number of jobs were found in cable and other program distribution.

Employment is spread around the country, but jobs in radio and television stations and large, well-known publications are concentrated in metropolitan areas. Media representative firms also are concentrated in large cities with many advertising agencies, such as New York City.

Job Outlook

Employment is projected to increase about as fast as average. Growth in new media outlets, such as the Internet, will be partially offset by a decline in print media. Applicants who have sales experience and a college degree should have the best opportunities, but keen competition for jobs is expected during downturns in advertising spending.

Employment change. Employment of advertising sales agents is expected to increase by 7 percent from 2008 to 2018, about as fast as the average for all occupations. Fast growth in the number of cable channels, online advertisers, and other advertising media will create many new opportunities for advertisers. This growth will be partially offset by the decline in print media, which will decrease the demand for advertising sales agents in these industries.

Advertising as an industry is expected to grow over the 2008–2018 period. Changes in technology will create new and more efficient ways for advertisers to reach customers, which will increase the need for advertising sales agents. Growth should be particularly high in online advertising sales, in cable television, and for consolidated media firms.

At the same time, the industries employing large shares of advertising sales agents, particularly the newspaper, periodical, and directory publishing industries, have suffered significant declines in recent years. As a result, there are likely to be fewer opportunities for advertising sales agents within these areas compared to other industries over the next decade.

Although advances in technology have made advertising sales agents more productive, allowing agents to take on additional duties and improve the quality of the services they provide, technological advances have not substantially decreased overall demand for these workers. Productivity gains have had the largest effect on the miscellaneous services that these workers provide, such as accounting, the formulation of proposals, and customer service duties, allowing them to provide faster, improved services to their clients. For example, the use of e-mail has considerably shortened the time it takes to negotiate a sale and place an ad. Sales agents may accomplish more in less time, but many work more hours than in the past, spending additional time on follow-up and service calls. Thus, although productivity gains will temper the growth of advertising sales agents, who can now manage more accounts, the increasing growth in advertising across all industries will ensure that new advertising sales agents will continue to be needed in the future.

Job prospects. Applicants who have sales experience and a college degree should have the best opportunities. For those with a proven sales record in advertising sales, opportunities should be excellent. In addition to the job openings generated by employment growth, openings will occur each year because of the need to replace sales representatives who transfer to other occupations or leave the labor force. Each year, many advertising sales agents discover that they are unable to earn enough money; as a result, they leave the occupation. Advertising revenues are sensitive to economic downturns, which cause the industries and companies that advertise to reduce both the frequency of campaigns and the overall level of spending on advertising. Advertising sales agents must work hard to get the most out of every dollar spent on advertising under these conditions. Therefore, the number of opportunities for advertising sales agents fluctuates with the business cycle. Applicants can expect keen competition for job openings during downturns in advertising spending.

Earnings

Including commissions, median annual wages for all advertising sales agents were $43,360 per year in May 2009. The middle 50 percent earned between $30,550 and $64,500 a year. The lowest 10 percent earned less than $22,610, and the highest 10 percent earned more than $94,100 a year. Median annual wages for sales agents in the industries in which they were concentrated were as follows:

Projections Data from the National Employment Matrix

Occupational title	SOC Code	Employment, 2008	Projected employment, 2018	Change, 2008–2018	
				Number	Percent
Advertising sales agents 41-3011		166,800	178,900	12,100	7

NOTE: Data in this table are rounded.

Motion picture and video industries	$62,030
Cable and other subscription programming	46,270
Advertising, public relations, and related services	47,870
Radio and television broadcasting	41,820
Newspaper, periodical, book, and directory publishers	37,810

Performance-based pay, including bonuses and commissions, can make up a large portion of an advertising sales agent's earnings. Most employers pay some combination of salaries, commissions, and bonuses. Commissions are usually based on individual sales numbers, whereas bonuses may depend on individual performance, on the performance of all sales workers in a group or district, or on the performance of the entire company. For agents covering multiple areas or regions, commissions also may be based on the difficulty in making a sale in that particular area. Sales revenue is affected by the economic conditions and business expectations facing the industries that tend to advertise. Earnings from commissions are likely to be high when these industries are doing well and low when companies decide not to advertise as frequently.

In addition to their earnings, advertising sales agents are usually reimbursed for entertaining clients and for other business expenses, such as the costs of transportation, meals, and hotel stays. They often receive benefits such as health and life insurance, pension plans, vacation and sick leave, personal use of a company car, and frequent-flier mileage. Some companies offer incentives such as free vacation trips or gifts for outstanding sales workers.

Related Occupations

Advertising sales agents market services to clients in order to increase sales revenue. Other workers with similar duties include advertising, marketing, promotions, public relations, and sales managers; insurance sales agents; real estate brokers and sales agents; sales engineers; sales representatives, wholesale and manufacturing; and securities, commodities, and financial services sales agents.

Sources of Additional Information

To learn about opportunities for employment as an advertising sales agent, contact local broadcasters, radio stations, and publishers for advertising sales representative positions or look for media representative firms in your area.

For information about advertising sales careers in newspaper publishing, contact

▸ The Newspaper Association of America, 4401 Wilson Blvd., Suite 900, Arlington, VA 22203. Internet: www.naa.org

Aircraft and Avionics Equipment Mechanics and Service Technicians

(O*NET 49-2091.00 and 49-3011.00)

Significant Points

■ Most workers learn their jobs in one of about 170 schools certified by the Federal Aviation Administration (FAA).

■ Job opportunities should be favorable for persons who have completed an aircraft mechanic training program, but keen competition is likely for jobs at major airlines, which offer the best pay and benefits.

■ Job opportunities are likely to continue to be best at small commuter and regional airlines, at FAA repair stations, and in general aviation.

Nature of the Work

Today's airplanes are highly complex machines with parts that must function within extreme tolerances for them to operate safely. To keep aircraft in peak operating condition, *aircraft and avionics equipment mechanics and service technicians* perform scheduled maintenance, make repairs, and complete inspections required by the FAA.

Many aircraft mechanics specialize in preventive maintenance. They inspect aircraft engines, landing gear, instruments, pressurized sections, accessories—brakes, valves, pumps, and air-conditioning systems, for example—and other parts of the aircraft and do the necessary maintenance and replacement of parts. They also keep records related to the maintenance performed on the aircraft. Mechanics and technicians conduct inspections following a schedule based on the number of hours the aircraft has flown, calendar days since the last inspection, cycles of operation, or a combination of these factors. In large, sophisticated planes equipped with aircraft monitoring systems, mechanics can gather valuable diagnostic information from electronic boxes and consoles that monitor the aircraft's basic operations. In planes of all sorts, aircraft mechanics examine engines by working through specially designed openings while standing on ladders or scaffolds or by using hoists or lifts to remove the entire engine from the craft. After taking an engine apart, mechanics use precision instruments to measure parts for wear and use X-ray and magnetic inspection equipment to check for invisible cracks. They repair or replace worn or defective parts. Mechanics also may repair sheet metal or composite surfaces; measure the tension of control cables; and check for corrosion, distortion, and cracks in the fuselage, wings, and tail. After completing all repairs, they must test the equipment to ensure that it works properly.

Other mechanics specialize in repair work rather than inspection. They find and fix problems that pilots describe. For example, during a preflight check, a pilot may discover that the aircraft's fuel gauge does not work. To solve the problem, mechanics may troubleshoot the electrical system, using electrical test equipment to make sure that no wires are broken or shorted out, and replace any defective electrical or electronic components. Mechanics work as fast as safety permits so that the aircraft can be put back into service quickly.

Some mechanics work on one or many different types of aircraft, such as jets, propeller-driven airplanes, and helicopters. Others specialize in one section of a particular type of aircraft, such as the engine, hydraulics, or electrical system. In small, independent repair shops, mechanics usually inspect and repair many different types of aircraft.

Airframe mechanics are authorized to work on any part of the aircraft except the instruments, power plants, and propellers. *Powerplant mechanics* are authorized to work on engines and do limited work on propellers. Combination airframe-and-powerplant mechanics—called *A&P mechanics*—work on all parts of the plane except the instruments. Most mechanics working on civilian aircraft today are A&P mechanics.

Avionics systems—components used for aircraft navigation and radio communications, weather radar systems, and other instruments and computers that control flight, engine, and other primary functions—are now an integral part of aircraft design and have vastly increased aircraft capability. *Avionics technicians* repair and maintain these systems. Because of the increasing use of technology, more time is spent repairing electronic systems, such as computerized controls. Technicians also may be required to analyze and develop solutions to complex electronic problems.

Work environment. Mechanics work in hangars, repair stations, or out on the airfield on the "flight lines" where aircraft park. Mechanics often work under time pressure to maintain flight schedules or, in general aviation, to keep from inconveniencing customers. At the same time, mechanics have a tremendous responsibility to maintain safety standards, and this can cause the job to be stressful.

Frequently, mechanics must lift or pull objects weighing more than 70 pounds. They often stand, lie, or kneel in awkward positions and occasionally must work in precarious positions, such as on scaffolds or ladders. Noise and vibration are common when engines are being tested, so ear protection is necessary. According to BLS data, full-time aircraft mechanics and service technicians experienced a higher than average work-related injury and illness rate. Aircraft mechanics usually work 40 hours a week on 8-hour shifts around the clock. Overtime and weekend work is frequent.

Training, Other Qualifications, and Advancement

Most mechanics who work on civilian aircraft are certified by the FAA, which requires mechanics to be at least 18 years of age, fluent in English, and have a high school diploma or its equivalent in addition to having the needed technical skills. Most mechanics learn their skills in an FAA-certified Aviation Maintenance Technician School.

Education and training. Although a few people become mechanics through on-the-job training, most learn the skills needed to do their jobs in 1 of about 170 Aviation Maintenance Technician schools certified by the FAA. By law, FAA standards require that certified mechanic schools offer students a minimum of 1,900 class-hours. Coursework in schools normally lasts from 12 to 24 months and provides training with the tools and equipment used on the job. About one-third of these schools award 2-year and 4-year degrees in avionics, aviation technology, or aviation maintenance management.

Aircraft trade schools are placing more emphasis on technologies such as turbine engines, composite materials, and aviation electronics, which are increasingly being used in the construction of new aircraft. Technological advances have also affected aircraft maintenance, meaning mechanics must have an especially strong background in computers and electronics to get or keep jobs in this field.

Courses in mathematics, physics, chemistry, electronics, computer science, and mechanical drawing are helpful because they demonstrate many of the principles involved in the operation of aircraft, and knowledge of these principles is often necessary to make repairs. Courses that develop writing skills also are important because mechanics are often required to submit reports. Mechanics must be able to read, write, and understand English.

A few mechanics are trained on the job by experienced mechanics. Their work must be supervised and documented by certified mechanics until they have FAA certificates.

Licensure. The FAA requires that all maintenance work on aircraft be performed by certified mechanics or under the supervision of a certified mechanic. As a result, most airlines hire mechanics that have FAA certification. The FAA offers certification for airframe mechanics and powerplant mechanics, although most airlines prefer to hire mechanics with a combined A&P certificate.

Mechanics need at least 18 months of work experience before applying for an airframe or powerplant certificate, and 30 months of experience working with both engines and airframes for a combined A&P certificate, although completion of a program at an FAA-certified school can be substituted for these work experience requirements.

In addition to having experience or formal training, applicants for all certificates must pass written, oral, and practical tests that demonstrate that they can do the work authorized by the certificate. Written tests are administered at one of the many designated computer testing facilities worldwide, while the oral and practical tests are administered by a Designated Mechanic Examiner of the FAA. All tests must be passed within a 24- month period to receive certification.

FAA regulations require current work experience to keep certificates valid. Applicants must have at least 1,000 hours of work experience in the previous 24 months or take a refresher course. Mechanics also must take at least 16 hours of training every 24 months to keep their certificates current. Many mechanics take training courses offered by manufacturers or employers, usually through outside contractors.

The FAA allows certified airframe mechanics who are trained and qualified and who have the proper tools to work on avionics equipment. However, avionics technicians are not required to have FAA certification if they have avionics repair experience from the military or from working for avionics manufacturers. Avionics technicians who work on communications equipment must obtain a restricted radio-telephone operator license from the Federal Communications Commission.

Other qualifications. Aircraft mechanics must do careful and thorough work that requires a high degree of mechanical aptitude. Employers seek applicants who are self-motivated, hard working, enthusiastic, and able to diagnose and solve complex mechanical problems. Additionally, employers prefer mechanics who can perform a variety of tasks. Agility is important for the reaching and climbing necessary to do the job. Because they may work on the tops of wings and fuselages on large jet planes, aircraft mechanics must not be afraid of heights.

Advances in computer technology, aircraft systems, and the materials used to manufacture airplanes have made mechanics' jobs more highly technical. Aircraft mechanics must possess the skills necessary to troubleshoot and diagnose complex aircraft systems. They also must continually update their skills with knowledge of new technology and advances in aircraft technology.

Some aircraft mechanics in the Armed Forces acquire enough general experience to satisfy the work experience requirements for the FAA certificate. With additional study, they may pass the certifying exam. In general, however, jobs in the military services are too specialized to provide the broad experience required by the FAA. Most Armed Forces mechanics have to complete the entire FAA training program, although a few receive some credit for the material they learned in the service. In any case, military experience is a great advantage when seeking employment; employers consider applicants with formal training to be the most desirable applicants.

Advancement. As aircraft mechanics gain experience, they may advance to lead mechanic (or crew chief), inspector, lead inspector, or shop supervisor positions. Opportunities are best for those who have an aircraft inspector's authorization. To obtain an inspector's authorization, a mechanic must have held an A&P certificate for at least 3 years, with 24 months of hands-on experience.

In the airlines, where promotion often is determined by examination, supervisors sometimes advance to executive positions. Those with broad experience in maintenance and overhaul might become inspectors with the FAA. With additional business and management training, some open their own aircraft maintenance facilities. Mechanics with the necessary pilot licenses and flying experience may take the FAA examination for the position of flight engineer, with opportunities to become pilots.

Mechanics and technicians learn many different skills in their training that can be applied to other jobs, and some transfer to other skilled repairer occupations or electronics technician jobs. For example, some avionics technicians continue their education and become aviation engineers, electrical engineers (specializing in circuit design and testing), or communication engineers. Others become repair consultants, in-house electronics designers, or join research groups that test and develop products.

Employment

Aircraft and avionics equipment mechanics and service technicians held about 140,300 jobs in 2008; about 87 percent of these workers were aircraft mechanics and service technicians; the rest were avionics technicians.

Employment of aircraft and avionics equipment mechanics and service technicians primarily is concentrated in a small number of industries. Almost half of aircraft and avionics equipment mechan-

ics and service technicians worked in air transportation and support activities for air transportation. About 21 percent worked in aerospace product and parts manufacturing and about 15 percent worked for the federal government. Most of the rest worked for companies that operate their own planes to transport executives and cargo.

Most airline mechanics and service technicians work at major airports near large cities. Civilian mechanics employed by the U.S. Armed Forces work at military installations.

Job Outlook

Job growth for aircraft and avionics equipment mechanics and service technicians is expected to be about as fast as the average for all occupations. Job opportunities should be favorable for people who have completed an aircraft mechanic training program, but keen competition is likely for jobs at major airlines.

Employment change. Employment is expected to increase by 7 percent during the 2008–2018 period, which is about as fast as the average for all occupations. Passenger air traffic is expected to increase as the result of an expanding economy and a growing population, and the need for aircraft mechanics and service technicians will grow accordingly. Although there is an increasing trend for some large airlines to outsource aircraft and avionics equipment mechanic jobs overseas, most airline companies still prefer that aircraft maintenance be performed in the U.S. because overseas contractors may not comply with more stringent U.S. safety regulations.

Job prospects. Most job openings for aircraft mechanics through the year 2018 will stem from the need to replace the many mechanics expected to retire over the next decade. In addition, some mechanics will leave to work in related fields, such as automobile repair, as their skills are largely transferable to other maintenance and repair occupations.

Also contributing to favorable future job opportunities for mechanics is the long-term trend toward fewer students entering technical schools to learn skilled maintenance and repair trades. Many of the students who have the ability and aptitude to work on planes are choosing to go to college, work in computer-related fields, or go into other repair and maintenance occupations with better working conditions. If this trend continues, the supply of trained aviation mechanics may not keep up with the needs of the air transportation industry.

Job opportunities will continue to be the best at small commuter and regional airlines, at FAA repair stations, and in general aviation. Commuter and regional airlines are the fastest-growing segment of the air transportation industry, but wages in these airlines tend to be lower than those in the major airlines, so they attract fewer job applicants. Also, some jobs will become available as experienced mechanics leave for higher-paying jobs with the major airlines or transfer to other occupations. Mechanics will face more competition for jobs with large airlines because the high wages and travel benefits that these jobs offer generally attract more qualified applicants than there are openings.

Nonetheless, job opportunities with the airlines are expected to be better than they have been in the past. In general, prospects will be best for applicants with experience and an A&P certification. Mechanics who keep abreast of technological advances in electronics, composite materials, and other areas will be in greatest demand. Also, mechanics who are willing to relocate to smaller rural areas will have better job opportunities.

Projections Data from the National Employment Matrix

Occupational title	SOC Code	Employment, 2008	Projected employment, 2018	Change, 2008–2018	
				Number	Percent
Aircraft and avionics equipment mechanics and service technicians .... —		140,300	150,100	9,800	7
Avionics technicians 49-2091		18,800	20,800	2,000	11
Aircraft mechanics and service technicians 49-3011		121,500	129,300	7,800	6

NOTE: Data in this table are rounded.

Avionics technicians who are trained to work with complex aircraft systems, performing some duties normally performed by certified A&P mechanics, should have the best job prospects. Additionally, technicians with licensing that enables them to work on the airplane, either removing or reinstalling equipment, are expected to be in especially high demand.

Earnings

Median hourly wages of aircraft mechanics and service technicians were about $25.39 in May 2009. The middle 50 percent earned between $20.80 and $29.67. The lowest 10 percent earned less than $16.04, and the highest 10 percent earned more than $34.42. Median hourly wages in the industries employing the largest numbers of aircraft mechanics and service technicians in May 2009 were as follows:

Scheduled air transportation $27.94
Federal executive branch 25.84
Aerospace product and parts manufacturing 25.11
Nonscheduled air transportation 24.29
Support activities for air transportation 21.57

Median hourly wages of avionics technicians were about $23.31 in May 2009. The middle 50 percent earned between $20.54 and $28.28. The lowest 10 percent earned less than $16.65, and the highest 10 percent earned more than $31.55.

Mechanics who work on jets for the major airlines generally earn more than those working on other aircraft. Those who graduate from an aviation maintenance technician school often earn higher starting salaries than individuals who receive training in the Armed Forces or on the job. Airline mechanics and their immediate families receive reduced-fare transportation on their own and most other airlines.

Almost 3 in 10 aircraft and avionics equipment mechanics and service technicians are members of unions or covered by union agreements. The principal unions are the International Association of Machinists and Aerospace Workers and the Transport Workers Union of America. Some mechanics are represented by the International Brotherhood of Teamsters.

Related Occupations

Workers in some other occupations that involve similar mechanical and electrical work include automotive service technicians and mechanics; electrical and electronics installers and repairers; electricians; and elevator installers and repairers.

Sources of Additional Information

Information about jobs with a particular airline can be obtained by writing to the personnel manager of the company.

For general information about aircraft and avionics equipment mechanics and service technicians, contact

▸ Professional Aviation Maintenance Association, 400 N. Washington St., Suite 300, Alexandria, VA 22314. Internet: www.pama.org

For information on jobs in a particular area, contact employers at local airports or local offices of the state employment service.

Information on obtaining positions as aircraft and avionics equipment mechanics and service technicians with the federal government is available from the Office of Personnel Management through USAJOBS, the federal government's official employment information system. This resource for locating and applying for job opportunities can be accessed through the Internet at www.usajobs.opm.gov or through an interactive voice response telephone system at (703) 724-1850 or TDD (978) 461-8404. These numbers are not toll free, and charges may result.

Animal Care and Service Workers

(O*NET 39-2011.00 and 39-2021.00)

Significant Points

■ Animal lovers get satisfaction in this occupation, but the work can be unpleasant, physically and emotionally demanding, and sometimes dangerous.

■ Most workers are trained on the job, but employers generally prefer to hire people who have experience with animals; some jobs require formal education.

■ Most positions will present excellent employment opportunities; however, keen competition is expected for jobs as zookeepers and marine mammal trainers.

■ Earnings are relatively low.

Nature of the Work

Many people like animals. But, as pet owners will admit, taking care of them is hard work. *Animal care and service workers*—who include *animal caretakers* and *animal trainers*—train, feed, water, groom, bathe, and exercise animals and clean, disinfect, and repair their cages. They also play with the animals, provide companionship, and observe behavioral changes that could indicate illness or injury. Boarding kennels, pet stores, animal shelters, rescue leagues, veterinary hospitals and clinics, stables, laboratories, aquariums and natural aquatic habitats, and zoological parks all house animals and employ animal care and service workers. Job titles and duties vary by employment setting.

Kennel attendants care for pets while their owners are working or traveling out of town. Beginning attendants perform basic tasks, such as cleaning both the cages and the dog runs, filling food and water dishes, and exercising animals. Experienced attendants may provide basic animal health care, as well as bathe animals, trim nails, and attend to other grooming needs. Attendants who work in kennels also may sell pet food and supplies, assist in obedience training, or prepare animals for shipping.

Groomers are animal caretakers who specialize in maintaining a pet's appearance. Most groom dogs and a few groom cats. Some groomers work in kennels, veterinary clinics, animal shelters, or pet supply stores. Others operate their own grooming business, typically at a salon or, increasingly, by making house calls. Such mobile services are growing rapidly because they offer convenience for pet owners, flexibility of schedules for groomers, and minimal trauma for pets resulting from their being in unfamiliar surroundings. Groomers clean and sanitize equipment to prevent the spread of disease, as well as maintain a clean and safe environment for the animals. Groomers also schedule appointments, discuss pets' grooming needs with clients, and collect general information on the pets' health and behavior. Groomers sometimes are the first to notice a medical problem, such as an ear or skin infection, that requires veterinary care.

Grooming the pet involves several steps: an initial brush-out is followed by a clipping of hair with combs and grooming shears; the groomer then cuts the animal's nails, cleans the ears, bathes and blow-dries the animal, and ends with a final trim and styling.

Animal caretakers in animal shelters work mainly with cats and dogs and perform a variety of duties typically determined by the worker's experience. In addition to attending to the basic needs of the animals, caretakers at shelters keep records of the animals, including information about any tests or treatments performed on them. Experienced caretakers may vaccinate newly admitted animals under the direction of a veterinarian or veterinary technician and euthanize (painlessly put to death) seriously ill, severely injured, or unwanted animals. Animal caretakers in animal shelters also interact with the public, answering telephone inquiries, screening applicants who wish to adopt an animal, or educating visitors on neutering and other animal health issues.

Pet sitters look after one or more animals when their owner is away. They do this by traveling to the pet owner's home to carry out the daily routine. Most pet sitters feed, walk, and play with the animal, but some more experienced sitters also may be required to bathe, train, or groom them. Most watch over dogs and a few take care of cats. By not removing the pet from its normal surroundings, trauma is reduced and the animal can maintain its normal diet and exercise regimen.

Grooms, or caretakers, care for horses in stables. They saddle and unsaddle horses, give them rubdowns, and walk them to cool them off after a ride. They also feed, groom, and exercise the horses; clean out stalls and replenish bedding; polish saddles; clean and organize the tack (harness, saddle, and bridle) room; and store supplies and feed. Experienced grooms may help train horses.

In zoos, animal care and service workers, called *keepers*, prepare the diets and clean the enclosures of animals and sometimes assist in raising them when they are very young. They watch for any signs of illness or injury, monitor eating patterns or any changes in behavior and record their observations. Keepers also may answer questions and ensure that the visiting public behaves responsibly toward the exhibited animals. Depending on the zoo, keepers may be assigned to work with a broad group of animals, such as mammals, birds, or reptiles, or they may work with a limited collection of animals such as primates, large cats, or small mammals.

Animal trainers train animals for riding, security, performance, obedience, or assisting people with disabilities. Animal trainers do this by accustoming the animal to the human voice and human contact and teaching the animal to respond to commands. The three most commonly trained animals are dogs, horses, and marine mammals, including dolphins and sea lions. Trainers use several techniques to help them train animals. One technique, known as a bridge, is a stimulus that a trainer uses to communicate the precise moment an animal does something correctly. When the animal responds correctly, the trainer gives positive reinforcement in a variety of ways: offering food, toys, play, and rubdowns or speaking the word "good." Animal training takes place in small steps and often takes months and even years of repetition. During the teaching process, trainers provide animals with mental stimulation, physical exercise, and husbandry. A relatively new form of training teaches animals to cooperate with workers giving medical care: Animals learn "veterinary" behaviors, such as allowing for the collection of blood samples; physical, X-ray, ultrasonic, and dental exams; physical therapy; and the administration of medicines and replacement fluids.

Training also can be a good tool for facilitating the relocation of animals from one habitat to another, easing, for example, the process of loading horses onto trailers. Trainers often work in competitions or shows, such as circuses, marine parks, and aquariums; many others work in animal shelters, dog kennels and salons, or horse farms. Trainers in shows work to display the talent and ability of an animal, such as a dolphin, through interactive programs to educate and entertain the public.

In addition to their hands-on work with the animals, trainers often oversee other aspects of animals' care, such as preparing their diet and providing a safe and clean environment and habitat.

Work environment. People who love animals get satisfaction from working with and helping them. However, some of the work may be unpleasant, physically or emotionally demanding, and, sometimes, dangerous. Data from the U.S. Bureau of Labor Statistics show that full-time animal care and service workers experienced a work-related injury and illness rate that was higher than the national average. Most animal care and service workers have to clean animal cages and lift, hold, or restrain animals, risking exposure to bites or scratches. Their work often involves kneeling, crawling, repeated bending, and, occasionally, lifting heavy supplies such as bales of hay or bags of feed. Animal caretakers must take precautions when treating animals with germicides or insecticides. They may work outdoors in all kinds of weather, and the work setting can be noisy. Caretakers of show and sports animals travel to competitions.

Animal care and service workers who witness abused animals or who assist in euthanizing unwanted, aged, or hopelessly injured animals may experience emotional distress. Those working for private humane societies and municipal animal shelters often deal with the public, some of whom may be hostile. Such workers must maintain a calm and professional demeanor while helping to enforce the laws regarding animal care.

Animal care and service workers often work irregular hours. Most animals are fed every day, so caretakers often work weekend and holiday shifts. In some animal hospitals, research facilities, and animal shelters, an attendant is on duty 24 hours a day, which means night shifts.

Training, Other Qualifications, and Advancement

On-the-job training is the most common way animal care and service workers learn their work; however, employers generally prefer to hire people who have experience with animals. Some jobs require formal education.

Education and training. Animal trainers often need a high school diploma or GED equivalent. Some animal training jobs may require a bachelor's degree and additional skills. For example, marine mammal trainers usually need a bachelor's degree in biology, marine biology, animal science, psychology, or a related field. An animal health technician degree also may qualify trainers for some jobs.

Most equine trainers learn their trade by working as a groom at a stable. Some study at an accredited private training school.

Many dog trainers attend workshops and courses at community colleges and vocational schools. Topics include basic study of canines, learning theory of animals, teaching obedience cues, problem solving methods, and safety. Many such schools also offer business training.

Pet sitters are not required to have any specific training, but knowledge of and some form of previous experience with animals often are recommended.

Many zoos require their caretakers to have a bachelor's degree in biology, animal science, or a related field. Most require experience with animals, preferably as a volunteer or paid keeper in a zoo.

Pet groomers typically learn their trade by completing an informal apprenticeship, usually lasting 6 to 10 weeks, under the guidance of an experienced groomer. Prospective groomers also may attend one of the 50 state-licensed grooming schools throughout the country, with programs varying in length from 2 to 18 weeks. Beginning groomers often start by taking on one duty, such as bathing and drying the pet. They eventually assume responsibility for the entire grooming process, from the initial brush-out to the final clipping.

Animal caretakers in animal shelters are not required to have any specialized training, but training programs and workshops are available through the Humane Society of the United States, the American Humane Association, and the National Animal Control Association. Workshop topics include investigations of cruelty, appropriate methods of euthanasia for shelter animals, proper guidelines for capturing animals, techniques for preventing problems with wildlife, and dealing with the public.

Beginning animal caretakers in kennels learn on the job and usually start by cleaning cages and feeding animals.

Certification and other qualifications. Certifications are available in many animal service occupations. For dog trainers, certification by a professional association or one of the hundreds of private vocational or state-approved trade schools can be advantageous. The National Dog Groomers Association of America offers certification for master status as a groomer. To earn certification, applicants must demonstrate their practical skills and pass two exams. The National Association of Professional Pet Sitters offers a two-stage,

home-study certification program for those who wish to become pet care professionals. Topics include business management, animal care, and animal health issues, and applicants must pass a written exam to earn certification. The Pet Care Services Association offers a three-stage, home-study program for individuals interested in pet care. Levels I and II focus on basic principles of animal care and customer service, while Level III spotlights management and professional aspects of the pet care business. Those who complete the third stage and pass oral and written examinations become Certified Kennel Operators (CKO).

All animal care and service workers need patience, sensitivity, and problem-solving ability. Those who work in shelters also need tact and communication skills, because they often deal with individuals who abandon their pets. The ability to handle emotional people is vital for workers at shelters.

Animal trainers especially need problem-solving skills and experience in animal obedience. Successful marine mammal trainers also should have good-public speaking skills, because presentations are a large part of the job. Usually four to five trainers work with a group of animals at one time; therefore, trainers should be able to work as part of a team. Marine mammal trainers must also be good swimmers; certification in SCUBA is a plus.

Most horse-training jobs have minimum weight requirements for candidates.

Advancement. With experience and additional training, caretakers in animal shelters may become adoption coordinators, animal control officers, emergency rescue drivers, assistant shelter managers, or shelter directors. Pet groomers who work in large retail establishments or kennels may, with experience, move into supervisory or managerial positions. Experienced groomers often choose to open their own salons or mobile grooming business. Advancement for kennel caretakers takes the form of promotion to kennel supervisor, assistant manager, and manager; those with enough capital and experience may open up their own kennels. Zookeepers may advance to senior keeper, assistant head keeper, head keeper, and assistant curator, but very few openings occur, especially for the higher level positions.

Employment

Animal care and service workers held 220,400 jobs in 2008. Nearly 4 out of 5 worked as nonfarm animal caretakers; the remainder worked as animal trainers. Nonfarm animal caretakers often worked in boarding kennels, animal shelters, rescue leagues, stables, grooming shops, pet stores, animal hospitals, and veterinary offices. A significant number of caretakers worked for animal humane societies, racing stables, dog and horse racetrack operators, zoos, theme parks, circuses, and other amusement and recreation services.

Employment of animal trainers is concentrated in animal services that specialize in training and in commercial sports, where racehorses and dogs are trained. About 54 percent of animal trainers were self-employed.

Job Outlook

Because many workers leave this occupation each year, there will be excellent job opportunities for most positions. Much faster than average employment growth also will add to job openings. However, keen competition is expected for jobs as zookeepers and marine mammal trainers.

Projections Data from the National Employment Matrix

Occupational title	SOC Code	Employment, 2008	Projected employment, 2018	Change, 2008–2018	
				Number	Percent
Animal care and service workers 39-2000		220,400	265,900	45,500	21
Animal trainers 39-2011		47,100	56,700	9,600	20
Nonfarm animal caretakers 39-2021		173,300	209,100	35,900	21

NOTE: Data in this table are rounded.

Employment change. Employment of animal care and service workers is expected to grow 21 percent over the 2008–2018 decade, much faster than the average for all occupations. The companion pet population, which drives employment of animal caretakers in kennels, grooming shops, animal shelters, and veterinary clinics and hospitals, is anticipated to increase. Pet owners—including a large number of baby boomers, whose disposable income is expected to increase as they age—are expected to increasingly purchase grooming services, daily and overnight boarding services, training services, and veterinary services, resulting in more jobs for animal care and service workers. As more pet owners consider their pets part of the family, demand for luxury animal services and the willingness to spend greater amounts of money on pets should continue to grow. Demand for marine mammal trainers, on the other hand, should grow slowly.

Demand for animal care and service workers in animal shelters is expected to grow as communities increasingly recognize the connection between animal abuse and abuse toward humans and continue to commit private funds to animal shelters, many of which are working hand in hand with social service agencies and law enforcement teams.

Job prospects. Due to employment growth and the need to replace workers who leave the occupation, job opportunities for most positions should be excellent. The need to replace pet sitters, dog walkers, kennel attendants, and animal control and shelter workers leaving the field will create the overwhelming majority of job openings. Many animal caretaker jobs require little or no training and have flexible work schedules, making them suitable for people seeking a first job or for temporary or part-time work. Prospective groomers also will face excellent opportunities as the companion dog population is expected to grow and services such as mobile grooming continue to grow in popularity. The outlook for caretakers in zoos and aquariums, however, is not favorable, due to slow job growth and keen competition for the few positions.

Prospective mammal trainers also will face keen competition as the number of applicants greatly exceeds the number of available positions. Prospective horse trainers should anticipate an equally challenging labor market because the number of entry-level positions is limited. Dog trainers, however, should experience conditions that are more favorable, driven by their owners' desire to instill obedience in their pet. Opportunities for dog trainers should be best in large metropolitan areas.

Job opportunities for animal care and service workers may vary from year to year because the strength of the economy affects demand for these workers. Pet owners tend to spend more on animal services when the economy is strong.

Earnings

Wages are relatively low. Median annual wages of nonfarm animal caretakers were $19,550 in May 2009. The middle 50 percent earned between $17,110 and $24,100. The bottom 10 percent earned less than $15,590, and the top 10 percent earned more than $31,660. Median annual wages in the industries employing the largest numbers of nonfarm animal caretakers in May 2009 were as follows:

Spectator sports	$20,520
Other personal services	19,930
Social advocacy organizations	18,640
Veterinary services	18,840
Other miscellaneous store retailers	18,510

Median annual wages of animal trainers were $26,930 in May 2009. The middle 50 percent earned between $19,710 and $37,540. The lowest 10 percent earned less than $16,920, and the top 10 percent earned more than $52,130.

Related Occupations

Others who work extensively with animals include agricultural workers, other; animal control workers; biological scientists; farmers, ranchers, and agricultural managers; veterinarians; veterinary assistants and laboratory animal caretakers; and veterinary technologists and technicians.

Sources of Additional Information

For career information and information on training, certification, and earnings of a related occupation—animal control officers—contact

▸ National Animal Control Association, P.O. Box 480851, Kansas City, MO 64148-0851. Internet: www.nacanet.org

For information on becoming an advanced pet care technician at a kennel, contact

▸ Pet Care Services Association, 2760 N. Academy Blvd., Suite 120, Colorado Springs, CO 80917. Internet: www.petcareservices.org

For general information on pet grooming careers, including workshops and certification information, contact

▸ National Dog Groomers Association of America, P.O. Box 101, Clark, PA 16113. Internet: www.nationaldoggroomers.com

For information on pet sitting, including certification information, contact

▸ National Association of Professional Pet Sitters, 15000 Commerce Pkwy., Suite C, Mount Laurel, NJ 08054. Internet: www.petsitters. org

Artists and Related Workers

(O*NET 27-1011.00, 27-1012.00, 27-1013.00, 27-1014.00, and 27-1019.00)

Significant Points

■ About 60 percent of artists and related workers are self-employed.

■ Keen competition is expected for both salaried jobs and freelance work because the arts attract many talented people with creative ability.

■ Artists usually develop their skills through a bachelor's degree program or other postsecondary training in art or design.

■ Earnings for self-employed artists vary widely; some well-established artists earn more than salaried artists, while others find it difficult to rely solely on income earned from selling art.

Nature of the Work

Artists create art to communicate ideas, thoughts, or feelings. They use a variety of methods—painting, sculpting, or illustration—and an assortment of materials, including oils, watercolors, acrylics, pastels, pencils, pen and ink, plaster, clay, and computers. Artists' works may be realistic, stylized, or abstract and may depict objects, people, nature, or events.

Artists generally fall into one of four categories. *Art directors* formulate design concepts and presentation approaches for visual communications. *Craft artists* create or reproduce handmade objects for sale or exhibition. *Fine artists, including painters, sculptors, and illustrators*, create original artwork, using a variety of media and techniques. *Multimedia artists and animators* create special effects, animation, or other visual images on film, on video, or with computers or other electronic media.

Art directors develop design concepts and review material that is to appear in periodicals, newspapers, and other printed or digital media. They control the overall visual direction of a project in fields such as advertising and publishing. They decide how best to present a concept visually so that it is organized, eye catching, and appealing. Art directors decide which photographs or artwork to use and oversee the design, layout, and production of material to be produced. They may direct workers engaged in artwork, design, layout, and copywriting.

Craft artists make a wide variety of objects, mostly by hand, that are sold in their own studios, in retail outlets, or at arts-and-crafts shows. Some craft artists display their works in galleries and museums. Craft artists work with many different materials, including ceramics, glass, textiles, wood, metal, and paper, to create unique pieces of art such as pottery, stained glass, quilts, tapestries, lace, candles, and clothing. Many craft artists also use fine-art techniques—for example, painting, sketching, and printing—to add finishing touches to their art.

Fine artists typically display their work in museums, commercial art galleries, corporate collections, and private homes. Some of their artwork may be commissioned (done on request from clients), but most is sold by the artist or through private art galleries or dealers. The gallery and the artist predetermine how much each will earn from the sale. Only the most successful fine artists are able to support themselves solely through the sale of their works. Most fine artists have at least one other job to support their art careers. Some work in museums or art galleries as fine-arts directors or as curators, planning and setting up art exhibits. A few artists work as art critics for newspapers or magazines or as consultants to foundations or institutional collectors. Other artists teach art classes or conduct workshops in schools or in their own studios. Some artists also hold full-time or part-time jobs unrelated to art and pursue fine art as a hobby or second career.

Usually, fine artists specialize in one or two art forms, such as painting, illustrating, sketching, sculpting, printmaking, and restoring. Painters, illustrators, cartoonists, and sketch artists work with two-dimensional art forms, using shading, perspective, and color to produce realistic scenes or abstractions.

Illustrators usually create pictures for books, magazines, and other publications and for commercial products such as textiles, wrapping paper, stationery, greeting cards, and calendars. Increasingly, illustrators are working in digital format—for example, creating scenery or objects for a video game. This has created new opportunities for illustrators to work with animators and in broadcast media.

Medical and scientific illustrators combine drawing skills with knowledge of biology or other sciences. Medical illustrators work digitally or traditionally to create images of human anatomy and surgical procedures as well as three-dimensional models and animations. Scientific illustrators draw animal and plant life, atomic and molecular structures, and geologic and planetary formations. These illustrations are used in medical and scientific publications and in audiovisual presentations for teaching purposes. Illustrators also work for lawyers, producing exhibits for court cases.

Cartoonists draw political, advertising, social, and sports cartoons. Some cartoonists work with others who create the idea or story and write captions. Some cartoonists write captions themselves. Most cartoonists have comic, critical, or dramatic talents in addition to drawing skills.

Sketch artists create likenesses of subjects with pencil, charcoal, or pastels. Sketches are used by law enforcement agencies to assist in identifying suspects, by the news media to depict courtroom scenes, and by individual patrons for their own enjoyment.

Sculptors design three-dimensional artworks, either by molding and joining materials such as clay, glass, wire, plastic, fabric, or metal, or by cutting and carving forms from a block of plaster, wood, or stone. Some sculptors combine various materials to create mixed-media installations. Some incorporate light, sound, and motion into their works.

Printmakers create printed images from designs cut or etched into wood, stone, or metal. After creating the design, the artist uses a printing press to roll the image onto paper or fabric. Some make prints by pressing the inked surface onto paper by hand or by graphically encoding and processing data, using a computer. The digitized images can then be printed onto paper.

Painting restorers preserve and restore damaged and faded paintings. They apply solvents and cleaning agents to clean the surfaces of the paintings, they reconstruct or retouch damaged areas, and they apply preservatives to protect the paintings. Restoration is highly detailed work and usually is reserved for experts in the field.

Multimedia artists and animators work primarily in motion picture and video industries, advertising, and computer systems design services. They draw by hand and use computers to create the series of pictures that form the animated images or special effects seen in movies, television programs, and computer games. Some draw storyboards for television commercials, movies, and animated features. Storyboards present television commercials in a series of scenes similar to a comic strip and allow an advertising agency to evaluate commercials proposed by advertising companies. Storyboards also serve as guides to placing actors and cameras on the television or motion picture set and to other production details. Many multimedia artists model objects in three dimensions by computer and work with programmers to make the images move.

Work environment. Many artists work in fine art or commercial art studios located in office buildings, warehouses, or lofts. Others work in private studios in their homes. Some fine artists share studio space, where they also may exhibit their work. Studio surroundings usually are well lighted and ventilated; however, fine artists may be exposed to fumes from glue, paint, ink, and other materials and to dust or other residue from filings, splattered paint, or spilled cleaners and other fluids. Artists who sit at drafting tables or who use computers for extended periods may experience back pain, eyestrain, or fatigue.

Artists employed by publishing companies, advertising agencies, and design firms generally work a standard workweek. During busy periods, they may work overtime to meet deadlines. Self-employed artists can set their own hours. They may spend much time and effort selling their artwork to potential customers or clients and building a reputation.

Training, Other Qualifications, and Advancement

Art directors usually have years of work experience and generally need at least a bachelor's degree. Because of the level of technical expertise demanded, multimedia artists and animators also need a bachelor's degree. Although formal schooling is not strictly required for craft and fine artists, it is very difficult to become skilled enough to make a living without some training.

Education and training. Many colleges and universities offer programs leading to a bachelor's or master's degree in fine arts. Courses usually include core subjects such as English, social science, and natural science, in addition to art history and studio art. Independent schools of art and design also offer postsecondary studio training in the craft, fine, and multimedia arts leading to certificates in the specialties or to an associate or bachelor's degree in fine arts. Typically, these programs focus more intensively on studio work than do the academic programs in a university setting. In 2009 the National Association of Schools of Art and Design accredited approximately 300 postsecondary institutions with programs in art and design; most of these schools award a degree in art.

Art directors usually begin as entry-level artists or designers in advertising, publishing, design, or motion picture production firms. An artist is promoted to art director after having demonstrated artistic and leadership abilities. Depending on the scope of their responsibilities, some art directors may pursue a degree in art administration or management, which teaches business skills such as project management and finance.

Many educational programs in art also provide training in computer techniques. Computers are used widely in the visual arts, and knowledge and training in computer graphics and other visual display software are critical elements of many jobs in these fields.

Medical illustrators must have both a demonstrated artistic ability and a detailed knowledge of living organisms, surgical and medical procedures, and human and animal anatomy. A bachelor's degree combining art and premedical courses usually is required. However, most medical illustrators also choose to pursue a master's degree in medical illustration. This degree is offered in four accredited schools in the United States.

Those who want to teach fine arts at public elementary or secondary schools usually must have a teaching certificate in addition to a bachelor's degree. An advanced degree in fine arts or arts administration is usually necessary for management or administrative positions in government or in foundations or for teaching in colleges and universities.

Other qualifications. Evidence of appropriate talent and skill, displayed in an artist's portfolio, is an important factor used by art directors, clients, and others in deciding whether to hire an individual or contract for his or her work. A portfolio is a collection of samples of the artist's best work. Assembling a successful portfolio requires skills usually developed through postsecondary training in art or visual communications. Internships also provide excellent opportunities for artists to develop and enhance their portfolios.

Advancement. Artists hired by firms often start with relatively routine work. While doing this work, however, they may observe other artists and practice their own skills.

Craft and fine artists advance professionally as their work circulates and as they establish a reputation for a particular style. Many of the most successful artists continually develop new ideas, and their work often evolves over time.

Many artists do freelance work while continuing to hold a full-time job until they are established. Others freelance part time while still in school to develop experience and to build a portfolio of published work.

Freelance artists try to develop a set of clients who regularly contract for work. Some freelance artists are widely recognized for their skill in specialties such as cartooning or children's book illustration. These artists may earn high incomes and can choose the type of work they do.

Employment

Artists held about 221,900 jobs in 2008. About 60 percent were self-employed. Employment was distributed as follows:

Art directors	84,200
Multimedia artists and animators	79,000
Fine artists, including painters, sculptors and illustrators	23,600
Craft artists	13,600
Artists and related workers, all other	21,500

Of the artists who were not self-employed, many worked for advertising and related services; newspaper, periodical, book, and software publishers; motion picture and video industries; specialized design services; and computer systems design and related services. Some self-employed artists offered their services to advertising agencies, design firms, publishing houses, and other businesses.

Job Outlook

Employment is projected to grow about as fast as the average. Competition for jobs is expected to be keen for both salaried and

Projections Data from the National Employment Matrix

Occupational title	SOC Code	Employment, 2008	Projected employment, 2018	Change, 2008–2018	
				Number	Percent
Artists and related workers.................................27-1010		221,900	247,700	25,800	12
Art directors 27-1011		84,200	94,000	9,800	12
Craft artists 27-1012		13,600	14,600	1,000	7
Fine artists, including painters, sculptors, and illustrators...27-1013		23,600	25,700	2,100	9
Multi-media artists and animators 27-1014		79,000	90,200	11,200	14
Artists and related workers, all other 27-1019		21,500	23,200	1,700	8

NOTE: Data in this table are rounded.

freelance jobs in all specialties because the number of people with creative ability and an interest in this career is expected to continue to exceed the number of available openings. Despite the competition, employers and individual clients are always on the lookout for talented and creative artists.

Employment change. Employment of artists and related workers is expected to grow 12 percent through 2018, about as fast as the average for all occupations. An increasing reliance on artists to create digital or multimedia artwork will drive growth.

Art directors will see an increase in jobs in advertising due to demand for the overall vision they bring to a project. However, declining opportunities in publishing will hold down job growth. With many magazines moving to an online-only format, art directors are used less in this field.

Demand for illustrators who work on a computer will increase as media companies use more detailed images and backgrounds in their designs. However, illustrators and cartoonists who work in publishing may see job opportunities decline as newspapers continue to cut staffs. Many are instead opting to post their work on political websites and online publications. The small number of medical illustrators will also be in greater demand as medical research continues to grow.

Demand for multimedia artists and animators will increase as consumers continue to demand more realistic video games, movie and television special effects, and 3D animated movies. Additional job openings will arise from an increasing need for computer graphics in the growing number of mobile technologies. The demand for animators is also increasing in alternative areas such as scientific research and design services. Some lower-priority animation has been offshored, negatively affecting employment of animators.

Job prospects. Competition for jobs as artists and related workers will be keen because there are more qualified candidates than available jobs. Employers in all industries should be able to choose from among the most qualified candidates.

Despite the competition, studios, galleries, and individual clients are always on the lookout for artists who display outstanding talent, creativity, and style. Among craft and fine artists, talented individuals who have developed a mastery of artistic techniques and skills will have the best job prospects. Multimedia artists and animators should have better job opportunities than other artists but still will experience competition. Despite an expanding number of opportunities, art directors should experience keen competition for the available openings. Craft and fine artists work mostly on a freelance or commission basis and may find it difficult to earn a living solely by selling their artwork. Only the most successful craft and fine art-

ists receive major commissions for their work. Competition among artists for the privilege of being shown in galleries is expected to remain intense, as will competition for grants from sponsors such as private foundations, state and local arts councils, and the National Endowment for the Arts. Because of their reliance on grants, and because the demand for artwork is dependent on consumers having disposable income, many of these artists will find that their income fluctuates with the overall economy.

Earnings

Median annual wages of salaried art directors were $78,580 in May 2009. The middle 50 percent earned between $56,250 and $111,300. The lowest 10 percent earned less than $41,670, and the highest 10 percent earned more than $160,060. Median annual wages were $80,220 in advertising, public relations and related services.

Median annual wages of salaried craft artists were $29,960. The middle 50 percent earned between $20,840 and $39,540. The lowest 10 percent earned less than $16,760, and the highest 10 percent earned more than $57,550.

Median annual wages of salaried fine artists, including painters, sculptors, and illustrators, were $44,160. The middle 50 percent earned between $29,270 and $64,180. The lowest 10 percent earned less than $19,680, and the highest 10 percent earned more than $86,650.

Median annual wages of salaried multimedia artists and animators were $58,520. The middle 50 percent earned between $43,170 and $77,410. The lowest 10 percent earned less than $32,360, and the highest 10 percent earned more than $99,130. Median annual wages were $64,990 in motion picture and video industries and $54,120 in advertising, public relations, and related services.

Earnings for self-employed artists vary widely. Some charge only a nominal fee while they gain experience and build a reputation for their work. Others, such as well-established freelance fine artists and illustrators, can earn more than salaried artists. Many, however, find it difficult to rely solely on income earned from selling paintings or other works of art. Like other self-employed workers, freelance artists must provide their own benefits.

Related Occupations

Other workers who apply artistic skills include archivists, curators, and museum technicians; commercial and industrial designers; fashion designers; graphic designers; jewelers and precious stone and metal workers; photographers; and woodworkers.

Some workers who use computers extensively and may require art skills are computer software engineers and computer programmers and desktop publishers.

Sources of Additional Information

For general information about art and design and a list of accredited college-level programs, contact

▸ National Association of Schools of Art and Design, 11250 Roger Bacon Dr., Suite 21, Reston, VA 20190. Internet: http://nasad.arts-accredit.org

For information on careers in the craft arts and for a list of schools and workshops, contact

▸ American Craft Council Library, 72 Spring St., 6th Floor, New York, NY 10012. Internet: www.craftcouncil.org

For information on careers in illustration, contact

▸ Society of Illustrators, 128 E. 63rd St., New York, NY 10065. Internet: www.societyillustrators.org

For information on careers in medical illustration, contact

▸ Association of Medical Illustrators, P.O. Box 1897, Lawrence, KS 66044. Internet: www.ami.org

For information on workshops, scholarships, internships, and competitions for art students interested in advertising careers, contact

▸ Art Directors Club, 106 W. 29th St., New York, NY 10001. Internet: www.adcglobal.org

Assemblers and Fabricators

(O*NET 51-2011.00, 51-2021.00, 51-2022.00, 51-2023.00, 51-2031.00, 51-2041.00, 51-2091.00, 51-2092.00, 51-2093.00, and 51-2099.00)

Significant Points

■ Most assemblers work on teams, making good communication skills and the ability to get along with others important.

■ A high school diploma is sufficient for most jobs, but experience and extra training are needed for more advanced assembly work.

■ Employment is projected to experience little or no change between 2008 and 2018.

■ Job opportunities are expected to be good in the manufacturing sector, particularly in growing high-technology industries.

Nature of the Work

Assemblers and fabricators play an important role in the manufacturing process. They assemble both finished products and the pieces that go into them. The products they assemble using tools, machines, and their hands range from entire airplanes to children's toys. They fabricate and assemble household appliances, automobiles, computers, electronic devices, and more.

Changes in technology have transformed the manufacturing and assembly process. Modern manufacturing systems use robots, computers, programmable motion control devices, and various sensing technologies. These systems change the way in which goods are made and affect the jobs of those who make them. The more advanced assemblers must be able to work with these new technologies and use them to produce goods.

The job of an assembler or fabricator ranges from very easy to very complicated, requiring a range of knowledge and skills. Skilled assemblers putting together complex machines, for example, begin by reading detailed schematics or blueprints that show how to assemble the machine. After determining how parts should connect, they use hand or power tools to trim, shim, cut, and make other adjustments to fit components together and align properly. Once the parts are properly aligned, they connect them with bolts and screws or by welding or soldering pieces together.

Careful quality control is important throughout the assembly process, so assemblers look for faulty components and mistakes in the assembly process. They help to fix problems before more defective products are produced.

Manufacturing techniques are evolving away from traditional assembly line systems toward "lean" manufacturing systems, which are causing the nature of assemblers' work to change. Lean manufacturing uses teams of workers to produce entire products or components. *Team assemblers* may still work on an assembly line, but they rotate through different tasks, rather than specializing in a single task. The team also may decide how the work is assigned and how different tasks are performed. This worker flexibility helps companies cover for absent workers, improves productivity, and increases companies' ability to respond to changes in demand by shifting labor from one product line to another. For example, if demand for a product drops, companies may reduce the total number of workers producing it, asking the remaining workers to perform more stages of the assembly process. Some aspects of lean production, such as rotating tasks and seeking worker input on improving the assembly process, are common to all assembly and fabrication occupations.

Although most assemblers and fabricators are classified as team assemblers, others specialize in producing one type of product or perform the same or similar tasks throughout the assembly process. These workers are classified according to the products they assemble or produce. *Electrical and electronic equipment assemblers*, for example, build products such as electric motors, computers, electronic control devices, and sensing equipment. Automated systems have been put in place as many small electronic parts are too small or fragile for human assembly. Much of the remaining work of electrical and electronic assemblers is manual assembly during the small-scale production of electronic devices used in avionic systems, military systems, and medical equipment. Manual production requires these workers to use devices such as soldering irons. *Electromechanical equipment assemblers* assemble and modify electromechanical devices such as household appliances, CT scanners, or vending machines. The workers use a variety of tools, such as rulers, rivet guns, and soldering irons. *Coil winders, tapers, and finishers* wind wire coil used in a variety of electric and electronic products, including resistors, transformers, generators, and electric motors.

Engine and other machine assemblers construct, assemble, or rebuild engines, turbines, and machines used in automobiles, construction and mining equipment, and power generators. *Aircraft structure, surfaces, rigging, and systems assemblers* assemble, fit, fasten, and install parts of airplanes, space vehicles, or missiles, including tails and wings, landing gear, and heating and ventilation systems. *Structural metal fabricators and fitters* cut, align, and fit together structural metal parts and may assist in welding or riveting the parts together. *Fiberglass laminators and fabricators* develop products made of fiberglass, mainly boat decks and hulls. *Timing device assemblers, adjusters, and calibrators* perform precision assembling or adjusting of timing devices within very narrow tolerances.

It has become more common to involve assemblers and fabricators in product development. Designers and engineers consult manufacturing workers during the design stage to improve product reliability and manufacturing efficiency. For example, an assembler may tell a designer that the dashboard of a new car design will be too difficult to install quickly and consistently. The designer could then redesign it to make it easier to install.

Some experienced assemblers work with designers and engineers to build prototypes or test products. These assemblers must be able to read and interpret complex engineering specifications from text, drawings, and computer-aided drafting systems. They also may need to use a variety of tools and precision measuring instruments.

Work environment. Most assemblers and manufacturers work in manufacturing plants. The working environment is improving, but varies by plant and by industry. Many physically difficult tasks have been automated or made easier through the use of power tools, such as tightening massive bolts or moving heavy parts into position. Assembly work, however, may still involve long periods of standing or sitting.

Most factories today are generally clean, well lit, and well ventilated, and depending on what type of work is being performed, they may also need to be dirt and dust-free. Electronic and electromechanical assemblers particularly must work in environments free of dust that could affect the operation of the products they build. Some assemblers may come into contact with potentially harmful chemicals or fumes, but ventilation systems and other safety precautions normally minimize any harmful effects. Other assemblers may come in contact with oil and grease, and their working areas may be quite noisy. Fiberglass laminators and fabricators are exposed to fiberglass, which may irritate the skin; these workers wear gloves and long sleeves and must use respirators for safety.

Most full-time assemblers work a 40-hour week, although overtime and shift work are common in some industries. Work schedules of assemblers may vary at plants with more than one shift.

Training, Other Qualifications, and Advancement

The education level and qualifications needed to enter these jobs vary depending on the industry and employer. While a high school diploma or GED is sufficient for most jobs, experience and extra training are needed for more advanced assembly work.

Education and training. Most applicants for assembler positions need only a high school diploma or GED, with workers learning the skills they need through on-the-job training, sometimes including employer-sponsored classroom instruction. Some employers may require specialized training or an associate degree for the most skilled assembly jobs. For example, jobs with electrical, electronic, and aircraft and motor vehicle products manufacturers typically require more formal education through technical schools.

Certification and other qualifications. Assembly workers must be able to follow instructions carefully, which may require some basic reading skills and the ability to follow diagrams and pictures. Manual dexterity and the ability to carry out complex, repetitive tasks quickly and methodically also are important. For some positions, the ability to lift heavy objects may be needed. Team assem-

blers also need good interpersonal and communication skills to be able to work well with their teammates. Good eyesight and manual dexterity are necessary for assemblers and fabricators who work with small parts. Plants that make electrical and electronic products may test applicants for color vision, because their products often contain many differently colored wires.

Certifications are not common for most types of assemblers and fabricators. However, many employers that hire electrical and electronic assembly workers, especially those in the aerospace and defense industries, require certifications in soldering, such as those offered by the IPC.

Advancement. As assemblers and fabricators become more experienced, they may progress to jobs that require greater skill and may be given more responsibility. Experienced assemblers may become product repairers if they have learned the many assembly operations and understand the construction of a product. These workers fix assembled pieces that operators or inspectors have identified as defective. Assemblers also can advance to quality control jobs or be promoted to supervisor. Experienced assemblers and fabricators also may become members of research and development teams, working with engineers and other project designers to design, develop, and build prototypes and test new product models.

Employment

Assemblers and fabricators held about 2.0 million jobs in 2008. They worked in many industries, but more than 75 percent worked in manufacturing. Within the manufacturing sector, assembly of transportation equipment, such as aircraft, autos, trucks, and buses, accounted for 20 percent of all jobs. Assembly of computers and electronic products accounted for another 11 percent of all jobs. Other industries that employ many assemblers and fabricators are machinery manufacturing and electrical equipment, appliance, and component manufacturing.

The following table shows the employment of assemblers and fabricators in the manufacturing industries that employed the most workers in 2008:

Motor vehicle parts manufacturing	134,900
Semiconductor and other electronic component manufacturing	94,800
Motor vehicle manufacturing	85,000
Navigational, measuring, electromedical, and control instruments manufacturing	72,400
Architectural and structural metals manufacturing	71,700

Assemblers and fabricators also work in many other nonmanufacturing industries. Twelve percent were employed by employment services firms, mostly as temporary workers; these temporary workers were mostly assigned to manufacturing plants. Wholesale and retail trade firms employed the next-highest number of assemblers and fabricators. Many of these assemblers perform the final assembly of goods before the item is delivered to the customer. For example, most imported furniture is shipped in pieces and assemblers for furniture wholesalers and retailers put together the furniture prior to delivery.

Team assemblers, the largest specialty, accounted for 57 percent of assembler and fabricator jobs. The distribution of employment among the various types of assemblers was as follows in 2008:

Projections Data from the National Employment Matrix

Occupational title	SOC Code	Employment, 2008	Projected employment, 2018	Change, 2008–2018	
				Number	Percent
Assemblers and fabricators	51-2000	1,950,900	1,913,100	−37,800	−2
Aircraft structure, surfaces, rigging, and systems assemblers	51-2011	44,100	48,200	4,100	9
Electrical, electronics, and electromechanical assemblers	51-2020	297,500	254,200	−43,200	−15
Coil winders, tapers, and finishers	51-2021	22,100	16,500	−5,600	−25
Electrical and electronic equipment assemblers	51-2022	213,300	182,000	−31,300	−15
Electromechanical equipment assemblers	51-2023	62,100	55,700	−6,400	−10
Engine and other machine assemblers	51-2031	39,900	36,700	−3,200	−8
Structural metal fabricators and fitters	51-2041	114,100	113,700	−400	0
Miscellaneous assemblers and fabricators	51-2090	1,455,400	1,460,200	4,900	0
Fiberglass laminators and fabricators	51-2091	30,300	28,900	−1,400	−5
Team assemblers	51-2092	1,112,300	1,112,700	400	0
Timing device assemblers, adjusters, and calibrators	51-2093	2,700	2,600	−100	−4
All other assemblers and fabricators	51-2099	309,900	316,000	6,000	2

NOTE: Data in this table are rounded.

Team assemblers	1,112,300
Electrical and electronic equipment assemblers	213,300
Structural metal fabricators and fitters	114,100
Electromechanical equipment assemblers	62,100
Aircraft structure, surfaces, rigging, and systems assemblers	44,100
Engine and other machine assemblers	39,900
Fiberglass laminators and fabricators	30,300
Coil winders, tapers, and finishers	22,100
Timing device assemblers, adjusters, and calibrators	2,700
Assemblers and fabricators, all other	309,900

Job Outlook

Employment is projected to experience little or no change, primarily reflecting productivity growth and strong foreign competition in manufacturing. Job opportunities are expected to be good for qualified applicants in the manufacturing sector, particularly in growing, high-technology industries.

Employment change. Employment of assemblers and fabricators is expected to experience little or no change between 2008 and 2018, declining by 2 percent. Within the manufacturing sector, employment of assemblers and fabricators will be determined largely by the growth or decline in the production of certain manufactured goods. In general, despite projected growth in the output of manufactured goods, overall employment is not expected to grow as the whole sector becomes more efficient and is able to produce more with fewer workers. However, some individual industries are projected to have more jobs than others. The aircraft products and parts industry is projected to gain jobs over the decade as demand for new commercial planes grows significantly. Thus, the need for aircraft structure, surfaces, rigging, and systems assemblers is expected to grow. Also, industries such as electromedical product manufacturing, which includes magnetic resonance imaging (MRI) machines, pacemakers, and other devices, should grow with an aging population requiring additional medical technology.

In most other manufacturing industries, employment of assemblers and fabricators will be negatively affected by increasing productivity, which will come from improved processes, tools, and, in some cases, automation. Automation is limited in assembly by intricate products and complicated techniques. Automation will replace workers in operations with a large volume of simple, repetitive work. Automation will have less effect on the assembly of products that are low in volume or very complicated.

The use of team production techniques has been one factor in the continuing success of the manufacturing sector, boosting productivity and improving the quality of goods. Thus, while the number of assemblers overall is expected to decline in manufacturing, the number of team assemblers should grow as more manufacturing plants convert to using team production techniques.

Some manufacturers have sent their assembly functions to countries where labor costs are lower. Decisions by U.S. corporations to move manufacturing to other nations may limit employment growth for assemblers in some industries.

The largest increase in the number of assemblers and fabricators is projected to be in the employment services industry, which supplies temporary workers to various industries. Temporary workers are gaining in importance in the manufacturing sector and elsewhere as companies facing cost pressures strive for a more flexible workforce to meet fluctuations in the market.

Job prospects. Job opportunities for assemblers are expected to be good for qualified applicants in the manufacturing sector, particularly in growing, high-technology industries, such as aerospace and electromedical devices. Some employers report difficulty finding qualified applicants looking for manufacturing employment. Many job openings will result from the need to replace workers leaving or retiring from this large occupational group.

Earnings

Wages vary by industry, geographic region, skill, educational level, and complexity of the machinery operated. Median hourly wages of team assemblers were $12.89 in May 2009. The middle 50 percent earned between $10.15 and $16.39. The lowest 10 percent earned less than $8.48, and the highest 10 percent earned more than $20.85. Median hourly wages in the manufacturing industries employing the largest numbers of team assemblers were as follows:

Motor vehicle manufacturing	$25.68
Motor vehicle body and trailer manufacturing	14.45
Motor vehicle parts manufacturing	14.22
Plastics product manufacturing	11.58
Employment services	9.83

Median hourly wages of electrical and electronic equipment assemblers were $13.77 in May 2009. The middle 50 percent earned between $10.93 and $17.63. The lowest 10 percent earned less than $9.17, and the highest 10 percent earned more than $22.35. Median hourly wages in the manufacturing industries employing the largest numbers of electrical and electronic equipment assemblers were as follows:

Navigational, measuring, electromedical, and control instruments manufacturing	$14.90
Electrical equipment manufacturing	13.71
Other electrical equipment and component manufacturing	13.06
Semiconductor and other electronic component manufacturing	13.43
Employment services	11.98

In May 2009, other assemblers and fabricators had the following median hourly wages:

Aircraft structure, surfaces, rigging, and systems assemblers	$21.86
Engine and other machine assemblers	16.58
Structural metal fabricators and fitters	16.29
Electromechanical equipment assemblers	14.75
Timing device assemblers, adjusters, and calibrators	13.50
Fiberglass laminators and fabricators	13.65
Coil winders, tapers, and finishers	13.48
Assemblers and fabricators, all other	13.39

Some assemblers and fabricators are members of labor unions. These unions include the International Association of Machinists and Aerospace Workers; the United Automobile, Aerospace and Agricultural Implement Workers of America; the International Brotherhood of Electrical Workers; and the United Steelworkers of America.

Related Occupations

Other occupations that involve operating machines and tools and assembling and checking products include industrial machinery mechanics and millwrights; inspectors, testers, sorters, samplers, and weighers; machine setters, operators, and tenders—metal and plastic; and welding, soldering, and brazing workers.

Sources of Additional Information

For information on certifications in electronics soldering, contact

▸ IPC, 3000 Lakeside Dr., 309 S, Bannockburn, IL 60015 Internet: www.ipc.org

Athletes, Coaches, Umpires, and Related Workers

(O*NET 27-2021.00, 27-2022.00, and 27-2023.00)

Significant Points

■ These jobs require immense overall knowledge of the game, usually acquired through years of experience at lower levels.

■ Career-ending injuries are always a risk for athletes.

■ Job opportunities will be best for part-time coaches, sports instructors, umpires, referees, and sports officials in high schools, sports clubs, and other settings.

■ Aspiring professional athletes will continue to face extremely keen competition.

Nature of the Work

Few people who dream of becoming paid professional *athletes*, *coaches*, or *sports officials* beat the odds and make a full-time living from professional athletics. Professional athletes often have short careers with little job security. Even though the chances of employment as a professional athlete are slim, there are many opportunities for at least a part-time job as a coach, instructor, referee, or umpire in amateur athletics or in high school, college, or university sports.

Athletes and *sports competitors* compete in organized, officiated sports events to entertain spectators. When playing a game, athletes are required to understand the strategies of their game while obeying the rules and regulations of the sport. The events in which they compete include both team sports, such as baseball, basketball, football, hockey, and soccer, and individual sports, such as golf, tennis, and bowling. The level of play varies from unpaid high school athletics to professional sports, in which the best from around the world compete in events broadcast on international television.

Being an athlete involves more than competing in athletic events. Athletes spend many hours each day practicing skills and improving teamwork under the guidance of a coach or a sports instructor. They view videotapes to critique their own performances and techniques and to learn their opponents' tendencies and weaknesses to gain a competitive advantage. Some athletes work regularly with strength trainers to gain muscle and stamina and to prevent injury. Many athletes push their bodies to the limit during both practice and play, so career-ending injury always is a risk; even minor injuries may put a player at risk of replacement. Because competition at all levels is extremely intense and job security is always precarious, many athletes train year round to maintain excellent form and technique and peak physical condition. Very little downtime from the sport exists at the professional level. Some athletes must conform to regimented diets to supplement any physical training program.

Coaches organize amateur and professional athletes and teach them the fundamental skills of individual and team sports. (In individual sports, *instructors* sometimes may fill this role.) Coaches train athletes for competition by holding practice sessions to perform drills that improve the athletes' form, technique, skills, and stamina. Along with refining athletes' individual skills, coaches are responsible for instilling good sportsmanship, a competitive spirit, and teamwork and for managing their teams during both practice sessions and competitions. Before competition, coaches evaluate or scout the opposing team to determine game strategies and practice specific plays. During competition, coaches may call specific plays intended to surprise or overpower the opponent, and they may substitute players for optimum team chemistry and success. Coaches' additional tasks may include selecting, storing, issuing, and taking inventory of equipment, materials, and supplies.

Many coaches in high schools are primarily teachers of academic subjects who supplement their income by coaching part time. College coaches consider coaching a full-time discipline and may be away from home frequently as they travel to competitions and to scout and recruit prospective players.

Sports instructors teach professional and nonprofessional athletes individually. They organize, instruct, train, and lead athletes in indoor and outdoor sports such as bowling, tennis, golf, and swimming. Because activities are as diverse as weight lifting, gymnastics, scuba diving, and karate, instructors tend to specialize in one or a few activities. Like coaches, sports instructors also may hold daily practice sessions and be responsible for any needed equipment and supplies. Using their knowledge of their sport and of physiology, they determine the type and level of difficulty of exercises, prescribe specific drills, and correct athletes' techniques. Some instructors also teach and demonstrate the use of training apparatus, such as trampolines or weights, for correcting athletes' weaknesses and enhancing their conditioning. Like coaches, sports instructors evaluate the athlete and the athlete's opponents to devise a competitive game strategy.

Coaches and sports instructors sometimes differ in their approaches to athletes because of the focus of their work. For example, while coaches manage the team during a game to optimize its chance for victory, sports instructors—such as those who work for professional tennis players—often are not permitted to instruct their athletes during competition. Sports instructors spend more of their time with athletes working one-on-one, which permits them to design customized training programs for each individual. Motivating athletes to play hard challenges most coaches and sports instructors but is vital for the athlete's success. Many coaches and instructors derive great satisfaction working with children or young adults, helping them to learn new physical and social skills, improve their physical condition, and achieve success in their sport.

Umpires, referees, and *other sports officials* officiate at competitive athletic and sporting events. They observe the play and impose penalties for infractions as established by the rules and regulations of the various sports. Umpires, referees, and sports officials anticipate play and position themselves to best see the action, assess the situation, and determine any violations. Some sports officials, such as boxing referees, may work independently, while others such as umpires work in groups. Regardless of the sport, the job is highly stressful because officials are often required to make a decision in a split second, sometimes resulting in strong disagreement among competitors, coaches, and spectators.

Professional *scouts* evaluate the skills of both amateur and professional athletes to determine talent and potential. As a sports intelligence agent, the scout's primary duty is to seek out top athletic candidates for the team he or she represents. At the professional level, scouts typically work for scouting organizations or as freelance scouts. In locating new talent, scouts perform their work in secrecy so as not to "tip off" their opponents about their interest in certain players. At the college level, the head scout often is an assistant coach, although freelance scouts may aid colleges by

reporting to coaches about exceptional players. Scouts at this level seek talented high school athletes by reading newspapers, contacting high school coaches and alumni, attending high school games, and studying videotapes of prospects' performances. They also evaluate potential players' backgrounds and personal characteristics, such as motivation and discipline, by talking to the players' coaches, parents, and teachers.

Work environment. Irregular work hours are common for athletes, coaches, umpires, referees, and other sports officials. They often work Saturdays, Sundays, evenings, and holidays. Athletes and full-time coaches usually work more than 40 hours a week for several months during the sports season, if not most of the year. High school coaches in educational institutions often coach more than one sport.

Athletes, coaches, and sports officials who participate in competitions that are held outdoors may be exposed to all weather conditions of the season. Athletes, coaches, and some sports officials frequently travel to sporting events. Scouts also travel extensively in locating talent. Athletes, coaches, and sports officials regularly encounter verbal abuse. Officials also face possible physical assault and, increasingly, lawsuits from injured athletes based on their officiating decisions.

Athletes and sports competitors had one of the highest rates of non-fatal on-the-job injuries. Coaches and sports officials also face the risk of injury, but the risk is not as great as that faced by athletes and sports competitors.

Training, Other Qualifications, and Advancement

Education and training requirements for athletes, coaches, umpires, and related workers vary greatly by the level and type of sport. Regardless of the sport or occupation, these jobs require immense overall knowledge of the game, usually acquired through years of experience at lower levels.

Education and training. Most athletes, coaches, umpires, and related workers get their training from having played in the sport at some level. All of these sports-related workers need to have an extensive knowledge of the way the sport is played, its rules and regulations, and strategies, which is often acquired by playing the sport in a school or recreation center, but also with the help of instructors or coaches, or in a camp that teaches the fundamentals of the sport.

Athletes get their training in several ways. For most team sports, athletes gain experience by competing in high school and collegiate athletics or on club teams. Although a high school or college degree may not be required to enter the sport, most athletes who get their training this way are often required to maintain specific academic standards to remain eligible to play, which often results in earning a degree. Other athletes, in gymnastics or tennis, for example, learn their sport by taking private or group lessons.

Although there may not be a specific education requirement, head coaches at public secondary schools and sports instructors at all levels usually must have a bachelor's degree. For high school coaching and sports instructor jobs, schools usually prefer, and may have to hire teachers willing to take on these part-time jobs. If no suitable teacher is found, schools hire someone from outside. College coaches also usually are required to have a bachelor's degree. Degree programs specifically related to coaching include exercise and sports science, physiology, kinesiology, nutrition and fitness, physical education, and sports medicine. Some entry-level positions for coaches or instructors require only experience derived as a participant in the sport or activity.

Each sport has specific requirements for umpires, referees, and other sports officials; some require these officials to pass a test of their knowledge of the sport. Umpires, referees, and other sports officials often begin their careers and gain needed experience by volunteering for intramural, community, and recreational league competitions. They are often required to attend some form of training course or academy.

Scouting jobs often require experience playing a sport at the college or professional level that makes it possible to spot young players who possess athletic ability and skills. Most beginning scouting jobs are as part-time talent spotters in a particular area or region.

Licensure and certification. The need for athletes, coaches, umpires, and related workers to be licensed or certified to practice varies by sport and by locality. For example, in drag racing, drivers need to graduate from approved schools in order to be licensed to compete in the various drag racing series. The governing body of the sport may revoke licenses and suspend players who do not meet the required performance, education, or training. In addition, athletes may have their licenses or certification suspended for inappropriate activity.

Most public high school coaches need to meet state requirements for certification to become a head coach. Certification, however, may not be required for coaching and sports instructor jobs in private schools. College coaches may be required to be certified. For those interested in becoming scuba, tennis, golf, karate, or other kind of instructor, certification is highly desirable and may be required. There are many certifying organizations specific to the various sports, and their requirements vary. Coaches' certification often requires that one must be at least 18 years old and certified in cardiopulmonary resuscitation (CPR). Participation in a clinic, camp, or school also usually is required for certification. Part-time workers and those in smaller facilities are less likely to need formal education or training and may not need certification.

To officiate at high school athletic events, umpires, referees, and other officials must register with the state agency that oversees high school athletics and pass an exam on the rules of the particular game. For college refereeing, candidates must be certified by an officiating school and be evaluated during a probationary period. Some larger college sports conferences require officials to have certification and other qualifications, such as residence in or near the conference boundaries, along with several years of experience officiating at high school, community college, or other college conference games.

Other qualifications. Athletes, coaches, umpires, and related workers often direct teams or compete on them. Thus these workers must relate well to others and possess good communication and leadership skills. They may need to pass a background check and applicable drug tests. Athletes who seek to compete professionally must have extraordinary talent, desire, and dedication to training. Coaches must be resourceful and flexible to successfully instruct and motivate individuals and groups of athletes. Officials need good vision, reflexes, and the ability to make decisions quickly.

Advancement. For most athletes, turning professional is the biggest advancement. They often begin to compete immediately, although some may spend more time "on the bench," as a reserve, to gain experience. In some sports, such as baseball, athletes may begin their professional career on a minor league team before moving up to the major leagues. Professional athletes generally advance in their sport by winning and achieving accolades and earning a higher salary.

Many coaches begin their careers as assistant coaches to gain the knowledge and experience needed to become a head coach. Head coaches at large schools and colleges that strive to compete at the highest levels of a sport require substantial experience as a head coach at another school or as an assistant coach. To reach the ranks of professional coaching, a person usually needs years of coaching experience and a winning record in the lower ranks or experience as an athlete in that sport.

Standards for umpires and other officials become more stringent as the level of competition advances. A local or state academy may be required to referee a school baseball game. Those seeking to officiate at minor or major league games must attend a professional umpire training school. To advance to umpiring in Major League Baseball, umpires usually need 7 to 10 years of experience in various minor leagues before being considered for major league jobs.

Finding talented players is essential for scouts to advance. Hard work and a record of success often lead to full-time jobs and responsibility for scouting in more areas. Some scouts advance to scouting director jobs or various administrative positions in sports.

Employment

Athletes, coaches, umpires, and related workers held about 258,100 jobs in 2008. Coaches and scouts held 225,700 jobs; athletes and sports competitors, 16,500; and umpires, referees, and other sports officials, 15,900. About half of all athletes, coaches, umpires, and related workers worked part time or maintained variable schedules. Many sports officials and coaches receive such small and irregular payments for their services—occasional officiating at club games, for example—that they may not consider themselves employed in these occupations, even part time.

Among those employed in wage and salary jobs, 52 percent held jobs in public and private educational services. About 13 percent worked in amusement, gambling, and recreation industries, including golf and tennis clubs, gymnasiums, health clubs, judo and karate schools, riding stables, swim clubs, and other sports and recreation facilities. Another 6 percent worked in the spectator sports industry.

About 16 percent of workers in this occupation were self-employed, earning prize money or fees for lessons, scouting, or officiating assignments. Many other coaches and sports officials, although technically not self-employed, have such irregular or tenuous working arrangements that their working conditions resemble those of self-employment.

Job Outlook

Employment of athletes, coaches, umpires, and related workers is expected to grow much faster than the average for all occupations through 2018. Very keen competition is expected for jobs at the highest levels of sports with progressively more favorable opportunities in lower levels of competition.

Employment change. Employment of athletes, coaches, umpires, and related workers is expected to increase by 23 percent from 2008 to 2018, which is much faster than the average for all occupations. A larger population overall that will continue to participate in organized sports for entertainment, recreation, and physical

Projections Data from the National Employment Matrix

Occupational title	SOC Code	Employment, 2008	Projected employment, 2018	Change, 2008–2018	
				Number	Percent
Athletes, coaches, umpires, and related workers 27-2020		258,100	317,700	59,600	23
Athletes and sports competitors 27-2021		16,500	18,400	1,900	12
Coaches and scouts 27-2022		225,700	281,700	56,000	25
Umpires, referees, and other sports officials 27-2023		15,900	17,600	1,700	10

NOTE: Data in this table are rounded.

conditioning will boost demand for these workers, particularly for coaches, umpires, sports instructors, and other related workers. Job growth also will be driven by the increasing number of retirees who are expected to participate more in leisure activities such as golf and tennis, which require instruction. Additionally, the demand for private sports instruction is expected to grow among young athletes as parents try to help their children reach their full potential. Future expansion of new professional teams and leagues may create additional openings for all of these workers.

Additional coaches and instructors are expected to be needed as school and college athletic programs expand. Population growth is expected to cause the construction of additional schools, but funding for athletic programs often is cut first when budgets become tight. Still, the popularity of team sports often enables shortfalls to be offset with the assistance from fundraisers, booster clubs, and parents. In colleges, most of the expansion is expected to be in women's sports.

Job prospects. Persons who are state-certified to teach academic subjects are likely to have the best prospects for obtaining coaching and instructor jobs in schools. The need to replace the many high school coaches will provide most coaching opportunities.

Competition for professional athlete jobs will continue to be extremely keen. In major sports, such as basketball and football, only about 1 in 5,000 high school athletes becomes professional in these sports. The expansion of nontraditional sports may create some additional opportunities. Because most professional athletes' careers last only a few years due to debilitating injuries and age, annual replacement needs for these jobs is high, creating some job opportunities. However, the talented young men and women who dream of becoming sports superstars greatly outnumber the number of openings.

Opportunities should be best for persons seeking part-time umpire, referee, and other sports official jobs at the high school level. Coaches in girls' and women's sports may have better opportunities and face less competition for positions. Competition is expected for higher paying jobs at the college level and will be even greater for jobs in professional sports. Competition should be keen for paying jobs as scouts, particularly for professional teams, because the number of available positions is limited.

Earnings

Median annual wages of athletes and sports competitors were $40,210 in May 2009. The middle 50 percent earned between $22,980 and $88,760. The highest paid professional athletes earn much more.

Median annual wages of umpires and related workers were $22,880 in May 2009. The middle 50 percent earned between $17,820 and

$33,710. The lowest-paid 10 percent earned less than $15,880, and the highest-paid 10 percent earned more than $48,080.

In May 2009, median annual wages of coaches and scouts were $28,380. The middle 50 percent earned between $18,600 and $43,690. The lowest-paid 10 percent earned less than $15,910, and the highest-paid 10 percent earned more than $62,750. However, the highest-paid professional coaches earn much more. Median annual wages in the industries employing the largest numbers of coaches and scouts in May 2009 are shown below:

Colleges, universities, and professional schools $39,690
Other amusement and recreation industries........... 29,090
Other schools and instruction 25,160
Elementary and secondary schools 22,300

Wages vary by level of education, certification, and geographic region. Some instructors and coaches are paid a salary, while others may be paid by the hour, per session, or based on the number of participants.

Related Occupations

Other occupations involved with athletes or sports include dietitians and nutritionists; fitness workers; physical therapists; recreation workers; and recreational therapists.

Other workers who teach and motivate students include teachers—kindergarten, elementary, middle, and secondary.

Sources of Additional Information

For information about sports officiating for team and individual sports, contact

▶ National Association of Sports Officials, 2017 Lathrop Ave., Racine, WI 53405. Internet: www.naso.org

For additional information related to individual sports, refer to the organization that represents the sport.

Automotive Body and Related Repairers

(O*NET 49-3021.00 and 49-3022.00)

Significant Points

■ Little or no change in the overall number of jobs is expected.

■ Repairers need good reading ability and basic mathematics and computer skills to use print and digital technical manuals.

■ Many repairers, particularly in urban areas, need a national certification to advance past entry-level work.

Nature of the Work

Most of the damage resulting from everyday vehicle collisions can be repaired, and vehicles can be refinished to look and drive like new. This damage may be relatively minor, such as scraped paint or a dented panel, or major, requiring the complex replacement of parts. Such repair services are performed by trained workers.

Automotive body and related repairers, often called *collision repair technicians*, straighten bent bodies, remove dents, and replace crumpled parts that cannot be fixed. They repair all types of vehicles, and although some work on large trucks, buses, or tractor-trailers, most work on cars and small trucks. They can work alone, with only general direction from supervisors, or as specialists on a repair team. In some shops, helpers or apprentices assist experienced repairers.

Each damaged vehicle presents different challenges for repairers. Using their broad knowledge of automotive construction and repair techniques, automotive body repairers must decide how to handle each job based on what the vehicle is made of and what needs to be fixed. They must first determine the extent of the damage and decide which parts can be repaired or need to be replaced.

If the car is heavily damaged, an automotive body repairer might start by measuring the frame to determine if there has been structural damage. Repairers would then attach or clamp frames and sections to structural machines that use hydraulic pressure to align damaged components. "Unibody" vehicles—designs built without frames—must be restored to precise factory specifications for the vehicle to operate correctly. For these vehicles, repairers use bench systems to accurately measure how much each section is out of alignment and hydraulic machinery to return the vehicle to its original shape.

Only once the frame is aligned properly can repairers begin to fix or replace other damaged body parts. If the vehicle or part is made of metal, body repairers will use a pneumatic metal-cutting gun or a plasma cutter to remove badly damaged sections of body panels and then weld or otherwise attach replacement sections. Less serious dents are pulled out with a hydraulic jack or hand prying bar or knocked out with hand tools or pneumatic hammers. Small dents and creases in the metal are smoothed by holding a small anvil against one side of the damaged area while hammering the opposite side. Repairers may also remove very small pits and dimples with pick hammers and punches in a process called metal finishing. Body repairers then use plastic or solder to fill small dents that cannot be worked out of plastic or metal panels. On metal panels, they sculpt the hardened filler to the original shape by filing, grinding and sanding the repair back to the shape that is desired.

Body repairers may also repair or replace the plastic body parts that are increasingly used on new vehicles. They remove damaged panels and identify the type and properties of the plastic used. Some types of plastic allow repairers to apply heat from a hot-air welding gun or immerse the panel in hot water and press the softened section back into shape by hand. In most cases, it is more cost effective for the plastic parts to be replaced rather than to be repaired. A few body repairers specialize in fixing fiberglass car bodies.

Some body repairers specialize in installing and repairing glass in automobiles and other vehicles. *Automotive glass installers and repairers* remove broken, cracked, or pitted windshields and window glass. Glass installers apply a moisture-proofing compound along the edges of the glass, place the glass in the vehicle, and install rubber strips around the sides of the windshield or window to make it secure and weatherproof.

Many large shops make repairs using an assembly-line approach where vehicles are fixed by a team of repairers who each specialize in several types of repair. One worker might straighten frames while another repairs doors and fenders, for example. In most shops, automotive painters do the priming and refinishing, but in small shops, workers often do both body repairing and painting. (Automotive painters are discussed in the section on painting and coating workers, except construction and maintenance elsewhere in this book.)

Work environment. Repairers work indoors in body shops where noise from the clatter of hammers against metal and the whine of power tools is prevalent. Most shops are well ventilated to disperse dust and paint fumes. Body repairers may also be required to work in awkward or cramped positions, and much of their work can be physically challenging. Hazards include cuts from sharp metal edges, burns from torches and heated metal, injuries from power tools. However, serious accidents usually are avoided when the shop is kept clean and orderly and safety practices are observed.

Most automotive body repairers work a standard 40-hour week. More than 40 hours a week may be required when there is a backlog of repair work to be completed. This may include working on weekends.

Training, Other Qualifications, and Advancement

As automotive technology rapidly becomes more sophisticated, most employers prefer applicants who have completed a formal training program in automotive body repair or refinishing. Most new repairers complete at least part of this training on the job, while continuing to receive training from industry vendors or suppliers throughout their careers. Many repairers, particularly in urban areas, need a national certification to advance past entry-level work.

Education and training. A high school diploma or GED is often all that is required to enter this occupation, but more specific education and training is needed to learn how to repair newer automobiles. Collision repair programs may be offered in high school or in postsecondary vocational schools and community colleges. Courses in electronics, physics, chemistry, English, computers, and mathematics provide a good background for a career as an automotive body repairer. Training programs combine classroom instruction and hands-on practice.

Trade and technical school programs typically award certificates to graduates after 6 months to a year of collision repair study. Some community colleges offer 2-year programs in collision repair. Many of these schools also offer certificates for individual courses, so that students are able to take classes incrementally or as needed.

New repairers begin by assisting experienced body repairers in tasks such as removing damaged parts and sanding body panels. Novices learn to remove small dents and make other minor repairs. They then progress to more difficult tasks, such as straightening body parts and installing either repaired or replaced bolt-on parts. Generally, it takes 3 to 4 years of hands-on training to become skilled in all aspects of body repair, some of which may be completed as part of a formal education program. Basic automotive glass installation and repair can be learned in as little as 6 months, but becoming fully qualified can take several years.

Continuing education and training are needed throughout a career in automotive body repair. Automotive parts composition, body materials, electronics, and airbags and other new safety components continue to change and to become more complex. To keep up with these technological advances, repairers must continue to gain new skills by reading technical manuals and furthering their education with classes and seminars. Many companies within the automotive body repair industry send employees to advanced training programs to brush up on old skills or to learn new techniques.

Other qualifications. Fully skilled automotive body repairers must have good reading ability and basic mathematics, including geometry, physics, and computer skills. Restoring unibody automobiles to their original specification requires repairers to follow instructions and diagrams in print and digital technical manuals and to make precise three-dimensional measurements of the position of one body section relative to another. In addition, repairers should enjoy working with their hands and be able to pay attention to detail while they work.

Certification and advancement. Certification by the National Institute for Automotive Service Excellence (ASE), although voluntary, is the pervasive industry credential for experienced automotive body repairers. Many repairers, particularly in urban areas, need a national certification to advance past entry-level work. Repairers may take up to four ASE Master Collision Repair and Refinish Exams. Repairers who pass at least one exam and have 2 years of hands-on work experience earn ASE certification. The completion of a post-secondary program in automotive body repair may be substituted for 1 year of work experience. Those who pass all four exams become ASE Master Collision Repair and Refinish Technicians. Automotive body repairers must retake the examination at least every 5 years to retain their certification. Ongoing training through the Inter-Industry Conference on Auto Collision Repair (I-CAR) can lead to additional recognition as a Platinum technician. Finally, many vehicle manufacturers and paint manufacturers also have product certification programs that can advance a repairer's career.

As beginners increase their skills, learn new techniques, earn certifications, and complete work more rapidly, their pay increases. An experienced automotive body repairer with managerial ability may advance to shop supervisor, and some workers open their own body repair shops. Other repairers become automobile damage appraisers for insurance companies.

Employment

Automotive body and related repairers held about 185,900 jobs in 2008; about 10 percent specialized in automotive glass installation and repair. Around 62 percent of repairers worked for automotive repair and maintenance shops, while 17 percent worked for automobile dealers. A small number worked for wholesalers of motor vehicles, parts, and supplies. About 12 percent of automotive body repairers were self-employed.

Job Outlook

Employment is projected to see little or no change. Job opportunities will be excellent for people with formal training in automotive body repair and refinishing as older workers retire and need to be replaced; those without any training or experience will face competition.

Employment change. Employment of automotive body repairers is expected to grow by 1 percent over the 2008–2018 decade. The number of vehicles on the road is expected to continue increasing over the next decade. This will lead to overall growth in the demand for collision repair services. The increasing role of technology in vehicles also will mean new opportunities for workers with expertise or training in repairing particular makes and models of cars or working with specific materials.

However, several factors will limit the number of new jobs for automotive body repairers. The increasingly advanced technology used in vehicles has led to significant increases in the prices of new and replacement parts. Collision repair shop owners, in an effort to stay profitable, have adopted productivity-enhancing techniques. The result of this has also been consolidation within the industry, or a decreasing number of collision repair shops and limited total employment growth. In some cases, the use of new technology like airbags has led to more cars that are involved in accidents to be declared a total loss—where repairing a car costs more than the value of the vehicle. High insurance deductibles have meant that an increasing number of cars suffering minor collision damage are going unrepaired.

Job prospects. Although few jobs are expected to arise due to growth, the need to replace experienced repairers who transfer to other occupations or who retire or stop working for other reasons will provide many job openings over the next 10 years. Opportunities will be excellent for people with formal training in automotive body repair and refinishing. Those without any training or experience in automotive body refinishing or collision repair will face competition for these jobs.

Earnings

Median hourly wages of automotive body and related repairers, including incentive pay, were $18.26 in May 2009. The middle 50 percent earned between $14.24 and $24.05 an hour. The lowest 10 percent earned less than $11.12, and the highest 10 percent earned more than $30.76 an hour. Median hourly wages of automotive body and related repairers were $19.26 in automobile dealers and $17.95 in automotive repair and maintenance.

Median hourly wages of automotive glass installers and repairers, including incentive pay, were $15.91 in May 2009. The middle 50 percent earned between $12.71 and $19.30 an hour. The lowest 10 percent earned less than $10.09 and the highest 10 percent earned

Projections Data from the National Employment Matrix

Occupational title	SOC Code	Employment, 2008	Projected employment, 2018	Change, 2008–2018	
				Number	Percent
Automotive body and related repairers ....—		185,900	187,000	1,100	1
Automotive body and related repairers 49-3021		166,400	167,200	800	0
Automotive glass installers and repairers 49-3022		19,500	19,900	400	2

NOTE: Data in this table are rounded.

more than $23.76 an hour. Median hourly wages in automotive repair and maintenance shops, the industry employing the largest number of these workers, were $15.77.

The majority of body repairers employed by independent repair shops and automotive dealers are paid on an incentive basis. Under this system, body repairers are paid a set amount for various tasks, and earnings depend on both the amount of work assigned and how fast it is completed. Employers frequently guarantee workers a minimum weekly salary. Body repairers who work for trucking companies, bus lines, and other organizations that maintain their own vehicles usually receive an hourly wage.

Helpers and trainees typically earn between 30 percent and 60 percent of the earnings of skilled workers. They are paid by the hour until they are skilled enough to be paid on an incentive basis.

Employee benefits vary widely from business to business. However, industry sources report that benefits such as paid leave, health insurance, and retirement assistance are increasingly common in the collision repair industry. Automotive dealerships are the most likely to offer such incentives.

Related Occupations

Other occupations associated with vehicle maintenance and repair include automotive service technicians and mechanics; diesel service technicians and mechanics; glaziers; heavy vehicle and mobile equipment service technicians and mechanics; and painting and coating workers, except construction and maintenance.

Sources of Additional Information

Additional details about work opportunities may be obtained from automotive body repair shops, automobile dealers, or local offices of your state employment service. State employment service offices also are a source of information about training programs.

For general information about automotive body repairer careers, contact any of the following sources:

▸ Automotive Careers Today, 8400 Westpark Dr., MS #2, McLean, VA 22102. Internet: www.autocareerstoday.org

▸ Automotive Service Association, P.O. Box 929, Bedford, TX 76095. Internet: www.asashop.org

▸ Inter-Industry Conference on Auto Collision Repair Education Foundation (I-CAR), 5125 Trillium Blvd., Hoffman Estates, IL 60192. Internet: www.collisioncareers.org

▸ Society of Collision Repair Specialists, P.O. Box 909, Prosser, WA 99350. Internet: www.scrs.com

For general information about careers in automotive glass installation and repair, contact

▸ National Glass Association, 8200 Greensboro Dr., Suite 302, McLean, VA 22102. Internet: www.myglassclass.com

For information on how to become a certified automotive body repairer, write to

▸ National Institute for Automotive Service Excellence (ASE), 101 Blue Seal Dr. SE, Suite 101, Leesburg, VA 20175. Internet: www.asecert.org

For a directory of certified automotive body repairer programs, contact

▸ National Automotive Technician Education Foundation, 101 Blue Seal Dr. SE, Suite 101, Leesburg, VA 20175. Internet: www.natef.org

For a directory of accredited private trade and technical schools that offer training programs in automotive body repair, contact

▸ Accrediting Commission of Career Schools and Colleges, 2101 Wilson Blvd., Suite 302, Arlington, VA 22201. Internet: www.accsc.org/

Automotive Service Technicians and Mechanics

(O*NET 49-3023.00, 49-3023.01, and 49-3023.02)

Significant Points

■ Automotive service technicians and mechanics must continually adapt to changing technology and repair techniques.

■ Formal automotive technician training is the best preparation.

■ Opportunities should be very good for those who complete post-secondary automotive training programs; those without formal automotive training are likely to face competition for entry-level jobs.

Nature of the Work

Automotive service technicians inspect, maintain, and repair automobiles and light trucks that run on gasoline, electricity, or alternative fuels, such as ethanol. They perform basic care maintenance, such as oil changes and tire rotations, diagnose more complex problems, and plan and execute vehicle repairs. (Service technicians who work on diesel-powered trucks, buses, and equipment are discussed in the job description for diesel service technicians and mechanics.)

Automotive service technicians' and mechanics' responsibilities have evolved from simple mechanical repairs to high-level technology-related work. Today, integrated electronic systems and complex computers regulate vehicles and their performance while on the road. This increasing sophistication of automobiles requires workers who can use computerized shop equipment and work with electronic components while maintaining their skills with traditional hand tools. Technicians must have an increasingly broad knowledge of how vehicles' complex components work and interact. They also must be able to work with electronic diagnostic equipment and digital manuals and reference materials.

When mechanical or electrical troubles occur, technicians first get a description of the problem from the owner or, in a large shop, from the repair service estimator or service advisor who wrote the repair order. To locate the problem, technicians use a diagnostic approach. First, they test to see whether components and systems are secure and working properly. Then, they isolate the components or systems that might be the cause of the problem. For example, if an air conditioner malfunctions, the technician might check for a simple problem, such as a low coolant level, or a more complex issue, such as a bad drive-train connection that has shorted out the air conditioner. As part of their investigation, technicians may test drive the vehicle or use a variety of testing equipment, including onboard and hand-held diagnostic computers or compression gauges. These tests may indicate whether a component is salvageable or whether a new one is required. Accuracy and efficiency are critical in diagnosing and repairing vehicles, as parts are increasingly expensive, and timely repairs allow shops to take on more business.

During routine service inspections, technicians test and lubricate engines and other major components. Sometimes, technicians repair or replace worn parts before they cause breakdowns or damage the vehicle. Technicians usually follow a checklist to ensure that they examine every critical part. Belts, hoses, plugs, brakes, fuel systems, and other potentially troublesome items are watched closely.

Service technicians use a variety of tools in their work. They use power tools, such as pneumatic wrenches, to remove bolts quickly; machine tools like lathes and grinding machines to rebuild brakes; welding and flame-cutting equipment to remove and repair exhaust systems; and jacks and hoists to lift cars and engines. They also use common hand tools, such as screwdrivers, pliers, and wrenches, to work on small parts and in hard-to-reach places. Technicians usually provide their own hand tools, and many experienced workers have thousands of dollars invested in them. Employers furnish expensive power tools, engine analyzers, and other diagnostic equipment.

Computers are also commonplace in modern repair shops. Service technicians compare the readouts from computerized diagnostic testing devices with benchmarked standards given by the manufacturer. Deviations outside of acceptable levels tell the technician to investigate that part of the vehicle more closely. Through the Internet or from software packages, most shops receive automatic updates to technical manuals and access to manufacturers' service information, technical service bulletins, and other databases that allow technicians to keep up with common problems and to learn new procedures.

High-technology tools are needed to fix the computer equipment that operates everything from the engine to the radio in many cars. In fact, today, most automotive systems, such as braking, transmission, and steering systems, are controlled primarily by computers and electronic components. Additionally, luxury vehicles often have integrated global positioning systems, accident-avoidance systems, and other new features with which technicians will need to become familiar. Also, as more alternate-fuel vehicles are purchased, more automotive service technicians will need to learn the science behind these automobiles and how to repair them.

Automotive service technicians in large shops often specialize in certain types of repairs. For example, *transmission technicians and rebuilders* work on gear trains, couplings, hydraulic pumps, and other parts of transmissions. Extensive knowledge of computer controls, the ability to diagnose electrical and hydraulic problems, and other specialized skills are needed to work on these complex components, which employ some of the most sophisticated technology used in vehicles. *Tune-up technicians* adjust ignition timing and valves and adjust or replace spark plugs and other parts to ensure efficient engine performance. They often use electronic testing equipment to isolate and adjust malfunctions in fuel, ignition, and emissions control systems.

Automotive air-conditioning repairers install and repair air conditioners and service their components, such as compressors, condensers, and controls. These workers require special training in federal and state regulations governing the handling and disposal of refrigerants. *Front-end mechanics* align and balance wheels and repair steering mechanisms and suspension systems. They frequently use special alignment equipment and wheel-balancing machines. *Brake repairers* adjust brakes, replace brake linings and pads, and make other repairs on brake systems. Some technicians specialize in both brake and front-end work.

Work environment. While in 2008, most automotive service technicians worked a standard 40 hour week, 24 percent worked longer hours. Some may work evenings and weekends to satisfy customer service needs. Generally, service technicians work indoors in well-ventilated and well-lighted repair shops. However, some shops are drafty and noisy. Although many problems can be fixed with simple computerized adjustments, technicians frequently work with dirty and greasy parts and in awkward positions. They often lift heavy parts and tools. As a result, minor workplace injuries are not uncommon, but technicians usually can avoid serious accidents if safe practices are observed.

Training, Other Qualifications, and Advancement

Automotive technology is rapidly growing in sophistication, and employers are increasingly looking for workers who have completed a formal training program in high school or in a postsecondary vocational school or community college. Acquiring National Institute for Automotive Service Excellence (ASE) certification is important for those seeking work in large, urban areas.

Education and training. Most employers regard the successful completion of a vocational training program in automotive service technology as the best preparation for trainee positions. High school programs, while an asset, vary greatly in scope. Graduates of these programs may need further training to become qualified. Some of the more extensive high school programs participate in Automotive Youth Education Service (AYES), a partnership between high school automotive repair programs, automotive manufacturers, and franchised automotive dealers. All AYES high school programs are certified by the National Institute for Automotive Service Excellence. Students who complete these programs are well prepared to enter entry-level technician positions or to advance their technical education. Courses in automotive repair, electronics, physics, chemistry, English, computers, and mathematics provide a good educational background for a career as a service technician.

Postsecondary automotive technician training programs usually provide intensive career preparation through a combination of classroom instruction and hands-on practice. Schools update their curriculums frequently to reflect changing technology and equipment. Some trade and technical school programs provide concentrated training for 6 months to a year, depending on how many hours the student attends each week, and upon completion, award a certificate. Community college programs usually award a certificate or an associate degree. Some students earn repair certificates in a particular skill and leave to begin their careers. Associate degree programs, however, usually take 2 years to complete and include classes in English, basic mathematics, computers, and other subjects, as well as automotive repair. Recently, some programs have added classes on customer service, stress management, and other employability skills. Some formal training programs have alliances with tool manufacturers that help entry-level technicians accumulate tools during their training period.

Various automobile manufacturers and participating franchised dealers also sponsor 2-year associate degree programs at postsecondary schools across the nation. Students in these programs typically spend alternate 6-week to 12-week periods attending classes full time and working full time in the service departments of sponsoring dealers. At these dealerships, students work with an experienced worker who provides hands-on instruction and timesaving tips.

Those new to automotive service usually start as trainee technicians, technicians' helpers, or lubrication workers, and gradually acquire and practice their skills by working with experienced mechanics and technicians. In many cases, on-the-job training may be a part of a formal education program. With a few months' experience, beginners perform many routine service tasks and make simple repairs. While some graduates of postsecondary automotive training programs often are able to earn promotion to the journey level after only a few months on the job, it typically takes 2 to 5 years of experience to become a fully qualified service technician, who is expected to quickly perform the more difficult types of routine service and repairs. An additional 1 to 2 years of experience familiarizes technicians with all types of repairs. Complex specialties, such as transmission repair, require another year or two of training and experience. In contrast, brake specialists may learn their jobs in considerably less time because they do not need complete knowledge of automotive repair.

Employers increasingly send experienced automotive service technicians to manufacturer training centers to learn to repair new models or to receive special training in the repair of components, such as electronic fuel injection or air conditioners. Motor vehicle dealers and other automotive service providers may send promising beginners or experienced technicians to manufacturer-sponsored technician training programs to upgrade or maintain employees' skills. Factory representatives also visit many shops to conduct short training sessions.

Other qualifications. The ability to diagnose the source of a problem quickly and accurately requires good reasoning ability and a thorough knowledge of automobiles. Many technicians consider diagnosing hard-to-find troubles one of their most challenging and satisfying duties. For trainee automotive service technician jobs, employers look for people with strong communication and analytical skills. Technicians need good reading, mathematics, and computer skills to study technical manuals. They must also read to keep up with new technology and learn new service and repair procedures and specifications.

Training in electronics is vital because electrical components, or a series of related components, account for nearly all malfunctions in modern vehicles. Trainees must possess mechanical aptitude and knowledge of how automobiles work. Experience working on motor vehicles in the Armed Forces or as a hobby can be very valuable.

Certification and advancement. ASE certification has become a standard credential for automotive service technicians. While not mandatory for work in automotive service, certification is common for all experienced technicians in large, urban areas. Certification is available in eight different areas of automotive service, such as electrical systems, engine repair, brake systems, suspension and steering, and heating and air conditioning. For certification in each area, technicians must have at least 2 years of experience and pass the examination. Completion of an automotive training program in high school, vocational or trade school, or community or junior

college may be substituted for 1 year of experience. For ASE certification as a Master Automobile Technician, technicians must pass all eight examinations.

By becoming skilled in multiple auto repair services, technicians can increase their value to their employer and their pay. Experienced technicians who have administrative ability sometimes advance to shop supervisor or service manager. Those with sufficient funds many times open independent automotive repair shops. Technicians who work well with customers may become automotive repair service estimators. They may also find work as educators.

Employment

Automotive service technicians and mechanics held about 763,700 jobs in 2008. Automotive repair and maintenance shops and automobile dealers employed the majority of these workers, with 31 percent working in shops and 28 percent employed by dealers. In addition, automotive parts, accessories, and tire stores employed 7 percent of automotive service technicians. Others worked in gasoline stations; automotive equipment rental and leasing companies; federal, state, and local governments; and other organizations. About 16 percent of service technicians were self-employed, compared with 7 percent of all installation, maintenance, and repair occupations.

Job Outlook

The number of jobs for automotive service technicians and mechanics is projected to grow slower than the average for all occupations, although many job openings will arise as experienced technicians retire. Opportunities should be good for those who complete postsecondary automotive training programs, as some employers report difficulty finding workers with the right skills; those without formal automotive training are likely to face competition for entry-level jobs.

Employment change. Employment of automotive service technicians and mechanics is expected to increase by 5 percent between 2008 and 2018, slower than the average for all occupations. Continued growth in the number of vehicles in use in the United States will lead to new jobs for workers performing basic car maintenance and repair. More entry-level workers will be needed to perform these services, such as oil changes and replacing worn brakes. Additionally, the average lifespan of vehicles is increasing, which will further increase the demand for repair services, especially postwarranty work. The increasing use of advanced technology in automobiles will also lead to new opportunities for repair technicians, especially those with specialized skills or certifications. Workers with expertise in certain makes or models of vehicles, or with an advanced understanding of certain systems, such as hybrid-fuel technology, will be in demand. At the same time, consolidation in the automobile dealer industry, a significant employer of technicians, will limit the need for new workers.

Projections Data from the National Employment Matrix

Occupational title	SOC Code	Employment, 2008	Projected employment, 2018	Change, 2008–2018	
				Number	Percent
Automotive service technicians and mechanics 49-3023		763,700	799,600	35,900	5

NOTE: Data in this table are rounded.

Job prospects. In addition to openings from growth, many job openings will be created by the need to replace retiring technicians. Job opportunities are expected to be very good for those who complete postsecondary automotive training programs and who earn ASE certification. Some employers report difficulty in finding workers with the right skills. People with good diagnostic and problem-solving abilities, training in electronics, and computer skills are expected to have the best opportunities. Those without formal automotive training are likely to face competition for entry-level jobs.

Most new job openings will be in automobile dealerships and independent repair shops where most automobile service technicians currently work. However, the large-scale restructuring and closing of many automobile dealerships will lead to fewer openings in dealer service centers for the initial part of the next decade.

Earnings

Median hourly wages of automotive service technicians and mechanics, including commission, were $17.03 in May 2009. The middle 50 percent earned between $12.49 and $22.71 per hour. The lowest 10 percent earned less than $9.54, and the highest 10 percent earned more than $28.81 per hour. Median annual wages in the industries employing the largest numbers of service technicians were as follows:

Automotive repair and maintenance	15.65
Automobile dealers	19.71
Automotive parts, accessories, and tire stores	14.98
Gasoline stations	15.00
Local government	$20.83

Many experienced technicians employed by automobile dealers and independent repair shops receive a commission related to the labor cost charged to the customer. Under this system, weekly earnings depend on the amount of work completed. Employers frequently guarantee commissioned technicians a minimum weekly salary. Some employees offer health and retirement benefits, but such compensation packages are not universal and can vary widely.

Related Occupations

Other workers who repair and service motor vehicles include automotive body and related repairers; diesel service technicians and mechanics; heavy vehicle and mobile equipment service technicians and mechanics; and small engine mechanics.

Sources of Additional Information

For more details about work opportunities, contact local automobile dealers and repair shops or local offices of the state employment service. The state employment service also may have information about training programs.

For general information about a career as an automotive service technician, contact

▶ Automotive Careers Today, 8400 Westpark Dr., MS #2, McLean, VA 22102. Internet: www.autocareerstoday.org

▶ Career Voyages, U.S. Department of Labor, 200 Constitution Ave. NW, Washington, DC 20210. Internet: www.careervoyages.gov/automotive-main.cfm

A list of certified automotive service technician training programs can be obtained from

▶ National Automotive Technicians Education Foundation, 101 Blue Seal Dr. SE, Suite 101, Leesburg, VA 20175. Internet: www.natef.org

For a directory of accredited private trade and technical schools that offer programs in automotive service technician training, contact

▶ Accrediting Commission of Career Schools and Colleges, 2101 Wilson Blvd., Suite 302, Arlington, VA 22201. Internet: www.accsc.org

Information on automobile manufacturer-sponsored programs in automotive service technology can be obtained from

▶ Automotive Youth Educational Systems (AYES), 101 Blue Seal Dr. SE, Suite 101, Leesburg, VA, 20175. Internet: www.ayes.org

Information on how to become a certified automotive service technician is available from

▶ National Institute for Automotive Service Excellence (ASE), 101 Blue Seal Dr. SE, Suite 101, Leesburg, VA 20175. Internet: www.asecert.org

Barbers, Cosmetologists, and Other Personal Appearance Workers

(O*NET 39-5011.00, 39-5012.00, 39-5092.00, 39-5093.00, and 39-5094.00)

Significant Points

■ Employment is expected to grow much faster than the average for all occupations.

■ A state license is required for barbers, cosmetologists, and most other personal appearance workers, although qualifications vary by state.

■ About 44 percent of workers are self-employed; many also work flexible schedules.

Nature of the Work

Barbers and *cosmetologists* focus on providing hair care services to enhance the appearance of customers. Other personal appearance workers, such as *manicurists and pedicurists*, *shampooers*, and *skin care specialists*, provide specialized beauty services that help clients look and feel their best.

Barbers cut, trim, shampoo, and style hair mostly for male clients. They also may fit hairpieces and offer scalp treatments and facial shaving. In many states, barbers are licensed to color, bleach, and highlight hair, and to offer permanent-wave services. Barbers also may provide skin care and nail treatments.

Hairdressers, hairstylists, and cosmetologists offer a wide range of beauty services, such as shampooing, cutting, coloring, and styling of hair. They may advise clients on how to care for their hair at home. In addition, cosmetologists may be trained to give manicures, pedicures, and scalp and facial treatments; provide makeup analysis; and clean and style wigs and hairpieces.

A number of workers offer specialized services. Manicurists and pedicurists, called *nail technicians* in some states, work exclusively on nails and provide manicures, pedicures, polishing, and nail extensions to clients. Another group of specialists is skin care specialists, or *estheticians*, who cleanse and beautify the skin by giving facials, full-body treatments, and head and neck massages, as well as apply makeup. They also may remove hair through waxing or, if properly trained, with laser treatments. Finally, in larger salons, shampooers specialize in shampooing and conditioning hair.

In addition to working with clients, personal appearance workers may keep records of hair color or skin care regimens used by their regular clients. A growing number actively sell hair, skin, and nail care products. Barbers, cosmetologists, and other personal appearance workers who operate their own salons have managerial duties that may include hiring, supervising, and firing workers, as well as keeping business and inventory records, ordering supplies, and arranging for advertising.

Work environment. Many full-time barbers, cosmetologists, and other personal appearance workers put in a 40-hour week, but longer hours are common, especially among self-employed workers. Work schedules may include evenings and weekends, the times when beauty salons and barbershops are busiest. Many workers, especially those who are self-employed, determine their own schedules. In 2008, about 29 percent of barbers, hairstylists and cosmetologists worked part time, and 14 percent had variable schedules.

Barbers, cosmetologists, and other personal appearance workers usually work in clean, pleasant surroundings with good lighting and ventilation. Most work in a salon or barbershop, although some may work in a spa, hotel, or resort. Good health and stamina are important, because these workers are on their feet for most of their shift. Prolonged exposure to some hair and nail chemicals may cause irritation, so protective clothing, such as plastic gloves or aprons, may be worn.

Training, Other Qualifications, and Advancement

All states require barbers, cosmetologists, and other personal appearance workers to be licensed, with the exceptions of shampooers. To qualify for a license, most job seekers are required to graduate from a state-licensed barber or cosmetology school.

Education and training. A high school diploma or GED is required for some personal appearance workers in some states. In addition, most states require that barbers and cosmetologists complete a program in a state-licensed barber or cosmetology school. Programs in hairstyling, skin care, and other personal appearance services can be found in both high schools and in public or private postsecondary vocational schools.

Full-time programs in barbering and cosmetology usually last 9 months or more and may lead to an associate degree, but training for manicurists and pedicurists and skin care specialists requires significantly less time. Shampooers generally do not need formal training. Most professionals take advanced courses in hairstyling or other personal appearance services to keep up with the latest trends. They also may take courses in sales and marketing.

Licensure. All states require barbers, cosmetologists, and other personal appearance workers to be licensed, with the exception of shampooers. Qualifications for a license vary by state, but generally a person must have a high school diploma or GED, be at least 16 years old, and have graduated from a state-licensed barber or cosmetology school. After graduating from a state approved training program, students take a state licensing examination. The exam consists of a written test and, in some cases, a practical test of styling skills or an oral examination. In many states, cosmetology training may be credited toward a barbering license, and vice versa, and a few states combine the two licenses. Most states require separate licensing examinations for manicurists, pedicurists, and skin care specialists. A fee is usually required upon application for a license, and periodic license renewals may be necessary.

Some states have reciprocity agreements that allow licensed barbers and cosmetologists to obtain a license in another state without additional formal training, but such agreements are uncommon. Consequently, persons who wish to work in a particular state should review the laws of that state before entering a training program.

Other qualifications. Successful personal appearance workers should have an understanding of fashion, art, and technical design. They also must keep a neat personal appearance and a clean work area. Interpersonal skills, image, and attitude play an important role in career success. As client retention and retail sales become an increasingly important part of salons' revenue, the ability to be an effective salesperson becomes ever more vital for salon workers. Some cosmetology schools consider "people skills" to be such an integral part of the job that they require coursework in that area. Business skills are important for those who plan to operate their own salons.

Advancement. Advancement usually takes the form of higher earnings, as barbers and cosmetologists gain experience and build a steady clientele. Some barbers and cosmetologists manage salons, lease booth space in salons, or open their own salons after several years of experience. Others teach in barber or cosmetology schools or provide training through vocational schools. Still others advance to other related occupations, such as sales representatives for companies that sell salon-related products, image or fashion consultants, or examiners for state licensing boards.

Employment

Barbers, cosmetologists, and other personal appearance workers held about 821,900 jobs in 2008. Of these, barbers and cosmetologists held 684,200 jobs, manicurists and pedicurists 76,000, skin care specialists 38,800, and shampooers 22,900.

Most of these workers are employed in personal care services establishments, such as beauty salons, barbershops, nail salons, and day and resort spas. Others were employed in nursing and other residential care homes. Nearly every town has a barbershop or beauty salon, but employment in this occupation is concentrated in the most populous cities and states.

About 44 percent of all barbers, cosmetologists, and other personal appearance workers are self-employed. Many of these workers own their own salon, but a growing number of the self-employed lease booth space or a chair from the salon's owner. In this case, workers provide their own supplies, and are responsible for paying their own taxes and benefits. They may pay a monthly or weekly fee to the salon owner, who is responsible for utilities and maintenance of the building.

Job Outlook

Overall employment of barbers, cosmetologists, and other personal appearance workers is projected to grow much faster than the average for all occupations. Opportunities for entry-level workers should

Projections Data from the National Employment Matrix

Occupational title	SOC Code	Employment, 2008	Projected employment, 2018	Change, 2008–2018	
				Number	Percent
Barbers, cosmetologists, and other personal appearance workers .... —		821,900	987,400	165,500	20
Barbers and cosmetologists	39-5010	684,200	817,400	133,200	19
Barbers	39-5011	53,500	59,700	6,200	12
Hairdressers, hairstylists, and cosmetologists	39-5012	630,700	757,700	127,000	20
Manicurists and pedicurists..................................	39-5092	76,000	90,200	14,300	19
Shampooers...	39-5093	22,900	26,300	3,400	15
Skin care specialists	39-5094	38,800	53,500	14,700	38

NOTE: Data in this table are rounded.

be favorable, while job candidates at high-end establishments will face keen competition.

Employment change. Personal appearance workers will grow by 20 percent from 2008 to 2018, which is much faster than the average for all occupations.

Employment trends are expected to vary among the different occupational specialties. Employment of hairdressers, hairstylists, and cosmetologists will increase by about 20 percent, much faster than average, while the number of barbers will increase by 12 percent, about as fast as average. This growth will primarily come from an increasing population, which will lead to greater demand for basic hair services. Additionally, the demand for hair coloring and other advanced hair treatments has increased in recent years, particularly among baby boomers and young people. This trend is expected to continue, leading to a favorable outlook for hairdressers, hairstylists, and cosmetologists.

Continued growth in the number of full-service spas and nail salons will also generate numerous job openings for manicurists, pedicurists, and skin care specialists. Estheticians and other skin care specialists will see large gains in employment, and are expected to grow almost 38 percent, much faster than average, primarily due to the popularity of skin treatments for relaxation and medical well-being. Manicurists and pedicurists meanwhile will grow by 19 percent, faster than average.

Job prospects. Job opportunities generally should be good, particularly for licensed personal appearance workers seeking entry-level positions. A large number of job openings will come about from the need to replace workers who transfer to other occupations, retire, or leave the labor force for other reasons. However, workers can expect keen competition for jobs and clients at higher-paying salons, as these positions are relatively few and require applicants to compete with a large pool of licensed and experienced cosmetologists. Opportunities will generally be best for those with previous experience and for those licensed to provide a broad range of services.

Earnings

Median hourly wages in May 2009 for hairdressers, hairstylists, and cosmetologists, including tips and commission, were $11.21. The middle 50 percent earned between $8.79 and $15.12. The lowest 10 percent earned less than $7.68, and the highest 10 percent earned more than $20.79.

Median hourly wages in May 2009 for barbers, including tips, were $11.61. The middle 50 percent earned between $9.39 and $15.13.

The lowest 10 percent earned less than $7.90, and the highest 10 percent earned more than $20.48.

Among skin care specialists, median hourly wages, including tips, were $13.74, for manicurists and pedicurists $9.48, and for shampooers $8.61.

While earnings for entry-level workers usually are low, earnings can be considerably higher for those with experience. A number of factors, such as the size and location of the salon, determine the total income of personal appearance workers. They may receive commissions based on the price of the service or a salary based on the number of hours worked, and many receive commissions on the products they sell. In addition, some salons pay bonuses to employees who bring in new business. For many personal appearance workers, the ability to attract and hold regular clients is a key factor in determining earnings.

Although some salons offer paid vacations and medical benefits, many self-employed and part-time workers in this occupation do not enjoy such benefits. Some personal appearance workers receive free trial products from manufacturers in the hope that they will recommend the products to clients.

Related Occupations

Fitness workers; makeup artists, theatrical and performance; and massage therapists.

Sources of Additional Information

For details on state licensing requirements and approved barber or cosmetology schools, contact your state boards of barber or cosmetology examiners.

State licensing board requirements and a list of licensed training schools for cosmetologists may be obtained from

▸ National Accrediting Commission of Cosmetology Arts and Sciences, 4401 Ford Ave., Suite 1300, Alexandria, VA 22302. Internet: www.naccas.org

Information about a career in cosmetology is available from

▸ National Cosmetology Association, 401 N. Michigan Ave., Chicago, IL 60611. Internet: www.ncacares.org

For information on a career as a barber, contact

▸ National Association of Barber Boards of America, 2703 Pine St., Arkadelphia, AR 71923. Internet: www.nationalbarberboards.com

Bill and Account Collectors

(O*NET 43-3011.00)

Significant Points

■ Employment of bill and account collectors is projected to grow by about 19 percent over the 2008–2018 decade, which is faster than average for all occupations.

■ Most jobs in this occupation require only a high school diploma, though many employers prefer workers with some customer service experience.

■ Job prospects should be favorable, especially for those with related work experience.

Nature of the Work

Bill and account collectors, often called *collectors*, attempt to collect payment on overdue bills. Some are employed by third-party collection agencies, while others—known as *in-house collectors*—work directly for the original creditors, such as mortgage and credit card companies, health-care providers, and utilities.

The duties of bill and account collectors are similar across the many different organizations in which they work. First, collectors are called upon to locate and notify consumers or businesses with delinquent accounts, usually over the telephone, but sometimes by letter. When debtors move without leaving a forwarding address, collectors may check with the post office, telephone companies, credit bureaus, or former neighbors to obtain the new address. This is called "skip tracing." Computer systems assist in tracing by automatically tracking when individuals or companies change their addresses or contact information on any of their open accounts.

Once collectors find debtors, they inform them of the overdue accounts and solicit payment. If necessary, they review terms of sale, or credit contracts. Good collectors use their listening skills to attempt to learn the cause of delinquencies. They generally have the authority to offer repayment plans or other assistance to make it easier for debtors to pay their bills. In many cases, they are able to find payment solutions that will allow the debtors to pay off their accounts. They may also offer simple advice or refer customers to debt counselors.

If a consumer agrees to pay, the collector records this commitment and checks later to verify that the payment was made. If a consumer fails to pay, the collector prepares a statement indicating the consumer's delinquency for the credit department of the establishment. In more extreme cases, collectors may initiate repossession proceedings, disconnect service, or hand the account over to an attorney for legal action. Most collectors handle other administrative functions for the accounts assigned to them, including recording changes of address and purging the records of the deceased.

Because people are very sensitive about their financial problems, collectors must be careful to follow applicable federal and state laws that govern their work. The Federal Trade Commission requires that a collector positively identify the delinquent account holder before announcing that the purpose of the call is to collect a debt. The collector must then issue a statement—often called a "mini-Miranda"—that lets the customer know that he or she is a collector. Collectors also face many state laws that govern how they must proceed in doing their work. Most companies use electronic systems to help collectors remember all laws and regulations governing each call.

Collectors use computers and a variety of automated systems in their jobs. Companies keep records of their accounts using computers, and collectors can keep track of previous collection attempts and other information in computerized notes. Using this information puts them at an advantage when trying to negotiate with consumers. As with most call center workers, they use headsets instead of regular telephones. Many also use automatic dialing, which allows collectors to make calls quickly and efficiently, without the chance of dialing incorrectly.

Work environment. In-house bill and account collectors typically are employed in an office environment, and those who work for third-party collection agencies may work in a call-center environment. Workers spend most of their time on the phone tracking down and contacting people with debts. The work can be stressful, as many consumers are confrontational when pressed about their debts. Successful collectors must face regular rejection and still be ready to make the next call in a polite and positive voice. Fortunately, some consumers appreciate assistance in resolving their outstanding debts, and can be quite grateful.

As in most jobs where workers spend most of their time on the phone, collectors usually have goals they are expected to meet. Typically these include calls per hour and success rate goals. Additionally, because most workers are offered incentives for collecting, they may rely on a certain level of success to meet their own budgetary needs.

Bill and account collectors sometimes must work evenings and weekends. While some collectors work part-time, the majority work 40 hours per week. Flexible work schedules are common.

Training, Other Qualifications, and Advancement

Most employers require collectors to have at a least a high school diploma and prefer applicants with postsecondary education or customer service experience. Employers provide on-the-job training to new employees.

Education and training. Most bill and account collectors are required to have at least a high school diploma. However, employers prefer workers who have completed some college or who have experience in other occupations that involve contact with the public. Previous experience working in a call center is especially helpful.

Once hired, workers receive on-the-job training. New employees learn company procedures under the guidance of a supervisor or other senior worker. Some formal classroom training may also be necessary, such as training in specific computer software. Additional training topics usually include telephone techniques and negotiation skills. Workers also learn the laws governing the collection of debt as mandated by the Fair Debt Collection Practices Act and various state laws.

Other qualifications. Workers should have good communication and people skills because they need to speak to consumers daily, some of whom may be in stressful financial situations. They should be comfortable talking on the telephone with people they have never met. They must be mature and able to handle rejection. Computer literacy and experience with advanced telecommunications equipment are also useful.

Projections Data from the National Employment Matrix

Occupational title	SOC Code	Employment, 2008	Projected employment, 2018	Change, 2008–2018	
				Number	Percent
Bill and account collectors.....................43-3011		411,000	490,500	79,500	19

NOTE: Data in this table are rounded.

Advancement. As collectors gain experience, their success rates generally go up, leading them to earn more money in commissions. Successful collectors are usually given larger accounts with higher earning opportunities. Some become team leaders or supervisors. Workers who acquire additional skills, experience, and training improve their advancement opportunities.

Employment

Bill and account collectors held about 411,000 jobs in 2008. About one-quarter of collectors worked in business support services. Another 19 percent worked in finance and insurance, and 18 percent worked for health-care and social assistance providers.

Job Outlook

Employment of bill and account collectors is expected to grow faster than the average for all occupations. Job prospects are expected to be favorable, especially for those with related work experience.

Employment change. Employment of bill and account collectors is projected to grow by about 19 percent over the 2008–2018 decade, which is faster than average for all occupations. New jobs should be created in key industries such as health-care and financial services, which often have delinquent accounts. In-house bill collectors will take on some of these collections, while others will be sold to third-party collection agencies. In both cases, bill and account collectors will be responsible for recovering these debts, causing the occupation to grow.

Job growth will be tempered somewhat by continued outsourcing of collections work to offshore call centers. In recent years, many companies have chosen to use these call centers for some of their debt recovery efforts. Nevertheless, creditors will continue to hire collectors in the United States, as domestic workers tend to have greater success in negotiating with clients.

The occupation should see large growth in the health-care industry. The rapid growth projected in this industry, in combination with increasing prices, should result in many collections opportunities. This will affect both collectors who work in the health-care industry itself and those who work for collections agencies that accept accounts from health-care providers.

Job prospects. Opportunities for job seekers who are looking for bill and account collector jobs should be favorable due to continued job growth and the need to replace workers who leave the occupation. Those who have experience in a related occupation should have the best prospects. Companies prefer to hire workers who have worked in a call center before, or in another job that requires regular phone-based negotiations.

Unlike most occupations, the number of collections jobs tends to remain stable and even grow during economic downturns. When the economy suffers, individuals and businesses struggle to meet their financial obligations. While this increases the number of debts that must be collected, it also means that fewer people are able to pay their outstanding debt. Companies decide how many collectors to hire based on expected success rates. As a result, the number of collectors does not necessarily increase proportionally to the number of delinquent accounts. Nevertheless, the number of collections jobs tends to remain stable during downturns, although prospective employees may face increased competition for these jobs.

Earnings

Median hourly wages of bill and account collectors were $14.87 in May 2009. The middle 50 percent earned between $12.23 and $18.23. The lowest 10 percent earned less than $10.22, and the highest 10 percent earned more than $22.32. Most bill and account collectors earn commissions based on the amount of debt they recover.

Related Occupations

Bill and account collectors review and collect information on accounts. Other occupations with similar responsibilities include credit authorizers, checkers, and clerks; interviewers, except eligibility and loan; and loan officers.

Collectors spend most of their time on the telephone, speaking with customers. Other jobs that require regular telephone interaction include customer service representatives; and sales representatives, wholesale and manufacturing.

Sources of Additional Information

Career information on bill and account collectors is available from

▸ ACA International, The Association of Credit and Collection Professionals, P.O. Box 390106, Minneapolis, MN 55439. Internet: www.acainternational.org

Bookkeeping, Accounting, and Auditing Clerks

(O*NET 43-3031.00)

Significant Points

■ Bookkeeping, accounting, and auditing clerks held about 2.1 million jobs in 2008 and are employed in nearly every industry.

■ A high school degree is the minimum requirement; however, postsecondary education is increasingly important, and an associate degree in business or accounting is required for some positions.

■ The large size of this occupation ensures plentiful job openings, including many opportunities for temporary and part-time work.

Nature of the Work

Bookkeeping, accounting, and auditing clerks are financial record-keepers. They update and maintain accounting records, including those which calculate expenditures, receipts, accounts payable and receivable, and profit and loss. These workers have a wide range of skills from full-charge bookkeepers, who can maintain an entire company's books, to accounting clerks, who handle specific tasks. All these clerks make numerous computations each day and must be comfortable using computers to calculate and record data.

In small businesses, *bookkeepers and bookkeeping clerks* often have responsibility for some or all the accounts, known as the general ledger. They record all transactions and post debits (costs) and credits (income). They also produce financial statements and prepare reports and summaries for supervisors and managers. Bookkeepers prepare bank deposits by compiling data from cashiers; verifying and balancing receipts; and sending cash, checks, or other forms of payment to the bank. Additionally, they may handle payroll, make purchases, prepare invoices, and keep track of overdue accounts.

In large companies, *accounting clerks* have more specialized tasks. Their titles, such as *accounts payable clerk* or *accounts receivable clerk*, often reflect the type of accounting they do. In addition, their responsibilities vary by level of experience. Entry-level accounting clerks post details of transactions, total accounts, and compute interest charges. They also may monitor loans and accounts to ensure that payments are up to date. More advanced accounting clerks may total, balance, and reconcile billing vouchers; ensure the completeness and accuracy of data on accounts; and code documents according to company procedures.

Auditing clerks verify records of transactions posted by other workers. They check figures, postings, and documents to ensure that they are mathematically accurate, and properly coded. They also correct or note errors for accountants or other workers to fix.

As organizations continue to computerize their financial records, many bookkeeping, accounting, and auditing clerks use specialized accounting software, spreadsheets, and databases. Most clerks now enter information from receipts or bills into computers, and the information is then stored electronically. The widespread use of computers also has enabled bookkeeping, accounting, and auditing clerks to take on additional responsibilities, such as payroll, procurement, and billing. Many of these functions require these clerks to write letters and make phone calls to customers or clients.

Work environment. Bookkeeping, accounting, and auditing clerks work in an office environment. They may experience eye and muscle strain, backaches, headaches, and repetitive motion injuries from using computers on a daily basis. Clerks may have to sit for extended periods while reviewing detailed data.

Many bookkeeping, accounting, and auditing clerks work regular business hours and a standard 40-hour week, although some may work occasional evenings and weekends. About 1 out of 4 clerks worked part time in 2008.

Bookkeeping, accounting, and auditing clerks may work longer hours to meet deadlines at the end of the fiscal year, during tax time, or when monthly or yearly accounting audits are performed. Additionally, those who work in hotels, restaurants, and stores may put in overtime during peak holiday and vacation seasons.

Training, Other Qualifications, and Advancement

Employers usually require bookkeeping, accounting, and auditing clerks to have at least a high school diploma and some accounting coursework or relevant work experience. Clerks should also have good communication skills, be detail oriented, and be trustworthy.

Education and training. Most bookkeeping, accounting, and auditing clerks are required to have a high school degree at a minimum. However, having some postsecondary education is increasingly important and an associate degree in business or accounting is required for some positions. Although a bachelor's degree is rarely required, graduates may accept bookkeeping, accounting, and auditing clerk positions to get into a particular company or to enter the accounting or finance field with the hope of eventually being promoted.

Once hired, bookkeeping, accounting, and auditing clerks usually receive on-the-job training. Under the guidance of a supervisor or another experienced employee, new clerks learn company procedures. Some formal classroom training also may be necessary, such as training in specialized computer software.

Other qualifications. Bookkeeping, accounting, and auditing clerks must be careful, orderly, and detail oriented to avoid making errors and to recognize errors made by others. These workers also should be discreet and trustworthy, because they frequently come in contact with confidential material. They should also have good communication skills, because they increasingly work with customers. In addition, all bookkeeping, accounting, and auditing clerks should have a strong aptitude for numbers.

Experience in a related job and working in an office environment are recommended. Workers must be able to use computers, and knowledge of specialized bookkeeping or accounting software is especially valuable.

Certification and advancement. Bookkeeping, accounting, and auditing clerks, particularly those who handle all the recordkeeping for a company, may find it beneficial to become certified. The Certified Bookkeeper (CB) designation, awarded by the American Institute of Professional Bookkeepers, demonstrates that individuals have the skills and knowledge needed to carry out all bookkeeping functions, including overseeing payroll and balancing accounts, according to accepted accounting procedures. For certification, candidates must have at least 2 years of bookkeeping experience, pass a four-part examination, and adhere to a code of ethics. Several colleges and universities offer a preparatory course for certification; some offer courses online. Additionally, certified bookkeepers are required to meet a continuing education requirement every 3 years to maintain certification.

Bookkeeping, accounting, and auditing clerks usually advance by taking on more duties for higher pay or by transferring to a closely related occupation. Most companies fill office and administrative support supervisory and managerial positions by promoting individuals from within their organizations, so clerks who acquire additional skills, experience, and training improve their advancement opportunities. With appropriate experience and education, some bookkeeping, accounting, and auditing clerks may become accountants or auditors.

Projections Data from the National Employment Matrix

Occupational title	SOC Code	Employment, 2008	Projected employment, 2018	Change, 2008–2018	
				Number	Percent
Bookkeeping, accounting, and auditing clerks 43-3031		2,063,800	2,276,200	212,400	10

NOTE: Data in this table are rounded.

Employment

Bookkeeping, accounting, and auditing clerks held about 2.1 million jobs in 2008. They work in nearly all industries and at all levels of government. State and local government; educational services; health care; and the accounting, tax preparation, bookkeeping, and payroll services industries are among the individual industries employing the largest numbers of these clerks.

Job Outlook

Job growth is projected to be about as fast as the average. The large size of this occupation ensures plentiful job opportunities, as many bookkeeping, accounting, and auditing clerks are expected to retire or transfer to other occupations.

Employment change. Employment of bookkeeping, accounting, and auditing clerks is projected to grow by 10 percent during the 2008–2018 decade, which is about as fast as the average for all occupations. This occupation is one of the largest growth occupations in the economy, with about 212,400 new jobs expected over the projections decade.

A growing economy will result in more financial transactions and other activities that require recordkeeping by these workers. Additionally, an increased emphasis on accuracy, accountability, and transparency in the reporting of financial data for public companies will increase the demand for these workers. Also, new regulations and reporting methods, including the use of International Financial Reporting Standards, should result in additional demand for clerks involved in accounting and auditing. However, growth will be limited by improvements in accounting software and document-scanning technology that make it easier to record, track, audit, and file financial information, including transactions and reports. Moreover, companies will continue to outsource their bookkeeping, accounting, and, in some cases, auditing functions to third-party contractors located both domestically and abroad.

Job prospects. While many job openings are expected to result from job growth, even more openings will stem from the need to replace existing workers who leave. Each year, numerous jobs will become available, as clerks transfer to other occupations or leave the labor force. The large size of this occupation ensures plentiful job openings, including many opportunities for temporary and part-time work.

Clerks who can carry out a wider range of bookkeeping and accounting activities will be in greater demand than specialized clerks. For example, demand for full-charge bookkeepers is expected to increase, because they can perform a wider variety of financial transactions, including payroll and billing. Certified Bookkeepers (CBs) and those with several years of accounting or bookkeeping experience who have demonstrated that they can handle a range of tasks will have the best job prospects.

Earnings

In May 2009, the median annual wages of bookkeeping, accounting, and auditing clerks were $33,450. The middle half of the occupation earned between $26,910 and $41,280. The top 10 percent of bookkeeping, accounting, and auditing clerks earned more than $50,450, and the bottom 10 percent earned less than $21,280.

Related Occupations

Bookkeeping, accounting, and auditing clerks work with financial records. Other workers who perform similar duties include accountants and auditors; billing and posting clerks and machine operators; brokerage clerks; credit authorizers, checkers, and clerks; payroll and timekeeping clerks; and procurement clerks.

Sources of Additional Information

For information on the Certified Bookkeeper designation, contact

▶ American Institute of Professional Bookkeepers, 6001 Montrose Rd., Suite 500, Rockville, MD 20852. Internet: www.aipb.org

Brickmasons, Blockmasons, and Stonemasons

(O*NET 47-2021.00 and 47-2022.00)

Significant Points

- Job opportunities are expected to be good, especially for those with restoration skills.
- Some entrants learn informally on the job, but apprenticeship programs provide the most thorough training.
- The work is usually outdoors and involves lifting heavy materials and working on scaffolds.
- About 27 percent of brickmasons, blockmasons, and stonemasons are self-employed.

Nature of the Work

Brickmasons, blockmasons, and *stonemasons* create attractive, durable surfaces and structures. For thousands of years, these workers have built buildings, fences, roads, walkways, and walls using bricks, concrete blocks, and natural stone. The structures that they build will continue to be in demand for years to come.

The work varies in complexity, from laying a simple masonry walkway to installing an ornate exterior on a highrise building. Workers cut or break the materials used to create walls, floors, and other structures. Once their building materials are properly sized, they are laid with or without a binding material. Workers use their own perceptions and a variety of tools to ensure that the structure meets the desired standards. After they finish laying the bricks, blocks, or stone, the workers clean the finished product with a variety of cleaning agents.

Brickmasons and blockmasons—who often are called simply *bricklayers*—build and repair walls, floors, partitions, fireplaces, chimneys, and other structures with brick, precast masonry panels, concrete block, and other masonry materials. Some brickmasons specialize in installing firebrick linings in industrial furnaces.

When building a structure, brickmasons usually start in the corners. Because of the precision needed, corners are time-consuming to erect and require the skills of experienced bricklayers. To lay the brick, brickmasons spread a bed of mortar (a mixture of cement, lime, sand, and water) with a trowel (a flat, bladed metal tool with a handle), place the brick on the mortar bed, and press and tap the brick into place. Depending on blueprint specifications, brickmasons either cut bricks with a hammer and chisel or saw them to fit around windows, doors, and other openings. Mortar joints are then finished with jointing tools for a sealed, neat, uniform appearance. Although brickmasons typically use steel supports, or lintels, at window and door openings, they sometimes build brick arches, which support and enhance the beauty of the brickwork.

Refractory masons are brickmasons who specialize in installing firebrick and refractory tile in high-temperature boilers, furnaces, cupolas, ladles, and soaking pits in industrial establishments. Most of these workers are employed in steel mills, where molten materials flow on refractory beds from furnaces to rolling machines. They also are employed at oil refineries, glass furnaces, incinerators, and other locations requiring high temperatures during the manufacturing process.

After a structure is completed, there is often work that still needs to be done. *Pointing, cleaning, and caulking workers* can be the final workers on a job or the primary workers on a restoration project. These workers usually replace bricks or make repairs to brickwork on older structures where mortar has come loose. Special care is taken not to damage the main structural integrity or the bricks, blocks, or stone. Depending on how much mortar is being replaced, it may take several applications to allow the new mortar to cure properly. After laying the new bricks, the workers use chemicals to clean the brick and stone to give the structure a finished appearance.

Stonemasons build stone walls, as well as set stone exteriors and floors. They work with two types of stone—natural-cut stone, such as marble, granite, and limestone; and artificial stone, made from concrete, marble chips, or other masonry materials. Masons use a special hammer and chisel to cut stone. They cut stone along the grain to make various shapes and sizes, and valuable pieces are often cut with a saw that has a diamond blade. Stonemasons often work from a set of drawings in which each stone has been numbered for identification. Helpers may locate and carry these prenumbered stones to the masons. A derrick operator using a hoist may be needed to lift large stone pieces into place.

When building a stone wall, masons set the first course of stones into a shallow bed of mortar. They then align the stones with wedges, plumb lines, and levels, and work them into position with various tools. Masons continue to build the wall by alternating layers of mortar and courses of stone. As the work progresses, masons remove the wedges, fill the joints between stones, and use a pointed metal tool, called a tuck pointer, to smooth the mortar to an attractive finish. To hold large stones in place, stonemasons attach

brackets to the stones and weld or bolt these brackets to anchors in the wall. Finally, masons wash the stones with a cleansing solution to remove stains and dry the mortar.

When setting stone floors, which often consist of large and heavy pieces of stone, masons first use a trowel to spread a layer of damp mortar over the surface to be covered. They then use crowbars and hard rubber mallets for aligning and leveling to set the stone in the mortar bed. To finish, workers fill the joints and clean the stone slabs.

Some masons specialize in setting marble, which, in many respects, is similar to setting large pieces of stone. Brickmasons and stonemasons also repair imperfections and cracks and replace broken or missing masonry units in walls and floors.

Most nonresidential buildings are now built with walls made of some combination of any of the following: concrete block, brick veneer, stone, granite, marble, tile, and glass. In the past, masons doing nonresidential interior work mainly built block partition walls and elevator shafts, but because many types of masonry and stone are used in the interiors of today's nonresidential structures, these workers now must be more versatile. For example, some brickmasons and blockmasons now install structural insulated concrete units and wall panels. They also install a variety of masonry anchors and other masonry-associated accessories used in many high-rise buildings.

Work environment. Brickmasons, blockmasons, and stonemasons usually work outdoors; in contrast to the past when work slowed down in the winter months, new processes and materials are allowing these masons to work in a greater variety of weather conditions. Masons stand, kneel, and bend for long periods and often have to lift heavy materials. Common hazards include injuries from tools and falls from scaffolds, but these can often be avoided when proper safety equipment, such as a hardhat, is used and when proper safety practices are followed.

Many workers work a standard 40-hour week. Some, however, do work more. Earnings for workers in the construction trades can be reduced on occasion when poor weather and slowdowns in construction activity decrease the amount of time the laborers can work.

Training, Other Qualifications, and Advancement

Some brickmasons, blockmasons, and stonemasons pick up their skills informally, observing and learning from experienced workers. Many others receive initial training in vocational education schools or from industry-based programs common throughout the country. Others complete an apprenticeship, which provides the most thorough training.

Education and training. Individuals who learn the trade on the job usually start as helpers, laborers, or mason tenders. These workers carry materials, move or assemble scaffolds, and mix mortar. When the opportunity arises, they learn from experienced craftworkers how to mix and spread mortar, lay brick and block, or set stone. They also may learn restoration skills such as cleaning, pointing, and repointing. As they gain experience, they learn more difficult tasks and make the transition to full-fledged craftworkers. The learning period usually lasts longer for workers who learn the trade on the job than for those who have already been trained in an apprenticeship program. Registered apprenticeship programs usually last between 3 and 4 years.

Some workers learn the trade at technical schools that offer masonry courses. Entrance requirements and fees vary depending on the school and who is funding the program. Some people take courses before being hired, and some take them later as part of on-the-job training.

Apprenticeships for brickmasons, blockmasons, and stonemasons usually are sponsored by local union-management joint apprenticeship and training committees, local contractors, or trade associations. Apprenticeship programs usually require 3 to 4 years of on-the-job training, in addition to a minimum of 144 hours of classroom instruction each year in blueprint reading, mathematics, layout work, sketching, and other subjects. In the coming years, the focus of apprenticeships is likely to change from time served to demonstrated competence. This may result in apprenticeships of shorter average duration. Applicants for apprenticeships must be at least 17 years old and in good physical condition. A high school diploma is preferable, especially with courses in mathematics, mechanical drawing, and general shop.

Apprentices often start by working with laborers: carrying materials, mixing mortar, and building scaffolds for about a month. Next, apprentices learn to lay, align, and join brick and block. They may also learn to work with stone and concrete, which is important when using other masonry materials.

Bricklayers who work in nonresidential construction usually work for large contractors and receive well-rounded training—normally through an apprenticeship in all phases of brick or stone work. Those who work in residential construction usually work for small contractors and specialize in only one or two aspects of the job.

Other qualifications. The most desired qualities in workers are dependability and a strong work ethic. Knowledge of basic math, including measurement, volume, mixing proportions, algebra, plane geometry, and mechanical drawing are important in this trade.

Advancement. With additional training and experience, brickmasons, blockmasons, and stonemasons may become supervisors for masonry contractors. Some eventually become owners of businesses and may spend most of their time as managers. Others move into closely related areas such as construction management or building inspection. Many unionized Joint Apprenticeship and Training Committees offer "life-long learning" through continuing education courses that help those members who want to advance their technical knowledge and their careers.

Employment

Brickmasons, blockmasons, and stonemasons held 160,200 jobs in 2008. The vast majority were brickmasons and blockmasons. Workers in these crafts are employed in building construction or by specialty trade contractors.

About 27 percent of brickmasons, blockmasons, and stonemasons were self-employed. Many of the self-employed are contractors who work on small jobs, such as patios, walkways, and fireplaces.

Job Outlook

Brickmasons, blockmasons, and stonemasons should see as fast as average growth as the construction industry responds to the needs of a growing population. Job prospects should be better for workers with more thorough training who can work on complex structures.

Employment change. Jobs for brickmasons, blockmasons, and stonemasons are expected to increase by 12 percent over the 2008–2018 decade, as fast as the average for all occupations, as the rising population will create a need for schools, hospitals, apartment buildings, and other structures. Also stimulating demand for workers will be the need to build more energy-efficient industrial facilities and office buildings (some of which may be made from brick) and to restore a growing number of old brick buildings. Moreover, the federal government has indicated a willingness to spend more on repairing schools and on making government buildings more energy efficient, which should have a positive impact on the construction industry in general.

Because of demographic forces, the residential housing market is expected to eventually pick up again. Brick exteriors and, particularly, stone should remain popular, reflecting a growing preference for durable exterior materials requiring little maintenance. There is also an increased demand for durable homes that incorporate brick or stone in hurricane-prone areas.

Job prospects. Job opportunities for brickmasons, blockmasons, and stonemasons are expected to be in rough balance over the 2008–2018 period as laid-off workers and a reduced level of construction help balance out a need for skilled brickmasons, blockmasons, and stonemasons. The masonry workforce is growing older, and a large number of masons are expected to retire over the next decade, which will create many job openings. Applicants who take masonry-related courses at technical schools will improve their job prospects.

Employment of brickmasons, blockmasons, and stonemasons, like that of many other construction workers, is sensitive to changes in the economy. When the level of construction activity falls, workers in these trades can experience periods of unemployment. On the other hand, shortages of workers may occur in some areas during peak periods of building activity. Ongoing, however, is the need to repair and restore a large number of aging masonry buildings. This work will increase opportunities for workers with these types of skills.

New concerns over the costs of heating and cooling buildings of all types has led to a need to train construction workers of all types, including brickmasons, blockmasons, and stonemasons, in

Projections Data from the National Employment Matrix

Occupational title	SOC Code	Employment, 2008	Projected employment, 2018	Change, 2008–2018	
				Number	Percent
Brickmasons, blockmasons, and stonemasons 47-2020		160,200	178,600	18,500	12
Brickmasons and blockmasons...........................47-2021		135,800	151,500	15,600	12
Stonemasons 47-2022		24,300	27,100	2,800	12

NOTE: Data in this table are rounded.

the emerging field of green construction. Contractors familiar with this burgeoning area will have better job opportunities in the future.

Earnings

Median hourly wages of brickmasons and blockmasons in May 2009 were $22.47. The middle 50 percent earned between $17.11 and $29.43. The lowest 10 percent earned less than $13.45, and the highest 10 percent earned more than $36.98. In the two industries employing the largest numbers of brickmasons and blockmasons in May 2000—the foundation, structure, and building exterior contractors industry and the nonresidential building industry—median hourly wages were $21.01 and $25.08, respectively.

Median hourly wages of wage and salary stonemasons in May 2009 were $17.68. The middle 50 percent earned between $13.87 and $23.06. The lowest 10 percent earned less than $11.32, and the highest 10 percent earned more than $31.39.

Apprentices or helpers usually start at about 50 percent of the wage rate paid to experienced workers. Pay increases as apprentices gain experience and learn new skills. Employers usually increase apprentices' wages about every 6 months on the basis of specific advancement criteria.

About 18 percent of brickmasons, blockmasons, and stonemasons were members of unions, mainly the International Union of Bricklayers and Allied Craftsworkers.

Related Occupations

Brickmasons, blockmasons, and stonemasons combine a thorough knowledge of brick, concrete block, stone, and marble with manual skill to erect attractive, yet highly durable, structures. Workers in other occupations with similar skills include carpenters; carpet, floor, and tile installers and finishers; cement masons, concrete finishers, segmental pavers, and terrazzo workers; and drywall and ceiling tile installers, tapers, plasterers, and stucco masons.

Sources of Additional Information

For details about apprenticeships or other work opportunities in these trades, contact local bricklaying, stonemasonry, or marble-setting contractors; the Associated Builders and Contractors; a local office of the International Union of Bricklayers and Allied Craftsworkers; a local joint union-management apprenticeship committee; or the nearest office of a state employment service or apprenticeship agency. Apprenticeship information is also available from the U.S. Department of Labor's toll-free helpline: (877) 872-5627 and online at www.doleta.gov/OA/eta_default.cfm.

For general information on apprenticeships and how to get them, see the *Occupational Outlook Quarterly* article "Apprenticeships: Career training, credentials—and a paycheck in your pocket," online at www.bls.gov/opub/ooq/2002/summer/art01.pdf and in print in many libraries and career centers.

For information on training for brickmasons, blockmasons, and stonemasons, contact

▸ Mason Contractors Association of America, 33 South Roselle Rd., Schaumburg, IL 60193. Internet: www.masoncontractors.org

▸ National Association of Home Builders, Home Builders Institute, 1201 15th St. NW, Washington, DC 20005. Internet: www.hbi.org

For information about training, including a credential in green construction, contact

▸ International Union of Bricklayers and Allied Craftworkers, 620 F St. NW, Washington, DC 20004. Internet: www.bacweb.org

▸ National Center for Construction Education and Research, 3600 NW 43rd St., Bldg. G, Gainesville, FL 32606. Internet: www.nccer.org

For general information about the work of bricklayers, contact

▸ International Masonry Institute National Training Center, The James Brice House, 42 East St., Annapolis, MD 21401. Internet: www.imiweb.org

▸ Associated General Contractors of America, Inc., 2300 Wilson Blvd., Suite 400, Arlington, VA 22201. Internet: www.agc.org

▸ National Concrete Masonry Association, 13750 Sunrise Valley Dr., Herndon, VA 20171-4662. Internet: www.ncma.org

Building Cleaning Workers

(O*NET 37-1011.00, 37-2011.00, 37-2012.00, and 37-2019.00)

Significant Points

■ Entry-level workers need no formal education and learn on the job.

■ Most job openings result from the need to replace the many workers who leave this very large occupation.

■ Job prospects are expected to be good.

Nature of the Work

Building cleaning workers keep office buildings, hospitals, stores, apartment houses, hotels, and residences clean, sanitary, and in good condition. Some do only cleaning, while others have a wide range of duties.

Janitors and cleaners perform a variety of heavy cleaning duties, such as cleaning floors, shampooing rugs, washing walls and glass, and removing trash. They may fix leaky faucets, empty trash cans, do painting and carpentry, replenish bathroom supplies, mow lawns, and see that heating and air-conditioning equipment works properly. On a typical day, janitors may wet- or dry-mop floors, clean bathrooms, vacuum carpets, dust furniture, make minor repairs, and exterminate insects and rodents. They may also clean snow or debris from sidewalks in front of buildings and notify management of the need for major repairs. While janitors typically perform most of the duties mentioned, cleaners tend to work for companies that specialize in one type of cleaning activity, such as washing windows.

Maids and housekeeping cleaners perform any combination of light cleaning duties to keep private households or commercial establishments, such as hotels, restaurants, hospitals, and nursing homes, clean and orderly. In private households, they dust and polish furniture; sweep, mop, and wax floors; vacuum; and clean ovens, refrigerators, and bathrooms. They also may wash dishes, polish silver, and change and make beds. Some wash, fold, and iron clothes; a few wash windows. General houseworkers also may take clothes and laundry to the cleaners, buy groceries, and perform other errands. In hotels, aside from cleaning and maintaining the premises, maids and housekeeping cleaners may deliver ironing boards, cribs, and rollaway beds to guests' rooms. In hospitals, they also may wash bed frames, make beds, and disinfect and sanitize equipment and supplies with germicides. Janitors, maids, and cleaners use many kinds of equipment, tools, and cleaning materials. For one job, they may need standard cleaning implements; another may require an electric floor polishing machine and a special cleaning solution. Improved building materials, chemical cleaners, and power equipment have made many tasks easier and less time consuming, but cleaning workers must learn the proper use of equipment and cleaners to avoid harming floors, fixtures, building occupants, and themselves.

Cleaning supervisors coordinate, schedule, and supervise the activities of janitors and cleaners. They assign tasks and inspect building areas to see that work has been done properly; they also issue supplies and equipment and inventory stocks to ensure that supplies on hand are adequate. They may be expected to screen and hire job applicants; train new and experienced employees; and recommend promotions, transfers, or dismissals. Supervisors may prepare reports concerning the occupancy of rooms, hours worked, and department expenses. Some also perform cleaning duties.

Building cleaning workers in large office and residential buildings, and more recently in large hotels, often work in teams consisting of workers who specialize in vacuuming, picking up trash, and cleaning restrooms, among other things. Supervisors conduct inspections to ensure that the building is cleaned properly and the team is functioning efficiently. In hotels, one member of the team is responsible for reporting electronically to the supervisor when rooms are cleaned.

Work environment. Because office buildings generally are cleaned while they are empty, many cleaning workers work evening hours. Some, however, such as school and hospital custodians, work in the daytime. When there is a need for 24-hour maintenance, janitors may be assigned to shifts. Many full-time building cleaners worked about 40 hours a week in 2008, but a substantial number worked part time. Part-time cleaners usually work in the evenings and on weekends.

Most building cleaning workers work indoors, but some work outdoors part of the time, sweeping walkways, mowing lawns, or shoveling snow. Working with machines can be noisy, and some tasks, such as cleaning bathrooms and trash rooms, can be dirty and unpleasant. Building cleaning workers experience injuries more frequently than workers in most other occupations. They may suffer cuts, bruises, and burns from machines, handtools, and chemicals. They spend most of their time on their feet, sometimes lifting or pushing heavy furniture or equipment. Many tasks, such as dusting or sweeping, require constant bending, stooping, and stretching. Lifting the increasingly heavier mattresses at nicer hotels in order to change the linens can cause back injuries and sprains. ·

Training, Other Qualifications, and Advancement

Most building cleaning workers, except supervisors, do not need any formal education and mainly learn their skills on the job or in informal training sessions sponsored by their employers. Supervisors, though, generally have at least a high school diploma and often some college.

Education and training. No special education is required for most entry-level janitorial or cleaning jobs, but workers should be able to perform simple arithmetic and follow instructions. High school shop courses are helpful for jobs involving repair work. Most building cleaners learn their skills on the job. Beginners usually

work with an experienced cleaner, doing routine cleaning. As they gain more experience, they are assigned more complicated tasks. In some cities, programs run by unions, government agencies, or employers teach janitorial skills. Students learn how to clean buildings thoroughly and efficiently; how to select and safely use various cleansing agents; and how to operate and maintain machines, such as wet-and-dry vacuums, buffers, and polishers. Students learn to plan their work, to follow safety and health regulations, to interact positively with people in the buildings they clean, and to work without supervision. Instruction in minor electrical, plumbing, and other repairs also may be given.

Supervisors of building cleaning workers usually need at least a high school diploma, but many have completed some college or earned a degree, especially those who work at places where clean rooms and well-functioning buildings are a necessity, such as in hospitals and hotels. In many establishments, they are required to take some in-service training to improve their housekeeping techniques and procedures and to enhance their supervisory skills.

Other qualifications. Employers usually look for dependable, hardworking individuals who are in good health, follow directions well, and get along with other people.

Certification and advancement. A small number of cleaning supervisors and managers are members of the International Executive Housekeepers Association, which offers two kinds of certification programs for cleaning supervisors and managers: Certified Executive Housekeeper (CEH) and Registered Executive Housekeeper (REH). The CEH designation is offered to those with a high school education, while the REH designation is offered to those who have a 4-year college degree. Both designations are earned by attending courses and passing exams and both must be renewed every 3 years to ensure that workers keep abreast of new cleaning methods. Those with the REH designation usually oversee the cleaning services of hotels, hospitals, casinos, and other large institutions that rely on well-trained experts for their cleaning needs.

Advancement opportunities for workers usually are limited in organizations where they are the only maintenance worker. Where there is a large maintenance staff, however, cleaning workers can be promoted to supervisor or to area supervisor or manager. Some janitors open their own maintenance or cleaning businesses.

Employment

Building cleaning workers held about 4.1 million jobs in 2008. About 299,000 were self-employed.

Janitors and cleaners worked in nearly every type of establishment and held about 2.4 million jobs. Around 33 percent of janitors worked for firms supplying services to buildings and dwellings, about 20 percent were employed in educational services, and 6 percent worked in government. About 132,700 were self-employed.

Maids and housekeepers held about 1.5 million jobs. Private households employed about 30 percent of these workers, while hotels, motels, and other traveler accommodations employed 29 percent. Hospitals, nursing homes, and other residential care facilities employed about 17 percent. Although cleaning jobs can be found in all cities and towns, most located in highly populated areas where there are many office buildings, schools, apartment houses, nursing homes, and hospitals. About 106,900 maids and housekeeping cleaners were self-employed in 2008.

Projections Data from the National Employment Matrix

Occupational title	SOC Code	Employment, 2008	Projected employment, 2018	Change, 2008–2018	
				Number	Percent
Building cleaning workers...............................—		4,139,000	4,343,300	204,300	5
First-line supervisors/managers of housekeeping and janitorial workers....................................37-1011		251,100	263,900	12,800	5
Building cleaning workers 37-2010		3,887,900	4,079,400	191,500	5
Janitors and cleaners, except maids and housekeeping cleaners 37-2011		2,375,300	2,479,400	104,100	4
Maids and housekeeping cleaners 37-2012		1,498,200	1,583,700	85,600	6
Building cleaning workers, all other..............37-2019		14,500	16,200	1,700	12

NOTE: Data in this table are rounded.

First-line supervisors of housekeeping and janitorial workers held 251,100 jobs. Approximately 22 percent worked in firms supplying services to buildings and dwellings, while approximately 15 percent were employed in educational services. About 12 percent worked in hotels, motels, and all other traveler accommodations while about 9 percent worked in health-care organizations. About 58,400 were self-employed.

Job Outlook

Overall employment of building cleaning workers is expected to grow more slowly than average, and job opportunities are expected to be good.

Employment change. The number of building cleaning workers is expected to grow by 5 percent from 2008 to 2018, more slowly than the average for all occupations. Unlike some occupations, increased productivity is not expected to impact the employment of building cleaning workers. Despite small improvements in cleaning supplies, tools, and processes, roughly the same number of workers will be needed for any given building.

Employment of janitors and cleaners is projected to increase by 4 percent, more slowly than the average for all occupations. As the pace of construction contracts and fewer buildings are built, growth in this occupation should be relatively slow. Many new jobs are expected in health care, however, as this industry is expected to grow rapidly, and in administrative support firms as more claiming work is contracted out. Employment of maids and housekeeping cleaners is also expected to increase more slowly than the average, growing by 6 percent from 2008 to 2018. Many new jobs are expected in hotels as demand for accommodations increases, in private households as more people purchase residential cleaning services, and companies that supply maid services on a contract basis, as more of this work is contracted out. Employment of supervisors and managers of these workers, in addition, is projected to grow more slowly than the average, increasing by 5 percent. An increasing number of supervisors will be needed to manage the growing number of janitors, maids, and other cleaning workers.

Job prospects. Job prospects are expected to be good. Most job openings should result from the need to replace the many workers who leave this very large occupation.

Earnings

Median hourly wages of janitors and cleaners, except maids and housekeeping cleaners, were $10.56 in May 2009. The middle 50 percent earned between $8.63 and $13.70. The lowest 10 percent earned less than $7.63, and the highest 10 percent earned more than $17.53. Median hourly wages in May 2009 in the industries employing the largest numbers of janitors and cleaners, except maids and housekeeping cleaners, were as follows:

Services to buildings and dwellings.........................	$9.46
Elementary and secondary schools	12.82
Local government..	12.97
Colleges, universities, and professional schools	12.15
General medical and surgical hospitals	11.72

Median hourly wages of maids and housekeeping cleaners were $9.26 in May 2009. The middle 50 percent earned between $8.13 and $11.28. The lowest 10 percent earned less than $7.41, and the highest 10 percent earned more than $14.04. Median hourly wages in the traveler accommodation industry were $8.95, while median hourly wages in general medical and surgical hospitals were $10.51 in May 2009.

Median hourly wages of wage-and-salary first-line supervisors and managers of housekeeping and janitorial workers were $16.73 in May 2009. The middle 50 percent earned between $13.08 and $21.69. The lowest 10 percent earned less than $10.51, and the highest 10 percent earned more than $27.29. Median hourly wages in May 2009 in the industries employing the largest numbers of first-line supervisors and managers of housekeeping and janitorial workers were as follows:

Services to buildings and dwellings......................	$15.74
Traveler accommodation	14.50
Elementary and secondary schools	19.15
Nursing care facilities	16.18
General medical and surgical hospitals	17.80

Related Occupations

Workers who also specialize in one of the many job functions of janitors and cleaners include dishwashers and grounds maintenance workers.

Sources of Additional Information

Information about janitorial jobs may be obtained from state employment service offices.

For information on certification in executive housekeeping, contact

▶ International Executive Housekeepers Association, Inc., 1001 Eastwind Dr., Suite 301, Westerville, OH 43081-3361. Internet: www.ieha.org

Carpenters

(O*NET 47-2031.00, 47-2031.01, and 47-2031.02)

Significant Points

■ About 32 percent of all carpenters are self-employed.

■ Job opportunities should be best for those with the most training and skills.

■ Carpenters can learn their craft through on-the-job training, vocational schools or technical colleges, or formal apprenticeship programs, which often takes three to four years.

Nature of the Work

Carpenters construct, erect, install, and repair structures and fixtures made from wood and other materials. Carpenters are involved in many different kinds of construction, from the building of highways and bridges to the installation of kitchen cabinets.

Each carpentry task is somewhat different, but most involve the same basic steps. Working from blueprints or instructions from supervisors, carpenters first do the layout—measuring, marking, and arranging materials—in accordance with local building codes. They cut and shape wood, plastic, fiberglass, or drywall using hand and power tools, such as chisels, planes, saws, drills, and sanders. They then join the materials with nails, screws, staples, or adhesives. In the last step, carpenters do a final check of the accuracy of their work with levels, rules, plumb bobs, framing squares, and surveying equipment, and make any necessary adjustments. Some materials come prefabricated, allowing for easier and faster installation.

Carpenters may do many different carpentry tasks, or they may specialize in one or two. Carpenters who remodel homes and other structures, for example, need a broad range of carpentry skills. As part of a single job, they might frame walls and partitions, put in doors and windows, build stairs, install cabinets and molding, and complete many other tasks. Well-trained carpenters are able to switch from residential building to commercial construction or remodeling work, depending on which offers the best work opportunities.

Carpenters who work for large construction contractors or specialty contractors may perform only a few regular tasks, such as constructing wooden forms for pouring concrete, or erecting scaffolding. Some carpenters build tunnel bracing, or brattices, in underground passageways and mines to control the circulation of air through the passageways and to worksites. Others build concrete forms for tunnel, bridge, or sewer construction projects.

Carpenters employed outside the construction industry perform a variety of installation and maintenance work. They may replace panes of glass, ceiling tiles, and doors, as well as repair desks, cabinets, and other furniture. Depending on the employer, carpenters install partitions, doors, and windows; change locks; and repair broken furniture. In manufacturing firms, carpenters may assist in moving or installing machinery. (For more information on workers who install machinery, see the discussion of industrial machinery mechanics and millwrights, as well as maintenance and repair workers, general, elsewhere in this book.)

Work environment. As is true of other building trades, carpentry work is sometimes strenuous. Prolonged standing, climbing, bending, and kneeling often are necessary. Carpenters risk injury working with sharp or rough materials, using sharp tools and power equipment, and working in situations where they might slip or fall. Consequently, workers in this occupation experience a very high incidence of nonfatal injuries and illnesses. Additionally, carpenters who work outdoors are subject to variable weather conditions.

Many carpenters work a standard 40 hour week; however, some work more. About 7 percent worked part time.

Training, Other Qualifications, and Advancement

Carpenters can learn their craft through on-the-job training, vocational schools or technical colleges, or formal apprenticeship programs, which often take three to four years.

Education and training. Learning to be a carpenter can start in high school. Classes in English, algebra, geometry, physics, mechanical drawing, blueprint reading, and general shop will prepare students for the further training they will need.

After high school, there are a number of different ways to obtain the necessary training. Some people get a job as a carpenter's helper, assisting more experienced workers. At the same time, the helper might attend a trade or vocational school, or community college to receive further trade-related training and eventually become a carpenter.

Some employers offer employees formal apprenticeships. These programs combine on-the-job training with related classroom instruction. Apprentices usually must be at least 18 years old and meet local requirements. Apprenticeship programs usually last 3 to 4 years, but new rules may allow apprentices to complete programs sooner as competencies are demonstrated.

On the job, apprentices learn elementary structural design and become familiar with common carpentry jobs, such as layout, form building, rough framing, and outside and inside finishing. They also learn to use the tools, machines, equipment, and materials of the trade. In the classroom, apprentices learn safety, first aid, blueprint reading, freehand sketching, basic mathematics, and various carpentry techniques. Both in the classroom and on the job, they learn the relationship between carpentry and the other building trades.

The number of apprenticeship programs is limited, however, so only a small proportion of carpenters learn their trade through these programs. Most apprenticeships are offered by commercial and industrial building contractors, along with construction unions.

Some people who are interested in carpentry careers choose to receive classroom training before seeking a job. There are a number of public and private vocational-technical schools and training academies affiliated with unions and contractors that offer training to become a carpenter. Employers often look favorably upon these students and usually start them at a higher level than those without this training.

Other qualifications. Carpenters need manual dexterity, good eye-hand coordination, physical fitness, and a good sense of balance. The ability to solve mathematical problems quickly and accurately also is required. In addition, military service or a good work history is viewed favorably by employers.

Certification and advancement. Carpenters who complete formal apprenticeship programs receive certification as journeypersons. Some carpenters earn other certifications in scaffold building, high torque bolting, or pump work. These certifications prove that carpenters are able to perform these tasks, which can lead to additional responsibilities.

Carpenters usually have more opportunities than most other construction workers to become general construction supervisors, because carpenters are exposed to the entire construction process. For those who would like to advance, it is increasingly important to be able to communicate in both English and Spanish in order to relay instructions and safety precautions to workers; Spanish-speaking workers make up a large part of the construction workforce in many areas. Carpenters may advance to carpentry supervisor or general construction supervisor positions. Others may become independent contractors. Supervisors and contractors need good communication skills to deal with clients and subcontractors. They also should be able to identify and estimate the quantity of materials needed to complete a job and accurately estimate how long a job will take to complete and what it will cost.

Employment

Carpenters are employed throughout the country in almost every community and make up the second largest building trades occupation. They held about 1.3 million jobs in 2008.

About 32 percent worked in the construction of buildings industry, and about 22 percent worked for specialty trade contractors. Most of the rest of wage and salary carpenters worked for manufacturing firms, government agencies, retail establishments, and a wide variety of other industries. About 32 percent of all carpenters were self-employed. Some carpenters change employers each time they finish a construction job. Others alternate between working for a contractor and working as contractors themselves on small jobs, depending on where the work is available.

Job Outlook

As fast as average job growth, coupled with replacement needs, will create a large number of openings each year. Job opportunities should be best for those with the most training and skills.

Employment change. Employment of carpenters is expected to increase by 13 percent during the 2008–2018 decade, as fast as the average for all occupations. Population growth over the next decade will stimulate some growth in the construction industry over the long run to meet people's housing and other basic needs. Energy conservation will also stimulate demand for buildings that are more energy efficient, particularly in the industrial sector. The home remodeling market also will create demand for carpenters. Moreover, construction of roads and bridges should increase the demand for carpenters in the coming decade. Much will depend on spending by the federal and state governments, as they attempt to upgrade and repair existing infrastructure, such as highways, bridges, and public buildings.

Some of the demand for carpenters, however, will be offset by expected productivity gains resulting from the increasing use of prefabricated components and improved fasteners and tools. Prefabricated wall panels, roof assemblies, and stairs, as well as prehung doors and windows can be installed very quickly. Instead of having to be built on the worksite, prefabricated walls, partitions, and stairs can be lifted into place in one operation; beams and, in some cases, entire roof assemblies, are lifted into place using a crane. As prefabricated components become more standardized, builders will use them more often. New and improved tools, equipment, techniques, and materials also are making carpenters more versatile, allowing them to perform more carpentry tasks.

Job prospects. Job opportunities will be good for those with the most training and skills. The need to replace carpenters who retire or leave the occupation for other reasons should result in a large number of openings. Carpenters with specialized or all-around skills will have better opportunities for steady work than carpenters who can perform only a few relatively simple, routine tasks.

Employment of carpenters, like that of many other construction workers, is sensitive to the fluctuations of the economy. Workers in these trades may experience periods of unemployment when the overall level of construction falls. On the other hand, shortages of these workers may occur in some areas during peak periods of building activity.

Job opportunities for carpenters also vary by geographic area. Construction activity parallels the movement of people and businesses and reflects differences in local economic conditions. The areas with the largest population increases will also provide the best opportunities for jobs as carpenters and for apprenticeships for people seeking to become carpenters.

Earnings

In May 2009, median hourly wages of wage and salary carpenters were $18.98. The middle 50 percent earned between $14.62 and $25.76. The lowest 10 percent earned less than $11.83, and the highest 10 percent earned more than $34.01. Median hourly wages in the industries employing the largest numbers of carpenters were as follows:

Residential building construction	$18.15
Nonresidential building construction	21.38
Building finishing contractors	19.80
Foundation, structure, and building exterior contractors	17.64
Employment services	17.68

Earnings can be reduced on occasion, because carpenters lose work-time in bad weather and during recessions when jobs are unavailable. Earnings may be increased by overtime during busy periods.

Some carpenters are members of the United Brotherhood of Carpenters and Joiners of America. About 19 percent of all carpenters were members of unions or covered by union contracts, higher than the average for all occupations.

Projections Data from the National Employment Matrix

Occupational title	SOC Code	Employment, 2008	Projected employment, 2018	Change, 2008–2018	
				Number	Percent
Carpenters	47-2031	1,284,900	1,450,300	165,400	13

NOTE: Data in this table are rounded.

Related Occupations

Carpenters are skilled construction workers. Other skilled construction occupations include brickmasons, blockmasons, and stonemasons; cement masons, concrete finishers, segmental pavers, and terrazzo workers; construction equipment operators; drywall and ceiling tile installers, tapers, plasterers, and stucco masons; electricians; and plumbers, pipelayers, pipefitters, and steamfitters.

Sources of Additional Information

For information about carpentry apprenticeships or other work opportunities in this trade, contact local carpentry contractors, locals of the union mentioned above, local joint union-contractor apprenticeship committees, or the nearest office of the state employment service or apprenticeship agency. You can also find information on the registered apprenticeship system with links to state apprenticeship programs on the U.S. Department of Labor website: www. doleta.gov/OA/eta_default.cfm. Apprenticeship information is also available from the U.S. Department of Labor toll-free helpline: (877) 872-5627.

For information on training opportunities and carpentry in general, contact

▸ Associated Builders and Contractors, 4250 N. Fairfax Dr., 9th Floor, Arlington, VA 22203-1607. Internet: www.trytools.org

▸ Associated General Contractors of America, Inc., 2300 Wilson Blvd., Suite 400, Arlington, VA 22201-5426. Internet: www.agc.org

▸ National Center for Construction Education and Research, 3600 NW 43rd St., Bldg. G, Gainesville, FL 32606-8134. Internet: www.nccer.org

▸ National Association of Home Builders, Home Builders Institute, 1201 15th St. NW, Washington, DC 20005-2842. Internet: www.hbi.org

▸ United Brotherhood of Carpenters and Joiners of America, Carpenters Training Fund, 101 Constitution Ave. NW, Washington, DC 20001-2192. Internet: www.carpenters.org

For general information on apprenticeships and how to get them, see the *Occupational Outlook Quarterly* article "Apprenticeships: Career training, credentials—and a paycheck in your pocket," online at www.bls.gov/opub/ooq/2002/summer/art01.pdf and in print at many libraries and career centers.

Carpet, Floor, and Tile Installers and Finishers

(O*NET 47-2041.00, 47-2042.00, 47-2043.00, and 47-2044.00)

Significant Points

■ Most workers learn on the job.

■ About 35 percent of carpet, floor, and tile installers and finishers are self-employed.

■ Projected job growth varies by specialty; for example, tile and marble setters are expected to grow by 14 percent, while carpet installers are projected to decline by 1 percent.

■ Employment of carpet, floor, and tile installers and finishers is less sensitive to fluctuations in construction activity than is employment of workers in other construction trades.

Nature of the Work

Carpet, floor, and tile installers and finishers lay floor coverings in homes, offices, hospitals, stores, restaurants, and many other types of buildings. Tile also may be installed on walls and ceilings. Carpet, tile, and other types of floor coverings not only serve an important basic function in buildings, but their decorative qualities also contribute to the appeal of the buildings.

Before installing carpet, carpet installers first inspect the surface to be covered to determine its condition and, when necessary, correct any imperfections that could show through the carpet or cause the carpet to wear unevenly. They measure the area to be carpeted and plan the layout, keeping in mind likely traffic patterns and placement of seams for best appearance and maximum wear.

When installing wall-to-wall carpet without tacks, installers first fasten a tackless strip to the floor, next to the wall. They then install the padded cushion, or underlay. Next, they roll out, measure, mark, and cut the carpet, allowing for 2 to 3 inches of extra carpet for the final fitting. Using a device called a "knee kicker," they position the carpet, stretching it to fit evenly on the floor and snugly against each wall and door threshold. They then cut off the excess carpet. Finally, using a power stretcher, they stretch the carpet, hooking it to the tackless strip to hold it in place. The installers then finish the edges using a wall trimmer.

Because most carpet comes in 12-foot widths, wall-to-wall installations require installers to join carpet sections together for large rooms. The installers join the sections using heat-taped seams—seams held together by a special plastic tape that is activated by heat.

In commercial installations, carpet often is glued directly to the floor or to padding that has been glued to the floor. For special upholstery work, such as installing carpet on stairs, carpet may be held in place with staples.

Carpet installers use hand tools such as hammers, drills, staple guns, carpet knives, and rubber mallets. They also may use carpet-laying tools, such as carpet shears, knee kickers, wall trimmers, loop pile cutters, heat irons, and power stretchers.

Floor installers and *floor layers* lay floor coverings such as laminate, linoleum, vinyl, cork, and rubber for decorative purposes or to reduce noise, absorb shocks, or create air-tight environments. Although these workers also may install carpet, wood, or tile, that is not their main job. Before installing the floor, floor layers inspect the surface to be covered and, if necessary, correct any defects, such as a subfloor that is unleveled or contains rotted wood, in order to start with a strong, smooth, clean foundation. Then they measure and cut flooring materials. When installing linoleum or vinyl, they may use an adhesive to glue the material directly to the floor. For laminate floor installation, workers may unroll and install a polyethylene film that acts as a moisture barrier, along with a thicker, padded underlayer that helps reduce noise. Cork and rubber floors can often be installed directly on top of the subfloor without an underlayer. Finally, floor layers install the floor covering to form a tight fit.

After a carpenter installs a new hardwood floor or when a customer wants to refinish an old wood floor, floor sanders and finishers are called in to smooth any imperfections in the wood and apply coats of varnish or polyurethane. To remove imperfections and smooth the surface, they scrape and sand wood floors using floor-sanding machines. After sanding, they then examine the floor and remove excess glue from joints using a knife or wood chisel and may further sand the wood surfaces by hand, using sandpaper. Finally, they apply sealant using brushes or rollers, often applying multiple coats.

Tile installers, *tilesetters*, and *marble setters* apply hard tile and marble to floors, walls, ceilings, countertops, patios, and roof decks. Tile and marble are durable, impervious to water, and easy to clean, making them a popular building material in bathrooms, kitchens, hospitals, and commercial buildings.

Prior to installation, tilesetters use measuring devices, spacers, and levels to ensure that the tile is placed in a consistent manner. Tiles vary in color, shape, and size, with their sides ranging from 1 inch to 24 or more inches in length, so tilesetters sometimes prearrange tiles on a dry floor according to the planned design. This allows them to examine the pattern, check that they have enough of each type of tile, and determine where they will have to cut tiles to fit the design in the available space. Tilesetters cut tiles with a machine saw or a special cutting tool to cover all exposed areas, including corners and around pipes, tubs, and wash basins. To set tile on a flat, solid surface, such as drywall, concrete, plaster, or wood, tilesetters first use a tooth-edged trowel to spread "thinset"—a thin layer of either cement adhesive or "mastic," which is a very sticky paste. They then properly position the tile and gently tap the surface with the trowel handle, a rubber mallet, or a small block of wood to set the tile evenly and firmly. Spacers are used to maintain exact distance between tiles, and any excess thinset is wiped off the tile immediately after placement.

To apply tile to an area that lacks a solid surface, tilesetters nail a support of metal mesh or tile backer board to the wall or ceiling to be tiled. They use a trowel to apply a cement mortar—called a "scratch coat"—onto the metal screen and scratch the surface of the soft mortar with a small tool similar to a rake. After the scratch coat has dried, tilesetters apply a brown coat of mortar to level the surface and then apply mortar to the brown coat and begin to place tile onto the surface. Hard backer board also is used in areas where there is excess moisture, such as a shower stall.

When the cement or mastic has set, tilesetters fill the joints with "grout," which is very fine cement. Grout that is used for joints 1/8th of an inch and larger typically has sand in it. Tilesetters then apply the grout to the surface with a rubber-edged device called a "float" or a grouting trowel to fill the joints and remove excess grout. Before the grout sets, they wipe the tiles and smooth the joints with a wet sponge for a uniform appearance.

Marble setters cut and set marble slabs on floors and walls of buildings. They trim and cut marble to specified sizes using a power wet saw, other electric cutting equipment, or hand tools. After setting the marble in place, the workers polish the marble to a high luster using power tools or by hand.

Work environment. Carpet, floor, and tile installers and finishers usually work indoors and have regular daytime hours. However, when floor covering installers need to work in occupied stores or offices, they may work evenings and weekends to avoid disturbing customers or employees. By the time workers install carpets, flooring, or tile in a new structure, the majority of construction has been completed and the work area is relatively clean and uncluttered. Installing these materials is labor intensive; workers spend much of their time bending, kneeling, and reaching—activities that require endurance. The work can be very hard on workers' knees; therefore, safety regulations often require that they wear kneepads. Carpet installers frequently lift heavy rolls of carpet and may move heavy

furniture, which requires strength and can be physically exhausting and hard on workers' backs. Carpet and floor layers may be exposed to fumes from various kinds of glue and to fibers of certain types of carpet. Tile and floor installers are usually required to wear safety goggles when using certain equipment.

Workers are subject to cuts from tools or materials, falls from ladders, and strained muscles. Data from the U.S. Bureau of Labor Statistics show that full-time carpet, floor, and tile installers and finishers experienced a work-related injury and illness rate that was higher than the national average.

Training, Other Qualifications, and Advancement

The vast majority of carpet, floor, and tile installers and finishers learn their trade informally on the job. Some workers, mostly tile setters, learn through formal apprenticeship programs, which include classroom instruction and paid on-the-job training.

Education and training. Most carpet installers receive short-term on-the-job training, often sponsored by individual contractors; therefore, a high school diploma usually is not required. Workers start as helpers and begin with simple assignments, such as installing stripping and padding or helping to stretch newly installed carpet. With experience, helpers take on more difficult assignments, such as cutting and fitting.

Tile and marble setters learn their craft mostly through long-term on-the-job training. They start by helping carry materials and learning about the tools of the trade, and later they take on more difficult tasks, such as preparing the subsurface for tile or marble. As tile and marble setters progress, they learn to cut the tile and marble to fit the job. They also learn to apply grout and sealants to give the product its final appearance. Apprenticeship programs and some contractor-sponsored programs provide comprehensive training in all phases of the tilesetting and floor layer trades.

Other floor layers also learn on the job and begin by learning how to use the tools of the trade. As they progress, they learn how to cut and install the various floor coverings.

Other qualifications. Good manual dexterity, eye-hand coordination, physical fitness, and sense of balance and color are some of the skills needed to become carpet, floor, and tile installers and finishers. The ability to solve basic arithmetic problems quickly and accurately also is required. In addition, reliability and a good work history are viewed favorably by contractors.

Advancement. Carpet, floor, and tile installers and finishers sometimes advance to become supervisors, salespersons, or estimators. In these positions, they must be able to estimate the time, money, and quantity of materials needed to complete a job.

Some carpet installers may become managers for large installation firms. For those interested in advancement, it is increasingly important to be able to communicate in both English and Spanish because Spanish-speaking workers make up a large part of the construction workforce in many areas. Workers who want to advance to supervisor jobs or become independent contractors also need good English skills to deal with clients and subcontractors.

Many carpet, floor, and tile installers and finishers who begin working for someone else eventually go into business for themselves as independent contractors.

Projections Data from the National Employment Matrix

Occupational title	SOC Code	Employment, 2008	Projected employment, 2018	Change, 2008–2018	
				Number	Percent
Carpet, floor, and tile installers and finishers 47-2040		160,500	171,900	11,400	7
Carpet installers 47-2041		51,100	50,500	−600	−1
Floor layers, except carpet, wood, and hard tiles 47-2042		21,200	21,000	−200	−1
Floor sanders and finishers 47-2043		12,200	13,600	1,400	11
Tile and marble setters 47-2044		76,000	86,800	10,800	14

NOTE: Data in this table are rounded.

Employment

Carpet, floor, and tile installers and finishers held about 160,500 jobs in 2008. About 35 percent of all carpet, floor, and tile installers and finishers were self-employed. The following tabulation shows 2008 total employment by specialty:

Tile and marble setters....................................... 76,000
Carpet installers 51,100
Floor layers, except carpet, wood, and hard tiles ... 21,200
Floor sanders and finishers 12,200

Many carpet installers work for flooring contractors or floor covering retailers. Most salaried tilesetters are employed by tilesetting contractors who work mainly on nonresidential construction projects, such as schools, hospitals, and office buildings. Most self-employed tilesetters work on residential projects.

Although carpet, floor, and tile installers and finishers are employed throughout the nation, they tend to be concentrated in populated areas where there are high levels of construction activity.

Job Outlook

Employment of carpet, floor, and tile installers and finishers is expected to grow as fast as the average for all occupations. Job growth and opportunities, however, will differ among the individual occupations in this category.

Employment change. Overall employment is expected to grow by 7 percent between 2008 and 2018, about as fast as the average. Tile and marble setting, the largest specialty, will experience faster than average employment growth because population and business growth will result in more construction of shopping malls, hospitals, schools, restaurants, and other structures in which tile is used extensively. Tiles, including those made of glass, slate, and mosaic, and other less traditional materials, are also becoming more popular, particularly in the growing number of more expensive homes.

Employment of carpet installers, the second-largest specialty, will experience little or no change, declining by 1 percent, as residential investors and homeowners increasingly choose hardwood and tile floors because of their durability, neutral colors, and low maintenance and because owners feel these floors will add to the value of their homes. Carpets, on the other hand, stain and wear out faster than wood or tile, which contributes to the decreased demand for carpet installation. Nevertheless, carpet will continue to be used in nonresidential structures such as schools, offices, and hospitals. Also, many multifamily structures will require or recommend carpet because it provides sound dampening.

Workers who install other types of flooring, including laminate, cork, bamboo, rubber, and vinyl, should have little or no job growth because these materials are used less frequently and are often laid by other types of construction workers. Employment of floor sanders and finishers—a small specialty—is projected to grow by 11 percent, which is about as fast as average, because of the increasing use of prefinished hardwood flooring and because their work is heavily concentrated in the relatively small niche market of residential remodeling. There should also be some employment growth resulting from restoration of damaged hardwood floors, a procedure that is typically more cost effective than installing new floors.

Job prospects. In addition to employment growth, numerous job openings are expected for carpet, floor, and tile installers and finishers because of the need to replace workers who leave the occupation. The strenuous nature of the work leads to high replacement needs; many of these workers do not stay in the occupation long.

Few openings will arise for vinyl and linoleum floor installers because the number of these jobs is comparatively small and because homeowners can increasingly take advantage of easy application products, such as self-adhesive vinyl tiles.

Employment of carpet, floor, and tile installers and finishers is less sensitive to changes in construction activity than most other construction occupations because much of the work involves replacing worn carpet and other flooring in existing buildings. However, workers in these trades may still experience periods of unemployment when the overall level of construction falls. On the other hand, shortages of these workers may occur in some areas during peak periods of building activity.

Earnings

In May 2009, median hourly wages of carpet installers were $17.90. The middle 50 percent earned between $13.11 and $25.63. The lowest 10 percent earned less than $10.26, and the top 10 percent earned more than $34.03. Median hourly wages of carpet installers working for building finishing contractors were $18.53, and $16.77 for those working in home furnishings stores. Carpet installers are paid either on an hourly basis or by the number of yards of carpet installed.

Median hourly wages of wage and salary floor layers except carpet, wood, and hard tiles were $17.34 in May 2009. The middle 50 percent earned between $12.97 and $23.19. The lowest 10 percent earned less than $10.38, and the top 10 percent earned more than $30.57.

Median hourly wages of floor sanders and finishers were $15.76 in May 2009. The middle 50 percent earned between $12.99 and $20.07. The lowest 10 percent earned less than $10.71, and the top 10 percent earned more than $24.81.

Median hourly wages of tile and marble setters were $18.83 in May 2009. The middle 50 percent earned between $13.77 and $25.38.

The lowest 10 percent earned less than $10.53, and the top 10 percent earned more than $33.66.

Earnings of carpet, floor, and tile installers and finishers vary greatly by geographic location and by union membership status. Some carpet, floor, and tile installers and finishers belong to the United Brotherhood of Carpenters and Joiners of America. Some tilesetters belong to the International Union of Bricklayers and Allied Craftsmen, and some carpet installers belong to the International Brotherhood of Painters and Allied Trades.

Apprentices and other trainees usually start out earning about half of what an experienced worker earns; their wage rates increase as they advance through the training program.

Related Occupations

Carpet, floor, and tile installers and finishers measure, cut, and fit materials to cover a space. Workers in other occupations involving similar skills, but using different materials, include brickmasons, blockmasons, and stonemasons; carpenters; cement masons, concrete finishers, segmental pavers, and terrazzo workers; drywall and ceiling tile installers, tapers, plasterers, and stucco masons; painters and paperhangers; roofers; and sheet metal workers.

Sources of Additional Information

For details about apprenticeships or work opportunities, contact local flooring or tilesetting contractors or retailers, locals of the unions previously mentioned, or the nearest office of the state apprenticeship agency or employment service. Apprenticeship information is also available from the U.S. Department of Labor's toll-free helpline: 1 (877) 872-5627.

Additional information on training for carpet installers and floor layers is available from

▸ Finishing Trades Institute International, 7230 Parkway Dr., Hanover, MD 21076. Internet: www.finishingtradesinstitute.org

For general information about the work of tile installers and finishers, contact

▸ National Association of Home Builders, Home Builders Institute, 1201 15th St. NW, Washington, DC 20005. Internet: www.hbi.org and www.nahb.org

For more information about tile setting and tile training, contact

▸ National Tile Contractors Association, P.O. Box 13629, Jackson, MS 39236. Internet: www.tile-assn.com

For general information on apprenticeships and how to get them, see the *Occupational Outlook Quarterly* article "Apprenticeships: Career training, credentials—and a paycheck in your pocket," online at www.bls.gov/opub/ooq/2002/summer/art01.pdf and in print at many libraries and career centers.

Cashiers

(O*NET 41-2011.00)

Significant Points

■ Cashiers need little or no work experience; they are trained on the job.

■ Opportunities for full-time and part-time jobs are expected to be good because of the need to replace the large number of workers who leave cashier jobs.

■ Many cashiers start at the minimum wage.

Nature of the Work

Supermarkets, department stores, gasoline service stations, movie theaters, restaurants, and many other businesses employ cashiers to register the sale of their goods and services. Although specific job duties vary by employer, cashiers usually are assigned to a register at the beginning of their shifts and are given a drawer containing a specific amount of money with which to start—their "till." They must count their till to ensure that it contains the correct amount of money and adequate supplies of change. Some cashiers also handle returns and exchanges. When they do, they must ensure that returned merchandise is in good condition, and determine where and when it was purchased and what type of payment was used.

After entering charges for all items and subtracting the value of any coupons or special discounts, cashiers total the customer's bill and take payment. Forms of payment include cash; personal checks; and gift, credit, and debit cards. Cashiers must know the store's policies and procedures for each type of payment the store accepts. For checks and credit and debit card charges, they may request additional identification from the customer or call in for an authorization. They must verify the age of customers purchasing alcohol or tobacco. When the sale is complete, cashiers issue a receipt to the customer and return the appropriate change. They may also wrap or bag the purchase.

At the end of their shifts, cashiers once again count the drawers' contents and compare the totals with sales data. An occasional shortage of small amounts may be overlooked but, in many establishments, repeated shortages are grounds for dismissal. In addition to counting the contents of their drawers at the end of their shifts, cashiers usually separate and total charge forms, return slips, coupons, and any other noncash items.

Most cashiers use scanners and computers, but some establishments still require price and product information to be entered manually. In a store with scanners, a cashier passes a product's Universal Product Code over the scanning device, which transmits the code number to a computer. The computer identifies the item and its price. In other establishments, cashiers manually enter codes into computers and then descriptions of the items and their prices appear on the screen.

Depending on the type of establishment, cashiers may have other duties as well. In many supermarkets, for example, cashiers weigh produce and bulk food, as well as return unwanted items to the shelves. In convenience stores, cashiers may be required to know how to use a variety of machines other than cash registers, and how to furnish money orders and sell lottery tickets. Operating ticket-dispensing machines and answering customers' questions are common duties for cashiers who work at movie theaters and ticket agencies.

Work environment. Most cashiers work indoors, usually standing in booths or behind counters. Often, they are not allowed to leave their workstations without supervisory approval because they are responsible for large sums of money. The work of cashiers can be very repetitive, but improvements in workstation design in many stores are alleviating problems caused by repetitive motion. In addition, the work can sometimes be dangerous; the risk from robberies and homicides is much higher for cashiers than for other workers, although more safety precautions are being taken to help deter robbers.

About 47 percent of all cashiers worked part time in 2008. Hours of work often vary depending on the needs of the employer. Generally, cashiers are expected to work weekends, evenings, and holidays to accommodate customers' needs. However, many employers offer flexible schedules. Because the holiday season is the busiest time for most retailers, many employers restrict the use of vacation time from Thanksgiving through the beginning of January.

Training, Other Qualifications, and Advancement

Cashier jobs usually are entry-level positions requiring little or no previous work experience. They require good customer service skills.

Education and training. Although there are no specific educational requirements, employers filling full-time jobs often prefer applicants with high school diplomas.

Nearly all cashiers are trained on the job. In small businesses, an experienced worker often trains beginners. The trainee spends the first day observing the operation and becoming familiar with the store's equipment, policies, and procedures. After this, trainees are assigned to a register—frequently under the supervision of an experienced worker. In larger businesses, trainees spend several days in classes before being placed at cash registers. Topics typically covered in class include a description of the industry and the company, store policies and procedures, equipment operation, and security.

Training for experienced workers is not common, except when new equipment is introduced or when procedures change. In these cases, the employer or a representative of the equipment manufacturer trains workers on the job.

Other qualifications. People who want to become cashiers should be able to do repetitive work accurately. They also need basic mathematics skills and good manual dexterity. Because cashiers deal constantly with the public, they should be neat in appearance and able to deal tactfully and pleasantly with customers. In addition, some businesses prefer to hire workers who can operate specialized equipment or who have business experience, such as typing, selling, or handling money.

Advancement. Advancement opportunities for cashiers vary. For those working part time, promotion may be to a full-time position. Others advance to head cashier or cash-office clerk. In addition, this job offers a good opportunity to learn about an employer's business and can serve as a steppingstone to a more responsible position.

Employment

Cashiers held about 3.55 million jobs in 2008. Although cashiers are employed in almost every industry, 24 percent of all jobs were in grocery stores. Gasoline stations, department stores, and other retail establishments also employed large numbers of these workers. Outside of retail establishments, many cashiers worked in food services and drinking places.

Job Outlook

Cashiers are expected to grow more slowly than the average for all occupations. Opportunities for full-time and part-time jobs are expected to be good because of the need to replace the large number of workers who leave this occupation.

Employment change. Employment of cashiers is expected to grow by 4 percent between 2008 and 2018, which is slower than the average for all occupations. Continued growth in retail sales is expected, but the rising popularity of purchasing goods online will limit the employment growth of cashiers, although many customers still prefer the traditional method of purchasing goods at stores. Also, the growing use of self-service checkout systems in retail trade, especially at grocery stores, should have an adverse effect on employment of cashiers. These self-checkout systems may outnumber checkouts with cashiers in the future in many establishments. The impact on job growth for cashiers will largely depend on the public's acceptance of this self-service technology.

Job prospects. Opportunities for full-time and part-time cashier jobs should continue to be good because of the need to replace the large number of workers who transfer to other occupations or leave the labor force. There is substantial movement into and out of the occupation because education and training requirements are minimal and the predominance of part-time jobs is attractive to people seeking a short-term source of income rather than a full-time career. Historically, workers under the age of 25 have filled many of the openings in this occupation. In 2008, about 47 percent of all cashiers were 24 years of age or younger.

Because cashiers are needed in businesses and organizations of all types and sizes, job opportunities are found throughout the country. However, job opportunities may vary from year to year because the strength of the economy affects demand for cashiers. Companies tend to hire more cashiers when the economy is strong. Seasonal demand for cashiers also causes fluctuations in employment.

Earnings

Many cashiers start at the federal minimum wage, which was $7.25 an hour as of July 2009. Some state laws set the minimum wage higher, and establishments must pay at least that amount. Wages tend to be higher in areas where there is intense competition for workers.

Median hourly wages of cashiers, except gaming in May 2009 were $8.57. The middle 50 percent earned between $7.54 and $9.69 an hour. The lowest 10 percent earned less than $7.15, and the highest 10 percent earned more than $11.91 an hour. Median hourly wages in the industries employing the largest numbers of cashiers in May 2009 were as follows:

Projections Data from the National Employment Matrix

Occupational title	SOC Code	Employment, 2008	Projected employment, 2018	Change, 2008–2018	
				Number	Percent
Cashiers, except gaming 41-2011		3,550,000	3,675,500	125,500	4

NOTE: Data in this table are rounded.

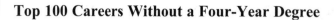

Grocery stores...$8.72
Gasoline stations...8.28
Other general merchandise stores 8.51
Department stores 8.37
Health and personal care stores............................8.74

Similar to other occupations, benefits for full-time cashiers tend to be better than those for cashiers working part time. In addition to typical benefits, those working in retail establishments often receive discounts on purchases, and cashiers in restaurants may receive free or low-cost meals. Some employers also offer employee stock option plans and education reimbursement plans.

Related Occupations

Cashiers accept payment for the purchase of goods and services. Other workers with similar duties include counter and rental clerks; food and beverage serving and related workers; gaming cage workers; postal service clerks; retail salespersons; and tellers.

Sources of Additional Information

General information on careers in grocery stores is available from

▶ Food Marketing Institute, 2345 Crystal Dr., Suite 800, Arlington, VA 22202. Internet: www.fmi.org

For information about employment opportunities as a cashier, contact

▶ The Association for Convenience and Petroleum Retailing, 1600 Duke St., Alexandria, VA 22314. Internet: www.nacsonline.com

▶ United Food and Commercial Workers International Union, Education Office, 1775 K St. NW, Washington, DC 20006.

Cement Masons, Concrete Finishers, Segmental Pavers, and Terrazzo Workers

(O*NET 47-2051.00, 47-2053.00, and 47-4091.00)

Significant Points

■ Job opportunities are expected to be good, especially for those with the most experience and skills.

■ Most workers learn on the job or through a combination of classroom and on-the-job training that can take three to four years.

■ Cement masons often have variable schedules and work overtime, with premium pay, because once concrete has been placed, the job must be completed quickly.

Nature of the Work

Cement masons, concrete finishers, and terrazzo workers all work with concrete, one of the most common and durable materials used in construction. Once set, concrete—a mixture of Portland cement, sand, gravel, and water—becomes the foundation for everything from decorative patios and floors to huge dams or miles of roadways.

Cement masons and *concrete finishers* place and finish concrete. They also may color concrete surfaces; expose aggregate (small stones) in walls and sidewalks; or fabricate concrete beams, columns, and panels. In preparing a site to place concrete, cement masons first set the forms for holding the concrete and properly align them. They then direct the casting of the concrete and supervise laborers who use shovels or special tools to spread it. Masons then guide a straightedge back and forth across the top of the forms to "screed," or level, the freshly placed concrete. Immediately after leveling the concrete, masons carefully float it—which means to smooth the concrete surface with a "bull float," a long-handled tool of about 8 by 48 inches that covers the coarser materials in the concrete and brings a rich mixture of fine cement paste to the surface.

After the concrete has been leveled and floated, concrete finishers press an edger between the forms and the concrete and guide it along the edge and the surface. This produces slightly rounded edges and helps prevent chipping or cracking. Concrete finishers use a special tool called a "groover" to make joints or grooves at specific intervals that help control cracking. Next, they smooth the surface using either a powered or hand trowel, which is a small, smooth, rectangular metal tool.

Sometimes, cement masons perform all the steps of laying concrete, including the finishing. As the final step, they retrowel the concrete surface back and forth with powered or hand trowels to create a smooth finish. For a coarse, nonskid finish, masons brush the surface with a broom or stiff-bristled brush. For a pebble finish, they embed small gravel chips into the surface. They then wash any excess cement from the exposed chips with a mild acid solution. For color, they use colored premixed concrete.

Throughout the entire process, cement masons must monitor how the wind, heat, or cold affects the curing of the concrete. They must have a thorough knowledge of concrete characteristics so that, by using sight and touch, they can determine what is happening to the concrete and take measures to prevent defects.

Segmental pavers lay out, cut, and install pavers—flat pieces of masonry made from compacted concrete or brick. This masonry is typically installed in patios, sidewalks, plazas, streets, crosswalks, parking lots, and driveways. Installers usually begin their work by preparing a base that has been graded to the proper depth and filled and leveled with a layer of sand. Installers then place the pavers in a pattern, normally by hand but sometimes by machine. Sand is then added to fill the joints between the pavers.

Terrazzo workers and *finishers* create attractive walkways, floors, patios, and panels by exposing marble chips and other fine aggregates on the surface of finished concrete. Much of the preliminary work of terrazzo workers is similar to that of cement masons. Depending on the type of terrazzo, they usually first build a solid, level concrete foundation that is 3 to 4 inches deep. Second, after the forms are removed from the foundation, workers add a 1-inch layer of sandy concrete. Terrazzo workers partially embed, or attach with adhesive, metal divider strips in the concrete wherever there is to be a joint or change of color in the terrazzo. For the third and final layer, terrazzo workers blend and place into each of the panels a fine marble chip mixture that may be color-pigmented. While the mixture is still wet, workers add additional marble chips of various colors into each panel and roll a lightweight roller over the entire surface.

When the terrazzo is thoroughly set, helpers grind it with a terrazzo grinder, which is somewhat like a floor polisher, only much heavier. Any depressions left by the grinding are filled with a matching grout material and hand-troweled for a smooth, uniform surface.

Terrazzo workers then clean, polish, and seal the dry surface for a lustrous finish.

Work environment. Concrete, segmental paving, and terrazzo work is fast paced and strenuous, and requires continuous physical effort. A workweek of 40 hours is the most common, although the number of hours can be increased or decreased by outside factors, such as the need to coordinate work with other jobs being done on the construction site. As a result, about 17 percent of workers have a variable schedule.

Because most finishing is done at floor level, workers must bend and kneel often. Many jobs are outdoors, and work is generally halted during inclement weather. The work, either indoors or outdoors, may be in areas that are muddy, dusty, or dirty. To avoid chemical burns from uncured concrete and sore knees from frequent kneeling, many workers wear kneepads. Workers usually also wear water-repellent boots while working with wet concrete.

Training, Other Qualifications, and Advancement

Most cement masons, concrete finishers, segmental pavers, and terrazzo workers learn their trades through on-the-job training, either as helpers or in apprenticeship programs. Some workers also learn their jobs by attending trade or vocational-technical schools.

Education and training. Many masons and finishers first gain experience as construction laborers. (See the section on construction laborers elsewhere in this book.) Most on-the-job training programs consist of informal instruction, in which experienced workers teach helpers to use the tools, equipment, machines, and materials of the trade. Trainees begin with tasks such as edging, jointing, and using a straightedge on freshly placed concrete. As training progresses, assignments become more complex, and trainees can usually do finishing work within a short time.

Some workers train in formal apprenticeship programs usually sponsored by local contractors, trade associations, or local union-management committees. These programs combine on-the-job training with a recommended minimum of 144 hours of classroom instruction each year. In the classroom, apprentices learn applied mathematics, blueprint reading, and safety. Apprentices generally receive special instruction in layout work and cost estimation. Apprenticeships may take 3 to 4 years to complete, although completion times are increasingly variable as apprenticeship progression based on demonstrated competence instead of time is gaining popularity. Applying for an apprenticeship may require a written test and a physical exam.

Many states have technical schools that offer courses in masonry which improve employment and advancement opportunities. Entrance requirements and fees vary depending on the school and who is funding the program. These schools may offer courses before hiring or after hiring as part of the on-the-job training.

Other qualifications. The most important qualities employers look for are dependability and a strong work ethic. When hiring helpers and apprentices, employers prefer high school graduates who are at least 18 years old, possess a driver's license, and are in good physical condition. The ability to get along with others is also important because cement masons frequently work in teams. High school courses in general science, mathematics, and vocational-technical subjects—such as blueprint reading and mechanical drawing—provide a helpful background. Cement masons, concrete finishers,

segmental pavers, and terrazzo workers should enjoy doing demanding work. They should take pride in craftsmanship and be able to work without close supervision.

Advancement. With additional training, cement masons, concrete finishers, segmental pavers, or terrazzo workers may become supervisors for masonry contractors or move into construction management, building inspection, or contract estimation. Certification programs offered through the National Concrete Masonry Association may allow workers to advance more quickly as they document higher levels of skill in working with concrete. Some workers eventually become owners of businesses, where they may spend most of their time managing rather than practicing their original trade. For those who want to own their own business, taking business classes will help to prepare.

Employment

Cement masons, concrete finishers, segmental pavers, and terrazzo workers held about 207,800 jobs in 2008; segmental pavers and terrazzo workers accounted for only a small portion of the total. Most cement masons and concrete finishers worked for specialty trade contractors, primarily foundation, structure, and building exterior contractors. They also worked for contractors in nonresidential and residential building construction and in heavy and civil engineering construction on projects such as highways, bridges, shopping malls, or large buildings such as factories, schools, and hospitals. A small number were employed by firms that manufacture concrete products. Most segmental pavers and terrazzo workers worked for specialty trade contractors who install decorative floors and wall panels.

Only about 5 percent of cement masons, concrete finishers, segmental pavers, and terrazzo workers were self-employed, a smaller proportion than in other building trades. Most self-employed masons specialize in small jobs, such as driveways, sidewalks, and patios.

Job Outlook

Average employment growth is expected, and job prospects are expected to be good, especially for those with the most experience and skills.

Employment change. Employment of cement masons, concrete finishers, segmental pavers, and terrazzo workers is expected to grow approximately 13 percent over the 2008–2018 decade, about as fast as the average for all occupations. Over the long run, more workers will likely be needed to build new highways, bridges, factories, and other residential and nonresidential structures to meet the demands of a growing population. Additionally, cement masons will be needed to repair and renovate existing highways and bridges and other aging structures. Additional funds for these projects are expected to come from the federal government, which plans to spend money on construction to stimulate the national economy by addressing necessary infrastructure repairs and renovating schools and other government buildings.

The use of concrete for buildings is increasing because its strength is an important asset in areas prone to severe weather. For example, residential construction in Florida is using more concrete as building requirements are changed in reaction to the increased frequency and intensity of hurricanes. Concrete use is likely to expand into other hurricane-prone areas as the durability of the Florida homes is demonstrated.

Projections Data from the National Employment Matrix

Occupational title	SOC Code	Employment, 2008	Projected employment, 2018	Change, 2008–2018	
				Number	Percent
Cement masons, concrete finishers, segmental pavers, and terrazzo workers.......................................	—	207,800	234,500	26,700	13
Cement masons, concrete finishers, and terrazzo workers	47-2050	206,600	233,200	26,600	13
Cement masons and concrete finishers..................	47-2051	201,000	226,800	25,900	13
Terrazzo workers and finishers	47-2053	5,600	6,300	700	13
Segmental pavers	47-4091	1,200	1,300	100	7

NOTE: Data in this table are rounded.

Job prospects. Opportunities for cement masons, concrete finishers, segmental pavers, and terrazzo workers are expected to be good, particularly for those with the most experience and skills. Employers report difficulty in finding workers with the right skills, as many qualified job seekers often prefer work that is less strenuous and has more comfortable working conditions. There are also expected to be a significant number of retirements over the next decade, which will create more job openings. Applicants who take masonry-related courses at technical schools will have better opportunities than those without these courses.

Employment of cement masons, concrete finishers, segmental pavers, and terrazzo workers, like that of many other construction workers, is sensitive to the fluctuations of the economy. Workers in these trades may experience periods of unemployment when the overall level of construction falls. On the other hand, shortages of these workers may occur in some areas during peak periods of building activity.

Earnings

In May 2009, the median hourly wage of cement masons and concrete finishers was $17.04. The middle 50 percent earned between $13.56 and $22.88. The bottom 10 percent earned less than $11.13, and the top 10 percent earned more than $30.64. Median hourly wages in the industries employing the largest numbers of cement masons and concrete finishers were as follows:

Foundation, structure, and building exterior contractors..	$16.80
Other specialty trade contractors..........................	17.06
Nonresidential building construction......................	18.03
Highway, street, and bridge construction................	17.02
Residential building construction...........................	17.73

In May 2009, the median hourly wage of terrazzo workers and finishers was $18.38. The middle 50 percent earned between $14.49 and $24.17. The bottom 10 percent earned less than $11.20, and the top 10 percent earned more than $31.36.

In May 2009, the median hourly wage of segmental pavers was $13.33. The middle 50 percent earned between $11.29 and $15.95. The bottom 10 percent earned less than $9.90, and the top 10 percent earned more than $18.87.

Like other construction trades workers who are paid by the hour, earnings of cement masons, concrete finishers, segmental pavers, and terrazzo workers may be reduced on occasion because poor weather and slowdowns in construction activity limit the amount of time they can work. Nonunion workers generally have lower wage rates than union workers. Apprentices usually start at 50 to 60 percent of the rate paid to experienced workers, and increases are generally achieved by meeting specified advancement requirements every 6 months. Cement masons often work overtime, with premium pay, because once concrete has been placed, the job must be completed.

About 14 percent of cement masons, concrete finishers, segmental pavers, and terrazzo workers belong to unions, the largest of which are the Operative Plasterers' and Cement Masons' International Association of the United States and Canada, and the International Union of Bricklayers and Allied Craftworkers. A few terrazzo workers belong to the United Brotherhood of Carpenters and Joiners of the United States.

Related Occupations

Other construction-related occupations requiring similar skills and knowledge include brickmasons, blockmasons, and stonemasons; carpet, floor, and tile installers and finishers; and drywall and ceiling tile installers, tapers, plasterers, and stucco masons.

An additional occupation in which workers use cement, segmental pavers, and terazzo in their work is grounds maintenance workers.

Sources of Additional Information

For information about apprenticeships and work opportunities, contact local concrete or terrazzo contractors, local offices of unions previously mentioned, a local joint union-management apprenticeship committee, or the nearest office of a state employment service or apprenticeship agency. Apprenticeship information is also available from the U.S. Department of Labor's toll-free helpline: (877) 872-5627. You may also check the U.S. Department of Labor's website for information on apprenticeships and links to state apprenticeship programs. Internet: www.doleta.gov/OA/eta_default.cfm

For general information about cement masons, concrete finishers, segmental pavers, and terrazzo workers, contact

▸ Associated Builders and Contractors, Workforce Development Division, 4250 N. Fairfax Dr., 9th Floor, Arlington, VA 22203-1607. Internet: www.trytools.org

▸ Associated General Contractors of America, Inc., 2300 Wilson Blvd., Suite 400, Arlington, VA 22201-5426. Internet: www.agc.org

▸ International Union of Bricklayers and Allied Craftworkers, International Masonry Institute, The James Brice House, 42 East St., Annapolis, MD 21401-1731. Internet: www.imiweb.org

▸ National Center for Construction Education and Research, 3600 NW 43rd St., Bldg. G, Gainesville, FL 32606-8127. Internet: www.nccer.org

▸ National Concrete Masonry Association, 13750 Sunrise Valley Dr., Herndon, VA 20171-4662. Internet: www.ncma.org

▸ National Terrazzo and Mosaic Association, 201 N. Maple, Suite 208, Purcellville, VA 20132-6102. Internet: www.ntma.com

▸ Operative Plasterers' and Cement Masons' International Association of the United States and Canada, 11720 Beltsville Dr., Suite 700, Beltsville, MD 20705-3104. Internet: www.opcmia.org

▸ Portland Cement Association, 5420 Old Orchard Rd., Skokie, IL 60077-1083. Internet: www.cement.org

For more information about careers and training as a mason, contact

▸ Mason Contractors Association of America, 33 South Roselle Rd., Schaumburg, IL 60193-1646. Internet: www.masoncontractors.org

For general information on apprenticeships and how to get them, see the *Occupational Outlook Quarterly* article "Apprenticeships: Career training, credentials—and a paycheck in your pocket," online at www.bls.gov/opub/ooq/2002/summer/art01.pdf and in print at many libraries and career centers.

Chefs, Head Cooks, and Food Preparation and Serving Supervisors

(O*NET 35-1011.00 and 35-1012.00)

Significant Points

■ Most workers in these occupations have prior experience in the food service or hospitality industries.

■ While most workers have some postsecondary training; many experienced workers with less education can still be promoted into these positions.

■ Job opportunities are expected to be good, largely because of high turnover; however, keen competition is expected for jobs at upscale restaurants that generally pay more.

Nature of the Work

Chefs, head cooks, and food preparation and serving supervisors oversee the daily food service operation of a restaurant or other food service establishment. *Chefs and head cooks* are usually responsible for directing cooks in the kitchen, dealing with food-related concerns, and providing leadership. They are also the most skilled cooks in the kitchen and use their creativity and knowledge of food to develop and prepare recipes.

Food preparation and serving supervisors oversee the kitchen and nonkitchen staff in a restaurant or food service facility. They may also oversee food preparation workers in fast food, cafeteria, or casual dining restaurants, where the menu is fairly standard from day to day, or in more formal restaurants, where a chef provides specific guidelines and exacting standards on how to prepare each item.

All of these workers—chefs, head cooks, and food preparation and serving supervisors—hire, train, and supervise staff, prepare cost estimates for food and supplies, set work schedules, order supplies, and ensure that the food service establishment runs efficiently and profitably. Additionally, these workers ensure that sanitation and safety standards are observed and comply with local regulations.

Fresh food must be stored and cooked properly, work surfaces and dishes clean and sanitary, and staff and customers safe from illness or injury to avoid being closed by the health department or law enforcement.

While all chefs have a role in preparing the food, developing recipes, determining serving sizes, planning menus, ordering food supplies, and overseeing kitchen operations to ensure uniform quality and presentation of meals, different types of chefs may have unique roles to perform or specialize in certain aspects of the job. *Executive chefs, head cooks, and chefs de cuisine* are primarily responsible for coordinating the work of the cooks and directing the preparation of meals. Executive chefs are in charge of all food service operations and also may supervise several kitchens of a hotel, restaurant, or corporate dining operation. A *sous chef*, or sub chef, is the second-in-command and runs the kitchen in the absence of the chef. Many chefs earn fame both for themselves and for their kitchens because of the quality and distinctive nature of the food they serve.

As a greater variety of establishments prepare and serve food, chefs and head cooks and first-line supervisors of food preparation and serving workers can be found in a greater variety of places. Grocery and specialty food stores employ these workers to develop recipes and prepare meals for customers to carry out. They increasingly work in residential care facilities, such as nursing homes, and in schools and hospitals. Some chefs and head cooks work for individuals rather than for restaurants, cafeterias, or food manufacturers. *Personal chefs* and *private household cooks* plan and prepare meals in private homes according to the client's tastes or dietary needs. They order groceries and supplies, clean the kitchen, and wash dishes and utensils. They also may serve meals. Personal chefs usually prepare a week's worth of meals in the client's home for the client to heat and serve according to directions. They may be self-employed or work as part of a team of personal chefs and employed by a company that provides this service. Private household cooks typically work full time for one client, such as corporate executives, university presidents, or diplomats, who regularly entertain as a part of their official duties.

While the work of chefs and head cooks is concentrated in the kitchen or in providing overall guidance, food preparation and serving supervisors oversee specific areas of operation in food service establishments or the kitchen and counter areas of quick service restaurants. In fast food and casual dining restaurants, they may share many of the same functions with food service managers. They are responsible for dealing with customer complaints, balancing the books at the end of the day, scheduling workers, and ordering supplies. They also supervise and train kitchen and food preparation staff and ensure that these workers know how to gather food supplies, operate equipment, and assemble orders.

Work environment. Restaurants and other food service facilities where these workers are employed are required to be clean and sanitary. Although the seating areas of eating places are often attractive, kitchens can be crowded and hot and filled with potential dangers, such as hot ovens and slippery floors. Job hazards for those working in kitchens include slips and falls, cuts, and burns, but these injuries are seldom serious. Chefs, head cooks, and supervisors are under constant pressure to get meals prepared quickly, while ensuring quality is maintained and safety and sanitation guidelines are observed. Because the pace can be hectic during peak dining times, workers must be able to communicate clearly so that food orders and service are done correctly.

Work hours in restaurants may include early mornings, late evenings, holidays, and weekends. Schedules for those working in offices, factories and school cafeterias may be more regular. In fine-dining restaurants, work schedules tend to be longer because of the time required to prepare ingredients in advance. Many executive chefs regularly work 12-hour days because they oversee the delivery of foodstuffs early in the day, plan the menu, and prepare those menu items that require the most skill. Depending upon the days of operation, some chefs or other supervisors may take less busy days off to offset the longer hours on other days.

Training, Other Qualifications, and Advancement

Most workers in these occupations have prior experience in the food service or hospitality industries. Most start as food preparation workers or line cooks in a full-service restaurant and work their way up to positions with more responsibility. Some attend cooking school or take vocational training classes and participate in internships or apprenticeship programs to acquire the additional skills needed to create menus and run a business.

Education and training. While most chefs, head cooks, and food preparation and serving supervisors have some postsecondary training, many experienced workers with less education can still be promoted. Formal training may take place at a community college, technical school, culinary arts school, or a 2-year or 4-year college with a degree in hospitality. A growing number of chefs participate in training programs sponsored by independent cooking schools, professional culinary institutes, 2-year or 4-year colleges with a hospitality or culinary arts department, or in the Armed Forces. Some large hotels and restaurants also operate their own training and job-placement programs for chefs and head cooks. Executive chefs, head cooks, and sous chefs who work in fine-dining restaurants require many years of training and experience.

For students in culinary training programs, most of their time is spent in kitchens learning to prepare meals by practicing cooking skills. They learn knife techniques and proper use and care of kitchen equipment. Training programs also include courses in nutrition, menu planning, portion control, purchasing and inventory methods, proper food storage procedures, and use of leftover food to minimize waste. Students also learn sanitation and public health rules for handling food. Training in food service management, computer accounting and inventory software, and banquet service are featured in some training programs. Most formal training programs also require students to get experience in a commercial kitchen through an internship, apprenticeship, or out-placement program.

Although formal training is an important way to enter the profession, many chefs are trained on the job, receiving real work experience and training from chef-mentors in the restaurants where they work. Others enter the profession through formal apprenticeship programs sponsored by professional culinary institutes, industry associations, and trade unions in coordination with the U.S. Department of Labor. The American Culinary Federation accredits more than 200 formal academic training programs and sponsors apprenticeship programs around the country. Typical apprenticeships last 2 years and combine classroom training and work experience. Accreditation is an indication that a culinary program meets recognized standards regarding course content, facilities, and quality of instruction.

Other qualifications. Chefs, head cooks, and food preparation and serving supervisors must demonstrate strong leadership and communication skills and have the ability to motivate others. Chefs and head cooks also must have an intense desire to cook, be creative, and have a keen sense of taste and smell. Personal cleanliness is essential because most states require health certificates indicating that workers are free from communicable diseases. Knowledge of a foreign language can be an asset because it may improve communication with other restaurant staff, vendors, and the restaurant's clientele.

Certification and advancement. The American Culinary Federation certifies pastry professionals, personal chefs, and culinary educators in addition to various levels of chefs. Certification standards are based primarily on experience and formal training. Although certification is not required, it can help to prove accomplishment and lead to advancement and higher-paying positions.

Advancement opportunities for chefs, head cooks, and food preparation and serving supervisors depend on their training, work experience, ability to perform more responsible and sophisticated tasks, and their leadership abilities.

Food preparation and serving supervisors may advance to become food service managers while some chefs and head cooks may go into business as caterers or personal chefs or open their own restaurant. Others may become instructors in culinary training programs, consultants on kitchen design, or food product or equipment sales representatives. A number of chefs and head cooks advance to executive chef positions or food service management positions. When staying in the restaurant business, advancement usually involves moving to a better, busier, or bigger restaurant or working at the corporate level overseeing several restaurants or food service facilities or testing new recipe, menu, or design concepts. (See the section on food service managers elsewhere in this book.)

Employment

Chefs, head cooks, and food preparation and serving supervisors held 941,600 jobs in 2008. Food preparation and serving supervisors held 88 percent of these jobs and chefs and head cooks held the remaining 12 percent. Nearly half of chefs and head cooks were employed at full-service restaurants (those that had table service). About 9 percent each were employed by hotels and the special food services industry that includes caterers and food service contractors. Eight percent were self-employed.

Forty-three percent of food preparation and serving supervisors were employed by limited-service eating places, made up mostly of cafeterias and fast food restaurants and other places that offer simple carry-out food items. Another 25 percent were employed by full-service restaurants. Supervisors are also found in schools, the special food services industry, and a wide variety of other places that serve food.

Job Outlook

Job opportunities are expected to be good, despite slower-than-average employment growth, due to the large numbers of workers who leave the occupation and need to be replaced. However, keen competition is expected for jobs at upscale restaurants that generally pay more.

Employment change. Employment of chefs, head cooks, and food preparation and serving supervisors is expected to increase by 6 percent over the 2008–2018 decade, which is more slowly than the

Projections Data from the National Employment Matrix

Occupational title	SOC Code	Employment, 2008	Projected employment, 2018	Change, 2008–2018	
				Number	Percent
Supervisors, food preparation and serving workers......	35-1000	941,600	997,000	55,400	6
Chefs and head cooks	35-1011	108,300	108,500	200	0
First-line supervisors/managers of food preparation and serving workers.......................	35-1012	833,300	888,500	55,100	7

NOTE: Data in this table are rounded.

average for all occupations. Growth will be generated by increases in population, a growing variety of dining venues, and continued demand for convenience. As more people opt for the timesaving ease of letting others do the cooking, the need for workers to oversee food preparation and serving will increase. Also, there is a growing consumer desire for healthier, made-from-scratch meals that chefs and head cooks can better prepare. Growth, however, may be tempered by slowing economic conditions as some restaurants and food preparation facilities close.

Job prospects. Job openings for chefs, head cooks, and food preparation and serving supervisors are expected to be good through 2018; however, competition should be keen for jobs at the more upscale restaurants that tend to pay more. Workers with a good business sense will have better job prospects, especially at restaurant chains where attention to costs is very important. Although job growth will create many new positions, the majority of job openings will stem from the need to replace workers who leave the occupation. The fast pace, long hours, and high energy levels required for these jobs often lead to high turnover.

Earnings

Earnings of chefs, head cooks, and food preparation and serving supervisors vary greatly by region and the type of employer. Earnings are usually highest in upscale restaurants and hotels, where many executive chefs are employed, and in major metropolitan and resort areas.

Median annual wage-and-salary earnings of chefs and head cooks were $40,090 in May 2009. The middle 50 percent earned between $30,080 and $53,510. The lowest 10 percent earned less than $22,860, and the highest 10 percent earned more than $69,560. Median annual wages in May 2009 in the industries employing the largest number of chefs and head cooks were as follows:

Full-service restaurants	$38,030
Traveler accommodation	46,710
Special food services...	42,000
Limited-service eating places	29,820
Other amusement and recreation industries...........	47,290

Median annual wage-and-salary earnings of food preparation and serving supervisors were $29,470 in May 2009. The middle 50 percent earned between $23,030 and $37,880. The lowest 10 percent earned less than $19,180, and the highest 10 percent earned more than $47,420. Median annual wages in May 2009 were $26,110 in limited-service restaurants and $32,890 in full-service eating places, the industries employing the largest numbers of food preparation and serving supervisors.

Some employers provide employees with uniforms and free meals, but federal law permits employers to deduct from their employees'

wages the cost or fair value of any meals or lodging provided, and some employers do so. Chefs, head cooks, and food preparation and serving supervisors who work full time often receive typical benefits, but part-time workers usually do not.

In some large hotels and restaurants, kitchen workers belong to unions. The principal unions are the Hotel Employees and Restaurant Employees International Union and the Service Employees International Union.

Related Occupations

Other people who prepare food items include cooks and food preparation workers, and food processing occupations.

Others who also work closely with these workers in the food service industry include food and beverage serving and related workers, and food service managers.

Sources of Additional Information

Information about job opportunities may be obtained from local employers and local offices of the state employment service.

Career information about chefs, cooks, and other kitchen workers, including a directory of 2-year and 4-year colleges that offer courses or training programs is available from

▸ National Restaurant Association, 1200 17th St. NW, Washington, DC 20036. Internet: www.restaurant.org

Information on the American Culinary Federation's culinary apprenticeship and certification programs and a list of accredited culinary programs is available from

▸ American Culinary Federation, 180 Center Place Way, St. Augustine, FL 32095. Internet: www.acfchefs.org

For information about becoming a personal or private chef, contact

▸ American Personal & Private Chef Association, 4572 Delaware St., San Diego, CA 92116. Internet: www.personalchef.com

For information about culinary apprenticeship programs registered with the U.S. Department of Labor, contact the local office of your state employment service agency, check the department's apprenticeship website: www.doleta.gov/OA/eta_default.cfm, or call the toll-free helpline: (877) 872-5627.

Child Care Workers

(O*NET 39-9011.00 and 39-9011.01)

Significant Points

■ About 33 percent of child care workers are self-employed, most of whom provide child care in their homes.

■ Training requirements range from a high school diploma to a college degree, although some jobs require less than a high school diploma.

■ Many workers leave these jobs every year, creating good job opportunities.

Nature of the Work

Child care workers nurture, teach, and care for children who have not yet entered kindergarten. They also supervise older children before and after school. These workers play an important role in children's development by caring for them when their parents are at work or are away for other reasons or when the parents place their children in care to help them socialize with children their age. In addition to attending to children's health, safety, and nutrition, child care workers organize activities and implement curricula that stimulate children's physical, emotional, intellectual, and social growth. They help children explore individual interests, develop talents and independence, build self-esteem, learn how to get along with others, and prepare for more formal schooling.

Child care workers generally are classified into three different groups based on where they work: private household workers, who care for children at the children's homes; family child care providers, who care for children in the providers' homes; and child care workers who work at child care centers, which include Head Start, Early Head Start, full-day and part-day preschool, and other early childhood programs.

Private household workers who are employed on an hourly basis usually are called babysitters. These child care workers bathe, dress, and feed children; supervise their play; wash their clothes; and clean their rooms. Babysitters also may put children to bed and wake them, read to them, involve them in educational games, take them for doctors' visits, and discipline them. Those who are in charge of infants prepare bottles and change diapers. Babysitters may work for many different families. Workers who are employed by one family are often called nannies. They generally take care of children from birth to age 12, tending to the children's early education, nutrition, health, and other needs. They also may perform the duties of a housekeeper, including cleaning and doing the laundry.

Family child care providers often work alone with a small group of children, although some work in larger settings they work in groups or teams. Child care centers generally have more than one adult per group of children; in groups of children aged 3 to 5 years, a child care worker may assist a more experienced preschool teacher.

Most child care workers perform a combination of basic care and teaching duties, but the majority of their time is spent on caregiving activities. However, there is an increasing focus on preparing children aged 3 to 5 years for school. Workers whose primary responsibility is teaching are classified as preschool teachers. (Preschool teachers are covered elsewhere in this book.) However, many basic care activities also are opportunities for children to learn. For example, a worker who shows a child how to tie a shoelace teaches the child while providing for that child's basic needs.

Child care workers spend most of their day working with children. However, they do maintain contact with parents or guardians through informal meetings or scheduled conferences to discuss each child's progress and needs. Many child care workers keep records of each child's progress and suggest ways in which parents can stimulate their child's learning and development at home. Some child care

centers and before- and after-school programs actively recruit parent volunteers to work with the children and participate in administrative decisions and program planning.

Young children learn mainly through playing, solving problems, questioning, and experimenting. Child care workers recognize that fact and capitalize on children's play and other experiences to further their language development (through storytelling and acting games), improve their social skills (by having them work together to build a neighborhood in a sandbox), and introduce scientific and mathematical concepts (by balancing and counting blocks when building a bridge or mixing colors when painting). Often, a less structured approach, including small-group lessons; one-on-one instruction; and creative activities such as art, dance, and music, is used to teach young children. Child care workers play a vital role in preparing children to build the skills they will need in school.

Child care workers in child care centers, schools, or family child care homes greet young children as they arrive, help them with their jackets, and select an activity of interest. When caring for infants, they feed and change them. To ensure a well-balanced program, child care workers prepare daily and long-term schedules of activities. Each day's activities balance individual and group play, as well as quiet time and time for physical activity. Children are given some freedom to participate in activities they are interested in. As children age, child care workers may provide more guided learning opportunities, particularly in the areas of math and reading.

Concern over school-aged children being home alone before and after school has spurred many parents to seek alternative ways for their children to spend their time constructively. The purpose of before- and after-school programs is to watch over school-aged children during the gap between school hours and the end of their parents' daily work hours. These programs also may operate during the summer and on weekends. Workers in before- and after-school programs may help students with their homework or engage them in extracurricular activities, including field trips, sports, learning about computers, painting, photography, and other subjects. Some child care workers are responsible for taking children to school in the morning and picking them up from school in the afternoon. Before- and after-school programs may be operated by public school systems, local community centers, or other private organizations.

Helping to keep children healthy is another important part of the job. Child care workers serve nutritious meals and snacks and teach good eating habits and personal hygiene. They ensure that children have proper rest periods. They identify children who may not feel well, and they may help parents locate programs that will provide basic health services. Child care workers also watch for children who show signs of emotional or developmental problems. Upon identifying such a child, they discuss the child's situation with their supervisor and the child's parents. Early identification of children with special needs—such as those with behavioral, emotional, physical, or learning disabilities—is important in improving their future learning ability. Special education teachers often work with preschool children to provide the individual attention they need.

Work environment. Helping children grow, learn, and gain new skills can be very rewarding. The work is sometimes routine, but new activities and challenges mark each day. Child care can be physically and emotionally taxing as workers constantly stand, walk, bend, stoop, and lift to attend to each child's interests and problems. These workers experienced a larger than average number of work-related injuries or illnesses.

States regulate child care facilities, the number of children per child care worker, the qualifications of the staff, and the health and safety of the children. To ensure that children in child care centers receive proper supervision, state or local regulations may require a certain ratio of workers to children. The ratio varies with the age of the children. For infants (children under 1 year old), child care workers may be responsible for 3 or 4 children. For toddler's (children 1 to 2 years old), workers may be responsible for 4 to 10 children, and for preschool-aged children (those between 3 and 5 years old), workers may be responsible for 8 to 25 children. However, these regulations vary greatly from state to state. In before- and after-school programs, workers may be responsible for many school-aged children at a time.

Family child care providers work out of their own homes, an arrangement that provides convenience, but also requires that their homes be accommodating to young children. Private household workers usually work in the homes or apartments of their employers. Most live in their own homes and travel to work, although some live in the home of their employer and generally are provided with their own room and bath. They often come to feel like part of their employer's family.

The work hours of child care workers vary widely. Child care centers usually are open year round, with long hours so that parents can drop off and pick up their children before and after work. Some centers employ full-time and part-time staff with staggered shifts to cover the entire day. Some workers are unable to take regular breaks during the day due to limited staffing. Public and many private preschool programs operate during the typical 9- or 10-month school year, employing both full-time and part-time workers. Family child care providers have flexible hours and daily routines, but they may work long or unusual hours to fit parents' work schedules. Live-in nannies usually work longer hours than do child care workers who live in their own homes. However, although nannies may work evenings or weekends, they usually get other time off. About 36 percent worked part time.

Training, Other Qualifications, and Advancement

Licensure and training requirements vary greatly by state, but some jobs require less than a high school diploma.

Education and training. The training and qualifications required of child care workers vary widely. Each state has its own licensing requirements that regulate caregiver training. These requirements range from less than a high school diploma, to a national Child Development Associate (CDA) credential, to community college courses or a college degree in child development or early childhood education. State requirements are generally higher for workers at child care centers than for family child care providers.

Child care workers in private settings who care for only a few children often are not regulated by states at all. Child care workers generally can obtain some form of employment with less than a high school diploma and little or no experience, but certain private firms and publicly funded programs have more demanding training and education requirements. Different public funding streams may set other education and professional development requirements. For example, many states have separate funding for prekindergarten programs for 4-year-old children. In accordance with the regulations that accompany the funding, these states typically set higher educa-

tion degree requirements for those workers than do ordinary state child care licensing requirements.

Some employers prefer workers who have taken secondary or postsecondary courses in child development and early childhood education or who have work experience in a child care setting. Other employers require their own specialized training. An increasing number of employers are requiring an associate degree in early childhood education

Licensure. Many states require child care centers, including those in private homes, to be licensed if they care for more than a few children. In order to obtain their license, child care centers may require child care workers to pass a background check, get immunizations, and meet a minimum training requirement.

Other qualifications. Child care workers must anticipate and prevent problems, deal with disruptive children, provide fair but firm discipline, and be enthusiastic and constantly alert. They must communicate effectively with the children and their parents, as well as with teachers and other child care workers. Workers should be mature, patient, understanding, and articulate and have energy and physical stamina. Skills in music, art, drama, and storytelling also are important. Self-employed child care workers must have business sense and management abilities.

Certification and advancement. Some employers prefer to hire child care workers who have earned a nationally recognized Child Development Associate (CDA) credential or the Child Care Professional (CCP) designation from the Council for Professional Recognition and the National Child Care Association, respectively. Requirements include child care experience and coursework, such as college courses or employer-provided seminars.

Opportunities for advancement are limited. However, as child care workers gain experience, some may advance to supervisory or administrative positions in large child care centers or preschools. Often, these positions require additional training, such as a bachelor's or master's degree. Other workers move on to work in resource and referral agencies, consulting with parents on available child care services. A few workers become involved in policy or advocacy work related to child care and early childhood education. With a bachelor's degree, workers may become preschool teachers or become certified to teach in public or private schools. Some workers set up their own child care businesses.

Employment

Child care workers held about 1.3 million jobs in 2008. About 33 percent of child care workers were self-employed; most of these were family child care providers.

Child day care services employed about 19 percent of all child care workers, and about 19 percent worked for private households. The remainder worked primarily in educational services; nursing and residential care facilities; amusement and recreation industries; civic and social organizations; and individual and family services. Some child care programs are for-profit centers, which may be affiliated with a local or national company. A very small percentage of private-industry establishments operate onsite child care centers for the children of their employees.

Job Outlook

Child care workers are expected to experience job growth that is about as fast as the average for all occupations. Job prospects will

Projections Data from the National Employment Matrix

Occupational title	SOC Code	Employment, 2008	Projected employment, 2018	Change, 2008–2018	
				Number	Percent
Child care workers	39-9011	1,301,900	1,443,900	142,100	11

NOTE: Data in this table are rounded.

be good because of the many workers who leave the occupation and need to be replaced.

Employment change. Employment of child care workers is projected to increase by 11 percent between 2008 and 2018, which is about as fast as the average for all occupations. An increasing emphasis on early childhood education programs will increase demand for these workers. Child care workers often work alongside preschool teachers as assistants. Therefore, increased demand for formal preschool programs will create growth for child care workers. Although only a few states currently provide targeted or universal preschool programs, many more are considering or starting such programs. A rise in enrollment in private preschools is likely as the value of formal education before kindergarten becomes more widely accepted. More states moving toward universal preschool education could increase employment growth for child care workers. However, growth will be moderated by relatively slow growth in the population of children under the age of five, who are generally cared for by these workers.

Job prospects. High replacement needs should create good job opportunities for child care workers. Qualified persons who are interested in this work should have little trouble finding and keeping a job. Many child care workers must be replaced each year as they leave the occupation to fulfill family responsibilities, to study, or for other reasons. Others leave because they are interested in pursuing other occupations or because of low wages.

Earnings

Pay depends on the educational attainment of the worker and the type of establishment. Although the pay generally is very low, more education usually means higher earnings. Median hourly wages of child care workers were $9.25 in May 2009. The middle 50 percent earned between $8.80 and $11.49. The lowest 10 percent earned less than $7.37, and the highest 10 percent earned more than $14.24. Median hourly wages in the industries employing the largest numbers of child care workers in May 2009 were as follows:

Child day care services	$8.62
Elementary and secondary schools	10.79
Other amusement and recreation industries..............	8.69
Other residential care facilities.............................	10.67
Civic and social organizations	8.71

Earnings of self-employed child care workers vary with the number of hours worked, the number and ages of the children, and the geographic location.

Benefits vary, but are minimal for most child care workers. Many employers offer free or discounted child care to employees. Some offer a full benefits package, including health insurance and paid vacations, but others offer no benefits at all. Some employers offer seminars and workshops to help workers learn new skills. A few are willing to cover the cost of courses taken at community colleges or technical schools. Live-in nannies receive free room and board.

Related Occupations

Child care work requires patience; creativity; an ability to nurture, motivate, teach, and influence children; and leadership, organizational, and administrative skills. Others who work with children and need these qualities and skills include teacher assistants; teachers—kindergarten, elementary, middle, and secondary; teachers—preschool, except special education; and teachers—special education.

Sources of Additional Information

For an electronic question-and-answer service on child care, for information on becoming a child care provider, and for information on other resources, contact

▸ National Child Care Information Center, 10530 Rosehaven St., Suite 400, Fairfax, VA 22030. Internet: www.nccic.org

For eligibility requirements and a description of the Child Development Associate credential, contact

▸ Council for Professional Recognition, 2460 16th St. NW, Washington, DC 20009-3547. Internet: www.cdacouncil.org

For eligibility requirements and a description of the Child Care Professional designation, contact

▸ National Child Care Association, 1325 G St. NW, Suite 500, Washington, DC 20005. Internet: www.nccanet.org

For information about early childhood education, contact

▸ National Association for the Education of Young Children, 1313 L St. NW, Suite 500 Washington, DC 20005. Internet: www.naeyc.org

For information about a career as a nanny, contact

▸ International Nanny Association, P.O. Box 1299, Hyannis, MA 02601. Internet: www.nanny.org

State departments of human services or social services can supply state regulations and training requirements for child care workers.

Claims Adjusters, Appraisers, Examiners, and Investigators

(O*NET 13-1031.00, 13-1031.01, 13-1031.02, and 13-1032.00)

Significant Points

■ Employment is concentrated in insurance-related industries.

■ Training and entry requirements vary widely.

■ College graduates and those with related experience should have the best opportunities for most types of jobs; competition will be keen for jobs as investigators.

■ Job opportunities should be best in health insurance companies and in regions susceptible to natural disasters.

Nature of the Work

Individuals and businesses purchase insurance policies to protect against monetary losses. In the event of a loss, policyholders submit claims, or requests for payment, seeking compensation for their loss. Adjusters, appraisers, examiners, and investigators deal with those claims. They work primarily for property and casualty insurance companies, for whom they handle a wide variety of claims alleging property damage, liability, or bodily injury. Their main role is to investigate claims, negotiate settlements, and authorize payments to claimants, who are the policyholders who make a claim. They must be mindful not to violate their rights under federal and state privacy laws. They must determine whether the customer's insurance policy covers the loss and how much of the loss should be paid. Although many adjusters, appraisers, examiners, and investigators have overlapping functions and may even perform the same tasks, the insurance industry generally assigns specific roles to each of these claims workers.

Adjusters plan and schedule the work required to process a claim. They might, for example, handle the claim filed after an automobile accident or after a storm damages a customer's home. Adjusters investigate claims by interviewing the claimant and witnesses, consulting police and hospital records, and inspecting property damage to determine how much the company should pay for the loss. Adjusters may consult with other professionals, such as accountants, architects, construction workers, engineers, lawyers, and physicians, who can offer a more expert evaluation of a claim. The information gathered—including photographs and statements, either written or recorded with audio or video—is set down in a report that is then used to evaluate the claim. When the policyholder's claim is approved, the claims adjuster negotiates with the claimant and settles the claim. When claims are contested, adjusters will work with attorneys and expert witnesses to defend the insurer's position.

Some large insurance companies centralize claims adjustment in a claims center, where the payout amount is estimated and a check is issued immediately. However, cases handled by independent adjusters, or those involving business losses or homeowner claims, such as hurricane or fire damage, all require a senior adjuster to physically inspect the damage and determine proper compensation.

When it comes to business or residential loss caused by, for example, vandalism or flooding, claimants can opt not to rely on the insurance company's adjuster and may instead choose to hire a public adjuster. Public adjusters are self-employed and work in the best interest of the client rather than the insurance company. In doing so, the adjuster prepares and presents claims to insurance companies, looking to negotiate the best possible settlement for the claimant. Insurance carriers also use the service of independent adjusters on a freelance basis, often in lieu of hiring them as regular employees. In this case, the independent adjusters work in the interest of the insurance company.

Claims examiners within property and casualty insurance firms may have duties similar to those of an adjuster, but often their primary job is to review claims after they are submitted in order to ensure that proper guidelines have been followed. They may assist adjusters with complicated claims or when, for instance, a natural disaster suddenly greatly increases the volume of claims.

Most claims examiners work for life or health insurance companies. In health insurance companies, examiners review health-related claims to see whether costs are reasonable given the diagnosis. They use guides that have information on the average period of disability, expected treatments, and average hospital stays for various ailments. Examiners check claim applications for completeness and accuracy, interview medical specialists, and consult policy files to verify the information reported in a claim. They then authorize appropriate payment, deny the claim, or refer the claim to an investigator for a more thorough review. Claims examiners usually specialize in group or individual insurance plans and in hospital, dental, or prescription drug claims.

In life insurance, claims examiners review the causes of death, particularly in the case of an accident, since most life insurance policies pay additional benefits if a death is accidental. Claims examiners also may review new applications for life insurance to make sure that the applicants have no serious illnesses that would make them a high risk to insure.

Another occupation that plays an important role in the accurate settlement of claims is that of the *appraiser*, whose role is to estimate the cost or value of an insured item. The majority of appraisers employed by insurance companies and independent adjusting firms are *auto damage appraisers*. These appraisers inspect damaged vehicles after an accident and estimate the cost of repairs. This information is then relayed to the adjuster, who incorporates the appraisal into the settlement.

Many claims adjusters and auto damage appraisers are equipped with laptop computers from which they can download the necessary forms and files from insurance company databases. Specialized software then generates estimates on standard forms. Adjusters also utilize digital cameras, which allow photographs of the damage to be sent to the company, allowing for faster and more efficient processing of claims.

When adjusters or examiners suspect fraud, they refer the claim to an investigator. *Insurance investigators* handle claims in which the company suspects fraudulent or criminal activity, such as arson, falsified workers' disability claims, staged accidents, or unnecessary medical treatments. The severity of insurance fraud cases can vary greatly, from claimants simply overstating damage to a vehicle to complicated fraud rings supported by dishonest doctors, lawyers, and even insurance personnel.

Investigators usually start with a database search to obtain background information on claimants and witnesses. Investigators can access personal information and identify Social Security numbers, aliases, driver's license numbers, addresses, phone numbers, criminal records, and past claims histories to establish whether a claimant has ever attempted insurance fraud. Then, investigators may visit claimants and witnesses to obtain an oral statement, take photographs, and inspect facilities, such as doctors' offices, to determine, for example, whether the doctors have a proper license. Investigators often consult with legal counsel and can be expert witnesses in court cases.

Often, investigators also perform surveillance work. For example, in a case involving fraudulent workers' compensation claims, an investigator may covertly observe the claimant for several days or even weeks. If the investigator observes the subject performing an activity that is ruled out by injuries stated in a workers' compensation claim, the investigator will take photos to document the activity and report it to the insurance company.

Work environment. Working environments of claims adjusters, appraisers, examiners, and investigators vary greatly. Many claims adjusters and auto damage appraisers often work outside the office, inspecting damaged buildings and automobiles. Adjusters who inspect damaged buildings must be wary of potential hazards, such as collapsed roofs and floors, as well as weakened structures.

Some adjusters report to the office every morning to get their assignments, while others simply call in from home and spend their days traveling to claim sites. Occasionally, experienced adjusters must be away from home for days—for example, when they travel to the scene of a disaster such as a tornado, hurricane, or flood—to work with local adjusters and government officials.

Most claims examiners employed by life and health insurance companies work a standard 5-day, 40-hour week in a typical office environment. In contrast, adjusters often must arrange their work schedules to accommodate evening and weekend appointments with clients. This sometimes results in adjusters working irregular schedules, especially when they have a lot of claims to scrutinize. Adjusters are often called to work in the event of emergencies and may have to work 50 or 60 hours a week until all claims are resolved.

Appraisers spend much of their time offsite at automotive body shops estimating vehicle damage costs. The remaining time may be spent working in the office. Many independent appraisers work from home, as continually improving valuation software has made estimating damage easier and more routine. Auto damage appraisers typically work regular hours and rarely work on the weekends. Self-employed appraisers also have the flexibility to make their own hours, as many appraisals are done by appointment.

Some days, investigators will spend all day in the office, searching databases, making telephone calls, and writing reports. Other times, they may be away, performing surveillance activities or interviewing witnesses. Some of the work can involve disagreements with claimants, so the job can be stressful and potentially confrontational. Insurance investigators often work irregular hours because of the need to conduct surveillance and contact people who are not available during normal working hours. Early morning, evening, and weekend work is common.

Training, Other Qualifications, and Advancement

Training and entry requirements vary widely. Although many in these occupations do not have a college degree, most companies prefer to hire college graduates or those with some insurance-related work experience or vocational training.

Education and training. There are no formal education requirements for any of these occupations, and a high school degree is typically the minimal requirement needed to obtain employment. However, most employers prefer to hire college graduates or people who have some insurance-related work experience or vocational training.

While a variety of degrees can be an asset, no specific college major is recommended. For example, a claims adjuster who has a business or an accounting background might be suited to specialize in claims of financial loss due to strikes, breakdowns of equipment, or damage to merchandise. College training in architecture or engineering is helpful in adjusting industrial claims, such as those involving damage from fires or other accidents. A legal background can be beneficial to someone handling workers' compensation and product liability cases. A medical background is useful for those examiners working on medical and life insurance claims.

While auto damage appraisers are not required to have a college education, most companies prefer to hire persons with formal training or previous experience or those with knowledge and technical skills who can identify and estimate the cost of repair. Many vocational colleges offer two-year programs in auto body repair and teach students how to estimate the costs to repair damaged vehicles.

For investigator jobs, most insurance companies prefer to hire people trained as law enforcement officers, private investigators, claims adjusters, or examiners because these workers have good interviewing and interrogation skills.

Beginning claims adjusters, appraisers, examiners, and investigators work on small claims under the supervision of an experienced worker. As they learn more about claims investigation and settlement, they are assigned larger, more complex claims. Trainees take on more responsibility as they demonstrate competence in handling assignments and progress in their coursework. Auto damage appraisers typically receive on-the-job training, which may last several months. This training usually involves working under close supervision while estimating damage costs until the employer decides the trainee is ready to perform estimates on his or her own.

Continuing education is very important for claims adjusters, appraisers, examiners, and investigators because federal and state laws and court decisions affect how claims are handled and the scope of insurance policies. Also, examiners working on life and health claims must be familiar with new medical procedures and prescription drugs. Examiners working on auto claims must be familiar with new car models and repair techniques.

Many companies offer training sessions to inform their employees of industry changes, and a number of schools and associations give courses and seminars on various topics having to do with claims. Online courses are also making distance learning possible.

Licensure. Licensing requirements for claims adjusters, appraisers, examiners, and investigators vary by state. Some states have few requirements, while others require either the completion of pre-licensing education, a satisfactory score on a licensing exam, or both. Earning a voluntary professional designation can sometimes substitute for completing an exam. In some states, claims adjusters employed by insurance companies can work under the company license and need not become licensed themselves. Public adjusters may need to meet separate or additional requirements. For example, some states require public adjusters to file a surety bond—a unique contract between at least three parties.

Some states that require licensing also require a certain number of continuing education credits per year in order to renew the license. Workers can fulfill their continuing education requirements by attending classes or workshops, by writing articles for claims publications, or by giving lectures and presentations.

Other qualifications. Claims adjusters, appraisers, and examiners often work closely with claimants, witnesses, and other insurance professionals, so they must be able to communicate effectively with others. Knowledge of computer applications also is very helpful. In addition, a valid driver's license and a good driving record are required for workers who must travel on the job. Some companies require applicants to pass a series of written tests designed to measure their communication, analytical, and general mathematical skills.

When hiring investigators, employers look for individuals who have ingenuity and who are persistent and assertive. Investigators should not be afraid of confrontation, should communicate well, and should be able to think on their feet. Good interviewing and interrogation skills also are important and usually are acquired in earlier careers in law enforcement.

Certification and advancement. Employees who demonstrate competence in claims work or administrative skills may be promoted to more responsible managerial or administrative jobs. Similarly, claims investigators may rise to become supervisor or manager of the investigations department. Once they achieve expertise, many choose to start their own independent adjusting or auto damage appraising firms.

Numerous examiners and adjusters choose to earn professional certifications and designations to demonstrate their expertise. Although requirements for these designations vary, some entail a minimum number of years of experience and the successful completion of an examination; in addition, a certain number of continuing education credits must be earned each year to retain the designation.

Employment

Adjusters, appraisers, examiners, and investigators held about 306,300 jobs in 2008. Insurance carriers employed 49 percent of claims adjusters, appraisers, examiners, and investigators; agencies, brokerages, and other insurance-related activities, such as private claims adjusting companies, employed another 24 percent. Less than 4 percent of these jobs were held by auto damage insurance appraisers. About 2 percent of adjusters, appraisers, examiners, and investigators were self-employed.

Job Outlook

Overall employment is expected to increase as fast as average. For claims adjusters and examiners, opportunities will be best with health insurance companies. For appraiser jobs, opportunities will be best for those who have some vocational training and previous auto body repair experience. Keen competition is expected for investigator jobs as the number of applicants typically outnumbers the number of positions available.

Employment change. Employment of claims adjusters, appraisers, examiners, and investigators is expected to grow by 7 percent over the 2008–2018 decade, as fast as the average for all occupations. Employment growth of adjusters and claims examiners will primarily stem from the growth of the health insurance industry. Rising health-care premiums and attempts by large insurance carriers to minimize costs will result in a greater need for claims examiners to more scrupulously review a growing number of medical claims. More claims being made by a growing elderly population also should spur demand for adjusters and claims examiners. Although technology is reducing the amount of time it takes for an adjuster to complete a claim, thereby increasing the number of claims that one adjuster can handle, demand for these jobs will increase anyway because many tasks cannot be easily automated.

Employment of insurance investigators is not expected to grow significantly, despite the expected increase in the number of claims in litigation and complexity of insurance fraud cases. Efficiencies gained through the Internet will continue to reduce the amount of time it takes investigators to perform background checks, allowing them to handle more cases.

Little to no change in employment of auto damage appraisers is expected. Despite a growing number of drivers and auto insurance policies being sold by insurance companies, the number of claims being filed is not expected to increase as much as the number of policies as efforts to make vehicles, roads, and highways safer will yield a decrease in the number of claims per policy.

Job prospects. Job opportunities for claims adjusters and examiners will be best in the health insurance industry as the industry seeks to minimize the number of paid claims and in areas susceptible to natural disasters, such as the Gulf Coast or West Coast. Hurricanes in Florida or wildfires in California, for example, will continue to spur demand, and opportunities with smaller independent firms will be particularly good. And while technology has made the work more efficient, workers will still be needed to contact policyholders, inspect damaged property, and consult with experts. Numerous job openings also will result from the need to replace workers who transfer to other occupations or leave the labor force. College graduates and those with previous related experience should have the best opportunities for jobs as claims adjusters, examiners, and investigators. Auto damage appraisers with related vocational training and auto body shop experience should have the best prospects. People entering these occupations with no formal training may find more opportunities with large insurance companies rather than small independent firms who prefer to hire experienced workers.

Competition for investigator jobs will remain keen because the occupation attracts many qualified people, including retirees from law enforcement, the military, and experienced claims adjusters and examiners who choose to get an investigator license. Heightened media and public awareness of insurance fraud also may attract qualified candidates to this occupation.

Earnings

Median annual wages of wage and salary claims adjusters, examiners, and investigators were $57,130 in May 2009. The middle 50 percent earned between $43,300 and $72,130. The lowest 10 percent earned less than $34,820, and the highest 10 percent earned more than $85,810.

Median annual wages of wage and salary auto damage insurance appraisers were $55,390 in May 2009. The middle 50 percent

Projections Data from the National Employment Matrix

Occupational title	SOC Code	Employment, 2008	Projected employment, 2018	Change, 2008–2018	
				Number	Percent
Claims adjusters, appraisers, examiners, and investigators... 13-1030		306,300	327,200	20,900	7
Claims adjusters, examiners, and investigators 13-1031		294,600	315,500	20,900	7
Insurance appraisers, auto damage 13-1032		11,700	11,700	100	1

NOTE: Data in this table are rounded.

earned between $46,040 and $65,060. The lowest 10 percent earned less than $37,580, and the highest 10 percent earned more than $77,380.

Many claims adjusters, especially those who work for insurance companies, receive additional bonuses or benefits as part of their job. Adjusters are often furnished with a laptop computer, a smart phone, and a company car or are reimbursed for the use of their own vehicle for business purposes.

Related Occupations

Property-casualty insurance adjusters and life and health insurance examiners must determine the validity of a claim and negotiate a settlement. They also are responsible for determining how much to reimburse the client. Occupations whose duties are related include bill and account collectors; billing and posting clerks and machine operators; bookkeeping, accounting, and auditing clerks; cost estimators; credit authorizers, checkers, and clerks; and medical records and health information technicians.

In determining the validity of a claim, insurance adjusters must inspect the damage to assess the magnitude of the loss. Workers who perform similar duties include construction and building inspectors and fire inspectors and investigators.

To ensure that company practices and procedures are followed, property and casualty examiners review insurance claims to which a claims adjuster has already proposed a settlement. Other workers who review documents for accuracy and compliance with a given set of rules and regulations are accountants and auditors and tax examiners, collectors, and revenue agents.

Auto damage appraisers must be familiar with the structure and functions of various automobiles and their parts. They must also be familiar with techniques to estimate value. The following workers have similar duties: appraisers and assessors of real estate, automotive body and related repairers, and automotive service technicians and mechanics.

Insurance investigators detect and investigate fraudulent claims and criminal activity. Their work is similar to that of private detectives and investigators.

Sources of Additional Information

General information about a career as a claims adjuster, appraiser, examiner, or investigator is available from the home offices of many insurance companies. Information about licensing requirements for claims adjusters may be obtained from the department of insurance in each state.

Information about the property-casualty insurance field can be obtained by contacting

▸ Insurance Information Institute, 110 William St., New York, NY 10038. Internet: www.iii.org

For information about professional designation and training programs, contact any of the following organizations:

▸ American Institute for Chartered Property Casualty Underwriters and the Insurance Institute of America, 720 Providence Rd., Suite 100, Malvern, PA 19355-3433. Internet: www.aicpcu.org

▸ International Claim Association, 1155 15th St. NW, Suite 500, Washington, DC 20005. Internet: www.claim.org

▸ National Association of Public Insurance Adjusters, 21165 Whitfield Place, Suite 105, Potomac Falls, VA 20165. Internet: www.napia.com

Information on careers in auto damage appraising can be obtained from

▸ Independent Automotive Damage Appraisers Association, P.O. Box 12291, Columbus, GA 31917-2291. Internet: www.iada.org

Clinical Laboratory Technologists and Technicians

(O*NET 29-2011.00, 29-2011.01, 29-2011.02, 29-2011.03, and 29-2012.00)

Significant Points

■ Excellent job opportunities are expected.

■ Clinical laboratory technologists usually have a bachelor's degree with a major in medical technology or in one of the life sciences; clinical laboratory technicians generally need either an associate degree or a certificate.

■ Most jobs will continue to be in hospitals, but employment will grow rapidly in other settings, as well.

Nature of the Work

Clinical laboratory testing plays a crucial role in the detection, diagnosis, and treatment of disease. *Clinical laboratory technologists*, also referred to as *clinical laboratory scientists* or *medical technologists*, and *clinical laboratory technicians*, also known as *medical technicians* or *medical laboratory technicians*, perform most of these tests.

Clinical laboratory personnel examine and analyze body fluids and cells. They look for bacteria, parasites, and other microorganisms; analyze the chemical content of fluids; match blood for transfusions; and test for drug levels in the blood that show how a patient is responding to treatment. Technologists also prepare specimens for examination, count cells, and look for abnormal cells in blood and body fluids. They use microscopes, cell counters, and other sophisticated laboratory equipment. They also use automated equipment and computerized instruments capable of performing a number of tests simultaneously. After testing and examining a specimen, they analyze the results and relay them to physicians.

With increasing automation and the use of computer technology, the work of technologists and technicians has become less hands-on and more analytical. The complexity of tests performed, the level of judgment needed, and the amount of responsibility workers assume depend largely on the amount of education and experience they have. Clinical laboratory technologists usually do more complex tasks than clinical laboratory technicians do.

Clinical laboratory technologists perform complex chemical, biological, hematological, immunologic, microscopic, and bacteriological tests. Technologists microscopically examine blood and other body fluids. They make cultures of body fluid and tissue samples, to determine the presence of bacteria, fungi, parasites, or other microorganisms. Technologists analyze samples for chemical content or a chemical reaction and determine concentrations of compounds such as blood glucose and cholesterol levels. They also type and cross match blood samples for transfusions.

Clinical laboratory technologists evaluate test results, develop and modify procedures, and establish and monitor programs, to ensure the accuracy of tests. Some technologists supervise clinical laboratory technicians.

Technologists in small laboratories perform many types of tests, whereas those in large laboratories generally specialize. *Clinical chemistry technologists*, for example, prepare specimens and analyze the chemical and hormonal contents of body fluids. *Microbiology technologists* examine and identify bacteria and other microorganisms. *Blood bank technologists*, or *immunohematology technologists*, collect, type, and prepare blood and its components for transfusions. *Immunology technologists* examine elements of the human immune system and its response to foreign bodies. *Cytotechnologists* prepare slides of body cells and examine these cells microscopically for abnormalities that may signal the beginning of a cancerous growth. *Molecular biology technologists* perform complex protein and nucleic acid testing on cell samples.

Clinical laboratory technicians perform less complex tests and laboratory procedures than technologists do. Technicians may prepare specimens and operate automated analyzers, for example, or they may perform manual tests in accordance with detailed instructions. They usually work under the supervision of medical and clinical laboratory technologists or laboratory managers. Like technologists, clinical laboratory technicians may work in several areas of the clinical laboratory or specialize in just one. *Phlebotomists* collect blood samples, for example, and *histotechnicians* cut and stain tissue specimens for microscopic examination by pathologists.

Work environment. Clinical laboratory personnel are trained to work with infectious specimens. When proper methods of infection control and sterilization are followed, few hazards exist. Protective masks, gloves, and goggles often are necessary to ensure the safety of laboratory personnel.

Working conditions vary with the size and type of employment setting. Laboratories usually are well lighted and clean; however, specimens, solutions, and reagents used in the laboratory sometimes produce fumes. Laboratory workers may spend a great deal of time on their feet.

Hours of clinical laboratory technologists and technicians vary with the size and type of employment setting. In large hospitals or in independent laboratories that operate continuously, personnel usually work the day, evening, or night shift and may work weekends and holidays. Laboratory personnel in small facilities may work on rotating shifts, rather than on a regular shift. In some facilities, laboratory personnel are on call several nights a week or on weekends, in case of an emergency.

Training, Other Qualifications, and Advancement

Clinical laboratory technologists generally require a bachelor's degree in medical technology or in one of the life sciences; clinical laboratory technicians usually need an associate degree or a certificate.

Education and training. The usual requirement for an entry-level position as a clinical laboratory technologist is a bachelor's degree with a major in medical technology or one of the life sciences; however, it is possible to qualify for some jobs with a combination of education and on-the-job and specialized training. Universities and hospitals offer medical technology programs.

Bachelor's degree programs in medical technology include courses in chemistry, biological sciences, microbiology, mathematics, and statistics, as well as specialized courses devoted to knowledge and skills used in the clinical laboratory. Many programs also offer or require courses in management, business, and computer applications. The Clinical Laboratory Improvement Act requires technologists who perform highly complex tests to have at least an associate degree.

Medical and clinical laboratory technicians generally have either an associate degree from a community or junior college or a certificate from a hospital, a vocational or technical school, or the Armed Forces. A few technicians learn their skills on the job.

The National Accrediting Agency for Clinical Laboratory Sciences (NAACLS) fully accredits about 479 programs for medical and clinical laboratory technologists, medical and clinical laboratory technicians, histotechnologists and histotechnicians, cytogenetic technologists, and diagnostic molecular scientists. NAACLS also approves about 60 programs in phlebotomy and clinical assisting. Other nationally recognized agencies that accredit specific areas for clinical laboratory workers include the Commission on Accreditation of Allied Health Education Programs and the Accrediting Bureau of Health Education Schools.

Licensure. Some states require laboratory personnel to be licensed or registered. Licensure of technologists often requires a bachelor's degree and the passing of an exam, but requirements vary by state and specialty. Information on licensure is available from state departments of health or boards of occupational licensing.

Certification and other qualifications. Many employers prefer applicants who are certified by a recognized professional association. Associations offering certification include the Board of Registry of the American Society for Clinical Pathology, the American Medical Technologists, the National Credentialing Agency for Laboratory Personnel, and the Board of Registry of the American Association of Bioanalysts. These agencies have different requirements for certification and different organizational sponsors.

In addition to certification, employers seek clinical laboratory personnel with good analytical judgment and the ability to work under pressure. Technologists in particular are expected to be good at problem solving. Close attention to detail is also essential for laboratory personnel because small differences or changes in test substances or numerical readouts can be crucial to a diagnosis. Manual dexterity and normal color vision are highly desirable, and with the widespread use of automated laboratory equipment, computer skills are important.

Advancement. Technicians can advance and become technologists through additional education and experience. Technologists may advance to supervisory positions in laboratory work or may become chief medical or clinical laboratory technologists or laboratory managers in hospitals. Manufacturers of home diagnostic testing kits and laboratory equipment and supplies also seek experienced technologists to work in product development, marketing, and sales.

Professional certification and a graduate degree in medical technology, one of the biological sciences, chemistry, management, or education usually speed advancement. A doctorate usually is needed to become a laboratory director. Federal regulation requires directors of moderately complex laboratories to have either a master's degree

Projections Data from the National Employment Matrix

Occupational title	SOC Code	Employment, 2008	Projected employment, 2018	Change, 2008–2018	
				Number	Percent
Clinical laboratory technologists and technicians 29-2010		328,100	373,600	45,600	14
Medical and clinical laboratory technologists 29-2011		172,400	193,000	20,500	12
Medical and clinical laboratory technicians 29-2012		155,600	180,700	25,000	16

NOTE: Data in this table are rounded.

or a bachelor's degree, combined with the appropriate amount of training and experience.

Employment

Clinical laboratory technologists and technicians held about 328,100 jobs in 2008. More than half of jobs were in hospitals. Most of the remaining jobs were in offices of physicians and in medical and diagnostic laboratories. A small proportion was in educational services and in all other ambulatory health-care services.

Job Outlook

Rapid job growth and excellent job opportunities are expected. Most jobs will continue to be in hospitals, but employment will grow rapidly in other settings, as well.

Employment change. Employment of clinical laboratory workers is expected to grow by 14 percent between 2008 and 2018, faster than the average for all occupations. The volume of laboratory tests continues to increase with both population growth and the development of new types of tests.

Technological advances will continue to have opposing effects on employment. On the one hand, new, increasingly powerful diagnostic tests and advances in genomics—the study of the genetic information of a cell or organism—will encourage additional testing and spur employment. On the other hand, research and development efforts targeted at simplifying and automating routine testing procedures may enhance the ability of nonlaboratory personnel—physicians and patients in particular—to perform tests now conducted in laboratories.

Although hospitals are expected to continue to be the major employer of clinical laboratory workers, employment is expected also to grow rapidly in medical and diagnostic laboratories, offices of physicians, and all other ambulatory health-care services.

Job prospects. Job opportunities are expected to be excellent because the number of job openings is expected to continue to exceed the number of job seekers. Although significant, job growth will not be the only source of opportunities. As in most occupations, many additional openings will result from the need to replace workers who transfer to other occupations, retire, or stop working for some other reason. Willingness to relocate will further enhance one's job prospects.

Earnings

Median annual wages of medical and clinical laboratory technologists were $55,140 in May 2009. The middle 50 percent earned between $45,810 and $65,050. The lowest 10 percent earned less than $37,540, and the highest 10 percent earned more than $75,960.

Median annual wages in the industries employing the largest numbers of medical and clinical laboratory technologists were as follows:

General medical and surgical hospitals	$55,700
Medical and diagnostic laboratories	54,610
Offices of physicians	51,090
Colleges, universities, and professional schools	50,990
Federal executive branch	61,630

Median annual wages of medical and clinical laboratory technicians were $36,030 in May 2009. The middle 50 percent earned between $28,770 and $45,420. The lowest 10 percent earned less than $23,850, and the highest 10 percent earned more than $55,210. Median annual wages in the industries employing the largest numbers of medical and clinical laboratory technicians were as follows:

General medical and surgical hospitals	$37,170
Medical and diagnostic laboratories	33,660
Offices of physicians	35,110
Other ambulatory health-care services	32,640
Colleges, universities, and professional schools	37,810

According to the American Society for Clinical Pathology, median hourly wages of staff clinical laboratory technologists and technicians, in various specialties and laboratory types, in 2007 were as follows:

Specialty	Hospital	Private clinic	Physician office laboratory
Cytotechnologist	$27.55	$28.75	$26.24
Histotechnologist	22.93	23.35	25.00
Medical technologist	23.45	23.00	20.00
Histotechnician	20.00	20.00	21.00
Medical laboratory technician	18.54	17.00	16.96
Phlebotomist	12.50	12.50	13.00

Related Occupations

Clinical laboratory technologists and technicians analyze body fluids, tissue, and other substances, using a variety of tests. Similar or related procedures are performed by chemists and materials scientists; science technicians; and veterinary technologists and technicians.

Sources of Additional Information

For a list of accredited and approved educational programs for clinical laboratory personnel, contact

▶ National Accrediting Agency for Clinical Laboratory Sciences, 5600 N. River Rd., Suite 720, Rosemont, IL 60018. Internet: www.naacls.org

Information on certification is available from

▶ American Association of Bioanalysts, Board of Registry, 906 Olive St., Suite 1200, St. Louis, MO 63101. Internet: www.aab.org

▶ American Medical Technologists, 10700 W. Higgins Rd., Suite 150, Rosemont, IL 60018. Internet: www.amt1.com

▶ American Society for Clinical Pathology, 33 W. Monroe St., Suite 1600, Chicago, IL 60603. Internet: www.ascp.org

▶ National Credentialing Agency for Laboratory Personnel, P.O. Box 15945-289, Lenexa, KS 66285. Internet: www.nca-info.org

Additional career information is available from

▶ American Association of Blood Banks, 8101 Glenbrook Rd., Bethesda, MD 20814. Internet: www.aabb.org

▶ American Society for Clinical Laboratory Science, 6701 Democracy Blvd., Suite 300, Bethesda, MD 20817. Internet: www.ascls.org

▶ American Society for Cytopathology, 100 W. 10th St., Suite 605, Wilmington, DE 19801. Internet: www.cytopathology.org

▶ Clinical Laboratory Management Association, 993 Old Eagle School Rd., Suite 405, Wayne, PA 19087. Internet: www.clma.org

Computer Control Programmers and Operators

(O*NET 51-4011.00 and 51-4012.00)

Significant Points

■ Manufacturing industries employ almost all of these workers.

■ Workers learn in apprenticeship programs, informally on the job, and in secondary, vocational, or postsecondary schools; many entrants have previously worked as machinists or machine setters, operators, and tenders.

■ Applicants are expected to face competition for jobs.

Nature of the Work

Computer control programmers and operators use computer numerically controlled (CNC) machines to produce a wide variety of products, from automobile engines to computer keyboards. CNC machines operate by reading the code included in a computer-controlled module, which drives the machine tool and performs the functions of forming and shaping a part formerly done by machine operators. CNC machines include tools such as lathes, laser cutting machines, roll forms, press brakes and printing presses. CNC machines use the same techniques as many other mechanical manufacturing machines but are controlled by a central computer instead of a human operator or electric switchboard. Many old-fashioned machines can be retrofitted with a computer control, which can greatly improve the productivity of a machine. Computer control programmers and operators normally produce large quantities of one part, although they may produce small batches or one-of-a-kind items. These machines are most commonly used in metalworking industries where precision is imperative, because computers can be more accurate than humans in this work.

CNC programmers—also referred to as *numerical tool and process control programmers*—develop the programs that run the machine

tools. They often review three-dimensional computer-aided/automated design (CAD) blueprints of a part and determine the sequence of events that will be needed to make the part. This may involve calculating where to cut or bore into the workpiece, how fast to feed the metal into the machine, and how much metal to remove.

Next, CNC programmers turn the planned machining operations into a set of instructions. These instructions are translated into a computer aided/automated manufacturing (CAM) program containing a set of commands for the machine to follow. On a CNC machine, commands normally are a series of numbers (hence, numerical control) that may describe where cuts should occur, where a roll should bend a piece, or the speed of the feed into the machine. After the program is developed, CNC programmers and operators check the programs to ensure that the machinery will function properly and that the output will meet specifications. Because a problem with the program could damage costly machinery and cutting tools or simply waste valuable time and materials, computer simulations may be used to check the program before a trial run. If errors are found, the program must be changed and retested until the problem is resolved. In addition, growing connectivity between CAD/CAM software and CNC machine tools is raising productivity by automatically translating designs into instructions for the computer controller on the machine tool. Many new machines take advantage of easy-to-use graphical user interface programs that use pictures and buttons, instead of long strings of a computer programming language. This improvement in usability has pushed many manufacturing companies to combine the jobs of CNC programmers and machine operators.

After the programming work is completed, CNC setup operators—also referred to as *computer-controlled machine tool operators, metal and plastic*—set up the machine for the job. They download the program into the machine, load the proper tools into the machine, position the workpiece on the CNC machine tool—spindle, lathe, milling machine, or other machine—and then start the machine. During the test run of a new program, the setup operator, who may also have some programming skills, or the CNC programmer closely monitors the machine for signs of problems, such as a vibrating work piece, the breakage of cutting tools, or an out-of-specification final product. If a problem is detected, a setup operator or CNC programmer will modify the program using the control module to eliminate the problems or to improve the speed and accuracy of the program.

Once a program is completed, the operation of the CNC machine may move from the more experienced setup operator to a less-skilled machine operator. Operators load workpieces and tools into a machine, press the start button, monitor the machine for problems, and measure the parts produced to check that they match specifications. If they encounter a problem that requires modification to the cutting program, they shut down the machine and wait for a more experienced CNC setup operator to fix the problem. Many CNC operators start at this basic level and gradually perform more setup tasks as they gain experience.

Regardless of skill level, all CNC operators detect some problems by listening for specific sounds—for example, a dull cutting tool that needs changing or excessive vibration. Machine tools rotate at high speeds, which can create problems with harmonic vibrations in the workpiece. Vibrations cause the machine tools to make minor cutting errors, hurting the quality of the product. Operators listen for vibrations and then adjust the cutting speed to compensate. For common errors in the machine, programmers write code that displays an error code to help operators, who are expected to make minor repairs, and machine mechanics fix a problem quickly. CNC operators also ensure that the workpiece is being properly lubricated and cooled, since the machining of metal products generates a significant amount of heat. Since CNC machines can operate with limited input from the operator, a single operator may monitor several machines simultaneously. Typically, an operator might monitor two machines cutting relatively simple parts from softer materials, while devoting most of his or her attention to a third machine cutting a much more difficult part from hard metal, such as stainless steel. Operators are often expected to carefully schedule their work so that all of the machines are always operating.

Work environment. Most machine shops are clean, well lit, and ventilated. Most modern CNC machines are partially or totally enclosed, minimizing the exposure of workers to noise, debris, and the lubricants used to cool workpieces during machining. People working in this occupation report fewer injuries than most other manufacturing jobs; nevertheless, working around machine tools can be noisy and presents certain dangers, and workers must follow safety precautions to minimize injuries. Computer-controlled machine tool operators, metal and plastic, wear protective equipment, such as safety glasses to shield against bits of flying metal and earplugs to dampen machinery noise. They also must exercise caution when handling hazardous coolants and lubricants. The job requires stamina, because operators stand most of the day and, at times, may need to lift moderately heavy workpieces.

Numerical tool and process control programmers work on desktop computers that may be in offices or on the shop floor. The office areas usually are clean, well lit, and free of machine noise. On the shop floor, CNC programmers encounter the same hazards and exercise the same safety precautions as do CNC operators.

Many computer control programmers and operators work a 40-hour week. CNC operators increasingly work evening and weekend shifts as companies justify investments in more expensive machinery by extending hours of operation. Overtime is common during peak production periods.

Training, Other Qualifications, and Advancement

Computer control programmers and operators train in various ways—in apprenticeship programs, informally on the job, and in secondary, vocational, or postsecondary schools. In general, the more skills needed for the job, the more education and training are needed to qualify. Many entrants have previously worked as machinists or machine setters, operators, and tenders.

Education and training. The amount and type of education and training needed depend on the type of job. Entry-level CNC machine operators may need at least a few months of on-the-job training to reach proficiency. Setup operators and programmers, however, may need years of experience or formal training to write or modify programs. Programmers and operators can receive their training in various ways—in apprenticeship programs, informally on the job, and in secondary, vocational, or postsecondary schools. A growing number of computer control programmers and more skilled operators receive their formal training from community or technical colleges. For some specialized types of programming, such as that needed to produce complex parts for the aerospace or shipbuilding industries, employers may prefer individuals with a degree in engineering.

For those interested in becoming computer control programmers or operators, high school or vocational school courses in mathematics (trigonometry and algebra), blueprint reading, computer programming, metalworking, and drafting are recommended. Apprenticeship programs consist of shop training and related classroom instruction. In shop training, apprentices learn filing, handtapping, and dowel fitting, as well as the operation of various machine tools. Classroom instruction includes math, physics, programming, blueprint reading, CAD software, safety, and shop practices. Skilled computer control programmers and operators need an understanding of the machining process, including the complex physics that occur at the cutting point. Thus, most training programs teach CNC operators and programmers to perform operations on manual machines prior to operating CNC machines.

As new technology is introduced, computer control programmers and operators normally receive additional training to update their skills. This training usually is provided by a representative of the equipment manufacturer or a local technical school. Many employers offer tuition reimbursement for job-related courses.

Certification and other qualifications. Employers prefer to hire workers who have a basic knowledge of computers and electronics and experience with machine tools. In fact, many entrants to these occupations have experience working as machine setters, operators, and tenders or machinists. Persons interested in becoming computer control programmers or operators should be mechanically inclined and able to work independently and do highly accurate work.

To boost the skill level of all metalworkers and to create a more uniform standard of competency, a number of training facilities and colleges have formed certification programs. Employers may pay for training and certification tests after hiring an entry-level worker.

Advancement. Computer control programmers and operators can advance in several ways. Experienced CNC operators may become CNC programmers or machinery mechanics, and some are promoted to supervisory or administrative positions in their firms. Some highly skilled workers move into tool and die making, and a few open their own shops.

Employment

Computer control programmers and operators held about 157,800 jobs in 2008. About 90 percent were computer-controlled machine tool operators, metal and plastic, and about 10 percent were numerical tool and process control programmers. The manufacturing industry employs almost all these workers. Employment was concentrated in fabricated metal products manufacturing, machinery manufacturing, plastics products manufacturing, and transportation equipment manufacturing making mostly aerospace and automobile parts. Although computer control programmers and operators work in all parts of the country, jobs are most plentiful in the areas where manufacturing is concentrated.

Job Outlook

Despite the projected increase in employment, applicants are expected to face competition for jobs, as there are more trained workers than available jobs.

Employment change. Overall employment of computer control programmers and operators is expected to increase by 4 percent over the 2008–2018 period, which is slower than average for all occupations. Employment of computer-controlled machine tool operators,

Projections Data from the National Employment Matrix

Occupational title	SOC Code	Employment, 2008	Projected employment, 2018	Change, 2008–2018	
				Number	Percent
Computer control programmers and operators............51-4010		157,800	164,500	6,700	4
Computer-controlled machine tool operators, metal and plastic...51-4011		141,000	150,300	9,300	7
Numerical tool and process control programmers ...51-4012		16,800	14,200	−2,600	−15

NOTE: Data in this table are rounded.

metal and plastic, is expected to increase by 7 percent, which is about as fast as the average for all occupations. The increasing use of CNC machine tools in all sectors of the manufacturing industry, replacing older mechanical metal and plastic working machines, will increase demand for computer-controlled machine tool operators. However, the demand for computer control programmers will be negatively affected by the increasing use of software (CAD/CAM) that automatically translates part and product designs into CNC machine tool instructions, and by simpler interfaces that allow machine operators to program the machines themselves. As a result, employment of numerical tool and process control programmers will decline by 15 percent over the projection period.

Job prospects. Computer control programmers and operators may face competition for jobs, as many workers currently operating mechanical machines will be retrained to operate computer-controlled machines and programming activities are increasingly done by these operators; however, workers with the ability to operate multiple CNC machine types should have better opportunities, as companies are increasingly demanding more versatile workers.

Earnings

Median hourly wages of computer-controlled machine tool operators, metal and plastic, were $16.57 in May 2009. The middle 50 percent earned between $13.23 and $20.11. The lowest 10 percent earned less than $10.82, whereas the top 10 percent earned more than $24.38. Median hourly wages in the manufacturing industries employing the largest numbers of computer-controlled machine tool operators, metal and plastic, in May 2009 were as follows:

Machine shops; turned product; and screw, nut, and bolt manufacturing............................	$15.92
Motor vehicle parts manufacturing.........................	15.80
Metalworking machinery manufacturing..................	18.78
Other fabricated metal product manufacturing.........	16.70
Plastics product manufacturing	14.83

Median hourly wages of numerical tool and process control programmers were $22.12 in May 2009. The middle 50 percent earned between $17.65 and $27.80. The lowest 10 percent earned less than $14.05, while the top 10 percent earned more than $34.40.

Many employers, especially those with formal apprenticeship programs, offer tuition assistance for training classes.

Related Occupations

Occupations most closely related to computer control programmers and operators are other metal and plastic working occupations, which include computer software engineers and computer programmers; industrial machinery mechanics and millwrights; machinists;

machine setters, operators, and tenders—metal and plastic; tool and die makers; and welding, soldering, and brazing workers.

Sources of Additional Information

For more information on training and new technology for computer control programmers and operators, contact

▸ Fabricators and Manufacturers Association, 833 Featherstone Rd., Rockford, IL 61107 Internet: www.fmanet.org

Computer Network, Systems, and Database Administrators

(O*NET 15-1061.00, 15-1071.00, 15-1071.01, 15-1081.00, 15-1081.01, 15-1099.00, 15-1099.01, 15-1099.02, 15-1099.03, 15-1099.04, 15-1099.05, 15-1099.06, 15-1099.07, 15-1099.08, 15-1099.09, 15-1099.10, 15-1099.11, 15-1099.12, 15-1099.13, and 15-1099.14)

Significant Points

■ Employment is projected to grow much faster than the average for all occupations and add 286,600 new jobs over the 2008–2018 decade.

■ Excellent job prospects are expected.

■ Workers can enter this field with many different levels of formal education, but relevant computer skills are always needed.

Nature of the Work

Information technology (IT) has become an integral part of modern life. Among its most important functions are the efficient transmission of information and the storage and analysis of information. The workers described in this section all help individuals and organizations share and store information through computer networks and systems, the Internet, and computer databases.

Network architects or *network engineers* are the designers of computer networks. They set up, test, and evaluate systems such as local area networks (LANs), wide area networks (WANs), the Internet, intranets, and other data communications systems. Systems are configured in many ways and can range from a connection between two offices in the same building to globally distributed networks, voice mail, and e-mail systems of a multinational organization. Network architects and engineers perform network modeling, analysis, and planning, which often require both hardware and software solutions. For example, setting up a network may involve the installation of several pieces of hardware, such as routers and hubs, wireless adaptors, and cables, as well as the installation and configuration of software, such as network drivers. These workers may also research related products and make necessary hardware and software recommendations, as well as address information security issues.

Network and computer systems administrators design, install, and support an organization's computer systems. They are responsible for LANs, WANs, network segments, and Internet and intranet systems. They work in a variety of environments, including large corporations, small businesses, and government organizations. They install and maintain network hardware and software, analyze problems, and monitor networks to ensure their availability to users. These workers gather data to evaluate a system's performance, identify user needs, and determine system and network requirements.

Systems administrators are responsible for maintaining system efficiency. They ensure that the design of an organization's computer system allows all of the components, including computers, the network, and software, to work properly together. Administrators also troubleshoot problems reported by users and by automated network monitoring systems and make recommendations for future system upgrades. Many of these workers are also responsible for maintaining network and system security.

Database administrators work with database management software and determine ways to store, organize, analyze, use, and present data. They identify user needs and set up new computer databases. In many cases, database administrators must integrate data from old systems into a new system. They also test and coordinate modifications to the system when needed and troubleshoot problems when they occur. An organization's database administrator ensures the performance of the system, understands the platform on which the database runs, and adds new users to the system. Because many databases are connected to the Internet, database administrators also must plan and coordinate security measures with network administrators. Some database administrators may also be responsible for database design, but this task is usually performed by *database designers* or *database analysts*.

Computer security specialists plan, coordinate, and maintain an organization's information security. These workers educate users about computer security, install security software, monitor networks for security breaches, respond to cyber attacks, and, in some cases, gather data and evidence to be used in prosecuting cyber crime. The responsibilities of computer security specialists have increased in recent years as cyber attacks have become more sophisticated.

Telecommunications specialists focus on the interaction between computer and communications equipment. These workers design voice, video, and data-communication systems; supervise the installation of the systems; and provide maintenance and other services to clients after the systems are installed. They also test lines and oversee equipment repair, and they may compile and maintain system records.

Web developers are responsible for the technical aspects of website creation. Using software languages and tools, they create applications for the Web. They identify a site's users and oversee its production and implementation. They determine the information that the site will contain and how it will be organized, and they may use Web development software to integrate databases and other information systems. Some of these workers may be responsible for the visual appearance of websites. Using design software, they create pages that appeal to the tastes of the site's users.

Webmasters or *Web administrators* are responsible for maintaining websites. They oversee issues such as availability to users and speed of access, and they are responsible for approving the content of the site. Webmasters also collect and analyze data on Web activity, traffic patterns, and other metrics, as well as monitor and respond to user feedback.

Work environment. Network and computer systems administrators, network architects, database administrators, computer security specialists, Web administrators, and Web developers normally work in well-lighted, comfortable offices or computer laboratories. Most work about 40 hours a week. However, about 15 percent of network and systems administrators, 14 percent of database administrators, and about 16 percent of network systems and data communications analysts (which includes network architects, telecommunications specialists, Web administrators, and Web developers) worked more than 50 hours per week in 2008. In addition, some of these workers may be required to be "on call" outside of normal business hours in order to resolve system failures or other problems.

As computer networks expand, more of these workers may be able to perform their duties from remote locations, reducing or eliminating the need to travel to the customer's workplace.

Injuries in these occupations are uncommon, but like other workers who spend long periods in front of a computer terminal typing on a keyboard, these workers are susceptible to eyestrain, back discomfort, and hand and wrist problems such as carpal tunnel syndrome.

Training, Other Qualifications, and Advancement

Training requirements vary by occupation. Workers can enter this field with many different levels of formal education, but relevant computer skills are always needed. Certification may improve an applicant's chances for employment and can help workers maintain adequate skill levels throughout their careers.

Education and training. Network and computer systems administrators often are required to have a bachelor's degree, although an associate degree or professional certification, along with related work experience, may be adequate for some positions. Most of these workers begin as computer support specialists before advancing into network or systems administration positions. (Computer support specialists are covered elsewhere in this book.) Common majors for network and systems administrators are computer science, information science, and management information systems (MIS), but a degree in any field, supplemented with computer courses and experience, may be adequate. A bachelor's degree in a computer-related field generally takes four years to complete and includes courses in computer science, computer programming, computer engineering, mathematics, and statistics. Most programs also include general education courses such as English and communications. MIS programs usually are part of the business school or college and contain courses such as finance, marketing, accounting, and management, as well as systems design, networking, database management, and systems security.

For network architect and database administrator positions, a bachelor's degree in a computer-related field generally is required, although some employers prefer applicants with a master's degree in business administration (MBA) with a concentration in information systems. MBA programs usually require two years of study beyond the undergraduate degree, and, like undergraduate business programs, include courses on finance, marketing, accounting, and management, as well as database management, electronic business, and systems management and design. In addition to formal education, network architects may be required to have several years of relevant work experience.

For Webmasters, an associate degree or certification is sufficient, although more advanced positions might require a computer-related bachelor's degree. For telecommunications specialists, employers prefer applicants with an associate degree in electronics or a related field, but for some positions, experience may substitute for formal education. Applicants for security specialist and Web developer positions generally need a bachelor's degree in a computer-related field, but for some positions, related experience and certification may be adequate.

Certification and other qualifications. Workers in these occupations must have strong problem-solving, analytical, and communication skills. Because they often deal with a number of tasks simultaneously, the ability to concentrate and pay close attention to detail also is important. Although these workers sometimes work independently, they frequently work in teams on large projects. As a result, they must be able to communicate effectively with other computer workers, such as programmers and managers, as well as with users or other staff who may have no computer background.

Job seekers can enhance their employment opportunities by earning certifications, which are offered through product vendors, computer associations, and other training institutions. Many employers regard these certifications as the industry standard, and some require their employees to be certified. In some cases, applicants without formal education may use certification and experience to qualify for some positions.

Because technology changes rapidly, computer specialists must continue to acquire the latest skills. Many organizations offer intermediate and advanced certification programs that pertain to the most recent technological advancements.

Advancement. Entry-level network and computer systems administrators are involved in routine maintenance and monitoring of computer systems. After gaining experience and expertise, they are often able to advance to more senior-level positions. They may also advance to supervisory positions.

Database administrators and network architects may advance into managerial positions, such as chief technology officer, on the basis of their experience. Computer specialists with work experience and considerable expertise in a particular area may find opportunities as independent consultants.

Computer security specialists can advance into supervisory positions or may move into other occupations, such as computer systems analysts.

Employment

Computer network, systems, and database administrators held about 961,200 jobs in 2008. Of these, 339,500 were network and computer systems administrators, 120,400 were database administrators, and 292,000 were network and data communications analysts. In addition, about 209,300 were classified as "computer specialists, all other," a residual category.

These workers were employed in a wide range of industries. About 14 percent of all computer network, systems, and database administrators were in computer systems design and related services. Substantial numbers of these workers were also employed in telecommunications companies, financial firms and insurance providers, business management organizations, schools, and government agencies. About 7 percent were self-employed.

Job Outlook

Employment is expected to grow much faster than the average, and job prospects should be excellent.

Employment change. Overall employment of computer network, systems, and database administrators is projected to increase by 30 percent from 2008 to 2018, much faster than the average for all occupations. In addition, this occupation will add 286,600 new jobs over that period. Growth, however, will vary by specialty.

Employment of network and computer systems administrators is expected to increase by 23 percent from 2008 to 2018, much faster than the average for all occupations. Computer networks are an integral part of business, and demand for these workers will increase as firms continue to invest in new technologies. The increasing adoption of mobile technologies means that more establishments will use the Internet to conduct business online. This growth translates into a need for systems administrators who can help organizations use technology to communicate with employees, clients, and consumers. Growth will also be driven by the increasing need for information security. As cyber attacks become more sophisticated, demand will increase for workers with security skills.

Employment of database administrators is expected to grow by 20 percent from 2008 to 2018, much faster than the average. Demand for these workers is expected to increase as organizations need to store, organize, and analyze increasing amounts of data. In addition, as more databases are connected to the Internet and as data security becomes increasingly important, a growing number of these workers will be needed to protect databases from attack.

Employment of network systems and data communications analysts is projected to increase by 53 percent from 2008 to 2018, which is much faster than the average and places it among the fastest growing of all occupations. This occupational category includes network architects and engineers, as well as Web administrators and developers. Demand for network architects and engineers will increase as organizations continue to upgrade their IT capacity and incorporate the newest technologies. The growing reliance on wireless networks will result in a need for many more of these workers. Workers with knowledge of information security also will be in demand as computer networks transmit an increasing amount of sensitive data.

Demand for Web administrators and Web developers will also be strong. More of these workers will be needed to accommodate the increasing amount of data sent over the Internet, as well as the growing number of Internet users. In addition, as the number of services provided over the Internet expands, Web administrators and developers will continue to see employment increases.

Growth in computer network, systems, and database administrators will be rapid in the computer systems design, data processing and hosting, software publishing, and technical consulting industries as these types of establishments utilize or provide an increasing array of IT services. Growth will also be rapid in health care as these organizations look to increase their efficiency and improve patient care through the use of information systems and other technology.

Growth in this occupation may be tempered somewhat by offshore outsourcing as firms transfer work to countries with lower-prevailing wages and highly skilled workforces. In addition, the consolidation of IT services may increase efficiency, reducing the demand for workers.

Job prospects. Computer network, systems, and database administrators should continue to enjoy excellent job prospects. In general, applicants with a college degree and certification will have the best

Projections Data from the National Employment Matrix

Occupational title	SOC Code	Employment, 2008	Projected employment, 2018	Change, 2008–2018	
				Number	Percent
Computer network, systems, and database administrators.. —		961,200	1,247,800	286,600	30
Database administrators 15-1061		120,400	144,700	24,400	20
Network and computer systems administrators 15-1071		339,500	418,400	78,900	23
Network systems and data communications analysts . 15-1081		292,000	447,800	155,800	53
All other computer specialists............................... 15-1099		209,300	236,800	27,500	13

NOTE: Data in this table are rounded.

opportunities. However, for some of these occupations, opportunities will be available for applicants with related work experience. Job openings in these occupations will be the result of strong employment growth, as well as the need to replace workers who transfer to other occupations or leave the labor force.

Earnings

Median annual wages of network and computer systems administrators were $67,710 in May 2009. The middle 50 percent earned between $52,940 and $85,830. The lowest 10 percent earned less than $41,940, and the highest 10 percent earned more than $105,970. Median annual wages in the industries employing the largest numbers of network and computer systems administrators in May 2009 were as follows:

Computer systems design and related services $72,190	
Management of companies and enterprises 71,070	
Wired telecommunications carriers 67,900	
Colleges, universities, and professional schools 59,790	
Elementary and secondary schools 57,320	

Median annual wages of database administrators were $71,550 in May 2009. The middle 50 percent earned between $53,470 and $93,260. The lowest 10 percent earned less than $40,780, and the highest 10 percent earned more than $114,200. In May 2009, median annual wages of database administrators employed in computer systems design and related services were $78,500, and for those in management of companies and enterprises, wages were $77,370.

Median annual wages of network systems and data communication analysts were $73,250 in May 2009. The middle 50 percent earned between $55,900 and $94,320. The lowest 10 percent earned less than $42,880, and the highest 10 percent earned more than $116,120. These wages encompass network architects, telecommunications specialists, Webmasters, and Web developers. Median annual wages in the industries employing the largest numbers of network systems and data communications analysts in May 2009 were as follows:

Computer systems design and related services $73,440	
Wired telecommunications carriers 77,850	
Management of companies and enterprises 77,020	
Insurance carriers... 75,710	
Local government.. 65,270	

Related Occupations

Other occupations that work with information technology include computer and information systems managers, computer scientists, computer software engineers and computer programmers, computer support specialists, and computer systems analysts.

Sources of Additional Information

For additional information about a career as a computer network, systems, or database administrator, contact

▶ The League of Professional System Administrators, 15000 Commerce Pkwy., Suite C, Mount Laurel, NJ 08054. Internet: www.lopsa.org

▶ Data Management International, 19239 N. Dale Mabry Hwy. #132, Lutz, FL 33548. Internet: www.dama.org

Additional information on a career in information technology is available from the following organizations:

▶ Association for Computing Machinery (ACM), 2 Penn Plaza, Suite 701, New York, NY 10121-0701. Internet: http://computingcareers.acm.org

▶ Institute of Electrical and Electronics Engineers Computer Society, Headquarters Office, 2001 L St. NW, Suite 700, Washington, DC 20036-4910. Internet: www.computer.org

▶ National Workforce Center for Emerging Technologies, 3000 Landerholm Circle SE, Bellevue, WA 98007. Internet: www.nwcet.org

▶ University of Washington Computer Science and Engineering Department, AC101 Paul G. Allen Center, Box 352350, 185 Stevens Way, Seattle, WA 98195-2350. Internet: www.cs.washington.edu/WhyCSE

▶ National Center for Women and Information Technology, University of Colorado, Campus Box 322 UCB, Boulder, CO 80309-0322. Internet: www.ncwit.org

Computer Support Specialists

(O*NET 15-1041.00)

Significant Points

■ Job growth is projected to be faster than the average for all occupations.

■ A bachelor's degree is required for some jobs, while an associate degree or certification is adequate for others.

■ Job prospects should be good, especially for college graduates with relevant skills and experience.

Nature of the Work

Computer support specialists provide technical assistance, support, and advice to individuals and organizations that depend on information technology. They work within organizations that use computer systems; for computer hardware or software vendors; or for third-party organizations that provide support services on a contract basis, such as help-desk service firms. Support specialists are usually differentiated between *technical support specialists* and *help-desk technicians.*

Technical support specialists respond to inquiries from their organizations' computer users and may run automatic diagnostics programs to resolve problems. In addition, they may write training manuals and train computer users in the use of new computer hardware and software. These workers also oversee the daily performance of their company's computer systems, resolving technical problems with local area networks (LAN), wide area networks (WAN), and other systems.

Help-desk technicians respond to telephone calls and e-mail messages from customers looking for help with computer problems. In responding to these inquiries, help-desk technicians must listen carefully to the customer, ask questions to diagnose the nature of the problem, and then patiently walk the customer through the problem-solving steps. They also install, modify, clean, and repair computer hardware and software. Many computer support specialists start out at the help desk.

Help-desk technicians deal directly with customer issues, and their employers value them as a source of feedback on their products and services. They are consulted for information about what gives customers the most trouble, as well as other customer concerns.

Work environment. Computer support specialists normally work in well-lighted, comfortable offices or computer laboratories. Most work about 40 hours a week. Those who work for third-party support firms often are away from their offices, spending considerable time working at a client's location. As computer networks expand, more computer support specialists may be able to provide technical support from remote locations. This capability would reduce or eliminate travel to the customer's workplace and may allow some support specialists to work from home.

Injuries in this occupation are uncommon, but like other workers who type on a keyboard for long periods, computer support specialists are susceptible to eyestrain, back discomfort, and hand and wrist problems such as carpal tunnel syndrome.

Training, Other Qualifications, and Advancement

A college degree is required for some computer support specialist positions, but an associate degree or certification may be sufficient for others. Strong problem-solving and communication skills are essential.

Education and training. Because of the wide range of skills required, there are many paths of entry to a job as a computer support specialist. Training requirements for computer support specialist positions vary, but many employers prefer to hire applicants with some formal college education. A bachelor's degree in computer science, computer engineering, or information systems is a prerequisite for some jobs; other jobs, however, may require only a computer-related associate degree. Some employers will hire

applicants with a college degree in any field, as long as the applicant has the necessary technical skills. For some jobs, relevant computer experience and certifications may substitute for formal education.

Most support specialists receive on-the-job training after being hired. This training can last anywhere from one week to one year, but a common length is about three months. Many computer support specialists, in order to keep up with changes in technology, continue to receive training throughout their careers by attending professional training programs offered by employers, hardware and software vendors, colleges and universities, and private training institutions.

Certification and other qualifications. For some jobs, professional certification may qualify an applicant for employment. Certification can demonstrate proficiency in a product or process and help applicants obtain some entry-level positions. Some hardware and software vendors require their computer support specialists to be certified, and many of these will fund this training after an applicant is hired. Voluntary certification programs are offered by a wide variety of organizations, including product vendors and training institutions, and are available across the nation.

People interested in becoming a computer support specialist must have strong problem-solving, analytical, and communication skills because troubleshooting and helping others are vital parts of the job. The constant interaction with other computer personnel, customers, and employees requires computer support specialists to communicate effectively via e-mail, over the phone, or in person. Strong writing skills are useful in writing e-mail responses and preparing manuals for employees and customers.

Advancement. Entry-level computer support specialists generally work directly with customers or in-house users. They may advance into positions that handle products or problems with higher levels of technical complexity. Some may advance into management roles. Some computer support specialists may find opportunities in other occupations, such as computer programmers or software engineers, designing products rather than assisting users. Promotions depend heavily on job performance, but formal education and professional certification can improve advancement opportunities. Advancement opportunities in hardware and software companies can occur quickly, sometimes within months.

Employment

Computer support specialists held about 565,700 jobs in 2008. Although they worked in a wide range of industries, about 18 percent were employed in the computer systems design and related services industry. Substantial numbers of these workers were also employed in administrative and support services companies, financial institutions, insurance companies, government agencies, educational institutions, software publishers, telecommunications organizations, and health-care organizations.

Job Outlook

Employment is expected to increase faster than the average. Job prospects should be good, especially for those with a college degree and relevant skills.

Employment change. Employment of computer support specialists is expected to increase by 14 percent from 2008 to 2018, which is faster than the average for all occupations. Demand for these workers will result as organizations and individuals continue to adopt the newest forms of technology. As technology becomes more

Projections Data from the National Employment Matrix

Occupational title	SOC Code	Employment, 2008	Projected employment, 2018	Change, 2008–2018	
				Number	Percent
Computer support specialists 15-1041		565,700	643,700	78,000	14

NOTE: Data in this table are rounded.

complex and widespread, support specialists will be needed in greater numbers to resolve the technical problems that arise. Businesses, especially, will demand greater levels of support, as information technology has become essential in the business environment.

Job growth will be fastest in several industries that rely heavily on technology. These include the computer systems design and related services industry; the data processing, hosting, and related services industry; the software publishing industry; and the management, scientific, and technical consulting industry. These industries will employ a growing number of support specialists as they utilize and provide an increasing array of IT services. Health-care and related establishments, in addition, may see substantial growth as these organizations look to improve their efficiency and patient care through the use of information systems and other technology.

Overall growth may be dampened, to a certain extent, as some jobs are outsourced to offshore locations. Advances in technology increasingly allow computer support specialists to provide assistance remotely. Some employers may seek to reduce expenses by hiring workers in areas that have lower prevailing wages.

Job prospects. Job prospects are expected to be good; those who possess a bachelor's degree, relevant technical and communication skills, and previous work experience should have even better opportunities than applicants with an associate degree or professional certification.

Earnings

Median annual wages of wage-and-salary computer support specialists were $44,300 in May 2009. The middle 50 percent earned between $34,320 and $57,290. The lowest 10 percent earned less than $27,200, and the highest 10 percent earned more than $72,690. Median annual wages in the industries employing the largest numbers of computer support specialists in May 2009 were as follows:

Computer systems design and related services $44,030
Elementary and secondary schools 41,170
Management of companies and enterprises 45,970
Colleges, universities, and professional schools 44,100
Professional and commercial equipment and
    supplies merchant wholesalers 49,230

Related Occupations

Other occupations that deal with technology or respond to customer inquiries include broadcast and sound engineering technicians and radio operators; computer and information systems managers; computer network, systems, and database administrators; computer software engineers and computer programmers; and customer service representatives.

Sources of Additional Information

For additional information about a career as a computer support specialist, contact

▸ Association of Support Professionals, 122 Barnard Ave., Watertown, MA 02472. Internet: http://asponline.com

▸ HDI, 102 S. Tejon, Suite 1200, Colorado Springs, CO, 80903. Internet: www.thinkhdi.com

For additional information about computer careers, contact

▸ Association for Computing Machinery, 2 Penn Plaza, Suite 701, New York, NY 10121-0701. Internet: http://computingcareers.acm.org

▸ Institute of Electrical and Electronics Engineers Computer Society, Headquarters Office, 2001 L St. NW, Suite 700, Washington, DC 20036-4910. Internet: www.computer.org

▸ National Workforce Center for Emerging Technologies, 3000 Landerholm Circle SE, Bellevue, WA 98007. Internet: www.nwcet.org

▸ University of Washington Computer Science and Engineering Department, AC101 Paul G. Allen Center, Box 352350, 185 Stevens Way, Seattle, WA 98195-2350. Internet: www.cs.washington.edu/WhyCSE

▸ National Center for Women and Information Technology, University of Colorado, Campus Box 322 UCB, Boulder, CO 80309-0322. Internet: www.ncwit.org

Computer, Automated Teller, and Office Machine Repairers

(O*NET 49-2011.00)

Significant Points

■ Employment is expected to decline slowly.

■ Job prospects will be best for applicants with knowledge of electronics, certification, formal training, and repair experience.

■ Workers qualify for these jobs by receiving training in electronics from associate degree programs, the military, vocational schools, equipment manufacturers, or employers.

Nature of the Work

Computer, automated teller, and office machine repairers install, fix, and maintain many of the machines that are used by businesses, households, and consumers. For large or stationary machines, repairers frequently perform the work on site. These workers—known as *field technicians*—often have assigned areas where they perform preventive maintenance on a regular basis. *Bench technicians* commonly repair smaller equipment and often work in repair shops located in stores, factories, or service centers. In small companies, repairers may work both in repair shops and at customer locations.

Computer repairers, also known as *computer service technicians* or *data processing equipment repairers*, service mainframe, server, and personal computers; printers; and auxiliary computer equipment. These workers primarily perform hands-on repair, maintenance, and installation of computers and related equipment. Workers who provide technical assistance, in person or by telephone, to computer system users are known as computer support specialists or computer support technicians. (See the section on computer support specialists elsewhere in this book.)

Computer repairers typically replace subsystems instead of repairing them. Commonly replaced subsystems include video cards, which transmit signals from the computer to the monitor; hard drives, which store data; and network cards, which allow communication over the network. Replacement is common because subsystems are usually inexpensive and businesses are reluctant to shut down their computers for time-consuming repairs. Defective modules may be given to bench technicians, who use software programs to diagnose the problem and who may repair the modules, if possible.

Office machine and *cash register servicers* work on photocopiers, cash registers, and fax machines. Newer models of office machinery include computerized components that allow them to function more reliably than earlier models and, therefore, require less maintenance.

Office machine repairers usually work on machinery at the customer's workplace. However, if the machines are small enough, customers may bring them to a repair shop for repair. Common malfunctions include paper jams caused by worn or dirty parts, and poor-quality copy resulting from problems with lamps, lenses, or mirrors. These malfunctions often can be resolved simply by cleaning the relevant components. Breakdowns also may result from the general wear and tear of commonly used parts. For example, heavy use of a photocopier may wear down the printhead, which applies ink to the final copy. In such cases, the repairer usually replaces the part instead of repairing it.

Automated teller machine servicers install and repair automated teller machines (ATMs) and, increasingly, electronic kiosks. In addition to performing bank transactions without the assistance of a teller, electric kiosks are being used for a variety of nontraditional services, including stamp, phone card, and ticket sales. A growing number of electronic kiosks also allow consumers to redeem movie tickets or airline and train boarding passes.

When ATMs malfunction, computer networks often recognize the problem and alert repairers. Common problems include worn magnetic heads on card readers, which prevent the equipment from recognizing customers' bank cards, and "pick failures," which prevent the equipment from dispensing the correct amount of cash. In such cases, field technicians travel to the locations of ATMs and repair equipment by removing and replacing defective components. Broken components may be taken to a repair shop, where bench technicians make the necessary repairs. Field technicians perform routine maintenance on a regular basis, replacing worn parts and running diagnostic tests to ensure that the equipment operates properly.

To install large equipment, such as mainframe computers and ATMs, repairers connect the equipment to power sources and communication lines that allow the transmission of information over computer networks. For example, when an ATM dispenses cash, it transmits the withdrawal information to the customer's bank. Workers may also install operating software and peripheral equipment, checking that all components are configured to operate together correctly.

Computer, automated teller, and office machine repairers use a variety of tools for diagnostic tests and repair. To diagnose malfunc-

tions, they use multimeters to measure voltage, current, resistance, and other electrical properties; signal generators to provide test signals; and oscilloscopes to monitor equipment signals. To diagnose computerized equipment, repairers use software programs. To repair or adjust equipment, workers use handtools, such as pliers, screwdrivers, and soldering irons.

Work environment. Repairers usually work in clean, well-lighted surroundings. Because computers and office machines are sensitive to extreme temperatures and humidity, repair shops usually are airconditioned and well ventilated. Field repairers must travel frequently to various locations to install, maintain, or repair customers' equipment. ATM repairers may have to perform their jobs in small, confined spaces that house the equipment.

Because computers and ATMs are critical for many organizations to function efficiently, data processing equipment repairers and ATM field technicians often work around the clock. Their schedules may include evening, weekend, and holiday shifts, sometimes assigned on the basis of seniority. Office machine and cash register servicers usually work regular business hours because the equipment they repair is not as critical. Most repairers work about 40 hours per week, but about 9 percent work more than 50 hours per week. Although their jobs are not strenuous, repairers often must lift equipment and work in a variety of postures. Repairers of computer monitors need to discharge voltage from the equipment to avoid electrocution.

Training, Other Qualifications, and Advancement

Knowledge of electronics is required, and employers prefer workers with formal training. Office machine and ATM repairers usually have an associate degree. Certification is available for entry-level workers and experienced workers seeking advancement.

Education and training. Knowledge of electronics is necessary for employment as a computer, automated teller, or office machine repairer. Employers prefer workers who are certified or who have training in electronics from an associate degree program, the military, a vocational school, or an equipment manufacturer. Employers generally provide some training to new repairers on specific equipment; however, workers are expected to arrive on the job with a basic understanding of equipment repair. Employers may send experienced workers to training sessions to keep up with changes in technology and service procedures.

Most office machine and ATM repairer positions require an associate degree in electronics. A basic understanding of mechanical equipment is also important because many of the parts that fail in office machines and ATMs, such as paper loaders, are mechanical. Entry-level employees at large companies normally receive on-the-job training lasting several months. Such training may include a week of classroom instruction, followed by a period of 2 weeks to several months assisting an experienced repairer.

Other qualifications. Field technicians work closely with customers and must have good communications skills and a neat appearance. Employers may require that field technicians have a driver's license.

Certification and advancement. Various organizations offer certification. For instance, the Electronics Technicians Association (ETA) offers more than 50 certification programs in numerous electronics specialties for varying levels of competence. The International

Projections Data from the National Employment Matrix

Occupational title	SOC Code	Employment, 2008	Projected employment, 2018	Change, 2008–2018	
				Number	Percent
Computer, automated teller, and office machine repairers..49-2011		152,900	146,200	–6,700	–4

NOTE: Data in this table are rounded.

Society of Certified Electronics Technicians also offers certification for several levels of competence, focusing on a broad range of topics, including basic electronics, multimedia systems, electronic systems, and appliance service. To become certified, applicants must meet several prerequisites and pass a comprehensive written or online examination. Certification demonstrates a level of competency. It can make an applicant more attractive to employers or increase an employee's opportunities for advancement.

Newly hired computer repairers may possibly work on personal computers or peripheral equipment. With experience, they can advance to positions maintaining more sophisticated systems, such as networking equipment and servers. Field repairers of ATMs may advance to bench technician positions responsible for more complex repairs. Experienced workers may become specialists who assist other repairers diagnose difficult problems or who work with engineers in designing equipment and developing maintenance procedures. Experienced workers may also move into management positions responsible for supervising other repairers.

Because of their familiarity with equipment, experienced repairers may also move into customer service or sales positions. Some experienced workers open their own repair shops or become wholesalers or retailers of electronic equipment.

Employment

Computer, automated teller, and office machine repairers held about 152,900 jobs in 2008. Wholesale trade establishments employed about 29 percent of the workers in this occupation; most of these establishments were wholesalers of professional and commercial equipment and supplies. Many workers also were employed in electronics and appliance stores and office supply stores. Others worked in electronic and precision equipment repair shops and computer systems design firms. About 20 percent of computer, automated teller, and office machine repairers were self-employed.

Job Outlook

Employment is expected to decline slowly. Opportunities will be best for applicants with knowledge of electronics, formal training, and repair experience. Employers increasingly prefer applicants who are certified.

Employment change. Employment of computer, automated teller, and office machine repairers is expected to decline by 4 percent from 2008 to 2018. Less expensive and more reliable computer equipment is expected to result in fewer computer repairers. Nonetheless, some computer repairers will be needed as malfunctions still occur and can cause severe problems for users, most of whom lack the knowledge to make repairs. Additionally, computers are critical to most businesses today and will become even more so as companies increasingly engage in electronic commerce, and as individuals continue to bank, shop, and pay bills online.

Employment growth of ATM repairers will be impeded as a result of newer technology which allows for the testing and resetting of machines remotely. The relatively slow rate at which new ATMs are installed will also limit demand for ATM repairers, despite a greater reliance on these machines by consumers.

Fewer office machine repairers will be needed as office equipment is often inexpensive and increasingly replaced instead of repaired. However, digital copiers and some newer office machines are more costly and complex. This equipment is often computerized, designed to work on a network, and capable of performing multiple functions. But because this equipment is becoming more reliable, the need for repairers will continue to decline.

Job prospects. Job prospects are expected to be limited as newer equipment continues to require less maintenance and repair. As a result, the vast majority of job openings will stem from the need to replace workers who retire or leave the occupation for other reasons. Those with knowledge of electronics, certification, formal training, and repair experience will have the best prospects.

A growing number of new ATMs called electronic kiosks offer non-traditional retail services, such as employee information processing and ticket redemption, in addition to banking transactions. Candidates who have expertise in the installation, maintenance, and repair of such equipment will also have better job prospects.

Earnings

Median hourly wages of computer, automated teller, and office machine repairers were $18.09 in May 2009. The middle 50 percent earned between $13.99 and $23.17. The lowest 10 percent earned less than $10.87, and the highest 10 percent earned more than $28.41. Median hourly wages in the industries employing the largest numbers of computer, automated teller, and office machine repairers in May 2009 were as follows:

Professional and commercial equipment and supplies merchant wholesalers	$19.26
Electronic and precision equipment repair and maintenance	17.01
Electronics and appliance stores	15.68
Computer systems design and related services	17.50
Office supplies, stationery, and gift stores	17.00

Related Occupations

Workers in other occupations who repair and maintain electronic equipment include broadcast and sound engineering technicians and radio operators; coin, vending, and amusement machine servicers and repairers; electrical and electronics installers and repairers; electricians; electronic home entertainment equipment installers and repairers; home appliance repairers; maintenance and repair workers, general; and radio and telecommunications equipment installers and repairers.

Sources of Additional Information

For information on electronics careers and certification, contact

▶ Electronics Technicians Association International, 5 Depot St., Greencastle, IN 46135. Internet: http://eta-i.org/

▶ International Society of Certified Electronics Technicians, 3608 Pershing Ave., Fort Worth, TX 76107-4527. Internet: www.iscet.org

Construction Equipment Operators

(O*NET 47-2071.00, 47-2072.00, and 47-2073.00)

Significant Points

■ Construction equipment operators are trained either through a formal apprenticeship program, through on-the-job training, through a paid training program, or a combination of these programs.

■ Job opportunities are expected to be good.

■ Hourly pay is relatively high, but operators of some types of equipment cannot work in inclement weather, so total annual earnings may be reduced.

Nature of the Work

Construction equipment operators use machinery to move construction materials, earth, and other heavy materials at construction sites and mines. They operate equipment that clears and grades land to prepare it for construction of roads, buildings, and bridges, as well as airport runways, power generation facilities, dams, levees, and other structures. They use machines to dig trenches to lay or repair sewer and other utilities, and hoist heavy construction materials. They even may work offshore constructing oil rigs. Construction equipment operators also operate machinery that spreads asphalt and concrete on roads and other structures.

These workers also help set up and inspect the equipment, make adjustments, and perform some maintenance and minor repairs. Construction equipment is more technologically advanced than it was in the past. For example, global positioning system (GPS) technology is now being used to help with grading and leveling activities.

Included in the construction equipment operator occupation are operating engineers and other construction equipment operators; paving and surfacing equipment operators; and pile-driver operators. *Operating engineers* and *other construction equipment operators* work with one or several types of power construction equipment. They may operate excavation and loading machines equipped with scoops, shovels, or buckets that dig sand, gravel, earth, or similar materials and load it into trucks or onto conveyors. In addition to operating the familiar bulldozers, they operate trench excavators, road graders, and similar equipment. Sometimes, they may drive and control industrial trucks or tractors equipped with forklifts or booms for lifting materials or with hitches for pulling trailers. They also may operate and maintain air compressors, pumps, and other power equipment at construction sites.

Paving and surfacing equipment operators operate machines that spread and level asphalt or spread and smooth concrete for roadways

or other structures. *Asphalt spreader operators* turn valves to regulate the temperature and flow of asphalt onto the roadbed. They must take care that the machine distributes the paving material evenly and without voids, and they must make sure that there is a constant flow of asphalt going into the hopper. Concrete paving machine operators control levers and turn handwheels to move attachments that spread, vibrate, and level wet concrete in forms. They must observe the surface of the concrete to identify low spots into which workers must add concrete. They use other attachments to smooth the surface of the concrete, spray on a curing compound, and cut expansion joints. Tamping equipment operators operate tamping machines that compact earth and other fill materials for roadbeds or other construction sites. They also may operate machines with interchangeable hammers to cut or break up old pavement and drive guardrail posts into the earth.

Pile-driver operators use large machines mounted on skids, barges, or cranes to hammer piles into the ground. Piles are long, heavy beams of wood or steel driven into the ground to support retaining walls, bulkheads, bridges, piers, or building foundations. Some pile-driver operators work on offshore oil rigs. Pile-driver operators move hand and foot levers and turn valves to activate, position, and control the pile-driving equipment.

Work environment. Construction equipment operators work outdoors in nearly every type of climate and weather condition, although in many areas of the country some types of construction operations must be suspended in winter. Bulldozers, scrapers, and especially pile-drivers are noisy and shake or jolt the operator. Operating heavy construction equipment can be dangerous, and this occupation incurs injuries and illnesses at a higher-than-average rate. As with most machinery, accidents generally can be avoided by observing proper operating procedures and safety practices. Construction equipment operators often get dirty, greasy, muddy, or dusty. Some operators work in remote locations on large construction projects, such as highways and dams, or in factory or mining operations.

Operators may have irregular hours because work on some construction projects continues around the clock or must be performed late at night or early in the morning.

Training, Other Qualifications, and Advancement

Construction equipment operators are trained either through a formal apprenticeship program, through on-the-job training, through a paid training program, or a combination of these programs.

Education and training. Employers of construction equipment operators generally prefer to hire high school graduates, although some employers may train nongraduates to operate some types of equipment. High school courses in automobile mechanics are helpful because workers may perform maintenance on their machines. Also useful are courses in science and mechanical drawing. With the development of GPS, construction equipment operators need more experience with computers than in the past.

On the job, workers may start by operating light equipment under the guidance of an experienced operator. Later, they may operate heavier equipment, such as bulldozers. Technologically advanced construction equipment with computerized controls and improved hydraulics and electronics requires more skill to operate. Operators of such equipment may need more training and some understanding of electronics.

It is generally accepted that formal training provides more comprehensive skills. Some construction equipment operators train in formal operating engineer apprenticeship programs administered by union-management committees of the International Union of Operating Engineers (IUOE). Because apprentices learn to operate a wider variety of machines than do other beginners, they usually have better job opportunities. Apprenticeship programs consist of at least 3 years, or 6,000 hours, of paid on-the-job training together with 144 hours of related classroom instruction each year.

Private vocational schools offer instruction in the operation of certain types of construction equipment. Completion of such programs may help a person get a job. However, people considering this kind of training should check the school's reputation among employers in the area and find out if the school offers the opportunity to work on actual machines in realistic situations. A large amount of information can be learned in classrooms, but to become a skilled construction equipment operator, a worker needs to actually perform the various tasks. Many training facilities, including IUOE apprenticeship programs, incorporate sophisticated simulators into their training, allowing beginners to familiarize themselves with the equipment in a controlled environment.

Certification and other qualifications. Mechanical aptitude and experience operating related mobile equipment, such as farm tractors or heavy equipment, in the Armed Forces or elsewhere is an asset. Construction equipment operators often need a commercial driver's license to haul their equipment to the various job sites. Commercial driver's licenses are issued by states according to each state's rules and regulations. Operators also need to be in good physical condition and have a good sense of balance, the ability to judge distance, and eye-hand-foot coordination. Some operator positions require the ability to work at heights.

Certification or training from the right school can improve opportunities for job seekers; some employers may require operators to be certified. While attending some vocational schools, or by fulfilling the requirements of related professional associations, operators can qualify for various certifications. These certifications prove to potential employers that an operator is able to handle specific types of equipment.

Advancement. Construction equipment operators can advance to become supervisors. Some operators choose to pass on their knowledge and teach in training facilities. Other operators start their own contracting businesses, although doing so may be difficult because of high startup costs.

Employment

Construction equipment operators held about 469,300 jobs in 2008. Jobs were found in every section of the country and were distributed among various types of operators as follows:

Operating engineers and other construction equipment operators	404,500
Paving, surfacing, and tamping equipment operators	60,200
Pile-driver operators	4,600

About 63 percent of construction equipment operators worked in the construction industry. Many equipment operators worked in heavy and civil engineering construction, building highways, bridges, or railroads. About 16 percent of construction equipment operators worked in local government. Others—mostly grader, bulldozer, and scraper operators—worked in mining. Some also worked for manufacturing or utility companies. About 3 percent of construction equipment operators were self-employed.

Job Outlook

Average job growth is projected. The need to fill jobs and replace workers who leave the occupation should result in good job opportunities for construction equipment operators.

Employment change. Employment of construction equipment operators is expected to increase 12 percent between 2008 and 2018, about as fast as the average for all occupations. The likelihood of increased spending by the federal government on infrastructure to improve roads and bridges, railroads, the electric transmission system, and water and sewer systems, which are in great need of repair across the country, will generate numerous jobs for construction equipment operators who work primarily in these areas. In addition, population increases and the need for construction projects, such as new roads and sewer lines to service the increased population, will generate more jobs. However, without the extra spending on infrastructure by the federal government, employment may be flat as states and localities struggle with reduced taxes and budget shortfalls to pay for road and other improvements.

An expected rise in energy production is expected to increase work on oil rigs, smart grids, windmill farms, pipeline construction, and other types of power-generating facilities. Also, increased output of mines and rock and gravel quarries will generate jobs in the mining industry.

Job prospects. Job opportunities for construction equipment operators are expected to be good because the occupation often does not attract enough qualified candidates to fill jobs. Some workers'

Projections Data from the National Employment Matrix

Occupational title	SOC Code	Employment, 2008	Projected employment, 2018	Change, 2008–2018	
				Number	Percent
Construction equipment operators	47-2070	469,300	525,500	56,200	12
Paving, surfacing, and tamping equipment operators	47-2071	60,200	67,200	6,900	12
Pile-driver operator	47-2072	4,600	5,200	600	13
Operating engineers and other construction equipment operators	47-2073	404,500	453,200	48,700	12

NOTE: Data in this table are rounded.

reluctance to work in construction makes it easier for willing workers to get operator jobs.

In addition, many job openings will arise from job growth and from the need to replace experienced construction equipment operators who transfer to other occupations, retire, or leave the job for other reasons. Construction equipment operators who can use a wide variety of equipment will have the best prospects. Operators with pipeline experience will have especially good opportunities if, as expected, natural-gas companies expand work on their infrastructure.

Employment of construction equipment operators, like that of many other construction workers, is sensitive to fluctuations in the economy. Workers in these trades may experience periods of unemployment when the overall level of construction falls. However, shortages of these workers may occur in some areas during peak periods of building activity.

Earnings

Wages for construction equipment operators vary. In May 2009, median hourly wages of wage and salary operating engineers and other construction equipment operators were $19.12. The middle 50 percent earned between $15.01 and $25.81. The lowest 10 percent earned less than $12.60, and the highest 10 percent earned more than $33.67. Median hourly wages in the industries employing the largest numbers of operating engineers were as follows:

Other specialty trade contractors	$18.82
Local government	17.69
Highway, street, and bridge construction	21.78
Utility system construction	20.27
Other heavy and civil engineering construction	19.62

Median hourly wages of wage and salary paving, surfacing, and tamping equipment operators were $16.36 in May 2009. The middle 50 percent earned between $13.20 and $21.47. The lowest 10 percent earned less than $11.12, and the highest 10 percent earned more than $28.45. Median hourly wages in the industries employing the largest numbers of paving, surfacing, and tamping equipment operators were as follows:

Other specialty trade contractors	$16.38
Highway, street, and bridge construction	16.66
Local government	16.35

In May 2009, median hourly wages of wage and salary pile-driver operators were $22.24. The middle 50 percent earned between $17.41 and $33.19. The lowest 10 percent earned less than $14.60, and the highest 10 percent earned more than $38.46. Median hourly wages in the industries employing the largest numbers of pile-driver operators were as follows:

Highway, street, and bridge construction	$21.13
Other specialty trade contractors	27.75
Other heavy and civil engineering construction	23.29
Utility system construction	18.10
Nonresidential building construction	20.69

Hourly pay is relatively high, particularly in large metropolitan areas. However, annual earnings of some workers may be lower than hourly rates would indicate because work time may be limited by bad weather. About 27 percent of construction equipment operators belong to a union.

Related Occupations

Other workers who operate mechanical equipment include the following: agricultural equipment operators; logging equipment operators; material moving occupations; and truck drivers, heavy and tractor-trailer.

Sources of Additional Information

For further information about apprenticeships or work opportunities for construction equipment operators, contact a local of the International Union of Operating Engineers, a local apprenticeship committee, or the nearest office of the state apprenticeship agency or employment service. You also can find information on the registered apprenticeship system, with links to state apprenticeship programs, on the U.S. Department of Labor's website: www.doleta.gov/OA/eta_default.cfm. In addition, apprenticeship information is available from the U.S. Department of Labor's toll-free help line: (877) 872-5627.

For general information about the work of construction equipment operators, contact

▸ Associated General Contractors of America, 2300 Wilson Blvd., Suite 400, Arlington, VA 22201-5426. Internet: www.agc.org

▸ International Union of Operating Engineers, 1125 17th St. NW, Washington, DC 20036-4786. Internet: www.iuoe.org

▸ National Center for Construction Education and Research, 3600 NW 43rd St., Building G, Gainesville, FL 32606-8134. Internet: www.nccer.org

▸ Pile Driving Contractors Association, P.O. Box 66208, Orange Park, FL 32065-0021. Internet: www.pile-drivers.org

For general information on apprenticeships and how to get them, see the *Occupational Outlook Quarterly* article "Apprenticeships: Career training, credentials—and a paycheck in your pocket," online at www.bls.gov/opub/ooq/2002/summer/art01.pdf and in print at many libraries and career centers.

Construction Laborers

(O*NET 47-2061.00)

Significant Points

■ Many construction laborer jobs require a variety of basic skills, but others require specialized training and experience.

■ Most construction laborers learn on the job, but formal apprenticeship programs provide the most thorough preparation.

■ Job opportunities vary by locality, but in many areas there will be competition, especially for jobs requiring limited skills.

■ Laborers who have specialized skills or who can relocate near new construction projects should have the best opportunities.

Nature of the Work

Construction laborers can be found on almost all construction sites, performing a wide range of tasks from the very easy to the hazardous. They can be found at building, highway, and heavy construction sites; residential and commercial sites; tunnel and shaft excavations; and demolition sites. Many of the jobs they perform require physical strength, training, and experience. Other jobs require little skill and can be learned quickly. Although most construction laborers specialize in a type of construction, such as highway or tunnel construction, some are generalists who perform many different tasks during all stages of construction. Construction laborers who work in underground construction, such as in tunnels, or in demolition are more likely to specialize in only those areas.

Construction laborers clean and prepare construction sites. They remove trees and debris; tend pumps, compressors, and generators; and erect and disassemble scaffolding and other temporary structures. They load, unload, identify, and distribute building materials to the appropriate location according to project plans and specifications. Laborers also tend machines; for example, they may use a portable mixer to mix concrete or tend a machine that pumps concrete, grout, cement, sand, plaster, or stucco through a spray gun for application to ceilings and walls. They often help other craftworkers, including carpenters, plasterers, operating engineers, and masons.

Construction laborers are responsible for the installation and maintenance of traffic control devices and patterns. At highway construction sites, this work may include clearing and preparing highway work zones and rights-of-way; installing traffic barricades, cones, and markers; and controlling traffic passing near, in, and around work zones. Construction laborers also dig trenches; install sewer, water, and storm drainpipes; and place concrete and asphalt on roads. Other highly specialized tasks include operating laser guidance equipment to place pipes; operating air, electric, and pneumatic drills; and transporting and setting explosives for the construction of tunnels, shafts, and roads.

Some construction laborers help with the removal of hazardous materials, such as asbestos, lead, or chemicals.

Construction laborers operate a variety of equipment, including pavement breakers; jackhammers; earth tampers; concrete, mortar, and plaster mixers; electric and hydraulic boring machines; torches; small mechanical hoists; laser beam equipment; and surveying and measuring equipment. They may use computers and other high-tech input devices to control robotic pipe cutters and cleaners. To perform their jobs effectively, construction laborers must be familiar with the duties of other craftworkers and with the materials, tools, and machinery they use, as all of these workers work as part of a team, jointly carrying out assigned construction tasks.

Work environment. Most construction laborers do physically demanding work. Some work at great heights or outdoors in all weather conditions. Some jobs expose workers to harmful materials or chemicals, fumes, odors, loud noises, or dangerous machinery. Some laborers may be exposed to lead-based paint, asbestos, or other hazardous substances during their work, especially when they work in confined spaces. Workers in this occupation experience one of the highest rates of nonfatal injuries and illnesses; consequently, the work requires constant attention to safety on the job. To avoid injury, workers in these jobs wear safety clothing, such as gloves, hardhats, protective chemical suits, and devices to protect their eyes, respiratory system, or hearing. While working underground, construction laborers must be especially alert in order to follow procedures safely and must deal with a variety of hazards.

A standard 40 hour workweek is the most common workweek for construction laborers. About 1 in 7 has a variable schedule, as overnight work may be required in highway work. In some parts of the country, construction laborers may work only during certain seasons. They also may experience weather-related work stoppages at any time of the year.

Training, Other Qualifications, and Advancement

Many construction laborer jobs require a variety of basic skills, but others require specialized training and experience. Most construction laborers learn on the job, but formal apprenticeship programs provide the most thorough preparation.

Education and training. Although some construction laborer jobs have no specific educational qualifications or entry-level training, apprenticeships for laborers usually require a high school diploma or the equivalent. High school classes in English, mathematics, physics, mechanical drawing, blueprint reading, welding, and general shop can be helpful.

Most workers start by getting a job with a contractor who provides on-the-job training. Increasingly, construction laborers are finding work through temporary-help agencies that send laborers to construction sites for short-term work. Entry-level workers generally help more experienced workers, by performing routine tasks such as cleaning and preparing the worksite and unloading materials. When the opportunity arises, they learn from experienced construction trades workers how to do more difficult tasks, such as operating tools and equipment. Construction laborers also may choose or be required to attend a trade or vocational school, association training class, or community college to receive further trade-related training.

Some laborers receive more formal training in the form of an apprenticeship. These programs include between 2 and 4 years of classroom and on-the-job training. In the first 200 hours, workers learn basic construction skills, such as blueprint reading, the correct use of tools and equipment, and safety and health procedures. The remainder of the curriculum consists of specialized skills training in three of the largest segments of the construction industry: building construction, heavy and highway construction, and environmental remediation, such as lead or asbestos abatement and mold or hazardous waste remediation. Training in "green," energy-efficient construction, an area of growth in the construction industry, is now available and can help workers find employment.

Workers who use dangerous equipment or handle toxic chemicals usually receive specialized safety training. Laborers who remove hazardous materials are required to take union- or employer-sponsored Occupational Safety and Health Administration safety training.

Apprenticeship applicants usually must be at least 18 years old and meet local requirements. Because the number of apprenticeship programs is limited, however, only a small proportion of laborers learn their trade in this way.

Other qualifications. Laborers need manual dexterity, eye-hand coordination, good physical fitness, a good sense of balance, and an ability to work as a member of a team. The ability to solve arithmetic problems quickly and accurately may be required. In addition, military service or a good work history is viewed favorably by contractors.

Certification and advancement. Laborers may earn certifications in welding, scaffold erecting, and concrete finishing. These certifications help workers prove that they have the knowledge to perform more complex tasks.

Through training and experience, laborers can move into other construction occupations. Laborers may also advance to become construction supervisors or general contractors. For those who would like to advance, it is increasingly important to be able to communicate in both English and Spanish in order to relay instructions and safety precautions to workers with limited understanding of English; Spanish-speaking workers make up a large part of the construction workforce in many areas. Supervisors and contractors need good communication skills to deal with clients and subcontractors.

In addition, supervisors and contractors should be able to identify and estimate the quantity of materials needed to complete a job and accurately estimate how long a job will take to complete and what it will cost. Computer skills also are important for advancement as construction becomes increasingly mechanized and computerized.

Employment

Construction laborers held about 1.2 million jobs in 2008. They worked throughout the country, but like the general population, were concentrated in metropolitan areas. About 62 percent of construction laborers worked in the construction industry, including 27 percent who worked for specialty trade contractors. About 21 percent were self-employed in 2008.

Job Outlook

Employment is expected to grow much faster than the average. In many areas, there will be competition for jobs, especially those requiring limited skills. Laborers who have specialized skills or who can relocate near new construction projects should have the best opportunities.

Employment change. Employment of construction laborers is expected to grow by 20 percent between 2008 and 2018, much faster than the average for all occupations. Because of the large variety of tasks that laborers perform, demand for laborers will mirror the level of overall construction activity. However, some jobs may be adversely affected by automation as they are replaced by new machinery and equipment that improves productivity and quality.

Increasing job prospects for construction laborers, however, is the expected additional government funding for the repair and reconstruction of the nation's infrastructure, such as roads, bridges, public buildings, and water lines. The occupation should experience an increase in demand because laborers make up a significant portion of workers on these types of projects.

New emphasis on green construction also should help lead to better employment prospects as many green practices require more labor on construction sites. Additional duties resulting from practicing green construction include having to segregate materials that can be used again from those which cannot, and the actual reuse of such materials. In addition, these workers will be needed for the construction of any new projects to harness wind or solar power.

Job prospects. In many geographic areas, construction laborers—especially for those with limited skills—will experience competition

because of a plentiful supply of workers who are willing to work as day laborers. Overall opportunities will be best for those with experience and specialized skills and for those who can relocate to areas with new construction projects. Opportunities also will be better for laborers specializing in road construction.

Employment of construction laborers, like that of many other construction workers, is sensitive to the fluctuations of the economy. On the one hand, workers in these trades may experience periods of unemployment when the overall level of construction falls. On the other hand, shortages of these workers may occur in some areas during peak periods of building activity.

Earnings

Median hourly wages of wage and salary construction laborers in May 2009 were $14.01. The middle 50 percent earned between $10.92 and $19.11. The lowest 10 percent earned less than $8.86, and the highest 10 percent earned more than $27.05. Median hourly wages in the industries employing the largest number of construction laborers were as follows:

Other specialty trade contractors $14.00
Nonresidential building construction 15.04
Foundation, structure, and building exterior
    contractors 13.47
Residential building construction 13.85
Highway, street, and bridge construction 15.15

Earnings for construction laborers can be reduced by poor weather or by downturns in construction activity, which sometimes result in layoffs. Apprentices or helpers usually start out earning about 60 percent of the wage paid to experienced workers. Pay increases as apprentices gain experience and learn new skills.

Some laborers—about 14 percent—belong to a union, mainly the Laborers' International Union of North America.

Related Occupations

The work of construction laborers is closely related to that of other construction occupations, as well as that of others who perform similar physical work, such as the following: assemblers and fabricators; brickmasons, blockmasons, and stonemasons; forest and conservation workers; grounds maintenance workers; highway maintenance workers; logging workers; material moving occupations; refractory materials repairers, except brickmasons; and roustabouts, oil and gas.

Sources of Additional Information

For information about jobs as a construction laborer, contact local building or construction contractors, local joint labor-management apprenticeship committees, apprenticeship agencies, or the local office of your State Employment Service. You also can find

Projections Data from the National Employment Matrix

Occupational title	SOC Code	Employment, 2008	Projected employment, 2018	Change, 2008–2018	
				Number	Percent
Construction laborers 47-2061		1,248,700	1,504,600	255,900	20

NOTE: Data in this table are rounded.

information on the registered apprenticeships, together with links to state apprenticeship programs, on the U.S. Department of Labor's website: www.doleta.gov/OA/eta_default.cfm. Apprenticeship information also is available from the U.S. Department of Labor's toll-free help line: (877) 872-5627.

For general information on apprenticeships and how to get them, see the *Occupational Outlook Quarterly* article "Apprenticeships: Career training, credentials—and a paycheck in your pocket," online at www.bls.gov/opub/ooq/2002/summer/art01.pdf and in print at many libraries and career centers.

For information on education programs for laborers, contact

▸ Laborers-AGC Education and Training Fund, 37 Deerfield Rd., P.O. Box 37, Pomfret Center, CT 06258-0037.

▸ National Center for Construction Education and Research, 3600 NW 43rd St., Bldg. G, Gainesville, FL 32606. Internet: www.nccer.org

Cooks and Food Preparation Workers

(O*NET 35-2011.00, 35-2012.00, 35-2013.00, 35-2014.00, 35-2015.00, 35-2019.00, and 35-2021.00)

Significant Points

■ Many cooks and food preparation workers are young—35 percent are below the age of 24.

■ One-third of these workers are employed part time.

■ Job openings are expected to be plentiful because many of these workers will leave the occupation for full-time employment or better wages.

Nature of the Work

Cooks and food preparation workers prepare, season, and cook a wide range of foods—from soups, snacks, and salads to entrees, side dishes, and desserts. They work in a variety of restaurants, as well as other places where food is served, such as grocery stores, schools and hospitals. Cooks prepare and cook meals while food preparation workers assist cooks by performing tasks, such as peeling and cutting vegetables, trimming meat, preparing poultry, and keeping work areas clean and monitoring temperatures of ovens and stovetops.

Specifically, *cooks* measure, mix, and cook ingredients according to recipes, using a variety of equipment, including pots, pans, cutlery, ovens, broilers, grills, slicers, grinders, and blenders. *Food preparation workers* perform routine, repetitive tasks under the direction of chefs, head cooks, or food preparation and serving supervisors. These workers prepare the ingredients for complex dishes by slicing and dicing vegetables, and making salads and cold items. They weigh and measure ingredients, retrieve pots and pans, and stir and strain soups and sauces. Food preparation workers may also cut and grind meats, poultry, and seafood in preparation for cooking. They also clean work areas, equipment, utensils, dishes, and silverware.

Larger restaurants and food service establishments tend to have varied menus and larger kitchen staffs. Teams of restaurant cooks, sometimes called *assistant or line cooks*, each work an assigned station that is equipped with the types of stoves, grills, pans, and ingredients needed for the foods prepared at that station. Job titles often reflect the principal ingredient prepared or the type of cooking performed—*vegetable cook*, *fry cook*, or *grill cook*, for example. Chefs, head cooks, or food preparation and serving supervisors generally direct the work of cooks and food preparation workers (information on chefs, head cooks, and food preparation and serving supervisors is found elsewhere in this book).

The number, type, and responsibilities of cooks vary depending on where they work, the size of the facility, and the complexity and level of service offered. *Institution and cafeteria cooks*, for example, work in the kitchens of schools, cafeterias, businesses, hospitals, and other institutions. For each meal, they prepare a large quantity of a limited number of entrees, vegetables, and desserts according to preset menus. Meals are generally prepared in advance so diners seldom get the opportunity to special order a meal. *Restaurant cooks* usually prepare a wider selection of dishes, cooking most orders individually. *Short-order cooks* prepare foods in restaurants and coffee shops that emphasize fast service and quick food preparation. They grill and garnish hamburgers, prepare sandwiches, fry eggs, and cook French fries, often working on several orders at the same time. *Fast food cooks* prepare a limited selection of menu items in fast food restaurants. They cook and package food, such as hamburgers and fried chicken, to be kept warm until served. (Combined food preparation and serving workers, who prepare and serve items in fast food restaurants, are included with the material on food and beverage serving and related workers elsewhere in this book.)

Work environment. Many restaurant and institutional kitchens have modern equipment, convenient work areas, and air conditioning, but kitchens in older and smaller eating places are often not as well designed. Kitchen staffs invariably work in small quarters against hot stoves and ovens. They are under constant pressure to prepare meals quickly, while ensuring quality is maintained and safety and sanitation guidelines are observed. Because the pace can be hectic during peak dining times, workers must be able to communicate clearly so that food orders are completed correctly.

Working conditions vary with the type and quantity of food prepared and the local laws governing food service operations. Workers usually must stand for hours at a time, lifting heavy pots and kettles, and working near hot ovens and grills. The incidence of reported injuries for institution and cafeteria cooks, restaurant cooks, and food preparation workers was comparatively high compared to all occupations, but job hazards, such as falls, cuts, and burns, are seldom serious.

Work hours in restaurants may include early mornings, late evenings, holidays, and weekends. Work schedules of cooks and food preparation workers in factory and school cafeterias may be more regular. In 2008, 31 percent of cooks and almost half of food preparation workers had part-time schedules, compared to 16 percent of workers throughout the economy. Work schedules in fine-dining restaurants, however, tend to be longer because of the time required to prepare ingredients in advance.

The wide range in dining hours and the need for fully staffed kitchens during all open hours create work opportunities for students, youth, and other individuals seeking supplemental income, flexible work hours, or variable schedules. Sixteen percent of cooks and food preparation workers were 16 to 19 years old in 2008 and another 18 percent were aged 20 to 24. Kitchen workers employed by schools may work during the school year only, usually for 9 or 10 months. Similarly, resort establishments usually only offer seasonal employment.

Training, Other Qualifications, and Advancement

On-the-job training is the most common method of learning for cooks and food preparation workers; however, restaurant cooks and other cooks who want to take on more advanced cooking duties often attend cooking school. Vocational training programs are available to many high school students and may lead to positions in restaurants. Experience, enthusiasm, and a desire to learn are the most common requirements for advancement to higher skilled cooking jobs or positions in higher paying restaurants.

Education and training. A high school diploma is not required for beginning jobs but is recommended for those planning a career in food services. Most fast food or short-order cooks and food preparation workers learn their skills on the job. Training generally starts with basic sanitation and workplace safety regulations and continues with instruction on food handling, preparation, and cooking procedures.

Although most cooks and food preparation workers learn on the job, students with an interest in food service may be able to take high school or vocational school courses in kitchen basics and food safety and handling procedures. Additional training opportunities are also offered by many state employment services agencies and local job counseling centers. For example, many school districts, in cooperation with state departments of education, provide on-the-job training and summer workshops for cafeteria kitchen workers who aspire to become cooks.

When hiring restaurant cooks, employers usually prefer applicants who have training after high school. These training programs range from a few months to 2 years or more. Vocational or trade-school programs typically offer basic training in food handling and sanitation procedures, nutrition, slicing and dicing methods for various kinds of meats and vegetables, and basic cooking techniques, such as baking, broiling, and grilling. Longer certificate or degree granting programs, through independent cooking schools, professional culinary institutes, or college degree programs, train cooks who aspire to more responsible positions in fine-dining or upscale restaurants. They offer a wider array of training specialties, such as advanced cooking techniques; cooking for banquets, buffets, or parties; and cuisines and cooking styles from around the world. Some large hotels, restaurants, and the Armed Forces operate their own training and job-placement programs.

Professional culinary institutes, industry associations, and trade unions may also sponsor formal apprenticeship programs for cooks in coordination with the U.S. Department of Labor. The American Culinary Federation accredits more than 200 formal academic training programs and sponsors apprenticeship programs around the country. Typical apprenticeships last 2 years and combine classroom training and work experience. Accreditation is an indication that a culinary program meets recognized standards regarding course content, facilities, and quality of instruction.

Other qualifications. Cooks and food preparation workers must be efficient, quick, and work well as part of a team. Manual dexterity is helpful for cutting, chopping, and plating. These workers also need creativity and a keen sense of taste and smell. Personal cleanliness is essential because most states require health certificates indicating that workers are free from communicable diseases. Knowledge of a foreign language can be an asset because it may improve communication with other restaurant staff, vendors, and the restaurant's clientele.

Certification and advancement. The American Culinary Federation certifies chefs in different skill levels. For cooks seeking certification and advancement to higher-level chef positions, certification can help to demonstrate accomplishment and lead to higher-paying positions.

Advancement opportunities for cooks and food preparation workers depend on their training, work experience, and ability to perform more responsible and sophisticated tasks. Many food preparation workers, for example, may move into assistant or line cook positions or take on more complex food preparation tasks. Cooks who demonstrate an eagerness to learn new cooking skills and to accept greater responsibility may also advance and be asked to train or supervise lesser skilled kitchen staff. Some may become head cooks, chefs, or food preparation and serving supervisors. (See the section on chefs, head cooks, and food preparation and serving supervisors is found elsewhere in this book.) Others may find it necessary to move to other restaurants, often larger or more prestigious ones, in order to advance.

Employment

Cooks and food preparation workers held 3.0 million jobs in 2008. The distribution of jobs among the various types of cooks and food preparation workers was as follows:

Cooks, restaurant	914,200
Food preparation workers	891,900
Cooks, fast food	566,000
Cooks, institution and cafeteria	391,800
Cooks, short order	171,400
Cooks, private household	4,900
Cooks, all other	18,000

Two-thirds of all cooks and food preparation workers were employed in restaurants and other food services and drinking places. About 16 percent worked in institutions such as schools, universities, hospitals, and nursing care facilities. Grocery stores and hotels employed most of the remainder.

Job Outlook

Job opportunities for cooks and food preparation workers are expected to be good because of high turnover and the need to replace the workers who leave these occupations. The enjoyment of eating out and a preference for ready-made meals from a growing population will cause employment of these workers to increase, but slower than the average rate for all occupations over the 2008–2018 decade.

Employment change. Employment of cooks and food preparation workers is expected to increase by 6 percent over the 2008–2018 decade, more slowly than the average for all occupations. People will continue to enjoy eating out and taking meals home. In response, more restaurants will open and nontraditional food service operations, such as those found inside grocery and convenience stores, will serve more prepared food items. Other places that have dining rooms and cafeterias—such as schools, hospitals, and residential care facilities for the elderly—will open new or expanded food service operations to meet the needs of their growing customer base.

Among food services and drinking places, special food services, which include caterers and food service operators who often provide meals in hospitals, office buildings, or sporting venues on a contract

Projections Data from the National Employment Matrix

Occupational title	SOC Code	Employment, 2008	Projected employment, 2018	Change, 2008–2018	
				Number	Percent
Cooks and food preparation workers 35-2000		2,958,100	3,149,600	191,500	6
Cooks 35-2010		2,066,200	2,220,000	153,800	7
Cooks, fast food 35-2011		566,000	608,400	42,400	7
Cooks, institution and cafeteria 35-2012		391,800	429,700	37,900	10
Cooks, private household 35-2013		4,900	5,100	200	4
Cooks, restaurant 35-2014		914,200	984,400	70,300	8
Cooks, short order 35-2015		171,400	171,500	100	0
Cooks, all other 35-2019		18,000	20,900	2,900	16
Food preparation workers 35-2021		891,900	929,600	37,800	4

NOTE: Data in this table are rounded.

basis, are expected to grow the fastest during the projection period. These companies typically employ large numbers of cafeteria and institution cooks and other cooks who perform cooking duties; employment in these occupations is expected to grow 10 percent (about as fast as the average) and 16 percent (faster than the average), respectively.

Full-service restaurants also will continue to attract patrons and grow in number, but not as fast as the previous decade. As restaurants increase their focus on the carryout business, cooks and food preparation workers will be needed to compete with limited service restaurants and grocery stores. Employment of restaurant cooks is expected to show average growth (8 percent).

Limited service eating places, such as fast food restaurants, sandwich and coffee shops, and other eating places without table service, also are expected to grow during the projection period, as people place greater emphasis on value, quick service, and carryout capability. This will generate greater demand for fast food cooks. Employment of fast food cooks is expected to increase by 7 percent (average growth).

Employment of private household cooks should grow 4 percent, or more slowly than the average for all occupations, and employment of short-order cooks is expected to grow by less than 1 percent, which represents little to no change.

Food preparation workers are expected to grow more slowly than the average for all occupations, or 4 percent. As restaurants and quick-service eating places find more efficient ways of preparing meals–such as at central kitchens that may serve multiple outlets or in wholesale and distribution facilities that wash, portion, and season ingredients—food preparation will become simpler, allowing these lower-skilled workers to take on more varied tasks in a growing number of eating places. Additionally, foods requiring simple preparation will increasingly be sold at convenience stores, snack shops, and in grocery stores, which also will employ food preparation workers.

Job prospects. In spite of slower-than-average employment growth, job opportunities for cooks and food preparation workers are expected to be good, primarily because of the very large number of workers that will need to be replaced because of high turnover. Because many of these jobs are part time, people often leave for full-time positions. Individuals seeking full-time positions at high-end restaurants might encounter competition as the number of job applicants exceeds the number of job openings. Generally, there is lower turnover for full-time jobs and at established restaurants that pay well.

Earnings

Earnings of cooks and food preparation workers vary greatly by region and the type of employer. Earnings usually are highest in fine-dining restaurants and nicer hotels that have more exacting work standards. These restaurants are usually found in greater numbers in major metropolitan and resort areas.

Median annual wages of cooks, private household were $24,700 in May 2009. The middle 50 percent earned between $19,410 and $31,110. The lowest 10 percent earned less than $16,720, and the highest 10 percent earned more than $42,880.

Median annual wages of institution and cafeteria cooks were $22,620 in May 2009. The middle 50 percent earned between $18,310 and $28,130. The lowest 10 percent earned less than $15,820, and the highest 10 percent earned more than $34,030. Median annual wages in the industries employing the largest numbers of institution and cafeteria cooks were as follows:

Elementary and secondary schools $21,040
Nursing care facilities 22,570
Special food services 23,860
General medical and surgical hospitals 25,620
Community care facilities for the elderly 23,150

Median annual wages of restaurant cooks were $22,170 in May 2009. The middle 50 percent earned between $18,430 and $26,590. The lowest 10 percent earned less than $16,140, and the highest 10 percent earned more than $31,770. Median annual wages in the industries employing the largest numbers of restaurant cooks were as follows:

Full-service restaurants $21,960
Traveler accommodation 26,250
Limited-service eating places 19,060
Other amusement and recreation industries 25,150
Drinking places (alcoholic beverages) 22,070
Special food services 24,310

Median annual wages of short-order cooks were $19,520 in May 2009. The middle 50 percent earned between $16,730 and $23,580. The lowest 10 percent earned less than $15,340, and the highest 10 percent earned more than $28,340. Median annual wages in the industries employing the largest numbers of short-order cooks were as follows:

Full-service restaurants $19,710
Limited-service eating places 18,620
Drinking places (alcoholic beverages)..................19,670
Other amusement and recreation industries...........19,040
Grocery stores..20,770

Median annual wages of food preparation workers were $19,020 in May 2009. The middle 50 percent earned between $16,680 and $22,970. The lowest 10 percent earned less than $15,380, and the highest 10 percent earned more than $28,280. Median annual wages in the industries employing the largest number of food preparation workers were as follows:

Full-service restaurants $18,920
Limited-service eating places 17,580
Grocery stores..19,920

Median annual wages of fast food cooks were $17,720 in May 2009. The middle 50 percent earned between $15,980 and $19,490. The lowest 10 percent earned less than $14,960, and the highest 10 percent earned more than $22,760. Median annual wages in the industries employing the largest number of fast food cooks were as follows:

Limited-service eating places 17,660
Full-service restaurants 17,860
Gasoline stations...17,370
Grocery stores..19,780

Some employers provide employees with uniforms and free meals, but federal law permits employers to deduct from their employees' wages the cost or fair value of any meals or lodging provided, and some employers do so. Cooks and food preparation workers who work full time often receive typical benefits, but part-time and hourly workers usually do not.

In some large hotels and restaurants, kitchen workers belong to unions. The principal unions are the Hotel Employees and Restaurant Employees International Union and the Service Employees International Union.

Related Occupations

Other occupations in the food service industry include bakers; butchers and meat cutters; chefs, head cooks, and food preparation and serving supervisors; food and beverage serving and related workers; and food service managers.

Sources of Additional Information

Information about job opportunities may be obtained from local employers and local offices of the state employment service.

Career information for cooks and other kitchen workers, including a directory of 2- and 4-year colleges that offer courses or training programs, is available from

▶ National Restaurant Association, 1200 17th St. NW, Washington, DC 20036. Internet: www.restaurant.org

Information on the American Culinary Federation's apprenticeship and certification programs for cooks and a list of accredited culinary programs is available from

▶ American Culinary Federation, 180 Center Place Way, St. Augustine, FL 32095. Internet: www.acfchefs.org

For information about culinary apprenticeship programs registered with the U.S. Department of Labor, contact the local office of your state employment service agency or check the department's apprenticeship website: www.doleta.gov/OA/eta_default.cfm, or call the toll-free helpline: (877) 872-5627.

Correctional Officers

(O*NET 33-1011.00, 33-3011.00, and 33-3012.00)

Significant Points

■ The work can be stressful and hazardous; correctional officers have one of the highest rates of nonfatal on-the-job injuries.

■ Most jobs are in state and local government prisons and jails.

■ Job opportunities are expected to be favorable.

Nature of the Work

Correctional officers, also known as *detention officers* when they work in pretrial detention facilities, are responsible for overseeing individuals who have been arrested and are awaiting trial or who have been convicted of a crime and sentenced to serve time in a jail, reformatory, or penitentiary.

The jail population changes constantly as some prisoners are released, some are convicted and transferred to prison, and new offenders are arrested and enter the system. Correctional officers in local jails admit and process about 13 million people a year, with nearly 800,000 offenders in jail at any given time. Correctional officers in state and federal prisons watch over the approximately 1.6 million offenders who are incarcerated there at any given time. Typically, offenders serving time at county jails are sentenced to a year or less. Those serving a year or more are usually housed in state or federal prisons.

Correctional officers maintain security and inmate accountability to prevent disturbances, assaults, and escapes. Officers have no law enforcement responsibilities outside of the institution where they work. (For more information on related occupations, see the statements on police and detectives elsewhere in this book.)

Regardless of the setting, correctional officers maintain order within the institution and enforce rules and regulations. To help ensure that inmates are orderly and obey rules, correctional officers monitor the activities and supervise the work assignments of inmates. Sometimes, officers must search inmates and their living quarters for contraband like weapons or drugs, settle disputes between inmates, and enforce discipline. Correctional officers periodically inspect the facilities, checking cells and other areas of the institution for unsanitary conditions, contraband, fire hazards, and any evidence of infractions of rules. In addition, they routinely inspect locks, window bars, grilles, doors, and gates for signs of tampering. Finally, officers inspect mail and visitors for prohibited items.

Correctional officers report orally and in writing on inmate conduct and on the quality and quantity of work done by inmates. Officers also report security breaches, disturbances, violations of rules, and any unusual occurrences. They usually keep a daily log or record of their activities. Correctional officers cannot show favoritism and must report any inmate who violates the rules. If a crime is committed within their institution or an inmate escapes, they help the responsible law enforcement authorities investigate or search for the escapee. In jail and prison facilities with direct supervision of cellblocks, officers work unarmed. They are equipped with communications devices so that they can summon help if necessary. These officers often work in a cellblock alone, or with another officer, among the 50 to 100 inmates who reside there. The officers enforce regulations primarily through their interpersonal communication skills and through the use of progressive sanctions, such as the removal of some privileges.

In the highest security facilities, where the most dangerous inmates are housed, correctional officers often monitor the activities of prisoners from a centralized control center with closed-circuit television cameras and a computer tracking system. In such an environment, the inmates may not see anyone but officers for days or weeks at a time and may leave their cells only for showers, solitary exercise time, or visitors. Depending on the offenders' security classification, correctional officers may have to restrain inmates in handcuffs and leg irons to safely escort them to and from cells and other areas and to see authorized visitors. Officers also escort prisoners between the institution and courtrooms, medical facilities, and other destinations.

Bailiffs, also known as *marshals* or *court officers*, are law enforcement officers who maintain safety and order in courtrooms. Their duties, which vary by location, include enforcing courtroom rules, assisting judges, guarding juries from outside contact, delivering court documents, and providing general security for courthouses.

Work environment. Working in a correctional institution can be stressful and hazardous. Every year, correctional officers are injured in confrontations with inmates. Correctional officers and jailers have one of the highest rates of nonfatal on-the-job injuries. First-line supervisors/managers of correctional officers also face the risk of work-related injury. Correctional officers may work indoors or outdoors. Some correctional institutions are well lighted, temperature controlled, and ventilated, but others are old, overcrowded, hot, and noisy. Although both jails and prisons can be dangerous places to work, prison populations are more stable than jail populations, and correctional officers in prisons know the security and custodial requirements of the prisoners with whom they are dealing. Consequently, they tend to be safer places to work.

Correctional officers usually work an 8-hour day, 5 days a week, on rotating shifts. Some correctional facilities have longer shifts and more days off between scheduled work weeks. Because prison and jail security must be provided around the clock, officers work all hours of the day and night, weekends, and holidays. In addition, officers may be required to work paid overtime.

Training, Other Qualifications, and Advancement

Correctional officers go through a training academy and then are assigned to a facility where they learn most of what they need to know for their work through on-the-job training. Qualifications vary by agency, but all agencies require a high school diploma or equivalent, and some also require some college education or full-time work experience. Military experience is often seen as a plus for corrections employment.

Education and training. A high school diploma or graduation equivalency degree is required by all employers. The Federal Bureau of Prisons requires entry-level correctional officers to have at least a bachelor's degree; three years of full-time experience in a

field providing counseling, assistance, or supervision to individuals; or a combination of the two. Some state and local corrections agencies require some college credits, but law enforcement or military experience may be substituted to fulfill this requirement.

Federal, state, and some local departments of corrections provide training for correctional officers based on guidelines established by the American Correctional Association and the American Jail Association. Some states have regional training academies that are available to local agencies. At the conclusion of formal instruction, all state and local correctional agencies provide on-the-job training, including training on legal restrictions and interpersonal relations. Many systems require firearms proficiency and self-defense skills. Officer trainees typically receive several weeks or months of training in an actual job setting under the supervision of an experienced officer. However, on-the-job training varies widely from agency to agency.

Academy trainees generally receive instruction in a number of subjects, including institutional policies, regulations, and operations, as well as custody and security procedures. New federal correctional officers must undergo 200 hours of formal training within the first year of employment. They also must complete 120 hours of specialized training at the U.S. Federal Bureau of Prisons residential training center at Glynco, Georgia, within 60 days of their appointment. Experienced officers receive annual in-service training to keep abreast of new developments and procedures.

Correctional officers that are members of prison tactical response teams are trained to respond to disturbances, riots, hostage situations, forced cell moves, and other potentially dangerous confrontations. Team members practice disarming prisoners wielding weapons, protecting themselves and inmates against the effects of chemical agents, and other tactics.

Other qualifications. All institutions require correctional officers to be at least 18 to 21 years of age, be a U.S. citizen or permanent resident, and have no felony convictions. New applicants for federal corrections positions must be appointed before they are 37 years old. Some institutions require previous experience in law enforcement or the military, but college credits can be substituted to fulfill this requirement. Others require a record of previous job stability; usually accomplished through 2 years of work experience, which need not be related to corrections or law enforcement.

Correctional officers must be in good health. Candidates for employment are generally required to meet formal standards of physical fitness, eyesight, and hearing. In addition, many jurisdictions use standard tests to determine applicant suitability to work in a correctional environment. Good judgment and the ability to think and act quickly are indispensable. Applicants are typically screened for drug abuse, subject to background checks, and required to pass a written examination.

Advancement. Qualified officers may advance to the position of correctional sergeant. Correctional sergeants supervise correctional officers and usually are responsible for maintaining security and directing the activities of other officers during an assigned shift or in an assigned area. Ambitious and qualified correctional officers can be promoted to supervisory or administrative positions all the way up to warden. In some jurisdictions, corrections officers are given the opportunity to "bid" for a specialty assignment, such as working in correctional industries, correctional health or correctional counseling, and receive additional training. Promotion prospects may be enhanced by attending college. Officers sometimes transfer

Projections Data from the National Employment Matrix

Occupational title	SOC Code	Employment, 2008	Projected employment, 2018	Change, 2008–2018	
				Number	Percent
Correctional officers .... —		518,200	566,500	48,300	9
First-line supervisors/managers of correctional officers...33-1011		43,500	47,200	3,700	9
Bailiffs, correctional officers, and jailers...............33-3010		474,800	519,400	44,600	9
Bailiffs...33-3011		20,200	21,900	1,700	8
Correctional officers and jailers........................33-3012		454,500	497,500	42,900	9

NOTE: Data in this table are rounded.

to related jobs, such as probation officer, parole officer, and correctional treatment specialist.

Employment

Correctional officers and jailers held about 454,500 jobs in 2008, while first-line supervisors and managers of correctional officers held about 43,500 jobs. An additional 20,200 workers were employed as bailiffs. The vast majority of correctional officers and jailers and their supervisors were employed by state and local government in correctional institutions such as prisons, prison camps, and youth correctional facilities.

Job Outlook

Employment growth is expected to be as fast as the average for all occupations, and job opportunities are expected to be favorable.

Employment change. Employment of correctional officers is expected to grow 9 percent between 2008 and 2018, about as fast as the average for all occupations. Increasing demand for correctional officers will stem from population growth and rising rates of incarceration. Mandatory sentencing guidelines calling for longer sentences and reduced parole for inmates are a primary reason for increasing incarceration rates. Some states are reconsidering mandatory sentencing guidelines because of budgetary constraints, court decisions, and doubts about their effectiveness. Some employment opportunities also will arise in the private sector, as public authorities contract with private companies to provide and staff corrections facilities. Both state and federal corrections agencies are increasingly using private prisons.

Job prospects. Job opportunities for correctional officers are expected to be favorable. The need to replace correctional officers who transfer to other occupations, retire, or leave the labor force, coupled with rising employment demand, will generate job openings. In the past, some local and state corrections agencies have experienced difficulty in attracting and keeping qualified applicants, largely because of low salaries, shift work, and the concentration of jobs in rural locations. This situation is expected to continue.

Earnings

Median annual wages of correctional officers and jailers were $39,050 in May 2009. The middle 50 percent earned between $31,210 and $52,240. The lowest 10 percent earned less than $25,960, and the highest 10 percent earned more than $64,850. Median annual wages in the public sector were $53,360 in the federal government, $39,100 in state government, and $38,810 in local government. In the facilities support services industry, where the

relatively small number of officers employed by privately operated prisons is classified, median annual wages were $28,660.

Median annual wages of first-line supervisors/managers of correctional officers were $57,690 in May 2009. The middle 50 percent earned between $42,870 and $73,500. The lowest 10 percent earned less than $34,640, and the highest 10 percent earned more than $90,140. Median annual wages were $57,030 in state government and $57,310 in local government.

Median annual wages of bailiffs were $37,950 in May 2009. The middle 50 percent earned between $26,740 and $53,730. The lowest 10 percent earned less than $18,340, and the highest 10 percent earned more than $66,210. Median annual wages were $34,080 in local government.

In March 2009, the average salary for federal correctional officers was $53,459. Federal salaries were slightly higher in areas where prevailing local pay levels were higher.

In addition to typical benefits, correctional officers employed in the public sector are usually provided with uniforms or a clothing allowance to purchase their own uniforms. Civil service systems or merit boards cover officers employed by the federal government and most state governments. Their retirement coverage entitles correctional officers to retire at age 50 after 20 years of service or at any age with 25 years of service. Unionized correctional officers often have slightly higher wages and benefits.

Related Occupations

Other protective service occupations include police and detectives; probation officers and correctional treatment specialists; and security guards and gaming surveillance officers.

Sources of Additional Information

Further information about correctional officers is available from

▸ American Correctional Association, 206 N. Washington St., Suite 200, Alexandria, VA 22314. Internet: www.aca.org

▸ American Jail Association, 1135 Professional Ct., Hagerstown, MD 21740. Internet: www.corrections.com/aja

▸ Information on entrance requirements, training, and career opportunities for correctional officers at the federal level may be obtained from the Federal Bureau of Prisons. Internet: www.bop.gov

Information on obtaining a position as a correctional officer with the federal government is available from the Office of Personnel Management through USAJOBS, the federal government's official employment information system. This resource for locating and applying for job opportunities can be accessed through the Internet at www.usajobs.opm.gov or through an interactive voice response telephone system at (703) 724-1850 or TDD (978) 461-8404. These numbers are not toll free, so charges may result.

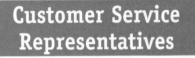

Customer Service Representatives

(O*NET 43-4051.00 and 43-4051.03)

Significant Points

■ Customer service representatives held about 2.3 million jobs in 2008, ranking among the largest occupations.

■ Most companies require a high school diploma and will provide job training.

■ Employment is projected to grow faster than average, and job prospects should be good.

Nature of the Work

Customer service representatives provide a valuable link between customers and the companies who produce the products they buy and the services they use. They are responsible for responding to customer inquiries and making sure that any problems they are experiencing are resolved. Although most customer service representatives do their work by telephone in call centers, some interact with customers by e-mail, fax, post, or face-to-face.

Many customer service inquiries involve simple questions or requests. For instance, a customer may want to know the status of an order or wish to change his or her address in the company's file. However, some questions may be somewhat more difficult, and may require additional research or help from an expert. In some cases, a representative's main function may be to determine who in the organization is best suited to answer a customer's questions.

Some customer inquiries are complaints, which generally must be handled in accordance with strict company policies. In some cases, representatives may try to fix problems or suggest solutions. They may have the authority to reverse erroneous fees or send replacement products. Other representatives act as gatekeepers who make sure that complaints are valid before accepting customer returns.

Although selling products and services is not the primary function of a customer service representative, some customer service representatives may provide information that helps customers to make purchasing decisions. For instance, a representative may point out a product or service that would fulfill a customer's needs. (For information on workers whose primary function is sales, see the statement on retail salespersons elsewhere in this book.)

Customer service representatives use computers, telephones, and other technology extensively in their work. When the customer has an account with the company, a representative will usually open his or her file in the company's computer system. Representatives use this information to solve problems and may be able to make specific changes as necessary. They also have access to responses for the most commonly asked questions and specific guidelines for dealing with requests or complaints. In the event that the representative does not know the answer or is unable to solve a specific problem, a supervisor or other experienced worker may provide assistance.

Many customer service workers are located in call centers, where they spend the entire day speaking on the telephone. Companies usually keep statistics on their workers to make sure they are working efficiently. This helps them to keep up with their call volume and ensures that customers do not have to wait on hold for extended periods of time. Supervisors may listen in on or tape calls to ensure customers are getting quality service.

Almost every industry employs customer service representatives, and their duties may vary greatly depending on the nature of the organization. For instance, representatives who work in banks may have similar duties to tellers, whereas those in insurance companies may be required to handle paperwork, such as changes to policies or renewals. Those who work for utility and communication companies may assist customers with service problems, such as outages. Representatives who work in retail stores often handle returns and help customers to find items in their stores.

Work environment. Although customer service representatives work in a variety of settings, most work in areas that are clean and well lit. Those who work in call centers generally have their own workstations or cubicle spaces equipped with telephones, headsets, and computers. Because many call centers are open extended hours or are staffed around the clock, these positions may require workers to take on early morning, evening, or late night shifts. Weekend or holiday work is also common. Because peak times may not last for a full shift, many workers are part-time or work a split shift. As a result, the occupation is well suited to flexible work schedules. Many companies hire additional employees at certain times of year when higher call volumes are expected.

Call centers may be crowded and noisy, and work may be repetitive and stressful, with little time between calls. Also, long periods spent sitting, typing, or looking at a computer screen may cause eye and muscle strain, backaches, headaches, and repetitive motion injuries. A growing number of employers are hiring telecommuters, who provide customer service from their own homes. Although this remains somewhat rare, it can be a major advantage for workers who need to remain in their homes during the day.

Customer service representatives working in retail stores may have customers approach them in person or contact them by telephone. They may be required to work later in the evenings or on weekends, as stores are generally open during those times. Evenings and weekends tend to be peak hours for customer traffic.

Customer service representatives may have to deal with difficult or irate customers, which can be challenging. However, the ability to resolve customers' problems has the potential to be very rewarding.

Training, Other Qualifications, and Advancement

Most jobs require at least a high school diploma. Employers provide training to workers before they begin serving customers.

Education and training. Most customer service representative jobs require a high school diploma. However, because employers are demanding a more skilled workforce, some customer service jobs now require associate or bachelor's degrees. High school and college-level courses in computers, English, or business are helpful in preparing for a job in customer service.

Training requirements vary by industry. Almost all customer service representatives are provided with some training prior to beginning work. This training generally focuses on the company and its products, the most commonly asked questions, the computer and telephone systems they will be using, and basic people skills. Length of training varies, but often lasts several weeks. Some customer service representatives are expected to update their training regularly. This is particularly true of workers in industries such as banking, in which regulations and products are continually changing.

Other qualifications. Because customer service representatives constantly interact with the public, good communication and problem-solving skills are essential. Verbal communication and listening skills are especially important. Companies prefer to hire individuals who have a pleasant speaking voice and are easy to understand. For workers who communicate through e-mail, good typing, spelling, and grammar skills are necessary. Basic to intermediate computer knowledge and good interpersonal skills are also important.

Customer service representatives play a critical role in providing an interface between customers and companies. As a result, employers seek out people who are friendly and possess a professional manner. The ability to deal patiently with problems and complaints and to remain courteous when faced with difficult or angry people is critical. Also, a customer service representative often must be able to work independently within specified time constraints.

Advancement. Customer service jobs are often good introductory positions into a company or an industry. In some cases, experienced workers can move into supervisory or managerial positions or they may move into areas such as product development, in which they can use their knowledge to improve products and services. Some people work in call centers with the hope of transferring to a position in another department.

Employment

Customer service representatives held about 2.3 million jobs in 2008, ranking among the largest occupations. They can be found in almost every industry, although about 23 percent worked in the finance and insurance industry. Another 15 percent worked in the administrative and support services industry, which includes third-party telephone call centers.

Job Outlook

Customer service representatives are expected to experience faster than average growth. Furthermore, job prospects should be good as many workers who leave this very large occupation will need to be replaced.

Employment change. Employment of customer service representatives is expected to grow by about 18 percent over the 2008–2018 period, faster than the average for all occupations. Providing quality customer service is important to nearly every company in the economy; in addition, companies are expected to place increasing

emphasis on customer relationships, resulting in increased demand for customer service representatives. This very large occupation is projected to provide about 400,000 new jobs over the next decade.

Customer service representatives are especially prevalent in the finance and insurance industry, as many customer interactions do not require physical contact. Employment of customer service representatives in this industry is expected to increase 9 percent over the 2008–2018 period.

Although technology has tempered growth of this occupation to some degree, it has also created many opportunities for growth. For instance, online banking has reduced the need for telephone banking services. At the same time, however, it has increased the need for customer service representatives who assist users with banking websites. Additionally, online services create many new opportunities for customer support representatives as companies that operate on the Internet provide customer service by telephone.

In the past, many companies chose to relocate their customer service call centers in foreign countries, which led to layoffs in some industries. Although many companies continue to offshore some of their customer service jobs, this is becoming less prevalent than in the past. While it continues to be less expensive to hire workers overseas, many companies have found that foreign workers do not have the same cultural sensitivity as those located within the United States.

Job prospects. Prospects for obtaining a job in this field are expected to be good, with more job openings than job seekers. In particular, bilingual job seekers should enjoy excellent opportunities. Rapid job growth, coupled with a large number of workers who leave the occupation each year, should make finding a job as a customer service representative relatively easy.

While jobs in some industries may be affected by economic downturns, customer service representatives are not as vulnerable to layoffs as some other workers. This is, in part, because many customer service representatives work in industries where customers have accounts. While customers may have less money to spend, and as a result may choose to purchase fewer goods or services, they continue to have customer service needs. For instance, during an economic downturn, individuals may have less money in their bank accounts, but they continue to need banking services and customer service from their banks. Nevertheless, companies do attempt to cut costs during such times, so downsizing is still a possibility.

Earnings

In May 2009, median hourly wages of customer service representatives were $14.56. The middle 50 percent earned between $11.53 and $18.50. The lowest 10 percent earned less than $9.33, and the highest 10 percent earned more than $23.57.

Earnings for customer service representatives vary according to level of skill required, experience, training, location, and size of

Projections Data from the National Employment Matrix

Occupational title	SOC Code	Employment, 2008	Projected employment, 2018	Change, 2008–2018	
				Number	Percent
Customer service representatives.............................43-4051		2,252,400	2,651,900	399,500	18

NOTE: Data in this table are rounded.

firm. Median hourly wages in the industries employing the largest numbers of these workers in May 2009 were as follows:

Business support services	$11.73
Insurance carriers	16.11
Depository credit intermediation	14.71
Agencies, brokerages, and other insurance-related activities	15.73
Employment services	13.31

In addition to receiving an hourly wage, full-time customer service representatives who work evenings, nights, weekends, or holidays may receive shift differential pay. Also, because call centers are often open during extended hours, or even 24 hours a day, some customer service representatives have the benefit of being able to work a schedule that does not conform to the traditional workweek. Other benefits can include life and health insurance, pensions, bonuses, employer-provided training, and discounts on the products and services the company offers.

Related Occupations

Customer service representatives interact with customers to provide information in response to inquiries about products and services and to handle and resolve complaints. Other occupations in which workers have similar dealings with customers and the public include bill and account collectors; computer support specialists; insurance sales agents; retail salespersons; securities, commodities, and financial services sales agents; and tellers.

Sources of Additional Information

For more information on customer service positions, contact your state employment office or

▸ International Customer Service Association. 24 Wernik Pl., Metuchen, NJ 08840. Internet: www.icsatoday.org

Dental Assistants

(O*NET 31-9091.00)

Significant Points

■ Job prospects should be excellent.

■ Dentists are expected to hire more assistants to perform routine tasks so dentists may devote their time to more complex procedures.

■ Many assistants learn their skills on the job, although an increasing number are trained in dental-assisting programs; most programs take one year or less to complete.

■ More than one-third of dental assistants worked part time in 2008.

Nature of the Work

Dental assistants perform a variety of patient care, office, and laboratory duties. They sterilize and disinfect instruments and equipment, prepare and lay out the instruments and materials required to treat each patient, and obtain and update patients' dental records. Assistants make patients comfortable in the dental chair and prepare them for treatment. During dental procedures, assistants work alongside the dentist to provide assistance. They hand instruments

and materials to dentists and keep patients' mouths dry and clear by using suction hoses or other devices. They also instruct patients on postoperative and general oral health care.

Dental assistants may prepare materials for impressions and restorations, and process dental X-rays as directed by a dentist. They also may remove sutures, apply topical anesthetics to gums or cavity-preventive agents to teeth, remove excess cement used in the filling process, and place dental dams to isolate teeth for treatment. Many states are expanding dental assistants' duties to include tasks such as coronal polishing and restorative dentistry functions for those assistants who meet specific training and experience requirements.

Dental assistants with laboratory duties make casts of the teeth and mouth from impressions, clean and polish removable appliances, and make temporary crowns. Those with office duties schedule and confirm appointments, receive patients, keep treatment records, send bills, receive payments, and order dental supplies and materials.

Dental assistants must work closely with, and under the supervision of, dentists. Additionally, dental assistants should not be confused with dental hygienists, who are licensed to perform a different set of clinical tasks. (See the statement on dental hygienists elsewhere in this book.)

Work environment. Dental assistants work in a well-lighted, clean environment. Their work area is usually near the dental chair so that they can arrange instruments, materials, and medication and hand them to the dentist when needed. Dental assistants must wear gloves, masks, eyewear, and protective clothing to protect themselves and their patients from infectious diseases. Assistants also follow safety procedures to minimize the risks associated with the use of X-ray machines.

Almost half of dental assistants had a 35- to 40-hour workweek in 2008. More than one-third worked part time, or less than 35 hours per week, and many others have variable schedules. Depending on the hours of the dental office where they work, assistants may have to work on Saturdays or evenings. Some dental assistants hold multiple jobs by working at dental offices that are open on different days or by scheduling their work at a second office around the hours they work at their primary office.

Training, Other Qualifications, and Advancement

Many assistants learn their skills on the job, although an increasing number are trained in dental-assisting programs offered by community and junior colleges, trade schools, technical institutes, or the Armed Forces. Most programs take 1 year to complete. For assistants to perform more advanced functions, or to have the ability to complete radiological procedures, many states require assistants to obtain a license or certification.

Education and training. In most states, there are no formal education or training requirements to become an entry-level dental assistant. High school students interested in a career as a dental assistant should take courses in biology, chemistry, health, and office practices. For those wishing to pursue further education, the Commission on Dental Accreditation (CODA) approved 281 dental-assisting training programs in 2009. Programs include classroom, laboratory, and preclinical instruction in dental-assisting skills and related theory. Most programs take close to 1 year to complete and lead to a certificate or diploma. Two-year programs offered in community and junior colleges lead to an associate degree. All programs

Projections Data from the National Employment Matrix

Occupational title	SOC Code	Employment, 2008	Projected employment, 2018	Change, 2008–2018	
				Number	Percent
Dental assistants	31-9091	295,300	400,900	105,600	36

NOTE: Data in this table are rounded.

require a high school diploma or its equivalent, and some require science or computer-related courses for admission. A number of private vocational schools offer 4- to 6-month courses in dental assisting, but the Commission on Dental Accreditation does not accredit these programs.

A large number of dental assistants learn through on-the-job training. In these situations, the employing dentist or other dental assistants in the dental office teach the new assistant dental terminology, the names of the instruments, how to perform daily duties, how to interact with patients, and other things necessary to help keep the dental office running smoothly. While some things can be picked up easily, it may be a few months before new dental assistants are completely knowledgeable about their duties and comfortable doing all their tasks without assistance.

A period of on-the-job training is often required even for those who have completed a dental-assisting program or have some previous experience. Different dentists may have their own styles of doing things that need to be learned before an assistant can be comfortable working with them. Office-specific information, such as where files and instruments are kept, will need to be learned at each new job. Also, as dental technology changes, dental assistants need to stay familiar with the instruments and procedures that they will be using or helping dentists to use. On-the-job training may be sufficient to keep assistants up to date on these matters.

Licensure and certification. Most states regulate the duties that dental assistants are allowed to perform. Some states require licensure or registration to perform expanded functions or to perform radiological procedures within a dentist's office. Licensure may include attending an accredited dental assisting program and passing a written or practical examination. Many states also require continuing education to maintain licensure or registration. However, a few states allow dental assistants to perform any function delegated to them by the dentist. Since requirements vary widely by state, it is recommended to contact the appropriate state board directly for specific requirements.

The Certified Dental Assistant (CDA) credential, administered by the Dental Assisting National Board (DANB), is recognized or required in more than 37 states toward meeting various requirements. Candidates may qualify to take the DANB certification examination by graduating from a CODA-accredited dental assisting education program or by having 2 years of full-time, or 4 years of part-time, experience as a dental assistant. In addition, applicants must have current certification in cardiopulmonary resuscitation. For annual recertification, individuals must earn continuing education credits. Other organizations offer registration, most often at the state level.

Individual states have also adopted different standards for dental assistants who perform certain advanced duties. In some states, dental assistants who perform radiological procedures must complete additional training distinct from that required to perform other expanded functions. Completion of the Radiation Health and Safety examination or the Certified Dental Assistant examination offered

by Dental Assisting National Board (DANB) meets the standards in 30 states and the District of Columbia. Some states require completion of a state-approved course in radiology as well. Twelve states have no formal requirements to perform radiological procedures.

Other qualifications. Dental assistants must be a second pair of hands for a dentist; therefore, dentists look for people who are reliable, work well with others, and have good manual dexterity.

Certification and advancement. Without further education, advancement opportunities are limited. Some dental assistants become office managers, dental-assisting instructors, dental product sales representatives, or insurance claims processors for dental insurance companies. Others go back to school to become dental hygienists. For many, this entry-level occupation provides basic training and experience and serves as a steppingstone to more highly skilled and higher-paying jobs. Assistants wishing to take on expanded functions or perform radiological procedures may choose to complete coursework in those functions allowed under state regulation or, if required, obtain a state-issued license.

Employment

Dental assistants held about 295,300 jobs in 2008. About 93 percent of all jobs for dental assistants were in offices of dentists. A small number of jobs were in the federal, state, and local governments or in offices of physicians.

Job Outlook

Employment is expected to increase much faster than average; job prospects are expected to be excellent.

Employment change. Employment is expected to grow 36 percent from 2008 to 2018, which is much faster than the average for all occupations. In fact, dental assistants are expected to be among the fastest growing occupations over the 2008–2018 projection period. Population growth, greater retention of natural teeth by middle-aged and older people, and an increased focus on preventative dental care for younger generations will fuel demand for dental services. Older dentists, who have been less likely to employ assistants or have employed fewer, are leaving the occupation and will be replaced by recent graduates, who are more likely to use one or more assistants. In addition, as dentists' workloads increase, they are expected to hire more assistants to perform routine tasks, so that they may devote their own time to more complex procedures.

Job prospects. Job prospects should be excellent, as dentists continue to need the aid of qualified dental assistants. There will be many opportunities for entry-level positions, but some dentists prefer to hire experienced assistants, those who have completed a dental-assisting program, or have met state requirements to take on expanded functions within the office.

In addition to job openings due to employment growth, some job openings will arise out of the need to replace assistants who transfer to other occupations, retire, or leave for other reasons.

Earnings

Median annual wages of dental assistants were $33,230 in May 2009. The middle 50 percent earned between $27,520 and $39,780. The lowest 10 percent earned less than $22,710, and the highest 10 percent earned more than $47,070.

Benefits vary substantially by practice setting and may be contingent upon full-time employment. According to a 2008 survey conducted by the Dental Assisting National Board (DANB), 86 percent of Certified Dental Assistants (CDA) reported receiving paid vacation from their employers, and more than half of CDAs received health benefits.

Related Occupations

Other workers support health practitioners, including dental hygienists; medical assistants; occupational therapist assistants and aides; pharmacy technicians and aides; physical therapist assistants and aides; and surgical technologists.

Sources of Additional Information

Information about career opportunities and accredited dental assistant programs is available from

▸ Commission on Dental Accreditation, American Dental Association, 211 E. Chicago Ave., Suite 1900, Chicago, IL 60611. Internet: www.ada.org/prof/ed/accred/commission/index.asp

For information on becoming a Certified Dental Assistant and a list of state boards of dentistry, contact

▸ Dental Assisting National Board, Inc., 444 N. Michigan Ave., Suite 900, Chicago, IL 60611. Internet: www.danb.org

For more information on a career as a dental assistant and general information about continuing education, contact

▸ American Dental Assistants Association, 35 E. Wacker Dr., Suite 1730, Chicago, IL 60601. Internet: www.dentalassistant.org

Dental Hygienists

(O*NET 29-2021.00)

Significant Points

■ A degree from an accredited dental hygiene school and a state license are required for this job.

■ Dental hygienists rank among the fastest-growing occupations.

■ Job prospects are expected to be favorable in most areas, but strong competition for jobs is likely in some areas.

■ About half of all dental hygienists work part time, and flexible scheduling is a distinctive feature of this job.

Nature of the Work

Dental hygienists remove soft and hard deposits from teeth, teach patients how to practice good oral hygiene, and provide other preventive dental care. They examine patients' teeth and gums, recording the presence of diseases or abnormalities.

Dental hygienists use an assortment of tools to complete their tasks. Hand and rotary instruments and ultrasonic devices are used to clean and polish teeth, which includes removing tartar, stains, and plaque. Hygienists use X-ray machines to take dental pictures, and some-times develop the film. They may use models of teeth to explain oral hygiene, perform root planning as a periodontal therapy, or apply cavity-preventative agents such as fluorides and pit and fissure sealants.

Other tasks hygienists may perform vary by state. In some states, hygienists are allowed to administer anesthetics, while in others they administer local anesthetics using syringes. Some states also allow hygienists to place and carve filling materials, temporary fillings, and periodontal dressings; remove sutures; and smooth and polish metal restorations.

Dental hygienists also help patients develop and maintain good oral health. For example, they may explain the relationship between diet and oral health or inform patients how to select toothbrushes and show them how to brush and floss their teeth.

Hygienists sometimes make a diagnosis and other times prepare clinical and laboratory diagnostic tests for the dentist to interpret. Hygienists sometimes work chair-side with the dentist during treatment.

Work environment. Dental hygienists work in clean, well-lighted offices. Important health safeguards include strict adherence to proper radiological procedures and the use of appropriate protective devices when administering anesthetic gas. Dental hygienists also wear safety glasses, surgical masks, and gloves to protect themselves and patients from infectious diseases. Dental hygienists also should be careful to avoid possible shoulder and neck injury from sitting for long periods of time while working with patients.

Flexible scheduling is a distinctive feature of this job. Full-time, part-time, evening, and weekend schedules are common. Dentists frequently hire hygienists to work only 2 or 3 days a week, so hygienists may hold jobs in more than one dental office. In 2008, about half of all dental hygienists worked part time—less than 35 hours a week.

Training, Other Qualifications, and Advancement

A degree from an accredited dental hygiene school and a state license are required for this job.

Education and training. A high school diploma and college entrance test scores are usually required for admission to a dental hygiene program. High school students interested in becoming dental hygienists should take courses in biology, chemistry, and mathematics. Some dental hygiene programs also require applicants to have completed at least one year of college. Specific entrance requirements typically vary from one school to another.

In 2008, there were 301 dental hygiene programs accredited by the Commission on Dental Accreditation. Most dental hygiene programs grant an associate degree, although some also offer a certificate, a bachelor's degree, or a master's degree. A minimum of an associate degree or certificate in dental hygiene is generally required for practice in a private dental office. A bachelor's or master's degree usually is required for research, teaching, or clinical practice in public or school health programs.

Schools offer laboratory, clinical, and classroom instruction in subjects such as anatomy, physiology, chemistry, microbiology, pharmacology, nutrition, radiography, histology (the study of tissue structure), periodontology (the study of gum diseases), pathology, dental materials, clinical dental hygiene, and social and behavioral sciences.

Projections Data from the National Employment Matrix

Occupational title	SOC Code	Employment, 2008	Projected employment, 2018	Change, 2008–2018	
				Number	Percent
Dental hygienists..	29-2021	174,100	237,000	62,900	36

NOTE: Data in this table are rounded.

Licensure. Dental hygienists must be licensed by the state in which they practice. Nearly all states require candidates to graduate from an accredited dental hygiene school and pass both a written and clinical examination. The American Dental Association's (ADA) Joint Commission on National Dental Examinations administers the written examination, which is accepted by all states and the District of Columbia. State or regional testing agencies administer the clinical examination. In addition, most states require an examination on the legal aspects of dental hygiene practice. Alabama is the only state that does not require candidates to take the ADA written exam. Instead, they require that candidates meet the requirements of the Alabama Dental Hygiene Program, which mandates taking courses, completing on-the-job training at a dentist's office, and passing a separate state administered licensing examination.

Other qualifications. Dental hygienists should work well with others because they work closely with dentists and dental assistants, as well as dealing directly with patients. Hygienists also need good manual dexterity, because they use dental instruments within patients' mouths, with little room for error.

Advancement. Advancement opportunities usually come from working outside a typical dentist's office, and usually require a bachelor's or master's degree in dental hygiene. Some dental hygienists may choose to pursue a career teaching at a dental hygiene program, working in public health, or working in a corporate setting.

Employment

Dental hygienists held about 174,100 jobs in 2008. Because multiple job holding is common in this field, the number of jobs exceeds the number of hygienists. About 51 percent of dental hygienists worked part time. Almost all jobs for dental hygienists—about 96 percent—were in offices of dentists. A very small number worked for employment services, in physicians' offices, or in other industries.

Job Outlook

Dental hygienists rank among the fastest growing occupations. Job prospects are expected to be favorable in most areas, but competition for jobs is likely in some areas.

Employment change. Employment of dental hygienists is expected to grow 36 percent through 2018, which is much faster than the average for all occupations. This projected growth ranks dental hygienists among the fastest growing occupations, in response to increasing demand for dental care and more use of hygienists.

The demand for dental services will grow because of population growth, older people increasingly retaining more teeth, and a growing emphasis on preventative dental care. To help meet this demand, facilities that provide dental care, particularly dentists' offices, will increasingly employ dental hygienists, often to perform services that have been performed by dentists in the past. Ongoing research indicating a link between oral health and general health also will spur the demand for preventative dental services, which are typically provided by dental hygienists.

Job prospects. Job prospects are expected to be favorable in most areas, but will vary by geographical location. Because graduates are permitted to practice only in the state in which they are licensed, hygienists wishing to practice in areas that have an abundance of dental hygiene programs may experience strong competition for jobs.

Older dentists, who have been less likely to employ dental hygienists, are leaving the occupation and will be replaced by recent graduates, who are more likely to employ one or more hygienists. In addition, as dentists' workloads increase, they are expected to hire more hygienists to perform preventive dental care, such as cleaning, so that they may devote their own time to more complex procedures.

Earnings

Median annual wages of dental hygienists were $67,340 in May 2009. The middle 50 percent earned between $55,620 and $79,990. The lowest 10 percent earned less than $44,900, and the highest 10 percent earned more than $92,860.

Earnings vary by geographic location, employment setting, and years of experience. Dental hygienists may be paid on an hourly, daily, salary, or commission basis.

Benefits vary substantially by practice setting and may be contingent upon full-time employment. According to a 2009 survey conducted by the American Dental Hygienist Association, about half of all hygienists reported receiving some form of employment benefits. Of those receiving benefits, paid vacation, sick leave, and retirement plans were the most common.

Related Occupations

Other workers supporting health practitioners in an office setting include dental assistants; medical assistants; occupational therapist assistants and aides; physical therapist assistants and aides; physician assistants; and registered nurses.

Others who work with radiation technology include radiation therapists.

Sources of Additional Information

For information on a career in dental hygiene, including educational requirements, and on available accredited programs, contact

▸ American Dental Hygienists Association, 444 N. Michigan Ave., Suite 3400, Chicago, IL 60611. Internet: www.adha.org

For information about accredited programs and educational requirements, contact

▸ Commission on Dental Accreditation, American Dental Association, 211 E. Chicago Ave., Chicago, IL 60611. Internet: www.ada.org/prof/ed/accred/commission/index.asp

The State Board of Dental Examiners in each state can supply information on licensing requirements.

Desktop Publishers

(O*NET 43-3021.00, 43-3021.01, 43-3021.02, and 43-3021.03)

Significant Points

■ About 38 percent work for newspaper, periodical, book, and directory publishers; another 21 percent work in the printing industry.

■ Employment is expected to decline rapidly.

■ Most employers prefer to hire experienced desktop publishers; among persons without experience, opportunities should be best for those with certificates or degrees in desktop publishing or graphic design.

Nature of the Work

Desktop publishers use computer software to format and combine text, data, photographs, charts, and other graphic art or illustrations into prototypes of pages and other documents that are to be printed. They then may print the document on a high-resolution printer or send the materials to a commercial printer. Examples of materials produced by desktop publishers include books, brochures, calendars, magazines, newsletters, newspapers, and forms.

Desktop publishers typically design and create the graphics that accompany text, find and edit photographs and other digital images, and manipulate the text and images to display information in an attractive and readable format. They design page layouts, develop presentations and advertising campaigns, and do color separation of pictures and graphics material. Some desktop publishers may write some of the text or headlines used in newsletters or brochures.

Desktop publishers use the appropriate software to enter and select formatting properties, such as the size and style of type, column width, and spacing. Print formats are stored in the computer and displayed on its monitor. New information, such as charts, pictures, or more text, can be added. An entire newspaper, catalog, or book page, complete with artwork and graphics, can be created on the screen exactly as it will appear in print. Then, digital files are used to produce printing plates. Like photographers and multimedia artists and animators, desktop publishers can create special effects or other visual images with the use of film, video, computers, or other electronic media. (Separate statements on photographers and on artists and related workers appear elsewhere in this book.)

Computer software and printing technology continue to advance, making desktop publishing more economical and efficient than before. Other innovations in the occupation include digital color page-makeup systems, electronic page-layout systems, and off-press color proofing systems. In addition, most materials are reproduced on the Internet as well as printed; therefore, desktop publishers may need to know electronic publishing software, such as Hypertext Markup Language (HTML), and may be responsible for converting text and graphics to an Internet-ready format.

Some desktop publishers may write and edit, as well as lay out and design pages. For example, in addition to laying out articles for a newsletter, desktop publishers may be responsible for copyediting content or for writing original content themselves. Desktop publishers' writing and editing responsibilities may vary widely from project to project and employer to employer. Smaller firms typically use desktop publishers to perform a wide range of tasks, while desktop publishers at larger firms may specialize in a certain part of the publishing process.

Desktop publishers also may be called publications specialists, electronic publishers, DTP operators, desktop publishing editors, electronic prepress technicians, electronic publishing specialists, image designers, typographers, compositors, layout artists, and Web publications designers. The exact name may vary with the specific tasks performed or simply by personal preference.

Work environment. Desktop publishers usually work in clean, air-conditioned office areas with little noise. They generally work a standard workweek; however, some may work night shifts, weekends, or holidays, depending upon the production schedule for the project or to meet deadlines.

These workers often are subject to stress and the pressures of short deadlines and tight work schedules. Like other workers who spend long hours working in front of a computer monitor, desktop publishers may be susceptible to eyestrain, back discomfort, and hand and wrist problems.

Training, Other Qualifications, and Advancement

Most desktop publishers learn their skills on the job. Experience is the best training, and many desktop publishers get started just by experimenting with the software and developing a knack for designing and laying out material for publication.

Education and training. There is generally no educational requirement for the job of desktop publisher. Most people learn on the job or by taking classes online or through local learning centers that teach the latest software. For those who are interested in pursuing a career in desktop publishing, an associate degree or a bachelor's degree in graphic arts, graphic communications, or graphic design is preferred. Graphic arts programs are a good way to learn about the desktop publishing software used to format pages, assign type characteristics, and import text and graphics into electronic page layouts. Courses in other aspects of printing also are available at vocational institutes and private trade and technical schools.

Other qualifications. Although formal training is not always required, those with certificates or degrees will have the best job opportunities. Most employers prefer to hire people who have at least a high school diploma and who possess good communication abilities, basic computer skills, and a strong work ethic. Desktop publishers should be able to deal courteously with people, because they have to interact with customers and clients and be able to express design concepts and layout options with them. In addition, they may have to do simple math calculations and compute ratios to scale graphics and artwork and estimate job costs. A basic understanding of, and facility with, computers, printers, scanners, and other office equipment and technologies also is needed to work as a desktop publisher.

Desktop publishers need good manual dexterity, and they must be able to pay attention to detail and work independently. In addition, good eyesight, including visual acuity, depth perception, a wide field of view, color vision, and the ability to focus quickly, are assets. Artistic ability often is a plus. Employers also seek persons who are even tempered and adaptable—important qualities for workers who frequently must meet deadlines and learn how to operate new equipment.

Projections Data from the National Employment Matrix

Occupational title	SOC Code	Employment, 2008	Projected employment, 2018	Change, 2008–2018	
				Number	Percent
Desktop publishers...43-9031		26,400	20,400	−5,900	−23

NOTE: Data in this table are rounded.

Advancement. Workers with limited training and experience assist more experienced staff on projects while they learn the software and gain practical experience. They advance on the basis of their demonstrated mastery of skills. Some may move into supervisory or management positions. Other desktop publishers may start their own companies or work as independent consultants, while those with more artistic talent and further education may find job opportunities in graphic design or commercial art.

Employment

Desktop publishers held about 26,400 jobs in 2008. Approximately 38 percent worked for newspaper, periodical, book, and directory publishers, while 21 percent worked in the printing and related support activities industry. Other desktop publishers work for professional, scientific, and technical services firms and in many other industries that produce printed or published materials.

The printing and publishing industries are two of the most geographically dispersed industries in the United States, and desktop publishing jobs are found throughout the country. Although most jobs are in large metropolitan cities, electronic communication networks and the Internet allow some desktop publishers to work from other locations.

Job Outlook

Employment is expected to decline rapidly because more people are learning basic desktop publishing skills as a part of their regular job functions in other occupations and because more organizations are formatting materials for display on the Internet rather than designing pages for print publication.

Employment change. Employment of desktop publishers is expected to decline 23 percent between 2008 and 2018. Desktop publishing has become a frequently used and common tool for designing and laying out printed matter, such as advertisements, brochures, newsletters, and forms. However, increased computer-processing capacity and the widespread availability of more elaborate desktop publishing software will make it easier and more affordable for nonprinting professionals to use. As a result, there will be less need for people to specialize in desktop publishing.

In addition, organizations are increasingly moving their published material to the Internet to save the cost of printing and distributing materials. This change will slow the growth of desktop publishers, especially in smaller membership and trade organizations, which publish newsletters and brief reports. Companies that produce more extensive reports and rely on high-quality, high-resolution color and graphics within their publications, however, will continue to use desktop publishers to lay out publications for offset printing.

Job prospects. There will be some job opportunities for desktop publishers because of the need to replace workers who move into managerial positions, transfer to other occupations, or leave the labor force. However, job prospects will be better for those with experience; many employers prefer to hire experienced desktop publishers because of the long time it takes to become good at this type of work. Among individuals with little or no experience, opportunities should be best for those with computer backgrounds, those with certification in desktop publishing, or those who have completed a postsecondary program in desktop publishing, graphic design, or Web design.

Earnings

Wages for desktop publishers vary according to level of experience, training, geographic location, and company size. Median annual wages of desktop publishers were $36,470 in May 2009. The middle 50 percent earned between $28,430 and $47,870. The lowest 10 percent earned less than $21,920, and the highest 10 percent earned more than $59,180 a year. Median annual wages of desktop publishers in May 2009 were $32,960 in newspaper, periodical, book, and directory publishers and $39,810 in printing and related support services.

Related Occupations

Desktop publishers use artistic and editorial skills in their work. These skills also are essential for the following workers: artists and related workers; commercial and industrial designers; graphic designers; and prepress technicians and workers.

Sources of Additional Information

Details about training programs may be obtained from local employers, such as newspapers and printing shops, or from local offices of the state employment service.

For information on careers and training in printing, desktop publishing, and graphic arts, write to

▶ Graphic Arts Education and Research Foundation, 1899 Preston White Dr., Reston, VA 20191-4367. Internet: www.gaerf.org

▶ Graphic Arts Information Network, 200 Deer Run Rd., Sewickley, PA 15143-2324. Internet: www.gain.net

Diesel Service Technicians and Mechanics

(O*NET 49-3031.00)

Significant Points

■ In addition to high school course offerings in automotive repair and electronics, programs in diesel engine repair are offered by many community colleges and trade and technical schools.

■ Opportunities are expected to be very good for people who complete formal training programs; applicants without formal training will face competition for jobs.

- National certification, the recognized standard of achievement, enhances a diesel service technician's advancement opportunities.

Nature of the Work

Diesel-powered engines are more efficient and durable than their gasoline-burning counterparts. These powerful engines are standard in our nation's trucks, locomotives, and buses and are becoming more prevalent in light vehicles, including passenger vehicles, pickups, and other work trucks.

Diesel service technicians and mechanics, including *bus and truck mechanics* and *diesel engine specialists*, repair and maintain the diesel engines that power transportation equipment. Other diesel technicians and mechanics work on other heavy vehicles and mobile equipment, including bulldozers, cranes, road graders, farm tractors, and combines. Others repair diesel-powered passenger automobiles, light trucks, or boats. (For information on technicians and mechanics working primarily on gasoline-powered automobiles, heavy vehicles and mobile equipment, or boat engines, see the job descriptions for automotive service technicians and heavy vehicle and mobile equipment service technicians and mechanics.)

Increasingly, diesel technicians must be versatile enough to adapt to customers' needs and to new technologies. It is common for technicians to handle all kinds of repairs, working on a vehicle's electrical system one day and doing major engine repairs the next. Diesel maintenance is becoming increasingly complex, as more electronic components are used to control the operation of an engine. For example, microprocessors now regulate and manage fuel injection and engine timing, increasing the engine's efficiency. Also, new emissions standards may require mechanics to retrofit engines with emissions control systems, such as emission filters and catalysts, to comply with pollution regulations. In modern shops, diesel service technicians use handheld or laptop computers to diagnose problems and adjust engine functions.

Technicians who work for organizations that maintain their own vehicles spend most of their time doing preventive maintenance. During a routine maintenance check, technicians follow a checklist that includes inspecting brake systems, steering mechanisms, wheel bearings, and other important parts. Following inspection, technicians repair or adjust parts that do not work properly or remove and replace parts that cannot be fixed.

Diesel service technicians use a variety of tools in their work, including power tools, such as pneumatic wrenches that remove bolts quickly; machine tools, such as lathes and grinding machines to rebuild brakes; welding and flame-cutting equipment to remove and repair exhaust systems; and jacks and hoists to lift and move large parts. Common hand tools—screwdrivers, pliers, and wrenches—are used to work on small parts and get at hard-to-reach places. Diesel service technicians and mechanics also use a variety of computerized testing equipment to pinpoint and analyze malfunctions in electrical systems and engines. Employers typically furnish expensive power tools, computerized engine analyzers, and other diagnostic equipment, but workers usually accumulate their own hand tools over time.

Work environment. Technicians normally work in well-lighted and ventilated areas. However, some shops are drafty and noisy. Many employers provide lockers and shower facilities. Diesel technicians usually work indoors, although they occasionally repair vehicles on the road or at the job site. Diesel technicians may lift heavy parts and tools, handle greasy and dirty parts, and stand or lie in awkward positions while making repairs. Minor cuts, burns, and bruises are common, although serious accidents can usually be avoided when safety procedures are followed. Technicians may work as a team or be assisted by an apprentice or helper when doing heavy work, such as removing engines and transmissions.

Most service technicians work a standard 40-hour week, although some work longer hours, particularly if they are self-employed. A growing number of shops have expanded their hours to speed repairs and offer more convenience to customers. Some truck and bus firms provide maintenance and repair service around the clock and on weekends.

Training, Other Qualifications, and Advancement

Employers prefer to hire graduates of formal training programs because those workers are able to advance quickly to the journey level of diesel service. Other workers who learn diesel engine repair through on-the-job training need 3 to 4 years of experience before becoming journey-level technicians.

Education and training. High school courses in automotive repair, electronics, English, mathematics, and physics provide a strong educational background for a career as a diesel service technician or mechanic. Many mechanics have additional training after high school.

A large number of community colleges and trade and vocational schools offer programs in diesel engine repair. These programs usually last from 6 months to 2 years and may lead to a certificate of completion or an associate degree. Some offer about 30 hours per week of hands-on training with equipment; others offer more lab or classroom instruction. Formal training provides a foundation in the latest diesel technology and instruction in the service and repair of the equipment that technicians will encounter on the job. Training programs also teach technicians to interpret technical manuals and to communicate well with coworkers and customers. Increasingly, employers work closely with representatives of educational programs, providing instructors with the latest equipment, techniques, and tools and offering jobs to graduates.

Although formal training programs lead to the best prospects, some technicians and mechanics learn through on-the-job training. Unskilled beginners generally are assigned tasks such as cleaning parts, fueling and lubricating vehicles, and driving vehicles into and out of the shop. Beginners are usually promoted to trainee positions as they gain experience and as vacancies become available.

After a few months' experience, most trainees can perform routine service tasks and make minor repairs. These workers advance to increasingly difficult jobs as they improve their ability and competence. After technicians master the repair and service of diesel engines, they learn to work on related components, such as brakes, transmissions, and electrical systems. Generally, technicians with at least three to four years of on-the-job experience will qualify as journey-level diesel technicians.

Employers often send experienced technicians and mechanics to special training classes conducted by manufacturers and vendors, in which workers learn about the latest technology and repair techniques.

Other qualifications. Employers usually look for applicants who have mechanical aptitude and strong problem-solving skills and

Projections Data from the National Employment Matrix

Occupational title	SOC Code	Employment, 2008	Projected employment, 2018	Change, 2008–2018	
				Number	Percent
Bus and truck mechanics and diesel engine specialists 49-3031		263,100	278,000	14,900	6

NOTE: Data in this table are rounded.

who are at least 18 years old and in good physical condition. Technicians need a state commercial driver's license to test-drive trucks or buses on public roads. Many companies also require applicants to pass a drug test. Practical experience in automobile repair at an automotive service station, in the Armed Forces, or as a hobby is valuable as well.

Certification and advancement. Experienced diesel service technicians and mechanics with leadership ability may advance to shop supervisor or service manager, and some open their own repair shops. Technicians and mechanics with sales ability sometimes become sales representatives.

Although national certification is not required for employment, many diesel engine technicians and mechanics find that it increases their ability to advance. Certification by the National Institute for Automotive Service Excellence (ASE) is the recognized industry credential for diesel and other automotive service technicians and mechanics. Diesel service technicians may be certified in specific areas of truck repair, such as drivetrains, brakes, suspension and steering, electrical and electronic systems, or preventive maintenance and inspection. For certification in each area, a technician must pass one or more of the ASE-administered exams and present proof of 2 years of relevant work experience. To become what's known as a master technician, all the tests in a given series must be passed. To remain certified, technicians must be retested every 5 years.

Employment

Diesel service technicians and mechanics held about 263,100 jobs in 2008. These workers were employed in almost every industry, particularly those that use trucks, buses, and equipment to haul, deliver, and transport materials, goods, and people. The largest employer, the truck transportation industry, employed about 17 percent of diesel service technicians and mechanics. About 8 percent were employed by automotive repair and maintenance facilities. The rest were employed throughout the economy, including construction, manufacturing, retail and wholesale trade, and automotive leasing. About 6 percent were self-employed. Nearly every area of the country employs diesel service technicians and mechanics, although most work is found in towns and cities where trucking companies, bus lines, and other fleet owners have large operations.

Job Outlook

The number of jobs for diesel service technicians and mechanics is projected to grow slower than the average for all occupations. Opportunities should be very good for people who complete formal training in diesel mechanics; applicants without formal training will face competition for jobs.

Employment change. Employment of diesel service technicians and mechanics is expected to grow by 6 percent from 2008 to 2018, slower than the average for all occupations. The diesel

engine, because of its durability and fuel efficiency, is the preferred engine for heavy-duty trucks, buses, and other large vehicles. As more freight is shipped across the country, additional trucks, and corresponding truck repairers, will be needed. Despite this trend, the increasing durability of new vehicles will limit the need for additional workers. Most new jobs will continue to be in the freight trucking and automotive repair and maintenance industries. Beyond the growth in the number of vehicles that need to be serviced, there will be additional demand for diesel engines mechanics to retrofit and modernize existing vehicles to comply with environmental regulations.

Due to higher fuel efficiency requirements for automakers, diesel engines are expected to be used in a small but increasing number of cars and light trucks. This will create additional jobs for diesel service technicians, specifically in the automotive repair and maintenance and automobile dealer industries.

Job prospects. People who enter diesel engine repair will find favorable opportunities, especially as the need to replace workers who retire increases over the next decade. Opportunities should be very good for people with strong technical skills and who complete formal training in diesel mechanics at community colleges or vocational schools. Applicants without formal training will face competition for jobs.

Earnings

Median hourly wages of bus and truck mechanics and diesel engine specialists, including incentive pay, were $19.35 in May 2009. The middle 50 percent earned between $15.70 and $23.89 an hour. The lowest 10 percent earned less than $12.78, and the highest 10 percent earned more than $28.70 an hour. Median hourly wages in the industries employing the largest numbers of bus and truck mechanics and diesel engine specialists in May 2009 were as follows:

General freight trucking	$18.07
Local government	22.49
Automotive repair and maintenance	18.37
Motor vehicle and motor vehicle parts and supplies merchant wholesalers	19.49
Specialized freight trucking	17.28

Because many experienced technicians employed by truck fleet dealers and independent repair shops receive a commission related to the labor cost charged to the customer, weekly earnings depend on the amount of work completed. Beginners usually earn from 50 to 75 percent of the rate of skilled workers and receive increases as they become more skilled.

About 23 percent of diesel service technicians and mechanics are members of labor unions, including the International Association of Machinists and Aerospace Workers; the Amalgamated Transit Union; the International Union, United Automobile, Aerospace and Agricultural Implement Workers of America; the Transport

Workers Union of America; the Sheet Metal Workers' International Association; and the International Brotherhood of Teamsters. Labor unions may provide additional benefits for their members.

Related Occupations

Diesel service technicians and mechanics repair trucks, buses, and other diesel-powered equipment. Related technician and mechanic occupations include aircraft and avionics equipment mechanics and service technicians; automotive body and related repairers; automotive service technicians and mechanics; heavy vehicle and mobile equipment service technicians and mechanics; and small engine mechanics.

Sources of Additional Information

More details about work opportunities for diesel service technicians and mechanics may be obtained from local employers such as trucking companies, truck dealers, or bus lines; locals of the unions previously mentioned; and local offices of your state employment service. Local state employment service offices also may have information about training programs. State boards of postsecondary career schools have information on licensed schools with training programs for diesel service technicians and mechanics.

For general information about a career as a diesel service technician or mechanic, write to

▸ Association of Diesel Specialists, 400 Admiral Blvd., Kansas City, MO 64106. Internet: www.diesel.org

Information on how to become a certified diesel technician of medium to heavy-duty vehicles or a certified bus technician is available from

▸ National Institute for Automotive Service Excellence (ASE), 101 Blue Seal Dr. SE, Suite 101, Leesburg, VA 20175. Internet: www.asecert.org

For a directory of accredited private trade and technical schools with training programs for diesel service technicians and mechanics, contact

▸ Accrediting Commission of Career Schools and Colleges, 2101 Wilson Blvd., Suite 302, Arlington, VA 22201. Internet: www.accsc.org

▸ National Automotive Technicians Education Foundation, 101 Blue Seal Dr. SE, Suite 101, Leesburg, VA 20175. Internet: www.natef.org

Drafters

(O*NET 17-3011.00, 17-3011.01, 17-3011.02, 17-3012.00, 17-3012.01, 17-3012.02, 17-3013.00, and 17-3019.00)

Significant Points

■ Opportunities should be best for individuals with at least two years of postsecondary training in drafting.

■ Overall employment is projected to grow more slowly than average, but growth will vary by specialty.

■ Demand for various types of drafters depends on the needs of local industry.

Nature of the Work

Drafters prepare technical drawings and plans, which are used by production and construction workers to build everything from microchips to skyscrapers.

Drafters' drawings provide visual guidelines and show how to construct a product or structure. Drawings include technical details and specify dimensions, materials, and procedures. Drafters fill in technical details using drawings, rough sketches, specifications, and calculations made by engineers, surveyors, architects, or scientists. For example, many drafters use their knowledge of standardized building techniques to draw in the details of structures. Some use their understanding of engineering and manufacturing theory and standards to draw the parts of a machine; they determine design elements, such as the numbers and kinds of fasteners needed to assemble the machine. Drafters use technical handbooks, tables, calculators, and computers to complete their work.

Most drafters use Computer-Aided Design and Drafting (CADD) systems to prepare drawings. Consequently, some drafters may be referred to as *CADD operators*. With CADD systems, drafters can create and store drawings electronically so that they can be viewed, printed, or programmed directly into automated manufacturing systems. CADD systems also permit drafters to quickly prepare variations of a design. Although drafters use CADD extensively, they still need knowledge of traditional drafting techniques in order to fully understand and explain concepts.

Drafting work has many specialties; the most common types of drafters are the following:

Aeronautical drafters prepare engineering drawings that detail plans and specifications used in the manufacture of aircraft, missiles, and related parts.

Architectural drafters draw architectural and structural features of buildings for new construction projects. These workers may specialize in a type of building, such as residential or commercial, or in a kind of material used, such as reinforced concrete, masonry, steel, or timber.

Civil drafters prepare drawings and topographical and relief maps used in major construction or civil engineering projects, such as highways, bridges, pipelines, flood-control projects, and water and sewage systems.

Electrical drafters prepare wiring and layout diagrams used by workers who erect, install, and repair electrical equipment and wiring in communication centers, power plants, electrical distribution systems, and buildings.

Electronics drafters draw wiring diagrams, circuit board assembly diagrams, schematics, and layout drawings used in the manufacture, installation, and repair of electronic devices and components.

Mechanical drafters prepare drawings showing the detail and method of assembly of a wide variety of machinery and mechanical devices, indicating dimensions, fastening methods, and other requirements.

Process piping or pipeline drafters prepare drawings used in the layout, construction, and operation of oil and gas fields, refineries, chemical plants, and process piping systems.

Work environment. Drafters usually work in comfortable offices. Because they spend long periods in front of computers doing detailed work, drafters may be susceptible to eyestrain, back discomfort, and hand and wrist problems. Most drafters work a standard 40-hour week; only a small number work part time.

Training, Other Qualifications, and Advancement

Employers prefer applicants who have completed postsecondary school training in drafting, which is offered by technical institutes, community colleges, and some 4-year colleges and universities. Employers are most interested in applicants with well-developed drafting and mechanical drawing skills; knowledge of drafting standards, mathematics, science, and engineering technology; and a solid background in CADD techniques.

Education and training. High school courses in mathematics, science, computer technology, design, computer graphics, and, where available, drafting are useful for people considering a drafting career. Employers prefer applicants who have also completed training after high school at a technical institute, community college, or 4-year college or university. Prospective students should contact prospective employers to ask which schools they prefer and contact schools to ask for information about the kinds of jobs their graduates have, the type and condition of instructional facilities and equipment, and teacher qualifications.

Technical institutes offer intensive technical training, but they provide a less general education than do community colleges. Either certificates or diplomas may be awarded, and programs can vary considerably in length and in the types of courses offered. Many technical institutes offer 2-year associate degree programs.

Community colleges offer programs similar to those in technical institutes but include more classes in drafting theory and also often require general education classes. Courses taken at community colleges are more likely to be accepted for credit at 4-year colleges. After completing a 2-year associate degree program, graduates may obtain jobs as drafters or continue their education in a related field at a 4-year college. Most 4-year colleges do not offer training in drafting, but they do offer classes in engineering, architecture, and mathematics that are useful for obtaining a job as a drafter.

Technical training obtained in the Armed Forces also can be applied in civilian drafting jobs. Some additional training may be necessary, depending on the technical area or military specialty.

Training differs somewhat within the drafting specialties, although the basics, such as mathematics, are similar. In an electronics drafting program, for example, students learn how to depict electronic components and circuits in drawings. In architectural drafting, they learn the technical specifications of buildings.

Certification and other qualifications. Mechanical ability and visual aptitude are important for drafters. Prospective drafters should be able to draw well and perform detailed work accurately. Artistic ability is helpful in some specialized fields, as is knowledge of manufacturing and construction methods. In addition, prospective drafters should have good interpersonal skills because they work closely with engineers, surveyors, architects, and other professionals and, sometimes, with customers.

The American Design Drafting Association (ADDA) has established a certification program for drafters. Although employers usually do not require drafters to be certified, certification demonstrates knowledge and an understanding of nationally recognized practices. Individuals who wish to become certified must pass the Drafter Certification Test, which is administered periodically at ADDA-

authorized sites. Applicants are tested on basic drafting concepts, such as geometric construction, working drawings, and architectural terms and standards.

Advancement. Entry-level or junior drafters usually do routine work under close supervision. After gaining experience, they may become intermediate drafters and progress to more difficult work with less supervision. At the intermediate level, they may need to exercise more judgment and perform calculations when preparing and modifying drawings. Drafters may eventually advance to senior drafter, designer, or supervisor. Many employers pay for continuing education; with appropriate college degrees, drafters may go on to become engineering technicians, engineers, or architects.

Employment

Drafters held about 251,900 jobs in 2008. Architectural and civil drafters held 47 percent of these jobs, mechanical drafters held about 31 percent, and electrical and electronics drafters held about 13 percent.

About 52 percent of all jobs for drafters were in architectural, engineering, and related services firms that design construction projects or do other engineering work on a contract basis for other industries. Another 24 percent of jobs were in manufacturing industries such as machinery, fabricated metal products, computer and electronic products, and transportation-equipment manufacturing. Approximately 3 percent of drafters were self-employed in 2008.

Job Outlook

Drafters can expect slower than average employment growth, with the best opportunities expected for those with at least two years of postsecondary training.

Employment change. Employment of drafters is expected to grow by 4 percent between 2008 and 2018, which is slower than the average for all occupations. However, growth will vary by specialty.

Architectural and civil drafting is expected to be the fastest growing specialty, increasing by 9 percent, which is about as fast as the average. Increases in overall construction activity stemming from U.S. population growth and the related need to improve the nation's infrastructure should spur demand for drafters trained in architectural and civil design.

In contrast to employment of architectural and civil drafters, little or no change in employment is expected of mechanical drafters and of electronic and electrical drafters. Many of these workers are concentrated in slow-growing or declining manufacturing industries that offer few opportunities for growth related to expansion. However, increasingly complex design problems associated with new products and manufacturing processes will increase the demand for mechanical drafters and electronic and electrical drafters employed in engineering and drafting services firms that will be charged with finding solutions to these problems.

Across all specialties, CADD systems that are more powerful and easier to use will allow many tasks to be done by other technical professionals, thus curbing demand for drafters. Job growth also should be slowed as some drafting work, which can be done by sending CADD files over the Internet, is outsourced offshore to countries that pay lower wages.

Job prospects. Opportunities should be best for individuals with at least two years of postsecondary training in a drafting program that

Projections Data from the National Employment Matrix

Occupational title	SOC Code	Employment, 2008	Projected employment, 2018	Change, 2008–2018	
				Number	Percent
Drafters..	17-3010	251,900	262,500	10,700	4
Architectural and civil drafters............................	17-3011	118,400	129,100	10,800	9
Electrical and electronics drafters.......................	17-3012	33,600	33,900	300	1
Mechanical drafters	17-3013	78,700	77,800	–900	–1
Drafters, all other..	17-3019	21,200	21,700	500	2

NOTE: Data in this table are rounded.

provides strong technical skills and considerable experience with CADD systems. CADD has increased the complexity of drafting applications while enhancing the productivity of drafters. It also has enhanced the nature of drafting by creating more possibilities for design and drafting. As technology continues to advance, employers will look for drafters with a strong background in fundamental drafting principles, a high level of technical sophistication, and the ability to apply their knowledge to a broader range of responsibilities. Most job openings are expected to arise from the need to replace drafters who transfer to other occupations or leave the labor force completely.

Employment of drafters remains tied to industries that are sensitive to cyclical changes in the economy, primarily construction and manufacturing. During recessions, drafters may be laid off. However, a growing number of drafters should continue to find employment on a temporary or contract basis as more companies turn to the employment services industry to meet their changing needs.

Demand for particular drafting specialties varies throughout the country because employment usually is contingent on the needs of local industry.

Earnings

Drafters' earnings vary by specialty, location, and level of responsibility. Median annual wages of architectural and civil drafters were $45,600 in May 2009. The middle 50 percent earned between $36,170 and $55,420. The lowest 10 percent earned less than $29,050, and the highest 10 percent earned more than $69,610. Median annual wages for architectural and civil drafters in architectural, engineering, and related services were $45,420.

Median annual wages of mechanical drafters were $47,790 in May 2009. The middle 50 percent earned between $37,840 and $59,740. The lowest 10 percent earned less than $30,640, and the highest 10 percent earned more than $73,050. Median annual wages for mechanical drafters in architectural, engineering, and related services were $48,920.

Median annual wages of electrical and electronics drafters were $52,080 in May 2009. The middle 50 percent earned between $41,190 and $66,280. The lowest 10 percent earned less than $33,140, and the highest 10 percent earned more than $80,960. In architectural, engineering, and related services, median annual wages for electrical and electronics drafters were $50,340.

Related Occupations

Other workers who prepare or analyze detailed drawings and make precise calculations and measurements include architects, except landscape and naval; commercial and industrial designers; engineers; engineering technicians; landscape architects; and surveyors,

cartographers, photogrammetrists, and surveying and mapping technicians.

Sources of Additional Information

Information on schools offering programs in drafting and related fields is available from

▸ Accrediting Commission of Career Schools and Colleges, 2101 Wilson Blvd., Suite 302, Arlington, VA 22201. Internet: www.accsc.org

Information about certification is available from

▸ American Design Drafting Association, 105 E. Main St., Newbern, TN 38059. Internet: www.adda.org

Drywall and Ceiling Tile Installers, Tapers, Plasterers, and Stucco Masons

(O*NET 47-2081.00, 47-2082.00, and 47-2161.00)

Significant Points

- Most workers learn their trade through informal training programs or through an apprenticeship.
- Work is physically demanding.
- Job prospects are expected to be good.
- Workers may be idled when downturns in the economy slow construction activity.

Nature of the Work

Drywall and *ceiling tile installers, tapers, plasterers*, and *stucco masons* are specialty construction workers who build, apply, or fasten interior and exterior wallboards or wall coverings in residential, commercial, and other structures. Specifically, drywall and ceiling tile installers and tapers work indoors, installing wallboards to ceilings or to interior walls of buildings; plasterers and stucco masons, on the other hand, work both indoors and outdoors—applying plaster to interior walls and cement or stucco to exterior walls. While most work is performed for functionality, such as fireproofing and sound dampening, some applications are intended purely for decorative purposes.

Drywall consists of a thin layer of gypsum between two layers of heavy paper. It is used to make walls and ceilings in most buildings today because it is faster and cheaper to install than plaster.

There are two kinds of drywall workers—installers and tapers—although many workers do both types of work. Installers, also called *framers* or *hangers*, fasten drywall panels to the inside framework of houses and other buildings. Tapers or *finishers*, prepare these panels for painting by taping and finishing joints and imperfections. In addition to drywall workers, ceiling tile installers also help to build walls and ceilings.

Because drywall panels are manufactured in standard sizes—usually 4 feet by 8 feet—drywall installers must measure, cut, fit, and fasten them to the inside framework of buildings. Installers saw, drill, or cut holes in panels for electrical outlets, air-conditioning units, and plumbing. After making these alterations, installers typically screw the wallboard panels to the wood or metal framework, called studs. Because drywall is heavy and cumbersome, another worker usually helps the installer to position and secure the panel. Installers often use a lift when placing ceiling panels.

After the drywall is installed, tapers fill joints between panels with a joint compound, also called spackle or "mud." Using the wide, flat tip of a special trowel, they spread the compound into and along each side of the joint. They immediately use the trowel to press a paper tape—used to reinforce the drywall and to hide imperfections—into the wet compound and to smooth away excess material. Nail and screw depressions also are covered with this compound, as are imperfections caused by the installation of air-conditioning vents and other fixtures. Using increasingly wider trowels, tapers apply second and third coats of the compound, sanding the treated areas after each coat to make them smooth and devoid of seams.

Ceiling tile installers, or *acoustical carpenters*, apply or mount acoustical tiles or blocks, strips, or sheets of shock-absorbing materials to ceilings and walls of buildings to reduce deflection of sound or to decorate rooms. First, they measure and mark the surface according to blueprints and drawings. Then, they nail or screw moldings to the wall to support and seal the joint between the ceiling tile and the wall. Finally, they mount the tile, either by applying a cement adhesive to the back of the tile and then pressing the tile into place, or by nailing, screwing, or wire-tying the lath directly to the structural framework.

Plasterers apply plaster to interior walls and ceilings to form fire-resistant and relatively soundproof surfaces. They also apply plaster veneer over drywall to create smooth or textured abrasion-resistant finishes. In addition, plasterers install prefabricated exterior insulation systems over existing walls—for good insulation and interesting architectural effects—and cast ornamental designs in plaster. Stucco masons apply durable plasters, such as polymer-based acrylic finishes and stucco, to exterior surfaces.

Plasterers can plaster either solid surfaces, such as concrete block, or supportive wire mesh called lath. When plasterers work with hard interior surfaces, such as concrete block and concrete, they first apply a brown coat of gypsum plaster that provides a base, which is followed by a second, or finish coat, also called "white coat." When plastering metal-mesh lath foundations, they apply a preparatory "scratch coat" with a trowel. They spread this rich plaster mixture into and over the metal lath. Before the plaster sets, plasterers scratch its surface with a rake-like tool to produce ridges so that the subsequent brown coat will bond tightly. They then apply the brown coat and the white finish coat.

When plastering on nonsolid surfaces, *lathers* are needed to help build supportive walls out of wire. This support base is put on walls, ceilings, ornamental frameworks, and partitions of buildings before plaster and other coatings are added.

Applying different types of plaster coating requires different techniques. When applying the brown coat, plasterers spray or trowel the mixture onto the surface, then smooth it to an even, level surface. For the finish, or white coat, plasterers usually prepare a mixture of plaster and water. They quickly apply this using a "hawk," which is a light, metal plate with a handle, along with a trowel, brush, and water. This mixture, which sets very quickly, produces a very smooth, durable finish.

Plasterers create decorative interior surfaces as well. One way that they do this is by pressing a brush or trowel firmly against a wet plaster surface and using a circular hand motion to create decorative swirls. Plasterers sometimes do more complex decorative and ornamental work that requires special skill and creativity. For example, they may mold intricate wall and ceiling designs, such as cornice pieces and chair rails. Following an architect's blueprint, plasterers pour or spray a special plaster into a mold and allow it to set. Workers then remove the molded plaster and put it in place, according to the plan.

Stucco masons usually apply stucco—a mixture of Portland cement, lime, and sand—over cement, concrete, masonry or wire lath. Stucco also may be applied directly to a wire lath with a scratch coat, followed by a brown coat, and then a finish coat. Stucco masons may also embed marble or gravel chips into the finish coat to achieve a pebble-like, decorative finish.

When required, stucco masons apply insulation to the exteriors of new and old buildings. They cover the outer wall with rigid foam insulation board and reinforcing mesh, and then trowel on a base coat. They may apply an additional coat of this material with a decorative finish.

Work environment. As in many other construction trades, this work is physically demanding. Drywall and ceiling tile installers, tapers, plasterers, and stucco masons spend most of the day on their feet, either standing, bending, stretching, or kneeling. Some workers need to use stilts; others may have to lift and maneuver heavy, cumbersome materials, such as oversized wallboards. The work also can be dusty and dirty, irritating the skin, eyes, and lungs, unless protective masks, goggles, and gloves are used. Hazards include falls from ladders and scaffolds, and injuries from power tools and from working with sharp tools, such as utility knives.

Most work indoors, except for the relatively few stucco masons who apply exterior finishes.

Training, Other Qualifications, and Advancement

Most workers learn their trade through informal training programs or through an apprenticeship. It can take 3 to 4 years of paid on-the-job training to become a fully skilled worker, but many skills can be learned within the first year. In general, the more formal the training process, the more skilled the individual becomes, and the more in demand by employers.

Education and training. A high school education, or its equivalent, is helpful, as are courses in basic math, mechanical drawing, and blueprint reading. The most common way to get a first job is to find an employer who will provide on-the-job training. Entry-level workers generally start as helpers, assisting more experienced workers. Employers may also send new employees to a trade or vocational school or community college to receive classroom training.

Some employers, particularly large nonresidential construction contractors with unionized workforces, offer employees formal apprenticeships. These programs combine on-the-job training with related classroom instruction—at least 144 hours of instruction each year for drywall and ceiling tile installers and tapers, and 166 hours for plasterers and stucco masons. The length of the apprenticeship program, usually 3 to 4 years, varies with the apprentice's skill. Because the number of apprenticeship programs is limited, however, only a small proportion of these workers learn their trade this way.

Helpers and apprentices start by carrying materials, lifting and cleaning up debris. They also learn to use the tools, machines, equipment, and materials of the trade. Within a few weeks, they learn to measure, cut, apply, and install materials. Eventually, they become fully experienced workers. At the end of their training, workers learn to estimate the cost of completing a job.

Other job seekers may choose to obtain their training before seeking a job. There are a number of vocational-technical schools and training academies affiliated with the industry's unions and contractors that offer training in these occupations. Employers often look favorably upon graduates of these training programs and usually start them at a higher level than those without the training.

Other qualifications. Workers need to be in good physical condition and have good eye-hand coordination, a sense of balance and manual dexterity. For drywall and ceiling tile installers and tapers, the ability to solve basic arithmetic problems quickly and accurately is required. They also should be able to identify and estimate the quantity of materials needed to complete a job, and accurately estimate how long a job will take to complete and at what cost.

Artistic creativity is helpful for plasterers and stucco masons who apply decorative finishes. In addition, a good work history is viewed favorably by contractors.

Apprentices usually must be at least 18 years old and have a high school diploma or GED. Those who complete apprenticeships registered with the federal or state government receive a journey worker certificate that is recognized nationwide.

Certification and advancement. Some organizations related to masonry trades offer training and certification intended to enhance the skills of their members. For example, the International Union of Bricklayers and Allied Craftworkers International Masonry Institute confers designations in several areas of specialization, including one for plastering. Candidates who complete a 12-week certification program can earn a designation as a "journey level plasterer" by passing a competency-based exam. Experienced candidates can become trainers and earn a designation as "Certified Instructor or Journeyworkers and Apprentices in the Trowel Trades."

Drywall and ceiling tile installers, tapers, plasterers, and stucco masons may advance to supervisor or general construction supervisor positions. However, it is increasingly important to be able to communicate in both English and Spanish in order to relay instructions and safety precautions to workers with limited understanding of English because Spanish-speaking workers make up a large part of the construction workforce in many areas. Knowing English well also makes it easier to advance. Many workers become independent contractors. Others become building inspectors.

Employment

Drywall and ceiling tile installers, tapers, plasterers, and stucco masons held about 237,700 jobs in 2008. About 19 percent were self-employed independent contractors. The following tabulation shows 2008 wage-and-salary employment by specialty:

Drywall and ceiling tile installers	151,300
Plasterers and stucco masons	49,000
Tapers	37,400

Most workers are employed in populous areas. In other areas, where there may not be enough work to keep them employed full time, carpenters and painters usually do the work.

Job Outlook

Employment of drywall and ceiling tile installers, tapers, plasterers, and stucco masons is expected to grow about as fast as average for all occupations. Job growth, however, will differ among the individual occupations in this category. Good job prospects are expected overall.

Employment change. Overall employment is expected to grow by 12 percent between 2008 and 2018. Employment of drywall and ceiling tile installers—the largest specialty—is expected to grow 14 percent, reflecting growth of new construction and remodeling projects. New residential construction projects are expected to provide the majority of jobs during the projection decade, but home improvement and renovation projects are also expected to create jobs because existing residential and nonresidential buildings are getting old and need repair.

Employment of tapers is expected to grow 13 percent, which is as fast as the average. Demand for tapers, which often mirrors demand for drywall installers, also will be driven by the overall growth of construction activity.

Employment of plasterers and stucco masons, on the other hand, is expected to grow 7 percent. Despite an increased appreciation for the attractiveness and durability that plaster provides, growing use of cheaper and easier to install alternatives, such as drywall, will impede employment growth for these workers. Nonetheless, stucco masons will experience some employment growth due to demand for new polymer-based exterior insulating finishes that are gaining popularity, particularly in the South and Southwest regions of the country.

Job prospects. Job opportunities for drywall and ceiling tile installers, tapers, plasterers, and stucco masons are expected to be good overall. Many potential workers are not attracted to this occupation because they prefer work that is less strenuous and has more comfortable working conditions. Experienced workers will have especially favorable opportunities.

Besides opportunities resulting from job growth, many drywall and ceiling tile installer and taper jobs will open up each year because of the need to replace workers who transfer to other occupations or leave the labor force. Skilled, experienced plasterers with artistic ability should have excellent opportunities, especially with restoration projects. Decorative custom finishes, expensive homes, and large-scale restoration projects will further result in opportunities for plasterers in the Northeast, particularly in urban areas. For stucco masons, the best employment opportunities should continue to be in Florida, California, and the Southwest, where the use of stucco is expected to remain popular.

Like many other construction workers, employment in these occupations is sensitive to the fluctuations of the economy. Workers in these trades may experience periods of unemployment when the overall level of construction falls. On the other hand, shortages

Projections Data from the National Employment Matrix

Occupational title	SOC Code	Employment, 2008	Projected employment, 2018	Change, 2008–2018	
				Number	Percent
Drywall and ceiling tile installers, tapers, plasterers, and stucco masons ....—		237,700	266,200	28,500	12
Drywall installers, ceiling tile installers, and tapers 47-2080		188,700	214,000	25,300	13
Drywall and ceiling tile installers............................47-2081		151,300	171,700	20,500	14
Tapers 47-2082		37,400	42,300	4,900	13
Plasterers and stucco masons 47-2161		49,000	52,200	3,200	7

NOTE: Data in this table are rounded.

of these workers may occur in some areas during peak periods of building activity.

Earnings

The median hourly wages of wage and salary drywall and ceiling tile installers were $17.88 in May 2009. The middle 50 percent earned between $14.17 and $23.91. The lowest 10 percent earned less than $11.63, and the highest 10 percent earned more than $32.43.

Median hourly wages of wage and salary tapers were $21.37 in May 2009. The middle 50 percent earned between $15.87 and $28.85. The lowest 10 percent earned less than $13.00, and the highest 10 percent earned more than $35.50.

Median hourly wages of wage and salary plasterers and stucco masons were $18.16 in May 2009. The middle 50 percent earned between $14.54 and $23.60. The lowest 10 percent earned less than $12.13, and the top 10 percent earned more than $31.45.

Related Occupations

Drywall and ceiling tile installers, tapers, plasterers, and stucco masons combine strength and dexterity with precision and accuracy to make materials fit according to a plan. Other occupations that require similar abilities include brickmasons, blockmasons, and stonemasons; carpenters; carpet, floor, and tile installers and finishers; cement masons, concrete finishers, segmental pavers, and terrazzo workers; and insulation workers.

Sources of Additional Information

For information about work opportunities in this field, contact local drywall installation, ceiling tile installation, plaster and stucco mason contractors, a local joint union-management apprenticeship committee, a state or local chapter of the Associated Builders and Contractors, or the nearest office of the state employment service or apprenticeship agency. You can also find information on the registered apprenticeship system with links to state apprenticeship programs on the U.S. Department of Labor's website: www.doleta. gov/OA/eta_default.cfm. Apprenticeship information is also available from the U.S. Department of Labor's toll-free helpline: (877) 282-5627.

For details about job qualifications and training programs in drywall application and finishing and ceiling tile installation, contact

▸ Associated Builders and Contractors, 4250 N. Fairfax Dr., 9th Floor, Arlington, VA 22203. Internet: www.abc.org/

▸ Association of Wall and Ceiling Industries International, 513 W. Broad St., Suite 210, Falls Church, VA 22046. Internet: www.awci.org

▸ Finishing Trades Institute, International Union of Painters and Allied Trades, 1750 New York Ave. NW, Washington, DC 20006. Internet: www.finishingtradesinstitute.org

▸ National Association of Home Builders, Home Builders Institute, 1201 15th St. NW, 6th Floor, Washington, DC 20005. Internet: www.hbi.org

▸ National Center for Construction Education and Research, 3600 NW 43rd St., Building G, Gainesville, FL 32606. Internet: www.nccer.org

For information about plasterers, contact

▸ Operative Plasterers' and Cement Masons' International Association of the United States and Canada, 11720 Beltsville Dr., Suite 700, Beltsville, MD 20705. Internet: www.opcmia.org

For general information on apprenticeships and how to get them, see the *Occupational Outlook Quarterly* article "Apprenticeships: Career training, credentials—and a paycheck in your pocket," online at www.bls.gov/opub/ooq/2002/summer/art01.pdf and in print at many libraries and career centers.

Electrical and Electronics Installers and Repairers

(O*NET 49-2092.00, 49-2093.00, 49-2094.00, 49-2095.00, and 49-2096.00)

Significant Points

■ Knowledge of electrical equipment and electronics is necessary for employment; employers often prefer applicants with an associate degree in electronics, and professional certification often is required.

■ Job opportunities will be best for applicants with an associate degree, certification, or related experience.

■ Overall employment is projected to grow more slowly than the average for all occupations.

Nature of the Work

Businesses and other organizations depend on complex electronic equipment for a variety of functions. Industrial controls automatically monitor and direct production processes on the factory floor. Transmitters and antennae provide communication links for many organizations. Electric power companies use electronic equipment to operate and control generating plants, substations, and monitoring equipment. The federal government uses radar and missile control systems to provide for the national defense and to direct commercial air traffic. Such complex pieces of electronic equipment are installed, maintained, and repaired by *electrical and electronics installers and repairers.*

Installers and repairers, known as *field technicians,* often travel to factories or other locations to repair equipment. These workers usually have assigned areas in which they perform preventive maintenance on a regular basis. When equipment breaks down, field technicians go to a customer's site to repair the equipment. *Bench technicians* work in repair shops located in factories and service centers, fixing components that cannot be repaired on the factory floor.

Electrical and electronic equipment are two distinct types of industrial equipment, although a great deal of equipment contains both electrical and electronic components. In general, electrical parts provide the power for the equipment, whereas electronic components control the device.

Some industrial electronic equipment is self-monitoring and alerts repairers to malfunctions. When equipment breaks down, repairers will first check for common causes of trouble, such as loose connections or obviously defective components. If routine checks do not locate the trouble, repairers may refer to schematics and manufacturers' specifications that show connections and provide instructions on how to trace problems. Automated electronic control systems are becoming increasingly complex, making diagnosis more challenging. With these systems, repairers use software programs and testing equipment to diagnose malfunctions. Among their diagnostic tools are multimeters, which measure voltage, current, and resistance, and advanced multimeters, which measure capacitance, inductance, and current gain of transistors. Repairers also use signal generators, which provide test signals, and oscilloscopes, which display signals graphically. Finally, repairers use handtools such as pliers, screwdrivers, soldering irons, and wrenches to replace faulty parts and adjust equipment.

Because repairing components is a complex activity and factories cannot allow production equipment to stand idle, repairers on the factory floor usually remove and replace defective units, such as circuit boards, instead of fixing them. Defective units are discarded or returned to the manufacturer or a specialized shop for repair. Bench technicians at these locations have the training, tools, and parts needed to thoroughly diagnose and repair circuit boards or other complex components. These workers also locate and repair circuit defects, such as poorly soldered joints, blown fuses, or malfunctioning transistors.

Electrical and electronics installers often retrofit older manufacturing equipment with new automated control devices. Older manufacturing machines are frequently in good working order, but are limited by inefficient control systems for which replacement parts are no longer available. As a result, installers sometimes replace old electronic control units with new programming logic controls (PLCs). Setting up and installing a new PLC involves connecting it to different sensors and electrically powered devices (electric motors, switches, and pumps) and writing a computer program to operate the PLC. Electronics installers often coordinate their efforts with those of other workers who are installing and maintaining equipment. (See the section on industrial machinery mechanics and millwrights elsewhere in this book.)

Electrical and electronics installers and repairers, transportation equipment install, adjust, or maintain mobile electronic communication equipment, including sound, sonar, security, navigation, and surveillance systems on trains, watercraft, or other vehicles.

Electrical and electronics repairers, powerhouse, substation, and relay inspect, test, maintain, or repair electrical equipment used in generating stations, substations, and in-service relays. These workers may be known as powerhouse electricians, relay technicians, or power transformer repairers. *Electric motor, power tool, and related repairers*—such as armature winders, generator mechanics, and electric golf cart repairers—specialize in installing, maintaining, and repairing electric motors, wiring, or switches.

Electronic equipment installers and repairers, motor vehicles have a significantly different job. They install, diagnose, and repair communication, sound, security, and navigation equipment in motor vehicles. Most installation work involves either new alarm or sound systems. New sound systems vary significantly in cost and complexity of installation. For instance, replacing a head unit (radio) with a new CD player is simple, requiring the removal of a few screws and the connection of a few wires. Installing a new sound system with a subwoofer, amplifier, and fuses is far more complicated. The installer builds a custom fiberglass or wood box designed to hold the subwoofer and to fit inside the unique dimensions of the automobile. Installing sound-deadening material, which often is necessary with more powerful speakers, requires an installer to remove many parts of a car (for example, seats, carpeting, or interiors of doors), add sound-absorbing material in empty spaces, and reinstall the interior parts. The installer also runs new speaker and electrical cables. The new system may require additional fuses, a new electrical line to be run from the battery through a newly drilled hole in the firewall into the interior of the vehicle, or a more powerful alternator or battery. Motor vehicle installers and repairers work with an increasingly complex range of electronic equipment, including DVD players, satellite navigation equipment, passive security systems, and active security systems.

Work environment. Many electrical and electronics installers and repairers work on factory floors, where they are subject to noise, dirt, vibration, and heat. Bench technicians primarily work in repair shops, where the surroundings are reasonably quiet, comfortable, and well lighted.

Installers and repairers may have to do heavy lifting and work in a variety of positions. They must follow safety guidelines and often wear protective goggles and hardhats. When working on ladders or on elevated equipment, repairers must wear harnesses to avoid falls. Before repairing a piece of machinery, these workers must follow procedures to ensure that others cannot start the equipment during the repair process. They also must take precautions against electric shock by locking off power to the unit under repair.

Motor vehicle electronic equipment installers and repairers normally work indoors in well-ventilated and well-lighted repair shops. Minor cuts and bruises are common, but serious accidents usually are avoided when safety practices are observed.

Training, Other Qualifications, and Advancement

Applicants with an associate degree in electronics are preferred, and professional certification often is required.

Education and training. Knowledge of electrical equipment and electronics is necessary for employment. Employers often prefer applicants with an associate degree from a community college or technical school, although a high school diploma may be sufficient for some jobs. Entry-level repairers may begin by working with

Projections Data from the National Employment Matrix

Occupational title	SOC Code	Employment, 2008	Projected employment, 2018	Change, 2008–2018	
				Number	Percent
Electrical and electronics installers and repairers	—	160,900	168,400	7,500	5
Electric motor, power tool, and related repairers	49-2092	23,700	24,900	1,200	5
Electrical and electronics installers and repairers, transportation equipment	49-2093	16,100	16,700	700	4
Electrical and electronics repairers, commercial and industrial equipment	49-2094	78,000	81,000	2,900	4
Electrical and electronics repairers, powerhouse, substation, and relay	49-2095	23,400	26,100	2,700	12
Electronic equipment installers and repairers, motor vehicles	49-2096	19,700	19,700	0	0

NOTE: Data in this table are rounded.

experienced technicians who provide technical guidance, and work independently only after developing the necessary skills.

Other qualifications. Installers and repairers should have good eyesight and color perception to work with the intricate components used in electronic equipment. Field technicians work closely with customers and should have good communication skills and a neat appearance. Employers also may require that field technicians have a driver's license.

Certification and advancement. Various organizations offer certification. For instance, the Electronics Technicians Association (ETA) offers over 50 certification programs in numerous electronics specialties for varying levels of competence. The International Society of Certified Electronics Technicians also offers certification for several levels of competence, focusing on a broad range of topics, including basic electronics, electronic systems, and appliance service. To become certified, applicants must meet several prerequisites and pass a comprehensive written or online examination. Certification demonstrates a level of competency and can make an applicant more attractive to employers, as well as increase one's opportunities for advancement.

Experienced repairers with advanced training may become specialists or troubleshooters who assist other repairers diagnose difficult problems. Workers with leadership skills may become supervisors of other repairers. Some experienced workers open their own repair shops.

Employment

Electrical and electronics installers and repairers held about 160,900 jobs in 2008. The following tabulation breaks down their employment by occupational specialty:

Electrical and electronics installers and repairers, commercial and industrial equipment..................78,000
Electric motor, power tool, and related repairers......23,700
Electrical and electronics repairers, powerhouse, substation, and relay.......................23,400
Electrical equipment installers and repairers, motor vehicles..............................19,700
Electrical and electronics installers and repairers, transportation equipment..................16,100

Many repairers worked for repair and maintenance establishments.

Job Outlook

Overall employment is expected to grow more slowly than the average through the year 2018. Job prospects should be best for applicants with an associate degree, certification, and related experience.

Employment change. Overall employment of electrical and electronics installers and repairers is expected to grow by 5 percent through the year 2018, which is slower than the average for all occupations. Growth rates, however, will vary by occupational specialty.

Employment of electrical and electronics installers and repairers of commercial and industrial equipment is expected to grow 4 percent, which is slower than the average for all occupations. As equipment becomes more sophisticated, businesses will strive to lower costs by increasing and improving automation. Companies will install electronic controls, robots, sensors, and other equipment to automate processes such as assembly and testing. Improved reliability of equipment, however, may constrain employment growth of installers; on the other hand, companies will increasingly rely on repairers because malfunctions that idle commercial and industrial equipment will continue to be costly.

Little or no employment change is expected for motor vehicle electronic equipment installers and repairers. As motor vehicle manufacturers install more and better sound, security, entertainment, and navigation systems in new vehicles, and as newer electronic systems require progressively less maintenance, employment growth for aftermarket electronic equipment installers will be limited.

Employment of electric motor, power tool, and related repairers is expected to grow 5 percent, which is slower than the average for all occupations. Retrofitting electrical generators in public buildings to reduce emissions and energy consumption will spur some employment growth. However, improvements in electrical and electronic equipment design, as well as the increased use of disposable tool parts should suppress job growth.

Employment of electrical and electronic installers and repairers of transportation equipment is expected to grow 4 percent, which is slower than the average for all occupations. Declining employment in the rail transportation industry will dampen growth in this occupational specialty.

Employment of electrical and electronics installers and repairers, powerhouse, substation, and relay is also expected to grow 12 percent, about as fast as the average for all occupations. While privatization in utilities industries should improve productivity and hinder employment growth, installation of newer, energy efficient green technologies will spur demand for employment.

Job prospects. Job opportunities should be best for applicants with an associate degree in electronics, certification, and related experience. In addition to employment growth, the need to replace workers who transfer to other occupations or leave the labor force will result in some job openings.

Earnings

Median hourly wages of electrical and electronics repairers, commercial and industrial equipment were $24.39 in May 2009. The middle 50 percent earned between $19.34 and $29.53. The lowest 10 percent earned less than $15.12, and the highest 10 percent earned more than $34.76. In May 2009, median hourly wages were $25.90 in the federal government and $22.79 in building equipment contractors, the industries employing the largest numbers of electrical and electronics repairers, commercial and industrial equipment.

Median hourly wages of electric motor, power tool, and related repairers were $17.44 in May 2009. The middle 50 percent earned between $13.79 and $22.16. The lowest 10 percent earned less than $10.62, and the highest 10 percent earned more than $27.88. In May 2009, median hourly wages were $17.25 in commercial and industrial machinery and equipment (except automotive and electronic) repair, the industry employing the largest number of electronic motor, power tool, and related repairers.

Median hourly wages of electrical and electronics repairers, powerhouse, substation, and relay were $29.94 in May 2009. The middle 50 percent earned between $25.82 and $34.33. The lowest 10 percent earned less than $20.90, and the highest 10 percent earned more than $39.21. In May 2009, median hourly wages were $30.34 in electric power generation, transmission, and distribution, the industry employing the largest number of these repairers.

Median hourly wages of electronics installers and repairers, motor vehicles were $13.49 in May 2009. The middle 50 percent earned between $10.81 and $16.94. The lowest 10 percent earned less than $9.01, and the highest 10 percent earned more than $21.33.

Median hourly wages of electrical and electronics repairers, transportation equipment were $22.03 in May 2009. The middle 50 percent earned between $17.43 and $26.72. The lowest 10 percent earned less than $13.78, and the highest 10 percent earned more than $31.23.

Related Occupations

Workers in other occupations who install and repair electronic equipment include aircraft and avionics equipment mechanics and service technicians; broadcast and sound engineering technicians and radio operators; coin, vending, and amusement machine servicers and repairers; computer, automated teller, and office machine repairers; electricians; electronic home entertainment equipment installers and repairers; elevator installers and repairers; maintenance and repair workers, general; and radio and telecommunications equipment installers and repairers.

Sources of Additional Information

For information on careers and certification, contact any of the following organizations:

▸ ACES International, 5381 Chatham Lake Dr., Virginia Beach, VA 23464. Internet: www.acesinternational.org

▸ Electronics Technicians Association International, 5 Depot St., Greencastle, IN 46135. Internet: http://eta-i.org/

▸ International Society of Certified Electronics Technicians, 3608 Pershing Ave., Fort Worth, TX 76107. Internet: www.iscet.org

Electricians

(O*NET 47-2111.00)

Significant Points

■ Job opportunities should be good, especially for those with the broadest range of skills.

■ Most electricians acquire their skills by completing an apprenticeship program usually lasting four years.

■ About 79 percent of electricians work in the construction industry or are self-employed, but there also will be opportunities for electricians in other industries.

Nature of the Work

Electricians install and maintain all of the electrical and power systems for our homes, businesses, and factories. They install and maintain the wiring and control equipment through which electricity flows. They also install and maintain electrical equipment and machines in factories and a wide range of other businesses.

Electricians generally focus on either construction or maintenance, although many do both. Electricians specializing in construction primarily install wiring systems into factories, businesses, and new homes. Electricians specializing in maintenance fix and upgrade existing electrical systems and repair electrical equipment. All electricians must follow state and local building codes and the National Electrical Code when performing their work.

Electricians usually start their work by reading blueprints— technical diagrams that show the locations of circuits, outlets, load centers, panel boards, and other equipment. After determining where all the wires and components will go, electricians install and connect the wires to circuit breakers, transformers, outlets, or other components and systems.

When installing wiring, electricians use handtools such as conduit benders, screwdrivers, pliers, knives, hacksaws, and wire strippers, as well as power tools such as drills and saws. Later, they use ammeters, ohmmeters, voltmeters, harmonics testers, and other equipment to test connections and ensure the compatibility and safety of components.

Maintenance electricians repair or replace electric and electronic equipment when it breaks. They make needed repairs as quickly as possible in order to minimize inconvenience. They may replace items such as circuit breakers, fuses, switches, electrical and electronic components, or wire.

Electricians also periodically inspect all equipment to ensure that it is operating properly and to correct problems before breakdowns occur.

Maintenance work varies greatly, depending on where an electrician works. Electricians who focus on residential work perform a wide variety of electrical work for homeowners. They may rewire a home and replace an old fuse box with a new circuit breaker box to accommodate additional appliances, or they may install new lighting and other electric household items, such as ceiling fans. These electricians also might do some construction and installation work.

Electricians in large factories usually do maintenance work that is more complex. These kinds of electricians may repair motors, transformers, generators, and electronic controllers on machine tools and industrial robots. They also advise management as to whether the continued operation of certain equipment could be hazardous. When working with complex electronic devices, they may consult with engineers, engineering technicians, line installers and repairers, or industrial machinery mechanics and maintenance workers. (Descriptions for all of these occupations except engineers appear elsewhere in this book.)

Work environment. Electricians work indoors and out, at construction sites, in homes, and in businesses or factories. The work may be strenuous at times and may include bending conduit; lifting heavy objects; and standing, stooping, and kneeling for long periods. Electricians risk injury from electrical shock, falls, and cuts, and must follow strict safety procedures to avoid injuries. Data from the U.S. Bureau of Labor Statistics show that full-time electricians experienced a work-related injury and illness rate that was higher than the national average. When working outdoors, they may be subject to inclement weather. Some electricians may have to travel long distances to job sites.

Most electricians work a standard 40-hour week, although overtime may be required. Those who do maintenance work may work nights or weekends and be on call to go to the work site when needed. Electricians in industrial settings may have periodic extended overtime during scheduled maintenance or retooling periods. Companies that operate 24 hours a day may employ three shifts of electricians.

Training, Other Qualifications, and Advancement

Most electricians learn their trade through apprenticeship programs that combine on-the-job training with related classroom instruction.

Education and training. Apprenticeship programs combine paid on-the-job training with related classroom instruction. Joint training committees made up of local unions of the International Brotherhood of Electrical Workers and local chapters of the National Electrical Contractors Association, individual electrical contracting companies, or local chapters of the Associated Builders and Contractors and the Independent Electrical Contractors Association usually sponsor apprenticeship programs.

Because of the comprehensive training received, those who complete apprenticeship programs qualify to do both maintenance and construction work. Apprenticeship programs usually last 4 years. Each year includes at least 144 hours of classroom instruction and 2,000 hours of on-the-job training. In the classroom, apprentices learn electrical theory, blueprint reading, mathematics, electrical code requirements, and safety and first aid practices. They also may

receive specialized training in soldering, communications, fire alarm systems, and cranes and elevators.

On the job, apprentices work under the supervision of experienced electricians. At first, they drill holes, set anchors and attach conduit. Later, they measure, fabricate, and install conduit and install, connect, and test wiring, outlets, and switches. They also learn to set up and draw diagrams for entire electrical systems. Eventually, they practice and master all of an electrician's main tasks.

Some people start their classroom training before seeking an apprenticeship. A number of public and private vocational-technical schools and training academies offer training to become an electrician. Employers often hire students who complete these programs and usually start them at a more advanced level than those without this training. A few people become electricians by first working as helpers—assisting electricians by setting up job sites, gathering materials, and doing other nonelectrical work—before entering an apprenticeship program. All apprentices need a high school diploma or a General Equivalency Diploma (GED). Electricians also may need additional classes in mathematics because they solve mathematical problems on the job.

Education continues throughout an electrician's career. Electricians may need to take classes to learn about changes to the National Electrical Code, and they often complete regular safety programs, manufacturer-specific training, and management training courses. Classes on such topics as low-voltage voice and data systems, telephone systems, video systems, and alternative energy systems such as solar energy and wind energy increasingly are being given as these systems become more prevalent. Other courses teach electricians how to become contractors.

Licensure. Most states and localities require electricians to be licensed. Although licensing requirements vary from state to state, electricians usually must pass an examination that tests their knowledge of electrical theory, the National Electrical Code, and local and state electric and building codes.

Electrical contractors who do electrical work for the public, as opposed to electricians who work for electrical contractors, often need a special license. In some states, electrical contractors need certification as master electricians. Most states require master electricians to have at least 7 years of experience as an electrician or a bachelor's degree in electrical engineering or a related field.

Other qualifications. Applicants for apprenticeships usually must be at least 18 years old and have a high school diploma or a GED. They also may have to pass a test and meet other requirements.

Other skills needed to become an electrician include manual dexterity, eye-hand coordination, physical fitness, and a good sense of balance. Electricians also need good color vision because workers frequently must identify electrical wires by color. In addition, apprenticeship committees and employers view a good work history or military service favorably.

Advancement. Experienced electricians can advance to jobs as supervisors. In construction, they also may become project managers or construction superintendents. Those with sufficient capital and management skills can start their own contracting business, although doing so often requires a special electrical contractor's license. Supervisors and contractors should be able to identify and estimate costs and prices and the time and materials needed to complete a job. Many electricians also become electrical inspectors.

For those who seek to advance, it is increasingly important to be able to communicate in both English and Spanish in order to relay instructions and safety precautions to workers with limited understanding of English; Spanish-speaking workers make up a large part of the construction workforce in many areas. Spanish-speaking workers who want to advance in this occupation need very good English skills to understand electrician classes and installation instructions, which are usually written in English and are highly technical.

Employment

Electricians held about 694,900 jobs in 2008. About 65 percent of wage and salary workers were employed by electrical contracting firms, and the remainder worked as electricians in a variety of other industries. In addition, about 9 percent of electricians were self-employed.

Job Outlook

Average employment growth is expected. Job prospects should be good, particularly for workers with the widest range of skills, including voice, data, and video wiring.

Employment change. Employment of electricians should increase 12 percent between 2008 and 2018, about as fast as the average for all occupations. As the population grows, electricians will be needed to wire new homes, restaurants, schools, and other structures that will be built to accommodate the growing population. In addition, older buildings will require improvements to their electrical systems to meet modern codes and accommodate higher electricity consumption due to the greater use of electronic equipment in houses and workplaces.

New technologies also are expected to continue to spur demand for these workers. Robots and other automated manufacturing systems in factories will require the installation and maintenance of more complex wiring systems. In addition, efforts to boost conservation of energy in public buildings and in new construction will boost demand for electricians because electricians are key to installing some of the latest energy savers, such as solar panels and motion sensors for turning on lights.

Job prospects. In addition to jobs created by the increased demand for electrical work, openings are expected over the next decade as electricians retire. This will create good job opportunities, especially for those with the widest range of skills, including voice, data, and video wiring. Job openings for electricians will vary by location and specialty, however, and will be best in the fastest growing regions of the country.

Employment of electricians, like that of many other construction workers, is sensitive to the fluctuations of the economy. On the one hand, workers in these trades may experience periods of unemployment when the overall level of construction falls. On the other hand,

shortages of these workers may occur in some areas during peak periods of building activity.

Although employment of maintenance electricians is steadier than that of construction electricians, those working in the automotive and other manufacturing industries that are sensitive to cyclical swings in the economy may experience layoffs during recessions. In addition, in many industries opportunities for maintenance electricians may be limited by increased contracting out for electrical services in an effort to reduce operating costs. However, increased job opportunities for electricians in electrical contracting firms should partially offset job losses in other industries.

Earnings

In May 2009, median hourly wages of wage and salary electricians were $22.68. The middle 50 percent earned between $17.30 and $30.35. The lowest 10 percent earned less than $13.79, and the highest 10 percent earned more than $38.59. Median hourly wages in the industries employing the largest numbers of electricians were as follows:

Building equipment contractors............................ $22.12
Local government.. 25.83
Employment services.. 19.09
Nonresidential building construction....................... 22.81
Electric power generation, transmission and
    distribution.. 27.97

Apprentices usually start at between 30 and 50 percent of the rate paid to fully trained electricians, depending on experience. As apprentices become more skilled, they receive periodic pay increases throughout their training.

About 32 percent of all electricians are members of a union, especially the International Brotherhood of Electrical Workers. Among unions representing maintenance electricians are the International Brotherhood of Electrical Workers; the International Union of Electronic, Electrical, Salaried, Machine, and Furniture Workers; the International Association of Machinists and Aerospace Workers; the International Union, United Automobile, Aircraft and Agricultural Implement Workers of America; and the United Steelworkers of America.

Related Occupations

Other occupations that combine manual skill and knowledge of electrical materials and concepts include the following computer, automated teller, and office machine repairers; electrical and electronics drafters; electrical and electronics engineering technicians; electrical and electronics installers and repairers; electronic home entertainment equipment installers and repairers; elevator installers and repairers; heating, air-conditioning, and refrigeration mechanics and installers; and line installers and repairers.

Projections Data from the National Employment Matrix

Occupational title	SOC Code	Employment, 2008	Projected employment, 2018	Change, 2008–2018	
				Number	Percent
Electricians...47-2111		694,900	777,900	83,000	12

NOTE: Data in this table are rounded.

Sources of Additional Information

For details about apprenticeships or other work opportunities in this trade, contact the offices of the state employment service, the state apprenticeship agency, local electrical contractors or firms that employ maintenance electricians, or local union-management electrician apprenticeship committees. Apprenticeship information is available from the U.S. Department of Labor's toll-free help line: (877) 872-5627. Internet: www.doleta.gov/OA/eta_default.cfm

Information may be available as well from local chapters of the Independent Electrical Contractors, Inc.; the National Electrical Contractors Association; the Home Builders Institute; the Associated Builders and Contractors trade association; and the International Brotherhood of Electrical Workers.

For information about union apprenticeship and training programs, contact

▸ National Joint Apprenticeship Training Committee, 301 Prince George's Blvd., Upper Marlboro, MD 20774-7410. Internet: www.njatc.org

▸ National Electrical Contractors Association, 3 Bethesda Metro Center, Suite 1100, Bethesda, MD 20814-6302. Internet: www.necanet.org

▸ International Brotherhood of Electrical Workers, 900 Seventh St. NW, Washington, DC 20001-3886. Internet: www.ibew.org

For information about independent apprenticeship programs, contact

▸ Associated Builders and Contractors, Workforce Development Department, 4250 N. Fairfax Dr., 9th Floor, Arlington, VA 22203-1607. Internet: www.trytools.org

▸ Independent Electrical Contractors, Inc., 4401 Ford Ave., Suite 1100, Alexandria, VA 22302-1464. Internet: www.ieci.org

▸ National Association of Home Builders, Home Builders Institute, 1201 15th St. NW, 6th Floor, Washington, DC 20005-2842. Internet: www.hbi.org

▸ National Center for Construction Education and Research, 3600 NW 43rd St., Bldg. G, Gainesville, FL 32606-8134. Internet: www.nccer.org

For general information on apprenticeships and how to get them, see the *Occupational Outlook Quarterly* article "Apprenticeships: Career training, credentials—and a paycheck in your pocket," online at www.bls.gov/opub/ooq/2002/summer/art01.pdf and in print at many libraries and career centers.

Emergency Medical Technicians and Paramedics

(O*NET 29-2041.00)

Significant Points

■ Employment is projected to grow as fast as the average for all occupations.

■ Emergency medical technicians and paramedics need formal training and certification or licensure, but requirements vary by state.

■ Emergency services function 24 hours a day, so emergency medical technicians and paramedics have irregular working hours.

■ Opportunities will be best for those who have earned advanced certifications.

Nature of the Work

People's lives often depend on the quick reaction and competent care of *emergency medical technicians (EMTs) and paramedics*. Incidents as varied as automobile accidents, heart attacks, slips and falls, childbirth, and gunshot wounds require immediate medical attention. EMTs and paramedics provide this vital service as they care for and transport the sick or injured to a medical facility.

In an emergency, EMTs and paramedics are typically dispatched by a 911 operator to the scene, where they often work with police and fire fighters. (Police and fire fighters are discussed elsewhere in this book.) Once they arrive, EMTs and paramedics assess the nature of the patient's condition, while trying to determine whether the patient has any pre-existing medical conditions. Following protocols and guidelines, they provide emergency care and transport the patient to a medical facility. EMTs and paramedics operate in emergency medical services systems where a physician provides medical direction and oversight.

EMTs and paramedics use special equipment, such as backboards, to immobilize patients before placing them on stretchers and securing them in the ambulance for transport to a medical facility. These workers generally work in teams. During the transport of a patient, one EMT or paramedic drives, while the other monitors the patient's vital signs and gives additional care, as needed. Some paramedics work as part of a helicopter's flight crew to quickly transport critically ill or injured patients to hospital trauma centers.

At the medical facility, EMTs and paramedics help transfer patients to the emergency department, report their observations and actions to emergency department staff, and may provide additional emergency treatment. After each run, EMTs and paramedics document the trip, replace used supplies and check equipment. If a transported patient has a contagious disease, EMTs and paramedics decontaminate the interior of the ambulance and report cases to the proper authorities.

EMTs and paramedics also provide transportation for patients from one medical facility to another, particularly if they work for private ambulance services. Patients often need to be transferred to a hospital that specializes in treating their injury or illness or to facility that provides long-term care, like nursing homes.

Beyond these general duties, the specific responsibilities of EMTs and paramedics depend on their level of qualification and training. The National Registry of Emergency Medical Technicians (NREMT) certifies emergency medical service providers at five levels: First Responder; EMT-Basic; EMT-Intermediate (which has two levels called 1985 and 1999) and Paramedic. Some states, however, have their own certification programs and use distinct names and titles.

The *EMT-Basic* represents the first response of the emergency medical system. An EMT trained at this level is prepared to care for patients at the scene of an accident and while transporting patients by ambulance to the hospital under the direction of more highly trained medical personnel. The EMT-Basic has the emergency skills to assess a patient's condition and manage respiratory, cardiac, and trauma emergencies.

The *EMT-Intermediate* has more advanced training. However, the specific tasks that those certified at this level are allowed to perform vary greatly from state to state.

Paramedics provide more extensive pre-hospital care than do EMTs. In addition to carrying out the procedures of the other levels, paramedics administer medications orally and intravenously, interpret electrocardiograms (EKGs), perform endotracheal intubations, and use monitors and other complex equipment. However, like the EMT-Intermediate level, what paramedics are permitted to do varies by state.

Work environment. EMTs and paramedics work both indoors and out, in all types of weather. They are required to do considerable kneeling, bending, and heavy lifting. These workers are at a higher risk for contracting illnesses or experiencing injuries on the job than workers in other occupations. They risk noise-induced hearing loss from sirens and back injuries from lifting patients. In addition, EMTs and paramedics may be exposed to communicable diseases, such as hepatitis-B and AIDS, as well as to violence from mentally unstable or combative patients. The work is not only physically strenuous but can be stressful, sometimes involving life-or-death situations and suffering patients. Nonetheless, many people find the work exciting and challenging and enjoy the opportunity to help others. These workers experienced a larger than average number of work-related injuries or illnesses

Many EMTs and paramedics are required to work more than 40 hours a week. Because emergency services function 24 hours a day, EMTs and paramedics may have irregular working hours.

Training, Other Qualifications, and Advancement

Generally, a high school diploma is required to enter a training program to become an EMT or paramedic. Workers must complete a formal training and certification process.

Education and training. A high school diploma is usually required to enter a formal emergency medical technician training program. Training is offered at progressive levels: EMT-Basic, EMT-Intermediate, and Paramedic.

At the EMT-Basic level, coursework emphasizes emergency skills, such as managing respiratory, trauma, and cardiac emergencies, and patient assessment. Formal courses are often combined with time in an emergency department or ambulance. The program provides instruction and practice in dealing with bleeding, fractures, airway obstruction, cardiac arrest, and emergency childbirth. Students learn how to use and maintain common emergency equipment, such as backboards, suction devices, splints, oxygen delivery systems, and stretchers. Graduates of approved EMT-Basic training programs must pass a written and practical examination administered by the state licensing agency or the NREMT.

At the EMT-Intermediate level, training requirements vary by state. The nationally defined levels, EMT-Intermediate 1985 and EMT-Intermediate 1999, typically require 30 to 350 hours of training based on scope of practice. Students learn advanced skills such the use of advanced airway devices, intravenous fluids, and some medications.

The most advanced level of training for this occupation is Paramedic. At this level, the caregiver receives training in anatomy and physiology as well as advanced medical skills. Most commonly, the training is conducted in community colleges and technical schools

and may result in an associate degree. These programs may take up to one to two years. Such education prepares the graduate to take the NREMT examination to become certified as a paramedic. Extensive related coursework and clinical and field experience are required. Refresher courses and continuing education are available for EMTs and paramedics at all levels.

Licensure. All 50 states require EMTs and paramedics to be licensed, but the levels and titles vary from state to state. In most states and the District of Columbia certification by the NREMT is required at some or all levels. Some states administer their own certification examination or provide the option of taking either the NREMT or state examination. In most states, licensure renewal is required every two to three years and generally, EMTs and paramedics must take refresher training courses or complete continuing education requirements. Many states restrict licensure based on an individual's criminal history.

Other qualifications. EMTs and paramedics should be emotionally stable; have good dexterity, agility, and physical coordination; and be able to lift and carry heavy loads. They also need good eyesight (corrective lenses may be used) with accurate color vision. Many employers require a criminal background check.

Advancement. Paramedics can become supervisors, operations managers, administrative directors, or executive directors of emergency services. Some EMTs and paramedics become instructors, dispatchers, or physician assistants; others move into sales or marketing of emergency medical equipment. A number of people become EMTs and paramedics to test their interest in health care before training as registered nurses, physicians, or other health workers.

Employment

EMTs and paramedics held about 210,700 jobs in 2008. Most career EMTs and paramedics work in metropolitan areas. Volunteer EMTs and paramedics are more common in small cities, towns, and rural areas. These individuals volunteer for fire departments, emergency medical services, or hospitals and may respond to only a few calls per month.

Paid EMTs and paramedics were employed in a number of industries. About 45 percent worked as employees of ambulance services. About 29 percent worked in local government. Another 20 percent worked in hospitals.

Job Outlook

Employment for EMTs and paramedics is expected to grow about as fast as the average for all occupations through 2018. Job prospects should be good, particularly in cities and private ambulance services.

Employment change. Employment of emergency medical technicians and paramedics is expected to grow 9 percent between 2008 and 2018, which is about as fast as the average for all occupations. Growth in this occupation is due in large part to increasing call volume due to aging population. As a large segment of the population—aging members of the baby boom generation—becomes more likely to have medical emergencies, demand will increase for EMTs and paramedics. In addition, the time that EMTs and paramedics must spend with each patient is increasing as emergency departments across the country are experiencing overcrowding. As a result, when an ambulance arrives, it takes longer to transfer the patient from the care of the EMTs and paramedics to the staff of the

Projections Data from the National Employment Matrix

Occupational title	SOC Code	Employment, 2008	Projected employment, 2018	Change, 2008–2018	
				Number	Percent
Emergency medical technicians and paramedics 29-2041		210,700	229,700	19,000	9

NOTE: Data in this table are rounded.

emergency department. In addition, some emergency departments divert ambulances to other hospitals when they are too busy to take on new patients. As a result, ambulances may not be able to go to the nearest hospital, which increases the amount of time spent in transit. Both these factors result in EMTs and paramedics spending more time with each patient, which means more workers are needed to meet demand.

In addition, hospitals are increasingly specializing in treating a particular illness or injury. This results in more patients needing to be transferred to the hospital best able to treat them. Most patients must be transferred by ambulance, so their condition can be monitored en route. Therefore, more demand for transfers between hospitals increases the demand for the services of EMTs and paramedics.

There also still will be demand for part-time, volunteer EMTs and paramedics in rural areas and smaller metropolitan areas.

Job prospects. Job prospects should be favorable. Many job openings will arise from growth and from the need to replace workers who leave the occupation because of the limited potential for advancement, as well as the modest pay and benefits in private-sector jobs. In addition, full-time paid EMTs and paramedics will be needed to replace unpaid volunteers. Emergency medical service agencies find it increasingly difficult to recruit and retain unpaid volunteers because of the amount of training and the large time commitment these positions require. As a result, more paid EMTs and paramedics are needed.

Competition will be greater for jobs in local government, including fire, police, and independent third-service rescue squad departments that tend to have better salaries and benefits. EMTs and paramedics who have advanced education and certifications should enjoy the most favorable job prospects, as clients and patients demand higher levels of care before arriving at the hospital.

Earnings

Earnings of EMTs and paramedics depend on the employment setting and geographic location of their jobs, as well as their training and experience. Median hourly wages of EMTs and paramedics were $14.42 in May 2009. The middle 50 percent earned between $11.37 and $18.87. The lowest 10 percent earned less than $9.31, and the highest 10 percent earned more than $24.74. Median hourly wages in the industries employing the largest numbers of EMTs and paramedics in May 2009 were $13.43 in other ambulatory health-care services and $15.74 in local government.

In 2008, about 27 percent of EMTs and paramedics belonged to a union or were covered by a union contract.

Related Occupations

Other workers in occupations that require quick and level-headed reactions to life-or-death situations are air traffic controllers; fire fighters; physician assistants; police and detectives; and registered nurses.

Sources of Additional Information

General information about emergency medical technicians and paramedics is available from

▸ National Association of Emergency Medical Technicians, P.O. Box 1400, Clinton, MS 39060-1400. Internet: www.naemt.org

▸ National Highway Traffic Safety Administration, Office of Emergency Medical Services, 1200 New Jersey Ave., SE, NTI-140, Washington, DC 20590. Internet: www.ems.gov

▸ National Registry of Emergency Medical Technicians, Rocco V. Morando Bldg., 6610 Busch Blvd., P.O. Box 29233, Columbus, OH 43229. Internet: www.nremt.org

Engineering Technicians

(O*NET 17-3021.00, 17-3022.00, 17-3023.00, 17-3023.01, 17-3023.03, 17-3024.00, 17-3024.01, 17-3025.00, 17-3026.00, 17-3027.00, 17-3027.01, 17-3029.00, 17-3029.01, 17-3029.02, 17-3029.03, 17-3029.04, 17-3029.05, 17-3029.06, 17-3029.07, 17-3029.08, 17-3029.09, 17-3029.10, 17-3029.11, and 17-3029.12)

Significant Points

■ Electrical and electronic engineering technicians make up 33 percent of all engineering technicians.

■ Employment of engineering technicians is influenced by economic conditions similar to those which affect engineers; as a result, job outlook varies by specialty.

■ Opportunities will be best for individuals with an associate degree or other postsecondary training in engineering technology.

Nature of the Work

Engineering technicians use the principles and theories of science, engineering, and mathematics to solve technical problems in research and development, manufacturing, sales, construction, inspection, and maintenance. Their work is more narrowly focused and application-oriented than that of scientists and engineers. Many engineering technicians assist engineers and scientists, especially in research and development. Others work in quality control, inspecting products and processes, conducting tests, or collecting data. In manufacturing, they may assist in product design, development, or production.

Engineering technicians who work in research and development build or set up equipment, prepare and conduct experiments, collect data, calculate or record results, and help engineers or scientists in other ways, such as making prototype versions of newly designed equipment. They also assist in design work, often using computer-aided design and drafting (CADD) equipment.

Most engineering technicians specialize, learning skills and working in the same disciplines as engineers. Occupational titles, therefore, tend to reflect this similarity. This book does not cover in detail some branches of engineering technology, such as chemical engineering technology (the development of new chemical products and processes) and bioengineering technology (the development and implementation of biomedical equipment), for which there are accredited programs of study.

Aerospace engineering and operations technicians operate and maintain equipment used to test aircraft and spacecraft. New aircraft designs are subjected to years of testing before they are put into service, since failure of key components during flight can be fatal. Technicians may calibrate test equipment, such as wind tunnels, and determine causes of equipment malfunctions. They may also program and run computer simulations that test new designs virtually. Using computer and communications systems, aerospace engineering and operations technicians often record and interpret test data.

Civil engineering technicians help civil engineers plan and oversee the construction of highways, buildings, bridges, dams, wastewater treatment systems, and other structures. Some estimate construction costs and specify materials to be used, and some may even prepare drawings or perform land-surveying duties. Others may set up and monitor instruments used to study traffic conditions.

Electrical and electronic engineering technicians help design, develop, test, and manufacture electrical and electronic equipment such as communication equipment, medical monitoring devices, navigational equipment, and computers. They may work in product evaluation and testing, using measuring and diagnostic devices to adjust, test, and repair equipment. (Workers whose jobs primarily involve repairing electrical and electronic equipment often are referred to as electronics technicians, but they are included with electrical and electronics installers and repairers elsewhere in this book.)

Electro-mechanical engineering technicians combine knowledge of mechanical engineering technology with knowledge of electrical and electronic circuits to design, develop, test, and manufacture electronic and computer-controlled mechanical systems, such as robotic assembly machines. They also operate these machines in factories and other work sites. Their work often overlaps that of both electrical and electronic engineering technicians and mechanical engineering technicians.

Environmental engineering technicians work closely with environmental engineers and scientists in developing methods and devices used in the prevention, control, or remediation of environmental hazards. They inspect and maintain equipment related to air pollution and recycling. Some inspect water and wastewater treatment systems to ensure that pollution control requirements are met.

Industrial engineering technicians study the efficient use of personnel, materials, and machines in factories, stores, repair shops, and offices. Working under the direction of industrial engineers, they prepare layouts of machinery and equipment, plan the flow of work, conduct statistical studies of production time or quality, and analyze production costs.

Mechanical engineering technicians help engineers design, develop, test, and manufacture industrial machinery, consumer products, and other equipment. They may assist in product tests by, for example, setting up instrumentation for auto crash tests. They may make sketches and rough layouts, record and analyze data, make calculations and estimates, and report on their findings. When planning production, mechanical engineering technicians prepare layouts and drawings of the assembly process and of parts to be manufactured.

They estimate labor costs, equipment life, and plant space. Some test and inspect machines and equipment or work with engineers to eliminate production problems.

Work environment. Most engineering technicians work 40 hours a week in laboratories, in offices, in manufacturing or industrial plants, or on construction sites. Some may be exposed to hazards from equipment, chemicals, or toxic materials, but incidents are rare as long as proper procedures are followed.

Training, Other Qualifications, and Advancement

Most employers prefer to hire engineering technicians with an associate degree or other postsecondary training in engineering technology. Training is available at technical institutes, at community colleges, at extension divisions of colleges and universities, at public and private vocational-technical schools, and in the Armed Forces.

Education and training. Although it may be possible to qualify for certain engineering technician jobs without formal training, most employers prefer to hire someone with a two-year associate degree or other postsecondary training in engineering technology. Workers with less formal engineering technology training need more time to learn skills while on the job. Prospective engineering technicians should take as many high school science and math courses as possible to prepare for programs in engineering technology after high school.

Most two-year associate degree programs accredited by the Technology Accreditation Commission of the Accreditation Board for Engineering and Technology (ABET) include at least college algebra and trigonometry and one or two basic science courses. Depending on the specialty, more math or science may be required. About 700 ABET-accredited programs are offered in engineering technology specialties.

The types of technical courses required depend on the specialty. For example, prospective mechanical engineering technicians may take courses in fluid mechanics, thermodynamics, and mechanical design; prospective electrical engineering technicians may need classes in electrical circuits, microprocessors, and digital electronics; and those preparing to work in environmental engineering technology need courses in environmental regulations and safe handling of hazardous materials.

Technical institutes offer intensive technical training through application and practice, but they provide less theory and general education than do community colleges. Many technical institutes offer two-year associate degree programs and are similar to or part of a community college or state university system. Other technical institutes are run by private organizations, with programs that vary considerably in length and types of courses offered.

Community colleges offer curriculums that are similar to those in technical institutes but include more theory and liberal arts. There may be little or no difference between programs at technical institutes and community colleges, as both offer associate degrees. After completing the two-year program, some graduates get jobs as engineering technicians, whereas others continue their education at four-year colleges. However, an associate degree in pre-engineering is different from one in engineering technology. Students who enroll in a two-year pre-engineering program may find it difficult to find work as an engineering technician if they decide not to enter a four-year engineering program because pre-engineering programs usually focus less on hands-on applications and more on academic preparatory work. Conversely, graduates of two-year engineering technology programs may not receive credit for some of the courses they have taken if they choose to transfer to a four-year engineering program. Colleges having four-year programs usually do not offer engineering technician training, but college courses in science, engineering, and mathematics are useful for obtaining a job as an engineering technician. Many four-year colleges offer bachelor's degrees in engineering technology, but graduates of these programs often are hired to work as technologists or applied engineers, not technicians.

Vocational-technical schools, another source of technical training, include postsecondary public institutions that serve local students and emphasize training needed by local employers. Most schools that offer training to become an engineering technician require a high school diploma or its equivalent for admission.

Other training in technical areas may be obtained in the Armed Forces. Many military technical training programs are highly regarded by employers. However, skills acquired in military programs are often narrowly focused and may be less applicable in civilian industry, which often requires broader training. Therefore, some additional training may be needed, depending on the acquired skills and the kind of job.

Other qualifications. Because many engineering technicians assist in design work, creativity is desirable. Good communication skills and the ability to work well with others also are important because engineering technicians are typically part of a team of engineers and other technicians.

Certification and advancement. Engineering technicians usually begin by performing routine duties under the close supervision of an experienced technician, technologist, engineer, or scientist. As they gain experience, they are given more difficult assignments with only general supervision. Some engineering technicians eventually become supervisors.

Employment

Engineering technicians held 497,300 jobs in 2008. Approximately 33 percent were electrical and electronic engineering technicians, as indicated by the following tabulation.

Electrical and electronic engineering technicians	164,000
Civil engineering technicians	91,700
Industrial engineering technicians	72,600
Mechanical engineering technicians	46,100
Environmental engineering technicians	21,200
Electro-mechanical technicians	16,400
Aerospace engineering and operations technicians	8,700
Engineering technicians, except drafters, all other	76,600

About 34 percent of all engineering technicians worked in manufacturing. Another 25 percent worked in professional, scientific, and technical service industries, mostly in engineering or business services companies that do engineering work on contract for government, manufacturing firms, or other organizations.

In 2008, the federal government employed 35,300 engineering technicians. State governments employed 31,300, and local governments employed 25,100.

Job Outlook

Overall employment of engineering technicians is expected to grow slower than the average for all occupations, but projected growth and job prospects vary by specialty. Opportunities will be best for individuals with an associate degree or other postsecondary training in engineering technology.

Employment change. Overall employment of engineering technicians is expected to grow by 5 percent between 2008 and 2018, slower than the average for all occupations. Competitive pressures will force companies to improve and update manufacturing facilities and product designs, although increased efficiencies and automation of many support activities will curtail job growth for engineering technicians.

Employment of engineering technicians in some design functions may also be affected by increasing globalization of the development process. To reduce costs and speed project completion, some companies may relocate part of their development operations to facilities overseas, affecting both engineers and engineering technicians—particularly in electronics and computer-related specialties. However, some aspects of the work of engineering technicians require on-site presence, particularly in the environmental, civil, and industrial specialties, so demand for these engineering technicians within the United States should continue to grow.

Because engineering technicians work closely with engineers, employment of engineering technicians is often influenced by the same local and national economic conditions that affect engineers. As a result, the employment outlook varies with industry and specialization.

Aerospace engineering and operations technicians are expected to have 2 percent employment growth between 2008 and 2018, signifying little or no change. Although demand for aerospace products will continue to grow, increased use of computer simulations for designing and testing new products will diminish the need for new aerospace engineering technicians.

Civil engineering technicians are expected to have 17 percent employment growth between 2008 and 2018, faster than the average for all occupations. Spurred by population growth and the related need to improve the nation's infrastructure, more civil engineering technicians will be needed to expand transportation, water supply, and pollution control systems, as well as large buildings and building complexes. They also will be needed to repair or replace existing roads, bridges, and other public structures.

The number of electrical and electronic engineering technician jobs is expected to decline by 2 percent between 2008 and 2018, signifying little or no change. Despite rising demand for electronic goods—including communications equipment, defense-related equipment, medical electronics, and consumer products—foreign competition in design and manufacturing, together with increased efficiencies in the design process, will reduce demand for these workers.

The number of electro-mechanical technician jobs is expected to decline moderately by 5 percent between 2008 and 2018. As with the closely related electrical and electronic engineering technicians and mechanical engineering technicians, job losses will be caused by increased productivity in the design and manufacture of

Projections Data from the National Employment Matrix

Occupational title	SOC Code	Employment, 2008	Projected employment, 2018	Change, 2008–2018	
				Number	Percent
Engineering technicians, except drafters...................... 17-3020		497,300	523,100	25,800	5
Aerospace engineering and operations technicians ... 17-3021		8,700	8,900	200	2
Civil engineering technicians 17-3022		91,700	107,200 1	5,500	17
Electrical and electronic engineering technicians...... 17-3023		164,000	160,400	–3,600	–2
Electro-mechanical technicians 17-3024		16,400	15,600	–800	–5
Environmental engineering technicians 17-3025		21,200	27,500	6,400	30
Industrial engineering technicians.......................... 17-3026		72,600	77,400	4,800	7
Mechanical engineering technicians........................ 17-3027		46,100	45,500	–700	–1
Engineering technicians, except drafters, all other.... 17-3029		76,600	80,600	4,000	5

NOTE: Data in this table are rounded.

electro-mechanical products such as unmanned aircraft and robotic equipment.

Environmental engineering technicians are expected to have 30 percent employment growth between 2008 and 2018, much faster than the average for all occupations. More environmental engineering technicians will be needed to comply with environmental regulations and to develop methods of cleaning up existing hazards. A shift in emphasis toward preventing problems rather than controlling those which already exist, as well as increasing public health concerns resulting from population growth, also will spur demand.

Industrial engineering technicians are expected to have 7 percent employment growth between 2008 and 2018, about as fast as average. As firms continue to seek new means of reducing costs and increasing productivity, demand for industrial engineering technicians to analyze and improve production processes should increase. This should lead to some job growth even in manufacturing industries with slowly growing or declining employment.

Mechanical engineering technicians are expected to decline by 1 percent between 2008 and 2018, which represents little or no change. Increased foreign competition in both design services and manufacturing, together with improved efficiencies in design and testing, will reduce the need for mechanical engineering technicians.

Job prospects. Job prospects will vary by specialty and location, as employment is influenced by economic conditions similar to those which affect engineers. In general, opportunities will be best for individuals with an associate degree or other postsecondary training in engineering technology. As technology becomes more sophisticated, employers will continue to look for technicians who are skilled in new technology and who require little additional training. Even in specialties that are expected to experience job declines, there will still be job openings resulting from the need to replace technicians who retire or leave the labor force for any other reason.

Earnings

Median annual wages in May 2009 of engineering technicians by specialty are shown in the following tabulation.

Aerospace engineering and operations
  technicians $56,960
Electrical and electronic engineering
  technicians 54,820
Mechanical engineering technicians 48,970
Industrial engineering technicians...................... 46,760

Electro-mechanical technicians........................... 48,010
Civil engineering technicians 45,970
Environmental engineering technicians................ 42,350

Median annual wages of wage and salary electrical and electronic engineering technicians were $54,820 in May 2009. The middle 50 percent earned between $42,610 and $65,470. The lowest 10 percent earned less than $33,380, and the highest 10 percent earned more than $77,660. Median annual earnings in the industries employing the largest numbers of electrical and electronic engineering technicians were as follows:

Architectural, engineering, and related services....$52,590
Semiconductor and other electronic component
  manufacturing 49,500
Navigational, measuring, electromedical, and
  control instruments manufacturing 49,070

In May 2009, median annual wages for aerospace engineering and operations technicians in the aerospace products and parts manufacturing industry were $53,280, and the median annual salary for environmental engineering technicians in the architectural, engineering, and related services industry was $39,910. Median annual wages for civil engineering technicians in the architectural, engineering, and related services industry were $45,630. The median annual wage for industrial engineering technicians in the semiconductor and other electronic component manufacturing industry was $44,980. In the architectural, engineering, and related services industry, the median annual wage for mechanical engineering technicians was $48,730. Electro-mechanical technicians earned a median annual wage of $45,920 in the semiconductor and other electronic component manufacturing industry.

Related Occupations

Engineering technicians apply scientific and engineering skills that are usually gained in postsecondary programs below the bachelor's degree level. Similar occupations include broadcast and sound engineering technicians and radio operators; drafters; and science technicians.

Sources of Additional Information

Information about careers in engineering technology is available from

▶ JETS (Junior Engineering Technical Society), 1420 King St., Suite 405, Alexandria, VA 22314. Internet: www.jets.org

▶ Pathways to Technology. Internet: www.pathwaystotechnology.org

Information on engineering technology programs accredited by the Accreditation Board for Engineering and Technology is available from

▶ ABET, Inc., 111 Market Place, Suite 1050, Baltimore, MD 21202. Internet: www.abet.org

Farmers, Ranchers, and Agricultural Managers

(O*NET 11-9011.00, 11-9011.01, 11-9011.02, 11-9011.03, and 11-9012.00)

Significant Points

- Modern farming requires knowledge of new developments in agriculture, often gained through growing up on a farm or through postsecondary education.

- Overall employment is projected to decline because of increasing productivity and consolidation of farms.

- Small-scale, local farming, particularly horticulture and organic farming, offers the best opportunities for entering the occupation.

Nature of the Work

American farmers, ranchers, and agricultural managers direct the activities of one of the world's largest and most productive agricultural sectors. They produce enough food and fiber to meet the needs of the United States and for export. *Farmers and ranchers* own and operate mainly family-owned farms. They also may lease land from a landowner and operate it as a working farm. *Agricultural managers* manage the day-to-day activities of one or more farms, ranches, nurseries, timber tracts, greenhouses, or other agricultural establishments for farmers, absentee landowners, or corporations. While their duties and responsibilities vary widely, all farmers, ranchers, and agricultural managers focus on the business aspects of running a farm. On small farms, they may oversee the entire operation; on larger farms, they may oversee a single activity, such as marketing.

Farm output and income are strongly influenced by the weather, disease, fluctuations in prices of domestic farm products, and federal farm programs. In crop-production operations, farmers and managers usually determine the best time to plant seed, apply fertilizer and chemicals, and harvest and market the crops. Many carefully plan the combination of crops they grow so that if the price of one crop drops, they will have sufficient income from another crop to make up the loss. Farmers, ranchers, and managers monitor the constantly changing prices for their products. They use different strategies to protect themselves from unpredictable changes in the markets for agricultural products. If they plan ahead, they may be able to store their crops or keep their livestock to take advantage of higher prices later in the year. Those who participate in the futures market enter contracts on future delivery of agricultural goods. These contracts can minimize the risk of sudden price changes by guaranteeing a certain price for farmers' and ranchers' agricultural goods when they are ready to sell.

While most farm output is sold to food-processing companies, some farmers—particularly operators of smaller farms—may choose to sell their goods directly to consumers through farmers' markets.

Some use cooperatives to reduce their financial risk and to gain a larger share of the prices consumers pay. For example, in community-supported agriculture, cooperatives sell shares of a harvest to consumers prior to the planting season. This frees the farmer from having to bear all the financial risks and ensures a market for the produce of the coming season. Farmers, ranchers, and agricultural managers also negotiate with banks and other credit lenders to get the best financing deals for their equipment, livestock, and seed.

Like other businesses, farming operations have become more complex in recent years, so many farmers use computers to keep financial and inventory records. They also use computer databases and spreadsheets to manage breeding, dairy, and other farm operations.

The type of farm managers operate determines their specific tasks. On crop farms—farms growing grain, cotton, other fibers, fruit, and vegetables—farmers are responsible for preparing, tilling, planting, fertilizing, cultivating, spraying, and harvesting. After the harvest, they make sure that the crops are properly packaged, stored, and marketed. Livestock, dairy, and poultry farmers and ranchers feed and care for animals and keep barns, pens, coops, and other farm buildings clean and in good condition. They also plan and oversee breeding and marketing activities. Both farmers and ranchers operate machinery and maintain equipment and facilities, and both track technological improvements in animal breeding and seeds and choose new or existing products.

The size of the farm or ranch often determines which of these tasks farmers and ranchers handle themselves. Operators of small farms usually perform all tasks, physical and administrative. They keep records for management and tax purposes, service machinery, maintain buildings, and grow vegetables and raise animals. Operators of large farms, by contrast, have employees who help with the physical work. Although employment on most farms is limited to the farmer and one or two family workers or hired employees, some large farms have 100 or more full-time and seasonal workers. Some of these employees are in nonfarm occupations, working as truck drivers, sales representatives, bookkeepers, and computer specialists.

Agricultural managers usually do not plant, harvest, or perform other production activities; instead, they hire and supervise farm and livestock workers, who perform most daily production tasks. Managers may establish output goals; determine financial constraints; monitor production and marketing; hire, assign, and supervise workers; determine crop transportation and storage requirements; and oversee maintenance of the property and equipment.

Horticultural specialty farmers oversee the production of fruits, vegetables, flowers, and ornamental plants used in landscaping, including turf. They also grow nuts, berries, and grapes for wine. *Aquaculture farmers* raise fish and shellfish in marine, brackish, or fresh water, usually in ponds, floating net pens, raceways, or recirculating systems. They stock, feed, protect, and otherwise manage aquatic life sold for consumption or used for recreational fishing.

Work environment. Farmers and farm managers on crop farms usually work from sunrise to sunset during the planting and harvesting seasons. The rest of the year, they plan next season's crops, market their output, and repair machinery.

On livestock-producing farms and ranches, work goes on throughout the year. Animals, unless they are grazing, must be fed and watered every day, and dairy cows must be milked two or three times a day. Many livestock and dairy farmers monitor and attend to the health of their herds, which may include assisting in the birthing of animals.

Such farmers and farm managers rarely get the chance to get away unless they hire an assistant or arrange for a temporary substitute.

Farmers and farm managers who grow produce and perishables have different demands on their time depending on the crop grown and the season. They may work very long hours during planting and harvesting season, but shorter hours at other times. Some farmers maintain cover crops during the cold months, which keep them busy beyond the typical growing season.

On very large farms, farmers and farm managers spend substantial time meeting farm supervisors in charge of various activities. Professional farm managers overseeing several farms may divide their time between traveling to meet farmers or landowners and planning the farm operations in their offices. As farming practices and agricultural technology become more sophisticated, farmers and farm managers are spending more time in offices and on computers, where they electronically manage many aspects of their businesses. Some farmers also attend conferences exchanging information, particularly during the winter months.

Farm work can be hazardous. Tractors and other farm machinery can cause serious injury, and workers must be constantly alert on the job. The proper operation of equipment and handling of chemicals are necessary to avoid accidents, safeguard health, and protect the environment.

Training, Other Qualifications, and Advancement

Experience gained from growing up on or working on a family farm is the most common way farmers learn their trade. However, modern farming requires making increasingly complex scientific, business, and financial decisions, so postsecondary education in agriculture is important, even for people who were raised on farms.

Education and training. Most farmers receive their training on the job, often by being raised on a farm. However, the completion of a two-year associate degree or a four-year bachelor's degree at a college of agriculture is becoming increasingly important for farm managers and for farmers and ranchers who expect to make a living at farming.

Students should select the college most appropriate to their interests and location. All state university systems have at least one land-grant college or university with a school of agriculture. Common programs of study include business with a concentration in agriculture, farm management, agronomy, dairy science, agricultural economics and business, horticulture, crop and fruit science, and animal science. For students interested in aquaculture, formal programs are available and include coursework in fisheries biology, fish culture, hatchery management and maintenance, and hydrology.

Agricultural colleges teach technical knowledge of crops, growing conditions, and plant diseases. They also teach prospective ranchers and dairy farmers the basics of veterinary science and animal husbandry. Students also study how the environment is affected by farm operations, such as the impact of various pesticides on local animals.

New farmers, ranchers, and agricultural managers often spend time working under an experienced farmer to learn how to apply the skills learned through academic training. Those without academic training often take many years to learn how weather, fertilizers, seed, feeding, or breeding affect the growth of crops or the raising of animals in addition to other aspects of farming. A small number of farms offer formal apprenticeships to help young people learn the practical skills of farming and ranching.

Other qualifications. Farmers, ranchers, and agricultural managers need managerial skills to organize and operate a business. A basic knowledge of accounting and bookkeeping is essential in keeping financial records, and knowledge of credit sources is vital for buying seed, fertilizer, and other needed inputs. Workers must also be familiar with safety regulations and requirements of governmental agricultural support programs. Computer skills are becoming increasingly important, especially on large farms, where they are widely used for recordkeeping and business analysis. In addition, skills in personnel management, communication, and conflict resolution are important in the operation of a farm or ranch business.

Mechanical aptitude and the ability to work with tools of all kinds also are valuable skills for a small-farm operator who often maintains and repairs machinery or farm structures.

Certification and advancement. Because of rapid changes in the industry, farmers, ranchers, and agricultural managers need to stay informed about continuing advances in agricultural methods, both in the United States and abroad. They need to monitor changes in governmental regulations that may affect production methods or markets for particular crops. Agricultural managers can enhance their professional status through voluntary certification as an Accredited Farm Manager (AFM) by the American Society of Farm Managers and Rural Appraisers. Accreditation requires several years of farm management experience, the appropriate academic background—a bachelor's degree or, preferably, a master's degree in a field of agricultural science—and passing courses and examinations related to the business, financial, and legal aspects of farm and ranch management.

Employment

Farmers, ranchers, and agricultural managers held more than 1.2 million jobs in 2008. Nearly 80 percent were self-employed farmers and ranchers, and the remainder were wage and salary agricultural managers. Most farmers, ranchers, and agricultural managers oversee crop production activities, while others manage livestock and dairy production.

The soil, topography of the land, and climate often determine the type of farming and ranching done in a particular area. California, Texas, Iowa, Nebraska, and Minnesota are the leading agricultural states in terms of agricultural output measured in dollars. Texas, Missouri, Iowa, Oklahoma, and Kentucky are the leading agricultural states in terms of numbers of farms.

Job Outlook

Overall employment is projected to decline, reflecting the decline of self-employed farmers because of the consolidation of farms and increasing productivity; however, employment of salaried agricultural managers is expected to increase.

Employment change. Employment of self-employed farmers is expected to decline moderately by 8 percent over the 2008–2018 decade. The continuing ability of the agriculture sector to produce more with fewer workers will cause some farmers to go out of business as market pressures leave little room for the marginally successful farmer. As land, machinery, seed, and chemicals become more expensive, only well-capitalized farmers and corporations will be able to buy many of the farms that become available. These

Projections Data from the National Employment Matrix

Occupational title	SOC Code	Employment, 2008	Projected employment, 2018	Change, 2008–2018	
				Number	Percent
Agricultural managers................................ 11-9010		1,234,000	1,169,400	–64,600	–5
Farm, ranch, and other agricultural managers........ 11-9011		248,100	262,700	14,600	6
Farmers and ranchers.. 11-9012		985,900	906,700	–79,200	–8

NOTE: Data in this table are rounded.

larger, more productive farms are better able to withstand the adverse effects of climate and price fluctuations on farm output and income. Larger farms also have advantages in obtaining government subsidies and payments because these payments are usually based on acreage owned and per-unit production.

In contrast, agricultural managers are projected to gain jobs, growing by about 6 percent, slower than the average for all occupations. Owners of large tracts of land, who often do not live on the property they own, increasingly will seek the expertise of agricultural managers to run their farms and ranches in a business-like manner.

Despite the expected continued consolidation of farmland and the projected decline in overall employment of this occupation, an increasing number of small-scale farmers have developed successful market niches that involve personalized, direct contact with their customers. Many are finding opportunities in horticulture and organic food production, which are among the fastest-growing segments of agriculture. Others use farmers' markets that cater directly to urban and suburban consumers, allowing the farmers to capture a greater share of consumers' food dollars. Some small-scale farmers belong to collectively owned marketing cooperatives that process and sell their product. Other farmers participate in community-supported agriculture cooperatives that allow consumers to buy a share of the farmer's harvest directly.

Job prospects. Fewer jobs are expected for farmers and ranchers than in the past; better prospects are expected for wage and salary agricultural managers. Small-scale, local farming, particularly horticulture and organic farming, offer the best opportunities for entering the occupation. With fewer people wanting to become farmers and a large number of farmers expected to retire or give up their farms in the next decade, there will be some opportunities to own or lease a farm. Additionally, the market for agricultural products is projected to be good for most products over the next decade, so many farmers who retire will need to be replaced. Farmers who grow crops used in landscaping, such as trees, shrubs, turf, and other ornamentals, also will have better job prospects as people put more money into landscaping their homes and businesses.

Some private organizations are helping to make farmland available and affordable for new farmers through a variety of institutional innovations. Land Link programs, coordinated by the International Farm Transition Network, operate in 20 states. They help match up young farmers with farmers approaching retirement so that arrangements can be made to pass along their land to young farmers wishing to keep the land under cultivation. Often beginning farmers lease some or all of their farmland. Sometimes a new farmer will work on a farm for a few years while the farm owner gradually transfers ownership to the new farmer.

Earnings

Incomes of farmers and ranchers vary greatly from year to year because prices of farm products fluctuate with weather conditions and other factors that influence the quantity and quality of farm output and the demand for those products. In addition to farm business income, farmers often receive government subsidies or other payments that supplement their incomes and reduce some of the risk of farming. Many farmers—primarily operators of small farms—have recently been relying more and more on off-farm sources of income.

Full-time, salaried farmers and ranchers had median weekly earnings of $622 in 2009. The middle half earned between $503 and $903 per week. The highest-paid 10 percent earned more than $1,764, and the lowest-paid 10 percent earned less than $364 per week.

Self-employed farmers must procure their own health and life insurance. As members of farm organizations, they may receive group discounts on health and life insurance premiums.

Related Occupations

Farmers, ranchers, and agricultural managers strive to improve the quality of agricultural products and the efficiency of farms. Others whose work relates to agriculture include agricultural and food scientists; agricultural inspectors; agricultural workers, other; engineers; farm and home management advisors; and purchasing managers, buyers, and purchasing agents.

Sources of Additional Information

For general information about farming and agricultural occupations, contact

▶ National FFA Organization, Attention: Career Information Requests, P.O. Box 68690, Indianapolis, IN 46268-0960. Internet: www.ffa.org

For information about certification as an accredited farm manager, contact

▶ American Society of Farm Managers and Rural Appraisers, 950 Cherry St., Suite 508, Denver, CO 80246-2664. Internet: www.asfmra.org

For information on the USDA's program to help small farmers get started, contact

▶ Family and Small Farm Program, U.S. Department of Agriculture, National Institute of Food and Agriculture, 1400 Independence Ave. SW, Stop 2201, Washington, DC 20250-2201. Internet: www.csrees.usda.gov/smallfarms.cfm

For information on Land Link programs, contact

▶ The Beginning Farm Center, 10861 Douglas Ave., Suite B, Urbandale, IA 50322-2042. Internet: www.farmtransition.org/netwpart.html

▸ Center for Rural Affairs, 145 Main St., P.O. Box 136, Lyons, NE 68038-2677. Internet: www.cfra.org/resources/beginning_farmer

For information on organic farming, horticulture, and internships, contact

▸ Alternative Farming System Information Center, NAL, 10301 Baltimore Ave., Room 132, Beltsville, MD 20705-2326. Internet: www.nal.usda.gov

▸ ATTRA, National Sustainable Agriculture Information Service, P.O. Box 3657, Fayetteville, AR 72702-3657. Internet: www.attra.ncat.org

Fire Fighters

(O*NET 33-1021.00, 33-1021.01, 33-1021.02, 33-2011.00, 33-2011.01, and 33-2011.02)

Significant Points

■ Fire fighting involves hazardous conditions and long, irregular hours.

■ About 9 out of 10 fire fighters are employed by local governments.

■ Applicants generally must pass written, physical, and medical examinations, and candidates with some postsecondary education are increasingly preferred.

■ Keen competition for jobs is expected because this occupation attracts many qualified candidates.

Nature of the Work

Every year, fires and other emergencies take thousands of lives and destroy property worth billions of dollars. *Fire fighters* help protect the public against these dangers by responding to fires and a variety of other emergencies. Although they put out fires, fire fighters more frequently respond to other emergencies. They are often the first emergency personnel at the scene of a traffic accident or medical emergency and may be called upon to treat injuries or perform other vital functions.

During duty hours, fire fighters must be prepared to respond immediately to a fire or other emergency. Fighting fires is complex and dangerous and requires organization and teamwork. At every emergency scene, fire fighters perform specific duties assigned by a superior officer. At fires, they connect hose lines to hydrants and operate a pump to send water to high-pressure hoses. Some carry hoses, climb ladders, and enter burning buildings—using systematic and careful procedures—to put out fires. At times, they may need to use tools to make their way through doors, walls, and debris, sometimes with the aid of information about a building's floor plan. Some find and rescue occupants who are unable to leave the building safely without assistance. They also provide emergency medical attention, ventilate smoke-filled areas and attempt to salvage the contents of buildings. Fire fighters' duties may change several times while the company is in action. Sometimes they remain at the site of a disaster for days at a time, rescuing trapped survivors, and assisting with medical treatment.

Fire fighters work in a variety of settings, including metropolitan areas, rural areas, airports, chemical plants and other industrial sites. They also have assumed a range of responsibilities, including providing emergency medical services. In fact, most calls to which fire fighters respond involve medical emergencies. In addition, some fire fighters work in hazardous materials units that are specially trained for the control, prevention, and cleanup of hazardous materials, such as oil spills or accidents involving the transport of chemicals.

Workers specializing in forest fires utilize methods and equipment different from those of other fire fighters. When fires break out, crews of fire fighters are brought in to suppress the blaze with heavy equipment and water hoses. Fighting forest fires, like fighting urban fires, is rigorous work. One of the most effective means of fighting a forest fire is creating fire lines—cutting down trees and digging out grass and all other combustible vegetation in the path of the fire in order to deprive it of fuel. Elite fire fighters called *smoke jumpers* parachute from airplanes to reach otherwise inaccessible areas. This tactic, however, can be extremely hazardous.

When they aren't responding to fires and other emergencies, fire fighters clean and maintain equipment, learn additional skills related to their jobs, conduct practice drills, and participate in physical fitness activities. They also prepare written reports on fire incidents and review fire science literature to stay informed about technological developments and changing administrative practices and policies.

Work environment. Fire fighters spend much of their time at fire stations, which are usually similar to dormitories. When an alarm sounds, fire fighters respond, regardless of the weather or hour. Fire fighting involves a high risk of death or injury. Common causes include floors caving in, walls toppling, traffic accidents, and exposure to flame and smoke. Fire fighters also may come into contact with poisonous, flammable, or explosive gases and chemicals and radioactive materials, all of which may have immediate or long-term effects on their health. For these reasons, they must wear protective gear that can be very heavy and hot.

Work hours of fire fighters are longer and more varied than the hours of most other workers. Many fire fighters work about 50 hours a week, and sometimes they may work longer. In some agencies, fire fighters are on duty for 24 hours, then off for 48 hours, and receive an extra day off at intervals. In others, they work a day shift of 10 hours for 3 or 4 days, work a night shift of 14 hours for 3 or 4 nights, have 3 or 4 days off, and then repeat the cycle. In addition, fire fighters often work extra hours at fires and other emergencies and are regularly assigned to work on holidays. Fire lieutenants and fire captains frequently work the same hours as the fire fighters they supervise.

Training, Other Qualifications, and Advancement

Applicants for fire fighting jobs usually are required to have at least a high school diploma, but candidates with some postsecondary education are increasingly being preferred. Most municipal jobs require passing written and physical tests. All fire fighters receive extensive training after being hired.

Education and training. Most fire fighters have a high school diploma; however, the completion of community college courses or, in some cases, an associate degree, in fire science may improve an applicant's chances for a job. A number of colleges and universities offer courses leading to two-year or four-year degrees in fire engineering or fire science. In recent years, an increasing proportion of new fire fighters have had some education after high school.

As a rule, entry-level workers in large fire departments are trained for several weeks at the department's training center or academy. Through classroom instruction and practical training, the recruits study fire fighting techniques, fire prevention, hazardous materials control, local building codes, and emergency medical procedures, including first aid and cardiopulmonary resuscitation (CPR). They also learn how to use axes, chain saws, fire extinguishers, ladders, and other fire fighting and rescue equipment. After successfully completing training, the recruits are assigned to a fire company, where they undergo a period of probation.

Many fire departments have accredited apprenticeship programs lasting up to four years, including programs in fighting forest fires. These programs combine formal instruction with on-the-job training under the supervision of experienced fire fighters.

Almost all departments require fire fighters to be certified as emergency medical technicians. (For more information, see the job description in this book for emergency medical technicians and paramedics.) Although most fire departments require the lowest level of certification, Emergency Medical Technician-Basic (EMT-Basic), larger departments in major metropolitan areas increasingly are requiring paramedic certification. Some departments include this training in the fire academy, whereas others prefer that recruits earn EMT certification on their own, but will give them up to 1 year to do it.

In addition to participating in training programs conducted by local fire departments, some fire fighters attend training sessions sponsored by the U.S. National Fire Academy. These training sessions cover topics such as executive development, antiarson techniques, disaster preparedness, hazardous materials control, and public fire safety and education. Some states also have mandatory or voluntary fire fighter training and certification programs. Many fire departments offer fire fighters incentives, such as tuition reimbursement or higher pay, for completing advanced training.

Other qualifications. Applicants for municipal fire fighting jobs usually must pass a written exam; tests of strength, physical stamina, coordination, and agility; and a medical examination that includes a drug screening. Workers may be monitored on a random basis for drug use after accepting employment. Examinations are generally open to people who are at least 18 years of age and have a high school education or its equivalent. Those who receive the highest scores in all phases of testing have the best chances of being hired.

Among the personal qualities fire fighters need are mental alertness, self-discipline, courage, mechanical aptitude, endurance, strength, and a sense of public service. Initiative and good judgment also are extremely important, because fire fighters make quick decisions in emergencies. Members of a crew live and work closely together under conditions of stress and danger for extended periods, so they must be dependable and able to get along well with others. Leadership qualities are necessary for officers, who must establish and maintain discipline and efficiency, as well as direct the activities of the fire fighters in their companies.

Advancement. Most experienced fire fighters continue studying to improve their job performance and prepare for promotion examinations. To progress to higher level positions, they acquire expertise in advanced fire fighting equipment and techniques, building construction, emergency medical technology, writing, public speaking, management and budgeting procedures, and public relations.

Opportunities for promotion depend upon the results of written examinations, as well as job performance, interviews, and seniority.

Hands-on tests that simulate real-world job situations also are used by some fire departments.

Usually, fire fighters are first promoted to engineer, then lieutenant, captain, battalion chief, assistant chief, deputy chief, and, finally, chief. For promotion to positions higher than battalion chief, many fire departments now require a bachelor's degree, preferably in fire science, public administration, or a related field. An associate degree is required for executive fire officer certification from the National Fire Academy.

Employment

In 2008, total paid employment in fire fighting occupations was about 365,600. Fire fighters held about 310,400 jobs, and first-line supervisors/managers of fire fighting and prevention workers held about 55,200. These employment figures include only paid career fire fighters—they do not cover volunteer fire fighters, who perform the same duties and may constitute the majority of fire fighters in a residential area. According to the U.S. Fire Administration, about 70 percent of fire companies were staffed entirely by volunteer fire fighters in 2007.

About 91 percent of fire fighting workers were employed by local governments. Some local and regional fire departments are being consolidated into countywide establishments to reduce administrative staffs, cut costs, and establish consistent training standards and work procedures. Some large cities have thousands of career fire fighters, while many small towns have only a few. Most of the fire fighters not employed by local governments worked in fire departments on federal and state installations, including airports. Private fire fighting companies employ a small number of fire fighters.

Job Outlook

Although employment is expected to grow faster than the average for all jobs, candidates for these positions are expected to face keen competition because these positions are highly attractive and sought after.

Employment change. Employment of fire fighters is expected to grow by 19 percent over the 2008–2018 decade, which is faster than the average for all occupations. Most job growth will stem from volunteer fire fighting positions being converted to paid positions. In recent years, it has become more difficult for volunteer fire departments to recruit and retain volunteers, perhaps because of the considerable amount of training and time commitment required. Furthermore, a trend toward more people living in and around cities has increased the demand for fire fighters. When areas develop and become more densely populated, emergencies and fires affect more buildings and more people and, therefore, require more fire fighters.

Job prospects. Prospective fire fighters are expected to face keen competition for available job openings. Many people are attracted to fire fighting because it is challenging and provides the opportunity to perform an essential public service, a high school education is usually sufficient for entry, and a pension is usually guaranteed after 25 years of service. Consequently, the number of qualified applicants in most areas far exceeds the number of job openings, even though the written examination and physical requirements eliminate many applicants. This situation is expected to persist in coming years. Applicants with the best chances are those who are physically fit and score the highest on physical-conditioning and mechanical aptitude

Projections Data from the National Employment Matrix

Occupational title	SOC Code	Employment, 2008	Projected employment, 2018	Change, 2008–2018	
				Number	Percent
Fire fighting occupations ....—		365,600	427,600	62,100	17
First-line supervisors/managers of fire fighting and prevention workers....................................33-1021		55,200	59,700	4,500	8
Fire fighters...33-2011		310,400	367,900	57,500	19

NOTE: Data in this table are rounded.

exams. Those who have completed some fire fighter education at a community college and have EMT or paramedic certification will have an additional advantage.

Earnings

Median annual wages of fire fighters were $45,050 in May 2009. The middle 50 percent earned between $32,000 and $59,650. The lowest 10 percent earned less than $22,990, and the highest 10 percent earned more than $74,390. Median annual wages were $45,710 in local government, $46,580 in the federal government, $25,620 in other support services, and $36,480 in state governments.

Median annual wages of first-line supervisors/managers of fire fighting and prevention workers were $68,250 in May 2009. The middle 50 percent earned between $53,820 and $87,190. The lowest 10 percent earned less than $41,680, and the highest 10 percent earned more than $109,750. First-line supervisors/managers of fire fighting and prevention workers employed in local government earned a median of about $69,500 a year.

According to the International City-County Management Association, average salaries in 2008 for sworn full-time positions were as follows:

Position	Minimum annual base salary	Maximum annual base salary
Fire chief	$78,672	$104,780
Deputy chief..............................	69,166	88,571
Battalion chief...........................	66,851	81,710
Assistant fire chief	65,691	83,748
Fire captain	60,605	72,716
Fire lieutenant	50,464	60,772
Engineer	48,307	62,265

Fire fighters who average more than a certain number of work hours per week are required to be paid overtime. The threshold is determined by the department. Fire fighters often work extra shifts to maintain minimum staffing levels and during special emergencies.

In 2008, 66 percent of all fire fighters were union members or covered by a union contract. Fire fighters receive benefits that usually include medical and liability insurance, vacation and sick leave, and some paid holidays. Almost all fire departments provide protective clothing (helmets, boots, and coats) and breathing apparatus, and many also provide dress uniforms. Fire fighters generally are covered by pension plans, often offering retirement at half pay after 25 years of service or if the individual is disabled in the line of duty.

Related Occupations

Other occupations that involve protecting the public and property are emergency medical technicians and paramedics; fire inspectors and investigators; and police and detectives.

Sources of Additional Information

Information about a career as a fire fighter may be obtained from local fire departments and from either of the following organizations:

▸ International Association of Fire Fighters, 1750 New York Ave. NW, Washington, DC 20006. Internet: www.iaff.org

▸ U.S. Fire Administration, 16825 S. Seton Ave., Emmitsburg, MD 21727. Internet: www.usfa.dhs.gov

Information about professional qualifications and a list of colleges and universities offering two-year or four-year degree programs in fire science or fire prevention may be obtained from

▸ National Fire Academy, 16825 S. Seton Ave., Emmitsburg, MD 21727. Internet: www.usfa.dhs.gov/nfa

Fitness Workers

(O*NET 39-9031.00)

Significant Points

■ Many fitness and personal training jobs are part time, but many workers increase their hours by working at several different facilities or at clients' homes.

■ Most fitness workers need to be certified.

■ Employment is expected to grow much faster than the average.

■ Job prospects are expected to be good.

Nature of the Work

Fitness workers lead, instruct, and motivate individuals or groups in exercise activities, including cardiovascular exercise, strength training, and stretching. They work in health clubs, country clubs, hospitals, universities, yoga and Pilates studios, resorts, and clients' homes. Fitness workers also are found in workplaces, where they organize and direct health and fitness programs for employees. Although gyms and health clubs offer a variety of exercise activities, such as weight lifting, yoga, cardiovascular training, and karate, fitness workers typically specialize in only a few areas.

Personal trainers work one-on-one or with two or three clients, either in a gym or in the clients' homes. They help clients assess their level of physical fitness and set and reach fitness goals. *Trainers* also demonstrate various exercises and help clients improve their exercise techniques. They may keep records of their clients' exercise sessions to monitor the clients' progress toward physical fitness. They also may advise their clients on how to modify their lifestyles outside of the gym to improve their fitness.

Group exercise instructors conduct group exercise sessions that usually include aerobic exercise, stretching, and muscle conditioning. Cardiovascular conditioning classes often are set to music. *Instructors* select the music and choreograph a corresponding exercise sequence. Two increasingly popular conditioning methods taught in exercise classes are Pilates and yoga. In these classes, instructors demonstrate the different moves and positions of the particular method; they also observe students and correct those who are doing the exercises improperly. Group exercise instructors are responsible for ensuring that their classes are motivating, safe, and challenging, yet not too difficult for the participants.

Fitness directors oversee the fitness-related aspects of a health club or fitness center. They create and oversee programs that meet the needs of the club's members, including new-member orientations, fitness assessments, and workout incentive programs. They also select fitness equipment; coordinate personal training and group exercise programs; hire, train, and supervise fitness staff; and carry out administrative duties.

Fitness workers in smaller facilities with few employees may perform a variety of functions in addition to their fitness duties, such as tending the front desk, signing up new members, giving tours of the fitness center, writing newsletter articles, creating posters and flyers, and supervising the weight-training and cardiovascular equipment areas. In larger commercial facilities, personal trainers often are required to sell their services to members and to make a specified number of sales. Some fitness workers may combine the duties of group exercise instructors and personal trainers; in smaller facilities, the fitness director may teach classes and do personal training.

Work environment. Most fitness workers spend their time indoors at fitness or recreation centers and health clubs. Fitness directors and supervisors, however, typically spend most of their time in an office. In some fitness centers, workers may split their time among doing office work, engaging in personal training, and teaching classes. Nevertheless, fitness workers at all levels risk suffering injuries during physical activities.

Since most fitness centers are open long hours, fitness workers often work nights and weekends and even occasional holidays. In 2008, about 40 percent of fitness workers were part-time employees. Some may travel from place to place throughout the day, to different gyms or to clients' homes, to maintain a full work schedule.

Fitness workers generally enjoy a lot of autonomy. Group exercise instructors choreograph or plan their own classes, and personal trainers have the freedom to design and implement their clients' workout routines.

Training, Other Qualifications, and Advancement

For most fitness workers, certification is critical. Personal trainers usually must be certified to begin working with clients or with members of a fitness facility. Group fitness instructors may begin without a certification, but they are often encouraged or required by their employers to become certified.

Education and training. The education and training required depends on the specific type of fitness work: personal training,

group fitness, and a specialization such as Pilates or yoga each need different preparation. Personal trainers often start out by taking classes to become certified. Then they may begin by working alongside an experienced trainer before being allowed to train clients alone. Group fitness instructors often get started by participating in exercise classes until they are ready to audition as instructors and, if the audition is successful, begin teaching classes. They also may improve their skills by taking training courses or attending fitness conventions. Most employers require instructors to work toward becoming certified.

Fitness workers usually do not receive much on-the-job training; they are expected to know how to do their jobs when they are hired. Workers may receive some organizational training to learn about the operations of their new employer. Occasionally, they receive specialized training if they are expected to teach or lead a specific method of exercise or focus on a particular age or ability group. Because requirements vary from employer to employer, before pursuing training it may be helpful to contact local fitness centers or other potential employers to find out what background they prefer.

An increasing number of employers are requiring fitness workers to have a bachelor's degree in a field related to health or fitness, such as exercise science or physical education. Some employers allow workers to substitute a college degree for certification, but most employers who require a bachelor's degree also require certification.

Training for *Pilates* and *yoga instructors* has changed. When interest in these forms of exercise exploded, the demand for teachers grew faster than the ability to train them properly. Inexperienced teachers contributed to student injuries, leading to a push toward more standardized, rigorous requirements for teacher training.

Pilates and *yoga teachers* now need specialized training in their particular method of exercise. For Pilates, training options range from weekend-long workshops to yearlong programs, but the trend is toward requiring even more training. The Pilates Method Alliance has established training standards that recommend at least 200 hours of training; the group also has standards for training schools and maintains a list of training schools that meet the requirements. However, some Pilates teachers are certified group exercise instructors who attend short Pilates workshops; currently, many fitness centers hire people with minimal Pilates training if the applicants have a fitness certification and group fitness experience.

Training requirements for yoga teachers are similar to those for Pilates teachers. Training programs range from a few days to more than 2 years. Many people get their start by taking yoga; eventually, their teachers may consider them ready to assist or to substitute teach. Some students may begin teaching their own classes when their yoga teachers think that they are ready; the teachers may even provide letters of recommendation. Those who wish to pursue teaching more seriously usually seek formal teacher training.

Currently, there are many training programs throughout the yoga community, as well as programs throughout the fitness industry. The Yoga Alliance has established training standards requiring at least 200 training hours, with a specified number of hours in techniques, teaching methodology, anatomy, physiology, philosophy, and other areas. The Yoga Alliance also registers schools that train students to its standards. Because some schools may meet the standards but not be registered, prospective students should check the requirements and decide whether particular schools meet them.

Certification and other qualifications. The most important characteristic that an employer looks for in a new fitness instructor is the ability to plan and lead a class that is motivating and safe. Group fitness instructors do not necessarily require certification to begin working. However, most organizations encourage their group instructors to become certified over time, and many require it.

In the fitness field, there are many organizations that offer certification. Getting certified by one of the top certification organizations is becoming increasingly important, especially for personal trainers. One way to ensure that a certifying organization is reputable is to make sure that it is accredited by the National Commission for Certifying Agencies.

Most certifying organizations require candidates to have a high school diploma, be certified in cardiopulmonary resuscitation (CPR), and pass an exam. All certification exams have a written component, and some also have a practical component. The exams measure knowledge of human physiology, understanding of proper exercise techniques, assessment of client fitness levels, and development of appropriate exercise programs. There is no particular training program required for certification; candidates may prepare however they prefer. Certifying organizations do offer study materials, including books, CD-ROMs, other audio and visual materials, and exam preparation workshops and seminars, but candidates are not required to purchase materials to take exams.

Certification generally is good for 2 years, after which workers must become recertified by attending continuing education classes or conferences, writing articles, or giving presentations. Some organizations offer more advanced certification that requires an associate or bachelor's degree in an exercise-related subject for individuals who are interested in training athletes, working with people who are injured or ill, or advising clients on general health.

Pilates and yoga instructors usually do not need group exercise certification to maintain their employment. It is more important that they have specialized training in their particular method of exercise. However, the Pilates Method Alliance does offer certification. Pilates certification requires 450 hours of documented training or 720 hours of full-time work the previous 12 months.

People planning fitness careers should be outgoing, excellent communicators, good at motivating people, and sensitive to the needs of others. Excellent health and physical fitness are important because of the physical nature of the job. Those who wish to be personal trainers in a large commercial fitness center should have strong sales skills. All personal trainers should have the personality and motivation to attract and retain clients.

Advancement. A bachelor's degree in exercise science, physical education, kinesiology (the study of the mechanics of human motion, including the role of the muscles), or a related area, along with experience, usually is required to advance to management positions in a health club or fitness center. Some organizations require a master's degree. As in other occupations, managerial skills also are needed to advance to supervisory or managerial positions. College courses in management, business administration, accounting, and personnel management may be helpful, but many fitness companies have corporate universities in which they train employees for management positions.

Personal trainers may advance to head trainer, with responsibility for hiring and overseeing the personal training staff and for bringing in new personal-training clients. Group fitness instructors may be promoted to group exercise director, a position responsible for hiring instructors and coordinating exercise classes. Later, a worker might become the fitness director of an organization, managing the fitness budget and staff. A worker also might become the general manager, whose main focus is the financial aspects of the organization, particularly setting and achieving sales goals; in a small fitness center, however, the general manager usually is involved with all aspects of running the facility. Some workers go into business for themselves and open their own fitness centers.

Employment

Fitness workers held about 261,100, jobs in 2008. About 61 percent of all personal trainers and group exercise instructors worked in fitness and recreational sports centers, including health clubs. Another 13 percent worked in civic and social organizations. About 9 percent of fitness workers were self-employed; many of these were personal trainers, while others were group fitness instructors working on a contract basis with fitness centers. Many fitness jobs are part time, and many workers hold multiple jobs, teaching or doing personal training at several different fitness centers and at clients' homes.

Job Outlook

Jobs for fitness workers are expected to increase much faster than the average for all occupations. Fitness workers should have good opportunities because of continued job growth in health clubs, fitness facilities, and other settings in which fitness workers are concentrated.

Employment change. Employment of fitness workers is expected to increase 29 percent over the 2008–2018 decade, which is much faster than the average for all occupations. These workers are expected to gain jobs because an increasing number of people are spending time and money on fitness and more businesses are recognizing the benefits of health and fitness programs for their employees.

Aging baby boomers, one group that increasingly is becoming concerned with staying healthy and physically fit, will be the main driver of employment growth in fitness workers. An additional factor is the combination of a reduction in the number of physical education programs in schools with parents' growing concern about childhood obesity. This factor will increase the need for fitness workers to work with children in nonschool settings, such as health clubs. Increasingly, parents also are hiring personal trainers for their children, and the number of weight-training gyms for children is expected to continue to grow. Health club membership among young adults has grown steadily as well, driven by concern with physical fitness and by rising incomes.

As health clubs strive to provide more personalized service to keep their members motivated, they will continue to offer personal training and a wide variety of group exercise classes. Participation in yoga and Pilates is expected to continue to increase, driven partly by the aging population, which demands low-impact forms of exercise and seeks relief from arthritis and other ailments.

Job prospects. Opportunities are expected to be good for fitness workers because demand for these workers is expected to remain strong in health clubs, fitness facilities, and other settings in which fitness workers are concentrated. In addition, many job openings will stem from the need to replace the large numbers of workers who leave these occupations each year. Part-time jobs will be easier to find than full-time jobs. People with degrees in fitness-related subjects will have better opportunities because clients prefer to

Projections Data from the National Employment Matrix

Occupational title	SOC Code	Employment, 2008	Projected employment, 2018	Change, 2008–2018	
				Number	Percent
Fitness trainers and aerobics instructors 39-9031		261,100	337,900	76,800	29

NOTE: Data in this table are rounded.

work with people they perceive as higher-quality trainers. Trainers who incorporate new technology and wellness issues as part of their services may be in more demand.

Earnings

Median annual wages of fitness trainers and aerobics instructors in May 2009 were $30,670. The middle 50 percent earned between $19,860 and $45,720. The bottom 10 percent earned less than $16,430, while the top 10 percent earned $62,120 or more. These figures do not include the earnings of the self-employed. Earnings of successful self-employed personal trainers can be much higher. Median annual wages in the industries employing the largest numbers of fitness workers in May 2009 were as follows:

Other amusement and recreation industries..........$32,320
Civic and social organizations 25,090
Other schools and instruction 24,440
Local government... 30,840
General medical and surgical hospitals 33,680

Because many fitness workers work part time, they often do not receive benefits such as health insurance or retirement plans from their employers. They are able to use fitness facilities at no cost, however.

Related Occupations

Other occupations that focus on health and physical fitness include the following: athletes, coaches, umpires, and related workers; dietitians and nutritionists; physical therapists; and recreation workers.

Sources of Additional Information

For more information about fitness careers and about universities and other institutions offering programs in health and fitness, contact

▸ National Strength and Conditioning Association, 1885 Bob Johnson Dr., Colorado Springs, CO 80906. Internet: www.nsca-lift.org

For information about personal trainer and group fitness instructor certifications, contact

▸ American College of Sports Medicine, P.O. Box 1440, Indianapolis, IN 46206-1440. Internet: www.acsm.org

▸ American Council on Exercise, 4851 Paramount Dr., San Diego, CA 92123. Internet: www.acefitness.org

▸ National Academy of Sports Medicine, 26632 Agoura Rd., Calabasas, CA 91302. Internet: www.nasm.org

▸ NSCA Certification Commission, 1885 Bob Johnson Dr., Colorado Springs, CO 80906. Internet: www.nsca-cc.org

For information about Pilates certification and training programs, contact

▸ Pilates Method Alliance, P.O. Box 37096, Miami, FL 33137-0906. Internet: www.pilatesmethodalliance.org

For information on yoga teacher training programs, contact

▸ Yoga Alliance, 1701 Clarendon Boulevard, Suite 110, Arlington, VA 22209. Internet: www.yogaalliance.org

For information about health clubs and sports clubs, contact

▸ International Health, Racquet, and Sportsclub Association, Seaport Center, 70 Fargo St., Boston, MA 02210. Internet: http://cms.ihrsa.org

Food and Beverage Serving and Related Workers

(O*NET 35-3011.00, 35-3021.00, 35-3022.00, 35-3022.01, 35-3031.00, 35-3041.00, 35-9011.00, 35-9021.00, 35-9031.00, and 35-9099.00)

Significant Points

■ Most jobs are part time and have few educational requirements, attracting many young people to the occupation—21 percent of these workers were 16 to 19 years old in 2008, about six times the proportion for all workers.

■ Job openings are expected to be abundant through 2018, which will create excellent opportunities for job seekers.

■ Tips comprise a major portion of earnings for servers, so keen competition is expected for jobs in fine dining and more popular restaurants where potential tips are greatest.

Nature of the Work

Food and beverage serving and related workers are the front line of customer service in full-service restaurants, casual dining eateries, and other food service establishments. These workers greet customers, escort them to seats and hand them menus, take food and drink orders, and serve food and beverages. They also answer questions, explain menu items and specials, and keep tables and dining areas clean and set for new diners. Most work as part of a team, helping coworkers to improve workflow and customer service.

Waiters and waitresses, also called *servers,* are the largest group of these workers. They take customers' orders, serve food and beverages, prepare itemized checks, and sometimes accept payment. Their specific duties vary considerably, depending on the establishment. In casual-dining restaurants serving routine, straightforward fare, such as salads, soups, and sandwiches, servers are expected to provide fast, efficient, and courteous service. In fine dining restaurants, where more complicated meals are prepared and often served over several courses, waiters and waitresses provide more formal service emphasizing personal, attentive treatment at a more leisurely pace. Waiters and waitresses may meet with managers and chefs before each shift to discuss the menu and any new items or specials, review ingredients for potential food allergies, or talk about any food safety concerns. They also discuss coordination between the kitchen and the dining room and any customer service issues from the previous day or shift. In addition, waiters and waitresses usually check the identification of patrons to ensure they meet the minimum age requirement for the purchase of alcohol and tobacco products wherever those items are sold.

Waiters and waitresses sometimes perform the duties of other food and beverage service workers, including escorting guests to tables, serving customers seated at counters, clearing and setting up tables, or operating a cash register. However, full-service restaurants frequently hire other staff, such as hosts and hostesses, cashiers, or dining room attendants, to perform these duties.

Bartenders fill drink orders either taken directly from patrons at the bar or through waiters and waitresses who place drink orders for dining room customers. Bartenders check the identification of customers seated at the bar to ensure they meet the minimum age requirement for the purchase of alcohol and tobacco products. They prepare mixed drinks, serve bottled or draught beer, and pour wine or other beverages. Bartenders must know a wide range of drink recipes and be able to mix drinks accurately, quickly, and without waste. Some establishments, especially those with higher volume, use equipment that automatically measures, pours, and mixes drinks at the push of a button. Bartenders who use this equipment, however, still must work quickly to handle a large volume of drink orders and be familiar with the ingredients for special drink requests. Much of a bartender's work still must be done by hand.

Besides mixing and serving drinks, bartenders stock and prepare garnishes for drinks; maintain an adequate supply of ice, glasses, and other bar supplies; and keep the bar area clean for customers. They also may collect payment, operate the cash register, wash glassware and utensils, and serve food to customers who dine at the bar. Bartenders usually are responsible for ordering and maintaining an inventory of liquor, mixers, and other bar supplies.

Hosts and hostesses welcome guests and maintain reservation and waiting lists. They may direct patrons to coatrooms, restrooms, or to a place to wait until their table is ready. Hosts and hostesses assign guests to tables suitable for the size of their group, escort patrons to their seats, and provide menus. They also enter reservations, arrange parties, and assist with other special requests. In some restaurants, they act as cashiers.

Dining room and cafeteria attendants and bartender helpers— sometimes referred to collectively as the bus staff—assist waiters, waitresses, and bartenders by cleaning and setting tables, removing dirty dishes, and keeping serving areas stocked with supplies. They may also assist waiters and waitresses by bringing meals out of the kitchen, distributing dishes to individual diners, filling water glasses, and delivering condiments. *Cafeteria attendants* stock serving tables with food, trays, dishes, and silverware. They may carry trays to dining tables for patrons. *Bartender helpers* keep bar equipment clean and glasses washed. *Dishwashers* clean dishes, cutlery, and kitchen utensils and equipment.

Food also is prepared and served in limited-service eateries, which don't employ servers and specialize in simpler preparations that often are made in advance. Two occupations with large numbers of workers are common in these types of establishments: *combined food preparation and serving workers, including fast food*; and *counter attendants, cafeteria, food concession, and coffee shop.* Combined food preparation and serving workers are employed primarily by fast food restaurants. They take food and beverage orders, retrieve items when ready, fill drink cups, and accept payment. They also may heat food items and assemble salads and sandwiches, which constitutes food preparation. Counter attendants take orders

and serve food in snack bars, cafeterias, movie theaters, and coffee shops over a counter or steam table. They may fill cups with coffee, soda, and other beverages and may prepare fountain specialties, such as milkshakes and ice cream sundaes. Counter attendants take carryout orders from diners and wrap or place items in containers. They clean counters, write itemized bills, and sometimes accept payment. Other workers, referred to as *food servers, nonrestaurant*, serve food to patrons outside of a restaurant environment. They might deliver room service meals in hotels or meals to hospital rooms or act as carhops, bringing orders to parked cars.

Work environment. Food and beverage service workers are on their feet most of the time and often carry heavy trays of food, dishes, and glassware. During busy dining periods, they are under pressure to serve customers quickly and efficiently. The work is relatively safe, but injuries from slips, cuts, and burns often result from hurrying or mishandling sharp tools. Three occupations—food servers, nonrestaurant; dining room and cafeteria attendants and bartender helpers; and dishwashers—reported higher incident rates than many occupations throughout the economy.

Part-time work is more common among food and beverage serving and related workers than among workers in almost any other occupation. In 2008, those on part-time schedules included half of all waiters and waitresses and almost three-fourths of all hosts and hostesses.

Food service and drinking establishments typically maintain long dining hours and offer flexible and varied work opportunities. Many food and beverage serving and related workers work evenings, weekends, and holidays. The long business hours allow for more flexible schedules that appeal to many teenagers who can gain valuable work experience. More than one-fifth of all food and beverage serving and related workers were 16 to 19 years old in 2008—about six times the proportion for all workers.

Training, Other Qualifications, and Advancement

Most food and beverage service jobs are entry level and require a high school diploma or less. Generally, training is received on the job; however, those who wish to work at more upscale restaurants, where income from tips is greater and service standards are higher, may need previous experience or vocational training.

Education and training. There are no specific educational requirements for most food and beverage service jobs. Many employers prefer to hire high school graduates for waiter and waitress, bartender, and host and hostess positions, but completion of high school usually is not required for fast food workers, counter attendants, dishwashers, and dining room attendants and bartender helpers. Many entrants to these jobs are in their late teens or early twenties and have a high school education or less. Usually, they have little or no work experience. Food and beverage service jobs are a major source of part-time employment for high school and college students, multiple job holders, and those seeking supplemental incomes.

All new employees receive some training from their employer. They learn safe food handling procedures and sanitation practices, for example. Some employers, particularly those in fast food restaurants, teach new workers using self-study programs, online programs, audiovisual presentations, and instructional booklets that explain food preparation and service skills. But most food and beverage serving and related workers pick up their skills by observing and working with more experienced workers. Some full-service restaurants also provide new dining room employees with some form of classroom training that alternates with periods of on-the-job work experience. These training programs communicate the operating philosophy of the restaurant, help establish a personal rapport with other staff, teach formal serving techniques, and instill a desire to work as a team. They also provide an opportunity to discuss customer service situations and the proper ways to handle unpleasant circumstances or unruly patrons.

Some food serving workers can acquire more skills by attending relevant classes offered by public or private vocational schools, restaurant associations, or large restaurant chains. Some bartenders acquire their skills through formal vocational training either by attending a school for bartending or a vocational and technical school where bartending classes are taught. These programs often include instruction on state and local laws and regulations, cocktail recipes, proper attire and conduct, and stocking a bar. Some of these schools help their graduates find jobs. Although few employers require any minimum level of educational attainment, some specialized training is usually needed in food handling and legal issues surrounding serving alcoholic beverages. Employers are more likely to hire and promote employees based on people skills and personal qualities than education.

Other qualifications. Restaurants rely on good food and customer service to retain loyal customers and succeed in a competitive industry. Food and beverage serving and related workers who exhibit excellent personal qualities—such as a neat appearance, an ability to work as part of a team, and a natural rapport with customers—will be highly sought after. Most states require workers who serve alcoholic beverages to be at least 18 years of age, but some states require servers to be older. For bartender jobs, many employers prefer to hire people who are 25 or older. All servers that serve alcohol need to be familiar with state and local laws concerning the sale of alcoholic beverages.

Waiters and waitresses need a good memory to avoid confusing customers' orders and to recall faces, names, and preferences of frequent patrons. Knowledge of a foreign language can be helpful to communicate with a diverse clientele and staff. Restaurants and hotels that have rigid table service standards often offer higher wages and have greater income potential from tips, but they may also have stiffer employment requirements, such as prior table service experience or higher education attainment than other establishments.

Advancement. Due to the relatively small size of most food serving establishments, opportunities for promotion are limited. After gaining experience, some dining room and cafeteria attendants and bartender helpers advance to waiter, waitress, or bartender jobs. For waiters, waitresses, and bartenders, advancement usually is limited to finding a job in a busier or more expensive restaurant or bar where prospects for tip earnings are better. Some bartenders, hosts and hostesses, and waiters and waitresses advance to supervisory jobs, such as dining room supervisor, maitre d', assistant manager, or restaurant general manager. A few bartenders open their own businesses. In larger restaurant chains, food and beverage service workers who excel often are invited to enter the company's formal management training program. (For more information, see food service managers elsewhere in this book.)

Employment

Food and beverage serving and related workers held 7.7 million jobs in 2008. The distribution of jobs among the various food and beverage serving occupations was as follows:

Combined food preparation and serving workers, including fast food	2,701,700
Waiters and waitresses	2,381,600
Counter attendants, cafeteria, food concession, and coffee shop	525,400
Dishwashers	522,900
Bartenders	508,700
Dining room and cafeteria attendants and bartender helpers	420,700
Hosts and hostesses, restaurant, lounge, and coffee shop	350,700
Food servers, nonrestaurant	189,800
All other food preparation and serving related workers	50,900

The overwhelming majority of jobs for food and beverage serving and related workers were found in food services and drinking places, such as restaurants, fast food outlets, bars, and catering or contract food service operations. Other jobs were in hotels, motels, and other traveler accommodation establishments; amusement, gambling, and recreation establishments; educational services; nursing care facilities; and civic and social organizations.

Jobs are located throughout the country but are more plentiful in larger cities and tourist areas. Vacation resorts offer seasonal employment.

Job Outlook

Average employment growth is expected, and job opportunities should be excellent for food and beverage serving and related workers as turnover is generally very high among these workers, but job competition is often keen for jobs at upscale restaurants.

Employment change. Overall employment of these workers is expected to increase by 10 percent over the 2008–2018 decade, which is about as fast as the average for all occupations. Food and beverage serving and related workers are projected to have one of the largest numbers of new jobs arise, about 761,000, over this period. The growth in jobs is expected to increase as the population continues to expand. However, employment will grow more slowly than in the past as people change their dining habits. The growing popularity of take-out food and the growing number and variety of places that offer carryout options, including at many full-service restaurants, will slow the growth of waiters and waitresses and other serving workers.

Projected employment growth will vary by job type. Employment of combined food preparation and serving workers, which includes fast food workers, is expected to increase faster than the average for all occupations. The limited service segment of the food services and drinking places industry has a low price advantage, fast service, and has been adding healthier foods. Slower-than-average employment growth is expected for waiters and waitresses, hosts and hostesses, and dining room and cafeteria attendants and bartender helpers, as more people use take-out service. Employment of bartenders, dishwashers, and counter attendants, cafeteria, food concession, and coffee shop will grow about as fast as average. Nonrestaurant servers, such as those who deliver food trays in hotels, hospitals,

Projections Data from the National Employment Matrix

Occupational title	SOC Code	Employment, 2008	Projected employment, 2018	Change, 2008–2018	
				Number	Percent
Food and beverage serving and related workers.................—		7,652,400	8,413,100	760,700	10
Food and beverage serving workers......................35-3000		6,307,200	6,962,300	655,100	10
Bartenders...35-3011		508,700	549,500	40,800	8
Fast food and counter workers.........................35-3020		3,227,100	3,670,400	443,300	14
Combined food preparation and serving workers, including fast food.....................35-3021		2,701,700	3,096,000	394,300	15
Counter attendants, cafeteria, food concession, and coffee shop.....................35-3022		525,400	574,400	49,000	9
Waiters and waitresses 35-3031		2,381,600	2,533,300	151,600	6
Food servers, nonrestaurant...........................35-3041		189,800	209,100	19,300	10
Other food preparation and serving related workers...35-9000		1,345,200	1,450,800	105,600	8
Dining room and cafeteria attendants and bartender helpers 35-9011		420,700	444,000	23,300	6
Dishwashers...35-9021		522,900	583,400	60,400	12
Hosts and hostesses, restaurant, lounge, and coffee shop 35-9031		350,700	373,400	22,800	6
Food preparation and serving related workers, all other 35-9099		50,900	50,000	−900	−2

NOTE: Data in this table are rounded.

residential care facilities, or catered events, are expected to have average employment growth.

Job prospects. Job opportunities at most eating and drinking places will be excellent because many people in these occupations change jobs frequently, which creates a large number of openings. Keen competition is expected, however, for jobs in popular restaurants and fine dining establishments, where potential earnings from tips are greatest.

Earnings

Food and beverage serving and related workers derive their earnings from a combination of hourly wages and customer tips. Earnings vary greatly, depending on the type of job and establishment. For example, fast food workers and hosts and hostesses usually do not receive tips, so their wage rates may be higher than those of waiters and waitresses and bartenders in full-service restaurants, but their overall earnings might be lower. In many full-service restaurants, tips are higher than wages. In some restaurants, workers contribute all or a portion of their tips to a tip pool, which is distributed among qualifying workers. Tip pools allow workers who don't usually receive tips directly from customers, such as dining room attendants, to feel a part of a team and to share in the rewards of good service.

In May 2009, median hourly wages (including tips) of waiters and waitresses were $8.50. The middle 50 percent earned between $7.60 and $10.62. The lowest 10 percent earned less than $7.17, and the highest 10 percent earned more than $14.48 an hour. For most waiters and waitresses, higher earnings are primarily the result of receiving more in tips rather than higher hourly wages. Tips usually average between 10 percent and 20 percent of guests' checks; waiters and waitresses working in busy or expensive restaurants earn the most.

Bartenders had median hourly wages (including tips) of $8.82. The middle 50 percent earned between $7.76 and $11.09. The lowest 10 percent earned less than $7.33, and the highest 10 percent earned more than $15.11 an hour. Like waiters and waitresses, bartenders employed in public bars may receive more than half of their earnings as tips. Service bartenders often are paid higher hourly wages to offset their lower tip earnings.

Median hourly wages (including tips) of dining room and cafeteria attendants and bartender helpers were $8.51. The middle 50 percent earned between $7.65 and $9.61. The lowest 10 percent earned less than $7.24, and the highest 10 percent earned more than $12.00 an hour. Most received over half of their earnings as wages; the rest of their income was a share of the proceeds from tip pools.

Median hourly wages of hosts and hostesses were $8.71. The middle 50 percent earned between $7.75 and $9.89. The lowest 10 percent earned less than $7.26, and the highest 10 percent earned more than $12.13 an hour. Wages comprised the majority of their earnings. In some cases, wages were supplemented by proceeds from tip pools.

Median hourly wages of combined food preparation and serving workers, including fast food, were $8.28. The middle 50 percent earned between $7.55 and $9.26. The lowest 10 percent earned less than $7.13, and the highest 10 percent earned more than $11.02 an hour. Although some combined food preparation and serving workers receive a part of their earnings as tips, fast food workers usually do not.

Median hourly wages of counter attendants in cafeterias, food concessions, and coffee shops (including tips) were $8.74. The middle 50 percent earned between $7.79 and $9.77 an hour. The lowest 10 percent earned less than $7.31, and the highest 10 percent earned more than $11.83 an hour.

Median hourly wages of dishwashers were $8.54. The middle 50 percent earned between $7.70 and $9.47. The lowest 10 percent earned less than $7.27, and the highest 10 percent earned more than $11.03 an hour.

Median hourly wages of food servers outside of restaurants were $9.42. The middle 50 percent earned between $8.14 and $11.74. The lowest 10 percent earned less than $7.46, and the highest 10 percent earned more than $14.75 an hour.

Many beginning or inexperienced workers earn the federal minimum wage ($7.25 per hour as of July 24, 2009), but many states set minimum wages higher than the federal minimum. Also, various minimum wage exceptions apply under specific circumstances to disabled workers, full-time students, youth under age 20 in their first 90 days of employment, tipped employees, and student-learners. Tipped employees are those who customarily and regularly receive more than $30 a month in tips. The employer may consider tips as part of wages, but the employer must pay at least $2.13 an hour in direct wages.

Many employers provide free meals and furnish uniforms, but some may deduct from wages the cost, or fair value, of any meals or lodging provided. Food and beverage service workers who work full time often receive typical benefits, but part-time workers usually do not. In some large restaurants and hotels, food and beverage serving and related workers belong to unions—principally the Unite HERE and the Service Employees International Union.

Related Occupations

Other workers who prepare or serve food and drink for diners include cashiers; chefs, head cooks, and food preparation and serving supervisors; cooks and food preparation workers; flight attendants; and retail salespersons.

Sources of Additional Information

Information about job opportunities may be obtained from local employers and local offices of state employment services agencies.

A guide to careers in restaurants plus a list of two- and four-year colleges offering food service programs and related scholarship information is available from

▸ National Restaurant Association, 1200 17th St. NW, Washington, DC 20036. Internet: www.restaurant.org

For general information on hospitality careers, contact

▸ International Council on Hotel, Restaurant, and Institutional Education, 2810 N. Parham Rd., Suite 230, Richmond, VA 23294. Internet: www.chrie.org

Food Processing Occupations

(O*NET 51-3011.00, 51-3021.00, 51-3022.00, 51-3023.00, 51-3091.00, 51-3092.00, and 51-3093.00)

Significant Points

■ Most workers in manual food processing jobs require little or no training prior to being hired.

■ As more jobs involving cutting and processing meat shift from retail stores to food processing plants, job growth will be concentrated among lesser-skilled workers, who are employed primarily in manufacturing.

■ Highly skilled bakers should be in demand.

Nature of the Work

Food processing occupations include many different types of workers who process raw food products into the finished goods sold by grocers, wholesalers, restaurants, or institutional food services. These workers perform a variety of tasks and are responsible for producing many of the food products found in every household. Some of these workers are bakers, others slaughter or process meat, and still others operate food processing equipment.

Bakers mix and bake ingredients according to recipes to produce varying types and quantities of breads, pastries, and other baked goods. Bakers commonly are employed in commercial bakeries that distribute breads and pastries through established wholesale and retail outlets, mail order, or manufacturers' outlets. In these manufacturing facilities, bakers produce mostly standardized baked goods in large quantities, using high-volume mixing machines, ovens, and other equipment. Grocery stores and specialty shops produce smaller quantities of breads, pastries, and other baked goods for consumption on their premises or for sale as specialty baked goods. Although the quantities prepared and sold in these stores are often small, they often come in a wide variety of flavors and sizes.

Other food processing workers convert animal carcasses into manageable pieces of meat, known as boxed meat or case-ready meat, suitable for sale to wholesalers and retailers. The nature of their jobs varies significantly depending on the stage of the process in which they are involved. In animal slaughtering and processing plants, *slaughterers and meat packers* slaughter cattle, hogs, and sheep, and cut carcasses into large wholesale cuts, such as rounds, loins, ribs, tenders, and chucks, to facilitate the handling, distribution, marketing, and sale of meat. In most plants, some slaughterers and meat packers further process the large parts into case-ready cuts that are ready for retail stores. Retailers and grocers increasingly prefer such prepackaged meat products because a butcher isn't needed to further portion the cuts for sale. Slaughterers and meat packers also produce hamburger meat and meat trimmings, and prepare sausages, luncheon meats, and other fabricated meat products. They usually work on assembly lines, with each individual responsible for only a few of the many cuts needed to process a carcass. Depending on the type of cut, these workers use knives; cleavers; meat saws; bandsaws; or other potentially dangerous equipment.

Poultry cutters and trimmers slaughter and cut up chickens, turkeys, and other types of poultry. Although the packaging end of the poultry processing industry is becoming increasingly automated, many jobs, such as slaughtering, trimming, and deboning, are still done manually. Most poultry cutters and trimmers perform routine cuts on poultry as it moves along production lines.

Meat, poultry, and fish cutters and trimmers also prepare ready-to-cook foods, often at processing plants, but increasingly at grocery and specialty food stores. This preparation often entails filleting meat, poultry, or fish; cutting it into bite-sized pieces or tenders; preparing and adding vegetables; and applying sauces and flavorings, marinades, or breading. These case-ready products are gaining in popularity as they offer quick and easy preparation for consumers while, in many cases, also offering healthier options.

Manufacturing and retail establishments are both likely to employ fish cutters and trimmers, also called *fish cleaners*. These workers primarily scale, cut, and dress fish by removing the head, scales, and other inedible portions and then cut the fish into steaks or fillets. In retail markets, these workers also may wait on customers and clean fish to order. Some fish processing is done aboard ships where fish can be caught, processed, and often flash frozen to preserve freshness.

Butchers and meat cutters generally process meat at later stages of production, although some are employed at meat processing plants. Most work for grocery stores, wholesale establishments that supply meat to restaurants, or institutional food service facilities that separate wholesale cuts of meat into retail cuts or smaller pieces, known as primals. These butchers cut meat into steaks and chops, shape and tie roasts, and grind beef for sale as chopped meat. Boneless cuts are prepared using knives, slicers, or power cutters, while bandsaws and cleavers are required to cut bone-in pieces of meat. Butchers and meat cutters in retail food stores also may weigh, wrap, and label the cuts of meat; arrange them in refrigerated cases for display; and prepare special cuts to fill orders by customers.

Others who work in food processing include *food batchmakers*, who set up and operate equipment that mixes, blends, or cooks ingredients used in the manufacture of food products according to formulas or recipes; *food cooking machine operators and tenders*, who operate or tend cooking equipment, such as steam-cooking vats, deep-fry cookers, pressure cookers, kettles, and boilers to prepare a wide range of cooked food products, and *food and tobacco roasting, baking, and drying machine operators and tenders*, who use equipment to reduce the moisture content of food or tobacco products or to prepare food for canning. The machines they use include hearth ovens, kiln driers, roasters, char kilns, steam ovens, and vacuum drying equipment. These workers monitor equipment for temperature, humidity, or other factors and make the appropriate adjustments to ensure proper cooking and processing.

All workers who work with food must regularly clean and sanitize utensils, work surfaces, and equipment used to process food to comply with health and sanitation guidelines to prevent the spread of disease.

Work environment. Working conditions vary by occupation and by type and size of establishment, but all employees are required to maintain good personal hygiene and keep equipment clean. Facilities that process food, regardless of industry or location, are regularly inspected to ensure that equipment and employees comply with health and sanitation regulations.

Most bakers work in bakeries, grocery stores, and restaurants. Bakeries are often hot and noisy. Bakers typically work under strict order deadlines and critical time-sensitive baking requirements, both of which can induce stress. Bakers usually work odd hours and may work early mornings, evenings, weekends, and holidays.

Butchers and meat cutters in animal slaughtering and processing plants and in large grocery stores work in large meat cutting rooms equipped with power machines, extremely sharp knives, and conveyors. In smaller retail shops, butchers or fish cleaners may work in a cramped space behind the meat or fish counter where they also can keep track of customers.

Butchers and meat cutters, poultry and fish cutters and trimmers, and slaughterers and meatpackers often work in cold, damp rooms where meat is kept to prevent spoiling. In addition, long periods of standing and repetitive physical tasks make the work tiring. Working with sharp knives on slippery floors makes butchers and meat cutters more susceptible to injury than almost all other workers in the economy; however, injury rates for the animal slaughtering and processing industry have been declining. Injuries include cuts and occasional amputations, which occur when knives, cleavers, or power tools are used improperly. Also, repetitive slicing and lifting often lead to cumulative trauma injuries, such as carpal tunnel syndrome and back strains. To reduce the incidence of cumulative trauma injuries, some employers have reduced employee workloads, added prescribed rest periods, redesigned jobs and tools, and promoted increased awareness of early warning signs as steps to prevent further injury. Nevertheless, workers in the occupation still face the potential threat that some injuries may be disabling.

Workers who operate food processing machinery typically work in production areas that are specially designed for food preservation or processing. Food batchmakers, in particular, work in kitchen-type, assembly-line production facilities. The ovens, as well as the motors of blenders, mixers, and other equipment, often make work areas very warm and noisy. Hazards created by the equipment that these workers use can cause injuries such as cuts and scrapes from cleaning and handling sharp tools and utensils and burns from being in contact with hot surfaces and liquids.

Food batchmakers; food and tobacco roasting, baking, and drying machine operators; and food cooking machine operators and tenders spend a great deal of time on their feet and generally work a regular 40-hour week that may include night and early morning shifts.

Training, Other Qualifications, and Advancement

No formal education is required for most food processing jobs. Employers generally provide most of the training for these occupations upon being hired.

Education and training. Bakers need to become skilled in baking, icing, and decorating. They often start their careers as apprentices or trainees. Apprentice bakers usually start in craft bakeries, while trainees usually begin in store bakeries, such as those in supermarkets. Many apprentice bakers participate in correspondence study and may work towards a certificate in baking.

The skills needed to be a baker are often underestimated. Bakers need to learn how to combine ingredients and to learn how ingredients are affected by heat. They need to learn how to operate and maintain a range of equipment used in the production process. Courses in nutrition are helpful for those selling baked goods or developing new recipes. If running a small business, they need to know how to operate a business. All bakers must follow government health and sanitation regulations.

Most butchers and meat, poultry, and fish cutters and trimmers acquire their skills through on-the-job training programs. The length of training varies significantly. Simple cutting operations require a few days to learn, while more complicated tasks, such as eviscerating slaughtered animals, generally require several months of training. The training period for highly skilled butchers at the retail level may be 1 or 2 years.

Generally, trainees begin by doing less difficult jobs, such as making simple cuts or removing bones. Under the guidance of experienced workers, trainees learn the proper use and care of tools and equipment, while also learning how to prepare various cuts of meat. After demonstrating skill with various meat cutting tools, trainees learn to divide carcasses into wholesale cuts and wholesale cuts into retail and individual portions. Trainees also may learn to roll and tie roasts, prepare sausage, and cure meat. Those employed in retail food establishments often are taught to perform basic business operations, such as inventory control, meat buying, and recordkeeping. In addition, growing concern about food-borne pathogens in meats has led employers to offer numerous safety seminars and extensive training in food safety to employees.

On-the-job training is common among food machine operators and tenders. They learn to run the different types of equipment by watching and helping other workers. Training can last anywhere from a month to a year, depending on the complexity of the tasks and the number of products involved. A degree in an appropriate area—dairy processing for those working in dairy product operations, for example—is helpful for advancement to a lead worker or a supervisory role. Most food batchmakers participate in on-the-job training, usually from about a month to a year. Some food batchmakers learn their trade through an approved apprenticeship program.

Other qualifications. Bakers need to be able to follow instructions, have an eye for detail, and communicate well with others. Meat, poultry, and fish cutters and trimmers need manual dexterity, good depth perception, color discrimination, and good hand-eye coordination. They also need physical strength to lift and move heavy pieces of meat. Butchers and fish cleaners who wait on customers should have a pleasant personality, a neat appearance, and the ability to communicate clearly. In some states, a health certificate is required for employment.

Certification and advancement. Bakers have the option of obtaining certification through the Retail Bakers of America. While not mandatory, obtaining certification assures the public and prospective employers that the baker has sufficient skills and knowledge to work at a retail baking establishment.

The Retail Bakers of America offers certification for four levels of competence with a focus on several broad areas, including baking sanitation, management, retail sales, and staff training. Those who wish to become certified must satisfy a combination of education and experience requirements prior to taking an examination. The education and experience requirements vary by the level of certification desired. For example, a certified journey baker requires no formal education but a minimum of 1 year of work experience. By contrast, a certified master baker must have earned the certified baker designation, and must have completed 30 hours of sanitation coursework approved by a culinary school or government agency, 30 hours of professional development courses or workshops, and a minimum of 8 years of commercial or retail baking experience.

Food processing workers in retail or wholesale establishments may progress to supervisory jobs, such as department managers or team leaders in supermarkets. A few of these workers may become buyers for wholesalers or supermarket chains. Some food processing workers go on to open their own markets or bakeries. In processing plants, workers may advance to supervisory positions or become team leaders.

Employment

Food processing workers held 706,700 jobs in 2008. Employment among the various types of food processing occupations was distributed as follows:

Meat, poultry, and fish cutters and trimmers	169,600
Bakers	151,600
Butchers and meat cutters	129,100
Food batchmakers	100,500
Slaughterers and meat packers	98,400
Food cooking machine operators and tenders	39,300
Food and tobacco roasting, baking, and drying machine operators and tenders	18,100

Fifty-eight percent of all food processing workers were employed in food manufacturing, including animal slaughtering and processing plants, the largest industry component. Food and beverage stores, which include grocery and specialty food stores, employed another 27 percent. Butchers, meat cutters, and bakers are employed in stores in almost every city and town in the nation, while most other food processing jobs are concentrated in communities with food processing plants.

Job Outlook

Increased demand for processed food and meat by a growing population will increase the need for food processing workers; however, processing plant and distribution efficiencies will offset growing output and cause employment of these workers to grow more slowly than the average between 2008 and 2018. In addition, job opportunities should be good as the need to replace experienced workers who transfer to other occupations or leave the labor force should generate additional job openings.

Employment change. Overall employment in the food processing occupations is projected to increase 4 percent during the 2008–2018 decade, more slowly than the average for all occupations. As the nation's population grows the demand for meat, poultry, and seafood; baked goods; and other processed foods will increase, requiring additional people to work in these occupations. Additionally, consumers are increasingly seeking out more convenient methods of preparing meals, which is driving up demand for convenient ready-to-eat or heat foods. These foods are increasingly being prepared at the factory, as well as the local grocery store for carry-out, thus increasing the need for workers in both locations. However, increasing productivity at meat and food processing plants should offset some of the need for more workers at these plants.

Slaughterers and meat packers; meat, poultry, and fish cutters and trimmers; and butchers and meat cutters are all expected to experience some growth in employment. For these occupations in particular, faster growth will take place at the processing plant and away from retail stores, as meats are increasingly processed at processing plants or centralized facilities for delivery to stores. This shift from retail stores to food processing plants will cause demand for lesser-skilled workers, who are employed primarily in meat packing manufacturing plants, to be greater than for butchers and meat cutters.

Many of these same reasons apply to employment in food processing jobs; however, these jobs are more automated than the meat processing occupations, thus productivity improvements will likely impact these workers more. Food batchmakers will experience average employment growth largely due to improved packaging and distribution operations; employment of food cooking machine operators and tenders will grow more slowly than the average; and food and tobacco roasting, baking, and drying machine operators and tenders will show little or no growth.

A growing number of stores that sell cookies, bread, and other specialty baked goods will spur demand for bakers, particularly in grocery and other specialty stores, but increased use of off-site contract bakers with larger baking capacities will offset increased demand and cause employment to show little or no change.

Job prospects. Jobs should be available in all food processing specialties because of the need to replace experienced workers who transfer to other occupations or leave the labor force. Highly skilled bakers should be especially in demand because of growing demand for specialty products and the time it takes to learn to make these products.

Projections Data from the National Employment Matrix

Occupational title	SOC Code	Employment, 2008	Projected employment, 2018	Change, 2008–2018	
				Number	Percent
Food processing occupations	51-3000	706,700	734,000	27,400	4
Bakers	51-3011	151,600	151,900	300	0
Butchers and other meat, poultry, and fish processing workers	51-3020	397,100	413,900	16,800	4
Butchers and meat cutters	51-3021	129,100	131,000	1,900	1
Meat, poultry, and fish cutters and trimmers	51-3022	169,600	180,400	10,800	6
Slaughterers and meat packers	51-3023	98,400	102,500	4,100	4
Miscellaneous food processing workers	51-3090	157,900	168,200	10,300	7
Food and tobacco roasting, baking, and drying machine operators and tenders	51-3091	18,100	18,200	100	0
Food batchmaker	51-3092	100,500	109,200	8,800	9
Food cooking machine operators and tenders	51-3093	39,300	40,800	1,500	4

NOTE: Data in this table are rounded.

Earnings

Earnings vary by industry, skill, geographic region, and educational level. Median annual wages of bakers were $23,630 in May 2009. The middle 50 percent earned between $19,040 and $30,140. The lowest 10 percent earned less than $16,600, and the highest 10 percent earned more than $37,520. Median annual wages in the industries employing the largest numbers of bakers in May 2009 were as follows:

Bakeries and tortilla manufacturing	$24,510
Grocery stores	24,170
Limited-service eating places	20,920
Other general merchandise stores	22,560
Full-service restaurants	22,320

Median annual wages of butchers and meat cutters were $28,850 in May 2009. The middle 50 percent earned between $22,120 and $37,370. The lowest 10 percent earned less than $17,940, and the highest 10 percent earned more than $45,470. Butchers and meat cutters employed at the retail level typically earned more than those in manufacturing. Median annual wages in the industries employing the largest numbers of butchers and meat cutters in May 2009 were as follows:

Grocery stores	$29,550
Specialty food stores	26,350
Animal slaughtering and processing	25,270
Other general merchandise stores	31,960
Grocery and related products merchant wholesalers	28,690

Meat, poultry, and fish cutters and trimmers typically earn less than butchers and meat cutters. In May 2009, median annual wages for these lower skilled workers were $22,130. The middle 50 percent earned between $19,040 and $25,480. The lowest 10 percent earned less than $16,860, while the highest 10 percent earned more than $30,750. Median annual wages in the industries employing the largest numbers of meat, poultry, and fish cutters and trimmers in May 2009 were as follows:

Animal slaughtering and processing	$22,370
Grocery stores	22,300
Seafood product preparation and packaging	18,620

Grocery and related product merchant wholesalers	23,020
Specialty food stores	20,050

In May 2009, median annual wages for slaughterers and meat packers were $23,490. The middle 50 percent earned between $19,870 and $27,400. The lowest 10 percent earned less than $17,070, and the highest 10 percent earned more than $31,290. Median annual wages in animal slaughtering and processing, the industry employing the largest number of slaughterers and meat packers, were $23,600 in May 2009.

In May 2009, median annual wages for food and tobacco roasting, baking, and drying machine operators and tenders were $27,270. The middle 50 percent earned between $21,340 and $35,660. The lowest 10 percent earned less than $17,580, and the highest 10 percent earned more than $43,130. Median annual wages in bakeries and tortilla manufacturing, the industry employing the largest number of food and tobacco roasting, baking, and drying machine operators and tenders, were $28,200 in May 2009.

Median annual earnings of food batchmakers were $24,290 in May 2009. The middle 50 percent earned between $19,160 and $32,220. The lowest 10 percent earned less than $16,740, and the highest 10 percent earned more than $40,910. Median annual wages in the industries employing the largest numbers of food batchmakers in May 2009 were as follows:

Bakeries and tortilla manufacturing	$22,760
Other food manufacturing	23,920
Fruit and vegetable preserving and specialty food manufacturing	24,800
Dairy product manufacturing	31,680
Sugar and confectionery product manufacturing	23,960

Median annual wages for food cooking machine operators and tenders were $23,100 in May 2009. The middle 50 percent earned between $18,960 and $29,080. The lowest 10 percent earned less than $16,610, and the highest 10 percent earned more than $35,440. Median annual wages in the industries employing the largest numbers of food cooking machine operators and tenders in May 2009 were as follows:

Fruit and vegetable preserving and specialty
food manufacturing...$25,810
Animal slaughtering and processing...................... 22,390
Other food manufacturing.................................. 25,980
Bakeries and tortilla manufacturing 22,730
Grocery stores.. 20,100

Food processing workers generally received typical benefits, including pension plans for union members or those employed by grocery stores. However, poultry workers rarely earned substantial benefits. In 2008, 16 percent of all food processing workers were union members or were covered by a union contract. Many food processing workers are members of the United Food and Commercial Workers International Union.

Related Occupations

Food processing workers must be skilled at both hand machine work and must have some knowledge of processes and techniques that are involved in handling and preparing food. Other occupations that require similar skills and knowledge include chefs, head cooks, and food preparation and serving supervisors; and cooks and food preparation workers.

Sources of Additional Information

See your state employment service offices for information about job openings for food processing occupations.

For information on various levels of certification as a baker, contact

▸ Retail Bakers of America, 8400 Westpark Dr., 2nd Floor, McLean, VA 22102

Food Service Managers

(O*NET 11-9051.00)

Significant Points

■ Although most food service managers qualify for their position based on their restaurant-related experience, an increasing number of employers prefer managers with a two- or four-year degree in a related field.

■ Food service managers coordinate a wide range of activities, but their most difficult tasks may be dealing with irate customers and motivating employees.

■ Job opportunities for food service managers should be good, as the number of managers who change jobs or leave this occupation is typically high and, in the long run, more will be hired to meet the growing demand for convenient food service.

Nature of the Work

Food service managers are responsible for the daily operations of restaurants and other establishments that prepare and serve meals and beverages to customers. Besides coordinating activities among various departments, such as kitchen, dining room, and banquet operations, food service managers ensure that customers are satisfied with their dining experience. In addition, they oversee the inventory and ordering of food, equipment, and supplies and arrange for the routine maintenance and upkeep of the restaurant's equipment and facilities. Managers are generally responsible for

all administrative and human-resource functions of the business, including recruiting new employees and monitoring employee performance and training.

Managers interview, hire, train, and when necessary, fire employees. Retaining good employees is a major challenge facing food service managers. Managers recruit employees at career fairs and at schools that offer academic programs in hospitality management or culinary arts and arrange for newspaper advertising to attract additional applicants. Managers oversee the training of new employees and explain the establishment's policies and practices. They schedule work hours, making sure that enough workers are present to cover each shift. If employees are unable to work, managers may have to call in alternates to cover for them or fill in themselves. Some managers may help with cooking, clearing tables, or other tasks when the restaurant becomes extremely busy.

Food service managers ensure that diners are served properly and in a timely manner. They investigate and resolve customers' complaints about food quality and service. They monitor orders in the kitchen to determine where backups may occur, and they work with the chef to remedy any delays in service. Managers direct the cleaning of the dining areas and the washing of tableware, kitchen utensils, and equipment to comply with company and government sanitation standards. Managers also monitor the actions of their employees and patrons on a continual basis to ensure the personal safety of everyone. They make sure that health and safety standards and local liquor regulations are obeyed.

In addition to their regular duties, food service managers perform a variety of administrative assignments, such as keeping employee work records; preparing the payroll; and completing paperwork to comply with licensing, tax, wage and hour, unemployment compensation, and Social Security laws. Some of this work may be delegated to an assistant manager or bookkeeper, or it may be contracted out, but most general managers retain responsibility for the accuracy of business records. Managers also maintain records of supply and equipment purchases and ensure that accounts with suppliers are paid.

Managers tally the cash and charge receipts received and balance them against the record of sales, securing them in a safe place. Finally, managers are responsible for locking up the establishment; checking that ovens, grills, and lights are off; and switching on alarm systems.

Technology influences the jobs of food service managers in many ways, enhancing efficiency and productivity. Many restaurants use computers and business software to place orders and track inventory and sales. They also allow food service managers to monitor expenses, employee schedules, and payroll matters more efficiently.

In most full-service restaurants and institutional food service facilities, the management team consists of a *general manager*, one or more *assistant managers*, and an *executive chef*. The executive chef is responsible for all food preparation activities, including running kitchen operations, planning menus, and maintaining quality standards for food service. In some cases, the executive chef is also the general manager or owner of the restaurant. General managers may employ several assistant managers that oversee certain areas, such as the dining or banquet rooms, or supervise different shifts of workers. In limited-service eating places, such as sandwich and coffee shops or fast food restaurants, managers or food preparation or serving supervisors, not executive chefs, are responsible for supervising routine food preparation operations. (For additional information on these other workers, see material on chefs, head cooks, and food preparation and serving supervisors elsewhere in this book.)

In restaurants, mainly full-service independent ones where there are both food service managers and executive chefs, the managers often help the chefs select menu items. Managers or executive chefs at independent restaurants select menu items, taking into account the past popularity of dishes, the ability to reuse any food not served the previous day, the need for variety, and the seasonal availability of foods. Managers or executive chefs analyze the recipes of the dishes to determine food, labor, and overhead costs; work out the portion size and nutritional content of each plate; and assign prices to various menu items. Menus must be developed far enough in advance that supplies can be ordered and received in time.

Managers or executive chefs estimate food needs, place orders with distributors, and schedule the delivery of fresh food and supplies. They plan for routine services or deliveries, such as linen services or the heavy cleaning of dining rooms or kitchen equipment, to occur during slow times or when the dining room is closed. Managers also arrange for equipment maintenance and repairs and coordinate a variety of services such as waste removal and pest control. Managers or executive chefs receive deliveries and check the contents against order records. They inspect the quality of fresh meats, poultry, fish, fruits, vegetables, and baked goods to ensure that expectations are met. They meet with representatives from restaurant supply companies and place orders to replenish stocks of tableware, linens, paper products, cleaning supplies, cooking utensils, and furniture and fixtures.

Work environment. Many food service managers work long hours—12 to 15 per day, 50 or more per week, and sometimes 7 days a week. Such schedules are common for fine dining restaurants and those, such as fast food restaurants, that operate extended hours. Managers of institutional food service facilities, such as school, factory, or office cafeterias, work more regular hours because the operating hours of these establishments usually conform to the operating hours of the business or facility they serve. However, many managers oversee multiple locations of a chain or franchise or may be called in on short notice, making hours unpredictable.

Managers should be calm; flexible; and able to work through emergencies, such as a fire or flood, to ensure everyone's safety. They also should be able to fill in for absent workers on short notice. Managers often experience the pressures of simultaneously coordinating a wide range of activities. When problems occur, it is the manager's responsibility to resolve them with minimal disruption to customers. The job can be hectic, and dealing with irate customers or uncooperative employees can be stressful.

Managers also may experience the typical minor injuries of other restaurant workers, such as muscle aches, cuts, or burns. Although injuries generally do not require prolonged absences from work, the incidence of injuries requiring at least one day's absence from work exceeds that of about 60 percent of all occupations.

Training, Other Qualifications, and Advancement

Experience in the food services industry, whether as a cook, waiter or waitress, or counter attendant, is the most common training for food service managers. Many restaurant and food service manager positions, particularly self-service and fast food, are filled by promoting experienced food and beverage preparation and service workers.

Education and training. Most food service managers have less than a bachelor's degree; however, some postsecondary education, including a college degree, is increasingly preferred for many food service manager positions. Many food service management companies and national or regional restaurant chains recruit management trainees from two- and four-year college hospitality or food service management programs, which require internships and real-life experience to graduate. While these specialized degrees are often preferred, graduates with degrees in other fields who have demonstrated experience, interest, and aptitude are also recruited.

Most restaurant chains and food service management companies have rigorous training programs for management positions. Through a combination of classroom and on-the-job training, trainees receive instruction and gain work experience in all aspects of the operation of a restaurant or institutional food service facility. Areas include food preparation, nutrition, sanitation, security, company policies and procedures, personnel management, recordkeeping, and preparation of reports. Training on the use of the restaurant's computer system is increasingly important as well. Usually, after several months of training, trainees receive their first permanent assignment as an assistant manager.

Almost 1,000 colleges and universities offer four-year programs in restaurant and hospitality management or institutional food service management; a growing number of university programs offer graduate degrees in hospitality management or similar fields. For those not interested in pursuing a four-year degree, community and junior colleges, technical institutes, and other institutions offer programs in the field leading to an associate degree or other formal certification.

Both two- and four-year programs provide instruction in subjects such as nutrition, sanitation, and food planning and preparation, as well as accounting, business law and management, and computer science. Some programs combine classroom and laboratory study with internships providing on-the-job experience. In addition, many educational institutions offer culinary programs in food preparation. Such training can lead to careers as cooks or chefs and provide a foundation for advancement to executive chef positions.

Many larger food service operations will provide or offer to pay for technical training, such as computer or business courses, so that employees can acquire the business skills necessary to read spreadsheets or understand the concepts and practices of running a business. Generally, this requires a long-term commitment on the employee's part to both the employer and to the profession.

Other qualifications. Most employers emphasize personal qualities when hiring managers. Workers who are reliable, show initiative, and have leadership qualities are highly sought after for promotion. Other qualities that managers look for are good problem-solving skills and the ability to concentrate on details. A neat and clean appearance is important because food service managers must convey self-confidence and show respect in dealing with the public. Because food service management can be physically demanding, good health and stamina are important.

Managers must be good communicators as they deal with customers, employees, and suppliers for most of the day. They must be able to motivate employees to work as a team to ensure that food and service meet appropriate standards. Additionally, the ability to speak multiple languages is helpful to communicate with staff and patrons.

Certification and advancement. The certified Foodservice Management Professional (FMP) designation is a measure of professional

Projections Data from the National Employment Matrix

Occupational title	SOC Code	Employment, 2008	Projected employment, 2018	Change, 2008–2018	
				Number	Percent
Food service managers 11-9051		338,700	356,700	18,000	5

NOTE: Data in this table are rounded.

achievement for food service managers. Although not a requirement for employment or necessary for advancement, voluntary certification can provide recognition of professional competence, particularly for managers who acquired their skills largely on the job. The National Restaurant Association Educational Foundation awards the FMP designation to managers who achieve a qualifying score on a written examination, complete a series of courses that cover a range of food service management topics, and meet standards of work experience in the field.

Willingness to relocate is often essential for advancement to positions with greater responsibility. Managers typically advance to larger or more prominent establishments or regional management positions within restaurant chains. Some may open their own food service establishments or franchise operations.

Employment

Food service managers held about 338,700 jobs in 2008. The majority of managers are salaried, but 42 percent are self-employed as owners of independent restaurants or other small food service establishments. Forty-one percent of all salaried jobs for food service managers are in full-service restaurants or limited-service eating places, such as fast food restaurants and cafeterias. Other salaried jobs are in special food services, an industry that includes food service contractors who supply food services at institutional, governmental, commercial, or industrial locations, and educational services, which primarily supply elementary and secondary schools. A smaller number of salaried jobs are in hotels; amusement, gambling, and recreation industries; nursing care facilities; and hospitals. Jobs are located throughout the country, with large cities and resort areas providing more opportunities for full-service dining positions.

Job Outlook

Food service manager jobs are expected to grow 5 percent, or more slowly than the average for all occupations through 2018. However, job opportunities should be good because many openings will arise from the need to replace managers who leave the occupation.

Employment change. Employment of food service managers is expected to grow 5 percent, or more slowly than the average for all occupations, during the 2008–2018 decade, as the number of eating and drinking establishments opening is expected to decline from the previous decade. Despite these reductions in the number of new eating and drinking places, new employment opportunities for food service managers will emerge in grocery and convenience stores and other retail and recreation industries to meet the growing demand for quick food in a variety of settings. Employment growth is projected to vary by industry. Most new jobs will be in full-service restaurants and limited-service eating places. Manager jobs will also increase in health-care and elder care facilities. Self-employment of these workers will generate nearly 40 percent of new jobs.

Job prospects. In addition to job openings from employment growth, the need to replace managers who transfer to other occupations or stop working will create good job opportunities. Although

practical experience is an integral part of finding a food service management position, applicants with a degree in restaurant, hospitality, or institutional food service management will have an edge when competing for jobs at upscale restaurants and for advancement in a restaurant chain or into corporate management.

Earnings

Median annual wages of salaried food service managers were $47,210 in May 2009. The middle 50 percent earned between $37,410 and $61,070. The lowest 10 percent earned less than $29,810, and the highest 10 percent earned more than $78,910. Median annual wages in the industries employing the largest numbers of food service managers were as follows:

Limited-service eating places	$42,160
Full-service restaurants	50,460
Special food services	52,480
Traveler accommodation	54,930

In addition to receiving typical benefits, most salaried food service managers are provided free meals and the opportunity for additional training, depending on their length of service. Some food service managers, especially those in full-service restaurants, may earn bonuses depending on sales volume or revenue.

Related Occupations

Other managers and supervisors in hospitality-related businesses include first-line supervisors or managers of food preparation and serving workers; gaming services occupations; lodging managers; and sales worker supervisors.

Sources of Additional Information

Information about a career as a food service manager, two- and four-year college programs in restaurant and food service management, and certification as a Foodservice Management Professional is available from

▸ National Restaurant Association Educational Foundation, 175 W. Jackson Blvd., Suite 1500, Chicago, IL 60604-2702. Internet: www.nraef.org

Career information about food service managers, as well as a directory of two- and four-year colleges that offer courses or programs that prepare persons for food service careers is available from

▸ National Restaurant Association, 1200 17th St. NW, Washington, DC 20036-3097. Internet: www.restaurant.org

General information on hospitality careers may be obtained from

▸ The International Council on Hotel, Restaurant, and Institutional Education, 2810 N. Parham Rd., Suite 230, Richmond, VA 23294. Internet: www.chrie.org

Additional information about job opportunities in food service management may be obtained from local employers and from local offices of state employment services agencies.

Grounds Maintenance Workers

(O*NET 37-1012.00, 37-3011.00, 37-3012.00, 37-3013.00, and 37-3019.00)

Significant Points

■ Most grounds maintenance workers need no formal education and are trained on the job; however, some workers may require formal education.

■ Occupational characteristics include full-time and part-time jobs, seasonal jobs, physically demanding work, and low earnings.

■ Job opportunities are expected to be good.

Nature of the Work

Grounds maintenance workers perform a variety of tasks necessary to achieve a pleasant and functional outdoor environment. They mow lawns, rake leaves, trim hedges and trees; plant flowers; and otherwise ensure that the grounds of houses, businesses, and parks are attractive, orderly, and healthy. They also care for indoor gardens and plantings in commercial and public facilities, such as malls, hotels, and botanical gardens.

These workers use hand tools such as shovels, rakes, pruning and handsaws, hedge and brush trimmers, and axes. They also use power lawnmowers, chain saws, leaf blowers, and electric clippers. Some use equipment such as tractors and twin-axle vehicles.

Grounds maintenance workers can be divided into several specialties, including landscaping workers, groundskeeping workers, pesticide handlers, tree trimmers, and grounds maintenance supervisors. In general, these specialties have varying job duties, but in many cases their responsibilities overlap.

Landscaping workers create new functional outdoor areas and upgrade existing landscapes, but also may help maintain landscapes. Their duties include planting bushes, trees, sod, and other forms of vegetation, as well as, edging, trimming, fertilizing, watering, and mulching lawns and grounds. They also grade property by creating or smoothing hills and inclines; install lighting or sprinkler systems; and build walkways, terraces, patios, decks, and fountains. Landscaping workers provide their services in a variety of residential and commercial settings, such as homes, apartment buildings, office buildings, shopping malls, and hotels and motels.

Groundskeeping workers, also called *groundskeepers,* usually focus on maintaining existing grounds. In addition to caring for sod, plants, and trees, they rake and mulch leaves, clear snow from walkways and parking lots, and use irrigation methods to adjust water consumption and prevent waste. These individuals work on athletic fields, golf courses, cemeteries, university campuses, and parks, as well as many of the same settings as landscaping workers. They also see to the proper upkeep and repair of sidewalks, parking lots, groundskeeping equipment, pools, fountains, fences, planters, and benches.

Groundskeeping workers who care for athletic fields keep natural and artificial turf in top condition, mark out boundaries, and paint turf with team logos and names before events. They mow, water, fertilize, and aerate the fields regularly. They must make sure that the underlying soil on fields with natural turf has the required

composition to allow proper drainage and to support the grasses used on the field. In sports venues, they vacuum and disinfect synthetic turf after its use to prevent the growth of harmful bacteria, and they remove the turf and replace the cushioning pad periodically.

Groundskeepers in parks and recreation facilities care for lawns, trees, and shrubs; maintain playgrounds; clean buildings; and keep parking lots, picnic areas, and other public spaces free of litter. They also may erect and dismantle snow fences, and maintain swimming pools. These workers inspect buildings and equipment, make needed repairs, and keep everything freshly painted.

Workers who maintain golf courses are called *greenskeepers.* Greenskeepers do many of the same things as other groundskeepers, but they also periodically relocate the holes on putting greens to prevent uneven wear of the turf and to add interest and challenge to the game. Greenskeepers also keep canopies, benches, ball washers, and tee markers repaired and freshly painted.

Some groundskeepers specialize in caring for cemeteries and memorial gardens. They dig graves to specified depths, generally using a backhoe. They mow grass regularly, apply fertilizers and other chemicals, prune shrubs and trees, plant flowers, and remove debris from graves.

Pesticide handlers, sprayers, and applicators, vegetation mix herbicides, fungicides, or insecticides and apply them through sprays, dusts, or vapors into the soil or onto plants. Those working for chemical lawn service firms are more specialized, inspecting lawns for problems and applying fertilizers, pesticides, and other chemicals to stimulate growth and prevent or control weeds, diseases, or insect infestation. Many practice integrated pest-management techniques.

Tree trimmers and pruners, sometimes called *arborists,* cut away dead or excess branches from trees or shrubs to clear roads, sidewalks, or utilities' equipment, or to improve the appearance, health, and value of trees. Some specialize in diagnosing and treating tree diseases, and in performing preventive measures to keep trees healthy. Some may plant trees. Some of these workers also specialize in pruning, trimming and shaping ornamental trees and shrubs for private residences, golf courses, or other institutional grounds. Tree trimmers and pruners use handsaws, pole saws, shears, and clippers. When trimming near power lines, they usually work on truck-mounted lifts and use power pruners.

Supervisors of landscaping and groundskeeping workers oversee grounds maintenance work. They prepare cost estimates, schedule work for crews on the basis of weather conditions or the availability of equipment, perform spot checks to ensure the quality of the service, and suggest changes in work procedures. In addition, supervisors train workers; keep employees' time records and record work performed; and may assist workers when deadlines are near. Supervisors who own their own business are also known as *landscape contractors.* They also often call themselves *landscape designers* if they create landscape design plans. Landscape designers also design exterior floral displays by planting annual or perennial flowers. Some work with landscape architects. Supervisors of workers on golf courses are known as *superintendents.*

Work environment. Many grounds maintenance jobs are seasonal, available mainly in the spring, summer, and fall, when most planting, mowing, trimming, and cleanup are necessary. Most of the work is performed outdoors in all kinds of weather. It can be physically demanding and repetitive, involving bending, lifting, and shoveling. This occupation offers opportunities for both part-time and full-time work.

According to BLS data, full-time landscaping and groundskeeping workers, tree trimmers and pruners, and the supervisors of these workers experienced a much higher than average rate of work-related injury and illness. Those who work with pesticides, fertilizers, and other chemicals, as well as dangerous equipment and tools such as power lawnmowers and chain saws, must exercise safety precautions. Workers who use motorized equipment must take care to protect their hearing.

Training, Other Qualifications, and Advancement

Most grounds maintenance workers need no formal education and are trained on the job. However, some workers may require formal education in areas such as landscape design, horticulture, or business management.

Education and training. There usually are no minimum educational requirements for entry-level positions in grounds maintenance. In 2008, most workers had no education beyond high school. A short period of on-the-job training generally is sufficient to teach new hires the necessary skills, which often include planting and maintenance procedures; the operation of mowers, trimmers, leaf blowers, small tractors and other equipment; and proper safety procedures. Large institutional employers such as golf courses or municipalities may supplement on-the-job training with coursework in subjects like horticulture or small engine repair. A bachelor's degree may be needed for those who want to become specialists.

Supervisors may need a high school diploma, and may receive several months of on-the-job training. Formal training in landscape design, horticulture, arboriculture, or business may improve an applicant's chances for employment. Landscape designers may be required to obtain such training.

Licensure. Most states require licensure or certification for workers who apply pesticides. Requirements vary but usually include passing a test on the proper use and disposal of insecticides, herbicides, and fungicides. Some states also require that landscape contractors be licensed.

Other qualifications. Employers look for responsible, self-motivated individuals because grounds maintenance workers often work with little supervision. Employers want people who can learn quickly and follow instructions accurately so that time is not wasted and plants are not damaged. Driving a vehicle is often needed for these jobs. If driving is required, preference is given to applicants with a driver's license, a good driving record, and experience driving a truck.

Certification and advancement. Laborers who demonstrate a proficiency in the work and have good communication skills may advance to crew leader or other supervisory positions. Becoming a grounds manager or landscape contractor may require some formal education beyond high school in addition to several years of experience. Some workers with groundskeeping backgrounds may start their own businesses after several years of experience.

Certification from a professional organization may improve a worker's chances for advancement. The Professional Grounds Management Society offers voluntary certification to grounds managers who have a bachelor's degree in a relevant major with at least four years of experience, including two years as a supervisor; an associate degree in a relevant major with six years of experience,

including three years as a supervisor; or eight years of experience including four years as a supervisor, and no degree. Additionally, candidates for certification must pass two examinations covering subjects such as insects and diseases, soils, trees and shrubs, turf management, irrigation, and budgets and finances. This organization also offers certification for grounds technicians. Candidates for this program must have a high school diploma or GED as well as two years of work experience as a grounds technician.

The Professional Landcare Network offers six certifications for individuals with varying levels of experience, in landscaping and grounds maintenance. Each of these programs requires applicants to pass an examination, and some require self-study course work. The Tree Care Industry Association offers five levels of credentials. Currently available credentials include Tree Care Apprentice, Ground Operations Specialist, Tree Climber Specialist, Aerial Lift Specialist and Tree Care Specialist, as well as a certification program in safety. These programs are available to individuals with varying levels of experience, and require applicants to pass training courses.

Employment

Grounds maintenance workers held about 1.5 million jobs in 2008. Employment was distributed as follows:

Landscaping and groundskeeping workers 1,205,800
First-line supervisors/managers of landscaping,
    lawn service, and groundskeeping workers 217,900
Tree trimmers and pruners 45,000
Pesticide handlers, sprayers, and applicators,
    vegetation 30,800
Grounds maintenance workers, all other 21,100

About 36 percent of all grounds maintenance workers were employed in companies providing landscaping services to buildings and dwellings. Others worked for educational institutions, public and private. Some were employed by local governments, installing and maintaining landscaping for parks, hospitals, and other public facilities. Around 402,000 grounds maintenance workers were self-employed, providing landscape maintenance directly to customers on a contract basis.

Job Outlook

Employment is expected to grow faster than average, and job opportunities should be good.

Employment change. Employment of grounds maintenance workers is expected to increase by 18 percent during the 2008–2018 decade, which is faster than the average for all occupations. In addition, grounds maintenance workers will be among the occupations with largest numbers of new jobs, with around 269,200. More workers will be needed to keep up with increasing demand for lawn care and landscaping services both from large institutions and from individual homeowners.

Major institutions, such as universities and corporate headquarters, recognize the importance of good landscape design in attracting personnel and clients and are expected to continue to use grounds maintenance services to maintain and upgrade their properties. Homeowners are also a growing source of demand for grounds maintenance workers. Many two-income households lack the time to take care of their lawns so they increasingly hire people to

Projections Data from the National Employment Matrix

Occupational title	SOC Code	Employment, 2008	Projected employment, 2018	Change, 2008–2018	
				Number	Percent
Grounds maintenance workers .... —		1,520,600	1,789,900	269,200	18
First-line supervisors/managers of landscaping, lawn service, and groundskeeping workers 37-1012		217,900	250,300	32,400	15
Grounds maintenance workers 37-3000		1,302,700	1,539,500	236,800	18
Landscaping and groundskeeping workers 37-3011		1,205,800	1,422,900	217,100	18
Pesticide handlers, sprayers, and applicators, vegetation... 37-3012		30,800	36,300	5,400	18
Tree trimmers and pruners 37-3013		45,000	56,800	11,800	26
Grounds maintenance workers, all other.............. 37-3019		21,100	23,600	2,500	12

NOTE: Data in this table are rounded.

maintain them. Also, as the population ages, more elderly home-owners will require lawn care services to help maintain their yards.

Employment of tree trimmers and pruners should grow by 26 percent from 2008 to 2018, which is much faster than the average. In order to improve the environment, municipalities across the country are planting more trees in urban areas, increasing demand for these workers.

Job prospects. Job opportunities are expected to be good. Openings will arise from faster-than-average growth and the need to replace workers who leave this large occupation.

Job opportunities for nonseasonal work are best in regions with temperate climates, where landscaping and lawn services are required all year. Opportunities may vary with local economic conditions.

Earnings

Wages of grounds maintenance workers are low. Median hourly wages of landscaping and groundskeeping workers were $11.29 in May 2009. The middle 50 percent earned between $9.24 and $14.24 per hour. The lowest 10 percent earned less than $8.06 per hour, and the highest 10 percent earned more than $17.82. Median hourly wages in the largest employing industries of landscaping and groundskeeping workers in May 2009 were as follows:

Services to buildings and dwellings...................... $11.23
Other amusement and recreation industries............. 10.16
Local government.. 12.91
Elementary and secondary schools 14.16
Employment services... 10.23

Median hourly wages of pesticide handlers, sprayers, and applicators, vegetation were $14.39 in May 2009. The middle 50 percent earned between $11.81 and $17.73 per hour. The lowest 10 percent earned less than $9.77 per hour, and the highest 10 percent earned more than $21.44. Median hourly wages in the services to buildings and dwellings industry were $14.64 in May 2009.

Median hourly wages of tree trimmers and pruners were $14.57 in May 2009. The middle 50 percent earned between $11.64 and $18.37 per hour. The lowest 10 percent earned less than $9.83 per hour, and the highest 10 percent earned more than $22.91. Median hourly wages in the services to buildings and dwellings industry were $14.18 in May 2009.

Median hourly wages of first-line supervisors/managers of landscaping, lawn service, and groundskeeping workers were $19.69 in May 2009. The middle 50 percent earned between $15.61 and

$25.61 per hour. The lowest 10 percent earned less than $12.82 per hour, and the highest 10 percent earned more than $32.22. Median hourly wages in the largest employing industries of first-line supervisors/managers of landscaping, lawn service, and groundskeeping workers in May 2009 were as follows:

Services to buildings and dwellings...................... $18.89
Local government.. 23.23
Other amusement and recreation industries............. 21.39

Related Occupations

Other occupations that work with plants and soils include agricultural workers, other; farmers, ranchers, and agricultural managers; forest and conservation workers; landscape architects; and logging workers.

Sources of Additional Information

For career and certification information on tree trimmers and pruners, contact

▸ Tree Care Industry Association, 136 Harvey Rd., Suite 101, Londonderry, NH 03053. Internet: www.treecareindustry.org

For information on work as a landscaping and groundskeeping worker, contact the following organizations:

▸ Professional Grounds Management Society, 720 Light St., Baltimore, MD 21230. Internet: www.pgms.org

▸ Professional Landcare Network, 950 Herndon Pkwy., Suite 450, Herndon, VA 20170. Internet: www.landcarenetwork.org

For information on becoming a licensed pesticide applicator, contact your state's Department of Agriculture or Department of Environmental Protection or Conservation.

Heating, Air-conditioning, and Refrigeration Mechanics and Installers

(O*NET 49-9021.00, 49-9021.01, and 49-9021.02)

Significant Points

■ Job prospects are expected to be excellent.

■ Employment is projected to grow much faster than the average.

- Employers prefer to hire those who have completed technical school training or a formal apprenticeship.

Nature of the Work

Heating and air-conditioning systems control the temperature, humidity, and the total air quality in residential, commercial, industrial, and other buildings. By providing a climate-controlled environment, refrigeration systems make it possible to store and transport food, medicine, and other perishable items. *Heating, air-conditioning, and refrigeration mechanics and installers*—also called *technicians*—install, maintain, and repair such systems. Because heating, ventilation, air-conditioning, and refrigeration systems often are referred to as HVACR systems, these workers also may be called HVACR technicians.

Heating, air-conditioning, and refrigeration systems consist of many mechanical, electrical, and electronic components, such as motors, compressors, pumps, fans, ducts, pipes, thermostats, and switches. In central forced air heating systems, for example, a furnace heats air, which is then distributed through a system of metal or fiberglass ducts. Technicians maintain, diagnose, and correct problems throughout the entire system. To do this, they adjust system controls to recommended settings and test the performance of the system using special tools and test equipment.

Technicians often specialize in either installation or maintenance and repair, although they are trained to do both. They also may specialize in doing heating work or air-conditioning or refrigeration work. Some specialize in one type of equipment—for example, hydronics (water-based heating systems), solar panels, or commercial refrigeration.

Technicians are often required to sell service contracts to their clients. Service contracts provide for regular maintenance of the heating and cooling systems, and they help to reduce the seasonal fluctuations of this type of work.

Technicians follow blueprints or other specifications to install oil, gas, electric, solid-fuel, and multiple-fuel heating systems and air-conditioning systems. After putting the equipment in place, they install fuel and water supply lines, air ducts and vents, pumps, and other components. They may connect electrical wiring and controls and check the unit for proper operation. To ensure the proper functioning of the system, furnace installers often use combustion test equipment, such as carbon dioxide testers, carbon monoxide testers, combustion analyzers, and oxygen testers. These tests ensure that the system will operate safely and at peak efficiency.

After a furnace or air-conditioning unit has been installed, technicians often perform routine maintenance and repair work to keep the systems operating efficiently. They may adjust burners and blowers and check for leaks. If the system is not operating properly, technicians check the thermostat, burner nozzles, controls, or other parts to diagnose and correct the problem.

Technicians also install and maintain heat pumps, which are similar to air conditioners but can be reversed so that they both heat and cool a home. Because of the added complexity, and the fact that they run both in summer and winter, these systems often require more maintenance and need to be replaced more frequently than traditional furnaces and air conditioners.

During the summer, when heating systems are not being used, heating equipment technicians do maintenance work, such as replacing filters, ducts, and other parts of the system that may accumulate dust and impurities during the operating season. During the winter, air-conditioning mechanics inspect the systems and do required maintenance, such as overhauling compressors.

Refrigeration mechanics install, service, and repair industrial and commercial refrigerating systems and a variety of refrigeration equipment. They follow blueprints, design specifications, and manufacturers' instructions to install motors, compressors, condensing units, evaporators, piping, and other components. They connect this equipment to the ductwork, refrigerant lines, and electrical power source. After making the connections, refrigerator mechanics charge the system with refrigerant, check it for proper operation and leaks, and program control systems.

When air-conditioning and refrigeration technicians service equipment, they must use care to conserve, recover, and recycle the refrigerants used in air-conditioning and refrigeration systems. The release of these refrigerants can be harmful to the environment. Technicians conserve the refrigerant by making sure that there are no leaks in the system; they recover it by venting the refrigerant into proper cylinders; they recycle it for reuse with special filter-dryers; or they ensure that the refrigerant is properly disposed of.

Heating, air-conditioning, and refrigeration mechanics and installers are adept at using a variety of tools to work with refrigerant lines and air ducts, including hammers, wrenches, metal snips, electric drills, pipe cutters and benders, measurement gauges, and acetylene torches. They use voltmeters, thermometers, pressure gauges, manometers, and other testing devices to check airflow, refrigerant pressure, electrical circuits, burners, and other components.

Other craft workers sometimes install or repair cooling and heating systems. For example, on a large air-conditioning installation job, especially where workers are covered by union contracts, ductwork might be done by sheet metal workers and duct installers; electrical work by electricians; and installation of piping, condensers, and other components by plumbers, pipelayers, pipefitters, and steamfitters. Home appliance repairers usually service room air conditioners and household refrigerators. (Additional information about each of these occupations appears elsewhere in this book.)

Work environment. Heating, air-conditioning, and refrigeration mechanics and installers work in homes, retail establishments, hospitals, office buildings, and factories—anywhere there is climate-control equipment that needs to be installed, repaired, or serviced. They may be assigned to specific job sites at the beginning of each day or may be dispatched to a variety of locations if they are making service calls.

Technicians may work outside in cold or hot weather, or in buildings that are uncomfortable because the air-conditioning or heating equipment is broken. In addition, technicians might work in awkward or cramped positions, and sometimes they are required to work in high places. Hazards include electrical shock, burns, muscle strains, and other injuries from handling heavy equipment. Appropriate safety equipment is necessary when handling refrigerants because contact can cause skin damage, frostbite, or blindness. When they are working in tight spaces, inhalation of refrigerant is a possible hazard.

The majority of mechanics and installers work at least 40 hours per week. During peak seasons, they often work overtime or irregular hours. Maintenance workers, including those who provide maintenance services under contract, often work evening or weekend shifts and are on call. Most employers try to provide a full workweek year-round by scheduling both installation and maintenance work, and many manufacturers and contractors now provide or even require year-round service contracts. In most shops that service both heating and air-conditioning equipment, employment is stable throughout the year.

Training, Other Qualifications, and Advancement

Because of the increasing sophistication of heating, air-conditioning, and refrigeration systems, employers prefer to hire those who have completed technical school training or a formal apprenticeship. Some mechanics and installers, however, still learn the trade informally on the job.

Education and training. Many heating, air-conditioning, and refrigeration mechanics and installers receive their primary training in secondary and postsecondary technical and trade schools and junior and community colleges that offer programs in heating, air conditioning, and refrigeration. These programs can take between six months and two years to complete. Others get their training in the Armed Forces.

High school students interested in some initial training for this industry should take courses in shop math, mechanical drawing, applied physics and chemistry, electronics, blueprint reading, and computer applications. Some knowledge of plumbing or electrical work and a basic understanding of electronics are beneficial for an HVACR technician. Secondary and postsecondary students studying HVACR learn about theory of temperature control, equipment design and construction, and electronics. They also learn the basics of installation, maintenance, and repair.

Three accrediting agencies have set academic standards for HVACR programs: HVAC Excellence; the National Center for Construction Education and Research; and the Partnership for Air-Conditioning, Heating, and Refrigeration Accreditation. After completing these programs, new technicians generally need between six months and two years of field experience before they are considered proficient.

Many other technicians train through apprenticeships. Apprenticeship programs frequently are run by joint committees representing local chapters of the Air-Conditioning Contractors of America, the Mechanical Contractors Association of America, Plumbing-Heating-Cooling Contractors—National Association, and locals of the Sheet Metal Workers' International Association or the United Association of Journeymen and Apprentices of the Plumbing and Pipefitting Industry of the United States and Canada. Local chapters of the Associated Builders and Contractors and the National Association of Home Builders sponsor other apprenticeship programs. Formal apprenticeship programs normally last three to five years and combine paid on-the-job training with classroom instruction. Classes include subjects such as safety practices, the use and care of tools, blueprint reading, and the theory and design of heating, ventilation, air-conditioning, and refrigeration systems. In addition to understanding how systems work, technicians must learn about refrigerant products and the legislation and regulations that govern their use.

Applicants for apprenticeships must have a high school diploma or equivalent. Math and reading skills are essential. After completing an apprenticeship program, technicians are considered skilled trades workers and capable of working alone. These programs are also a pathway to certification and, in some cases, college credits.

Those who acquire their skills on the job usually begin by assisting experienced technicians. They may begin by performing simple tasks such as carrying materials, insulating refrigerant lines, or cleaning furnaces. In time, they move on to more difficult tasks, such as cutting and soldering pipes and sheet metal and checking electrical and electronic circuits.

Licensure. Heating, air-conditioning, and refrigeration mechanics and installers are required to be licensed by some states and localities. Requirements for licensure vary greatly, but all states or localities that require a license have a test that must be passed. The contents of these tests vary by state or locality, with some requiring extensive knowledge of electrical codes and others focusing more on HVACR-specific knowledge. Completion of an apprenticeship program or two to five years of experience are also common requirements.

In addition, all technicians who purchase or work with refrigerants must be certified in their proper handling. To become certified to purchase and handle refrigerants, technicians must pass a written examination specific to the type of work in which they specialize. The three possible areas of certification are: Type I—servicing small appliances; Type II—high-pressure refrigerants; and Type III—low-pressure refrigerants. Exams are administered by organizations approved by the U.S. Environmental Protection Agency, such as trade schools, unions, contractor associations, or building groups.

Other qualifications. Because technicians frequently deal directly with the public, they should be courteous and tactful, especially when dealing with an aggravated customer. They should be in good physical condition because they sometimes have to lift and move heavy equipment.

Certification and advancement. Throughout the learning process, technicians may have to take a number of tests that measure their skills. For those with relevant coursework and less than two years of experience, the industry has developed a series of exams to test basic competency in residential heating and cooling, light commercial heating and cooling, and commercial refrigeration. These are referred to as "Entry-level" certification exams and are commonly conducted at both secondary and postsecondary technical and trade schools.

Additionally, HVACR technicians who have at least one year of experience performing installations and two years of experience performing maintenance and repair can take a number of different tests to certify their competency in working with specific types of equipment, such as oil-burning furnaces. The Air Conditioning, Heating, and Refrigeration Institute offers an Industry Competency Exam; HVAC Excellence offers both a Secondary Employment Ready Exam and Secondary Heat and Heat Plus exams; the National Occupational Competency Testing Institute offers a secondary exam; and the Refrigeration Service Engineers Society offers two levels of certification, as well. Employers increasingly recommend taking and passing these tests and obtaining certification; doing so may increase advancement opportunities.

Another way to increase advancement opportunities is to take advantage of any courses that will improve competency with computers; these courses are useful because of the increasing complexity of automated computer controls in larger buildings.

Advancement usually takes the form of higher wages. Some technicians, however, may advance to positions as supervisor or service manager. Others may move into sales and marketing. Still others may become building superintendents, cost estimators, system test and balance specialists, or, with the necessary certification, teachers. Those with sufficient money and managerial skill can open their own contracting business.

Projections Data from the National Employment Matrix

Occupational title	SOC Code	Employment, 2008	Projected employment, 2018	Change, 2008–2018	
				Number	Percent
Heating, air-conditioning, and refrigeration mechanics and installers	49-9021	308,200	394,800	86,600	28

NOTE: Data in this table are rounded.

Employment

Heating, air-conditioning, and refrigeration mechanics and installers held about 308,200 jobs in 2008; about 54 percent worked for plumbing, heating, and air-conditioning contractors. The rest were employed in a variety of industries throughout the country, reflecting a widespread dependence on climate-control systems. Some worked for refrigeration and air-conditioning service and repair shops, schools, and stores that sell heating and air-conditioning systems. Local governments, the federal government, hospitals, office buildings, and other organizations that operate large air-conditioning, refrigeration, or heating systems also employed these workers. About 16 percent of these workers were self-employed.

Job Outlook

With much faster than average job growth and numerous expected retirements, heating, air-conditioning, and refrigeration mechanics and installers should have excellent employment opportunities.

Employment change. Employment of heating, air-conditioning, and refrigeration mechanics and installers is projected to increase 28 percent during the 2008–2018 decade, much faster than the average for all occupations. As the population and stock of buildings grows, so does the demand for residential, commercial, and industrial climate-control systems. Residential HVACR systems generally need replacement after 10 to 15 years; the large number of homes built in recent years will enter this replacement time frame by 2018. The increased complexity of HVACR systems, which increases the possibility that equipment may malfunction, also will create opportunities for service technicians. A growing focus on improving indoor air quality and the increasing use of refrigerated equipment by a rising number of stores and gasoline stations that sell food should also create more jobs for heating, air-conditioning, and refrigeration technicians.

Concern for the environment and the need to reduce energy consumption overall has prompted the development of new energy-saving heating and air-conditioning systems. This emphasis on better energy management is expected to lead to the replacement of older systems and the installation of newer, more efficient systems in existing homes and buildings. Also, demand for maintenance and service work should rise as businesses and homeowners strive to keep increasingly complex systems operating at peak efficiency. Regulations prohibiting the discharge and production of older types of refrigerants that pollute the atmosphere should continue to result in the need to replace many existing air-conditioning systems or to modify them to use new environmentally safe refrigerants. The pace of replacement in the commercial and industrial sectors will quicken if Congress or individual states change tax rules designed to encourage companies to buy new HVACR equipment.

Job prospects. Job prospects for heating, air-conditioning, and refrigeration mechanics and installers are expected to be excellent, particularly for those who have completed training from an accredited technical school or a formal apprenticeship. A growing number of retirements of highly skilled technicians are expected to generate many more job openings. Many contractors have reported problems finding enough workers to meet the demand for service and installation of HVACR systems.

Technicians who specialize in installation work may experience periods of unemployment when the level of new construction activity declines, but maintenance and repair work usually remains relatively stable. People and businesses depend on their climate-control or refrigeration systems and must keep them in good working order, regardless of economic conditions.

In light of the complexity of new computer-controlled HVACR systems in modern high-rise buildings, prospects should be best for those who can acquire and demonstrate computer competency. Training in new techniques that improve energy efficiency will also make it much easier to enter the occupation.

Earnings

Median hourly wages of heating, air-conditioning, and refrigeration mechanics and installers were $19.76 in May 2009. The middle 50 percent earned between $15.42 and $25.80 an hour. The lowest 10 percent earned less than $12.38, and the top 10 percent earned more than $31.53. Median hourly wages in the industries employing the largest numbers of heating, air-conditioning, and refrigeration mechanics and installers were as follows:

Building equipment contractors...........................	$18.89
Direct selling establishments................................	20.82
Hardware, and plumbing and heating equipment and supplies merchant wholesalers......	22.08
Commercial and industrial machinery and equipment (except automotive and electronic) repair and maintenance	20.78
Local government..	22.73

Apprentices usually earn about 50 percent of the wage rate paid to experienced workers. As they gain experience and improve their skills, they receive periodic increases until they reach the wage rate of experienced workers.

Heating, air-conditioning, and refrigeration mechanics and installers generally receive a variety of employer-sponsored benefits. In addition to typical benefits such as health insurance and pension plans, some employers pay for work-related training and provide uniforms, company vans, and tools.

About 15 percent of heating, air-conditioning, and refrigeration mechanics and installers are members of a union. The unions to which the greatest numbers of mechanics and installers belong are the Sheet Metal Workers International Association and the United Association of Journeymen and Apprentices of the Plumbing and Pipefitting Industry of the United States and Canada.

Related Occupations

Heating, air-conditioning, and refrigeration mechanics and installers work with sheet metal and piping, and repair machinery, such as electrical motors, compressors, and burners. Other workers who have similar duties include boilermakers; electricians; home appliance repairers; plumbers, pipelayers, pipefitters, and steamfitters; and sheet metal workers.

Sources of Additional Information

For more information about opportunities for training, certification, and employment in this trade, contact local vocational and technical schools; local heating, air-conditioning, and refrigeration contractors; a local of the unions or organizations previously mentioned; a local joint union-management apprenticeship committee; or the nearest office of the state employment service or apprenticeship agency. You can also find information on the registered apprenticeship system with links to state apprenticeship programs on the U.S. Department of Labor's website: www.doleta.gov/OA/eta_default.cfm. Apprenticeship information is also available from the U.S. Department of Labor's toll-free helpline: (877) 872-5627.

For information on career opportunities, training, and technician certification, contact

- Air-Conditioning Contractors of America, 2800 Shirlington Rd., Suite 300, Arlington, VA 22206-3607. Internet: www.acca.org
- Air-Conditioning, Heating, and Refrigeration Institute, 2111 Wilson Blvd., Suite 500, Arlington, VA 22201-3001. Internet: www.ahrinet.org
- Associated Builders and Contractors, Workforce Development Department, 4250 N. Fairfax Dr., 9th Floor, Arlington, VA 22203-1607. Internet: www.trytools.org
- Carbon Monoxide Safety Association, P.O. Box 669, Eastlake, CO 80614-0669. Internet: www.cosafety.org
- Green Mechanical Council, 1701 Pennsylvania Ave. NW, Suite 300, Washington, DC 20006-5813. Internet: www.greenmech.org
- Home Builders Institute, National Association of Home Builders, 1201 15th St. NW, 6th Floor, Washington, DC 20005-2842. Internet: www.hbi.org
- HVAC Excellence, P.O. Box 491, Mt. Prospect, IL 60056-0521. Internet: www.hvacexcellence.org
- Mechanical Contractors Association of America, Mechanical Service Contractors of America, 1385 Piccard Dr., Rockville, MD 20850-4329. Internet: www.mcaa.org
- National Center for Construction Education and Research, 3600 NW 43rd St., Bldg. G, Gainesville, FL 32606-8134. Internet: www.nccer.org
- National Occupational Competency Testing Institute, 500 N. Bronson Ave., Big Rapids, MI 49307-2737. Internet: www.nocti.org
- North American Technician Excellence, 2111 Wilson Blvd., Suite 510, Arlington, VA 22201-3051. Internet: www.natex.org
- Plumbing-Heating-Cooling Contractors, 180 S. Washington St., P.O. Box 6808, Falls Church, VA 22046-6808. Internet: www.phccweb.org
- Radiant Panel Association, P.O. Box 717, Loveland, CO 80539-0717. Internet: www.radiantpanelassociation.org
- Refrigeration Service Engineers Society, 1666 Rand Rd., Des Plaines, IL 60016-3552. Internet: www.rses.org
- Sheet Metal and Air-Conditioning Contractors National Association, 4201 Lafayette Center Dr., Chantilly, VA 20151-1209. Internet: www.smacna.org

- United Association of Journeymen and Apprentices of the Plumbing and Pipefitting Industry, United Association Bldg., 3 Park Place, Annapolis, MD 21401-3687. Internet: www.ua.org

Heavy Vehicle and Mobile Equipment Service Technicians and Mechanics

(O*NET 49-3041.00, 49-3042.00, and 49-3043.00)

Significant Points

- Opportunities should be excellent for people with formal post-secondary training in heavy equipment repair; those without formal training will face competition.
- Generally, a service technician with at least three to four years of on-the-job experience is accepted as fully qualified.
- Wages for mobile heavy equipment mechanics are higher than the average for all installation, maintenance, and repair workers.

Nature of the Work

Heavy vehicles and mobile equipment are indispensable to many industrial activities, from construction to railroad transportation. Various types of equipment move materials, till land, lift beams, and dig earth to pave the way for development and production. *Heavy vehicle and mobile equipment service technicians and mechanics* repair and maintain engines and hydraulic, transmission, and electrical systems for this equipment. Farm machinery, cranes, bulldozers, and rail cars are all examples of heavy vehicles that require such service. (For information on service technicians specializing in diesel engines, see the section on diesel service technicians and mechanics elsewhere in this book.)

Service technicians perform routine maintenance checks on agricultural, industrial, construction, and rail equipment. They service fuel, brake, and transmission systems to ensure peak performance, safety, and longevity of the equipment. Maintenance checks and comments from equipment operators usually alert technicians to problems. After locating the problem, these technicians rely on their training and experience to use the best possible technique to solve it.

With many types of modern equipment, technicians can use diagnostic computers to diagnose components needing adjustment or repair. If necessary, they may partially dismantle affected components to examine parts for damage or excessive wear. Then, using handheld tools, they repair, replace, clean, and lubricate parts as necessary. In some cases, technicians recalibrate systems by typing codes into the onboard computer. After reassembling the component and testing it for safety, they put it back into the equipment and return the equipment to the field.

Many types of heavy and mobile equipment use hydraulic systems to raise and lower movable parts. When hydraulic components malfunction, technicians examine them for fluid leaks, ruptured hoses, or worn gaskets on fluid reservoirs. Occasionally, the equipment requires extensive repairs, as when a defective hydraulic pump needs replacing.

Service technicians diagnose electrical problems and adjust or replace defective components. They also disassemble and repair undercarriages and track assemblies. Occasionally, technicians weld broken equipment frames and structural parts, using electric or gas welders.

Technicians use a variety of tools in their work: power tools, such as pneumatic wrenches to remove bolts quickly, machine tools, like lathes and grinding machines, to rebuild brakes, welding and flame-cutting equipment to remove and repair exhaust systems, and jacks and hoists to lift and move large parts. Service technicians also use common hand tools—screwdrivers, pliers, and wrenches—to work on small parts and to get at hard-to-reach places. They may use a variety of computerized testing equipment to pinpoint and analyze malfunctions in electrical systems and other essential systems. Tachometers and dynamometers, for example, can be used to locate engine malfunctions. Service technicians also use ohmmeters, ammeters, and voltmeters when working on electrical systems. Employers typically furnish expensive power tools, computerized engine analyzers, and other diagnostic equipment, but hand tools are normally accumulated with experience, and many experienced technicians have thousands of dollars invested in them.

It is common for technicians in large shops to specialize in one or two types of repair. For example, a shop may have individual specialists in major engine repair, transmission work, electrical systems, and suspension or brake systems. Technicians in smaller shops, on the other hand, generally perform multiple functions.

Technicians also specialize in types of equipment. *Mobile heavy equipment mechanics and service technicians*, for example, keep construction and surface mining equipment, such as bulldozers, cranes, graders, and excavators in working order. Typically, these workers are employed by equipment wholesale distribution and leasing firms, large construction and mining companies, local and federal governments, and other organizations operating and maintaining heavy machinery and equipment fleets. Service technicians employed by the federal government may work on tanks and other armored military equipment.

Farm equipment mechanics service, maintain, and repair farm equipment, as well as smaller lawn and garden tractors sold to homeowners. What once was a general repairer's job around the farm has evolved into a specialized technical career. Farmers have increasingly turned to farm equipment dealers to service and repair their equipment because the machinery has grown in complexity. Modern equipment uses more computers, electronics, and hydraulics, making it difficult to perform repairs without specialized training and tools.

Rail car repairers specialize in servicing railroad locomotives and other rolling stock, streetcars and subway cars, or mine cars. Most rail car repairers work for railroads, public and private transit companies, and rail car manufacturers.

Work environment. Heavy vehicle and mobile equipment service technicians usually work indoors. To repair vehicles and equipment, technicians often lift heavy parts and tools, handle greasy and dirty parts, and stand or lie in awkward positions. Minor cuts, burns, and bruises are common. However, serious accidents normally can be avoided as long as safety practices are observed. Although some shops are drafty and noisy, technicians usually work in well-lighted and ventilated areas. Many employers provide uniforms, locker rooms, and shower facilities. Mobile heavy equipment mechanics and rail car repairers generally work a standard 40-hour week.

When heavy or mobile equipment breaks down at a construction site, it may be too difficult or expensive to bring into a repair shop, so the shop will send a field service technician to the site to make repairs. Field service technicians work outdoors and spend much of their time away from the shop. Generally, more experienced service technicians specialize in field service. They drive trucks specially equipped with replacement parts and tools. On occasion, they must travel many miles to reach disabled machinery.

The hours of work for farm equipment mechanics vary according to the season of the year. During the busy planting and harvesting seasons, farm equipment mechanics often work 6 or 7 days a week, 10 to 12 hours daily. In slow winter months, however, they may work fewer than 40 hours a week.

Training, Other Qualifications, and Advancement

Although industry experts recommend that applicants complete a formal diesel or heavy equipment mechanic training program after graduating from high school, many people qualify for service technician jobs by training on the job. Employers seek people with mechanical aptitude who are knowledgeable about diesel engines, transmissions, electrical systems, computers, and hydraulics.

Education and training. High school courses in automobile repair, physics, chemistry, and mathematics provide a strong foundation for a career as a service technician or mechanic. After high school, those interested in heavy vehicle repair can choose to attend community colleges or vocational schools that offer programs in diesel technology. Some of these schools tailor programs to heavy equipment mechanics. These programs teach the basics of analytical and diagnostic techniques, electronics, and hydraulics. The increased use of electronics and computers makes training in electronics essential for new heavy and mobile equipment mechanics. Some one-year to two-year programs lead to a certificate of completion, while others lead to an associate degree in diesel or heavy equipment mechanics. Formal training programs enable trainee technicians to advance to the journey, or experienced worker, level sooner than with informal ones.

Entry-level workers with no formal background in heavy vehicle repair begin to perform routine service tasks and make minor repairs after a few months of on-the-job training. As they prove their ability and competence, workers advance to harder jobs. Generally, a service technician with at least three to four years of on-the-job experience is accepted as fully qualified.

Many employers send trainee technicians to training sessions conducted by heavy equipment manufacturers. The sessions, which typically last up to one week, provide intensive instruction in the repair of the manufacturer's equipment. Some sessions focus on particular components found in the equipment, such as diesel engines, transmissions, axles, or electrical systems. Other sessions focus on particular types of equipment, such as crawler-loaders and crawler-dozers. When appropriate, experienced technicians attend training sessions to gain familiarity with new technology or equipment.

Other qualifications. Technicians must read and interpret service manuals, so reading ability and communication skills are both important. The technology used in heavy equipment is becoming more sophisticated, and technicians should feel comfortable with computers and electronics because handheld diagnostic computers are often used to make engine adjustments and diagnose problems. Experience in the Armed Forces working on diesel engines and heavy equipment provides valuable background for these positions.

Certification and advancement. There is no one certification that is recognized throughout the various industries that employ heavy vehicle mobile equipment service technicians. Rather, graduation or completion of an accredited postsecondary program in heavy vehicle repair is seen as the best credential for employees to have. Manufacturers also offer certificates in specific repairs or working with particular equipment. Such credentials allow employees to take on more responsibilities and advance faster.

Experienced technicians may advance to field service jobs, where they have a greater opportunity to tackle problems independently and earn additional pay. Field positions may require a commercial driver's license and a clean driving record. Technicians with administrative ability may become shop supervisors or service managers. Some technicians open their own repair shops or invest in a franchise.

Employment

Heavy vehicle and mobile equipment service technicians and mechanics held about 190,700 jobs in 2008. Approximately 136,300 were mobile heavy equipment mechanics, 31,200 were farm equipment mechanics, and 23,100 were rail car repairers.

About 29 percent were employed by machinery, equipment, and supplies merchant wholesalers. About 13 percent worked in construction, primarily for specialty trade contractors and highway, street, and bridge construction companies; another 11 percent were employed by federal, state, and local governments. Other service technicians worked in mining; rail transportation; and commercial and industrial machinery and equipment rental, leasing, and repair. A small number repaired equipment for machinery and railroad rolling stock manufacturers. About 6 percent of service technicians were self-employed.

Nearly every area of the country employs heavy and mobile equipment service technicians and mechanics, although most work in towns and cities where equipment dealers, equipment rental and leasing companies, and construction companies have repair facilities.

Job Outlook

The number of heavy vehicle and mobile equipment service technicians and mechanics is expected to grow about as fast as the average for all occupations. Those who have completed postsecondary training programs should find excellent opportunities, as employers report difficulty finding candidates with this training to fill available positions. Those without a formal background in diesel engine or heavy vehicle repair will face competition.

Employment change. Employment of heavy vehicle and mobile equipment service technicians and mechanics is expected to grow by 8 percent through the year 2018, about as fast as the average for all occupations. Demand will be driven primarily by growth in the use of heavy equipment in the construction industry, although growth will be slower in this industry than in recent years. In addition, the increasing sophistication of the technology used in heavy vehicles and mechanics should lead to greater demand for technicians and mechanics with specialized skills.

Growth in other industries that use heavy equipment, such as energy exploration and mining, will also contribute to the need for new workers. The need to feed a growing population, and the increased use of agriculture products to make biofuels, will lead to additional farm mechanic jobs, while the continued expansion of railways for freight shipping and transportation will lead to new openings for rail car repairers. Many new mobile heavy equipment and farm equipment mechanic positions are expected to be in firms that sell, rent, or lease such machines, as their repair services make up an important part of their business. Employment of mobile heavy equipment mechanics is expected to grow by 9 percent from 2008 to 2018, while jobs for farm equipment mechanics and rail car repairers are expected to increase by 7 percent.

Job prospects. Opportunities for heavy vehicle and mobile equipment service technicians and mechanics should be excellent for those who have completed formal training programs in diesel or heavy equipment mechanics. Employers report difficulty finding candidates with formal postsecondary training to fill available service technician positions. People without formal training are expected to encounter growing difficulty entering these jobs. Most job openings for mobile, rail, and farm equipment technicians will arise from the need to replace experienced repairers who retire or change occupations.

Construction and mining operations, which use large numbers of heavy vehicles and mobile equipment, are particularly sensitive to changes in the level of economic activity. While the increased use of such equipment increases the need for periodic service and repair, heavy and mobile equipment may be idle during downturns. As a result, opportunities for service technicians who work on construction and mining equipment may fluctuate with the cyclical nature of these industries. In addition, opportunities for farm equipment mechanics are seasonal and are best in warmer months.

Earnings

Median hourly wages of mobile heavy equipment mechanics were $21.21 in May 2009, higher than the $19.04 per hour median for all installation, maintenance, and repair occupations. The middle 50 percent earned between $17.14 and $25.67. The lowest 10 percent

Projections Data from the National Employment Matrix

Occupational title	SOC Code	Employment, 2008	Projected employment, 2018	Change, 2008–2018	
				Number	Percent
Heavy vehicle and mobile equipment service technicians and mechanics 49-3040		190,700	206,100	15,500	8
Farm equipment mechanics..............................49-3041		31,200	33,400	2,100	7
Mobile heavy equipment mechanics, except engines 49-3042		136,300	148,100	11,800	9
Rail car repairers..49-3043		23,100	24,600	1,500	7

NOTE: Data in this table are rounded.

earned less than $14.06, and the highest 10 percent earned more than $31.18. Median hourly wages in the industries employing the largest numbers of mobile heavy equipment mechanics were as follows:

Machinery, equipment, and supplies merchant wholesalers	$21.19
Local government	22.37
Commercial and industrial machinery and equipment rental and leasing	20.10
Other specialty trade contractors	20.33
Commercial and industrial machinery and equipment (except automotive and electronic) repair and maintenance	19.22

Median hourly wages of farm equipment mechanics were $15.85 in May 2009. The middle 50 percent earned between $12.93 and $19.17. The lowest 10 percent earned less than $10.52, and the highest 10 percent earned more than $23.11. In machinery, equipment, and supplies merchant wholesalers, the industry employing the largest number of farm equipment mechanics, median wages were $16.17.

Median hourly wages of rail car repairers were $22.33 in May 2009. The middle 50 percent earned between $17.31 and $27.18. The lowest 10 percent earned less than $13.88, and the highest 10 percent earned more than $31.11. Median hourly wages were $24.82 in rail transportation, the industry employing the largest number of rail car repairers.

About 23 percent of heavy vehicle and mobile equipment service technicians and mechanics are members of unions, including the International Association of Machinists and Aerospace Workers, the International Union of Operating Engineers, and the International Brotherhood of Teamsters. Members may enjoy job benefits in addition to what employers provide.

Related Occupations

Workers in related repair occupations include aircraft and avionics equipment mechanics and service technicians; automotive service technicians and mechanics; diesel service technicians and mechanics; industrial machinery mechanics and millwrights; and small engine mechanics.

Sources of Additional Information

More details about job openings for heavy vehicle and mobile equipment service technicians and mechanics may be obtained from local heavy and mobile equipment dealers and distributors, construction contractors, and government agencies. Local offices of the state employment service also may have information on job openings and training programs.

For general information about a career as a heavy vehicle and mobile equipment service technician or mechanic, contact

▶ Associated Equipment Distributors, 615 W. 22nd St., Oak Brook, IL 60523. Internet: www.aedcareers.com

A list of certified diesel service technician training programs can be obtained from

▶ National Automotive Technician Education Foundation (NATEF), 101 Blue Seal Dr. SE, Suite 101, Leesburg, VA 20175. Internet: www.natef.org

Information on certification as a heavy-duty diesel service technician is available from

▶ National Institute for Automotive Service Excellence (ASE), 101 Blue Seal Dr. SE, Suite 101, Leesburg, VA 20175. Internet: www.asecert.org

Home Health Aides and Personal and Home Care Aides

(O*NET 31-1011.00 and 39-9021.00)

Significant Points

■ Job opportunities are expected to be excellent because of rapid growth in home health care and high replacement needs.

■ Training requirements vary from state to state, the type of home services agency, and funding source covering the costs of services.

■ Many of these workers work part time and weekends or evenings to suit the needs of their clients.

Nature of the Work

Home health aides and personal and home care aides help people who are disabled, chronically ill, or cognitively impaired and older adults, who many need assistance, live in their own homes or in residential facilities instead of in health facilities or institutions. They also assist people in hospices and day programs and help individuals with disabilities go to work and remain engaged in their communities. Most aides work with elderly or physically or mentally disabled clients who need more care than family or friends can provide. Others help discharge hospital patients who have relatively short-term needs.

Aides provide light housekeeping and homemaking tasks such as laundry, change bed linens, shop for food, plan and prepare meals. Aides also may help clients get out of bed, bathe, dress, and groom. Some accompany clients to doctors' appointments or on other errands.

Home health aides and personal and home care aides provide instruction and psychological support to their clients. They may advise families and patients on nutrition, cleanliness, and household tasks.

Aides' daily routine may vary. They may go to the same home every day or week for months or even years and often visit four or five clients on the same day. However, some aides may work solely with one client who is in need of more care and attention. In some situations, this may involve working with other aides in shifts so that the client has an aide throughout the day and night. Aides also work with clients, particularly younger adults at schools or at the client's work site.

In general, home health aides and personal and home care aides have similar job duties. However, there are some small differences.

Home health aides typically work for certified home health or hospice agencies that receive government funding and therefore must comply with regulations to receive funding. This means that they must work under the direct supervision of a medical professional, usually a nurse. These aides keep records of services performed and of clients' condition and progress. They report changes in the client's condition to the supervisor or case manager. Aides also work with therapists and other medical staff.

Home health aides may provide some basic health-related services, such as checking patients' pulse rate, temperature, and respiration rate. They also may help with simple prescribed exercises and assist with medications administration. Occasionally, they change simple dressings, give massage, provide skin care, or assist with braces and artificial limbs. With special training, experienced home health aides also may assist with medical equipment such as ventilators, which help patients breathe.

Personal and home care aides—also called homemakers, caregivers, companions, and personal attendants—work for various public and private agencies that provide home care services. In these agencies, caregivers are likely supervised by a licensed nurse, social worker, or other nonmedical managers. Aides receive detailed instructions explaining when to visit clients and what services to perform for them. However, personal and home care aides work independently, with only periodic visits by their supervisors. These caregivers may work with only one client each day or five or six clients once a day every week or every two weeks.

Some aides are hired directly by the patient or the patient's family. In these situations, personal and home care aides are supervised and assigned tasks directly by the patient or the patient's family.

Aides may also work with individuals who are developmentally or intellectually disabled. These workers are often called direct support professionals and they may assist in implementing a behavior plan, teaching self-care skills and providing employment support, as well as providing a range of other personal assistance services.

Work environment. Work as an aide can be physically demanding. Aides must guard against back injury because they may have to move patients into and out of bed or help them to stand or walk. Aides also may face hazards from minor infections and exposure to communicable diseases, such as hepatitis, but can avoid infections by following proper procedures. Because mechanical lifting devices available in institutional settings are not as frequently available in patients' homes, home health aides must take extra care to avoid injuries resulting from overexertion when they assist patients. These workers experienced a larger than average number of work-related injuries or illnesses

Aides also perform tasks that some may consider unpleasant, such as emptying bedpans and changing soiled bed linens. The patients they care for may be disoriented, irritable, or uncooperative. Although their work can be emotionally demanding, many aides gain satisfaction from assisting those in need.

Most aides work with a number of different patients, each job lasting a few hours, days, or weeks. They often visit multiple patients on the same day. Surroundings differ by case. Some homes are neat and pleasant, whereas others are untidy and depressing. Some clients are pleasant and cooperative; others are angry, abusive, depressed, or otherwise difficult.

Home health aides and personal and home care aides generally work alone, with periodic visits from their supervisor. They receive detailed instructions explaining when to visit patients and what services to perform. Aides are responsible for getting to patients' homes, and they may spend a good portion of the work day traveling from one patient to another.

Many of these workers work part time and weekends or evenings to suit the needs of their clients.

Training, Other Qualifications, and Advancement

Home health aides must receive formal training and pass a competency test to work for certified home health or hospice agencies that receive reimbursement from Medicare or Medicaid. Personal and home care aides, however, face a wide range of requirements, which vary from state to state.

Education and training. Home health aides and personal and home care aides are generally not required to have a high school diploma. They usually are trained on the job by registered nurses, licensed practical nurses, experienced aides, or their supervisor. Aides are instructed on how to cook for a client, including on special diets. Furthermore, they may be trained in basic housekeeping tasks, such as making a bed and keeping the home sanitary and safe for the client. Generally, they are taught how to respond to an emergency, learning basic safety techniques. Employers also may train aides to conduct themselves in a professional and courteous manner while in a client's home. Some clients prefer that tasks are done a certain way and will teach the aide. A competency evaluation may be required to ensure that the aide can perform the required tasks.

Licensure. Home health aides who work for agencies that receive reimbursement from Medicare or Medicaid must receive a minimum level of training. They must complete both a training program consisting of a minimum of 75 hours and a competency evaluation or state certification program. Training includes information regarding personal hygiene, safe transfer techniques, reading and recording vital signs, infection control, and basic nutrition. Aides may take a competency exam to become certified without taking any of the training. At a minimum, 16 hours of supervised practical training are required before an aide has direct contact with a resident. These certification requirements represent the minimum, as outlined by the federal government. Some states may require additional hours of training to become certified.

Personal and home care aides are not required to be certified.

Other qualifications. Aides should have a desire to help people. They should be responsible, compassionate, patient, emotionally stable, and cheerful. In addition, aides should be tactful, honest, and discreet, because they work in private homes. Aides also must be in good health. A physical examination, including state-mandated tests for tuberculosis and other diseases, may be required. A criminal background check and a good driving record also may be required for employment.

Certification and advancement. The National Association for Home Care and Hospice (NAHC) offers national certification for aides. Certification is a voluntary demonstration that the individual has met industry standards. Certification requires the completion of 75 hours of training; observation and documentation of 17 skills for competency, assessed by a registered nurse; and the passing of a written exam developed by NAHC.

Advancement for home health aides and personal and home care aides is limited. In some agencies, workers start out performing homemaker duties, such as cleaning. With experience and training, they may take on more personal care duties. Some aides choose to receive additional training to become nursing aides, licensed practical nurses, or registered nurses. Some may start their own home care agency or work as a self-employed aide. Self-employed aides have no agency affiliation or supervision and accept clients, set fees, and arrange work schedules on their own.

Projections Data from the National Employment Matrix

Occupational title	SOC Code	Employment, 2008	Projected employment, 2018	Change, 2008–2018	
				Number	Percent
Home health aides and personal and home care aides........... —		1,738,800	2,575,600	836,700	48
Home health aides 31-1011		921,700	1,382,600	460,900	50
Personal and home care aides................................ 39-9021		817,200	1,193,000	375,800	46

NOTE: Data in this table are rounded.

Employment

Home health aides and personal and home care aides held about 1.7 million jobs in 2008. The majority of jobs were in home health-care services, individual and family services, residential care facilities, and private households.

Job Outlook

Excellent job opportunities are expected for this occupation because rapid employment growth and high replacement needs are projected to produce a large number of job openings.

Employment change. Employment of home health aides is projected to grow by 50 percent between 2008 and 2018, which is much faster than the average for all occupations. Employment of personal and home care aides is expected to grow by 46 percent from 2008 to 2018, which is much faster than the average for all occupations. For both occupations, the expected growth is due, in large part, to the projected rise in the number of elderly people, an age group that often has mounting health problems and that needs some assistance with daily activities. The elderly and other clients, such as the mentally disabled, increasingly rely on home care.

This trend reflects several developments. Inpatient care in hospitals and nursing homes can be extremely expensive, so more patients return to their homes from these facilities as quickly as possible in order to contain costs. Patients who need assistance with everyday tasks and household chores rather than medical care can reduce medical expenses by returning to their homes. Furthermore, most patients—particularly the elderly—prefer care in their homes rather than in nursing homes or other inpatient facilities. This development is aided by the realization that treatment can be more effective in familiar surroundings.

Job prospects. In addition to job openings created by the increased demand for these workers, replacement needs are expected to lead to many openings. The relatively low skill requirements, low pay, and high emotional demands of the work result in high replacement needs. For these same reasons, many people are reluctant to seek jobs in the occupation. Therefore, persons who are interested in and suited for this work—particularly those with experience or training as personal care, home health, or nursing aides—should have excellent job prospects.

Earnings

Median hourly wages of wage-and-salary personal and home care aides were $9.46 in May 2009. The middle 50 percent earned between $8.14 and $11.08 an hour. The lowest 10 percent earned less than $7.36, and the highest 10 percent earned more than $12.45 an hour. Median hourly wages in the industries employing the largest numbers of personal and home care aides were as follows:

Individual and family services	$9.81
Home health-care services	8.55
Vocational rehabilitation services	9.95
Residential mental retardation, mental health and substance abuse facilities	10.01
Employment services	9.92

Median hourly wages of home health aides were $9.85 in May 2009. The middle 50 percent earned between $8.52 and $11.67 an hour. The lowest 10 percent earned less than $7.67, and the highest 10 percent earned more than $14.13 an hour. Median hourly wages in the industries employing the largest numbers of home health aides in May 2009 were as follows:

Home health-care services	$9.49
Residential mental retardation, mental health and substance abuse facilities	10.25
Community care facilities for the elderly	9.60
Individual and family services	9.42
Nursing care facilities	10.31

Aides receive slight pay increases with experience and added responsibility. Usually, they are paid only for the time worked in the home, not for travel time between jobs, and must pay for their travel costs from their earnings. Most employers hire only on-call hourly workers.

Related Occupations

Home health aides and personal and home care aides combine the duties of caregivers and social service workers. Workers in related occupations that involve personal contact to help others include child care workers; licensed practical and licensed vocational nurses; medical assistants; nursing and psychiatric aides; occupational therapist assistants and aides; physical therapist assistants and aides; radiation therapists; registered nurses; and social and human service assistants.

Sources of Additional Information

Information on licensing requirements for nursing and home health aides, as well as lists of state-approved nursing aide programs, are available from state departments of public health, departments of occupational licensing, boards of nursing, and home care associations.

For information about voluntary credentials for personal and home care aides, contact

▸ National Association for Home Care and Hospice, 228 Seventh St. SE, Washington, DC 20003. Internet: www.nahc.org

Industrial Machinery Mechanics and Millwrights

(O*NET 49-9041.00, 49-9043.00, and 49-9044.00)

Significant Points

■ Most workers are employed in manufacturing.

■ Machinery maintenance workers learn on the job, industrial machinery mechanics usually need some education after high school, and millwrights typically learn through formal apprenticeship programs.

■ Applicants with broad skills in machine repair and maintenance should have favorable job prospects.

Nature of the Work

Imagine an automobile assembly line: a large conveyor system moves unfinished automobiles down the line, giant robotic welding arms bond the different body panels together, hydraulic lifts move the motor into the body of the car, and giant presses stamp body parts from flat sheets of steel. All these complex machines need workers to install them and service them to make sure they function properly. Assembling and setting up these machines on the factory floor is the job of millwrights, while industrial machinery mechanics and machinery maintenance workers maintain and repair these machines.

Millwrights are the highly skilled workers who install, assemble, and, when necessary, dismantle machinery in factories, power plants, and construction sites. These workers consult with engineers and managers to determine the best location to place a machine. Millwrights then transport the machine parts to the desired location, using fork lifts, hoists, winches, cranes and other equipment. Machines do not arrive in one piece, and millwrights need to assemble them from their component parts. Millwrights must understand how a machine functions to assemble and disassemble it properly; this may involve knowledge of electronics, pneumatics, and computer systems. They use complex instruction books that detail the assembly of the machinery and use tools such as levels, welding machines, hydraulic torque wrenches. Millwrights use micrometers, precision measuring devices, to achieve the extreme tolerances required by modern machines. On large projects, the use of cranes and trucks is common.

Assembly of a machine can take a few days or several weeks. Aside from assembly, millwrights are also involved in major repairs and disassembly of machines. If a manufacturing plant needs to clear floor space for new machinery, it can sell or trade-in old equipment. The breaking down of a machine is normally just as complicated as assembling it; all parts must be carefully taken apart, categorized and packaged for shipping.

While major repairs may require the assistance of a millwright, keeping machines in good working order is the primary responsibility of *industrial machinery mechanics*, also called industrial machinery repairers or maintenance machinists. To do this effectively, these workers must be able to detect minor problems and correct them before they become larger problems. Machinery mechanics use technical manuals, their understanding of the equipment, and careful observation to discover the cause of the problem. For example, after hearing a vibration from a machine, the mechanic must decide whether it is due to worn belts, weak motor bearings, or some other problem. Mechanics often need years of training and experience to fully diagnose all problems, but computerized diagnostic systems and vibration analysis techniques provide aid in determining the nature of the problem.

After diagnosing the problem, the industrial machinery mechanic may disassemble the equipment to repair or replace the necessary parts. Increasingly, mechanics are expected to have the electrical, electronics, and computer programming skills to repair sophisticated equipment on their own. Once a repair is made, mechanics perform tests to ensure that the machine is running smoothly. Primary responsibilities of industrial machinery mechanics also include preventive maintenance; for example, they adjust and calibrate automated manufacturing equipment, such as industrial robots.

The most basic maintenance and repair tasks are performed by *machinery maintenance workers*. These employees are responsible for cleaning and lubricating machinery, performing basic diagnostic tests, checking performance, and testing damaged machine parts to determine whether major repairs are necessary. In carrying out these tasks, maintenance workers must follow machine specifications and adhere to maintenance schedules. Maintenance workers may perform minor repairs, but major repairs generally are left to machinery mechanics.

Industrial machinery mechanics and machinery maintenance workers use a variety of tools to perform repairs and preventive maintenance. They may use hand tools to adjust a motor or a chain hoist to lift a heavy printing press off the ground. When replacements for broken or defective parts are not readily available, or when a machine must be returned quickly to production, mechanics may create a new part using lathes, grinders, or drill presses. Mechanics use catalogs to order replacement parts and often follow blueprints, technical manuals, and engineering specifications to maintain and fix equipment. By keeping complete and up-to-date records, mechanics try to anticipate trouble and service equipment before factory production is interrupted. If an industrial machinery mechanic is unable to repair a machine and a major overhaul is needed, a millwright with expertise on the machine may be hired to make the repair.

Work environment. In production facilities, these workers are subject to common shop injuries such as cuts, bruises, and strains. In the construction setting, workers must be careful of heavy equipment. They also may work in awkward positions, including on top of ladders or in cramped conditions under large machinery, which exposes them to additional hazards. To avoid injuries, workers must follow safety precautions and use protective equipment, such as hardhats, safety glasses, steel-tipped shoes, hearing protectors, and belts.

Because factories and other facilities cannot afford to have industrial machinery out of service for long periods, mechanics may be on call or assigned to work nights or on weekends. Overtime is common among these occupations, as about 30 percent of employees worked over 40 hours per week, on average, in 2008.

Millwrights are typically employed on a contract basis and may only spend a few days or weeks at a single site. As a result, schedules of work can be unpredictable, and workers may experience downtime in between jobs.

Training, Other Qualifications, and Advancement

Millwrights typically go through formal apprenticeship programs that last a few years and involve both classroom and on-the-job training. Industrial machinery mechanics usually need some education after high school plus experience working on specific machines before they can be considered a mechanic. Machinery maintenance workers can usually get a job with little more than a high school diploma or its equivalent; most workers learn on the job.

Education and training. All machinery maintenance and millwright worker positions generally require a high school diploma, GED, or its equivalent. However, employers increasingly prefer to hire machinery maintenance workers with some training in industrial technology. Employers also prefer to hire those who have taken high school or postsecondary courses in mechanical drawing, mathematics, blueprint reading, computer programming, or electronics.

Most millwrights, and some industrial machinery mechanics, enter the occupation through an apprenticeship program that typically lasts about 4 years. Apprenticeships can be sponsored by local union chapters, employers, or the state labor department. Training in these apprenticeships involves a combination of on-the-job training and classroom learning. Job seekers can apply for union apprenticeships, and qualified applicants may begin training in local training facilities and factories.

Industrial machinery mechanics usually need a year or more of formal education and training after high school to learn the growing range of mechanical and technical skills that they need. While mechanics used to specialize in one area, such as hydraulics or electronics, many factories now require every mechanic to have knowledge of electricity, electronics, hydraulics, and computer programming.

Workers can get this training in a number of different ways. A 2-year associate degree program in industrial maintenance provides good preparation. Other mechanics may start as helpers or in other factory jobs and learn the skills of the trade informally and by taking courses offered through their employer. It is common for experienced production workers to move into maintenance positions if they show good mechanical abilities. Employers may offer on-site classroom training or send workers to local technical schools while they receive on-the-job training. Classroom instruction focuses on subjects such as shop mathematics, blueprint reading, welding, electronics, and computer training. In addition to classroom training, it is important that mechanics train on the specific machines they will repair. They can get this training on the job, through dealer or manufacturer's representatives, or in a classroom.

Machinery maintenance workers typically receive on-the-job training lasting a few months to a year to perform routine tasks, such as setting up, cleaning, lubricating, and starting machinery. This training may be offered by experienced workers, professional trainers, or representatives of equipment manufacturers.

Other qualifications. Machinery mechanics must have good problem-solving abilities, as it is important for them to be able to discover the cause of a problem to repair it. Mechanical aptitude and manual dexterity are also important. Good reading comprehension is necessary to understand the technical manuals of a wide range of machines; and good communications skills are also essential in order for millwrights, mechanics, and maintenance workers to understand the needs of other workers and managers. In addition, good physical conditioning and agility are necessary because repairers sometimes have to lift heavy objects or climb to reach equipment.

Advancement. Opportunities for advancement vary by specialty. Machinery maintenance workers, if they take classes and gain additional skills, may advance to industrial machinery mechanic or supervisor. Industrial machinery mechanics also advance by working with more complicated equipment and gaining additional repair skills. The most highly skilled repairers can be promoted to supervisor, master mechanic, or millwright. Experienced millwrights can advance into team leading roles.

Employment

Industrial machinery mechanics, machinery maintenance workers, and millwrights held about 408,300 jobs in 2008; 45,200 of these jobs were held by millwrights, with the largest concentration of workers in manufacturing and construction industries. In manufacturing, many of these workers are employed in the transportation equipment, wood product, and paper manufacturing industries. In construction, most workers were employed in the nonresidential building and building equipment contractors industries. Also, some millwrights work in the utilities industry.

Industrial machinery mechanics held about 287,700 jobs, while machinery maintenance workers accounted for 75,400 jobs. Many of both types of workers were employed in the manufacturing sector in industries such as food processing and chemical, fabricated metal product, machinery, and motor vehicle and parts manufacturing. Additionally, about 10 percent work in wholesale trade, mostly for dealers of industrial equipment. Manufacturers often rely on these dealers to make complex repairs to specific machines. About 9 percent of mechanics work for the commercial and industrial machinery and equipment repair and maintenance industry, often making site visits to companies to repair equipment.

Job Outlook

Employment is projected to grow more slowly than average, and applicants with broad skills in machine repair and maintenance should have favorable job prospects.

Employment change. Employment of industrial machinery mechanics and millwrights is expected to grow 6 percent from 2008 to 2018, more slowly than the average for all occupations. The increased use of machinery in manufacturing will require more millwrights to install this equipment and more mechanics and maintenance workers to keep it in good working order.

Employment of millwrights is expected to grow 1 percent from 2008 to 2018, the equivalent of little or no change. The demand for millwrights is driven by the purchasing of machinery in the construction and manufacturing industries. Cost-cutting pressures will drive manufacturers to further automate production and increase machinery presence on the factory floor. The growth of the power industry will also generate work for millwrights, as they install and repair turbines on wind mills, coal plants, and hydroelectric dams.

Employment of industrial machinery mechanics and maintenance workers is expected to grow 7 percent from 2008 to 2018, which is slower than average. As factories become increasingly automated, these workers will be needed to maintain and repair the automated equipment. However, many new computer-controlled machines are capable of diagnosing problems quickly, resulting in faster and easier repair, which somewhat slows the growth of these occupations.

Projections Data from the National Employment Matrix

Occupational title	SOC Code	Employment, 2008	Projected employment, 2018	Change, 2008–2018	
				Number	Percent
Industrial machinery mechanics and millwrights .... —		408,300	433,300	25,000	6
Industrial machinery mechanics 49-9041		287,700	308,600	20,900	7
Maintenance workers, machinery 49-9043		75,400	78,800	3,400	5
Millwrights 49-9044		45,200	45,900	600	1

NOTE: Data in this table are rounded.

Job prospects. Applicants with broad skills in machine repair and maintenance should have favorable job prospects. In addition to job openings from growth, there will be a need to replace the many older workers who are expected to retire, and those who leave the occupation for other reasons. Some employers have reported difficulty in recruiting young workers with the necessary skills.

Mechanics and millwrights are not as affected by changes in production levels as other manufacturing workers, as mechanics and millwrights often are retained during production downtime to complete major equipment overhaul and to keep expensive machinery in working order.

Earnings

Median hourly wages of millwrights were $23.14 in May 2009. The middle 50 percent earned between $18.24 and $29.79. The lowest 10 percent earned less than $14.92, and the highest 10 percent earned more than $36.00.

Median hourly wages of industrial machinery mechanics were $21.38 in May 2009. The middle 50 percent earned between $17.21 and $26.40. The lowest 10 percent earned less than $14.02, and the highest 10 percent earned more than $32.05.

Machinery maintenance workers earned somewhat less than the higher skilled industrial machinery mechanics. Median hourly wages of machinery maintenance workers were $18.16 in May 2009. The middle 50 percent earned between $14.16 and $23.32. The lowest 10 percent earned less than $11.14, and the highest 10 percent earned more than $28.41.

Earnings vary by industry and geographic region. Median hourly wages in the industries employing the largest numbers of industrial machinery mechanics in May 2009 were as follows:

Commercial and industrial machinery and equipment (except automotive and electronic) repair and maintenance...................	$18.93
Machinery, equipment, and supplies merchant wholesalers	20.47
Animal slaughtering and processing	17.32
Local government..	21.76
Plastics product manufacturing	20.45

In 2008, almost half of all millwrights belonged to unions, while about 19 percent of industrial machinery mechanics were union members.

Related Occupations

Other workers do installation, maintenance, and repair, including electrical and electronics installers and repairers; electricians; machinists; maintenance and repair workers, general; plumbers, pipelayers, pipefitters, and steamfitters; and welding, soldering, and brazing workers.

Sources of Additional Information

For information about millwright training and apprenticeships, contact

▸ United Brotherhood of Carpenters/Millwrights, 6801 Placid St., Las Vegas, NV 89119. Internet: www.ubcmillwrights.org

For further information on apprenticeship programs, write to the Apprenticeship Council of your state's labor department or local firms that employ machinery mechanics and repairers. You can also find information on registered apprenticeships, together with links to state apprenticeship programs, on the U.S. Department of Labor website: www.doleta.gov/OA/eta_default.cfm. Apprenticeship information is also available from the U.S. Department of Labor toll-free helpline: (877) 872-5627.

Industrial Production Managers

(O*NET 11-3051.00, 11-3051.01, 11-3051.02, 11-3051.03, 11-3051.04, 11-3051.05, and 11-3051.06)

Significant Points

■ Industrial production managers coordinate all the people and equipment involved in the manufacturing process.

■ Most employers prefer to hire workers with a college degree; experience in some part of production operations usually is required as well.

■ Employment is expected to decline as overall employment in manufacturing declines.

Nature of the Work

Industrial production managers plan, direct, and coordinate the production activities required to produce the vast array of goods manufactured every year in the United States. They make sure that production meets output and quality goals while remaining within budget. Depending on the size of the manufacturing plant, industrial production managers may oversee the entire plant or just one area of it.

Industrial production managers devise methods to use the plant's personnel and capital resources to best meet production goals. They may determine which machines will be used, whether new machines need to be purchased, whether overtime or extra shifts are necessary, and what the sequence of production will be. They monitor the production run to make sure that it stays on schedule, and they correct any problems that may arise.

Part of an industrial production manager's job is to come up with ways to make the production process more efficient. Traditional factory methods, such as mass assembly lines, have given way to "lean" production techniques, which give managers more flexibility. In a traditional assembly line, each worker was responsible for only a small portion of the assembly, repeating that task on every product. Lean production, by contrast, employs teams to build and assemble products in stations or cells. Thus, rather than specializing in a specific task, workers are capable of performing all jobs within a team. Without the constraints of the traditional assembly line, industrial production managers can more easily change production levels and staffing on different product lines to minimize inventory levels and more quickly react to changing customer demands.

Industrial production managers also monitor product standards and implement quality control programs. They make sure that the finished product meets a certain level of quality, and if it doesn't, they try to find out what the problem is and solve it. Although traditional quality control programs reacted only to problems that reached a certain significant level, newer management techniques and programs, such as ISO 9000, Total Quality Management (TQM), or Six Sigma, emphasize continuous quality improvement. If the problem relates to the quality of work performed in the plant, the manager may implement better training programs or reorganize the manufacturing process, often on the basis of the suggestions of employee teams. If the cause is substandard materials or parts from outside suppliers, the industrial production manager may work with the suppliers to improve their quality.

Industrial production managers work closely with other managers of the firm to implement the company's policies and goals. They also must work with the firm's financial departments in order to come up with a budget and spending plan. They work the closest with the heads of the sales, procurement, and logistics departments. Sales managers relay the client's needs and the price the client is willing to pay to the production department, which must then fill the order. The logistics or distribution department handles the delivery of the goods, often coordinating with the production department. The procurement department orders the supplies that the production department needs to make its products. The procurement department also is responsible for making sure that the inventories of supplies are maintained at proper levels so that production proceeds without interruption. A breakdown in communications between the production manager and the procurement department can cause slowdowns and a failure to meet production schedules. Just-in-time production techniques have reduced inventory levels, making constant communication among managers, suppliers, and procurement departments even more important.

Work environment. Most industrial production managers divide their time between production areas and their offices. While in the production area, they must follow established health and safety practices and wear the required protective clothing and equipment. The time in the office, which often is located near production areas, usually is spent meeting with subordinates or other department managers, analyzing production data, and writing and reviewing reports.

Many industrial production managers work extended hours, especially when production deadlines must be met. In 2008, about a third of all workers worked more than 50 hours a week on average.

In facilities that operate around the clock, managers often work late shifts and may be called at any hour to deal with emergencies. This could mean going to the plant to resolve the problem, regardless of the hour, and staying until the situation is under control. Dealing with production workers as well as superiors when working under the pressure of production deadlines or emergency situations can be stressful. Corporate restructuring has eliminated levels of management and support staff, thus shifting more responsibilities to production managers and compounding the stress.

Training, Other Qualifications, and Advancement

Because of the diversity of manufacturing operations and job requirements, there is no standard preparation for this occupation. Most employers prefer to hire workers with a college degree. Experience in some part of production operations is also usually required.

Education and training. Many industrial production managers have a college degree in business administration, management, industrial technology, or industrial engineering. However, although employers may prefer candidates with a business or engineering background, some companies will hire well-rounded graduates from other fields who are willing to spend time in a production-related job because experience in some aspect of production operations is needed before one advances to upper-management positions.

Some industrial production managers enter the occupation after working their way up through the ranks, starting as production workers and then advancing to supervisory positions before being selected for management. These workers already have an intimate knowledge of the production process and the firm's organization. To increase their chances of promotion, workers can expand their skills by obtaining a college degree, demonstrating leadership qualities, or taking company-sponsored courses to learn the additional skills needed in management positions.

As production operations become more sophisticated, an increasing number of employers are looking for candidates with graduate degrees in industrial management or business administration, particularly for positions at larger plants where managers have more oversight responsibilities. Combined with an undergraduate degree in engineering, either of these graduate degrees is considered particularly good preparation. Managers who do not have graduate degrees often take courses in decision sciences, which provide them with techniques and statistical formulas that can be used to maximize efficiency and improve quality.

Those who enter the field directly from college or graduate school often are unfamiliar with the firm's production process. As a result, they may spend their first few months in the company's training program. These programs familiarize trainees with the production process, company policies, and the requirements of the job. In larger companies, they also may include assignments to other departments, such as purchasing and accounting. A number of companies hire college graduates as first-line supervisors and promote them to management positions later.

Other qualifications. Today, companies are placing greater importance on a candidate's interpersonal skills. Because the job requires the ability to compromise, persuade, and negotiate, successful production managers must be well rounded and have excellent communication skills. Strong computer skills also are essential.

Projections Data from the National Employment Matrix

Occupational title	SOC Code	Employment, 2008	Projected employment, 2018	Change, 2008–2018	
				Number	Percent
Industrial production managers 11-3051		156,100	144,100	−11,900	−8

NOTE: Data in this table are rounded.

Industrial production managers must continually keep informed of new production technologies and management practices. Many belong to professional organizations and attend trade shows or industry conferences where new equipment is displayed and new production methods and technologies discussed.

Certification and advancement. Some industrial production managers earn certifications that show their competency in various quality and management systems. Although certification is not required for industrial production manager jobs, it may improve job prospects.

One credential, Certified in Production and Inventory Management (CPIM), is offered by APICS, the Association for Operations Management, and requires passing a series of exams that cover supply chain management, resource planning, scheduling, production operations, and strategic planning. Those certified must complete a set number of professional development activities every three years to maintain their certification.

The American Society for Quality offers the Certified Manager of Quality/Organizational Excellence (CMQ/OE) credential. This certification is open to managers who pass an exam and who have at least 10 years of experience or education, five of which must be in a decision-making position. It is intended for managers who lead process improvement initiatives. To maintain certification, workers must complete a set number of professional development units every three years.

Industrial production managers with a proven record of superior performance may advance to plant manager or vice president of manufacturing. Others transfer to jobs with more responsibilities at larger firms. Opportunities also exist for managers to become consultants.

Employment

Industrial production managers held about 156,100 jobs in 2008. About 80 percent are employed in manufacturing industries, including fabricated metal product, transportation equipment, and computer and electronic product manufacturing. Production managers work in all parts of the country, but jobs are most plentiful in areas where manufacturing is concentrated.

Job Outlook

Employment is expected to decline moderately. Applicants with experience in production occupations, along with a college degree in industrial engineering, management, or a related field, will enjoy the best job prospects.

Employment change. Employment of industrial production managers is expected to decline moderately by 8 percent over the 2008–2018 decade. Overall manufacturing employment is expected to decline as the production process becomes more automated. However, because industrial production managers coordinate the use of both workers and machines in the production process, they will not be as affected as other occupations by automation. Nevertheless,

the employment decline will result from improved productivity and increased imports of manufactured goods.

Efforts to increase efficiency at the management level have led companies to ask production managers to assume more responsibilities, particularly as computers and production management software allow managers to coordinate scheduling, planning, and communication more easily among departments. In addition, more emphasis on quality in the production process has redistributed some of the production manager's oversight responsibilities to supervisors and workers on the production line. However, most of the decision-making work of production managers cannot be automated, a factor that will limit the decline in their employment.

Job prospects. Despite the projected employment decline, a number of jobs are expected to open because of the need to replace workers who retire or transfer to other occupations. Applicants with experience in production occupations, along with a college degree in industrial engineering, management, or business administration (particularly those with an undergraduate engineering degree and a master's degree in business administration or industrial management), will enjoy the best job prospects. Employers also are likely to seek candidates who have excellent communication skills and related work experience and who are personable, flexible, and eager to enhance their knowledge and skills through ongoing training.

Earnings

Median annual wages for industrial production managers were $85,080 in May 2009. The middle 50 percent earned between $65,680 and $111,790. The lowest 10 percent earned less than $51,290, and the highest 10 percent earned more than $146,030. Median annual wages in the manufacturing industries employing the largest numbers of industrial production managers were as follows:

Plastics product manufacturing	$78,640
Printing and related support activities	80,260
Navigational, measuring, electromedical, and control instruments manufacturing	97,920
Pharmaceutical and medicine manufacturing	95,430
Motor vehicle parts manufacturing	83,430

Related Occupations

Industrial production managers oversee production staff and equipment, ensure that production goals and quality standards are met, and implement company policies. Other managerial occupations with similar responsibilities include advertising, marketing, promotions, public relations, and sales managers; construction managers; and top executives.

Occupations requiring comparable training and problem-solving skills include engineers, management analysts, and operations research analysts.

Sources of Additional Information

General information on careers in industrial production management is available from local manufacturers and schools with programs in industrial management.

For more information on careers in production management and information on the CPIM certification, contact

▸ APICS, the Association for Operations Management, 8430 W. Bryn Mawr Ave., Suite 1000, Chicago, IL 60631. Internet: www.apics.org

For more information on quality management and the CMQ/OE certification, contact

▸ American Society for Quality, 600 N. Plankinton Ave., Milwaukee, WI 53203. Internet: www.asq.org

Inspectors, Testers, Sorters, Samplers, and Weighers

(O*NET 51-9061.00)

Significant Points

■ About 69 percent are employed in manufacturing establishments.

■ Although a high school diploma is sufficient for the basic testing of products, complex precision-inspecting positions are filled by experienced workers.

■ Employment is expected to decline slowly.

Nature of the Work

Inspectors, testers, sorters, samplers, and weighers, often called *quality-control inspectors* or another, similar name, ensure that your food will not make you sick, that your car will run properly, and that your pants will not split the first time you wear them. These workers monitor or audit quality standards for virtually all manufactured products, including foods, textiles, clothing, glassware, motor vehicles, electronic components, computers, and structural steel. As product quality becomes increasingly important to the success of many manufacturing firms, daily duties of inspectors place more focus on this aspect of their jobs.

Regardless of title, all inspectors, testers, sorters, samplers, and weighers work to guarantee the quality of the goods their firms produce. Specific job duties vary across the wide range of industries in which these workers are found. Materials inspectors may check products by sight, sound, feel, smell, or even taste to locate imperfections such as cuts, scratches, missing pieces, or crooked seams. These workers may verify dimensions, color, texture, strength, or other physical characteristics of objects. Mechanical inspectors generally verify that parts fit, move correctly, and are properly lubricated; check the pressure of gases and the level of liquids; test the flow of electricity; and do a test run to check for proper operation of a machine or piece of equipment. Some jobs involve only a quick visual inspection; others require a longer, detailed one. Sorters may separate goods according to length, size, fabric type, or color, while samplers test or inspect a sample taken from a batch or production run for malfunctions or defects. Weighers weigh quantities of materials for use in production. Testers repeatedly test existing products or prototypes under real-world conditions. Through these tests, companies determine how long a product will last, what parts will break down first, and how to improve durability.

Quality-control workers are involved at every stage of the production process. Some examine materials received from a supplier before sending them to the production line. Others inspect components and assemblies or perform a final check on the finished product. Depending on their skill level, inspectors also may set up and test equipment, calibrate precision instruments, repair defective products, or record data.

These workers rely on a number of tools to perform their jobs. Although some still use handheld measurement devices such as micrometers, calipers, and alignment gauges, it is more common for them to operate electronic inspection equipment, such as coordinate-measuring machines (CMMs). These machines use sensitive probes to measure a part's dimensional accuracy and allow the inspector to analyze the results with computer software. Inspectors testing electrical devices may use voltmeters, ammeters, and ohmmeters to test potential difference, current flow, and resistance, respectively. All the tools that inspectors use are maintained by calibration technicians, who ensure that they work properly and generate accurate readings.

Inspectors mark, tag, or note problems. They may reject defective items outright, send them for repair, or fix minor problems themselves. If the product is acceptable, the inspector will certify it. Quality-control workers record the results of their inspections, compute the percentage of defects and other statistical measures, and prepare inspection and test reports. Some electronic inspection equipment automatically provides test reports containing these inspection results. When defects are found, inspectors notify supervisors and help to analyze and correct the production problems.

The emphasis on finding the root cause of defects is a basic tenet of modern management and production philosophies. Current philosophies emphasize constant quality improvement through analysis and correction of the causes of defects. The nature of inspectors' work has changed from merely checking for defects to determining the cause of those defects.

This increased emphasis on quality means that companies now have integrated teams of inspection and production workers who jointly review and improve product quality. In addition, many companies use self-monitoring production machines to ensure that the output is produced within quality standards. These machines not only can alert inspectors to production problems, but also sometimes automatically repair defects.

Some firms have completely automated inspection with the help of advanced vision inspection systems using machinery installed at one or several points in the production process. Inspectors in these firms monitor the equipment, review output, and perform random product checks.

Work environment. Working conditions vary by industry and establishment size. As a result, some inspectors examine similar products for an entire shift, whereas others examine a variety of items.

In manufacturing, it is common for most inspectors to remain at one workstation. Inspectors in some industries may be on their feet all day and may have to lift heavy objects, whereas in other industries they sit during most of their shift and read electronic printouts of data. Workers in heavy manufacturing plants may be exposed to the noise and grime of machinery; in other plants, inspectors work in clean, air-conditioned environments suitable for carrying out controlled tests. As a result of these varied working conditions, injuries are not uncommon for this occupation, and workers must follow proper procedures to minimize risks.

Some inspectors work evenings, nights, or weekends. Shift assignments generally are made on the basis of seniority. Overtime may be required to meet production goals.

Training, Other Qualifications, and Advancement

Although a high school diploma is sufficient for the basic testing of products, complex precision-inspecting positions are filled by experienced workers.

Education and training. Training requirements vary with the responsibilities of the quality-control worker. For workers who perform simple "pass/fail" tests of products, a high school diploma generally is sufficient, together with limited in-house training. Training for new inspectors may cover the use of special meters, gauges, computers, and other instruments; quality-control techniques; blueprint reading; safety; and reporting requirements. There are some postsecondary training programs, but many employers prefer to train inspectors on the job.

The chances of finding work in this occupation can be improved by studying industrial trades, including computer-aided design, in high school or in a postsecondary vocational program. Laboratory work in the natural or biological sciences also may improve one's analytical skills and increase one's chances of finding work in medical or pharmaceutical labs, where many of these workers are employed.

As companies implement more automated inspection techniques that require less manual inspection, workers in this occupation will have to learn to operate and program more sophisticated equipment and learn software applications. Because these operations require additional skills, the need for higher education may be necessary. To address this need, some colleges are offering associate degrees in fields such as quality control management.

Other qualifications. In general, inspectors, testers, sorters, samplers, and weighers need mechanical aptitude, math and communication skills, and good hand-eye coordination and vision. Another important skill is the ability to analyze and interpret blueprints, data, manuals, and other material to determine specifications, inspection procedures, formulas, and methods for making adjustments.

Certification and advancement. The American Society for Quality offers 15 different types of certifications for workers in quality control. These certifications may assist workers in advancing within the occupation. They generally require a certain number of years of experience in the field and passage of an exam.

Advancement for workers with the necessary skills frequently takes the form of additional duties and responsibilities. Complex inspection positions are filled by experienced assemblers, machine operators, or mechanics who already have a thorough knowledge of the products and production processes. To advance to these positions, experienced workers may need training in statistical process control, new automation, or the company's quality assurance policies. Because automated inspection equipment and electronic recording of results are becoming common, computer skills also are important.

Employment

Inspectors, testers, sorters, samplers, and weighers held about 464,700 jobs in 2008. About 69 percent worked in manufacturing establishments that produced such products as motor vehicle parts, plastics products, semiconductor and other electronic components, and aerospace products and parts. Inspectors, testers, sorters, samplers, and weighers also were found in employment services; wholesale trade; and professional, scientific, and technical services.

Job Outlook

Like many other occupations concentrated in manufacturing industries, employment is expected to decline slowly, primarily because of the growing use of automated inspection and the redistribution of some quality-control responsibilities from inspectors to production workers.

Employment change. Employment of inspectors, testers, sorters, samplers, and weighers is expected to decline by 4 percent between 2008 and 2018. Because the majority of these employees work in the manufacturing sector, their outlook is greatly affected by what happens to manufacturing companies. The emphasis on improving quality and productivity has led many manufacturers to invest in automated inspection equipment and to take a more systematic approach to quality inspection. Continued improvements in technologies allow firms to automate inspection tasks, increasing workers' productivity and reducing the demand for inspectors.

In addition, work in many manufacturing companies continues to move abroad. As more production moves offshore, the number of quality-control workers is expected to decline as well.

Firms increasingly are integrating quality control into the production process. Many inspection duties are being redistributed from specialized inspectors to fabrication and assembly workers, who monitor quality at every stage of the production process. In addition, the growing implementation of statistical process control is resulting in "smarter" inspection. Using this system, firms survey the sources and incidence of defects so that they can better focus their efforts on reducing the number of defective products manufactured.

In some industries, however, automation is not a feasible alternative to manual inspection. Where key inspection elements are oriented toward size, such as length, width, or thickness, automation will become more important in the future. But where taste, smell, texture, appearance, complexity of fabric, or performance of

Projections Data from the National Employment Matrix

Occupational title	SOC Code	Employment, 2008	Projected employment, 2018	Change, 2008–2018	
				Number	Percent
Inspectors, testers, sorters, samplers, and weighers	51-9061	464,700	447,800	−16,900	−4

NOTE: Data in this table are rounded.

the product is important, inspection will continue to be done by workers.

Job prospects. Although numerous job openings will arise through the need to replace workers who move out of this large occupation, many of these jobs will be open only to experienced workers with advanced skills. There will be better opportunities in the employment services industry, as more manufacturers use contract inspection workers, and in growing manufacturing industries, such as medical equipment and pharmaceuticals.

Earnings

Median hourly wages of inspectors, testers, sorters, samplers, and weighers were $15.54 in May 2009. The middle 50 percent earned between $12.02 and $20.08 an hour. The lowest 10 percent earned less than $9.61 an hour, and the highest 10 percent earned more than $26.06 an hour. Median hourly wages in the industries employing the largest numbers of inspectors, testers, sorters, samplers, and weighers in May 2009 were as follows:

Employment services	$12.14
Aerospace product and parts manufacturing	22.45
Plastics product manufacturing	14.35
Semiconductor and other electronic component manufacturing	14.69
Motor vehicle parts manufacturing	16.19

Related Occupations

Other workers who conduct inspections include the following agricultural inspectors; construction and building inspectors; fire inspectors and investigators; occupational health and safety specialists; occupational health and safety technicians; and transportation inspectors,

Sources of Additional Information

For general information about inspection, testing, and certification, contact

▸ American Society for Quality, 600 N. Plankinton Ave., Milwaukee, WI 53203. Internet: www.asq.org

Insurance Sales Agents

(O*NET 41-3021.00)

Significant Points

■ In addition to offering insurance policies, agents increasingly sell mutual funds, annuities, and securities and offer comprehensive financial planning services, including retirement and estate planning services, some designed specifically for the elderly.

■ Agents must obtain a license in the states where they sell.

■ Job opportunities should be best for college graduates who have sales ability, excellent interpersonal skills, and expertise in a wide range of insurance and financial services.

Nature of the Work

Most people have their first contact with an insurance company through an insurance sales agent. These workers help individuals, families, and businesses select insurance policies that provide the best protection for their lives, health, and property.

Insurance sales agents, commonly referred to as "producers" in the insurance industry, sell one or more types of insurance, such as property and casualty, life, health, disability, and long-term care. Property and casualty insurance agents sell policies that protect individuals and businesses from financial loss resulting from automobile accidents, fire, theft, storms, and other events that can damage property. For businesses, property and casualty insurance can also cover injured workers' compensation, product liability claims, or medical malpractice claims.

Life insurance agents specialize in selling policies that pay beneficiaries when a policyholder dies. Depending on the policyholder's circumstances, a cash-value policy can be designed to provide retirement income, funds for the education of children, and other benefits, as well. Life insurance agents also sell annuities that promise a retirement income. Health insurance agents sell health insurance policies that cover the costs of medical care and loss of income due to illness or injury. They also may sell dental insurance and short-term and long-term-disability insurance policies. Agents may specialize in any one of these products, or function as generalists, providing multiple products to a single customer.

An increasing number of insurance sales agents offer their clients advice on how to minimize risk as well as comprehensive financial planning services, especially to those approaching retirement. These services include retirement planning, estate planning, and assistance in setting up pension plans for businesses. As a result, many insurance agents are involved in "cross-selling" or "total account development." Besides offering insurance, these agents may become licensed to sell mutual funds, variable annuities, and other securities. This practice is most common with life insurance agents who already sell annuities, but many property and casualty agents also sell financial products.

Insurance sales agents also prepare reports, maintain records, and seek out new clients. In the event that policyholders experience a loss, agents help them settle their insurance claims. Insurance sales agents working exclusively for one insurance company are referred to as *captive agents*. These agents typically have a contractual agreement with the carrier, and are usually an employee of the carrier. Independent insurance agents, or *brokers*, are mostly facilitators who represent several companies. They match insurance policies for their clients with the company that offers the best rate and coverage.

Technology—specifically, the Internet—has greatly affected the insurance business, making the tasks of obtaining price quotes and processing applications and service requests faster and easier. The Internet has made it easier for agents to take on more clients and to be better informed about new products. It has also altered the relationship between agent and client. Agents formerly used to devote much of their time to marketing and selling products to new clients. Now, clients are increasingly obtaining insurance quotes from a company's website and then contacting the company directly to purchase policies. This interaction gives the clients a more active role in selecting their policy while reducing the amount of time agents spend seeking new clients. Insurance sales agents also obtain many new accounts through referrals, so it is important that they maintain regular contact with their clients to ensure that the clients' financial needs are being met. Developing a satisfied clientele that will recommend an agent's services to other potential customers is a key to success for agents.

Increasing competition in the insurance industry has spurred carriers to find new ways to keep their clients satisfied. One solution is hiring customer service representatives who are accessible 24 hours a day, 7 days a week to handle routine tasks such as answering questions, making changes in policies, processing claims, and selling more products to clients. The opportunity to cross-sell new products to clients will help an agent's business grow. The use of customer service representatives also allows agents to concentrate their efforts on seeking out new clients and maintaining relationships with old ones. (See the statements on customer service representatives; and claims adjusters, appraisers, examiners, and investigators elsewhere in this book.)

Work environment. Most insurance sales agents work in offices. Since some agencies are small, agents may work alone or with only a few others. Some independent agents, or brokers, however, may spend much of their time traveling to meet with clients, close sales, or investigate claims. Agents usually determine their own hours of work and often schedule evening and weekend appointments for the convenience of clients. Some sales agents meet with clients during business hours and then spend evenings doing paperwork and preparing presentations to prospective clients. Although most agents work a 40-hour week, some may work much longer.

Training, Other Qualifications, and Advancement

Every sales agent involved in the solicitation, selling, or negotiation of insurance must have a state-issued license. Licensure requirements vary by state but typically require some insurance-related coursework and the passing of several exams. Although some agents are hired right out of college, many are hired by insurance companies as customer service representatives and are later promoted to sales agent.

Education and training. For insurance sales agent jobs, many companies and independent agencies prefer to hire college graduates—especially those who have majored in business, finance, or economics. High school graduates may be hired if they have proven sales ability or have been successful in other types of work.

College training can help agents grasp the technical aspects of insurance policies as well as the fundamentals of the insurance industry. Many colleges and universities offer courses in insurance, and a few schools offer a bachelor's degree in the field. College courses in finance, mathematics, accounting, economics, business law, marketing, and business administration enable insurance sales agents to understand how social and economic conditions relate to the insurance industry. Courses in psychology, sociology, and public speaking can prove useful in improving sales techniques. In addition, familiarity with popular software packages has become very important because computers provide instantaneous information on a wide variety of financial products and greatly improve an agent's efficiency.

Agents learn many of their job duties on the job from other agents. Many employers have their new agents shadow an experienced agent for a period of time. This allows the agent to learn how to conduct their business, how the agency interacts with clients, and how to write policies.

Employers also are placing greater emphasis on continuing professional education as the diversity of financial products sold by insurance agents increases. It is important for insurance agents to keep up to date on issues concerning clients. Changes in tax laws, government benefits programs, and other state and federal regulations can affect the insurance needs of clients and the way in which agents conduct business. Agents can enhance their selling skills and broaden their knowledge of insurance and other financial services by taking courses at colleges and universities and by attending institutes, conferences, and seminars sponsored by insurance organizations.

Licensure. Insurance sales agents must obtain a license in the states where they plan to work. Separate licenses are required for agents to sell life and health insurance and property and casualty insurance. In most states, licenses are issued only to applicants who complete specified prelicensing courses and who pass state examinations covering insurance fundamentals and state insurance laws. Most state licensing authorities also have mandatory continuing education requirements every two years, focusing on insurance laws, consumer protection, ethics, and the technical details of various insurance policies.

As the demand for financial products and financial planning increases, many insurance agents choose to gain the proper licensing and certification to sell securities and other financial products. Doing so, however, requires substantial study and passing an additional examination—either the Series 6 or Series 7 licensing exam, both of which are administered by the National Association of Securities Dealers (NASD). The Series 6 exam is for individuals who wish to sell only mutual funds and variable annuities, whereas the Series 7 exam is the main NASD series license that qualifies agents as general securities sales representatives.

Other qualifications. Previous experience in sales or insurance jobs can be very useful in becoming an insurance sales agent. In selling commercial insurance, technical experience in a particular field can help sell policies to those in the same profession. As a result, these agents tend to be older than entrants in many other occupations.

Insurance sales agents should be flexible, enthusiastic, confident, disciplined, hard working, and willing to solve problems. They should communicate effectively and inspire customer confidence. Because they usually work without supervision, sales agents must have good time-management skills and the initiative to locate new clients.

Certification and advancement. A number of organizations offer professional designation programs that certify an agent's expertise in specialties such as life, health, and property and casualty insurance, as well as financial consulting. For example, The National Alliance for Insurance Education and Research offers a wide variety of courses in health, life and property, and casualty insurance for independent insurance agents. Although voluntary, such programs assure clients and employers that an agent has a thorough understanding of the relevant specialty. Agents who complete certification are usually required to fulfill a specified number of hours of continuing education to retain their designation, as determined by the Alliance.

In the area of financial planning, many agents find it worthwhile to demonstrate competency by earning the certified financial planner or chartered financial consultant designation. The Certified Financial Planner credential, issued by the Certified Financial Planner Board of Standards, requires relevant experience, completion of education requirements, passing a comprehensive examination, and adherence to an enforceable code of ethics. The exam tests the candidate's knowledge of the financial planning process, insurance and risk

Projections Data from the National Employment Matrix

Occupational title	SOC Code	Employment, 2008	Projected employment, 2018	Change, 2008–2018	
				Number	Percent
Insurance sales agents	41-3021	434,800	486,400	51,600	12

NOTE: Data in this table are rounded.

management, employee benefits planning, taxes and retirement planning, and investment and estate planning.

The Chartered Financial Consultant (ChFC) and the Chartered Life Underwriter (CLU) designations, issued by the American College in Bryn Mawr, Pennsylvania, typically require professional experience and the completion of an eight-course program of study. For those new to the industry, however, the American College offers the Life Underwriter Training Council Fellow (FUTCF), an introductory course that teaches basic insurance concepts. Many property and casualty insurance agents obtain the Chartered Property Casualty Underwriter (CPCU) designation, offered by the American Institute for Chartered Property Casualty Underwriter. The majority of professional designations in insurance have continuing education requirements.

An insurance sales agent who shows ability and leadership may become a sales manager in a local office. A few advance to managerial or executive positions. However, many who have established a client base prefer to remain in sales work. Some—particularly in the property and casualty field—launch their own independent agencies or brokerage firms.

Employment

Insurance sales agents held about 434,800 jobs in 2008. About 51 percent of insurance sales agents work for insurance agencies and brokerages. About 21 percent work directly for insurance carriers. Although most insurance agents specialize in life and health insurance or property and casualty insurance, a growing number of "multiline" agents sell all lines of insurance. A small number of agents work for banks and securities brokerages as a result of the increasing integration of the finance and insurance industries. Approximately 22 percent of insurance sales agents are self-employed.

The majority of insurance sales agents are employed in local offices or independent agencies, but some work in the headquarters of insurance companies.

Job Outlook

Employment is expected to grow about as fast as average for all occupations. Opportunities will be best for college graduates who have sales ability, excellent interpersonal skills, and expertise in a wide range of insurance and financial services.

Employment change. Employment of insurance sales agents is expected to increase by 12 percent over the 2008–2018 period, which is about as fast as average for all occupations. Future demand for insurance sales agents depends largely on the variety of financial products and volume of sales. Sales of health insurance, long-term-care insurance, and other comprehensive financial planning services designed specifically for the elderly are expected to rise sharply as the population ages. In addition, a growing population will increase demand for insurance for automobiles, homes, and high-priced valuables and equipment. As new businesses emerge and existing firms expand their insurance coverage, sales of commercial insurance also should increase, including coverage such as product liability, workers' compensation, employee benefits, and pollution liability insurance.

Employment of agents will not keep up with the rising level of insurance sales, however. Many insurance carriers are trying to contain costs and are shedding their captive agents—those agents working directly for insurance carriers. Instead carriers are relying more on independent agents or brokers.

It is unlikely that the Internet will threaten the jobs of these agents. The automation of policy and claims processing allows insurance agents to take on more clients. Most clients value their relationship with their agent and prefer personal service, discussing their policies directly with their agents, rather than through a computer. Insurance law and investments are becoming more complex, and many people and businesses lack the time and expertise to buy insurance without the advice of an agent.

Job prospects. College graduates who have sales ability, excellent interpersonal skills, and expertise in a wide range of insurance and financial services should enjoy the best prospects. Multilingual agents should have an advantage, because they can serve a wider range of customers. Additionally, insurance language tends to be quite technical, so agents who have a firm understanding of relevant technical and legal terms will also be desirable to employers. Many beginning agents fail to earn enough from commissions to meet their income goals and eventually transfer to other careers. Many job openings are likely to result from the need to replace agents who leave the occupation or retire.

Agents may face some competition from traditional securities brokers and bankers, as they also sell insurance policies. Insurance sales agents will need to expand the products and services they offer as consolidation increases among insurance companies, banks, and brokerage firms and as demands increase from clients for more comprehensive financial planning.

Independent agents who incorporate new technology into their existing businesses will remain competitive. Agents who use the Internet to market their products will reach a broader client base and expand their business. Agents who offer better customer service also will remain competitive.

Earnings

The median annual wages of wage and salary insurance sales agents were $45,500 in May 2009. The middle 50 percent earned between $32,810 and $69,540. The lowest 10 percent had earnings of $25,800 or less, while the highest 10 percent earned more than $114,910. Median annual wages in May 2009 in the two industries employing the largest number of insurance sales agents were $44,700 for agencies, brokerages, and other insurance-related activities, and $48,150 for insurance carriers.

Many independent agents are paid by commission only, whereas sales workers who are employees of an agency or an insurance carrier may be paid in one of three ways: salary only, salary plus commission, or salary plus bonus. In general, commissions are the most common form of compensation, especially for experienced agents. The amount of the commission depends on the type and amount of insurance sold and on whether the transaction is a new policy or a renewal. Bonuses usually are awarded when agents meet their sales goals or when an agency meets its profit goals. Some agents involved with financial planning receive a fee for their services, rather than a commission.

Company-paid benefits to insurance sales agents usually include continuing education, training to qualify for licensing, group insurance plans, office space, and clerical support services. Some companies also may pay for automobile and transportation expenses, attendance at conventions and meetings, promotion and marketing expenses, and retirement plans. Independent agents working for insurance agencies receive fewer benefits, but their commissions may be higher to help them pay for marketing and other expenses.

Related Occupations

Other workers who provide or sell financial products or services include financial analysts; financial managers; personal financial advisors; real estate brokers and sales agents; and securities, commodities, and financial services sales agents.

Other sales workers include advertising sales agents; customer service representatives; and sales representatives, wholesale and manufacturing.

Other occupations in the insurance industry include claims adjusters, appraisers, examiners, and investigators; and insurance underwriters.

Sources of Additional Information

Occupational information about insurance sales agents is available from the home office of many insurance companies. Information on state licensing requirements may be obtained from the department of insurance at any state capital.

For information about insurance sales careers and training, contact

▸ National Association of Professional Insurance Agents, 400 N. Washington St., Alexandria, VA 22314. Internet: www.pianet.org

For information about health insurance sales careers, contact

▸ National Association of Health Underwriters, 2000 N. 14th St., Suite 450, Arlington, VA 22201. Internet: www.nahu.org

For general information on the property and casualty field, contact

▸ Insurance Information Institute, 110 William St., New York, NY 10038. Internet: www.iii.org

For information about professional designation programs, contact

▸ The American Institute for Chartered Property and Casualty Underwriters/Insurance Institute of America, 720 Providence Rd., Suite 100, Malvern, PA 19355-3433. Internet: www.aicpcu.org

▸ The American College, 270 S. Bryn Mawr Ave., Bryn Mawr, PA 19010-2195. Internet: www.theamericancollege.edu

For information on financial planning careers, contact

▸ Certified Financial Planner Board of Standards, Inc., 1425 K St. NW, Suite 500, Washington, DC 20005. Internet: www.cfp.net

Library Technicians and Library Assistants

(O*NET 25-4031.00 and 43-4121.00)

Significant Points

■ Improved technology enables library technicians to perform tasks once done by librarians.

■ Training requirements range from a high school diploma to an associate degree, but computer skills are necessary for all workers.

■ Job prospects should be good.

Nature of the Work

Library technicians and assistants help librarians acquire, prepare, and organize materials and assist users in locating the appropriate resources. These workers usually work under the supervision of a librarian, although they sometimes work independently. In small libraries, they handle a range of duties, while those in large libraries usually specialize. The duties of technicians and assistants are expanding and evolving as libraries increasingly use the Internet and other technologies to share information. They are increasingly responsible for daily library operations. Depending on where they work, these workers can have other titles, such as *library technical assistant, media aide, library media assistant, library aide,* or *circulation assistant.*

In some libraries, library technicians may have more responsibilities than library assistants. Technicians may be responsible for administering library programs, working with librarians to acquire new materials, and overseeing lower level staff. Assistants may be assigned more clerical duties, like shelving books, checking in returned material and assisting patrons with basic questions and requests.

Library technicians and assistants direct library users to standard references, organize and maintain periodicals, prepare volumes for binding, handle interlibrary loan requests, prepare invoices, perform routine cataloguing and coding of library materials, and retrieve information from computer databases. Some of these workers may supervise other support staff.

At the circulation desk, library technicians and assistants loan and collect books, periodicals, videotapes, and other materials. When an item is borrowed, assistants scan it and the patron's library card to record the transaction in the library database; they then stamp the due date on the item or print a receipt with the due date. When an item is returned, assistants inspect it for damage and scan it to record its return. Electronic circulation systems automatically generate notices reminding patrons that their materials are overdue, but library assistants may review the record for accuracy before sending out the notice. Library assistants also register new patrons and issue them library cards. They answer patrons' questions or refer them to a librarian.

The automation of recordkeeping has reduced the amount of clerical work performed by library technicians and assistants. Many libraries now offer self-service registration and circulation areas, where patrons can register for library cards and check out materials themselves. These technologies decrease the time library technicians spend recording and inputting records. At the same time, these systems require more of the technicians' time to ensure they continue to operate smoothly.

Throughout the library, assistants and technicians sort returned books, periodicals, and other items and put them on their designated shelves, in the appropriate files, or in storage areas. Before reshelving returned materials, they look for any damage and try to make repairs. For example, they may use tape or paste to repair torn pages or book covers and use other specialized processes to repair more valuable materials.

These workers may also locate materials being loaned to a patron or another library. Because nearly all library catalogs are computerized, they must be familiar with computers. They sometimes help patrons with computer searches.

Some library technicians and assistants specialize in helping patrons who have vision problems. Sometimes referred to as *braille-and-talking-books clerks*, these assistants review the borrower's list of desired reading materials, and locate those materials or close substitutes from the library collection of large-type or braille volumes and books on tape. They then give or mail the materials to the borrower.

Technicians and assistants also market library services. They participate in and help plan reader advisory programs, used-book sales, and outreach programs. They may also design posters, bulletin boards, or displays to inform patrons of library events and services.

As libraries increasingly use the Internet, virtual libraries, and other electronic resources, the duties of library technicians and assistants are changing. In fact, new technologies allow some of these workers to assume responsibilities which were previously performed only by librarians. They now catalog most new acquisitions and oversee the circulation of all library materials. They often maintain, update, and help customize electronic databases. They also may help to maintain the library's website and instruct patrons how to use the library's computers.

Some of these workers operate and maintain audiovisual equipment, such as projectors, tape and CD players, and DVD and videocassette players. They also assist users with microfilm or microfiche readers.

In school libraries, technicians and assistants encourage and teach students to use the library and media center. They also help teachers obtain instructional materials, and they assist students with assignments.

Some work in special libraries maintained by government agencies, corporations, law firms, advertising agencies, museums, professional societies, medical centers, or research laboratories. These technicians conduct literature searches, compile bibliographies, and prepare abstracts, usually on subjects of particular interest to the organization.

To extend library services to more patrons, many libraries operate bookmobiles that are often run by library technicians and assistants. They take bookmobiles—trucks stocked with books—to shopping centers, apartment complexes, schools, nursing homes, and other places. They may operate a bookmobile alone or with other library employees. Those who drive bookmobiles are responsible for answering patrons' questions, receiving and checking out books, collecting fines, maintaining the book collection, shelving materials, and occasionally operating audiovisual equipment to show slides or movies. They keep track of mileage and sometimes are responsible for maintenance of the vehicle and any equipment, such as

photocopiers, in it. Many bookmobiles are equipped with personal computers linked to the main library Internet system, allowing patrons access to electronic resources.

Work environment. Library technicians and assistants who prepare library materials sit at desks or computer terminals for long periods and can develop headaches or eyestrain. They may lift and carry books, climb ladders to reach high stacks, and bend low to shelve books on bottom shelves. Workers who work in bookmobiles may assist handicapped or elderly patrons to the bookmobile or shovel snow to ensure their safety. They may enter hospitals or nursing homes to deliver books.

Workers in school libraries work regular school hours. Those in public libraries and college and university libraries may work weekends, evenings, and some holidays. In corporate libraries, workers usually work normal business hours, although they often work overtime as well. The schedules of workers who drive bookmobiles often depend on the size of the area being served. About 61 percent of library assistants work part time, making the job appealing to retirees, students, and others interested in flexible schedules.

Training, Other Qualifications, and Advancement

Training requirements for library technicians vary widely, ranging from a high school diploma to specialized postsecondary training. Some employers only hire individuals who have library work experience or college training related to libraries; others train inexperienced workers on the job.

Library assistants receive most of their training on the job. No formal education is required, although familiarity with computers is helpful.

Education and training. Most libraries prefer to hire technicians who have earned a certificate or associate degree, but some smaller libraries may hire individuals with only a high school diploma.

Many library technicians in public schools must meet the same requirements as teacher assistants. Those in Title 1 schools—schools that receive special funding because of the high percentage of low income students enrolled—must hold an associate or higher degree, have a minimum of two years of college, or pass a rigorous state or local exam.

Associate degree and certificate programs for library technicians include courses in liberal arts and subjects related to libraries. Students learn about library organization and operation and how to order, process, catalogue, locate, and circulate library materials and media. They often learn to use library automation systems. Libraries and associations offer continuing education courses to inform technicians of new developments in the field.

Training requirements for library assistants are generally minimal; most libraries prefer to hire workers with a high school diploma or GED, although libraries also hire high school students for these positions. No formal postsecondary training is expected. Some employers hire individuals with experience in other clerical jobs; others train inexperienced workers on the job.

Other qualifications. Given the rapid spread of automation in libraries, computer skills are a necessity. Knowledge of databases, library automation systems, online library systems, online public access systems, and circulation systems is particularly valuable. Many bookmobile drivers must have a commercial driver's license.

Projections Data from the National Employment Matrix

Occupational title	SOC Code	Employment, 2008	Projected employment, 2018	Change, 2008–2018	
				Number	Percent
Library technicians and library assistants .... —		242,500	266,700	24,200	10
Library technicians 25-4031		120,600	131,200	10,600	9
Library assistants, clerical 43-4121		122,000	135,500	13,500	11

NOTE: Data in this table are rounded.

Knowledge of databases and other library automation systems is especially useful. These workers should be able to pay close attention to detail, as the proper shelving or storage of materials is essential.

Advancement. Library technicians and assistants usually advance by assuming added responsibilities. For example, they often start at the circulation desk, checking books in and out. After gaining experience, they may become responsible for storing and verifying information. As they advance, they may become involved in budget and personnel matters. Some advance to supervisory positions and are in charge of the day-to-day operation of their departments or, sometimes, a small library. Those who earn a graduate degree in library sciences can become librarians.

Employment

Library technicians held about 120,600 jobs in 2008; about 51 percent were employed by local governments. The federal government employs library technicians primarily at the U.S. Department of Defense.

Library assistants held about 122,000 jobs in 2008. About 52 percent of these workers were employed by local governments.

Job Outlook

Employment of library technicians and assistants is expected to grow about 10 percent, which is about as fast as the average for all occupations. Opportunities will be best for those with specialized postsecondary library training. Prospects should be good, because many workers leave these jobs and need to be replaced.

Employment change. Between 2008 and 2018, the number of library technicians is expected to grow about 9 percent, which is about as fast as the average for all occupations and the number of library assistants is expected to grow by about 11 percent, which is about as fast as the average for all occupations. Increasing use of library automation creates more opportunities for these workers. Electronic information systems have simplified some tasks, enabling them to be performed by technicians, rather than librarians, and spurring demand for technicians. However, job growth in educational institutions will be limited by slowing enrollment growth. In addition, public libraries often face budget pressures, which hold down overall growth in library services. However, this may result in the hiring of more of these workers, because they are paid less than librarians and, thus, represent a lower-cost way to offer some library services. Employment should grow more rapidly in special libraries because increasing numbers of professionals and other workers use those libraries. Because these workers are largely employed by public institutions, they are not directly affected by the ups and downs of the business cycle, but they may be affected by changes in the level of government funding for libraries.

Job prospects. Job prospects should be favorable. In addition to job openings from employment growth, some openings will result from the need to replace library technicians who transfer to other occupations or leave the labor force. Opportunities will be best for library technicians with specialized postsecondary library training. Each year, many people leave this relatively low-paying occupation for other occupations that offer higher pay or full-time work. This creates good job opportunities for those who want to become library assistants.

Earnings

Median hourly wages of library technicians in May 2009 were $14.22. The middle 50 percent earned between $10.91 and $18.21. The lowest 10 percent earned less than $8.44, and the highest 10 percent earned more than $22.47. Median hourly wages in the industries employing the largest numbers of library technicians in May 2009 were as follows:

Local government... $13.66
Elementary and secondary schools 13.24
Colleges, universities, and professional schools 16.07
Other information services................................... 14.65
Junior colleges.. 15.66

Salaries of library technicians in the federal government averaged $44,265 in March 2009.

Median hourly wages of library assistants were $11.05 in May 2009. The middle 50 percent earned between $8.79 and $14.32. The lowest 10 percent earned less than $7.69, and the highest 10 percent earned more than $17.82.

Median hourly wages in the industries employing the largest numbers of library assistants in May 2009 were as follows:

Local government... $10.41
Elementary and secondary schools 12.04
Colleges, universities and professional schools 13.39
Other information services...................................9.49
Junior colleges.. 12.25

Related Occupations

Library technicians and assistants perform organizational and administrative duties. Workers in other occupations with similar duties include librarians; medical records and health information technicians; receptionists and information clerks; and teacher assistants.

Sources of Additional Information

For general career information on library technicians, including information on training programs, contact

▶ American Library Association, Office for Human Resource Development and Recruitment, 50 E. Huron St., Chicago, IL 60611. Internet: www.ala.org/ala/educationcareers/index.cfm

Information concerning requirements and application procedures for positions in the Library of Congress can be obtained directly from

▶ Human Resources Office, Library of Congress, 101 Independence Ave. SE, Washington, DC 20540-2231. Internet: www.loc.gov/hr

State library agencies can furnish information on requirements for technicians and general information about career prospects in the state. Several of these agencies maintain job hotlines that report openings for library technicians.

State departments of education can furnish information on requirements and job opportunities for school library technicians.

Licensed Practical and Licensed Vocational Nurses

(O*NET 29-2061.00)

Significant Points

■ Most training programs last about one year and are offered by vocational or technical schools or community or junior colleges.

■ Overall job prospects are expected to be very good, but job outlook varies by industry.

■ Replacement needs will be a major source of job openings as many workers leave the occupation permanently.

Nature of the Work

Licensed practical nurses (*LPNs*), or *licensed vocational nurses* (*LVNs*), care for people who are sick, injured, convalescent, or disabled under the direction of physicians and registered nurses. (The work of registered nurses is described elsewhere in this book.) The nature of the direction and supervision required varies by state and job setting.

LPNs care for patients in many ways. Often, they provide basic bedside care. Many LPNs measure and record patients' vital signs such as height, weight, temperature, blood pressure, pulse, and respiration. They also prepare and give injections and enemas, monitor catheters, dress wounds, and give alcohol rubs and massages. To help keep patients comfortable, they assist with bathing, dressing, and personal hygiene, moving in bed, standing, and walking. They might also feed patients who need help eating. Experienced LPNs may supervise nursing assistants and aides.

As part of their work, LPNs collect samples for testing, perform routine laboratory tests, and record food and fluid intake and output. They clean and monitor medical equipment. Sometimes, they help physicians and registered nurses perform tests and procedures. Some LPNs help to deliver, care for, and feed infants.

LPNs also monitor their patients and report adverse reactions to medications or treatments. LPNs gather information from patients, including their health history and how they are currently feeling. They may use this information to complete insurance forms, preauthorizations, and referrals, and they share information with registered nurses and doctors to help determine the best course of care

for a patient. LPNs often teach family members how to care for a relative or teach patients about good health habits.

Most LPNs are generalists and will work in any area of health care. However, some work in a specialized setting, such as a nursing home, a doctor's office, or in home health care. LPNs in nursing care facilities help to evaluate residents' needs, develop care plans, and supervise the care provided by nursing aides. In doctors' offices and clinics, they may be responsible for making appointments, keeping records, and performing other clerical duties. LPNs who work in home health care may prepare meals and teach family members simple nursing tasks.

In some states, LPNs are permitted to administer prescribed medicines, start intravenous fluids, and provide care to ventilator-dependent patients.

Work environment. Most licensed practical nurses work a 40-hour week. In some work settings where patients need round-the-clock care, LPNs may have to work nights, weekends, and holidays. About 18 percent of LPNs and LVNs worked part-time in 2008. They often stand for long periods and help patients move in bed, stand, or walk.

LPNs may face hazards from caustic chemicals, radiation, and infectious diseases. They are subject to back injuries when moving patients. They often must deal with the stress of heavy workloads. In addition, the patients they care for may be confused, agitated, or uncooperative.

Training, Other Qualifications, and Advancement

Most practical nursing training programs last about 1 year, and are offered by vocational and technical schools or community or junior colleges. LPNs must be licensed to practice.

Education and training. LPNs must complete a state-approved training program in practical nursing to be eligible for licensure. Contact your state's board of nursing for a list of approved programs. Most training programs are available from technical and vocational schools or community and junior colleges. Other programs are available through high schools, hospitals, and colleges and universities. A high school diploma or its equivalent usually is required for entry, although some programs accept candidates without a diploma, and some programs are part of a high school curriculum.

Most year-long practical nursing programs include both classroom study and supervised clinical practice (patient care). Classroom study covers basic nursing concepts and subjects related to patient care, including anatomy, physiology, medical-surgical nursing, pediatrics, obstetrics nursing, pharmacology, nutrition, and first aid. Clinical practice usually is in a hospital but sometimes includes other settings.

Licensure. The National Council Licensure Examination, or NCLEX-PN, is required in order to obtain licensure as an LPN. The exam is developed and administered by the National Council of State Boards of Nursing. The NCLEX-PN is a computer-based exam and varies in length. The exam covers four major *Client Needs* categories: safe and effective care environment, health promotion and maintenance, psychosocial integrity, and physiological integrity. Eligibility for licensure may vary by state; for details, contact your state's board of nursing.

Projections Data from the National Employment Matrix

Occupational title	SOC Code	Employment, 2008	Projected employment, 2018	Change, 2008–2018	
				Number	Percent
Licensed practical and licensed vocational nurses	29-2061	753,600	909,200	155,600	21

NOTE: Data in this table are rounded.

Other qualifications. LPNs should have a caring, sympathetic nature. They should be emotionally stable because working with the sick and injured can be stressful. They also need to be observant, and to have good decision-making and communication skills. As part of a health-care team, they must be able to follow orders and work under close supervision.

LPNs should enjoy learning because continuing education credits are required by some states and/or employers at regular intervals. Career-long learning is a distinct reality for LPNs.

Advancement. In some employment settings, such as nursing homes, LPNs can advance to become charge nurses who oversee the work of other LPNs and nursing aides.

LPNs may become credentialed in specialties like IV therapy, gerontology, long-term care, and pharmacology.

Some LPNs also choose to become registered nurses through LPN-to-RN training programs.

Employment

Licensed practical and licensed vocational nurses held about 753,600 jobs in 2008. About 25 percent of LPNs worked in hospitals, 28 percent in nursing care facilities, and another 12 percent in offices of physicians. Others worked for home health-care services; employment services; residential care facilities; community care facilities for the elderly; outpatient care centers; and federal, state, and local government agencies.

Job Outlook

Employment of LPNs is projected to grow much faster than average. Overall job prospects are expected to be very good, but job outlook varies by industry. The best job opportunities will occur in nursing care facilities and home health-care services.

Employment change. Employment of LPNs is expected to grow by 21 percent between 2008 and 2018, much faster than the average for all occupations, in response to the long-term care needs of an increasing elderly population and the general increase in demand for health-care services.

Demand for LPNs will be driven by the increase in the share of the older population. Older persons have an increased incidence of injury and illness, which will increase their demand for health-care services. In addition, with better medical technology, people are living longer, increasing the demand for long-term health care. Job growth will occur over all health-care settings but especially those that service the geriatric population like nursing care facilities, community care facilities, and home health-care services.

In order to contain health-care costs, many procedures once performed only in hospitals are being performed in physicians' offices and in outpatient care centers, largely because of advances in technology. As a result, the number of LPNs should increase faster in these facilities than in hospitals. Nevertheless, hospitals will continue to demand the services of LPNs and will remain one of the largest employers of these workers.

Job prospects. In addition to projected job growth, job openings will result from replacement needs, as many workers leave the occupation permanently. Very good job opportunities are expected. Rapid employment growth is projected in most health-care industries, with the best job opportunities occurring in nursing care facilities and in home health-care services. There is a perceived inadequacy of available health care in many rural areas, so LPNs willing to locate in rural areas should have good job prospects.

Earnings

Median annual wages of licensed practical and licensed vocational nurses were $39,820 in May 2009. The middle 50 percent earned between $33,920 and $47,220. The lowest 10 percent earned less than $28,890, and the highest 10 percent earned more than $55,090. Median annual wages in the industries employing the largest numbers of licensed practical and licensed vocational nurses in May 2009 were as follows:

Nursing care facilities	$41,310
General medical and surgical hospitals	38,750
Offices of physicians	35,760
Home health-care services	40,370
Community care facilities for the elderly	41,140

Related Occupations

LPNs work closely with people while helping them. Other health-care occupations that work closely with patients include athletic trainers; emergency medical technicians and paramedics; home health aides and personal and home care aides; medical assistants; nursing and psychiatric aides; and registered nurses.

Sources of Additional Information

For information about practical nursing and specialty credentialing, contact the following organizations:

▶ National Association for Practical Nurse Education and Service, Inc., 1940 Duke St., Suite 200, Alexandria, VA 22314. Internet: www.napnes.org

▶ National Federation of Licensed Practical Nurses, Inc., 605 Poole Dr., Garner, NC 27529. Internet: www.nflpn.org

▶ National League for Nursing, 61 Broadway, 33rd Floor, New York, NY 10006. Internet: www.nln.org

Information on the NCLEX-PN licensing exam is available from

▶ National Council of State Boards of Nursing, 111 E. Wacker Dr., Suite 2900, Chicago, IL 60601. Internet: www.ncsbn.org

Lists of state-approved LPN programs are available from individual state boards of nursing.

Line Installers and Repairers

(O*NET 49-9051.00 and 49-9052.00)

Significant Points

- Earnings are higher in this occupation than in many other occupations that do not require postsecondary education.

- A growing number of retirements should create very good job opportunities, especially for electrical power-line installers and repairers.

- Line installers and repairers often work outdoors, and conditions can be hazardous.

- Most positions require several years of long-term on-the-job training.

Nature of the Work

Every time you turn on your lights, call someone on the phone, watch cable television, or access the Internet, you are connecting to complex networks of lines and cables that provide you with electricity and connect you with the outside world. *Line installers and repairers*, also known as *line workers* or *linemen*, are the people who install and maintain these networks.

Because these systems are so complicated, most line workers specialize in certain skill areas; the areas in which they specialize depend on their employers and on what part of the network the workers service. Line workers can be divided into two categories: *electrical power-line installers and repairers*, and *telecommunications line installers and repairers*. Workers can further specialize in either installation or repair. Electrical line workers can also be divided into workers who install and maintain the multistate power grids, and those who work for local utilities. Similarly, telecommunications line workers specialize in telephone, cable, fiber-optic, and other networks. Each of these specializations requires specific skills, and it may be difficult to transfer skills learned in one area to another. In many cases, two or more skills sets will be combined, especially for experienced workers and supervisors.

Electrical power-line installers and repairers install and maintain the power grid—the network of power lines that moves electricity from generating plants to customers. They routinely work with high voltage electricity, which requires extreme caution. This can range from hundreds of thousands of volts for long-distance transmission lines that make up the power grid to less than 10,000 volts for distribution lines that supply electricity to homes and businesses. Line workers who maintain the interstate power grid work in crews that travel to work locations throughout a large region to maintain transmission lines and towers. Workers employed by local utilities work mainly with lower voltage distribution lines, maintaining equipment such as transformers, voltage regulators, and switches. They may also work on traffic lights and streetlights.

In contrast, telecommunications line installers and repairers install and maintain the lines and cables used by local and long-distance telephone services, cable television, the Internet, and other communications networks. These services use a variety of different types of cables, including fiber-optic cables. Unlike metallic cables that carry electricity, fiber-optic cables are made of glass or plastic and transmit signals using light. Working with fiber optics requires special skills, such as splicing and terminating optical cables.

Additionally, workers must be able to test and troubleshoot cables and networking equipment.

Line installers are workers who install new cable. They may work for construction contractors, utilities, or telecommunications companies. They generally start a new job by digging underground trenches or erecting utility poles and towers to carry the wires and cables. They use a variety of construction equipment, including digger derricks, which are trucks equipped with augers and cranes used to dig holes in the ground and set poles in place. Line installers also use trenchers, cable plows, and borers, which are used to cut openings in the earth for the laying of underground cables. Once the infrastructure is in place, line installers string cable along poles and towers or through tunnels and trenches.

Line repairers are employed by utilities and telecommunications companies that maintain existing power and telecommunications lines. Maintenance needs may be identified in a variety of ways, including remote monitoring equipment, inspections by airplane or helicopter, and customer reports of service outages. Workers may also replace aging or outdated equipment. Many of these workers have installation duties in addition to their repair duties.

When a problem is reported, line repairers must identify its cause and fix it. This usually involves testing equipment and replacing it as necessary. In order to work on poles, line installers usually use bucket trucks to elevate themselves to the top of the structure, although all line workers must be adept at climbing poles when necessary. Workers use special safety equipment to keep them from falling when climbing utility poles. Storms and other natural disasters can cause extensive damage to networks of lines. When a connection goes out, line repairers must work quickly to restore service to customers.

Work environment. The work of line installers and repairers can be very physically demanding. Line installers must be comfortable working both at heights and in confined spaces. While bucket trucks have reduced the amount of climbing workers must do, all line workers must be able to climb utility poles and balance while working on them. They must also be able to lift equipment and work in a variety of positions, such as stooping or kneeling. Their work often requires that they drive utility vehicles, travel long distances, and work outdoors under poor weather conditions.

Line workers encounter serious hazards on their jobs and must follow safety procedures to minimize potential danger. They wear safety equipment when entering utility holes and test for the presence of gas before going underground. Electric power-line workers have somewhat hazardous jobs. High-voltage power lines can instantly electrocute a worker who comes in contact with a live cable. When possible, workers arrange for lines to be de-energized and test to make sure that any remaining voltage has been neutralized. When workers must work with live wires, they use electrically insulated protective devices and tools to ensure their safety. Power lines are typically higher than telephone and cable television lines, increasing the risk of severe injury due to falls. To prevent injuries, line installers must use fall-protection equipment when working on poles or towers.

While safety procedures and training have significantly reduced the danger that line workers face, the job is still among the most dangerous jobs in the American economy. Both telecommunications and electrical line workers have relatively high rates of nonfatal occupational injuries. In the early days of electricity, one in four line workers suffered fatal injuries on the job. Today, however, fatalities are extremely rare.

Workers on the interstate power grid or on long-distance communications systems are often required to travel extensively as part of their jobs. Since line installers and repairers fix damage from storms, they may be asked to work long and irregular hours during unpleasant weather. They can expect to frequently be on call and work overtime. When performing normal maintenance and constructing new lines, line installers work more traditional hours.

Training, Other Qualifications, and Advancement

Most line installers and repairers require several years of long-term on-the-job training and some classroom work to become proficient. Formal apprenticeships are common.

Education and training. Most companies require that line installers and repairers have a high school diploma or the equivalent. Employers look for people with basic knowledge of algebra and trigonometry and good reading and writing skills. Technical knowledge of electricity or electronics obtained through military service, vocational programs, or community colleges can be helpful, but it is rarely required for new employees.

Many community colleges offer programs in telecommunications, electronics, or electricity. Some programs work with local companies to offer one-year certificates that emphasize hands-on field work. More advanced two-year associate degree programs provide students with a broader knowledge of the technology used in telecommunications and electrical utilities. They offer courses in electricity, electronics, fiber optics, and microwave transmission.

Line installers and repairers receive most of their training on the job. Electrical line installers and repairers often must complete formal apprenticeships or other employer training programs. These programs, which can last up to five years, combine on-the-job training with formal classroom courses and are sometimes administered jointly by the employer and the union representing the workers. Safety regulations strictly define the training and educational requirements for apprentice electrical line installers, but licensure is not required.

Line installers and repairers working for telephone and cable television companies receive several years of on-the-job training. They also may attend training or take online courses provided by equipment manufacturers, schools, unions, or industry training organizations.

Other qualifications. Physical fitness is important because line workers must be able to climb; lift heavy objects (many employers require applicants to be able to lift at least 50 pounds); and do other physical activity that requires stamina, strength, and coordination. They often must work at a considerable height above the ground, so they cannot be afraid of heights. They must also work underground and in bucket trucks, so they must also be comfortable working in confined spaces. Normal ability to distinguish colors is necessary because wires and cables are often color coded. In addition, line workers usually need commercial driver's licenses to operate company-owned vehicles, and a good driving record is important.

Line installers and repairers must also be able to read instructions, write reports, and solve problems. They should also be mechanically inclined and like working with computers and new technology. Workers often rely on their fellow crew members for their safety, so teamwork is critical. Being able to get along with other people is very important in this job.

Advancement. Entry-level line workers generally begin with classroom training and begin an apprenticeship. Their on-the-job training begins with basic tasks, such as ground work and tree trimming. As they continue to learn additional skills from more experienced workers, they may advance to stringing cable and performing service installations. In time, they advance to more sophisticated maintenance and repair positions in which they are responsible for increasingly larger portions of the network.

After about three to five years of working, qualified line workers reach the journeyman level. A journeyman line worker is no longer considered apprenticed and can do most tasks without supervision. Journeyman line workers may also qualify for positions at other companies. Workers with many years of experience may become first-line supervisors or may advance to trainer positions.

Employment

Line installers and repairers held about 284,900 jobs in 2008. Approximately 171,000 were telecommunications line installers and repairers while the remaining 113,900 were electrical power-line installers and repairers. Nearly all line installers worked for telecommunications companies, including both cable television distribution and telecommunications companies; construction contractors; and electric power generation, transmission, and distribution companies.

Job Outlook

Little or no change in employment is expected. Retirements are expected to create very good job opportunities for new workers, particularly for electrical power-line installers and repairers.

Employment change. Overall employment of line installers and repairers will grow by 2 percent between 2008 and 2018. Despite employment declines in some of the major industries that employ these workers, some growth will occur as population growth and expansion of cities create increased need for power and communications lines. Further, the emphasis of both the electrical power and telecommunications industries on reliability will lead to reinforcement of these networks, which will require more workers.

Employment of telecommunications line installers and repairers will grow by about 1 percent over the 2008–2018 decade, the equivalent of little or no change. As the population grows, installers will continue to be needed to provide new telephone, cable, and Internet services for new developments. Additionally, the exponential growth of the Internet will require more long-distance fiber-optic lines, including interstate and undersea cables.

Employment of electrical power-line installers and repairers is expected to grow by about 4 percent between 2008 and 2018, slower than the average for all occupations. As with telecommunications line installers and repairers, growth will be largely attributable to the growing population and expansion of cities. With each new development, new lines are installed which will require maintenance. In addition, the interstate power grid will continue to grow in complexity to ensure reliability.

Job prospects. Very good job opportunities are expected, especially for electrical power-line installers and repairers. Because of layoffs in the 1990s, more of the electrical power industry is near retirement age than in most industries. This is of special concern for electrical line workers, who must be in good physical shape and cannot necessarily put off retirement in response to incentives.

Projections Data from the National Employment Matrix

Occupational title	SOC Code	Employment, 2008	Projected employment, 2018	Change, 2008–2018	
				Number	Percent
Line installers and repairers 49-9050		284,900	291,600	6,600	2
Electrical power-line installers and repairers 49-9051		113,900	119,000	5,100	4
Telecommunications line installers and repairers ... 49-9052		171,000	172,600	1,600	1

NOTE: Data in this table are rounded.

Telecommunications line workers face a similar demographic challenge. Additionally, technically skilled workers who do not have a college degree have an increasing number of employment opportunities, creating competition among employers. As a result, opportunities for new entrants should be very good.

Earnings

Earnings for line installers and repairers are above the average for occupations that do not require postsecondary education. In May 2009, median annual wages for electrical power-line installers and repairers were $56,670. The middle 50 percent earned between $43,050 and $66,080. The lowest 10 percent earned less than $32,170, and the highest 10 percent earned more than $80,310. Median annual wages in the industries employing the largest numbers of electrical power-line installers and repairers in May 2009 are shown below:

Electric power generation, transmission and
  distribution $59,990
Utility system construction 48,320
Local government 54,990
Building equipment contractors 53,280
Natural gas distribution 82,790

Median annual wages for telecommunications line installers and repairers were $49,110 in May 2009. The middle 50 percent earned between $34,470 and $62,160. The lowest 10 percent earned less than $26,520, and the highest 10 percent earned more than $70,230. Median annual wages in the industries employing the largest numbers of telecommunications line installers and repairers in May 2009 are shown below:

Wired telecommunications carriers $55,430
Building equipment contractors 38,630
Utility system construction 36,340
Cable and other subscription programming 45,140
Other telecommunications 59,790

Many line installers and repairers belong to unions, principally the Communications Workers of America, the International Brotherhood of Electrical Workers, and the Utility Workers Union of America. For these workers, union contracts set wage rates and wage increases and determine the time needed to advance from one wage level to the next.

Good health, education, and vacation benefits are common in the occupation.

Related Occupations

Other workers who install and repair electrical and electronic equipment include electrical and electronics installers and repairers;

electricians; power plant operators, distributors, and dispatchers; and radio and telecommunications equipment installers and repairers.

Sources of Additional Information

For more details about employment opportunities, contact the telephone, cable television, or electrical power companies in your community. For general information and educational resources on line installer and repairer jobs, contact

▶ American Public Power Association, 1875 Connecticut Ave. NW, Suite 1200, Washington, DC 20009-5715. Internet: www.appanet.org

▶ Center for Energy Workforce Development, 701 Pennsylvania Ave. NW, Washington, DC 20004-2696. Internet: www.cewd.org

▶ The Fiber Optic Association, 1119 S Mission Rd. #355, Fallbrook, CA 92028. Internet: www.thefoa.org

▶ International Brotherhood of Electrical Workers, 900 Seventh St. NW, Washington, DC 20001. Internet: www.ibew.org

▶ National Joint Apprenticeship and Training Committee (NJATC), 301 Prince Georges Blvd., Suite D, Upper Marlboro, MD 20774. Internet: www.njatc.org

Loan Officers

(O*NET 13-2072.00)

Significant Points

■ Nearly 9 out of 10 loan officers work for commercial banks, savings institutions, credit unions, and related financial institutions.

■ Educational requirements range from a high school diploma for many loan officers to a bachelor's degree for commercial loan officers; previous banking, lending, or sales experience is highly valued.

■ Good job opportunities are expected for mortgage and consumer loan officers and excellent opportunities are expected for commercial loan officers.

■ Earnings often fluctuate with the number of loans generated, rising substantially when the economy is strong and interest rates are low.

Nature of the Work

Many individuals take out loans to buy a house or car or pay for a college education. Businesses use loans to start companies, purchase inventory, or invest in capital equipment. *Loan officers* facilitate this lending by finding potential clients and helping them to apply for loans. Loan officers gather information to determine the likelihood that individuals and businesses will repay the loan. Loan officers may also provide guidance to prospective borrowers who have problems qualifying for traditional loans. For example, loan officers might determine the most appropriate type of loan for a particular customer and explain specific requirements and restrictions associated with the loan.

Loan officers usually specialize in commercial, consumer, or mortgage loans. Commercial or business loans help companies pay for new equipment or expand operations. Consumer loans include home equity, automobile, and personal loans. Mortgage loans are loans made to purchase real estate or to refinance an existing mortgage.

Loan officers guide clients through the process of applying for a loan. The process begins with the client contacting the bank through a phone call, visiting a branch, or filling out a Web-based loan application. The loan officer obtains basic information from the client about the purpose of the loan and the applicant's ability to pay the loan. The loan officer may need to explain the different types of loans and credit terms available to the applicant. Loan officers answer questions about the process and sometimes assist clients in filling out the application.

After a client completes an application, the loan officer begins the process of analyzing and verifying the information on the application to determine the client's creditworthiness. Often, loan officers can quickly access the client's credit history by using underwriting software that determines if a client is eligible for the loan. When a credit history is not available or when unusual financial circumstances are present, the loan officer may request additional financial information from the client or, in the case of commercial loans, copies of the company's financial statements. Commercial loans are often too complex for a loan officer to rely solely on underwriting software. The variety in companies' financial statements and varying types of collateral require human judgment. Collateral is any asset, such as a factory, house, or car, owned by the borrower that becomes the property of the bank if the loan is not repaid. Loan officers comment on and verify the information of a loan application in a loan file, which is used to analyze whether the prospective loan meets the lending institution's requirements. Loan officers then decide, in consultation with their managers, whether to grant the loan.

Commercial loans are sometimes so large—for example, the loan needed to build a new shopping mall—that a single bank will not lend all of the money. In this case, a commercial loan officer may work with other banks or investment bankers to put together a package of loans from multiple sources to finance the project.

In many instances, loan officers act as salespeople. Commercial loan officers, for example, contact firms to determine their needs for loans. If a firm is seeking new funds, the loan officer will try to persuade the company to obtain the loan from his or her institution. Similarly, mortgage loan officers develop relationships with commercial and residential real estate agencies so that when an individual or firm buys a property, the real estate agent might recommend contacting a specific loan officer for financing.

Some loan officers, called *loan underwriters*, specialize in evaluating a client's creditworthiness and may conduct a financial analysis or other risk assessment.

Other loan officers, referred to as *loan collection officers*, contact borrowers with delinquent loan accounts to help them find a method of repayment to avoid their defaulting on the loan. If a repayment plan cannot be developed, the loan collection officer initiates collateral liquidation, in which the lender seizes the collateral used to secure the loan—a home or car, for example—and sells it to repay the loan.

Work environment. Working as a loan officer usually involves considerable work outside the office. For example, commercial and mortgage loan officers frequently work away from their offices and rely on laptop computers and cellular telephones to keep in contact with their employers and clients. Mortgage loan officers often work out of their home or car, visiting offices or homes of clients to complete loan applications. Commercial loan officers sometimes travel to other cities to prepare complex loan agreements. Consumer loan officers, however, are likely to spend most of their time in an office.

Most loan officers work a standard 40-hour week, but many work longer, depending on the number of clients and the demand for loans. Mortgage loan officers can work especially long hours because they are free to take on as many customers as they choose. Loan officers are especially busy when interest rates are low, causing a surge in loan applications.

Training, Other Qualifications, and Advancement

Loan officers need a high school diploma and receive on-the-job training. Commercial loan officer positions often require a bachelor's degree in finance, economics, or a related field. Previous banking, lending, or sales experience is also highly valued by employers.

Education and training. Loan officer positions generally require a high school degree. Loan officers receive on-the-job training consisting of some formal company-sponsored training and informal training on the job over their first few months of employment. Commercial loan officer positions often require a bachelor's degree in finance, economics, or a related field. Because commercial loan officers analyze the finances of businesses applying for credit, they need to understand business accounting, financial statements, and cash flow analysis. Loan officers often advance to their positions after gaining experience in various other related occupations, such as teller or customer service representative.

Licensure. Recent federal legislation requires that all mortgage loan officers be licensed. Licensing requirements include at least 20 hours of coursework, passing a written exam, passing a background check, and having no felony convictions. There are also continuing education requirements for mortgage loan officers to maintain their licenses. There are currently no specific licensing requirements for other loan officers.

Other qualifications. People planning a career as a loan officer should be good at working with others, confident, and highly motivated. Loan officers must be willing to attend community events as representatives of their employer. Sales ability, good interpersonal and communication skills, and a strong desire to succeed also are important qualities for loan officers. Banks generally require their employees to pass a background check. Most employers also prefer applicants who are familiar with computers and banking and financial software.

Certification and advancement. Capable loan officers may advance to larger branches of their firms or to managerial positions. Some loan officers advance to supervise other loan officers and clerical staff.

Projections Data from the National Employment Matrix

Occupational title	SOC Code	Employment, 2008	Projected employment, 2018	Change, 2008–2018	
				Number	Percent
Loan officers 13-2072		327,800	360,900	33,000	10

NOTE: Data in this table are rounded.

Various banking associations and private schools offer courses and programs for students interested in lending and for experienced loan officers who want to keep their skills current. For example, the Bank Administration Institute, an affiliate of the American Banker's Association, offers the Loan Review Certificate Program for people who review and approve loans.

The Mortgage Bankers Association offers the Certified Mortgage Banker (CMB) designation to loan officers in real estate finance. The association offers three CMB designations—residential, commerce, and master—to candidates who have three years of experience, earn educational credits, and pass an exam. Completion of these courses and programs generally enhances employment and advancement opportunities.

Employment

Loan officers held about 327,800 jobs in 2008. Nearly 9 out of 10 loan officers were employed by commercial banks, savings institutions, credit unions, and related financial institutions. Loan officers are employed throughout the nation, but most work in urban and suburban areas. At some banks, particularly in rural areas, the branch or assistant manager often handles the loan application process.

Job Outlook

Loan officers can expect average employment growth. Good job opportunities should exist for loan officers.

Employment change. Employment of loan officers is projected to grow 10 percent between 2008 and 2018, which is about as fast as the average for all occupations. Employment growth will be driven by economic expansion and population increases, factors that generate demand for loans. Growth will be partially offset by increased automation that speeds the lending process and by the growing use of the Internet to apply for and obtain loans. However, these changes have also reduced the cost and complexity associated with refinancing loans, which could increase the number of loans originated.

The use of automated underwriting software has made the loan evaluation process much simpler than in the past. Underwriting software allows loan officers—particularly loan underwriters—to evaluate many more loans in less time. In addition, the mortgage application process has become highly automated and standardized, a simplification that has enabled mortgage loan vendors to offer their services over the Internet. Online vendors accept loan applications from customers over the Internet and determine which lenders have the best interest rates for particular loans. With this knowledge, customers can go directly to the lending institution, thereby bypassing mortgage loan brokers. Shopping for loans on the Internet is expected to become more common in the future and to slow job growth for loan officers.

Job prospects. Most job openings will result from the need to replace workers who retire or otherwise leave the occupation permanently. Good job opportunities should exist for mortgage and consumer loan officers. College graduates and those with banking, lending, or sales experience should have the best job prospects. Excellent opportunities should exist for commercial loan officers as banks report having a hard time finding qualified candidates.

Job opportunities for loan officers are influenced by the volume of applications, which is determined largely by interest rates and by the overall level of economic activity. Although loans remain a major source of revenue for banks, demand for new loans fluctuates and affects the income and employment opportunities of loan officers. An upswing in the economy or a decline in interest rates often results in a surge in real estate buying and mortgage refinancing, requiring loan officers to work long hours processing applications and inducing lenders to hire additional loan officers. Loan officers often are paid by commission on the value of the loans they place, and when the real estate market slows, they often suffer a decline in earnings and may even be subject to layoffs. The same applies to commercial loan officers, whose workloads increase during good economic times as companies seek to invest more in their businesses. In difficult economic conditions, an increase in the number of delinquent loans results in more demand for loan collection officers.

Earnings

Median annual wages of wage and salary loan officers were $54,880 in May 2009. The middle 50 percent earned between $39,990 and $76,610. The lowest 10 percent earned less than $31,030, while the top 10 percent earned more than $105,330. Median annual wages in the industries employing the largest numbers of loan officers were as follows:

Depository credit intermediation	$54,300
Nondepository credit intermediation	53,600
Activities related to credit intermediation	53,960
Management of companies and enterprises	57,110
Federal executive branch	69,920

The form of compensation for loan officers varies. Most are paid a commission based on the number of loans they originate. Some institutions pay only salaries, while others pay their loan officers a salary plus a commission or bonus based on the number of loans or the performance of the loans that they originated. Loan officers who are paid on commission usually earn more than those who earn only a salary, and those who work for smaller banks generally earn less than those employed by larger institutions.

Earnings often fluctuate with the number of loans generated, rising substantially when the economy is strong and interest rates are low.

Related Occupations

Loan officers help people manage financial assets and secure loans. Occupations that involve similar functions include financial analysts; insurance sales agents; insurance underwriters; loan counselors; personal financial advisors; real estate brokers and sales agents; and securities, commodities, and financial services sales agents.

Sources of Additional Information

Information about a career as a mortgage loan officer can be obtained from

▶ Mortgage Bankers Association, 1331 L St. NW, Washington, DC 20005. Internet: www.mortgagebankers.org

State bankers' associations can furnish specific information about job opportunities in their state. Also, individual banks can supply information about job openings and the activities, responsibilities, and preferred qualifications of their loan officers.

Machine Setters, Operators, and Tenders—Metal and Plastic

(O*NET 51-4021.00, 51-4022.00, 51-4023.00, 51-4031.00, 51-4032.00, 51-4033.00, 51-4034.00, 51-4035.00, 51-4051.00, 51-4052.00, 51-4061.00, 51-4062.00, 51-4071.00, 51-4072.00, 51-4081.00, 51-4191.00, 51-4192.00, 51-4193.00, 51-4194.00, and 51-4199.00)

Significant Points

■ Manufacturing industries employ more than 90 percent of workers.

■ A few weeks of on-the-job training is sufficient for most workers to learn basic machine tending operations, but a year or more is required to become a highly skilled operator or setter.

■ Employment is projected to decline rapidly.

■ Those who can operate multiple machines will have the best opportunities for advancement and for gaining jobs with more long-term potential.

Nature of the Work

Consider the parts of a toaster, such as the metal or plastic housing or the lever that lowers the toast. These parts, and many other metal and plastic products, are produced by machines that are controlled by machine setters, operators, and tenders—metal and plastic. In fact, machine operators in the metalworking and plastics industries play a major role in producing most of the consumer products on which we rely daily.

In general, these workers can be separated into two groups—those who set up machines for operation and those who operate the machines during production. *Machine setters*, or setup workers, prepare the machines prior to production, perform initial test runs producing a part, and may adjust and make minor repairs to the machinery during its operation. *Machine operators and tenders* primarily monitor the machinery during its operation; sometimes they load or unload the machine or make minor adjustments to the controls. Many workers both set up and operate equipment.

Setup workers prepare machines for production runs. Most machines can make a variety of products, and these different items are made by using different inputs or tooling. For instance, a single machine may use different sized tools to produce both large and small wheels for cars. The tools inside the machine must be changed and maintained by setup workers. On some machines, tools may become dull after extended use and must be sharpened. It is common for a setter to remove the tool, use a grinder or file to sharpen the tool, and place the tool back in the machine. New tools are produced by tool and die makers. After installing the tools into a machine, setup workers often produce the initial batch of goods, inspect the products, and turn the machine over to an operator.

Machine operators and tenders are responsible for running machines in manufacturing plants. After a setter prepares a machine for production, an operator observes the machine and the objects it produces. Operators may have to load the machine with materials for production or adjust machine speeds during production. Operators must periodically inspect the parts a machine produces by comparing the parts to a blueprint using rulers, micrometers, and other specialized measuring devices. If the products do not meet design parameters, the machine is shut down; if it is a common, minor error, the operator may fix the machine, but if it is more serious, an industrial machinery mechanic is called to make a repair. (See the statement on industrial machinery mechanics and millwrights elsewhere in this book.) Some machines don't require constant input or attention, so the operator may oversee multiple machines at a given time. In many cases, operators must document production numbers in a notebook or computer database at the end of every hour or shift.

Setters, operators, and tenders usually are identified by the type of machine with which they work. Some examples of specific titles are drilling-machine and boring-machine setup workers, milling-machine and planing-machine tenders, and lathe-machine and turning-machine tool operators. Job duties usually vary with the size of the firm and the type of machine being operated. Although some workers specialize in one or two types of machinery, many are trained to set up or operate a variety of machines. Increasing automation allows machine setters to operate multiple machines simultaneously. In addition, newer production techniques, such as team-oriented "lean" manufacturing, require machine operators to rotate between different machines. Rotating assignments results in more varied work, but also requires workers to have a wider range of skills.

Work environment. Most machine setters, operators, and tenders—metal and plastic work in areas that are clean, well lit, and well ventilated. Nevertheless, stamina is required, because machine operators and setters are on their feet much of the day and may do moderately heavy lifting. Also, these workers operate powerful, high-speed machines that can be dangerous if strict safety rules are not observed. Most operators wear protective equipment, such as safety glasses, earplugs, and steel-toed boots, to protect against flying particles of metal or plastic, noise from the machines, and heavy objects that could be dropped. Many modern machines are enclosed, minimizing the exposure of workers to noise, dust, and lubricants used during machining. Other required safety equipment varies by work setting and machine. For example, those in the plastics industry who work near materials that emit dangerous fumes or dust must wear respirators.

Overtime is common during periods of increased production for most machine setters, operators, and tenders—metal and plastic, but they usually work a 40-hour week. Because many metalworking and plastics working shops operate more than one shift daily, some operators work nights and weekends.

Training, Other Qualifications, and Advancement

A few weeks of on-the-job training are sufficient for most workers to learn basic machine operations, but a year or more is required to become a highly skilled operator or setter.

Education and training. Employers generally prefer workers who have a high school diploma or equivalent for jobs as machine setters, operators, and tenders. Those interested in this occupation can improve their employment opportunities by completing high school courses in shop and blueprint reading and by gaining a working knowledge of the properties of metals and plastics. A solid math background, including courses in algebra, geometry, trigonometry, and basic statistics, also is useful, along with experience working with computers.

Machine operator trainees begin by observing and assisting experienced workers, sometimes in formal training programs or apprenticeships. Under supervision, they may start by supplying materials, starting and stopping the machine, or removing finished products from it. Then they advance to the more difficult tasks performed by operators, such as adjusting feed speeds, changing cutting tools, or inspecting a finished product for defects. Eventually, some develop the skills and experience to set up machines and assist newer operators.

The complexity of the equipment largely determines the time required to become an operator. Most operators learn the basic machine operations and functions in a few weeks, but a year or more may be needed to become skilled operators or to advance to the more highly skilled job of setter. Although many operators learn on the job, some community colleges and other educational institutions offer courses and certifications in operating metal and plastics machines. In addition to providing on-the-job training, some employers send promising machine operators to classes. Other employers prefer to hire workers who have completed, or currently are enrolled in, a training program.

Setters or technicians often plan the sequence of work, make the first production run, and determine which adjustments need to be made. As a result, these workers need a thorough knowledge of the machinery and of the products being manufactured. Strong analytical abilities are particularly important for this job. Some companies have formal training programs for operators and setters, which often combine classroom instruction with on-the-job training.

Other qualifications. As the machinery in manufacturing plants becomes more complex and with changes to shop-floor organization that require more teamwork among employees, employers increasingly look for persons with good communication and interpersonal skills. Mechanical aptitude, manual dexterity, and experience working with machinery also are helpful.

Certification and advancement. Job opportunities and advancement can be enhanced by becoming certified in a particular machine skill. There are many trade groups that offer certification for machine operators and setup workers, and certifications vary greatly depending upon the skill level involved. Certifications may allow operators and setters to switch jobs more easily because they can prove their skills to a potential employer.

Advancement usually takes the form of higher pay and a wider range of responsibilities. With experience and expertise, workers can become trainees for more highly skilled positions; for instance, it is common for machine operators to move into setup or

machinery maintenance positions. Setup workers may also move into maintenance, machinist, or tool and die maker roles. (See the job descriptions for industrial machinery mechanics and millwrights and machinists elsewhere in this book.) Skilled workers with good communication and analytical skills can move into supervisory positions.

Employment

Machine setters, operators, and tenders, metal and plastic held about 1.0 million jobs in 2008. About 9 out of 10 jobs were found in manufacturing—primarily in fabricated metal products, plastics and rubber products, primary metal, machinery, and motor vehicle parts manufacturing.

Job Outlook

Employment is expected to decline rapidly. Those who can operate multiple machines will have the best opportunities for advancement and for gaining jobs with more long-term potential.

Employment change. Employment in the various machine setter, operator, and tender occupations is expected to decline rapidly by 13 percent from 2008 to 2018. Employment will be affected by technological advances, changing demand for the goods they produce, foreign competition, and the reorganization of production processes.

One of the most important factors influencing employment change in this occupation is the implementation of labor-saving machinery. Many firms are adopting new technologies, such as computer-controlled machine tools and robots in order to improve quality, lower production costs, and remain competitive. The switch to computer-controlled machinery requires the employment of computer control programmers and operators instead of machine setters, operators, and tenders. The lower-skilled manual machine tool operators and tenders jobs are more likely to be eliminated by these new technologies, because the functions they perform may be more effectively completed with computer-controlled machinery.

The demand for machine setters, operators, and tenders—metal and plastic is also affected by the demand for the parts they produce. Both the plastic and metal manufacturing industries face stiff foreign competition that is limiting the demand for domestically produced parts. Some domestic firms have outsourced their production to foreign countries, which has limited employment of machine setters and operators. Another way domestic manufacturers compete with low-wage foreign competition is by increasing their use of automated systems, which can make manufacturing establishments more competitive by improving their productivity. This increased automation also limits employment growth.

Job prospects. Despite the overall projected employment decline, a number of machine setter, operator, and tender jobs will become available because of an expected surge in retirements, primarily baby boomers, in the coming years. Workers with a thorough background in machine operations, certifications from industry associations, exposure to a variety of machines, and a good working knowledge of the properties of metals and plastics will be better able to adjust to the changing environment. In addition, new shop-floor arrangements will reward workers with good basic mathematics and reading skills, good communication skills, and the ability and willingness to learn new tasks. As workers adapt to team-oriented production methods, those who can operate multiple machines will have the best opportunities for advancement and for gaining jobs with more long-term potential.

Projections Data from the National Employment Matrix

Occupational title	SOC Code	Employment, 2008	Projected employment, 2018	Change, 2008–2018	
				Number	Percent
Machine setters, operators, and tenders—metal and plastic .... —		1,028,400	899,000	–129,400	–13
Forming machine setters, operators, and tenders, metal and plastic 51-4020		153,200	137,700	–15,500	–10
Extruding and drawing machine setters, operators, and tenders, metal and plastic 51-4021		90,700	86,000	–4,700	–5
Forging machine setters, operators, and tenders, metal and plastic 51-4022		28,100	22,600	–5,500	–19
Rolling machine setters, operators, and tenders, metal and plastic 51-4023		34,400	29,000	–5,300	–16
Machine tool cutting setters, operators, and tenders, metal and plastic.................................. 51-4030		444,300	368,400	–75,900	–17
Cutting, punching, and press machine setters, operators, and tenders, metal and plastic 51-4031		236,800	203,500	–33,300	– 14
Drilling and boring machine tool setters, operators, and tenders, metal and plastic 51-4032		33,000	24,200	–8,900	–27
Grinding, lapping, polishing, and buffing machine tool setters, operators, and tenders, metal and plastic 51-4033		92,700	77,900	–14,800	–16
Lathe and turning machine tool setters, operators, and tenders, metal and plastic 51-4034		55,700	40,800	–14,900	–27
Milling and planing machine setters, operators, and tenders, metal and plastic 51-4035		26,200	22,000	–4,100	–16
Metal furnace and kiln operators and tenders........... 51-4050		34,100	31,000	–3,100	–9
Metal-refining furnace operators and tenders 51-4051		19,100	17,400	–1,600	–9
Pourers and casters, metal............................... 51-4052		15,100	13,600	–1,500	–10
Model makers and patternmakers, metal and plastic.. 51-4060		17,100	16,100	–1,000	–6
Model makers, metal and plastic...................... 51-4061		10,100	9,500	–600	–6
Patternmakers, metal and plastic..................... 51-4062		7,000	6,600	–400	–6
Molders and molding machine setters, operators, and tenders, metal and plastic............................. 51-4070		158,800	150,700	–8,200	–5
Foundry mold and coremakers 51-4071		15,000	13,200	–1,800	–12
Molding, coremaking, and casting machine setters, operators, and tenders, metal and plastic 51-4072		143,800	137,400	–6,400	–4
Multiple machine tool setters, operators, and tenders, metal and plastic.................................. 51-4081		86,000	73,400	–12,600	–15
Miscellaneous metalworkers and plastic workers 51-4190		134,900	121,800	–13,100	–10
Heat treating equipment setters, operators, and tenders, metal and plastic...................... 51-4191		23,200	20,700	–2,500	–11
Lay-out workers, metal and plastic.................... 51-4192		8,300	7,300	–1,000	–12
Plating and coating machine setters, operators, and tenders, metal and plastic 51-4193		39,500	34,600	–4,900	–12
Tool grinders, filers, and sharpeners.................. 51-4194		18,800	17,400	–1,400	–7
All other metal workers and plastic workers........ 51-4199		45,000	41,700	–3,300	–7

NOTE: Data in this table are rounded.

Earnings

Wages for machine operators can vary by size of the company, union status, industry, and skill level and experience of the operator. Also, temporary employees, who are being hired in greater numbers, usually get paid less than permanently employed workers. The median hourly wages in May 2009 for a variety of machine setters, operators, and tenders—metal and plastic were as follows:

Model makers, metal and plastic...........................$19.82
Patternmakers, metal and plastic...........................17.54
Metal-refining furnace operators and tenders...........18.22
Lay-out workers, metal and plastic........................17.77
Rolling machine setters, operators, and
    tenders, metal and plastic...............................17.03
Milling and planing machine setters, operators,
    and tenders, metal and plastic...........................16.69
Lathe and turning machine tool setters,
    operators, and tenders, metal and plastic............16.29
Pourers and casters, metal...................................16.24
Heat treating equipment setters, operators,
    and tenders, metal and plastic...........................15.70
Tool grinders, filers, and sharpeners.......................16.00
Forging machine setters, operators, and
    tenders, metal and plastic...............................15.62
Multiple machine tool setters, operators, and
    tenders, metal and plastic...............................15.01
Drilling and boring machine tool setters,
    operators, and tenders, metal and plastic............15.13
Extruding and drawing machine setters, operators,
    and tenders, metal and plastic...........................14.94
Grinding, lapping, polishing, and buffing
    machine tool setters, operators, and tenders,
    metal and plastic 14.56
Foundry mold and coremakers 14.41
Plating and coating machine setters, operators,
    and tenders, metal and plastic...........................13.75
Cutting, punching, and press machine setters,
    operators, and tenders, metal and plastic............14.02
Molding, coremaking, and casting machine setters,
    operators, and tenders, metal and plastic............13.40
Metal workers and plastic workers, all other............15.46

Related Occupations

Workers whose duties are closely related to machine setters, operators, and tenders—metal and plastic include assemblers and fabricators; computer control programmers and operators; machinists; painting and coating workers, except construction and maintenance; tool and die makers; and welding, soldering, and brazing workers.

Sources of Additional Information

For general information about careers and companies employing metal machine setters, operators, and tenders, contact

▸ Fabricators and Manufacturers Association, 833 Featherstone Rd., Rockford, IL 61107 Internet: www.fmanet.org

Machinists

(O*NET 51-4041.00)

Significant Points

■ Machinists learn their job skills in apprenticeship programs, informally on the job, in vocational high schools, and in community or technical colleges.

■ Many entrants previously have worked as machine setters, operators, or tenders.

■ Employment is projected to decline slowly, but job opportunities are expected to be good.

Nature of the Work

Machinists use machine tools, such as lathes, milling machines, and grinders, to produce precision metal parts. Although they may produce large quantities of one part, precision machinists often produce small batches or one-of-a-kind items. They use their knowledge of the working properties of metals and their skill with machine tools to plan and carry out the operations needed to make machined products that meet precise specifications. The parts that machinists make range from bolts to automobile pistons.

Machinists first review electronic or written blueprints or specifications for a job before they machine a part. Next, they calculate where to cut or bore into the workpiece—the piece of steel, aluminum, titanium, plastic, silicon, or any other material that is being shaped. They determine how fast to feed the workpiece into the machine and how much material to remove. They then select tools and materials for the job, plan the sequence of cutting and finishing operations, and mark the workpiece to show where cuts should be made.

After this layout work is completed, machinists perform the necessary machining operations. They position the workpiece on the machine tool—drill press, lathe, milling machine, or other type of machine—set the controls, and make the cuts. During the machining process, they must constantly monitor the feed rate and speed of the machine. Machinists also ensure that the workpiece is properly lubricated and cooled, because the machining of metal products generates a significant amount of heat. The temperature of the workpiece is a key concern, because most metals expand when heated; machinists must adjust the size of their cuts relative to the temperature.

During the cutting process, machinists detect problems by listening for specific sounds—for example, that of a dull cutting tool or excessive vibration. Dull cutting tools are removed and replaced. Cutting speeds are adjusted to compensate for harmonic vibrations, which can decrease the accuracy of cuts, particularly on newer high-speed spindles and lathes. After the work is completed, machinists use both simple and highly sophisticated measuring tools to check the accuracy of their work against the blueprints.

Some machinists, often called *production machinists*, may produce large quantities of one part, especially parts requiring the use of complex operations and great precision. Many modern machine tools are computer numerically controlled (CNC). CNC machines, following a computer program, control the cutting tool speed, change dull tools, and perform all necessary cuts to create a part. Frequently, machinists work with computer control programmers to determine how the automated equipment will cut a part. (See the section on computer control programmers and operators elsewhere in this book.) The machinist determines the cutting path, speed of the cut and the feed rate, and the programmer converts path, speed, and feed information into a set of instructions for the CNC machine tool. Many machinists must be able to use both manual and computer-controlled machinery in their job.

Because most machinists train in CNC programming, they may write basic programs themselves and often modify programs in response to problems encountered during test runs. Modifications, called offsets, not only fix problems, but they also improve efficiency by reducing manufacturing time and tool wear. After the production process is designed, computer control operators implement it by performing relatively simple and repetitive operations.

Some manufacturing techniques employ automated parts loaders, automatic tool changers, and computer controls, allowing machines to operate without anyone present. One production machinist, working 8 hours a day, might monitor equipment, replace worn cutting tools, check the accuracy of parts being produced, adjust offsets, and perform other tasks on several CNC machines that operate 24 hours a day. In the off-hours, during what is known as "lights out manufacturing," which is the practice of running machines while the operators are not present, a factory may need only a few workers to monitor the entire factory.

Maintenance machinists repair or make new parts for existing machinery. After an industrial machinery mechanic or maintenance worker discovers the broken part of a machine, he or she gives the broken part to the machinist. (See the section on industrial machinery mechanics and millwrights elsewhere in this book.) To replace broken parts, maintenance machinists refer to blueprints and perform the same machining operations that were needed to create the original part. While production machinists are concentrated in a few industries, maintenance machinists work in many manufacturing industries.

Because the technology of machining is changing rapidly, machinists must learn to operate a wide range of machines. Some newer machines use lasers, water jets, or electrified wires to cut the workpiece. While some of the computer controls are similar to other machine tools, machinists must understand the unique cutting properties of these different machines. As engineers create new types of machine tools and new materials to machine, machinists must constantly learn new machining properties and techniques.

Work environment. Today, many machine shops are relatively clean, well lit, and ventilated. Computer-controlled machines often are partially or totally enclosed, minimizing the exposure of workers to noise, debris, and the lubricants used to cool workpieces during machining. Nevertheless, working around machine tools presents certain dangers, and workers must follow safety precautions. Machinists wear protective equipment, such as safety glasses to shield against bits of flying metal, and earplugs to dampen machinery noise. They also must exercise caution when handling hazardous coolants and lubricants, although many common water-based lubricants present little hazard. The job requires stamina, because machinists stand most of the day and, at times, may need to lift moderately heavy workpieces. Modern factories use autoloaders and overhead cranes to reduce heavy lifting.

Many machinists work a 40-hour week. Evening and weekend shifts are becoming more common, as companies extend hours of operation to make better use of expensive machines. However, this trend is somewhat offset by lights-out manufacturing that uses fewer

machinists and the use of machine operators for less desirable shifts. Overtime work is common during peak production periods.

Training, Other Qualifications, and Advancement

Machinists train in apprenticeship programs, vocational schools, or community or technical colleges, or informally on the job. Many entrants previously have worked as machine setters, operators, or tenders.

Education and training. There are many different ways to become a skilled machinist. Many entrants previously have worked as machine setters, operators, or tenders. In high school, students should take math courses, especially trigonometry and geometry and, if available, courses in blueprint reading, metalworking, and drafting. Some advanced positions, such as those in the aircraft manufacturing industry, require the use of advanced applied calculus and physics. Due to the increasing use of computer-controlled machinery, basic computer skills are needed before entering a training program. After high school, some machinists learn entirely on the job, but most acquire their skills in a mix of classroom and on-the-job training. Formal apprenticeship programs, typically sponsored by a union or manufacturer, are an excellent way to learn the job of machinist, but are often hard to get into. Apprentices usually must have a high school diploma, GED, or the equivalent; and most have taken algebra and trigonometry classes.

Apprenticeship programs consist of paid shop training and related classroom instruction lasting up to four years. In shop training, apprentices work almost full time and are supervised by an experienced machinist, while learning to operate various machine tools. Classroom instruction includes math, physics, materials science, blueprint reading, mechanical drawing, and quality and safety practices. In addition, as machine shops have increased their use of computer-controlled equipment, training in the operation and programming of CNC machine tools has become essential. Apprenticeship classes are often taught in cooperation with local community colleges or vocational-technical schools. A growing number of machinists are learning the trade through two-year associate degree programs at community or technical colleges. Graduates of these programs still need significant on-the-job experience as machinists' assistants before they are fully qualified.

Certification and other qualifications. People interested in becoming machinists should be mechanically inclined, have good problem-solving abilities, be able to work independently, and be able to do highly accurate work (tolerances may reach 50/1,000,000ths of an inch) that requires concentration and physical effort. Experience working with machine tools is helpful. In fact, many entrants have worked as machine setters, operators, or tenders.

To boost the skill level of machinists and to create a more uniform standard of competency, a number of training facilities, state apprenticeship boards, and colleges offer certification programs. Completing a recognized certification program provides a machinist with better career opportunities and helps employers better judge the abilities of new hires. Journeyworker certification can be obtained from state apprenticeship boards after completing an apprenticeship; this certification is recognized by many employers and often leads to better career opportunities.

As new automation is introduced, machinists normally receive additional training to update their skills. This training usually is

Projections Data from the National Employment Matrix

Occupational title	SOC Code	Employment, 2008	Projected employment, 2018	Change, 2008–2018	
				Number	Percent
Machinists	51-4041	421,500	402,200	−19,300	−5

NOTE: Data in this table are rounded.

provided by a representative of the equipment manufacturer or a local technical school. Some employers offer tuition reimbursement for job-related courses.

Advancement. Machinists can advance in several ways. Experienced machinists may become CNC programmers, tool and die makers, or mold makers, or be promoted to supervisory or administrative positions in their firms. A few open their own machine shops.

Employment

Machinists held about 421,500 jobs in 2008. About 78 percent of machinists work in manufacturing industries, such as machine shops and machinery, motor vehicle and parts, aerospace products and parts, and other transportation equipment manufacturing. Maintenance machinists work in most industries that use production machinery.

Job Outlook

Although employment of machinists is projected to decline slowly, job prospects are expected to be good.

Employment change. Employment of machinists is projected to decline by 5 percent over the 2008–2018 decade, due to rising productivity among these workers and strong foreign competition in the manufacture of goods. Machinists are becoming more efficient as a result of the expanded use of and improvements in technologies such as CNC machine tools, autoloaders, high-speed machining, and lights out manufacturing. This allows fewer machinists to accomplish the same amount of work. Technology is not expected to affect the employment of machinists as significantly as that of some other production workers, however, because machinists monitor and maintain many automated systems. Due to modern production techniques, employers prefer workers, such as machinists, who have a wide range of skills and are capable of performing almost any task in a machine shop.

Job prospects. Despite the projected decline in employment, job opportunities for machinists should continue to be good, as employers value the wide-ranging skills of these workers. Also, many young people with the necessary educational and personal qualifications needed to become machinists prefer to attend college or may not wish to enter production occupations. Therefore, the number of workers learning to be machinists is expected to be less than the number of job openings arising each year from the need to replace experienced machinists who retire or transfer to other occupations. Employment levels in this occupation are influenced by economic cycles—as the demand for machined goods falls, machinists involved in production may be laid off or forced to work fewer hours.

Earnings

Median hourly wages of machinists were $18.10 in May 2009. The middle 50 percent earned between $14.27 and $22.60. The lowest 10 percent earned less than $11.34, while the top 10 percent earned more than $27.52. Median hourly wages in the manufacturing industries employing the largest number of machinists were as follows:

Machine shops; turned product; and screw,
nut, and bolt manufacturing $17.34
Employment services 14.25
Aerospace product and parts manufacturing 20.26
Metalworking machinery manufacturing 18.44
Motor vehicle parts manufacturing 17.19

Apprentices earn much less than experienced machinists, but earnings increase quickly as they improve their skills. Also, most employers pay for apprentices' training classes.

Related Occupations

Machinists share similar duties with these other manufacturing occupations: computer control programmers and operators; industrial machinery mechanics and millwrights; machine setters, operators, and tenders—metal and plastic; and tool and die makers.

Sources of Additional Information

For information on training and new technology for machinists, contact

▸ Fabricators and Manufacturers Association, 833 Featherstone Rd., Rockford, IL 61107 Internet: www.fmanet.org

Information on the registered apprenticeship system with links to state apprenticeship programs may also be found on the U.S. Department of Labor website: www.doleta.gov/OA/eta_default. cfm. Apprenticeship information is also available from the U.S. Department of Labor toll-free helpline: (877) 872-5627.

Maintenance and Repair Workers, General

(O*NET 49-9042.00)

Significant Points

■ General maintenance and repair workers are employed in almost every industry.

■ Many workers learn their skills informally on the job; obtaining certification may result in better advancement opportunities in higher-paying industries.

■ Job growth and turnover in this large occupation should result in excellent job opportunities, especially for people with experience in maintenance and related fields.

Nature of the Work

Most craft workers specialize in one kind of work, such as plumbing or carpentry. *General maintenance and repair workers*, however, have skills in many different crafts. They repair and maintain machines, mechanical equipment, and buildings and work on plumbing, electrical, and air-conditioning and heating systems. They build partitions; make plaster or drywall repairs; and fix or paint roofs, windows, doors, floors, woodwork, and other parts of building structures. They also maintain and repair specialized equipment and machinery found in cafeterias, laundries, hospitals, stores, offices, and factories.

Typical duties include troubleshooting and fixing faulty electrical switches, repairing air-conditioning motors, and unclogging drains. New buildings sometimes have computer-controlled systems that allow maintenance workers to make adjustments in building settings and monitor for problems from a central location. For example, they can remotely control light sensors that turn off lights automatically after a set amount of time or identify a broken ventilation fan that needs to be replaced.

General maintenance and repair workers inspect and diagnose problems and determine the best way to correct them, frequently checking blueprints, repair manuals, and parts catalogs. They obtain supplies and repair parts from distributors or storerooms. Using common hand and power tools such as screwdrivers, saws, drills, wrenches, and hammers, as well as specialized equipment and electronic testing devices, these workers replace or fix worn or broken parts, where necessary, or make adjustments to correct malfunctioning equipment and machines.

General maintenance and repair workers also perform routine preventive maintenance and ensure that machines continue to run smoothly, building systems operate efficiently, and the physical condition of buildings does not deteriorate. Following a checklist, they may inspect drives, motors, and belts; check fluid levels; replace filters; and perform other maintenance actions. Maintenance and repair workers keep records of their work.

Employees in small establishments, where they are often the only maintenance worker, make all repairs, except for very large or difficult jobs. In larger establishments, duties may be limited to the maintenance of everything in a single workshop or a particular area.

Work environment. General maintenance and repair workers often carry out many different tasks in a single day, at any number of locations, including indoor and outdoor. They may work inside a single building, such as a hotel or hospital, or be responsible for the maintenance of many buildings, such as those in an apartment complex or college campus. They may have to stand for long periods, lift heavy objects, and work in uncomfortably hot or cold environments, in awkward and cramped positions, or on ladders. Those employed in small establishments often work with only limited supervision. Those in larger establishments frequently work under the direct supervision of an experienced worker. Some tasks put workers at risk of electrical shock, burns, falls, cuts, and bruises. Data from the U.S. Bureau of Labor Statistics show that full-time general maintenance workers experienced a work-related injury and illness rate that was much higher than the national average. Most general maintenance workers work a 40-hour week. Some work evening, night, or weekend shifts or are on call for emergency repairs.

Training, Other Qualifications, and Advancement

Many general maintenance and repair workers learn their skills informally on the job as helpers to other repairers or to carpenters, electricians, and other construction workers. Certification is available for entry-level workers, as well as experienced workers seeking advancement.

Education and training. General maintenance and repair workers often learn their skills informally on the job. They start as helpers, watching and learning from skilled maintenance workers. Helpers begin by performing simple jobs, such as fixing leaky faucets and replacing light bulbs, and progress to more difficult tasks, such as overhauling machinery or building walls. Some learn their skills by working as helpers to other types of repair or construction workers, including machinery repairers, carpenters, or electricians.

Several months of on-the-job training are required to become fully qualified, depending on the skill level required. Some jobs require a year or more to become fully qualified. Because a growing number of new buildings rely on computers to control their systems, general maintenance and repair workers may need basic computer skills, such as how to log onto a central computer system and navigate through a series of menus. Companies that install computer-controlled equipment usually provide on-site training for general maintenance and repair workers.

Many employers prefer to hire high school graduates. High school courses in mechanical drawing, electricity, woodworking, blueprint reading, science, mathematics, and computers are useful. Because of the wide variety of tasks performed by maintenance and repair workers, technical education is an important part of their training. Maintenance and repair workers often need to do work that involves electrical, plumbing, and heating and air-conditioning systems, or painting and roofing tasks. Although these basic tasks may not require a license to do the work, a good working knowledge of many repair and maintenance tasks is required. Many maintenance and repair workers learn some of these skills in high school shop classes and postsecondary trade or vocational schools or community colleges.

Licensure. Licensing requirements vary by state and locality. In some cases, workers may need to be licensed in a particular specialty such as electrical or plumbing work.

Other qualifications. Technical and mechanical aptitude, the ability to use shop mathematics, and manual dexterity are important attributes. Good health is necessary because the job involves much walking, climbing, standing, reaching, and heavy lifting. Difficult jobs require problem-solving ability, and many positions require the ability to work without direct supervision.

Certification and advancement. The International Management Institute (IMI) offers certification for three levels of competence, focusing on a broad range of topics, including blueprints, mathematics, basic electricity, piping systems, landscape maintenance, and troubleshooting skills. The lowest level of certification is Certified Maintenance Technician, the second level is Certified Maintenance Professional, and the highest level of certification is Certified Maintenance Manager. To become certified, applicants must meet several prerequisites and pass a comprehensive written examination.

Many general maintenance and repair workers in large organizations advance to maintenance supervisor or become craftworkers such as electricians, heating and air-conditioning mechanics, or

Projections Data from the National Employment Matrix

Occupational title	SOC Code	Employment, 2008	Projected employment, 2018	Change, 2008–2018	
				Number	Percent
Maintenance and repair workers, general..................49-9042		1,361,300	1,509,200	147,900	11

NOTE: Data in this table are rounded.

plumbers. Within small organizations, promotion opportunities may be limited. Obtaining IMI certification may lead to better advancement opportunities in higher paying industries.

Employment

General maintenance and repair workers held about 1.4 million jobs in 2008. They were employed in almost every industry. Around 18 percent worked in manufacturing industries, while about 11 percent worked for government. Others worked for wholesale and retail firms and for real estate firms that operate office and apartment buildings.

Job Outlook

Average employment growth is expected. Job growth and the need to replace those who leave this large occupation should result in excellent job opportunities, especially for those with experience in maintenance and related fields.

Employment change. Employment of general maintenance and repair workers is expected to grow 11 percent during the 2008–2018 decade, about as fast as the average for all occupations. Employment is related to the number of buildings—for example, office and apartment buildings, stores, schools, hospitals, hotels, and factories—and the amount of equipment needing maintenance and repair. One factor limiting job growth is that computers allow buildings to be monitored more efficiently, partially reducing the need for workers.

Job prospects. Job opportunities should be excellent, especially for those with experience in maintenance or related fields. Those who obtain certification will also face excellent opportunities. General maintenance and repair is a large occupation, generating many job openings due to growth and the need to replace those who leave the occupation. Many job openings are expected to result from the retirement of experienced maintenance workers over the next decade.

Earnings

Median hourly wages of general maintenance and repair workers were $16.65 in May 2009. The middle 50 percent earned between $12.76 and $21.62. The lowest 10 percent earned less than $10.00, and the highest 10 percent earned more than $26.72. Median hourly wages in the industries employing the largest numbers of general maintenance and repair workers in May 2009 are shown in the following tabulation:

Lessors of real estate...	$14.37
Local government...	17.62
Activities related to real estate............................	14.91
Traveler accommodation......................................	13.27
Elementary and secondary schools	17.72

About 15 percent of general maintenance and repair workers are members of unions, including the American Federation of State, County, and Municipal Employees and the United Auto Workers.

Related Occupations

Some duties of general maintenance and repair workers are similar to those of boilermakers; carpenters; electricians; heating, air-conditioning, and refrigeration mechanics and installers; and plumbers, pipelayers, pipefitters, and steamfitters.

Other, more specific, duties are similar to those of coin, vending, and amusement machine servicers and repairers; electrical and electronics installers and repairers; electronic home entertainment equipment installers and repairers; and radio and telecommunications equipment installers and repairers.

Sources of Additional Information

Information about job opportunities may be obtained from local employers and local offices of the state.

For information related to training and certification, contact

▸ International Maintenance Institute, P.O. Box 751896, Houston, TX 77275-1896. Internet: www.imionline.org

▸ Society for Maintenance and Reliability Professionals, 8400 Westpark Dr., 2nd Floor, McLean, VA 22102-3570. Internet: www.smrp.org/

Material Moving Occupations

(O*NET 53-7011.00, 53-7021.00, 53-7031.00, 53-7032.00, 53-7033.00, 53-7041.00, 53-7051.00, 53-7061.00, 53-7062.00, 53-7063.00, 53-7064.00, 53-7071.00, 53-7072.00, 53-7073.00, 53-7081.00, 53-7111.00, 53-7121.00, and 53-7199.00)

Significant Points

■ Despite little or no change in employment, numerous job openings will be created by the need to replace workers who leave this very large occupation.

■ Most jobs require little work experience or training.

■ Pay is low for many positions, and the seasonal nature of the work may reduce earnings.

Nature of the Work

Think about a common bicycle; over the course of its creation many workers have to transport a variety of materials to get it to your local store. First, the raw metal must be produced, either from a mine where an *excavator operator* digs into the earth to gather rocks with the proper minerals and places them on a conveyor operated by a *conveyor tender*; or by a *recyclable material collector* that picks up unwanted metal household goods. Next, the metal is refined in a foundry, at which point a *crane operator* or *hoist and winch operator* may place it on a trailer for shipping. After arriving at a factory, an *industrial truck operator* unloads the metal and a *machine feeder* loads it into a machine for production. After being assembled, the bicycle is placed into a box by a *hand packager* and then moved into a tractor trailer by a *truck loader*. Many products, like this bicycle, are handled by a variety of workers because, even with the use of machinery, moving goods and materials around work sites still requires significant human effort. Material moving workers are generally categorized into two groups—operators, who control the machines that move materials, and laborers, who move materials by hand.

Operators use machinery to move construction materials, earth, petroleum products, and other heavy materials. Generally, they move materials over short distances—around construction sites, factories, or warehouses. Some move materials onto or off of trucks and ships. Operators control equipment by moving levers, wheels, or foot pedals; operating switches; or turning dials. They also may set up and inspect equipment, make adjustments, and perform minor maintenance or repairs.

Laborers and hand material movers move freight, stock, or other materials by hand; clean vehicles, machinery, and other equipment; feed materials into or remove materials from machines or equipment; and pack or package products and materials.

Industrial truck and tractor operators drive and control industrial trucks or tractors that move materials around warehouses, storage yards, factories, construction sites, or other work sites. A typical industrial truck, often called a forklift or lift truck, has a hydraulic lifting mechanism and forks for moving heavy and large objects. Industrial truck and tractor operators also may operate tractors that pull trailers loaded with materials, goods, or equipment within factories and warehouses or around outdoor storage areas.

Excavating and loading machine and dragline operators tend or operate machinery equipped with scoops, shovels, or buckets to dig and load sand, gravel, earth, or similar materials into trucks or onto conveyors. These machines are primarily used in the construction and mining industries. *Dredge operators* excavate waterways, removing sand, gravel, rock, or other materials from harbors, lakes, rivers, and streams. Dredges are used primarily to maintain navigable channels but also are used to restore wetlands and other aquatic habitats; reclaim land; and create and maintain beaches. *Underground mining loading machine operators* load coal, ore, or rock into shuttles and mine cars or onto conveyors. Loading equipment may include power shovels, hoisting engines equipped with cable-drawn scrapers or scoops, and machines equipped with gathering arms and conveyors.

Crane and tower operators use mechanical boom and cable or tower and cable equipment to lift and move materials, machinery, and other heavy objects. Operators extend and retract horizontally mounted booms and lower and raise hooks attached to load lines. Most operators are guided by other workers using hand signals or a radio. Operators position loads from an onboard console or from a remote console at the site. Although crane and tower operators are noticeable at office building and other construction sites, the biggest group works in manufacturing industries that use heavy, bulky materials. Operators also work at major ports, loading and unloading large containers on and off ships. *Hoist and winch operators* control movement of cables, cages, and platforms to move workers and materials for manufacturing, logging, and other industrial operations. They work in positions such as derrick operators and hydraulic boom operators. Many hoist and winch operators are found in manufacturing or construction industries.

Pump operators tend, control, and operate pump and manifold systems that transfer gases, oil, or other materials to vessels or equipment. They maintain the equipment and regulate the flow of materials according to a schedule set up by petroleum engineers or production supervisors. *Gas compressor and gas pumping station operators* operate steam, gas, electric motor, or internal combustion engine-driven compressors. They transmit, compress, or recover gases, such as butane, nitrogen, hydrogen, and natural gas. *Wellhead pumpers* operate pumps and auxiliary equipment to produce flows of oil or gas from extraction sites.

Tank car, truck, and ship loaders operate ship-loading and ship-unloading equipment, conveyors, hoists, and other specialized material-handling equipment such as railroad tank car-unloading equipment. They may gauge or sample shipping tanks and test them for leaks. *Conveyor operators and tenders* control and tend conveyor systems that move materials to or from stockpiles, processing stations, departments, or vehicles. *Shuttle car operators* run diesel or electric-powered shuttle cars in underground mines, transporting materials to mine cars or conveyors.

Laborers and hand freight, stock, and material movers manually move materials and perform other unskilled, general labor. These workers move freight, stock, and other materials to and from storage and production areas, loading docks, delivery vehicles, ships, and containers. Their specific duties vary by industry and work setting. In factories, they may move raw materials or finished goods between loading docks, storage areas, and work areas, as well as sort materials and supplies and prepare them according to their work orders. Specialized workers within this group include baggage and cargo handlers—who work in transportation industries—and truck loaders and unloaders.

Hand packers and packagers manually pack, package, or wrap a variety of materials. They may label cartons, inspect items for defects, stamp information on products, keep records of items packed, and stack packages on loading docks. This group also includes order fillers, who pack materials for shipment, as well as gift wrappers. In grocery stores, they may bag groceries, carry packages to customers' cars, and return shopping carts to designated areas.

Machine feeders and offbearers feed materials into or remove materials from equipment or machines tended by other workers.

Cleaners of vehicles and equipment clean machinery, vehicles, storage tanks, pipelines, and similar equipment using water and cleaning agents, vacuums, hoses, brushes, or cloths.

Refuse and recyclable material collectors gather refuse and recyclables from homes and businesses into their trucks for transport to a dump, landfill, or recycling center. They lift and empty garbage cans or recycling bins by hand or, using hydraulic lifts on their vehicles, pick up and empty dumpsters. Some in this group drive the large garbage or recycling truck along the scheduled routes.

(For information on operating engineers; paving, surfacing, and tamping equipment operators; and pile-driver operators, see the statement on construction equipment operators elsewhere in this book.)

Work environment. Material moving work tends to be repetitive and physically demanding. Workers may lift and carry heavy objects and stoop, kneel, crouch, or crawl in awkward positions. Some work at great heights and some work outdoors—regardless of weather and climate. Some jobs expose workers to fumes, odors, loud noises, harmful materials and chemicals, or dangerous machinery. To protect their eyes, respiratory systems, and hearing, these workers wear safety clothing, such as gloves, hardhats, and other safety devices such as respirators. These jobs have become less dangerous as safety equipment—such as overhead guards on lift trucks—has become common. Accidents usually can be avoided by observing proper operating procedures and safety practices.

Material movers generally work 8-hour shifts—though longer shifts are not uncommon. In industries that work around the clock, material movers may work overnight shifts. Some do this because their employers do not want to disturb customers during normal business hours. Refuse and recyclable material collectors often work shifts starting at 5 or 6 a.m. Some material movers work only during certain seasons, such as when the weather permits construction activity.

Training, Other Qualifications, and Advancement

Many material moving occupations require little or no formal training. Most training for these occupations is done on the job. For those jobs requiring physical exertion, employers may require that applicants pass a physical exam.

Education and training. Material movers generally learn skills informally, on the job, from more experienced workers or their supervisors. Many employers prefer applicants with a high school diploma or GED, but most simply require workers to be at least 18 years old and physically able to perform the work.

Workers who handle toxic chemicals or use industrial trucks or other dangerous equipment must receive specialized training in safety awareness and procedures. Many of the training requirements are standardized through the Occupational Safety and Health Administration (OSHA), but training for workers in mining is regulated by the Mine Safety and Health Administration (MSHA). This training is usually provided by the employer. Employers also must certify that each operator has received the training and evaluate each operator at least once every three years.

For other operators, such as crane operators and those working with specialized loads, there are some training and apprenticeship programs available, such as that offered by the International Union of Operating Engineers. Apprenticeships combine paid on-the-job training with classroom instruction.

Licensure. Seventeen states and six cities have laws requiring crane operators to be licensed. Licensing requirements typically include a written test as well as a skills test to demonstrate that the licensee can operate a crane safely.

Certification and other qualifications. Some types of equipment operators can become certified by professional associations, such as the National Commission for the Certification of Crane Operators, and some employers may require operators to be certified.

Material moving equipment operators need a good sense of balance, the ability to judge distances, and eye-hand-foot coordination. For jobs that involve dealing with the public, such as baggers or grocery store courtesy clerks, workers should be pleasant and courteous. Most jobs require basic arithmetic skills, the ability to read procedural manuals, and the capacity to understand orders and other billing documents. Experience operating mobile equipment—such as tractors on farms or heavy equipment in the Armed Forces—is an asset. As material moving equipment becomes more advanced, workers will need to be increasingly comfortable with technology.

Advancement. In many of these occupations, experience may allow workers to qualify or become trainees for jobs such as construction trades workers; assemblers or other production workers; or motor vehicle operators. In many workplaces, new employees gain experience in a material moving position before being promoted to a better paying and more highly skilled job. Some may eventually advance to become supervisors.

Employment

Material movers held 4.6 million jobs in 2008. They were distributed among the detailed occupations as follows:

Laborers and freight, stock, and material movers, hand	2,317,300
Packers and packagers, hand	758,800
Industrial truck and tractor operators	610,300
Cleaners of vehicles and equipment	348,900
Refuse and recyclable material collectors	149,000
Machine feeders and offbearers	140,600
Excavating and loading machine and dragline operators	75,700
Crane and tower operators	43,900
Conveyor operators and tenders	41,000
Wellhead pumpers	18,600
Tank car, truck, and ship loaders	12,000
Pump operators, except wellhead pumpers	9,700
Loading machine operators, underground mining	4,400
Gas compressor and gas pumping station operators	4,300
Shuttle car operators	3,100
Hoist and winch operators	2,800
Dredge operators	2,200
Material moving workers, all other	41,000

About 29 percent of all material movers worked in the wholesale trade or retail trade industries. Another 20 percent worked in manufacturing; 17 percent were in transportation and warehousing; 4 percent were in construction and mining; and 12 percent worked in the employment services industry, on a temporary or contract basis. For example, companies that need workers for only a few days, to move materials or to clean up a site, may contract with temporary help agencies specializing in providing suitable workers on a short-term basis. A small proportion of material movers were self-employed.

Material movers work in every part of the country. Some work in remote locations on large construction projects such as highways and dams, while others work in factories, warehouses, or mining operations.

Job Outlook

Despite little or no change in employment, numerous job openings will be created by the need to replace workers who leave this very large occupation.

Employment change. Employment in material moving occupations is projected to decline by 1 percent between 2008 and 2018. Improvements in equipment, such as automated storage and retrieval systems and conveyors, and in supply management processes, such as automatic identification and data collection (AIDC), will continue to raise productivity and reduce the demand for material movers.

Projections Data from the National Employment Matrix

Occupational title	SOC Code	Employment, 2008	Projected employment, 2018	Change, 2008–2018	
				Number	Percent
Material moving occupations	53-7000	4,583,700	4,537,200	−46,500	−1
Conveyor operators and tenders	53-7011	41,000	37,200	−3,800	−9
Crane and tower operators	53-7021	43,900	40,900	−3,000	−7
Dredge, excavating, and loading machine operators	53-7030	82,300	88,600	6,300	8
Dredge operators	53-7031	2,200	2,400	200	7
Excavating and loading machine and dragline operators	53-7032	75,700	82,100	6,500	9
Loading machine operators, underground mining	53-7033	4,400	4,100	−300	−7
Hoist and winch operators	53-7041	2,800	2,600	−200	−8
Industrial truck and tractor operators	53-7051	610,300	627,000	16,700	3
Laborers and material movers, hand	53-7060	3,565,700	3,485,400	−80,200	−2
Cleaners of vehicles and equipment	53-7061	348,900	352,500	3,600	1
Laborers and freight, stock, and material movers, hand	53-7062	2,317,300	2,298,600	−18,700	−1
Machine feeders and offbearers	53-7063	140,600	109,500	−31,200	−22
Packers and packagers, hand	53-7064	758,800	724,800	−34,000	−4
Pumping station operators	53-7070	32,500	24,500	−8,000	−25
Gas compressor and gas pumping station operators	53-7071	4,300	3,400	−900	−21
Pump operators, except wellhead pumpers	53-7072	9,700	7,800	−1,900	−20
Wellhead pumpers	53-7073	18,600	13,300	−5,300	−28
Refuse and recyclable material collectors	53-7081	149,000	176,700	27,800	19
Shuttle car operators	53-7111	3,100	3,000	−100	−4
Tank car, truck, and ship loaders	53-7121	12,000	11,200	−900	−7
Material moving workers, all other	53-7199	41,000	40,000	−1,000	−2

NOTE: Data in this table are rounded.

Job growth for material movers depends on the growth or decline of employing industries and the type of equipment the workers operate or the materials they handle. Employment should grow in the warehousing and storage industry as more firms contract out their warehousing functions to this industry. Opportunities for material movers should decline in manufacturing due to productivity improvements and outsourcing of warehousing and other activities that depend on material movers. Opportunities will vary by establishment size as well, as large establishments are more likely to have the resources to invest in automated systems for their material moving needs. Although increasing automation will eliminate some routine tasks, many jobs will remain to meet the need to operate and maintain new equipment.

Job prospects. Despite the projected employment decline, a relatively high number of job openings will be created by the need to replace workers who transfer to other occupations, retire, or leave this very large occupation for other reasons—characteristic of occupations requiring little prior or formal training. Many industries where material moving workers are employed are sensitive to changes in economic conditions, so the number of job openings fluctuates with the economy.

Earnings

Median hourly wages of material moving workers in May 2009 were relatively low, as indicated by the following tabulation:

Gas compressor and gas pumping station operators $23.49
Loading machine operators, underground mining 21.36
Shuttle car operators 21.91
Crane and tower operators 21.22
Pump operators, except wellhead pumpers 18.97
Wellhead pumpers 18.48
Tank car truck and ship loaders 18.76
Hoist and winch operators 17.89
Excavating and loading machine and dragline operators 17.28
Dredge operators 16.63
Refuse and recyclable material collectors 15.42
Industrial truck and tractor operators 13.98
Conveyor operators and tenders 14.21
Machine feeders and offbearers 12.64
Laborers and freight stock and material movers, hand 11.11
Cleaners of vehicles and equipment 9.47
Packers and packagers, hand 9.36
Material moving workers, all other 15.39

Wages vary according to experience and job responsibilities. Wages usually are higher in metropolitan areas. Seasonal peaks and lulls in workload can affect the number of hours scheduled, which affects earnings. Some crane operators, such as those unloading containers from ships at major ports, earn substantially more than their counterparts in other industries or establishments. Some material movers are union members, and these workers tend to earn higher wages.

Related Occupations

Other entry-level workers who perform physical work or operate machinery: agricultural workers, other; building cleaning workers; construction equipment operators; construction laborers; grounds maintenance workers; and logging workers.

Sources of Additional Information

Information on training and apprenticeships for industrial truck operators is available from

▸ International Union of Operating Engineers, 1125 17th St. NW, Washington, DC 20036. Internet: www.iuoe.org

Information on crane and derrick operator certification and licensure is available from

▸ National Commission for the Certification of Crane Operators, 2750 Prosperity Ave., Suite 505, Fairfax, VA 22031. Internet: www.nccco.org

Information on safety and training requirements is available from

▸ U.S. Department of Labor, Occupational Safety and Health Administration (OSHA), 200 Constitution Ave. NW, Washington, DC 20210. Internet: www.osha.gov

▸ Mine Safety and Health Administration, 1100 Wilson Blvd., Arlington, VA 22209-3939. Internet: www.msha.gov

For information about job opportunities and training programs, contact local state employment service offices, building or construction contractors, manufacturers, and wholesale and retail establishments.

Medical Assistants

(O*NET 31-9092.00)

Significant Points

■ Employment is projected to grow much faster than average, ranking medical assistants among the fastest growing occupations over the 2008–2018 decade.

■ Job prospects should be excellent.

■ About 62 percent of medical assistants work in offices of physicians.

■ Some medical assistants are trained on the job, but many complete one-year or two-year programs.

Nature of the Work

Medical assistants perform administrative and clinical tasks to keep the offices of physicians, podiatrists, chiropractors, and other health practitioners running smoothly. The duties of medical assistants vary from office to office, depending on the location and size of the practice and the practitioner's specialty. In small practices, medical assistants usually do many different kinds of tasks, handling both administrative and clinical duties and reporting directly to an office manager, physician, or other health practitioner. Those in large practices tend to specialize in a particular area, under the supervision of department administrators. Medical assistants should not be confused with physician assistants, who examine, diagnose, and treat patients under the direct supervision of a physician.

Administrative medical assistants update and file patients' medical records, fill out insurance forms, and arrange for hospital admissions and laboratory services. They also perform tasks less specific to medical settings, such as answering telephones, greeting patients, handling correspondence, scheduling appointments, and handling billing and bookkeeping.

Clinical medical assistants have various duties, depending on state law. Some common tasks include taking medical histories and recording vital signs, explaining treatment procedures to patients, preparing patients for examinations, and assisting physicians during examinations. Medical assistants collect and prepare laboratory specimens and sometimes perform basic laboratory tests, dispose of contaminated supplies, and sterilize medical instruments. As directed by a physician, they might instruct patients about medications and special diets, prepare and administer medications, authorize drug refills, telephone prescriptions to a pharmacy, draw blood, prepare patients for X-rays, take electrocardiograms, remove sutures, and change dressings. Medical assistants also may arrange examining room instruments and equipment, purchase and maintain supplies and equipment, and keep waiting and examining rooms neat and clean.

Ophthalmic medical assistants, *optometric assistants*, and *podiatric medical assistants* are examples of specialized assistants who have additional duties. Ophthalmic medical assistants help ophthalmologists provide eye care. They conduct diagnostic tests, measure and record vision, and test eye muscle function. They apply eye dressings and also show patients how to insert, remove, and care for contact lenses. Under the direction of the physician, ophthalmic medical assistants may administer eye medications. They also maintain optical and surgical instruments and may assist the ophthalmologist in surgery. Optometric assistants also help provide eye care, working with optometrists. They provide chair-side assistance, instruct patients about contact lens use and care, conduct preliminary tests on patients, and otherwise provide assistance while working directly with an optometrist. Podiatric medical assistants make castings of feet, expose and develop X-rays, and assist podiatrists in surgery.

Work environment. Medical assistants work in well-lighted, clean environments. They constantly interact with other people and may have to handle several responsibilities at once. Most full-time medical assistants work a regular 40-hour week. However, medical assistants may work part time, evenings, or weekends.

Training, Other Qualifications, and Advancement

Some medical assistants are trained on the job, but many complete one- or two-year programs. Almost all medical assistants have at least a high school diploma, although there are no formal education or training requirements.

Education and training. Medical assisting programs are offered in vocational-technical high schools, postsecondary vocational schools, and community and junior colleges. Postsecondary programs usually last either one year and result in a certificate or diploma or two years and result in an associate degree. Courses cover anatomy, physiology, and medical terminology, as well as keyboarding, transcription, recordkeeping, accounting, and insurance processing. Students learn laboratory techniques, clinical and diagnostic procedures, pharmaceutical principles, the administration of medications, and first aid. They study office practices, patient relations, medical law, and ethics. There are two accrediting bodies that accredit medical assisting programs. Accredited programs often include an internship that provides practical experience in physicians' offices or other health-care facilities.

Formal training in medical assisting, while generally preferred, is not required. Many medical assistants are trained on the job, and usually only need to have a high school diploma or the equivalent. Recommended high school courses include mathematics, health, biology, keyboarding, bookkeeping, computers, and office skills. Volunteer experience in the health-care field also is helpful. Medical assistants who are trained on the job usually spend their first few months attending training sessions and working closely with more experienced workers.

Some states allow medical assistants to perform more advanced procedures, such as giving injections or taking X-rays, after passing a test or taking a course.

Other qualifications. Medical assistants deal with the public; therefore, they must be neat and well groomed and have a courteous, pleasant manner and they must be able to put patients at ease and explain physicians' instructions. They must respect the confidential nature of medical information. Clinical duties require a reasonable level of manual dexterity and visual acuity.

Certification and advancement. Although not required, certification indicates that a medical assistant meets certain standards of knowledge. It may also help to distinguish an experienced or formally trained assistant from an entry-level assistant, which may lead to a higher salary or more employment opportunities. There are various associations—such as the American Association of Medical Assistants (AAMA) and Association of Medical Technologists (AMT)—that award certification credentials to medical assistants. The certification process varies by association. It is also possible to become certified in a specialty, such as podiatry, optometry, or ophthalmology.

Medical assistants may also advance to other occupations through experience or additional training. For example, some may go on to teach medical assisting, and others pursue additional education to become nurses or other health-care workers. Administrative medical assistants may advance to office managers, or qualify for a variety of administrative support occupations.

Employment

Medical assistants held about 483,600 jobs in 2008. About 62 percent worked in offices of physicians; 13 percent worked in public and private hospitals, including inpatient and outpatient facilities;

and 11 percent worked in offices of other health practitioners, such as chiropractors and optometrists. Most of the remainder worked in other health-care industries, such as outpatient care centers and nursing and residential care facilities.

Job Outlook

Employment is projected to grow much faster than average, ranking medical assistants among the fastest growing occupations over the 2008–2018 decade. Job opportunities should be excellent, particularly for those with formal training or experience, and certification.

Employment change. Employment of medical assistants is expected to grow 34 percent from 2008 to 2018, much faster than the average for all occupations. As the health-care industry expands because of technological advances in medicine and the growth and aging of the population, there will be an increased need for all health-care workers. The increasing prevalence of certain conditions, such as obesity and diabetes, also will increase demand for health-care services and medical assistants. Increasing use of medical assistants to allow doctors to care for more patients will further stimulate job growth.

Helping to drive job growth is the increasing number of group practices, clinics, and other health-care facilities that need a high proportion of support personnel, particularly medical assistants who can handle both administrative and clinical duties. In addition, medical assistants work mostly in primary care, a consistently growing sector of the health-care industry.

Job prospects. Job seekers who want to work as a medical assistant should find excellent job prospects. Medical assistants are projected to account for a very large number of new jobs, and many other opportunities will come from the need to replace workers leaving the occupation. Medical assistants with formal training or experience—particularly those with certification—should have the best job opportunities, since employers generally prefer to hire these workers.

Earnings

The earnings of medical assistants vary, depending on their experience, skill level, and location. Median annual wages of wage-and-salary medical assistants were $28,650 in May 2009. The middle 50 percent earned between $24,060 and $33,760. The lowest 10 percent earned less than $20,750, and the highest 10 percent earned more than $39,970. Median annual wages in the industries employing the largest numbers of medical assistants in May 2009 were as follows:

```
Offices of physicians .........................................$29,100
General medical and surgical hospitals ................. 29,730
Offices of other health practitioners.................... 25,680
Outpatient care centers ..................................... 29,090
Colleges, universities, and professional schools ..... 29,030
```

Projections Data from the National Employment Matrix

Occupational title	SOC Code	Employment, 2008	Projected employment, 2018	Change, 2008–2018	
				Number	Percent
Medical assistants..31-9092		483,600	647,500	163,900	34

NOTE: Data in this table are rounded.

Related Occupations

Medical assistants perform work similar to the tasks completed by other workers in medical support occupations. Administrative medical assistants do work similar to that of medical records and health information technicians; medical secretaries; and medical transcriptionists.

Clinical medical assistants perform duties similar to those of dental assistants; dental hygienists; licensed practical and licensed vocational nurses; nursing and psychiatric aides; occupational therapist assistants and aides; pharmacy technicians and aides; physical therapist assistants and aides; and surgical technologists.

Sources of Additional Information

Information about career opportunities and certification for medical assistants is available from

▸ American Association of Medical Assistants, 20 N. Wacker Dr., Suite 1575, Chicago, IL 60606. Internet: www.aama-ntl.org

▸ American Medical Technologists, 10700 W. Higgins Rd., Suite 150, Rosemont, IL 60018. Internet: www.amt1.com

▸ National Healthcareer Association, 7 Ridgedale Ave., Suite 203, Cedar Knolls, NJ 07927. Internet: www.nhanow.com

For lists of accredited educational programs in medical assisting, contact

▸ Accrediting Bureau of Health Education Schools, 7777 Leesburg Pike, Suite 314 N, Falls Church, VA 22043. Internet: www.abhes.org

▸ Commission on Accreditation of Allied Health Education Programs, 1361 Park St., Clearwater, FL 33756. Internet: www.caahep.org

Information about career opportunities, training programs, and certification for ophthalmic medical personnel is available from

▸ Joint Commission on Allied Health Personnel in Ophthalmology, 2025 Woodlane Dr., St. Paul, MN 55125. Internet: www.jcahpo.org

Information about career opportunities, training programs, and certification for optometric assistants is available from

▸ American Optometric Association, 243 N. Lindbergh Blvd., St. Louis, MO 63141. Internet: www.aoa.org

Information about certification for podiatric assistants is available from

▸ American Society of Podiatric Medical Assistants, 2124 S. Austin Blvd., Cicero, IL 60804. Internet: www.aspma.org

Medical Records and Health Information Technicians

(O*NET 29-2071.00)

Significant Points

■ Employment is expected to grow much faster than the average.

■ Job prospects should be very good, particularly for technicians with strong computer software skills.

■ Entrants usually have an associate degree.

■ This is one of the few health-related occupations in which there is no direct hands-on patient care.

Nature of the Work

Medical records and health information technicians assemble patients' health information including medical history, symptoms, examination results, diagnostic tests, treatment methods, and all other health-care provider services. Technicians organize and manage health information data by ensuring its quality, accuracy, accessibility, and security. They regularly communicate with physicians and other health-care professionals to clarify diagnoses or to obtain additional information.

The increasing use of electronic health records (EHR) will continue to broaden and alter the job responsibilities of health information technicians. For example, with the use of EHRs, technicians must be familiar with EHR computer software, maintaining EHR security, and analyzing electronic data to improve health-care information. Health information technicians use EHR software to maintain data on patient safety, patterns of disease, and disease treatment and outcome. Technicians also may assist with improving EHR software usability and may contribute to the development and maintenance of health information networks.

Medical records and health information technicians' duties vary with the size of the facility where they work. Technicians can specialize in many aspects of health information.

Some medical records and health information technicians specialize in codifying patients' medical information for reimbursement purposes. Technicians who specialize in coding are called *medical coders* or *coding specialists.* Medical coders assign a code to each diagnosis and procedure by using classification systems software. The classification system determines the amount for which health-care providers will be reimbursed if the patient is covered by Medicare, Medicaid, or other insurance programs using the system. Coders may use several coding systems, such as those required for ambulatory settings, physician offices, or long-term care.

Medical records and health information technicians also may specialize in cancer registry. *Cancer* (or tumor) *registrars* maintain facility, regional, and national databases of cancer patients. Registrars review patient records and pathology reports, and assign codes for the diagnosis and treatment of different cancers and selected benign tumors. Registrars conduct annual followups to track treatment, survival, and recovery. This information is used to calculate survivor rates and success rates of various types of treatment, to locate geographic areas with high incidences of certain cancers, and to identify potential participants for clinical drug trials.

Work environment. Medical records and health information technicians work in pleasant and comfortable offices. This is one of the few health-related occupations in which there is no direct hands-on patient care.

Medical records and health information technicians usually work a typical 40-hour week. Some overtime may be required. In health facilities that are open 24 hours a day, 7 days a week, technicians may work day, evening, and night shifts. About 14 percent of technicians worked part time in 2008.

Training, Other Qualifications, and Advancement

Entry-level medical records and health information technicians usually have an associate degree. Many employers favor technicians who have a Registered Health Information Technicians (RHIT) credential.

Education and training. Medical records and health information technicians generally have an associate degree. Typical coursework in health information technology includes medical terminology, anatomy and physiology, health data requirements and standards, clinical classification and coding systems, data analysis, health-care reimbursement methods, database security and management, and quality improvement methods. Applicants can improve their chances of admission into a postsecondary program by taking biology, math, chemistry, health, and computer science courses in high school.

Certification and other qualifications. Most employers prefer to hire credentialed medical record and health information technicians. A number of organizations offer credentials typically based on passing a credentialing exam. Most credentialing programs require regular recertification and continuing education to maintain the credential. Many coding credentials require an amount of time in coding experience in the work setting.

The American Health Information Management Association (AHIMA) offers credentialing as a Registered Health Information Technician (RHIT). To obtain the RHIT credential, an individual must graduate from a two-year associate degree program accredited by the Commission on Accreditation for Health Informatics and Information Management Education (CAHIIM) and pass an AHIMA-administered written examination. In 2008, there were more than 200 CAHIIM-accredited health information technology college and university programs.

The American Academy of Professional Coders (AAPC) offers coding credentials. The Board of Medical Specialty Coding (BMSC) and Professional Association of Healthcare Coding Specialists (PAHCS) both offer credentialing in specialty coding. The National Cancer Registrars Association (NCRA) offers a credential as a Certified Tumor Registrar (CTR). To learn more about the credentials available and their specific requirements, contact the credentialing organization.

Health information technicians and coders should possess good oral and written communication skills as they often serve as liaisons between health-care facilities, insurance companies, and other establishments. Candidates proficient with computer software and technology will be appealing to employers as health-care facilities continue to adopt electronic health records. Medical records and health information technicians should enjoy learning, as continuing education is important in the occupation.

Advancement. Experienced medical records and health information technicians usually advance their careers by obtaining a bachelor's or master's degree or by seeking an advanced specialty certification. Technicians with a bachelor's or master's degree can advance and become a health information manager. (See the statement on *medical and health services managers* for more information on health information managers). Technicians can also obtain advanced specialty certification. Advanced specialty certification is typically experience-based, but may require additional formal education depending on the certifying organization.

Employment

Medical records and health information technicians held about 172,500 jobs in 2008. About 39 percent of jobs were in hospitals. Health information technicians work at a number of health-care providers such as offices of physicians, nursing care facilities, outpatient care centers, and home health-care services. Technicians also may be employed outside of health-care facilities, such as in federal government agencies.

Job Outlook

Employment is expected to grow much faster than the average. Job prospects should be very good; technicians with a strong understanding of technology and computer software will be in particularly high demand.

Employment change. Employment of medical records and health information technicians is expected to increase by 20 percent, much faster than the average for all occupations through 2018. Employment growth will result from the increase in the number of medical tests, treatments, and procedures that will be performed. As the population continues to age, the occurrence of health-related problems will increase. Cancer registrars should experience job growth as the incidence of cancer increases from an aging population.

In addition, with the increasing use of electronic health records, more technicians will be needed to complete the new responsibilities associated with electronic data management.

Job prospects. Job prospects should be very good. In addition to job growth, numerous openings will result from the need to replace medical record and health information technicians who retire or leave the occupation permanently. Technicians that demonstrate a strong understanding of technology and computer software will be in particularly high demand.

Earnings

The median annual wage of medical records and health information technicians was $31,290 in May 2009. The middle 50 percent earned between $24,870 and $40,540. The lowest 10 percent earned less than $20,850, and the highest 10 percent earned more than $51,510. Median annual wages in the industries employing the largest numbers of medical records and health information technicians in May 2009 were as follows:

General medical and surgical hospitals	$33,480
Offices of physicians	26,630
Nursing care facilities	31,200
Outpatient care centers	29,060
Federal executive branch	44,460

Projections Data from the National Employment Matrix

Occupational title	SOC Code	Employment, 2008	Projected employment, 2018	Change, 2008–2018	
				Number	Percent
Medical records and health information technicians	29-2071	172,500	207,600	35,100	20

NOTE: Data in this table are rounded.

Related Occupations

Health-care occupations with similar responsibilities include medical and health services managers, and medical transcriptionists.

Sources of Additional Information

A list of accredited training programs is available from

▸ The Commission on Accreditation for Health Informatics and Information Management Education, 233 N. Michigan Ave, 21st Floor, Chicago, IL 60601-5800. Internet: www.cahiim.org

For information careers and credentialing, contact

▸ American Health Information Management Association, 233 N. Michigan Ave., 21st Floor, Chicago, IL 60601-5809. Internet: www.ahima.org or http://himcareers.ahima.org

▸ American Academy of Professional Coders, 2480 S. 3850 W., Suite B, Salt Lake City, UT 84120. Internet: www.aapc.com

▸ Practice Management Institute, 9501 Console Dr., Suite 100, San Antonio, TX 78229. Internet: www.pmimd.com

▸ Professional Association of Healthcare Coding Specialists, 218 E. Bearss Ave., #354, Tampa, FL 33613. Internet: www.pahcs.org

▸ National Cancer Registrars Association, 1340 Braddock Place, Suite 203, Alexandria, VA 22314. Internet: www.ncra-usa.org

Musicians, Singers, and Related Workers

(O*NET 27-2041.00, 27-2041.01, 27-2041.04, 27-2042.00, 27-2042.01, and 27-2042.02)

Significant Points

■ Part-time schedules—typically at night and on weekends—intermittent unemployment, and rejection when auditioning for work are common; many musicians and singers supplement their income with earnings from other sources.

■ Aspiring musicians and singers begin studying an instrument or training their voice at an early age.

■ Competition for jobs, especially full-time jobs, is keen; talented individuals who can play several instruments and perform a wide range of musical styles should enjoy the best job prospects.

Nature of the Work

Musicians, singers, and related workers play musical instruments, sing, compose or arrange music, or conduct groups in instrumental or vocal performances. They perform solo or as part of a group, mostly in front of live audiences in nightclubs, concert halls, and theaters. They also perform in recording or production studios for radio, TV, film, or video games. Regardless of the setting, they spend considerable time practicing alone and with their bands, orchestras, or other musical ensembles.

Musicians play one or more musical instruments. Many musicians learn to play several related instruments and can perform equally well in several musical styles. Instrumental musicians, for example, may play in a symphony orchestra, rock group, or jazz combo one night, appear in another ensemble the next, and work in a studio band the following day. Some play a variety of string, brass, woodwind, or percussion instruments or electronic synthesizers.

Singers use their knowledge of voice production, melody, and harmony to interpret music and text. They sing character parts or perform in their own individual styles. Singers often are classified according to their voice range—soprano, contralto, tenor, baritone, or bass—or by the type of music they sing, such as rock, pop, folk, opera, rap, or country.

Music directors and *conductors* conduct, direct, plan, and lead instrumental or vocal performances by musical groups such as orchestras, choirs, and glee clubs. These leaders audition and select musicians, choose the music most appropriate for their talents and abilities, and direct rehearsals and performances. *Choral directors* lead choirs and glee clubs, sometimes working with a band or an orchestra conductor. Directors audition and select singers and lead them at rehearsals and performances to achieve harmony, rhythm, tempo, shading, and other desired musical effects.

Composers create original music such as symphonies, operas, sonatas, radio and television jingles, film scores, and popular songs. They transcribe ideas into musical notation, using harmony, rhythm, melody, and tonal structure. Although most composers and songwriters practice their craft on instruments and transcribe the notes with pen and paper, some use computer software to compose and edit their music.

Arrangers transcribe and adapt musical compositions to a particular style for orchestras, bands, choral groups, or individuals. Components of music—including tempo, volume, and the mix of instruments needed—are arranged to express the composer's message. Although some arrangers write directly into a musical composition, others use computer software to make changes.

Work environment. Musicians typically perform at night and on weekends. They spend much additional time practicing or in rehearsal. Full-time musicians with long-term employment contracts, such as those with symphony orchestras or television and film production companies, enjoy steady work and less travel. Nightclub, solo, or recital musicians frequently travel to perform in a variety of local settings and may tour nationally or internationally. Because many musicians find only part-time or intermittent work and experience unemployment between engagements, they often supplement their income with other types of jobs. The stress of constantly looking for work leads many musicians to accept permanent full-time jobs in other occupations while working part time as musicians.

Most instrumental musicians work closely with a variety of other people, including colleagues, agents, employers, sponsors, and audiences. Although they usually work indoors, some perform outdoors for parades, concerts, and festivals. In some nightclubs and restaurants, smoke and odors may be present and lighting and ventilation may be poor.

Training, Other Qualifications, and Advancement

Long-term on-the-job training is the most common way people learn to become musicians or singers. Aspiring musicians begin studying an instrument at an early age. They may gain valuable experience playing in a school or community band or orchestra or with a group of friends. Singers usually start training when their voices mature. Participation in school musicals or choirs often provides good early training and experience. Composers and music directors usually require a bachelor's degree in a related field.

Projections Data from the National Employment Matrix

Occupational title	SOC Code	Employment, 2008	Projected employment, 2018	Change, 2008–2018	
				Number	Percent
Musicians, singers, and related workers 27-2040		240,000	259,600	19,600	8
Music directors and composers...........................27-2041		53,600	59,000	5,300	10
Musicians and singers.......................................27-2042		186,400	200,600	14,200	8

NOTE: Data in this table are rounded.

Education and training. Musicians need extensive and prolonged training and practice to acquire the skills and knowledge necessary to interpret music at a professional level. Like other artists, musicians and singers continually strive to improve their abilities. Formal training may be obtained through private study with an accomplished musician, in a college or university music program, or in a music conservatory. An audition generally is necessary to qualify for university or conservatory study. The National Association of Schools of Music is made up of 615 accredited college-level programs in music. Courses typically include music theory, music interpretation, composition, conducting, and performance, either with a particular instrument or a voice performance. Music directors, composers, conductors, and arrangers need considerable related work experience or advanced training in these subjects.

A master's or doctoral degree usually is required to teach advanced music courses in colleges and universities; a bachelor's degree may be sufficient to teach basic courses. A degree in music education qualifies graduates for a state certificate to teach music in public elementary or secondary schools. Musicians who do not meet public school music education requirements may teach in private schools and recreation associations or instruct individual students in private sessions.

Other qualifications. Musicians must be knowledgeable about a broad range of musical styles. Having a broader range of interest, knowledge, and training can help expand employment opportunities and musical abilities. Voice training and private instrumental lessons, especially when taken at a young age, also help develop technique and enhance one's performance.

Young persons considering careers in music should have musical talent, versatility, creativity, poise, and good stage presence. Self-discipline is vital because producing a quality performance on a consistent basis requires constant study and practice. Musicians who play in concerts or in nightclubs and those who tour must have physical stamina to endure frequent travel and an irregular performance schedule. Musicians and singers also must be prepared to face the anxiety of intermittent employment and of rejection when auditioning for work.

Advancement. Advancement for musicians usually means becoming better known, finding work more easily, and performing for higher earnings. Successful musicians often rely on agents or managers to find them performing engagements, negotiate contracts, and develop their careers.

Employment

Musicians, singers, and related workers held about 240,000 jobs in 2008, of which 186,400 were held by musicians and singers; 53,600 were music directors and composers. Around 43 percent worked part time; 50 percent were self-employed. Many found jobs in cities in which entertainment and recording activities are concentrated, such as New York, Los Angeles, Las Vegas, Chicago, and Nashville.

Musicians, singers, and related workers are employed in a variety of settings. Of those who earn a wage or salary, 33 percent were employed by religious, grantmaking, civic, professional, and similar organizations and 12 percent by performing arts companies, such as professional orchestras, small chamber music groups, opera companies, musical theater companies, and ballet troupes. Musicians and singers also perform in nightclubs and restaurants and for weddings and other events. Well-known musicians and groups may perform in concerts, appear on radio and television broadcasts, and make recordings and music videos. The U.S. Armed Forces also offer careers in their bands and smaller musical groups.

Job Outlook

Employment is expected to grow as fast as average. Keen competition for jobs, especially full-time jobs, is expected to continue. Talented individuals who are skilled in multiple instruments and musical styles will have the best job prospects.

Employment change. Employment of musicians, singers, and related workers is expected to grow 8 percent during the 2008–2018 decade, as fast as the average for all occupations. Most new wage-and-salary jobs for musicians will arise in religious organizations. Slower than average employment growth is expected for self-employed musicians, who generally perform in nightclubs, concert tours, and other venues. The Internet and other new forms of media may provide independent musicians and singers alternative methods for distributing music.

Job prospects. Growth in demand for musicians will generate a number of job opportunities, and many openings also will arise from the need to replace those who leave the field each year because they are unable to make a living solely as musicians or singers, as well as those who leave for other reasons.

Competition for jobs as musicians, singers, and related workers—especially full-time jobs—is expected to be keen. The vast number of people with the desire to perform will continue to greatly exceed the number of openings. New musicians or singers will have their best chance of landing a job with smaller, community-based performing arts groups or as freelance artists. Instrumentalists should have better opportunities than singers because of a larger pool of work. Talented individuals who are skilled in multiple instruments or musical styles will have the best job prospects. However, talent alone is no guarantee of success: many people start out to become musicians or singers but leave the profession because they find the work difficult, the discipline demanding, and the long periods of intermittent unemployment a hardship.

Earnings

Median hourly wages of wage-and-salary musicians and singers were $22.36 in May 2009. The middle 50 percent earned between $12.64 and $37.09. The lowest 10 percent earned less than $8.04, and the highest 10 percent earned more than $58.90. Median hourly wages were $24.27 in performing arts companies and $13.08 in religious organizations. Annual wage data for musicians and singers were not available because of the wide variation in the number of hours worked by musicians and singers and the short-term nature of many jobs. It is rare for musicians and singers to have guaranteed employment that exceeds 3 to 6 months.

Median annual wages of salaried music directors and composers were $45,090 in May 2009. The middle 50 percent earned between $32,210 and $61,630. The lowest 10 percent earned less than $21,480, and the highest 10 percent earned more than $85,020.

For self-employed musicians and singers, earnings typically reflect the number of jobs a freelance musician or singer played or the number of hours and weeks of contract work, in addition to a performer's professional reputation and setting. Performers who can fill large concert halls, arenas, or outdoor stadiums generally command higher pay than those who perform in local clubs. Soloists or headliners usually receive higher earnings than band members or opening acts. The most successful musicians earn performance or recording fees that far exceed the median earnings.

The American Federation of Musicians negotiates minimum contracts for major orchestras during the performing season. Each orchestra works out a separate contract with its local union, but individual musicians may negotiate higher salaries. In regional orchestras, minimum salaries often are less because fewer performances are scheduled. Regional orchestra musicians frequently are paid for their services without any guarantee of future employment. Community orchestras often have limited funding and offer salaries that are much lower for seasons of shorter duration.

Although musicians employed by some symphony orchestras work under master wage agreements, which guarantee a season's work up to 52 weeks, many other musicians face relatively long periods of unemployment between jobs. Even when employed, many musicians and singers work part time in unrelated occupations. Thus, their earnings for music usually are lower than earnings in many other occupations. Moreover, because they may not work steadily for one employer, some performers cannot qualify for unemployment compensation and few have typical benefits such as sick leave or paid vacations. For these reasons, many musicians give private lessons or take jobs unrelated to music to supplement their earnings as performers.

Many musicians belong to a local of the American Federation of Musicians. Professional singers who perform live often belong to a branch of the American Guild of Musical Artists; those who record for the broadcast industries may belong to the American Federation of Television and Radio Artists.

Related Occupations

Other occupations that require a technical knowledge of musical instruments include musical instrument repairers and tuners.

Musicians, singers, and related workers are involved in the performing arts, as are actors, producers, and directors; announcers; and dancers and choreographers.

Sources of Additional Information

For general information about music and music teacher education and a list of accredited college-level programs, contact

▶ National Association of Schools of Music, 11250 Roger Bacon Dr., Suite 21, Reston, VA 20190. Internet: http://nasm.arts-accredit.org

Nursing and Psychiatric Aides

(O*NET 31-1012.00 and 31-1013.00)

Significant Points

■ Numerous job openings and excellent job opportunities are expected.

■ Most jobs are in nursing and residential care facilities and in hospitals.

■ A high school diploma is required for many jobs; specific qualifications vary by occupation, state laws, and work setting.

■ This occupation is characterized by modest entry requirements, low pay, high physical and emotional demands, and limited advancement opportunities.

Nature of the Work

Nursing and psychiatric aides help care for physically or mentally ill, injured, disabled, or infirm individuals in hospitals, nursing care facilities, and mental health settings. Nursing aides and home health aides are among the occupations commonly referred to as direct care workers, due to their role in working with patients who need long-term care. The specific care they give depends on their specialty.

Nursing aides, also known as *nurse aides, nursing assistants, certified nursing assistants, geriatric aides, unlicensed assistive personnel, orderlies, or hospital attendants*, provide hands-on care and perform routine tasks under the supervision of nursing and medical staff. Specific tasks vary, with aides handling many aspects of a patient's care. They often help patients to eat, dress, and bathe. They also answer calls for help, deliver messages, serve meals, make beds, and tidy up rooms. Aides sometimes are responsible for taking a patient's temperature, pulse rate, respiration rate, or blood pressure. They also may help provide care to patients by helping them get out of bed and walk, escorting them to operating and examining rooms, or providing skin care. Some aides help other medical staff by setting up equipment, storing and moving supplies, and assisting with some procedures. Aides also observe patients' physical, mental, and emotional conditions and report any change to the nursing or medical staff.

Nursing aides employed in nursing care facilities often are the principal caregivers and have more contact with residents than do other members of the staff. Because some residents may stay in a nursing care facility for months or even years, aides develop positive, caring relationships with their patients.

Psychiatric aides, also known as mental health assistants or psychiatric nursing assistants, care for mentally impaired or emotionally disturbed individuals. They work under a team that may include psychiatrists, psychologists, psychiatric nurses, social workers, and therapists. In addition to helping patients to dress, bathe, groom themselves, and eat, psychiatric aides socialize with them and lead them in educational and recreational activities. Psychiatric aides may play card games or other games with patients, watch television with them, or participate in group activities, such as playing sports or going on field trips. They observe patients and report any physical or behavioral signs that might be important for the professional staff to know. They accompany patients to and from therapy and treatment. Because they have such close contact with patients, psychiatric aides can have a great deal of influence on their outlook and treatment.

Work environment. Work as an aide can be physically demanding. Aides spend many hours standing and walking, and they often face heavy workloads. Aides must guard against back injury, because they may have to move patients into and out of bed or help them stand or walk. It is important for aides to be trained in and to follow the proper procedures for lifting and moving patients. Aides also may face hazards from minor infections and major diseases, such as hepatitis, but can avoid infections by following proper procedures. Nursing aides, orderlies, and attendants and psychiatric aides have some of the highest nonfatal injuries and illness rates for all occupations, in the 98th and 99th percentiles in 2007.

Aides also perform tasks that some may consider unpleasant, such as emptying bedpans and changing soiled bed linens. The patients they care for may be disoriented, irritable, or uncooperative. Psychiatric aides must be prepared to care for patients whose illnesses may cause violent behavior. Although their work can be emotionally demanding, many aides gain satisfaction from assisting those in need.

Most full-time aides work about 40 hours per week, but because patients need care 24 hours a day, some aides work evenings, nights, weekends, and holidays. In 2008 about 24 percent of nursing aides, orderlies, and attendants and psychiatric aides worked part time.

Training, Other Qualifications, and Advancement

In many cases, a high school diploma or equivalent is necessary for a job as a nursing or psychiatric aide. Specific qualifications vary by occupation, state laws, and work setting. Advancement opportunities are limited.

Education and training. Nursing and psychiatric aide training is offered in high schools, vocational-technical centers, some nursing care facilities, and some community colleges. Courses cover body mechanics, nutrition, anatomy and physiology, infection control, communication skills, and resident rights. Personal care skills, such as how to help patients bathe, eat, and groom themselves, also are taught. Hospitals may require previous experience as a nursing aide or home health aide. Some states also require psychiatric aides to complete a formal training program. However, most psychiatric aides learn their skills on the job from experienced workers.

Some employers provide classroom instruction for newly hired aides, while others rely exclusively on informal on-the-job instruction by a licensed nurse or an experienced aide. Such training may last from several days to a few months. Aides also may attend lectures, workshops, and in-service training.

Licensure and certification. Federal government requirements exist for nursing aides who work in nursing care facilities. These aides must complete a minimum of 75 hours of state-approved training and pass a competency evaluation. Aides who complete the program are known as certified nurse assistants (CNAs) and are placed on the state registry of nurse aides. Additional requirements may exist, but

vary by state. Therefore, individuals should contact their state board directly for applicable information.

Other qualifications. Aides must be in good health. A physical examination, including state-regulated disease tests, may be required. A criminal background check also is usually required for employment.

Applicants should be tactful, patient, understanding, emotionally stable, and dependable and should have a desire to help people. They also should be able to work as part of a team, have good communication skills, and be willing to perform repetitive, routine tasks.

Advancement. Opportunities for advancement within these occupations are limited. Aides generally need additional formal training or education to enter other health occupations. The most common health-care occupations for former aides are licensed practical nurse, registered nurse, and medical assistant.

For some individuals, these occupations serve as entry-level jobs. For example, some high school and college students gain experience working in these occupations while attending school. And experience as an aide can help individuals decide whether to pursue a career in health care.

Employment

Nursing and psychiatric aides held about 1.5 million jobs in 2008. Nursing aides, orderlies, and attendants held the most jobs—approximately 1.5 million, and psychiatric aides held about 62,500 jobs. About 41 percent of nursing aides, orderlies, and attendants worked in nursing care facilities and another 29 percent worked in hospitals. About 50 percent of all psychiatric aides worked in hospitals. Others were employed in residential care facilities, government agencies, outpatient care centers, and individual and family services.

Job Outlook

Employment is projected to grow faster than the average. Excellent job opportunities are expected.

Employment change. Overall employment of nursing and psychiatric aides is projected to grow 18 percent between 2008 and 2018, faster than the average for all occupations. However, growth will vary for individual occupations. Employment for nursing aides, orderlies, and attendants will grow 19 percent, faster than the average for all occupations, predominantly in response to the long-term care needs of an increasing elderly population. Financial pressures on hospitals to discharge patients as soon as possible should boost admissions to nursing care facilities. As a result, new jobs will be more numerous in nursing and residential care facilities than in hospitals, and growth will be especially strong in community care facilities for the elderly. Modern medical technology will also drive demand for nursing aides, because as the technology saves and extends more lives, it increases the need for long-term care provided by aides. However, employment growth is not expected to be as fast as for other health-care support occupations, largely because nursing aides are concentrated in the relatively slower growing nursing and residential care facilities industry sector. In addition, growth will be hindered by nursing facilities' reliance on government funding, which does not increase as fast as the cost of patient care. Government funding limits the number of nursing aides nursing facilities can afford to have on staff.

Projections Data from the National Employment Matrix

Occupational title	SOC Code	Employment, 2008	Projected employment, 2018	Change, 2008–2018	
				Number	Percent
Nursing and psychiatric aides................................ —		1,532,300	1,811,800	279,600	18
Nursing aides, orderlies, and attendants............... 31-1012		1,469,800	1,745,800	276,000	19
Psychiatric aides... 31-1013		62,500	66,100	3,600	6

NOTE: Data in this table are rounded.

Psychiatric aides are expected to grow 6 percent, more slowly than average. Psychiatric aides are a small occupation compared to nursing aides, orderlies, and attendants. Most psychiatric aides currently work in hospitals, but the industries most likely to see growth will be residential facilities for people with developmental disabilities, mental illness, and substance abuse problems. There is a long-term trend toward treating psychiatric patients outside of hospitals, because it is more cost effective and allows patients greater independence. Demand for psychiatric aides in residential facilities will rise in response to increases in the number of older persons, many of whom will require mental health services. Demand for these workers will also grow as an increasing number of mentally disabled adults, formerly cared for by their elderly parents, will need care. Job growth also could be affected by changes in government funding of programs for the mentally ill.

Job prospects. High replacement needs for nursing and psychiatric aides reflect modest entry requirements, low pay, high physical and emotional demands, and limited opportunities for advancement within the occupation. For these same reasons, the number of people looking to enter the occupation will be limited. Many aides leave the occupation to attend training programs for other health-care occupations. Therefore, people who are interested in, and suited for, this work should have excellent job opportunities.

Earnings

Median hourly wages of nursing aides, orderlies, and attendants were $11.56 in May 2009. The middle 50 percent earned between $9.85 and $13.94 an hour. The lowest 10 percent earned less than $8.42, and the highest 10 percent earned more than $16.33 an hour. Median hourly wages in the industries employing the largest numbers of nursing aides, orderlies, and attendants in May 2009 were as follows:

Nursing care facilities	$11.24
General medical and surgical hospitals	12.26
Community care facilities for the elderly.................	10.99
Home health-care services	10.63
Local government...	12.70

Median hourly wages of psychiatric aides were $12.33 in May 2009. The middle 50 percent earned between $9.63 and $15.77 an hour. The lowest 10 percent earned less than $8.13, and the highest 10 percent earned more than $19.97 an hour. Median hourly wages in the industries employing the largest numbers of psychiatric aides in May 2009 were as follows:

Psychiatric and substance abuse hospitals	$13.50
Residential mental retardation, mental health and substance abuse facilities...........................	10.37
General medical and surgical hospitals	13.40
Individual and family services	10.46
Outpatient care center	12.88

Related Occupations

Other occupations that help people who need routine care or treatment include child care workers; home health aides and personal and home care aides; licensed practical and licensed vocational nurses; medical assistants; occupational therapist assistants and aides; registered nurses; and social and human service assistants.

Sources of Additional Information

Information about employment opportunities may be obtained from local hospitals, nursing care facilities, home health-care agencies, psychiatric facilities, state boards of nursing, and local offices of the state employment service. Information on licensing requirements for nursing aides, and lists of state-approved nursing aide programs are available from state departments of public health, departments of occupational licensing, and boards of nursing.

For more information on nursing aides, orderlies, and attendants, contact

▸ National Association of Health Care Assistants, 1201 L St. NW, Washington, DC 20005. Internet: www.nahcacares.org

▸ National Network of Career Nursing Assistants 3577 Easton Rd., Norton, OH 44203. Internet: www.cna-network.org

For more information on the assisted living, nursing facility, developmentally disabled, and subacute care provider industry, contact

▸ American Health Care Association, 1201 L St. NW, Washington, DC 20005. Internet: www.ahca.org/

Office Clerks, General

(O*NET 43-9061.00)

Significant Points

■ Employment growth and high replacement needs in this large occupation will result in numerous job openings.

■ Prospects should be best for those with knowledge of basic computer applications and office machinery.

■ Part-time and temporary positions are common.

Nature of the Work

Rather than performing a single specialized task, *general office clerks* have responsibilities that often change daily with the needs of the specific job and the employer. Some clerks spend their days filing or keyboarding. Others enter data at a computer terminal. They also operate photocopiers, fax machines, and other office equipment; prepare mailings; proofread documents; and answer telephones and deliver messages.

The specific duties assigned to clerks vary significantly, depending on the type of office in which they work. An office clerk in a doctor's office, for example, would not perform the same tasks that a clerk in a large financial institution or in the office of an auto parts wholesaler would. Although all clerks may sort checks, keep payroll records, take inventory, and access information, they also perform duties unique to their employer. For example, a clerk in a doctor's office may organize medications, a corporate office clerk may help prepare materials for presentations, and a clerk employed by a wholesaler may fill merchandise orders.

Clerks' duties also vary by level of experience. Inexperienced employees may make photocopies, stuff envelopes, or record inquiries. Experienced clerks are usually given additional responsibilities. For example, they may maintain financial or other records, set up spreadsheets, verify statistical reports for accuracy and completeness, handle and adjust customer complaints, work with vendors, make travel arrangements, take inventory of equipment and supplies, answer questions on departmental services and functions, or help prepare invoices or budgetary requests. Senior office clerks may also be expected to monitor and direct the work of lower-level clerks.

Work environment. For the most part, general office clerks work in comfortable office settings. Those on full-time schedules usually work a standard 40-hour week; however, some work shifts or overtime during busy periods. About 24 percent of clerks worked part time in 2008. Many clerks also work in temporary positions.

Training, Other Qualifications, and Advancement

General office clerks often need to know how to use computers, word processing, and other business software and office equipment. Experience working in an office is helpful, but office clerks also learn skills on the job.

Education and training. Employers usually require a high school diploma or equivalent, and some require basic computer skills, including familiarity with word processing software, as well as other general office skills. Although most general office clerk jobs are entry-level positions, employers may prefer or require previous office or business experience.

Training for this occupation is available through business education programs offered in high schools, community and junior colleges, and postsecondary vocational schools. Courses in office practices, word processing, and other computer applications are particularly helpful.

Other qualifications. Because general office clerks usually work with other office staff, they should be cooperative and able to work as part of a team. Employers prefer individuals who can perform a variety of tasks and satisfy the needs of the many departments

within a company. In addition, applicants should have good writing and other communication skills, be detail oriented, and be adaptable.

Advancement. General office clerks who exhibit strong communication, interpersonal, and analytical skills may be promoted to supervisory positions. Others may move into different, more senior administrative jobs, such as receptionist, secretary, or administrative assistant. After gaining some work experience or specialized skills, many workers transfer to jobs with higher pay or greater advancement potential. Advancement to professional occupations within an organization normally requires additional formal education, such as a college degree.

Employment

General office clerks held about 3.0 million jobs in 2008. Most are employed in relatively small businesses. Although they work in every sector of the economy, about one-quarter worked in educational services and in health care and social assistance.

Job Outlook

Employment growth and high replacement needs in this large occupation are expected to result in numerous job openings for general office clerks. Prospects should be best for those with knowledge of basic computer applications and office machinery.

Employment change. Employment of general office clerks is expected to grow by 12 percent between 2008 and 2018, which is about as fast as the average for all occupations. The employment outlook for these workers will continue to be affected by the increasing use of technology, expanding office automation, and the consolidation of administrative support tasks. These factors will lead to a consolidation of administrative support staffs and a diversification of job responsibilities. However, this consolidation will increase the demand for general office clerks because they perform a variety of administrative support tasks, as opposed to clerks with very specific functions. It will become increasingly common within businesses, especially those smaller in size, to find only general office clerks in charge of all administrative support work.

Job prospects. In addition to many full-time job openings for general office clerks, part-time and temporary positions are common. Prospects should be best for those who have knowledge of basic computer applications and office machinery—such as computers, fax machines, telephone systems, and scanners—and good writing and other communication skills. Office clerks with previous business or office experience should also have good job prospects. As general administrative support duties continue to be consolidated, employers will increasingly seek well-rounded individuals with highly developed communication skills and the ability to perform multiple tasks.

Job opportunities may vary from year to year because the strength of the economy affects demand for general office clerks. Companies tend to employ more workers when the economy is strong.

Projections Data from the National Employment Matrix

Occupational title	SOC Code	Employment, 2008	Projected employment, 2018	Change, 2008–2018	
				Number	Percent
Office clerks, general.............................	43-9061	3,024,400	3,383,100	358,700	12

NOTE: Data in this table are rounded.

Industries least likely to be affected by economic fluctuations tend to be the most stable places for employment.

Earnings

Median annual wages of general office clerks were $26,140 in May 2009; the middle 50 percent earned between $20,250 and $33,010 annually. The lowest 10 percent earned less than $16,590, and the highest 10 percent earned more than $41,100. Median annual wages in the industries employing the largest numbers of general office clerks in May 2009 were as follows:

Local government	$29,530
Colleges, universities, and professional schools	26,600
Employment services	24,610
Elementary and secondary schools	26,380
General medical and surgical hospitals	28,540

Related Occupations

The duties of general office clerks can include a combination of bookkeeping, keyboarding, office machine operation, and filing. Other office and administrative support workers who perform similar duties include bookkeeping, accounting, and auditing clerks; communications equipment operators; customer service representatives; data entry and information processing workers; order clerks; receptionists and information clerks; secretaries and administrative assistants; stock clerks and order fillers; and tellers.

Nonclerical entry-level workers who perform these duties include cashiers; counter and rental clerks; and food and beverage serving and related workers.

Sources of Additional Information

State employment service offices and agencies can provide information about job openings for general office clerks.

For information related to administrative occupations, including educational programs and certified designations, contact

▸ International Association of Administrative Professionals, P.O. Box 20404, Kansas City, MO 64195-0404. Internet: www.iaap-hq.org

▸ American Management Association, 1601 Broadway, New York, NY 10019. Internet: www.amanet.org

▸ Association of Professional Office Managers, P.O. Box 1926, Rockville, MD 20849. Internet: www.apomonline.org

Painters and Paperhangers

(O*NET 47-2141.00 and 47-2142.00)

Significant Points

■ Most workers learn informally on the job as helpers, but some experts recommend completion of an apprenticeship program.

■ Employment prospects for painters should be excellent due to the large numbers of workers who leave the occupation for other jobs; paperhangers will face very limited opportunities.

■ About 45 percent of painters and paperhangers are self-employed.

Nature of the Work

Paint and indoor wall coverings make surfaces clean, attractive, and vibrant. In addition, paints and other sealers protect exterior surfaces from erosion caused by exposure to the weather.

Painters apply paint, stain, varnish, and other finishes to buildings and other structures. They select the right paint or finish for the surface to be covered, taking into account durability, ease of handling, method of application, and customers' wishes. Painters first prepare the surfaces to be coated, so that the paint will adhere properly. This may require removing the old coat of paint by sanding, wire brushing, burning, or water and abrasive blasting. Painters also fill nail holes and cracks, sandpaper rough spots, and wash walls and trim to remove dirt, grease, and dust. On new surfaces, they apply a primer or sealer to prepare the surface for the top coat. Painters also mix paints and match colors, relying on knowledge of paint composition and color harmony. In most paint shops or hardware stores, mixing and matching are automated.

There are several ways to apply paint and similar coverings. Therefore, painters must be able to choose the appropriate paint applicator for each job, depending on the surface to be covered, the characteristics of the finish, and other factors. Some jobs need only a good bristle brush with a soft, tapered edge; others require a dip or fountain pressure roller; still, others are best done using a paint sprayer. Many jobs need several types of applicators. In fact, painters may use an assortment of brushes, edgers, and rollers for a single job. The right tools speed the painter's work and produce the most attractive finish.

Some painting artisans specialize in creating distinctive finishes by using one of many decorative techniques. These techniques frequently involve "broken color," a process created by applying one or more colors in broken layers over a different base coat to produce a speckled or textured effect. Often these techniques employ glazes or washes applied over a solid colored background. Glazes are made of oil-based paints and give a sleek glow to walls. Washes are made of latex-based paints that have been thinned with water which adds a greater sense of depth and texture. Other decorative painting techniques include sponging, rag-rolling, stippling, sheen striping, dragging, distressing, color blocking, marbling, and faux finishes.

Some painters specialize in painting industrial structures to prevent deterioration. One example is applying a protective coating to oil rigs or steel bridges to fight corrosion. The coating most commonly used is a waterborne acrylic solvent that is easy to apply and environmentally friendly, but other specialized and sometimes difficult-to-apply coatings may be used. Painters may also coat interior and exterior manufacturing facilities and equipment such as storage tanks, plant buildings, lockers, piping, structural steel, and ships.

When painting any industrial structure, workers must take necessary safety precautions depending on their project. Those who specialize in interior applications such as painting the inside of storage tanks, for example, must wear a full-body protective suit. When working on bridges, painters are often suspended by cables and may work at extreme heights. When working on tall buildings, painters erect scaffolding, including "swing stages," scaffolds suspended by ropes, or cables attached to roof hooks. When painting steeples and other pointed structures, they use a bosun's chair, a swing-like device.

Paperhangers cover walls with decorative coverings made of paper, vinyl, or fabric. They first prepare the surface to be covered by applying a compound, which seals the surface and makes the covering adhere better. When redecorating, they may first remove the old covering by soaking, steaming, or applying solvents. When necessary, they patch holes and take care of other imperfections before hanging the new wall covering.

After preparing the surface, paperhangers mix the adhesive unless they are using pretreated paper. They then measure the area to be covered, check the covering for flaws, cut the covering into strips of the proper size, and closely examine the pattern in order to match it when the strips are hung. A great deal of this process can now be handled by specialized equipment.

The next step is to brush or roll the adhesive onto the back of the covering, if needed, and to then place the strips on the wall, making sure the pattern is matched, the strips are straight, and the edges are butted together to make tight, closed seams. Finally, paperhangers smooth the strips to remove bubbles and wrinkles, trim the top and bottom with a utility knife, and wipe off any excess adhesive.

Work environment. Most painters and paperhangers work 40 hours a week or less; about 25 percent have variable schedules or work part time. Painters and paperhangers must stand for long periods, often working from scaffolding and ladders. Their jobs also require a considerable amount of climbing, bending, kneeling, and stretching. These workers must have good stamina because much of the work is done with their arms raised overhead. Painters, especially industrial painters, often work outdoors, almost always in dry, warm weather. Those who paint bridges or building infrastructure may be exposed to extreme heights and uncomfortable positions; some painters work suspended with ropes or cables.

Some painting jobs can leave a worker covered with paint. Drywall dust created by electric sanders prior to painting requires workers to wear protective safety glasses and a dust mask. Painters and paperhangers occasionally work with materials that are hazardous or toxic, such as when they are required to remove lead-based paints. In the most dangerous situations, painters work in a sealed self-contained suit to prevent inhalation of or contact with hazardous materials. Data from the U.S. Bureau of Labor Statistics show that full-time painters and paperhangers experienced a work-related injury and illness rate that was higher than the national average.

Training, Other Qualifications, and Advancement

Painting and paperhanging is learned mostly on the job, but some experts recommend completion of an apprenticeship program.

Education and training. Most painters and paperhangers learn through on-the-job training and by working as a helper for an experienced painter. However, there are a number of formal and informal training programs that provide more thorough instruction and a better career foundation. In general, the more formal the training received, the more likely the individual will enter the profession at a higher level and earn a higher salary. There are limited informal training opportunities for paperhangers because there are fewer paperhangers and helpers are usually not required.

A high school education or its equivalent usually is required to enter an apprenticeship program. Apprenticeships for painters and paperhangers consist of 2 to 4 years of paid on-the-job training, supplemented by a minimum of 144 hours of related classroom instruction each year. Apprentices receive instruction in color harmony, use and care of tools and equipment, surface preparation, application techniques, paint mixing and matching, characteristics of different finishes, blueprint reading, wood finishing, and safety.

Besides apprenticeships, some workers gain skills by attending technical or vocational schools that offer training prior to employment. These schools can take about a year to complete.

Whether a painter learns the trade through a formal apprenticeship or informally as a helper, on-the-job instruction covers similar skill areas. Under the direction of experienced workers, trainees carry supplies, erect scaffolds, and do simple painting and surface preparation tasks while they learn about paint and painting equipment. As they gain experience, trainees learn to prepare surfaces for painting and paperhanging, to mix paints, and to apply paint and wall coverings efficiently and neatly. Near the end of their training, they may learn decorating concepts, color coordination, and cost-estimating techniques. In addition to learning craft skills, painters must become familiar with safety and health regulations so that their work complies with the law.

Other qualifications. Painters and paperhangers should have good manual dexterity, vision, and color sense. They also need physical stamina and balance to work on ladders and platforms. Apprentices or helpers generally must be at least 18 years old, in addition to the high school diploma or GED that most apprentices need.

Certification and advancement. Some organizations offer training and certification to enhance the skills of their members. People interested in industrial painting, for example, can earn several designations from the National Association of Corrosion Engineers in several areas of specialization, including one for coating applicators, called Protective Coating Specialist. Courses range from 1 day to several weeks depending on the certification program and specialty, and applicants must usually satisfy work experience requirements.

Painters and paperhangers may advance to supervisory or estimating jobs with painting and decorating contractors. Many establish their own painting and decorating businesses. For those who would like to advance, it is increasingly important to be able to communicate in both English and Spanish in order to relay instructions and safety precautions to workers with limited English skills; Spanish-speaking workers make up a large segment of the construction workforce in many areas. Painting contractors need good English skills to deal with clients and subcontractors.

Employment

Painters and paperhangers held about 450,100 jobs in 2008 of which 98 percent were painters. Around 36 percent of painters and paperhangers work for painting and wall covering contractors engaged in new construction, repair, restoration, or remodeling work. In addition, organizations that own or manage large buildings—such as apartment complexes—may employ painters, as do some schools, hospitals, factories, and government agencies.

Job Outlook

Overall employment is expected to grow 7 percent, reflecting as fast as average growth among painters but a rapid decline in the number of paperhangers. Excellent employment opportunities are expected for painters due to the need to replace the large number of workers who leave the occupation; paperhangers will have very limited opportunities.

Employment change. Overall employment is expected to grow by 7 percent between 2008 and 2018, about as fast as the average for all occupations. Employment of painters will grow 7 percent, as retiring baby boomers either purchase second homes or otherwise leave their

Projections Data from the National Employment Matrix

Occupational title	SOC Code	Employment, 2008	Projected employment, 2018	Change, 2008–2018	
				Number	Percent
Painters and paperhangers......................................47-2140		450,100	479,900	29,800	7
Painters, construction and maintenance...............47-2141		442,800	473,600	30,900	7
Paperhangers...47-2142		7,400	6,300	−1,100	−14

NOTE: Data in this table are rounded.

existing homes that then require interior painting. Investors who sell properties or rent them out will also require the services of painters prior to completing a transaction. The relatively short life of exterior paints in residential homes as well as changing color and application trends will continue to support demand for painters. Painting is labor-intensive and not susceptible to technological changes that might make workers more productive and slow employment growth.

Growth of industrial painting will be driven by the need to prevent corrosion and deterioration of the many industrial structures by painting or coating them. Applying a protective coating to steel bridges, for example, is cost-effective and can add years to the life expectancy of a bridge.

Employment of paperhangers, on the other hand, should decline rapidly as many homeowners take advantage of easy application materials and resort to cheaper alternatives, such as painting.

Job prospects. Job prospects for painters should be excellent because of the need to replace workers who leave the occupation for other jobs. There are no strict training requirements for entry into these jobs, so many people with limited skills work as painters or helpers for a relatively short time and then move on to other types of work with higher pay or better working conditions.

Opportunities for industrial painters should be excellent as the positions available should be greater than the pool of qualified individuals to fill them. While industrial structures that require painting are located throughout the nation, the best employment opportunities should be in the Gulf Coast region, where strong demand and the largest concentration of workers exist.

Very few openings will arise for paperhangers because the number of these jobs is comparatively small and cheaper, more modern decorative finishes such as faux effects and sponge painting have gained in popularity at the expense of paper, vinyl, or fabric wall coverings.

Job seekers considering these occupations should expect some periods of unemployment, especially until they gain experience. Many construction projects are of short duration, and construction activity is cyclical in nature. Remodeling, restoration, and maintenance projects, however, should continue as homeowners undertake renovation projects and hire painters even in economic downturns. Nonetheless, workers in these trades may experience periods of unemployment when the overall level of construction falls. On the other hand, a shortage of these workers may occur in some areas during peak periods of building activity.

Earnings

In May 2009, median hourly wages of wage and salary painters, construction and maintenance, were $16.21, not including the earnings of the self-employed. The middle 50 percent earned between $13.25 and $21.21. The lowest 10 percent earned less than $10.89,

and the highest 10 percent earned more than $27.93. Median hourly wages in the industries employing the largest numbers of painters were as follows:

Building finishing contractors $15.79
Residential building construction.......................... 14.54
Local government.. 21.64

In May 2009, median hourly wages for wage and salary paperhangers were $18.00. The middle 50 percent earned between $14.79 and $25.02. The lowest 10 percent earned less than $12.36, and the highest 10 percent earned more than $34.03.

Earnings for painters may be reduced on occasion because of bad weather and the short-term nature of many construction jobs. Hourly wage rates for apprentices usually start at 40 to 50 percent of the rate for experienced workers and increase periodically.

Some painters and paperhangers are members of the International Brotherhood of Painters and Allied Trades. Some painters are members of other unions.

Related Occupations

Painters and paperhangers apply various coverings to decorate and protect wood, drywall, metal, and other surfaces. Other construction workers who do finishing work include carpenters; carpet, floor, and tile installers and finishers; drywall and ceiling tile installers, tapers, plasterers, and stucco masons; and painting and coating workers, except construction and maintenance.

Sources of Additional Information

For details about painting and paperhanging apprenticeships or work opportunities, contact local painting and decorating contractors, local trade organizations, a local of the International Union of Painters and Allied Trades, a local joint union-management apprenticeship committee, or an office of the state apprenticeship agency or employment service.

For information about the work of painters and paperhangers and training opportunities, contact

▶ Associated Builders and Contractors, Workforce Development Department, 4250 N. Fairfax Dr., 9th Floor, Arlington, VA 22203. Internet: www.trytools.org

▶ International Union of Painters and Allied Trades, 1750 New York Ave. NW, Washington, DC 20006. Internet: www.iupat.org

▶ National Center for Construction Education and Research, 3600 NW 43rd St., Bldg. G, Gainesville, FL 32606. Internet: www.nccer.org

▶ Painting and Decorating Contractors of America, 1801 Park 270 Dr., Suite 220, St. Louis, MO 63146. Internet: www.pdca.org

For general information about the work of industrial painters and opportunities for training and certification as a protective coating specialist, contact

▸ National Association of Corrosion Engineers, 1440 South Creek Dr., Houston, TX 77084. Internet: www.nace.org

Painting and Coating Workers, Except Construction and Maintenance

(O*NET 51-9121.00, 51-9122.00, and 51-9123.00)

Significant Points

■ About two out of three jobs are in manufacturing establishments.

■ Most workers acquire their skills on the job; training usually lasts from a few days to several months, but becoming skilled in all aspects of painting can require one to two years of experience and training.

■ Overall employment is projected to grow.

■ Good job prospects are expected for skilled workers with painting experience.

Nature of the Work

Millions of items ranging from cars to candy are covered by paint, plastic, varnish, chocolate, or some other type of coating solution. Painting or coating is used to make a product more attractive or protect it from the elements. The paint finish on an automobile, for example, makes the vehicle more attractive and provides protection from corrosion. Achieving this end result is the work of *painting and coating workers*.

Before painting and coating workers can begin to apply the paint or other coating, they often need to prepare the surface. A metal, wood, or plastic part may need to be sanded or ground to correct imperfections or rough up a surface so that paint will stick to it. After they prepare the surface, the product is carefully cleaned to prevent any dust or dirt from becoming trapped under the paint. Metal parts are often washed or dipped in chemical baths to prepare the surface for painting and protect against corrosion. If the product has more than one color or has unpainted parts, masking is required. Masking normally involves carefully covering portions of the product with tape and paper.

After the product is prepared for painting, coating, or varnishing, a number of techniques may be used to apply the paint. Perhaps the most straightforward technique is simply dipping an item in a large vat of paint or other coating. This is the technique used by *dippers*, who immerse racks or baskets of articles in vats of paint, liquid plastic, or other solutions by means of a power hoist. This technique is commonly used for small parts in electronic equipment, such as cell phones.

Spraying products with a solution of paint or some other coating is also quite common. *Spray machine operators* use spray guns to coat metal, wood, ceramic, fabric, paper, and food products with paint and other coating solutions. Following a formula, operators fill the machine's tanks with a mixture of paints or chemicals, adding prescribed amounts of solution. Then they adjust nozzles on the spray guns to obtain the proper dispersion of the spray and hold or position the guns to direct the spray onto the article. Operators also check the flow and viscosity of the paint or solution and visually inspect the quality of the coating. When products are drying, these workers often must regulate the temperature and air circulation in drying ovens.

Some factories use automated painting systems that are operated by *coating, painting, and spraying machine setters, operators, and tenders*. When setting up these systems, operators position the automatic spray guns, set the nozzles, and synchronize the action of the guns with the speed of the conveyor carrying articles through the machine and drying ovens. The operator also may add solvents or water to the paint vessel to prepare the paint for application. During the operation of the painting machines, these workers tend the equipment, observe gauges on the control panel, and check articles for evidence of any variation from specifications. The operator uses a manual spray gun to "touch up" flaws.

Individuals who paint, coat, or decorate articles such as furniture, glass, pottery, toys, cakes, and books are known as *painting, coating, and decorating workers*. Some workers coat confectionery, bakery, and other food products with melted chocolate, cheese, oils, sugar, or other substances. Paper is often coated to give it its gloss or finish and silver, tin, and copper solutions are often sprayed on glass to make mirrors.

The best known group of painting and coating workers are those who refinish old or damaged cars, trucks, and buses in automotive body repair and paint shops. *Transportation equipment painters* who work in repair shops are among the most highly skilled manual spray operators, because they perform intricate, detailed work and mix paints to match the original color, a task that is especially difficult if the color has faded. The preparation work on an old car is similar to painting other metal objects. The paint is normally applied with a manually controlled spray gun.

Transportation equipment painters who work on new cars oversee several automated steps. A modern car is first dipped in an anti-corrosion bath, then coated with colored paint, and then painted in several coats of clear paint, which prevents scratches from damaging the colored paint.

Most other transportation equipment painters either paint equipment too large to paint automatically—such as ships or giant construction equipment—or perform touch-up work to repair flaws in the paint caused either by damage during assembly or flaws during the automated painting process.

With all types of coating, it is common for the painting process to be repeated several times to achieve a thick, smooth, protective coverage.

Work environment. Painting and coating workers typically work indoors and may be exposed to dangerous fumes from paint and coating solutions, although in general, workers' exposure to hazardous chemicals has decreased because of regulations limiting emissions of volatile organic compounds and other hazardous air pollutants. Painting usually is done in special ventilated booths with workers typically wearing masks or respirators that cover their noses and mouths. More sophisticated paint booths and fresh-air systems are increasingly used to provide a safer work environment.

Operators have to stand for long periods, and when using a spray gun, they may have to bend, stoop, or crouch in uncomfortable positions to reach different parts of the products.

Projections Data from the National Employment Matrix

Occupational title	SOC Code	Employment, 2008	Projected employment, 2018	Change, 2008–2018	
				Number	Percent
Painting workers..51-9120	51-9120	192,700	199,900	7,300	4
Coating, painting, and spraying machine setters, operators, and tenders......................................51-9121	51-9121	107,800	111,300	3,500	3
Painters, transportation equipment......................51-9122	51-9122	52,200	52,600	400	1
Painting, coating, and decorating workers............51-9123	51-9123	32,700	36,000	3,300	10

NOTE: Data in this table are rounded.

Most painting and coating workers work a normal 40-hour week, but automotive painters in repair shops can work more than 50 hours a week, depending on the number of vehicles that need repainting.

Training, Other Qualifications, and Advancement

A high school diploma or equivalent is required for most workers; training for new workers usually lasts from a few days to several months, but becoming skilled in all aspects of painting can require one to two years of experience.

Education and training. Painting and coating workers employed in the manufacturing sector are usually required to have a high school degree or equivalent; employers in other sectors may be willing to hire workers without a high school diploma. Training for beginning painting and coating machine setters, operators, and tenders and for painting, coating, and decorating workers, may last from a few days to a couple of months. Coating, painting, and spraying machine setters, operators, and tenders who modify the operation of computer-controlled equipment may require additional training in computer operations and minor programming. Transportation equipment painters typically learn their jobs through either apprenticeships as helpers or postsecondary education in painting.

Becoming skilled in all aspects of painting usually requires one to two years of experience and sometimes requires some formal classroom instruction and on-the-job training. Beginning helpers usually remove trim, clean, and sand surfaces to be painted; mask surfaces they do not want painted; and polish finished work. As helpers gain experience, they progress to more complicated tasks, such as mixing paint to achieve a good match and using spray guns to apply primer coats or final coats to small areas.

Additional instruction in safety, equipment, and techniques is offered at some community colleges and vocational or technical schools. Employers also sponsor training programs to help their workers become more productive. Additional training is available from manufacturers of chemicals, paints, or equipment, explaining their products and giving tips about techniques.

Other qualifications. Painting and coating workers in factories need to be able to read and follow detailed plans or blueprints. Some workers also need artistic talent to paint furniture, decorate cakes, or make sure that the paint on a car or other object is the right color. Applicants should be able to breathe comfortably wearing a respirator.

Certification and advancement. Voluntary certification by the National Institute for Automotive Service Excellence (ASE) is recognized as the standard of achievement for automotive painters. For certification, painters must pass a written examination and have at least two years of experience in the field. High school, trade or vocational school, or community or junior college training in automotive refinishing that meets ASE standards may substitute for up to one year of experience. To retain the certification, painters must retake the examination at least every five years. Outside of automobile painters, few receive certifications.

Some automotive painters go to technical schools to learn the intricacies of mixing and applying different types of paint. Such programs can improve employment prospects and speed up promotion. Experienced painting and coating workers with leadership ability may become team leaders or supervisors. Many become paint and coating inspectors. Those who get practical experience or formal training may become sales or technical representatives for chemical or paint companies. Some automotive painters eventually open their own shops.

Employment

Painting and coating workers held about 192,700 jobs in 2008. Coating, painting, and spraying machine setters, operators, and tenders accounted for about 107,800 jobs, while transportation equipment painters constituted about 52,200. Another 32,700 jobs were held by painting, coating, and decorating workers.

Approximately 2 out of 3 workers were employed by manufacturing establishments, particularly those that manufacture fabricated metal products, transportation equipment, industrial machines, household and office furniture, and plastic, wood, and paper products. Outside manufacturing, workers were employed by independent automotive repair shops and by motor vehicle dealers. About 6 percent were self-employed.

Job Outlook

Overall employment is expected to grow slower than the average for all occupations, but employment change will vary by specialty. Good job prospects are expected for skilled workers with painting experience.

Employment change. Overall employment of painting and coating workers is expected to increase by 4 percent from 2008 to 2018, which is slower than the average for all occupations. This growth will be driven primarily by the increasing number of goods requiring painting or coating. However, growth will be limited by gains in efficiency from automation and other processes. For example, operators will be able to coat goods more rapidly as sophisticated industrial machinery moves and aims spray guns more efficiently. Much of the growth in these occupations will be seen in the retail sector, as automation is less common in this industry.

Job prospects. Like many manufacturing occupations, employers report difficulty finding qualified workers. Opportunities should be good for those with painting experience. Job openings will result from the need to replace workers who leave the occupation and from increased specialization in manufacturing.

Earnings

Median hourly wages of coating, painting, and spraying machine setters, operators, and tenders were $13.75 in May 2009. The middle 50 percent earned between $11.01 and $17.38 an hour. The lowest 10 percent earned less than $9.26, and the highest 10 percent earned more than $21.49 an hour.

Median hourly wages of transportation equipment painters were $18.38 in May 2009. The middle 50 percent earned between $14.45 and $24.42 an hour. The lowest 10 percent earned less than $11.55, and the highest 10 percent earned more than $30.41 an hour. Median hourly wages of transportation equipment painters were $18.35 in automotive repair and maintenance shops and $18.91 in automobile dealers.

Median hourly wages of painting, coating, and decorating workers were $11.44 in May 2009. The middle 50 percent earned between $9.33 and $14.68 an hour. The lowest 10 percent earned less than $8.08, and the highest 10 percent earned more than $18.36 an hour.

Many automotive painters employed by motor vehicle dealers and independent automotive repair shops receive a commission, based on the labor cost charged to the customer. Under this method, earnings depend largely on the amount of work a painter does and how fast it is completed. Employers frequently guarantee commissioned painters a minimum weekly salary. Helpers and trainees usually receive an hourly rate until they become sufficiently skilled to work on commission. Trucking companies, bus lines, and other organizations that repair and refinish their own vehicles usually pay by the hour.

Some painting and coating machine operators belong to unions, including the United Auto Workers and the International Brotherhood of Teamsters. Most union operators work for manufacturers and large motor vehicle dealers.

Related Occupations

The work performed by the following occupations is similar to the duties of painting and coating workers: automotive body and related repairers; machine setters, operators, and tenders—metal and plastic; and painters and paperhangers.

Sources of Additional Information

For more details about work opportunities, contact local manufacturers, automotive body repair shops, motor vehicle dealers, vocational schools, locals of unions representing painting and coating workers, or the local offices of your state employment service. The state employment service also may be a source of information about training programs.

For a directory of certified automotive painting programs, contact

▶ National Automotive Technician Education Foundation, 101 Blue Seal Dr., Suite 101, Leesburg, VA 20175. Internet: www.natef.org

Paralegals and Legal Assistants

(O*NET 23-2011.00)

Significant Points

■ Despite projected much-faster-than-average employment growth, competition for jobs is expected.

■ Formally trained, experienced paralegals should have the best employment opportunities.

■ Most entrants have an associate's degree in paralegal studies or a bachelor's degree in another field and a certificate in paralegal studies.

■ About 71 percent work for law firms.

Nature of the Work

Although lawyers assume ultimate responsibility for legal work, they often delegate many of their tasks to paralegals. In fact, *paralegals*—also called *legal assistants*—are continuing to assume new responsibilities in legal offices and perform many of the same tasks as lawyers. Nevertheless, they are explicitly prohibited from carrying out duties considered to be within the scope of practice of law, such as setting legal fees, giving legal advice, and presenting cases in court.

One of a paralegal's most important tasks is helping lawyers prepare for closings, hearings, trials, and corporate meetings. Paralegals might investigate the facts of cases and ensure that all relevant information is considered. They also identify appropriate laws, judicial decisions, legal articles, and other materials that are relevant to assigned cases. After they analyze and organize the information, paralegals may prepare written reports that attorneys use in determining how cases should be handled. If attorneys decide to file lawsuits on behalf of clients, paralegals may help prepare the legal arguments, draft pleadings and motions to be filed with the court, obtain affidavits, and assist attorneys during trials. Paralegals also organize and track files of all important case documents and make them available and easily accessible to attorneys.

In addition to this preparatory work, paralegals perform a number of other functions. For example, they help draft contracts, mortgages, and separation agreements. They also may assist in preparing tax returns, establishing trust funds, and planning estates. Some paralegals coordinate the activities of other law office employees and maintain financial office records.

Computer software packages and the Internet are used to search legal literature stored in computer databases and on CD-ROM. In litigation involving many supporting documents, paralegals usually use computer databases to retrieve, organize, and index various materials. Imaging software allows paralegals to scan documents directly into a database, while billing programs help them to track hours billed to clients. Computer software packages also are used to perform tax computations and explore the consequences of various tax strategies for clients.

Paralegals are found in all types of organizations, but most are employed by law firms, corporate legal departments, and various government offices. In these organizations, they can work in many different areas of the law, including litigation, personal injury, corporate law, criminal law, employee benefits, intellectual property, labor law, bankruptcy, immigration, family law, and real estate. As the law becomes more complex, paralegals become more specialized. Within specialties, functions are often broken down further. For example, paralegals specializing in labor law may concentrate exclusively on employee benefits. In small and medium-size law firms, duties are often more general.

The tasks of paralegals differ widely according to the type of organization for which they work. *Corporate paralegals* often assist attorneys with employee contracts, shareholder agreements, stock-option plans, and employee benefit plans. They also may help prepare and file annual financial reports, maintain corporate minutes' record resolutions, and prepare forms to secure loans for the corporation. Corporate paralegals often monitor and review government regulations to ensure that the corporation is aware of new requirements and is operating within the law. Increasingly, experienced corporate paralegals or paralegal managers are assuming additional supervisory responsibilities, such as overseeing team projects.

The duties of paralegals who work in the public sector usually vary by agency. In general, *litigation paralegals* analyze legal material for internal use, maintain reference files, conduct research for attorneys, and collect and analyze evidence for agency hearings. They may prepare informative or explanatory material on laws, agency regulations, and agency policy for general use by the agency and the public. Paralegals employed in community legal-service projects help the poor, the aged, and others who are in need of legal assistance. They file forms, conduct research, prepare documents, and, when authorized by law, may represent clients at administrative hearings.

Work environment. Paralegals handle many routine assignments, particularly when they are inexperienced. As they gain experience, paralegals usually assume more varied tasks with additional responsibility. Paralegals do most of their work in offices and law libraries. Occasionally, they travel to gather information and perform other duties.

Paralegals employed by corporations and government usually work a standard 40-hour week. Although most paralegals work year round, some are temporarily employed during busy times of the year. Paralegals who work for law firms sometimes work very long hours when they are under pressure to meet deadlines.

Training, Other Qualifications, and Advancement

Most entrants have an associate degree in paralegal studies, or a bachelor's degree in another field and a certificate in paralegal studies. Some employers train paralegals on the job.

Education and training. There are several ways to become a paralegal. The most common is through a community college paralegal program that leads to an associate degree. Another common method of entry, mainly for those who already have a college degree, is earning a certificate in paralegal studies. A small number of schools offer bachelor's and master's degrees in paralegal studies. Finally, some employers train paralegals on the job.

Associate and bachelor's degree programs usually combine paralegal training with courses in other academic subjects. Certificate programs vary significantly, with some taking only a few months to complete. Most certificate programs provide intensive paralegal training for individuals who already hold college degrees.

More than 1,000 colleges and universities, law schools, and proprietary schools offer formal paralegal training programs. Approximately 260 paralegal programs are approved by the American Bar Association (ABA). Although not required by many employers, graduation from an ABA-approved program can enhance employment opportunities. Admission requirements vary. Some schools require certain college courses or a bachelor's degree, while others accept high school graduates or those with legal experience. A few schools require standardized tests and personal interviews.

The quality of paralegal training programs varies; some programs may include job placement services. If possible, prospective students should examine the experiences of recent graduates before enrolling in a paralegal program. Training programs usually include courses in legal research and the legal applications of computers. Many paralegal training programs also offer an internship, in which students gain practical experience by working for several months in a private law firm, the office of a public defender or attorney general, a corporate legal department, a legal aid organization, a bank, or a government agency. Internship experience is a valuable asset in seeking a job after graduation.

Some employers train paralegals on the job, hiring college graduates with no legal experience or promoting experienced legal secretaries. Some entrants have experience in a technical field that is useful to law firms, such as a background in tax preparation or criminal justice. Nursing or health administration experience is valuable in personal-injury law practices.

Certification and other qualifications. Although most employers do not require certification, earning voluntary certification from a professional national or local paralegal organization may offer advantages in the labor market. Many national and local paralegal organizations offer voluntary paralegal certifications by requiring students to pass an exam. Other organizations offer voluntary paralegal certifications by meeting certain criteria such as experience and education.

The National Association of Legal Assistants (NALA), for example, has established standards for certification that require various combinations of education and experience. Paralegals who meet these standards are eligible to take a 2-day examination. Those who pass the exam may use the Certified Legal Assistant (CLA) or Certified Paralegal (CP) credential. NALA certification is for a period of five years and 50 hours of continuing education is required for recertification. According to the NALA, as of September 4, 2009, there were 15,652 Certified Paralegals in the United States. NALA also offers the Advanced Paralegal Certification for experienced paralegals who want to specialize. The Advanced Paralegal Certification program is a curriculum-based program offered on the Internet.

The American Alliance of Paralegals, Inc., offers the American Alliance Certified Paralegal (AACP) credential, a voluntary certification program. Paralegals seeking the AACP certification must possess at least five years of paralegal experience and meet one of three educational criteria. Certification must be renewed every two years, including the completion of 18 hours of continuing education.

In addition, the National Federation of Paralegal Associations (NFPA) offers the Registered Paralegal (RP) designation to paralegals with a bachelor's degree and at least two years of experience who pass an exam. To maintain the credential, workers must complete 12 hours of continuing education every two years. The National Association of Legal Secretaries (NALS) offers the Professional Paralegal (PP) certification to those who pass a four-part exam. Recertification requires 75 hours of continuing education.

Projections Data from the National Employment Matrix

Occupational title	SOC Code	Employment, 2008	Projected employment, 2018	Change, 2008–2018	
				Number	Percent
Paralegals and legal assistants 23-2011		263,800	337,900	74,100	28

NOTE: Data in this table are rounded.

Paralegals must be able to document and present their findings and opinions to their supervising attorney. They need to understand legal terminology and have good research and investigative skills. Familiarity with the operation and applications of computers in legal research and litigation support also is important. Paralegals should stay informed of new developments in the laws that affect their area of practice. Participation in continuing legal education seminars allows paralegals to maintain and expand their knowledge of the law. In fact, all paralegals in California must complete 4 hours of mandatory continuing education in either general law or a specialized area of law.

Because paralegals frequently deal with the public, they should be courteous and uphold the ethical standards of the legal profession. The NALA, the NFPA, and a few states have established ethical guidelines for paralegals to follow.

Advancement. Paralegals usually are given more responsibilities and require less supervision as they gain work experience. Experienced paralegals who work in large law firms, corporate legal departments, or government agencies may supervise and delegate assignments to other paralegals and clerical staff. Advancement opportunities also include promotion to managerial and other law-related positions within the firm or corporate legal department. However, some paralegals find it easier to move to another law firm when seeking increased responsibility or advancement.

Employment

Paralegals and legal assistants held about 263,800 jobs in 2008. Private law firms employed 71 percent; most of the remainder worked for corporate legal departments and various levels of government. Within the federal government, the U.S. Department of Justice is the largest employer, followed by the Social Security Administration and the U.S. Department of the Treasury. A small number of paralegals own their own businesses and work as freelance legal assistants, contracting their services to attorneys or corporate legal departments.

Job Outlook

Despite projected much faster than average employment growth, competition for jobs is expected to continue as many people seek to go into this profession; experienced, formally trained paralegals should have the best employment opportunities.

Employment change. Employment of paralegals and legal assistants is projected to grow 28 percent between 2008 and 2018, much faster than the average for all occupations. Employers are trying to reduce costs and increase the availability and efficiency of legal services by hiring paralegals to perform tasks once done by lawyers. Paralegals are performing a wider variety of duties, making them more useful to businesses.

Demand for paralegals also is expected to grow as an expanding population increasingly requires legal services, especially in areas such as intellectual property, health care, international law, elder issues, criminal law, and environmental law. The growth of prepaid legal plans also should contribute to the demand for legal services.

Private law firms will continue to be the largest employers of paralegals, but a growing array of other organizations, such as corporate legal departments, insurance companies, real estate and title insurance firms, and banks also hire paralegals. Corporations in particular are expected to increase their in-house legal departments to cut costs. The wide range of tasks paralegals can perform has helped to increase their employment in small and medium-size establishments of all types.

Job prospects. In addition to new jobs created by employment growth, more job openings will arise as people leave the occupation. There will be demand for paralegals who specialize in areas such as real estate, bankruptcy, medical malpractice, and product liability. Community legal service programs, which provide assistance to the poor, elderly, minorities, and middle-income families, will employ additional paralegals to minimize expenses and serve the most people. Job opportunities also are expected in federal, state, and local government agencies, consumer organizations, and the courts. However, this occupation attracts many applicants, creating competition for jobs. Experienced, formally trained paralegals should have the best job prospects.

To a limited extent, paralegal jobs are affected by the business cycle. During recessions, demand declines for some discretionary legal services, such as planning estates, drafting wills, and handling real estate transactions. Corporations are less inclined to initiate certain types of litigation when falling sales and profits lead to fiscal belt tightening. As a result, full-time paralegals employed in offices adversely affected by a recession may be laid off or have their work hours reduced. However, during recessions, corporations and individuals are more likely to face problems that require legal assistance, such as bankruptcies, foreclosures, and divorces. Paralegals, who provide many of the same legal services as lawyers at a lower cost, tend to fare relatively better in difficult economic conditions.

Earnings

Wages of paralegals and legal assistants vary greatly. Salaries depend on education, training, experience, the type and size of employer, and the geographic location of the job. In general, paralegals who work for large law firms or in large metropolitan areas earn more than those who work for smaller firms or in less populated regions. In May 2009, full-time wage-and-salary paralegals and legal assistants earned $46,980. The middle 50 percent earned between $36,760 and $60,620. The top 10 percent earned more than $75,700, and the bottom 10 percent earned less than $29,800. Median annual wages in the industries employing the largest numbers of paralegals were as follows:

Legal services $44,260
Federal executive branch 60,490
Local government.. 46,210
State government.. 41,430
Management of companies and enterprises 57,020

In addition to earning a salary, many paralegals receive bonuses, in part to compensate them for sometimes having to work long hours. Paralegals also receive vacation, paid sick leave, a savings plan, life insurance, personal paid time off, dental insurance, and reimbursement for continuing legal education.

Related Occupations

Among the other occupations that call for a specialized understanding of the law, but that do not require the extensive training of a lawyer are claims adjusters, examiners, and investigators; law clerks; occupational health and safety specialists; occupational health and safety technicians; and title examiners, abstractors, and searchers.

Sources of Additional Information

General information on a career as a paralegal can be obtained from

▸ Standing Committee on Paralegals, American Bar Association, 321 N. Clark St., Chicago, IL 60654. Internet: www.abanet.org/legalservices/paralegals

For information on the Certified Legal Assistant exam, schools that offer training programs in a specific state, and standards and guidelines for paralegals, contact

▸ National Association of Legal Assistants, Inc., 1516 S. Boston St., Suite 200, Tulsa, OK 74119. Internet: www.nala.org

Information on the Paralegal Advanced Competency Exam, paralegal careers, paralegal training programs, job postings, and local associations is available from

▸ National Federation of Paralegal Associations, P.O. Box 2016, Edmonds, WA 98020. Internet: www.paralegals.org

Information on paralegal training programs, including the pamphlet *How to Choose a Paralegal Education Program*, may be obtained from

▸ American Association for Paralegal Education, 19 Mantua Rd., Mt. Royal, NJ 08061. Internet: www.aafpe.org

Information on paralegal careers, certification, and job postings is available from

▸ American Alliance of Paralegals, Inc., Suite 134-146, 4001 Kennett Pike, Wilmington, DE 19807. Internet: www.aapipara.org

For information on the Professional Paralegal exam, schools that offer training programs in a specific state, and standards and guidelines for paralegals, contact

▸ National Association of Legal Secretaries, 8159 E. 41st St., Tulsa, OK 74145. Internet: www.nals.org

Information on obtaining positions as a paralegal or legal assistant with the federal government is available from the Office of Personnel Management through USAJOBS, the federal government's official employment information system. This resource for locating and applying for job opportunities can be accessed through the Internet at www.usajobs.opm.gov or through an interactive voice response telephone system at (703) 724-1850 or TDD (978) 461-8404. These numbers are not toll free, and charges may result. For advice on how to find and apply for federal jobs, see the *Occupational*

Outlook Quarterly article "How to get a job in the federal government," online at www.bls.gov/opub/ooq/2004/summer/art01.pdf.

Pharmacy Technicians and Aides

(O*NET 29-2052.00 and 31-9095.00)

Significant Points

■ Job opportunities are expected to be good, especially for those with certification or previous work experience.

■ Many technicians and aides work evenings, weekends, and holidays.

■ About 75 percent of jobs are in a retail setting.

Nature of the Work

Pharmacy technicians and aides help licensed pharmacists prepare prescription medications, provide customer service, and perform administrative duties within a pharmacy setting. *Pharmacy technicians* generally are responsible for receiving prescription requests, counting tablets, and labeling bottles, while *pharmacy aides* perform administrative functions such as answering phones, stocking shelves, and operating cash registers. In organizations that do not have aides, however, pharmacy technicians may be responsible for these clerical duties.

Pharmacy technicians who work in retail or mail-order pharmacies have various responsibilities, depending on state rules and regulations. Technicians receive written prescription requests from patients. They also may receive prescriptions sent electronically from doctors' offices, and in some states they are permitted to process requests by phone. They must verify that the information on the prescription is complete and accurate. To prepare the prescription, technicians retrieve, count, pour, weigh, measure, and sometimes mix the medication. Then they prepare the prescription labels, select the type of container, and affix the prescription and auxiliary labels to the container. Once the prescription is filled, technicians price and file the prescription, which must be checked by a pharmacist before it is given to the patient. Technicians may establish and maintain patient profiles, as well as prepare insurance claim forms. Technicians always refer any questions regarding prescriptions, drug information, or health matters to a pharmacist.

In hospitals, nursing homes, and assisted-living facilities, technicians have added responsibilities, including preparing sterile solutions and delivering medications to nurses or physicians. Technicians may also record the information about the prescribed medication onto the patient's profile.

Pharmacy aides work closely with pharmacy technicians. They primarily perform administrative duties such as answering telephones, stocking shelves, and operating cash registers. They also may prepare insurance forms and maintain patient profiles. Unlike pharmacy technicians, pharmacy aides do not prepare prescriptions or mix medications.

Work environment. Pharmacy technicians and aides work in clean, organized, well-lighted, and well-ventilated areas. Most of their workday is spent on their feet. They may be required to lift heavy boxes or to use stepladders to retrieve supplies from high shelves.

Technicians and aides often have varying schedules that include nights, weekends, and holidays. In facilities that are open 24 hours a day, such as hospital pharmacies, technicians and aides may be required to work nights. Many technicians and aides work part time.

Training, Other Qualifications, and Advancement

There is no national training standard for pharmacy technicians, but employers favor applicants who have formal training, certification, or previous experience. There also are no formal training requirements for pharmacy aides, but a high school diploma may increase an applicant's prospects for employment.

Education and training. There are no standard training requirements for pharmacy technicians, but some states require a high school diploma or its equivalent. Although most pharmacy technicians receive informal on-the-job training, employers favor those who have completed formal training and certification. On-the-job training generally ranges between 3 and 12 months.

Formal technician education programs are available through a variety of organizations, including community colleges, vocational schools, hospitals, and the military. These programs range from 6 months to 2 years and include classroom and laboratory work. They cover a variety of subject areas, such as medical and pharmaceutical terminology, pharmaceutical calculations, pharmacy recordkeeping, pharmaceutical techniques, and pharmacy law and ethics. Technicians also are required to learn the names, actions, uses, and doses of the medications they work with. Many training programs include internships, in which students gain hands-on experience in actual pharmacies. After completion, students receive a diploma, a certificate, or an associate degree, depending on the program.

There are no formal education requirements for pharmacy aides, but employers may favor applicants with a high school diploma or its equivalent. Experience operating a cash register, interacting with customers, managing inventory, and using computers may be helpful. Pharmacy aides also receive informal on-the-job training that generally lasts less than 3 months.

Certification and other qualifications. In most states, pharmacy technicians must be registered with the state board of pharmacy. Eligibility requirements vary, but in some states applicants must possess a high school diploma or its equivalent and pay an application fee.

Most states do not require technicians to be certified, but voluntary certification is available through several private organizations. The Pharmacy Technician Certification Board (PTCB) and the Institute for the Certification of Pharmacy Technicians (ICPT) administer national certification examinations. Certification through such programs may enhance an applicant's prospects for employment and is required by some states and employers. To be eligible for either exam, candidates must have a high school diploma or its equivalent and no felony convictions of any kind. In addition, applicants for the PTCB exam must not have had any drug-related or pharmacy-related convictions, including misdemeanors. Many employers will reimburse the cost of the exams.

Under these programs, technicians must be recertified every 2 years. Recertification requires 20 hours of continuing education within the 2-year certification period. Continuing education hours can be earned from several different sources, including colleges, pharmacy associations, and pharmacy technician training programs. Up to 10 hours of continuing education also can be earned on the job under the direct supervision and instruction of a pharmacist.

Good customer service and communication skills are needed because pharmacy technicians and aides interact with patients, coworkers, and health-care professionals. Basic mathematics, spelling, and reading skills also are important, as technicians must interpret prescription orders and verify drug doses. Technicians also must be precise: Details are sometimes a matter of life and death.

Advancement. Advancement opportunities generally are limited, but in large pharmacies and health systems pharmacy technicians and aides with significant training or experience can be promoted to supervisory positions. Some may advance into specialty positions such as chemotherapy technician or nuclear pharmacy technician. Others may move into sales. With a substantial amount of formal training, some technicians and aides go on to become pharmacists.

Employment

Pharmacy technicians and aides held about 381,200 jobs in 2008. Of these, about 326,300 were pharmacy technicians and about 54,900 were pharmacy aides. About 75 percent of jobs were in a retail setting, and about 16 percent were in hospitals.

Job Outlook

Employment is expected to increase much faster than the average, and job opportunities are expected to be good.

Employment change. Employment of pharmacy technicians and aides is expected to increase by 25 percent from 2008 to 2018, which is much faster than the average for all occupations. The increased number of middle-aged and elderly people—who use more prescription drugs than younger people—will spur demand for pharmacy workers throughout the projection period. In addition, as scientific advances lead to new drugs, and as more people obtain prescription drug coverage, pharmacy workers will be needed in growing numbers.

Employment of pharmacy technicians is expected to increase by 31 percent. As cost-conscious insurers begin to use pharmacies as patient-care centers and pharmacists become more involved in patient care, pharmacy technicians will continue to see an expansion of their role in the pharmacy. In addition, they will increasingly adopt some of the administrative duties that were previously performed by pharmacy aides, such as answering phones and stocking shelves. As a result of this development, demand for pharmacy aides should decrease, and employment is expected to decline moderately, decreasing by 6 percent over the projection period.

Job prospects. Job opportunities for pharmacy technicians are expected to be good, especially for those with previous experience, formal training, or certification. Job openings will result from employment growth, as well as the need to replace workers who transfer to other occupations or leave the labor force.

Despite declining employment, job prospects for pharmacy aides also are expected to be good. As people leave this occupation, new applicants will be needed to fill the positions that remain.

Earnings

Median hourly wages of wage and salary pharmacy technicians in May 2009 were $13.49. The middle 50 percent earned between

Projections Data from the National Employment Matrix

Occupational title	SOC Code	Employment, 2008	Projected employment, 2018	Change, 2008–2018	
				Number	Percent
Pharmacy technicians and aides .... —		381,200	477,500	96,300	25
Pharmacy technicians 29-2052		326,300	426,000	99,800	31
Pharmacy aides.. 31-9095		54,900	51,500	–3,500	–6

NOTE: Data in this table are rounded.

$11.07 and $16.26. The lowest 10 percent earned less than $9.36, and the highest 10 percent earned more than $19.31.

Median hourly wages of wage-and-salary pharmacy aides were $10.00 in May 2009. The middle 50 percent earned between $8.68 and $12.03. The lowest 10 percent earned less than $7.86, and the highest 10 percent earned more than $14.92.

Certified technicians may earn more than noncertified technicians. Some technicians and aides belong to unions representing hospital or grocery store workers.

Related Occupations

Other occupations related to health care include the following: dental assistants; medical assistants; medical records and health information technicians; medical transcriptionists; and pharmacists.

Sources of Additional Information

For information on pharmacy technician certification programs, contact

▸ Pharmacy Technician Certification Board, 2215 Constitution Ave. NW, Washington DC 20037-2985. Internet: www.ptcb.org

▸ Institute for the Certification of Pharmacy Technicians, 2536 S. Old Hwy. 94, Suite 224, St. Charles, MO 63303. Internet: www.nationaltechexam.org

For a list of accredited pharmacy technician training programs, contact

▸ American Society of Health-System Pharmacists, 7272 Wisconsin Ave., Bethesda, MD 20814. Internet: www.ashp.org

For pharmacy technician career information, contact

▸ National Pharmacy Technician Association, P.O. Box 683148, Houston, TX 77268. Internet: www.pharmacytechnician.org

Photographers

(O*NET 27-4021.00)

Significant Points

■ Competition for jobs is expected to be keen because the work is attractive to many people.

■ Technical expertise, a "good eye," and creativity are essential, and some photographers need a college degree.

■ More than half of all photographers are self-employed, a much higher proportion than for most occupations.

Nature of the Work

Photographers produce and preserve images that paint a picture, tell a story, or record an event. To create commercial-quality photographs, photographers need technical expertise, creativity, and the appropriate professional equipment. Producing a successful picture requires choosing and presenting a subject to achieve a particular effect, and selecting the right cameras and other photographic enhancing tools. For example, photographers may enhance the subject's appearance with natural or artificial light, shoot the subject from an interesting angle, draw attention to a particular aspect of the subject by blurring the background, or use various lenses to produce desired levels of detail at various distances from the subject.

Today, most photographers use digital cameras instead of traditional silver-halide film cameras, although some photographers use both types, depending on their own preference and the nature of the assignment. Regardless of the camera they use, photographers also employ an array of other equipment—from lenses, filters, and tripods to flash attachments and specially constructed lighting equipment—to improve the quality of their work.

Digital cameras capture images electronically, allowing them to be edited on a computer. Images can be stored on portable memory devices such as compact disks, memory cards, and flash drives. Once the raw image has been transferred to a computer, photographers can use processing software to crop or modify the image and enhance it through color correction and other specialized effects. As soon as a photographer has finished editing the image, it can be sent anywhere in the world over the Internet.

Photographers also can create electronic portfolios of their work and display them on their own Web page, allowing them to reach prospective customers directly. Digital technology also allows the production of larger, more colorful, and more accurate prints or images for use in advertising, photographic art, and scientific research. Photographers who process their own digital images need to be proficient in the use of computers, high-quality printers, and editing software.

Photographers who use cameras with silver-halide film often send their film to laboratories for processing. Color film requires expensive equipment and exacting conditions for correct processing and printing. Other photographers, especially those using black-and-white film or creating special effects, develop and print their own photographs using their own fully equipped darkrooms. Photographers who develop their own film must invest in additional developing and printing equipment and acquire the technical skills to operate it.

Some photographers specialize in areas such as portrait, commercial and industrial, scientific, news, or fine arts photography. *Portrait photographers* take pictures of individuals or groups of people and usually work in their own studios. Some specialize in weddings, religious ceremonies, or school photographs and they may work on location. Portrait photographers who own and operate their own business have many responsibilities in addition to taking pictures. They must arrange for advertising, schedule appointments, set and adjust equipment, purchase supplies, keep records, bill customers, pay bills, and—if they have employees—hire, train, and direct their workers. Many also process their own images, design albums, and mount and frame the finished photographs.

Commercial and industrial photographers take pictures of various subjects, such as buildings, models, merchandise, artifacts, and landscapes. These photographs are used in a variety of media, including books, reports, advertisements, and catalogs. Industrial photographers often take pictures of equipment, machinery, products, workers, and company officials. The pictures are used for various purposes—for example, analysis of engineering projects, publicity, or records of equipment development or deployment. This photography frequently is done on location.

Scientific photographers take images of a variety of subjects to record scientific or medical data or phenomena, using knowledge of scientific procedures. They typically possess additional knowledge in areas such as engineering, medicine, biology, or chemistry.

News photographers, also called *photojournalists*, photograph newsworthy people, places, and sporting, political, and community events for newspapers, journals, magazines, or television.

Fine arts photographers sell their photographs as fine artwork. In addition to technical proficiency, fine arts photographers need artistic talent and creativity.

Self-employed, or freelance, photographers usually specialize in one of the above fields. In addition to carrying out assignments under direct contract with clients, they may license the use of their photographs through stock-photo agencies or market their work directly to the public. Stock-photo agencies sell magazines and other customers the right to use photographs, and pay the photographer a commission. These agencies require an application from the photographer and a sizable portfolio of pictures. Once accepted, photographers usually are required to submit a large number of new photographs each year. Self-employed photographers must also have a thorough understanding of copyright laws in order to protect their work.

Most photographers spend only a small portion of their work schedule actually taking photographs. Their most common activities are editing images on a computer—if they use a digital camera—and looking for new business—if they are self-employed.

Work environment. Working conditions for photographers vary considerably. Some photographers may work a 5-day, 40-hour week. News photographers, however, often work long, irregular hours and must be available to work on short notice. Many photographers work part time or on variable schedules.

Portrait photographers usually work in their own studios but also may travel to take photographs at the client's location, such as a school, a company office, or a private home. News and commercial photographers frequently travel locally, stay overnight on assignments, or travel to distant places for long periods.

Some photographers work in uncomfortable or even dangerous surroundings, especially news photographers covering accidents, natural disasters, civil unrest, or military conflicts. Many photographers must wait long hours in all kinds of weather for an event to take place and stand or walk for long periods while carrying heavy equipment. News photographers often work under strict deadlines.

Self-employment allows for greater autonomy, freedom of expression, and flexible scheduling. However, income can be uncertain and the continuous, time-consuming search for new clients can be stressful. Some self-employed photographers hire assistants who help seek out new business.

Training, Other Qualifications, and Advancement

Employers usually seek applicants with a "good eye," imagination, and creativity, as well as a good technical understanding of photography. Photojournalists or industrial or scientific photographers generally need a college degree. Freelance and portrait photographers need technical proficiency, gained through a degree, training program, or experience.

Education and training. Entry-level positions in photojournalism or in industrial or scientific photography generally require a college degree in photography or in a field related to the industry in which the photographer seeks employment. Entry-level freelance or portrait photographers need technical proficiency. Some complete a college degree or vocational training programs.

Photography courses are offered by many universities, community and junior colleges, vocational-technical institutes, and private trade and technical schools. Basic courses in photography cover equipment, processes, and techniques. Learning good business and marketing skills is important and some bachelor's degree programs offer courses focusing on them. Art schools offer useful training in photographic design and composition.

Photographers may start out as assistants to experienced photographers. Assistants acquire the technical knowledge needed to be a successful photographer and also learn other skills necessary to run a portrait or commercial photography business.

Individuals interested in a career in photography should try to develop contacts in the field by subscribing to photographic newsletters and magazines, joining camera clubs, and seeking summer or part-time employment in camera stores, newspapers, or photo studios.

Other qualifications. Photographers need good eyesight, artistic ability, and good hand-eye coordination. They should be patient, accurate, and detail-oriented and should be able to work well with others, as they frequently deal with clients, graphic designers, and advertising and publishing specialists. Photographers need to know how to use computer software programs and applications that allow them to prepare and edit images, and those who market directly to clients should know how to use the Internet to display their work.

Portrait photographers need the ability to help people relax in front of the camera. Commercial and fine arts photographers must be imaginative and original. News photographers must not only be good with a camera, but also understand the story behind an event so that their pictures match the story. They must be decisive in recognizing a potentially good photograph and act quickly to capture it.

Many photographers have websites which highlight an online portfolio that they use to attract work from magazines or advertising agencies. For freelance photographers, maintaining their website is essential.

Photographers who operate their own business, or freelance, need business skills as well as talent. These individuals must know how to prepare a business plan; submit bids; write contracts; keep financial records; market their work; hire models, if needed; get permission to shoot on locations that normally are not open to the public; obtain releases to use photographs of people; license and price photographs; and secure copyright protection for their work. To protect their rights and their work, self-employed photographers require basic knowledge of licensing and copyright laws, as well as knowledge of contracts and negotiation procedures.

Projections Data from the National Employment Matrix

Occupational title	SOC Code	Employment, 2008	Projected employment, 2018	Change, 2008–2018	
				Number	Percent
Photographers.. 27-4021		152,000	169,500	17,500	12

NOTE: Data in this table are rounded.

Freelance photographers also should develop an individual style of photography to differentiate themselves from the competition.

Advancement. After several years of experience, magazine and news photographers may advance to photography or picture editor positions. Some photographers teach at technical schools, film schools, or universities.

Employment

Photographers held about 152,000 jobs in 2008. More than half were self-employed, a much higher proportion than for most occupations. Some self-employed photographers have contracts with advertising agencies, magazine publishers, or other businesses to do individual projects for a set fee, while others operate portrait studios or provide photographs to stock-photo agencies.

Most salaried photographers work in portrait or commercial photography studios; most of the others work for newspapers, magazines, and advertising agencies. Photographers work in all areas of the country, but most are employed in metropolitan areas.

Job Outlook

Employment is expected to grow as fast as the average for all occupations. Photographers can expect keen competition for job openings because the work is attractive to many people.

Employment change. Employment of photographers is expected to grow 12 percent over the 2008–2018 period, about as fast as the average for all occupations. Demand for portrait photographers should increase as the population grows. Moreover, growth of Internet versions of magazines, journals, and newspapers will require increasing numbers of commercial photographers to provide digital images. The Internet and improved data management programs also should make it easier for freelancers to market directly to their customers, increasing opportunities for self-employment and decreasing reliance on stock photo agencies.

Job growth, however, will be constrained somewhat by the widespread use of digital photography and the falling price of digital equipment. Improvements in digital technology reduce barriers of entry into this profession and allow more individual consumers and businesses to produce, store, and access photographic images on their own. News and commercial photographers may be the most adversely affected by this increase in amateur photographers and noncopyrighted photos. Declines in the newspaper industry also will reduce demand for news photographers to provide still images for print.

Job prospects. Photographers can expect keen competition for job openings because the work is attractive to many people. The number of individuals interested in positions as commercial and news photographers is usually much greater than the number of openings. Salaried jobs in particular may be difficult to find as more companies contract with freelancers rather than hire their own photographers. Those who succeed in landing a salaried job or attracting enough work to earn a living by freelancing are likely to be adept at operating a business and to be among the most creative. They will be able to find and exploit the new opportunities available from rapidly changing technologies. Related work experience, job-related training, or some unique skill or talent—such as a background in computers or electronics or knowledge of a second language—also improves a photographer's job prospects.

Earnings

Median annual wages of salaried photographers were $29,770 in May 2009. The middle 50 percent earned between $21,150 and $44,230. The lowest 10 percent earned less than $17,120, and the highest 10 percent earned more than $62,340. Median annual wages in the photographic services industry, which employed the largest numbers of salaried photographers, were $26,870.

Salaried photographers—most of whom work full time—tend to earn more than those who are self-employed. Because most freelance and portrait photographers purchase their own equipment, they incur considerable expense acquiring and maintaining cameras and accessories. Unlike news and commercial photographers, few fine arts photographers are successful enough to support themselves solely through their art.

Related Occupations

Other occupations requiring artistic talent and creativity include architects, except landscape and naval; artists and related workers; commercial and industrial designers; fashion designers; graphic designers; and television, video, and motion picture camera operators and editors.

Photojournalists are often required to cover news stories much the same as news analysts, reporters, and correspondents.

The processing work that photographers do on computers is similar to the work of desktop publishers; and prepress technicians and workers.

Sources of Additional Information

Career information on photography is available from

▸ Professional Photographers of America, Inc., 229 Peachtree St. NE, Suite 2200, Atlanta, GA 30303. Internet: www.ppa.com

▸ National Press Photographers Association, Inc., 3200 Croasdaile Dr., Suite 306, Durham, NC 27705. Internet: www.nppa.org

▸ American Society of Media Photographers, Inc., 150 N. Second St., Philadelphia, PA 19106. Internet: www.asmp.org

Plumbers, Pipelayers, Pipefitters, and Steamfitters

(O*NET 47-2151.00, 47-2152.00, 47-2152.01, and 47-2152.02)

Significant Points

■ Job opportunities should be very good.

■ These workers constitute one of the largest and highest paid construction occupations.

■ Most states and localities require plumbers to be licensed.

■ Most workers train in apprenticeship programs and in career or technical schools or community colleges.

Nature of the Work

Most people are familiar with plumbers who come to their home to unclog a drain or fix a leaking toilet. Plumbers, pipelayers, pipefitters, and steamfitters install, maintain, and repair many different types of pipe systems. Some of these systems move water from reservoirs to municipal water treatment plants and then to residential, commercial, and public buildings. Other systems dispose of waste, supply gas to stoves and furnaces, or provide for heating and cooling needs. Pipe systems in powerplants carry the steam that powers huge turbines. Pipes also are used in manufacturing plants to move material through the production process. Specialized piping systems are very important in both pharmaceutical and computer-chip manufacturing.

Although plumbing, pipelaying, pipefitting, and steamfitting are sometimes considered a single trade, workers generally specialize in one of five areas. *Plumbers* install and repair the water, waste disposal, drainage, and gas systems in homes and commercial and industrial buildings. Plumbers also install plumbing fixtures—bathtubs, showers, sinks, and toilets—and appliances such as dishwashers, waste disposers, and water heaters. *Pipelayers* lay clay, concrete, plastic, or cast-iron pipe for drains, sewers, water mains, and oil or gas lines. Before laying the pipe, pipelayers prepare and grade the trenches either manually or with machines. After laying the pipe, they weld, glue, cement, or otherwise join the pieces together. *Pipefitters* install and repair both high-pressure and low-pressure pipe systems used in manufacturing, in the generation of electricity, and in the heating and cooling of buildings. They also install automatic controls that are increasingly being used to regulate these systems. *Steamfitters* install pipe systems that move liquids or gases under high pressure. *Sprinklerfitters* install automatic fire sprinkler systems in buildings. Plumbers, pipelayers, pipefitters, and steamfitters use many different materials and construction techniques, depending on the type of project. Residential water systems, for example, incorporate copper, steel, and plastic pipe that can be handled and installed by one or two plumbers. Municipal sewerage systems, by contrast, are made of large cast-iron pipes; installation normally requires crews of pipefitters. Despite these differences, all plumbers, pipelayers, pipefitters, and steamfitters must be able to follow building plans or blueprints and instructions from supervisors, lay out the job, and work efficiently with the materials and tools of their trade. When plumbers working construction install piping in a new house, they work from blueprints or drawings that show the planned location of pipes, plumbing fixtures, and appliances. Recently, plumbers have become more involved in the design

process. Their knowledge of codes and the operation of plumbing systems can cut costs. First they lay out the job to fit the piping into the structure of the house with the least waste of material. Then they measure and mark areas in which pipes will be installed and connected. Construction plumbers also check for obstructions such as electrical wiring and, if necessary, plan the pipe installation around the problem.

Sometimes, plumbers have to cut holes in walls, ceilings, and floors of a house. With some systems, they may hang steel supports from ceiling joists to hold the pipe in place. To assemble a system, plumbers—using saws, pipe cutters, and pipe-bending machines—cut and bend lengths of pipe. They connect the lengths of pipe with fittings, using methods that depend on the type of pipe used. For plastic pipe, plumbers connect the sections and fittings with adhesives. For copper pipe, they slide a fitting over the end of the pipe and solder it in place with a torch.

After the piping is in place in the house, plumbers install the fixtures and appliances and connect the system to the outside water or sewer lines. Finally, using pressure gauges, they check the system to ensure that the plumbing works properly.

Work environment. Plumbers work in commercial and residential settings where water and septic systems need to be installed and maintained. Pipefitters and steamfitters most often work in industrial and power plants. Pipelayers work outdoors, sometimes in remote areas, laying pipes that connect sources of oil, gas, and chemicals with the users of these resources. Sprinklerfitters work in all buildings that require the use of fire sprinkler systems.

Because plumbers, pipelayers, pipefitters, and steamfitters frequently must lift heavy pipes, stand for long periods, and sometimes work in uncomfortable or cramped positions, they need physical strength and stamina. They also may have to work outdoors in inclement weather. In addition, they are subject to possible falls from ladders, cuts from sharp tools, and burns from hot pipes or soldering equipment. Consequently, this occupation experiences rates of nonfatal injuries and illnesses that are much higher than average.

Plumbers, pipelayers, pipefitters, and steamfitters often work more than 40 hours per week and can be on call for emergencies nights and weekends. Some pipelayers may need to travel to and from work sites.

Training, Other Qualifications, and Advancement

Most plumbers, pipelayers, pipefitters, and steamfitters train on the job through jointly administered apprenticeships and in career or technical schools or community colleges.

Education and training. Plumbers, pipelayers, pipefitters, and steamfitters enter into the occupation in a variety of ways. Most plumbers, pipefitters, and steamfitters get their training in jointly administered apprenticeships or in technical schools and community colleges. Pipelayers typically receive their training on the job.

Apprenticeship programs generally provide the most comprehensive training available for these jobs. Such programs are, for the most part, administered jointly by union locals and their affiliated companies or by nonunion contractor organizations. Organizations that sponsor apprenticeships include the United Association of Journeymen and Apprentices of the Plumbing and Pipefitting Industry of the United States and Canada; local employers of either the Mechanical Contractors Association of America or the National Association of

Plumbing-Heating-Cooling Contractors; a union associated with a member of the National Fire Sprinkler Association; the Associated Builders and Contractors; the National Association of Plumbing-Heating-Cooling Contractors; the American Fire Sprinkler Association; and the Home Builders Institute of the National Association of Home Builders.

Apprenticeships—both union and nonunion—consist of 4 or 5 years of paid on-the-job training and at least 144 hours of related classroom instruction per year. Classroom subjects include drafting and blueprint reading, mathematics, applied physics and chemistry, safety, and local plumbing codes and regulations. On the job, apprentices first learn basic skills, such as identifying grades and types of pipe, using the tools of the trade, and unloading materials safely. As apprentices gain experience, they learn how to work with various types of pipe and how to install different piping systems and plumbing fixtures. Apprenticeship gives trainees a thorough knowledge of all aspects of the trade. Although most plumbers, pipefitters, and steamfitters are trained through apprenticeships, some still learn their skills informally on the job or by taking classes on their own.

Licensure. Although there are no uniform national licensing requirements, most states and communities require plumbers to be licensed. Licensing requirements vary, but most localities require workers to have 2 to 5 years of experience and to pass an examination that tests their knowledge of the trade and of local plumbing codes before they are permitted to work independently. Several states require a special license to work on gas lines. A few states require pipefitters to be licensed. Licenses usually require a test, experience, or both.

Other qualifications. Applicants for union or nonunion apprentice jobs must be at least 18 years old and in good physical condition. A drug test may be required. Apprenticeship committees may require applicants to have a high school diploma or its equivalent. For jointly administered apprenticeships approved by the U.S. Department of Labor, a high school diploma is mandatory, because these programs can earn credit from community colleges and, in some cases, from 4-year colleges. Armed Forces training in plumbing, pipefitting, and steamfitting is considered very good preparation. In fact, people with this background may be given credit for previous experience when they enroll in a civilian apprenticeship program. High school or postsecondary courses in shop, plumbing, general mathematics, drafting, blueprint reading, computers, and physics also are good preparation.

Certification and advancement. With additional training, some plumbers, pipefitters, and steamfitters become supervisors for mechanical and plumbing contractors. Others, especially plumbers, go into business for themselves, often starting as a self-employed plumber working from home. Some eventually become owners of businesses employing many workers and may spend most of their time as managers rather than as plumbers. Others move into closely related areas such as construction management or building inspection.

For those who would like to advance, it is becoming increasingly important to be able to communicate in both English and Spanish in order to relay instructions and safety precautions to workers with limited understanding of English; Spanish-speaking workers make up a large part of the construction workforce in many areas. Supervisors and contractors need good communication skills to deal with clients and subcontractors.

In line with new opportunities arising from the growing need to conserve water, the Plumbing-Heating-Cooling Contractors—National

Association has formed a partnership with GreenPlumbers USA to train and certify plumbers across the nation on water-saving technologies and energy efficiency. Attainment of this certification may help people trained in this area to get more jobs and advance more quickly.

Employment

Plumbers, pipelayers, pipefitters, and steamfitters constitute one of the largest construction occupations, holding about 555,900 jobs in 2008. About 56 percent worked for plumbing, heating, and air-conditioning contractors engaged in new construction, repair, modernization, or maintenance work. Others were employed by a variety of industrial, commercial, and government employers. Pipefitters, for example, were employed in the petroleum and chemical industries to maintain the pipes that carry industrial liquids and gases. About 12 percent of plumbers, pipelayers, pipefitters, and steamfitters were self-employed.

Job Outlook

Faster than average employment growth is projected. Job opportunities are expected to be very good.

Employment change. Employment of plumbers, pipelayers, pipefitters, and steamfitters is expected to grow 16 percent between 2008 and 2018, faster than the average for all occupations. Demand for plumbers will stem from new construction and from renovation of buildings. In addition, repair and maintenance of existing residential systems will keep plumbers employed. A growing emphasis on water conservation, particularly in dryer parts of the country, that will require retrofitting in order to conserve water in new ways will increase demand for plumbers. Demand for pipefitters and steamfitters will be driven by maintenance and construction of places such as powerplants, water and wastewater treatment plants, office buildings, and factories, all of which have extensive pipe systems. The stimulus package aimed at repairing the nation's infrastructure should help the employment picture immediately; long-term growth of pipelayer jobs will stem from the building of new water and sewer lines and of pipelines to new oil and gas fields. Demand for sprinklerfitters also should increase, because of proposed changes to construction codes, set to take effect in 2011, that will require the installation of fire sprinkler systems in residential buildings where these systems had previously never been required.

Job prospects. Job opportunities are expected to be very good, with demand for skilled plumbers, pipelayers, pipefitters, and steamfitters expected to outpace the supply of well-trained workers in this craft. Some employers report difficulty finding workers with the right qualifications. In addition, many people currently working in these trades are expected to retire over the next 10 years, which will create additional job openings. Workers with welding experience should have especially good opportunities.

Traditionally, many organizations with extensive pipe systems have employed their own plumbers or pipefitters to maintain equipment and keep systems running smoothly. But, to reduce labor costs, a large number of these firms no longer employ full-time, in-house plumbers or pipefitters. Instead, when they need a plumber, they increasingly are relying on workers provided under service contracts by plumbing and pipefitting contractors.

Construction projects generally provide only temporary employment. When a project ends, some plumbers, pipelayers, pipefitters,

Projections Data from the National Employment Matrix

Occupational title	SOC Code	Employment, 2008	Projected employment, 2018	Change, 2008–2018	
				Number	Percent
Pipelayers, plumbers, pipefitters, and steamfitters......47-2150		555,900	642,100	86,300	16
Pipelayers 47-2151		61,200	71,700	10,500	17
Plumbers, pipefitters, and steamfitters 47-2152		494,700	570,500	75,800	15

NOTE: Data in this table are rounded.

and steamfitters may be unemployed until they can begin work on a new project, although most companies are trying to limit these periods of unemployment in order to retain workers. In addition, the jobs of plumbers, pipelayers, pipefitters, and steamfitters are generally less sensitive to changes in economic conditions than are jobs in other construction trades. Moreover, the coming emphasis on conservation of energy and water is opening up opportunities for those plumbers, pipefitters, and steamfitters who become proficient in new green technologies.

Earnings

Plumbers, pipelayers, pipefitters, and steamfitters are among the highest paid workers in construction occupations. Median hourly wages of wage-and-salary plumbers, pipefitters, and steamfitters were $22.27 in May 2009. The middle 50 percent earned between $16.81 and $30.01. The lowest 10 percent earned less than $13.27, and the highest 10 percent earned more than $38.21. Median hourly wages in the industries employing the largest numbers of plumbers, pipefitters, and steamfitters were as follows:

Building equipment contractors...........................	$22.29
Utility system construction	21.98
Nonresidential building construction......................	23.36
Local government..	20.79
Natural gas distribution......................................	$26.77

In May 2009, median hourly wages of wage and salary pipelayers were $16.12. The middle 50 percent earned between $13.00 and $21.27. The lowest 10 percent earned less than $10.87, and the highest 10 percent earned more than $27.97.

Apprentices usually begin at about 50 percent of the wage rate paid to experienced workers. Wages increase periodically as skills improve. After an initial waiting period, apprentices receive the same benefits as experienced plumbers, pipelayers, pipefitters, and steamfitters.

About 31 percent of plumbers, pipelayers, pipefitters, and steamfitters belonged to a union. Many of these workers are members of the United Association of Journeymen and Apprentices of the Plumbing and Pipefitting Industry of the United States and Canada.

Related Occupations

Other workers who install and repair mechanical systems in buildings include the following: boilermakers; electricians; elevator installers and repairers; heating, air-conditioning, and refrigeration mechanics and installers; industrial machinery mechanics and millwrights; sheet metal workers; and stationary engineers and boiler operators.

Other construction-related workers who need to know plumbing requirements include the following construction and building inspectors; and construction managers.

Sources of Additional Information

For information about apprenticeships or work opportunities in plumbing, pipelaying, pipefitting, and steamfitting, contact local plumbing, heating, and air-conditioning contractors; a local or state chapter of the Plumbing-Heating-Cooling Contractors; a local chapter of the Mechanical Contractors Association; a local chapter of the United Association of Journeymen and Apprentices of the Plumbing and Pipefitting Industry of the United States and Canada; or the nearest office of your state employment service or apprenticeship agency. Apprenticeship information also is available from the U.S. Department of Labor's toll-free help line: (877) 872-5627.

For information about apprenticeship opportunities for plumbers, pipefitters, and steamfitters, contact

▸ United Association of Journeymen and Apprentices of the Plumbing and Pipefitting Industry, Three Park Place, Annapolis, MD 21401-3687. Internet: www.ua.org

For general information about the work of pipelayers, plumbers, and pipefitters, contact

▸ Mechanical Contractors Association of America, 1385 Piccard Dr., Rockville, MD 20850-4329. Internet: www.mcaa.org

▸ National Center for Construction Education and Research, 3600 NW 43rd St., Bldg. G, Gainesville, FL 32606-8134. Internet: www.nccer.org

▸ Plumbing-Heating-Cooling Contractors—National Association, 180 S. Washington St., Falls Church, VA 22046-2935. Internet: www.phccweb.org

For general information about the work of sprinklerfitters, contact

▸ American Fire Sprinkler Association, Inc., 12750 Merit Dr., Suite 350, Dallas, TX 75251-1273. Internet: www.firesprinkler.org

▸ National Fire Sprinkler Association, 40 Jon Barrett Rd., Patterson, NY 12563-2164. Internet: www.nfsa.org

For general information on apprenticeships and how to get them, see the *Occupational Outlook Quarterly* article "Apprenticeships: Career training, credentials—and a paycheck in your pocket," online at www.bls.gov/opub/ooq/2002/summer/art01.pdf and in print at many libraries and career centers.

Police and Detectives

(O*NET 33-1012.00, 33-3021.00, 33-3021.01, 33-3021.02, 33-3021.03, 33-3021.05, 33-3021.06, 33-3031.00, 33-3051.00, 33-3051.01, 33-3051.03, and 33-3052.00)

Significant Points

■ Police work can be dangerous and stressful.

■ Education requirements range from a high school diploma to a college degree or higher.

- Job opportunities in most local police departments will be favorable for qualified individuals, while competition is expected for jobs in state and federal agencies.

- Bilingual applicants with college training in police science or with military police experience will have the best opportunities.

Nature of the Work

Police officers and *detectives* protect lives and property. *Law enforcement officers'* duties depend on the size and type of their organizations.

Police and detectives pursue and apprehend individuals who break the law and then issue citations or give warnings. A large proportion of their time is spent writing reports and maintaining records of incidents they encounter. Most police officers patrol their jurisdictions and investigate any suspicious activity they notice. They also respond to calls from individuals. Detectives, who often are called *agents* or *special agents*, perform investigative duties such as gathering facts and collecting evidence.

The daily activities of police and detectives vary with their occupational specialty—such as police officer, *game warden*, or detective—and whether they are working for a local, state, or federal agency. Duties also differ substantially among various federal agencies, which enforce different aspects of the law. Regardless of job duties or location, police officers and detectives at all levels must write reports and maintain meticulous records that will be needed if they testify in court.

State and Local Law Enforcement. *Uniformed police officers* have general law enforcement duties. They maintain regular patrols and respond to calls for service. Much of their time is spent responding to calls and doing paperwork. They may direct traffic at the scene of an accident, investigate a burglary, or give first aid to an accident victim. In large police departments, officers usually are assigned to a specific type of duty.

Many urban police agencies are involved in community policing—a practice in which an officer builds relationships with the citizens of local neighborhoods and mobilizes the public to help fight crime.

Police agencies are usually organized into geographic districts, with uniformed officers assigned to patrol a specific area. *Officers* in large agencies often patrol with a partner. They attempt to become familiar with their patrol area and remain alert for anything unusual. Suspicious circumstances and hazards to public safety are investigated or noted, and officers are dispatched to individual calls for assistance within their district. During their shift, they may identify, pursue, and arrest suspected criminals; resolve problems within the community; and enforce traffic laws.

Some agencies have special geographic jurisdictions and enforcement responsibilities. Public college and university police forces, public school district police, and agencies serving transportation systems and facilities are examples. Most law enforcement workers in special agencies are uniformed officers.

Some police officers specialize in a particular field, such as chemical and microscopic analysis, training and firearms instruction, or handwriting and fingerprint identification. Others work with special units, such as horseback, bicycle, motorcycle, or harbor patrol; canine corps; special weapons and tactics (SWAT); or emergency response teams. A few local and special law enforcement officers primarily perform jail-related duties or work in courts. (For information on other officers who work in jails and prisons, see correctional officers, described elsewhere in this book.)

Sheriffs and *deputy sheriffs* enforce the law on the county level. Sheriffs usually are elected to their posts and perform duties similar to those of a local or county police chief. Sheriffs' departments tend to be relatively small, most having fewer than 50 sworn officers. Deputy sheriffs have law enforcement duties similar to those of officers in urban police departments. Police and sheriffs' deputies who provide security in city and county courts are sometimes called *bailiffs*.

State police officers, sometimes called *state troopers* or *highway patrol officers*, arrest criminals statewide and patrol highways to enforce motor vehicle laws and regulations. State police officers often issue traffic citations to motorists. At the scene of accidents, they may direct traffic, give first aid, and call for emergency equipment. They also write reports used to determine the cause of the accident. State police officers frequently are called upon to render assistance to other law enforcement agencies, especially those in rural areas or small towns.

State highway patrols operate in every state except Hawaii. Most full-time sworn personnel are uniformed officers who regularly patrol and respond to calls for service. Others work as investigators, perform court-related duties, or carry out administrative or other assignments.

Detectives are plainclothes investigators who gather facts and collect evidence for criminal cases. Some are assigned to interagency task forces to combat specific types of crime. They conduct interviews, examine records, observe the activities of suspects, and participate in raids or arrests. Detectives usually specialize in investigating one type of violation, such as homicide or fraud. They are assigned cases on a rotating basis and work on them until an arrest and conviction are made or until the case is dropped.

Fish and game wardens enforce fishing, hunting, and boating laws. They patrol hunting and fishing areas, conduct search and rescue operations, investigate complaints and accidents, and aid in prosecuting court cases.

Federal Law Enforcement. *Federal Bureau of Investigation (FBI) agents* are the government's principal investigators, responsible for investigating violations of more than 200 categories of federal law and conducting sensitive national security investigations. Agents may conduct surveillance, monitor court-authorized wiretaps, examine business records, investigate white-collar crime, or participate in sensitive undercover assignments. The FBI investigates a wide range of criminal activity, including organized crime, public corruption, financial crime, bank robbery, kidnapping, terrorism, espionage, drug trafficking, and cybercrime.

There are many other federal agencies that enforce particular types of laws. *U.S. Drug Enforcement Administration (DEA) agents* enforce laws and regulations relating to illegal drugs. *U.S. marshals and deputy marshals* provide security for the federal courts and ensure the effective operation of the judicial system. *Bureau of Alcohol, Tobacco, Firearms, and Explosives agents* enforce and investigate violations of federal firearms and explosives laws, as well as federal alcohol and tobacco tax regulations. The U.S. Department of State *Bureau of Diplomatic Security special agents* are engaged in the battle against terrorism.

The *Department of Homeland Security* also employs numerous law enforcement officers within several different agencies, including Customs and Border Protection, Immigration and Customs Enforcement, and the U.S. Secret Service. *U.S. Border Patrol agents* protect more than 8,000 miles of international land and water boundaries.

Immigration inspectors interview and examine people seeking entry into the United States and its territories. *Customs inspectors* enforce laws governing imports and exports by inspecting cargo, baggage, and articles worn or carried by people, vessels, vehicles, trains, and aircraft entering or leaving the United States. *Federal Air Marshals* provide air security by guarding against attacks targeting U.S. aircraft, passengers, and crews. *U.S. Secret Service special agents* and *U.S. Secret Service uniformed officers* protect the president, the vice president, their immediate families, and other public officials. Secret Service special agents also investigate counterfeiting, forgery of government checks or bonds, and fraudulent use of credit cards.

Other federal agencies employ police and special agents with sworn arrest powers and the authority to carry firearms. These agencies include the Postal Service, the Bureau of Indian Affairs Office of Law Enforcement, the Forest Service, and the National Park Service.

Work environment. Police and detective work can be very dangerous and stressful. Police officers and detectives have one of the highest rates of on-the-job injury and illness. In addition to the obvious dangers of confrontations with criminals, police officers and detectives need to be constantly alert and ready to deal appropriately with a number of other threatening situations. Many law enforcement officers witness death and suffering resulting from accidents and criminal behavior. A career in law enforcement may take a toll on their private lives.

Uniformed officers, detectives, agents, and inspectors usually are scheduled to work 40-hour weeks, but paid overtime is common. Shift work is necessary because protection must be provided around the clock. Junior officers frequently work weekends, holidays, and nights. Police officers and detectives are required to work whenever they are needed and may work long hours during investigations. Officers in most jurisdictions, whether on or off duty, are expected to be armed and to exercise their authority when necessary.

The jobs of some federal agents, such as U.S. Secret Service and DEA special agents, require extensive travel, often on very short notice. These agents may relocate a number of times over the course of their careers. Some special agents, such as those in the U.S. Border Patrol, may work outdoors in rugged terrain and in all kinds of weather.

Training, Other Qualifications, and Advancement

Education requirements range from a high school diploma to a college degree or higher. Most police and detectives learn much of what they need to know on the job, often in their agency's training academy. Civil service regulations govern the appointment of police and detectives in most states, large municipalities, and special police agencies, as well as in many smaller jurisdictions. Candidates must be U.S. citizens, usually at least 21 years old, and meet rigorous physical and personal qualifications.

Education and training. Applicants usually must have at least a high school education, and some departments require 1 or 2 years of college coursework or, in some cases, a college degree. Physical education classes and participation in sports are also helpful in developing the competitiveness, stamina, and agility needed for many law enforcement positions. Knowledge of a foreign language is an asset in many federal agencies and urban departments.

State and local agencies encourage applicants to take courses or training related to law enforcement subjects after high school. Many entry-level applicants for police jobs have completed some formal postsecondary education, and a significant number are college graduates. Many junior colleges, colleges, and universities offer programs in law enforcement or administration of justice. Many agencies pay all or part of the tuition for officers to work toward degrees in criminal justice, police science, administration of justice, or public administration and pay higher salaries to those who earn one of those degrees.

Before their first assignments, officers usually go through a period of training. In state and large local police departments, recruits get training in their agency's police academy, often for 12 to 14 weeks. In small agencies, recruits often attend a regional or state academy. Training includes classroom instruction in constitutional law and civil rights, state laws and local ordinances, and accident investigation. Recruits also receive training and supervised experience in patrol, traffic control, use of firearms, self-defense, first aid, and emergency response. Police departments in some large cities hire high school graduates who are still in their teens as police cadets or trainees. They do clerical work and attend classes, usually for one to two years, until they reach the minimum age requirement and can be appointed to the regular force.

Fish and game wardens also must meet specific requirements. Most states require at least two years of college study. Once hired, fish and game wardens attend a training academy lasting from 3 to 12 months, sometimes followed by further training in the field.

Federal agencies require a bachelor's degree, related work experience, or a combination of the two. Federal law enforcement agents undergo extensive training, usually at the U.S. Marine Corps base in Quantico, Virginia, or the Federal Law Enforcement Training Center in Glynco, Georgia. The specific educational requirements, qualifications, and training information for a particular federal agency can be found on its website. Many of these agencies are listed as sources of additional information at the end of this statement.

To be considered for appointment as an FBI agent, an applicant must be a college graduate and have at least three years of professional work experience or must have an advanced degree plus two years of professional work experience. An applicant who meets these criteria also must have one of the following: a college major in accounting, electrical engineering, information technology, or computer science; fluency in a foreign language; a degree from an accredited law school; or three years of related full-time work experience. All new FBI agents undergo 18 weeks of training at the FBI Academy on the U.S. Marine Corps base in Quantico, Virginia.

Other qualifications. Civil service regulations govern the appointment of police and detectives in most states, large municipalities, and special police agencies, as well as in many smaller jurisdictions. Candidates must be U.S. citizens usually must be at least 21 years old, and must meet rigorous physical and personal qualifications. Physical examinations for entry into law enforcement often include tests of vision, hearing, strength, and agility. Eligibility for appointment usually depends on one's performance in competitive written examinations and previous education and experience.

Candidates should enjoy working with people and meeting the public. Because personal characteristics such as honesty, sound judgment, integrity, and a sense of responsibility are especially important in law enforcement, candidates are interviewed by senior officers and their character traits and backgrounds are investigated.

Projections Data from the National Employment Matrix

Occupational title	SOC Code	Employment, 2008	Projected employment, 2018	Change, 2008–2018	
				Number	Percent
Police and detectives	—	883,600	968,400	84,700	10
First-line supervisors/managers of police and detectives...	33-1012	97,300	105,200	7,800	8
Detectives and criminal investigators...................33-3021		112,200	130,900	18,700	17
Fish and game wardens......................................33-3031		8,300	9,000	700	8
Police officers...33-3050		665,700	723,300	57,500	9
Police and sheriff's patrol officers 33-3051		661,500	718,800	57,300	9
Transit and railroad police 33-3052		4,300	4,500	200	5

NOTE: Data in this table are rounded.

A history of domestic violence may disqualify a candidate. In some agencies, candidates are interviewed by a psychiatrist or a psychologist or given a personality test. Most applicants are subjected to lie detector examinations or drug testing. Some agencies subject sworn personnel to random drug testing as a condition of continuing employment.

Although similar in nature, the requirements for federal agents are generally more stringent and the background checks are more thorough. There are polygraph tests as well as interviews with references. Jobs that require security clearances have additional requirements.

Advancement. Police officers usually become eligible for promotion after a probationary period ranging from six months to three years. In large departments, promotion may enable an officer to become a detective or to specialize in one type of police work, such as working with juveniles. Promotions to corporal, sergeant, lieutenant, and captain usually are made according to a candidate's position on a promotion list, as determined by scores on a written examination and on-the-job performance.

Federal agents often are on the General Services (GS) pay scale. Most begin at the GS-5 or GS-7 level. As agents meet time-in-grade and knowledge and skills requirements, they move up the GS scale. Promotions at and above GS-13 are most often managerial positions. Many agencies hire internally for these supervisory positions. A few agents may be able to enter the Senior Executive Series ranks of upper management.

Continuing training helps police officers, detectives, and special agents improve their job performance. Through police department academies, regional centers for public safety employees established by the states, and federal agency training centers, instructors provide annual training in self-defense tactics, firearms, use-of-force policies, sensitivity and communications skills, crowd-control techniques, relevant legal developments, and advances in law enforcement equipment.

Employment

Police and detectives held about 883,600 jobs in 2008. About 79 percent were employed by local governments. State police agencies employed about 11 percent. Various federal agencies employ police and detectives.

According to the U.S. Bureau of Justice Statistics, police and detectives employed by local governments worked primarily in cities with more than 25,000 inhabitants. Some cities have very large police forces, while thousands of small communities employ fewer than 25 officers each.

Job Outlook

Job opportunities in most local police departments will be favorable for qualified individuals, whereas competition is expected for jobs in state and federal agencies. As fast as average employment growth is expected.

Employment change. Employment of police and detectives is expected to grow 10 percent over the 2008–2018 decade, about as fast as the average for all occupations. Population growth is the main source of demand for police services.

Job prospects. Overall opportunities in local police departments will be favorable for individuals who meet the psychological, personal, and physical qualifications. In addition to openings from employment growth, many openings will be created by the need to replace workers who retire and those who leave local agencies for federal jobs and private-sector security jobs. Jobs in local police departments that offer relatively low salaries, or those in urban communities in which the crime rate is relatively high, may be the easiest to get. Some smaller departments may have fewer opportunities as budgets limit the ability to hire additional officers. Bilingual applicants with military experience or college training in police science will have the best opportunities in local and state departments.

There will be more competition for jobs in federal and state law enforcement agencies than for jobs in local agencies. Bilingual applicants with a bachelor's degree and several years of law enforcement or military experience, especially investigative experience, will have the best opportunities in federal agencies.

The level of government spending determines the level of employment for police and detectives. The number of job opportunities, therefore, can vary from year to year and from place to place. Layoffs are rare because retirements enable most staffing cuts to be handled through attrition. Trained law enforcement officers who lose their jobs because of budget cuts usually have little difficulty finding jobs with other agencies.

Earnings

Police and sheriff's patrol officers had median annual wages of $53,210 in May 2009. The middle 50 percent earned between $40,450 and $67,990. The lowest 10 percent earned less than $31,400, and the highest 10 percent earned more than $83,550. Median annual wages were $47,010 in federal government; $56,570 in state government; $53,250 in local government; and $45,730 in colleges, universities, and professional schools.

In May 2009, median annual wages of police and detective supervisors were $76,500. The middle 50 percent earned between $60,420 and $94,560. The lowest 10 percent earned less than $46,780, and the highest 10 percent earned more than $116,340. Median annual wages were $93,800 in federal government, $78,920 in state government, and $75,310 in local government.

In May 2009, median annual wages of detectives and criminal investigators were $62,110. The middle 50 percent earned between $47,070 and $83,650. The lowest 10 percent earned less than $37,960, and the highest 10 percent earned more than $99,980. Median annual wages were $73,120 in federal government, $53,110 in state government, and $58,160 in local government.

In May 2009, median annual wages of fish and game wardens were $48,800. The middle 50 percent earned between $37,310 and $60,110. The lowest 10 percent earned less than $30,920, and the highest 10 percent earned more than $89,130. Median annual wages were $51,280 in federal government, $49,130 in state government, and $43,760 in local government.

In May 2009, median annual wages of parking enforcement workers were $34,810. The middle 50 percent earned between $26,750 and $43,070. The lowest 10 percent earned less than $21,170, and the highest 10 percent earned more than $50,030. Median annual wages were $35,240 in local government and $26,890 in colleges, universities, and professional schools.

In May 2009, median annual wages of transit and railroad police were $50,940. The middle 50 percent earned between $40,600 and $63,800. The lowest 10 percent earned less than $34,330, and the highest 10 percent earned more than $75,180. Median annual wages were $47,410 in state government, $48,040 in local government, and $60,780 in rail transportation.

Federal law provides special salary rates to federal employees who serve in law enforcement. Additionally, federal special agents and inspectors receive law enforcement availability pay (LEAP)—equal to 25 percent of the agent's grade and step—awarded because of the large amount of overtime that these agents are expected to work. Salaries were slightly higher in selected areas where the prevailing local pay level was higher. Because federal agents may be eligible for a special law enforcement benefits package, applicants should ask their recruiter for more information.

Total earnings for local, state, and special police and detectives frequently exceed the stated salary because of payments for overtime, which can be significant.

According to the International City-County Management Association's annual Police and Fire Personnel, Salaries, and Expenditures Survey, average salaries for sworn full-time positions in 2008 were as follows:

Position	Minimum salary	Maximum salary w/o longevity
Police chief	$90,570	$113,930
Deputy chief	74,834	96,209
Police captain	72,761	91,178
Police lieutenant	65,688	79,268
Police sergeant	58,739	70,349
Police corporal	49,421	61,173

In addition to the common benefits—paid vacation, sick leave, and medical and life insurance—most police and sheriffs' departments provide officers with special allowances for uniforms. Many police officers retire at half-pay after 20 years of service; others often are eligible to retire with 30 or fewer years of service.

Related Occupations

Other occupations that help protect and serve people are correctional officers; emergency medical technicians and paramedics; fire fighters; private detectives and investigators; probation officers and correctional treatment specialists; and security guards and gaming surveillance officers.

Sources of Additional Information

Information about entry requirements may be obtained from federal, state, and local law enforcement agencies.

To find federal, state, and local law enforcement job fairs and other recruiting events across the country, contact

▸ National Law Enforcement Recruiters Association, P.O. Box 17132, Arlington, VA 22216. Internet: www.nlera.org

For general information about sheriffs and to learn more about the National Sheriffs' Association scholarship, contact

▸ National Sheriffs' Association, 1450 Duke St., Alexandria, VA 22314. Internet: www.sheriffs.org

For information about chiefs of police, contact

▸ International Association of Chiefs of Police, 515 N. Washington St., Alexandria, VA 22314. Internet: www.theiacp.org

Information related to federal law enforcement:

▸ Information about qualifications for employment as a Federal Bureau of Investigation (FBI) Special Agent is available from the nearest state FBI office. The address and phone number are listed in the local telephone directory. Internet: www.fbi.gov

▸ Information on career opportunities, qualifications, and training for U.S. Secret Service Special Agents and Uniformed Officers is available from the Secret Service Personnel Division at (202) 406-5830, (888) 813-877, (888) 813-USSS, or U.S. Secret Services, Recruitment and Hiring Coordination Center, 245 Murray Dr., Building 410, Washington, DC 20223. Internet: www.secretservice.gov/join

▸ Information about qualifications for employment as a Drug Enforcement Administration (DEA) Special Agent is available from the nearest DEA office, DEA Office of Personnel, 8701 Morrissette Dr., Springfield, VA 22152, or call (800) DEA-4288. Internet: www.usdoj.gov/dea

Information about jobs in other federal law enforcement agencies is available from

▸ U.S. Marshals Service, Human Resources Division—Law Enforcement Recruiting, Washington, DC 20530-1000. Internet: www.usmarshals.gov

▸ U.S. Bureau of Alcohol, Tobacco, Firearms, and Explosives, Office of Governmental and Public Affairs, 99 New York Ave. NE Mail Stop 5S144, Washington, DC 20226. Internet: www.atf.gov

▸ U.S. Customs and Border Protection, 1300 Pennsylvania Ave. NW, Washington, DC 20229. Internet: www.cbp.gov

▸ U.S. Department of Homeland Security, Washington, DC 20528. Internet: www.dhs.gov

Postal Service Mail Carriers

(O*NET 43-5052.00)

Significant Points

■ Little or no change in employment is projected over the 2008–2018 period.

■ Keen competition for jobs is expected.

■ Qualification is based on an examination.

■ Applicants customarily wait one to two years or more after passing the examination before being hired.

Nature of the Work

Postal service mail carriers deliver mail to residences and businesses in cities, towns, and rural areas. Although carriers are classified by their type of route—either city or rural—duties of *city and rural carriers* are similar. Most travel established routes, delivering and collecting mail. Mail carriers start work at the post office early in the morning, when they arrange the mail in delivery sequence. Automated equipment has reduced the time that carriers need to sort the mail, allowing them to spend more of their time delivering it.

Mail carriers cover their routes on foot, by vehicle, or by a combination of both. On foot, they carry a heavy load of mail in a satchel or push it on a cart. In most urban and rural areas, they use a car or small truck. The postal service provides vehicles to city carriers; most rural carriers use their own vehicles and are reimbursed for that use. Deliveries are made to houses, to roadside mailboxes, and to large buildings such as offices or apartments, which generally have all of their tenants' mailboxes in one location.

Besides delivering and collecting mail, carriers collect money for postage-due and COD (cash-on-delivery) fees and obtain signed receipts for registered, certified, and insured mail. If a customer is not home, the carrier leaves a notice that tells where special mail is being held. After completing their routes, carriers return to the post office with mail gathered from homes, businesses, and sometimes street collection boxes, and turn in the mail, receipts, and money collected during the day.

Some city carriers may have specialized duties such as delivering only parcels or picking up mail only from mail collection boxes. In comparison with city carriers, rural carriers perform a wider range of postal services, in addition to delivering and picking up mail. For example, rural carriers may sell stamps and money orders and register, certify, and insure parcels and letters. All carriers, however, must be able to answer customers' questions about postal regulations and services and provide change-of-address cards and other postal forms when requested.

Work environment. Most carriers begin work early in the morning—those with routes in a business district can start as early as 4 a.m. Overtime hours are frequently required for urban carriers. Carriers spend most of their time outdoors, delivering mail in all kinds of weather. Though carriers face many natural hazards, such as extreme temperatures and wet and icy roads and sidewalks, serious injuries are often due to the nature of the work, which requires repetitive arm and hand movements, as well as constant lifting and bending. These activities can lead to repetitive stress injuries in various joints and muscles.

Training, Other Qualifications, and Advancement

All applicants for postal service mail carrier jobs are required to take an examination. After passing the exam, it may take one to two years or longer before being hired because the number of applicants generally exceeds the number of job openings.

Education and training. There are no specific education requirements to become a postal service mail carrier; however, all applicants must have a good command of the English language. Upon being hired, new carriers are trained on the job by experienced workers. Many post offices offer classroom instruction on safety and defensive driving. Workers receive additional instruction when new equipment or procedures are introduced. In these cases, usually another postal employee or a training specialist trains the workers.

Other qualifications. Postal service mail carriers must be at least 18 years old. They must be U.S. citizens or have been granted permanent resident-alien status in the United States, and males must have registered with the Selective Service upon reaching age 18.

All applicants must pass a written examination that measures speed and accuracy at checking names and numbers and the ability to memorize mail distribution procedures. Job seekers should contact the post office or mail processing center where they wish to work to determine when an exam will be given. Applicants' names are listed in order of their examination scores. Five points are added to the score of an honorably discharged veteran and 10 points are added to the score of a veteran who was wounded in combat or is disabled. When a vacancy occurs, the appointing officer chooses one of the top three applicants; the rest of the names remain on the list to be considered for future openings until their eligibility expires—usually two years after the examination date.

When accepted, applicants must undergo a criminal-history check and pass a physical examination and a drug test. Applicants also may be asked to show that they can lift and handle mail sacks weighing 70 pounds. A safe driving record is required for mail carriers who drive at work, and applicants must receive a passing grade on a road test.

Good interpersonal skills are important because mail carriers must be courteous and tactful when dealing with the public, especially when answering questions or receiving complaints. A good memory and the ability to read rapidly and accurately are also important.

Advancement. Postal service mail carriers may begin on a casual, transitional, part-time, or flexible basis and become regular or full-time employees in order of seniority, as vacancies occur. Carriers can look forward to obtaining preferred routes as their seniority increases. Postal service mail carriers can advance to supervisory positions on a competitive basis.

Employment

The U.S. Postal Service employed 343,300 mail carriers in 2008. The majority of mail carriers work in cities and suburbs, while the rest work in rural areas.

Postal service mail carriers are classified as casual, transitional, part-time flexible, part-time regular, or full time. Casuals are hired for 90 days at a time to help process and deliver mail during peak mailing or vacation periods in rural areas. Transitional carriers are hired on a temporary basis in cities for a period of one year. Part-time, flexible workers do not have a regular work schedule or weekly guarantee

Projections Data from the National Employment Matrix

Occupational title	SOC Code	Employment, 2008	Projected employment, 2018	Change, 2008–2018	
				Number	Percent
Postal service mail carriers......................................43-5052		343,300	339,400	−3,900	−1

NOTE: Data in this table are rounded.

of hours but are called as the need arises. Part-time regulars have a set work schedule of fewer than 40 hours per week, often replacing regular full-time workers on their scheduled day off. Few carriers are classified as part-time employees, especially among rural carriers. Full-time postal employees work a 40-hour week over a 5-day period and made up 85 percent of mail carriers in 2008.

Job Outlook

Employment of postal service mail carriers is expected to experience little or no change through 2018. Keen competition is expected for mail carrier jobs because of the attractive wages and benefits and relatively low entry requirements.

Employment change. Employment of mail carriers is expected to decline by about 1 percent through 2018. Employment will be adversely affected by several factors. The use of automated "delivery point sequencing" systems to sort letter mail and flat mail directly, according to the order of delivery, reduces the amount of time that carriers spend sorting their mail, allowing them to spend more time on the streets delivering mail. The amount of time carriers save on sorting letter mail and flat mail will allow them to increase the size of their routes, which will reduce the need to hire more carriers. Additionally, the postal service is moving toward more centralized mail delivery, such as the use of cluster mailboxes, to cut down on the number of door-to-door deliveries. However, as the population continues to rise and the number of addresses to which mail must be delivered increases, the demand for mail carriers in some areas of the country will grow.

Employment and schedules in the postal service fluctuate with the demand for its services. When mail volume is high, such as during holidays, full-time employees work overtime, part-time workers get additional hours, and casual workers may be hired.

Job prospects. Those seeking jobs as postal service mail carriers can expect to encounter keen competition. The number of applicants usually exceeds the number of job openings because of the occupation's low entry requirements and attractive wages and benefits. The best employment opportunities for mail carriers are expected to be in areas of the country with significant population growth as the number of addresses to which mail must be delivered continues to grow.

Earnings

Median annual wages of postal service mail carriers were $52,200 in May 2009. The middle 50 percent earned between $43,580 and 53,680. The lowest 10 earned less than $37,950, while the top 10 percent earned more than $53,700. Rural mail carriers are reimbursed for mileage put on their own vehicles while delivering mail.

Postal service mail carriers enjoy a variety of employer-provided benefits similar to those enjoyed by other federal government workers. The National Association of Letter Carriers and the National Rural Letter Carriers Association together represent most of these workers.

Related Occupations

Other occupations with duties similar to those of postal service mail carriers include couriers and messengers; and truck drivers and driver/sales workers.

Sources of Additional Information

Information on job requirements, entrance examinations, and specific employment opportunities for postal service mail carriers is available from local post offices and state employment service offices. This information also is available from the United States Post Office online at www.usps.com.

Printing Machine Operators

(O*NET 51-5023.00)

Significant Points

- Most printing machine operators are trained on the job.
- Retirements among older press operators are expected to create openings for skilled workers.
- Rising demand for customized print jobs will mean those skilled in digital printing operations will have the best job opportunities.

Nature of the Work

Printing machine operators, also known as *press operators*, prepare, operate, and maintain printing presses. Duties vary according to the type of press they operate. Traditional printing methods, such as offset lithography, gravure, flexography, and letterpress, use a plate or roller that carries the final image that is to be printed and copies the image to paper. In addition to the traditional printing processes, plateless or nonimpact processes are coming into general use. Plateless processes—including digital, electrostatic, and ink-jet printing—are used for copying, duplicating, and document and specialty printing, usually by quick printing shops and smaller in-house printing shops. Digital presses with longer run capabilities are increasingly being used by commercial printers for short-run or customized printing jobs. Digital presses also allow printers to transfer files, blend colors, and proof images electronically, thus avoiding the costly and time-consuming steps of making printing plates that are common to lithographic or off-set printing.

Printing machine operators' jobs differ from one shop to another because of differences in the types and sizes of presses. Small commercial shops with relatively small presses, those that print only one or two colors at a time, can be operated by one person, often an owner or manager who performs all business activities. To attract a wider range of clients, larger commercial print shops may run several presses with different size and color capacities. Press operators typically specialize in operating one type of press but may operate more than one press at a time. However, press operators who are trained on more than one type of printing press are valuable because they can work on multiple types of printing jobs. Large newspaper, magazine, and book printers use giant "in-line web" presses that require a crew of several press operators and press assistants.

After working with prepress technicians to identify and resolve any potential problems with a job, press operators prepare machines for printing. To prepare presses, operators install the printing plate with the images to be printed and adjust the pressure at which the machine prints. They then ink the presses, load paper, and adjust the press to the paper size. Operators ensure that paper and ink meet specifications, and adjust the flow of ink to the inking rollers accordingly. They then feed paper through the press cylinders and adjust feed and tension controls. New digital technology, in contrast, is able to automate much of this work.

While printing presses are running, press operators monitor their operation and keep the paper feeders well stocked. They make adjustments to manage ink distribution, speed, and temperature in the drying chamber, if the press has one. If paper tears or jams and the press stops, which can happen with some offset presses, operators quickly correct the problem to minimize downtime. Similarly, operators working with other high-speed presses constantly look for problems, and when necessary make quick corrections to avoid expensive losses of paper and ink. Throughout the run, operators must regularly pull sheets to check for any printing imperfections. Most printers have, or will soon have, presses with computers and sophisticated instruments to control press operations, making it possible to complete printing jobs in less time. With this equipment, press operators set up, monitor, and adjust the printing process on a control panel or computer monitor, which allows them to control the press electronically.

In most shops, press operators also perform preventive maintenance. They oil and clean the presses and make minor repairs.

Work environment. Operating a press can be physically and mentally demanding, and sometimes tedious. Press operators are on their feet most of the time. Operators often work under pressure to meet deadlines. Most printing presses are capable of high printing speeds, and adjustments must be made quickly to avoid waste. Pressrooms are noisy, and workers in certain areas wear ear protection. Working with press machinery can be hazardous, but the threat of serious accidents has decreased. Newer computerized presses are equipped with safety features and allow operators to make most adjustments from a control panel.

Many press operators, particularly those who work for newspapers, work weekends, nights, and holidays as many presses operate continuously. They also may work overtime to meet deadlines. Most operators worked 40 hours per week in 2008.

Training, Other Qualifications, and Advancement

Although employers prefer that beginners complete a formal apprenticeship or a postsecondary program in printing equipment operation, many press operators are trained on the job. Attention to detail and familiarity with electronics and computers are essential for operators.

Education and training. Beginning press operators load, unload, and clean presses. With time and training, they may become fully

qualified to operate that type of press. Operators can gain experience on more than one kind of printing press during the course of their career.

Experienced operators will periodically receive retraining and skill updating. For example, printing plants that change from sheet-fed offset presses to digital presses have to retrain the entire press crew because skill requirements for the two types of presses are different.

Apprenticeships for press operators, once the dominant method for preparing for this occupation, are becoming less prevalent. When they are offered by the employer, they include on-the-job instruction and related classroom training or correspondence school courses.

Formal postsecondary programs in printing equipment operation offered by technical and trade schools, community colleges, and universities are growing in importance. Postsecondary courses in printing provide the theoretical and technical knowledge needed to operate advanced equipment. Some postsecondary school programs require two years of study and award an associate degree.

Because of technical developments in the printing industry, courses in chemistry, electronics, color theory, and physics are helpful.

Other qualifications. Persons who wish to become press operators need mechanical aptitude to make press adjustments and repairs. Workers need good vision and attention to detail to locate and fix problems with print jobs. Oral and written communication skills also are required. Operators should possess the mathematical skills necessary to compute percentages, weights, and measures, and to calculate the amount of ink and paper needed to do a job. Operators now also need basic computer skills to work with newer printing presses.

Certification and advancement. As press operators gain experience, they may advance in pay and responsibility by working on more complex printing presses. For example, operators who have demonstrated their ability to work with one-color sheet-fed presses may be trained to operate four-color sheet-fed presses. Voluntarily earning formal certification may also help press operators advance. Operators also may advance to pressroom supervisors and become responsible for an entire press crew. In addition, press operators can draw on their knowledge of press operations to become cost estimators, providing estimates of printing jobs to potential customers, sales representatives, and instructors of printing-related courses, or move into other administrative or executive occupations.

Employment

Printing machine operators held about 195,600 jobs in 2008. Over half of all press operator jobs were in printing and related support activities. Paper manufacturing and newspaper publishers also were large employers. Additional jobs were in advertising, public relations, and related services and plastics product manufacturing.

The printing and newspaper publishing industries are two of the most geographically dispersed in the United States. While printing machine operators thus can find jobs throughout the country, large numbers of jobs are concentrated in large printing centers such as the Chicago, Los Angeles–Long Beach, New York, Minneapolis–St. Paul, Philadelphia, Boston, and Washington, D.C. metropolitan areas.

Projections Data from the National Employment Matrix

Occupational title	SOC Code	Employment, 2008	Projected employment, 2018	Change, 2008–2018	
				Number	Percent
Printing machine operators	51-5023	195,600	185,000	–10,700	–5

NOTE: Data in this table are rounded.

Job Outlook

Employment of printing machine operators is projected to decline moderately through 2018, as newer printing presses require fewer operators. Despite this, job opportunities are expected to be favorable because a large number of these workers are expected to retire or leave the occupation over the next decade. The best opportunities will be available to skilled press operators.

Employment change. Employment of press operators is expected to decline by 5 percent over the 2008–2018 period. Employment will fall because increasing printer speed and automation require fewer press operators to maintain production levels. This will be especially true among the large printing press operations such as those used by the newspaper industry. Expansion of digital printing technologies and related increases in production cost efficiencies, however, will allow printers to print smaller quantities more profitably and meet the growing interest in the print-on-demand and electronic publishing markets. This should widen the market for printed materials, offsetting some of the employment loss from increased productivity. Short-run print capabilities will permit printers to distribute a wider variety of catalogs, direct mail enclosures, newspaper inserts, and other kinds of print as advertisers are better able to identify the specific interests of a targeted market or audience.

Job prospects. Opportunities for employment in printing press operations should be favorable. Retirements of older printing machine operators and the need for workers trained on computerized printing equipment will create many job openings. For example, small printing jobs will increasingly be run on sophisticated high-speed digital printing equipment that requires a complex set of skills, such as knowledge of database management software. Those who complete postsecondary training programs in printing and who are comfortable with computers will have the best employment opportunities.

Earnings

Median hourly wages of printing machine operators were $15.85 in May 2009, compared to $14.41 per hour for all production occupations. The middle 50 percent earned between $12.05 and $20.55 an hour. The lowest 10 percent earned less than $9.54, and the highest 10 percent earned more than $25.63 an hour. Median hourly wages in May 2009 were $16.20 in printing and related support activities and $17.59 in newspaper, periodical, book and directory publishers, industries employing among the largest numbers of printing machine operators.

The basic wage rate for a printing machine operator depends on the geographic area in which the work is located and on the size and complexity of the printing press being operated.

Related Occupations

Other workers who set up and operate production machinery include bookbinders and bindery workers; machine setters, operators, and tenders—metal and plastic; and prepress technicians and workers.

Sources of Additional Information

Details about apprenticeships and other training opportunities may be obtained from local employers, such as newspapers and printing shops, local offices of the Graphic Communications Conference of the International Brotherhood of Teamsters, local affiliates of Printing Industries of America, or local offices of the state employment service. Apprenticeship information is also available from the U.S. Department of Labor's toll-free helpline: 1 (877) 282-5627.

For information on careers and training in printing and the graphic arts contact

▸ NPES The Association for Suppliers of Printing Publishing, and Converting Technologies, 1899 Preston White Dr., Reston, VA 20191. Internet: www.npes.org/education/index.html

▸ Printing Industries of America, 200 Deer Run Rd., Sewickley, PA 15143. Internet: www.printing.org/

▸ Graphic Arts Education and Research Foundation, 1899 Preston White Dr., Reston, VA 20191. Internet: www.gaerf.org

▸ NAPL National Association of Printing Leadership, 75 W. Century Rd., Suite 100, Paramus, NJ 07652. Internet: www.napl.org/

Purchasing Managers, Buyers, and Purchasing Agents

(O*NET 11-3061.00, 13-1021.00, 13-1022.00, and 13-1023.00)

Significant Points

■ About 42 percent of purchasing managers, buyers, and purchasing agents are employed in wholesale trade or manufacturing establishments.

■ Employment is projected to grow 7 percent, which is as fast as the average.

■ Opportunities should be best for those with a college degree in engineering, business, economics, or one of the applied sciences.

■ Prospects often need continuing education or certification to advance.

Nature of the Work

Purchasing managers, *buyers*, and *purchasing agents* buy a vast array of farm products, durable and nondurable goods, and services for companies and institutions. They attempt to get the best deal for their company—the highest-quality goods and services at the lowest possible cost. They accomplish this by studying sales records and inventory levels of current stock, identifying foreign and domestic suppliers, and keeping abreast of changes affecting both the supply of and demand for needed products and materials. Purchasing professionals consider price, quality, availability, reliability, and technical support when choosing suppliers and merchandise. To be effective, purchasing professionals must have a working technical knowledge of the goods or services to be purchased.

There are several major types of purchasing managers, buyers, and purchasing agents. *Wholesale and retail buyers* purchase goods, such as clothing or electronics, for resale. Purchasing agents buy goods and services for use by their own company or organization. *Purchasing agents and buyers of farm products* purchase goods such as grain, Christmas trees, and tobacco for further processing or resale. Purchasing managers usually handle more complicated purchases and may supervise a group of purchasing agents. Purchasing professionals employed by government agencies or manufacturing firms usually are called purchasing directors, managers, or agents; sometimes they are known as contract specialists. Purchasing professionals in government place solicitations for services and accept bids and offers through the Internet. Some purchasing managers, called contract or supply managers, specialize in negotiating and supervising supply contracts.

Purchasing specialists who buy finished goods for resale are employed by wholesale and retail establishments, where they commonly are known as buyers or *merchandise managers*. Wholesale and retail buyers are an integral part of a complex system of distribution and merchandising that caters to the vast array of consumer needs and desires. Wholesale buyers purchase goods directly from manufacturers or from other wholesale firms for resale to retail firms, commercial establishments, and other organizations. In retail firms, buyers purchase goods from wholesale firms or directly from manufacturers for resale to the public.

Buyers largely determine which products their establishment will sell. Therefore, it is essential that they have the ability to predict what will appeal to consumers. If they fail to purchase the right products for resale, buyers jeopardize the profits and reputation of their company. They keep track of inventories and sales levels, check competitors' sales activities, and watch general economic conditions to anticipate consumer buying patterns. Buyers working for large and medium-sized firms usually specialize in acquiring one or two lines of merchandise, whereas buyers working for small stores may purchase the establishment's complete inventory.

Evaluating suppliers is one of the most critical functions of a purchasing manager, buyer, or purchasing agent. Many firms now run on a lean manufacturing schedule and use just-in-time inventories, so any delays in the supply chain can shut down production and potentially cost the firm its customers. Purchasing professionals use many resources to find out all they can about potential suppliers. The Internet has become an effective tool for searching catalogs, trade journals, industry and company publications, and directories. Purchasing professionals attend meetings, trade shows, and conferences to learn of new industry trends and make contacts with suppliers. They often interview prospective suppliers and visit their plants and distribution centers to assess their capabilities. It is important to make certain that the supplier is capable of delivering the desired goods or services on time, in the correct quantities, and without sacrificing quality. Once all of the necessary information on suppliers is gathered, orders are placed and contracts are awarded to those suppliers who meet the purchaser's needs. Most of the transaction process is now automated through use of the Internet.

Purchasing professionals often work closely with other employees in a process called "team buying." For example, before submitting an order, the team may discuss the design of custom-made products with company design engineers, the problems involving the quality of purchased goods with production supervisors, or the issues in shipping with managers in the receiving department. This additional interaction improves the quality of buying by adding different perspectives to the process.

Work environment. Most purchasing managers, buyers, and purchasing agents work in comfortable offices. They frequently work more than the standard 40-hour week because of special sales, conferences, or production deadlines. Evening and weekend work also is common before holiday and back-to-school seasons for those working in retail trade. Consequently, many retail firms discourage the use of vacation time during peak periods. Travel is sometimes necessary. Purchasers for worldwide companies may even travel outside the United States.

Training, Other Qualifications, and Advancement

Workers may begin as trainees, purchasing clerks, junior buyers, or assistant buyers. Most employers prefer to hire applicants who have a college degree and who are familiar with the merchandise they sell and with wholesaling and retailing practices. Prospects often need continuing education or certification to advance.

Education and training. Educational requirements tend to vary with the size of the organization. Large stores and distributors prefer applicants who have completed a bachelor's degree program with a business emphasis. Many manufacturing firms put an even greater emphasis on formal training, preferring applicants with a bachelor's or master's degree in engineering, business, economics, or one of the applied sciences. A master's degree is essential for advancement to many top-level purchasing manager jobs.

Regardless of academic preparation, new employees must learn the specifics of their employer's business. Training periods vary in length, with most lasting one to five years. In manufacturing, new employees work with experienced purchasers to learn about commodities, prices, suppliers, and markets. In addition, they may be assigned to the production planning department to learn about the material requirements system and the inventory system the company uses to keep production and replenishment functions working smoothly.

In wholesale and retail establishments, most trainees begin by selling merchandise, checking invoices on material received, and keeping track of stock. As they progress, trainees are given increased buying-related responsibilities.

Other qualifications. Purchasing managers, buyers, and purchasing agents must know how to use various software packages and the Internet. Other important qualities include the ability to analyze technical data in suppliers' proposals; good communication, negotiation, and mathematical skills; knowledge of supply-chain management; and the ability to perform financial analyses.

People who wish to become wholesale or retail buyers should be good at planning and decision making. They also should have an interest in merchandising. In addition, marketing skills and the ability to identify products that will sell are very important. Employers often look for leadership ability, too, because buyers spend a large portion of their time supervising assistant buyers and dealing with manufacturers' representatives and store executives.

Certification and advancement. An experienced purchasing agent or buyer may become an assistant purchasing manager before advancing to purchasing manager, supply manager, or director of

Projections Data from the National Employment Matrix

Occupational title	SOC Code	Employment, 2008	Projected employment, 2018	Change, 2008–2018	
				Number	Percent
Purchasing managers, buyers, and purchasing agents .... —		527,400	565,900	38,500	7
Purchasing managers 11-3061		70,300	71,400	1,100	2
Buyers and purchasing agents............................... 13-1020		457,100	494,500	37,400	8
Purchasing agents and buyers, farm products 13-1021		14,100	14,000	–200	–1
Wholesale and retail buyers, except farm products.. 13-1022		147,700	144,400	–3,300	–2
Purchasing agents, except wholesale, retail, and farm products 13-1023		295,200	336,100	40,900	14

NOTE: Data in this table are rounded.

materials management. At the top levels, duties may overlap with other management functions, such as production, planning, logistics, and marketing.

Regardless of industry, continuing education is essential for advancement. Many purchasing managers, buyers, and purchasing agents participate in seminars offered by professional societies and take college courses in supply management. Professional certification is becoming increasingly important, especially for those just entering the occupation.

There are several recognized credentials for purchasing agents and purchasing managers. The Certified Purchasing Manager (CPM) designation was conferred by the Institute for Supply Management. In 2008, this certification was replaced by the Certified Professional in Supply Management (CPSM) credential, covering the wider scope of duties now performed by purchasing professionals. The Certified Purchasing Professional (CPP) and Certified Professional Purchasing Manager (CPPM) designations are conferred by the American Purchasing Society. The Certified Supply Chain Professional (CSCP) credential is conferred by APICS, the Association for Operations Management. For workers in federal, state, and local government, the National Institute of Governmental Purchasing offers the designations of Certified Professional Public Buyer (CPPB) and Certified Public Purchasing Officer (CPPO). These certifications are awarded only after work-related experience and education requirements are met and written or oral exams are successfully completed.

Employment

Purchasing managers, buyers, and purchasing agents held about 527,400 jobs in 2008. About 42 percent worked in the wholesale trade and manufacturing industries and another 10 percent worked in retail trade. The remainder worked mostly in service establishments, such as management of companies and enterprises or professional, scientific, and technical services. A small number were self-employed.

The following tabulation shows the distribution of employment by occupational specialty:

Purchasing agents, except wholesale, retail, and farm products...295,200
Wholesale and retail buyers, except farm products 147,700
Purchasing managers 70,300
Purchasing agents and buyers, farm products 14,100

Job Outlook

Employment of purchasing managers, buyers, and purchasing agents is expected to increase 7 percent through the year 2018. Job growth and opportunities, however, will differ among different occupations in this category.

Employment change. Overall employment of purchasing managers, buyers, and purchasing agents is expected to increase 7 percent during the 2008–2018 decade, which is as fast as the average for all occupations. Employment of purchasing agents, except wholesale, retail, and farm products—the largest employment group in the industry—will experience faster-than-average growth as more companies demand a greater number of purchased goods and services. Additionally, large companies are increasing the size of their purchasing departments to accommodate purchasing services contracts from smaller companies. Also, many purchasing agents are now charged with procuring services that traditionally had been done in-house, such as computer and IT (information technology) support, in addition to traditionally contracted services such as advertising. Nonetheless, demand for workers may be somewhat limited by technological improvements, such as software that has eliminated much of the paperwork involved in ordering and procuring supplies and the growing number of purchases being made electronically through the Internet and electronic data interchange (EDI). Demand will also be limited by offshoring of routine purchasing actions to other countries.

Employment of purchasing managers is expected to have little or no change. The use of the Internet to conduct electronic commerce has made information easier to obtain, thus increasing the productivity of purchasing managers. The Internet also allows both large and small companies to bid on contracts. Exclusive supply contracts and long-term contracting have allowed companies to negotiate with fewer suppliers less frequently. Still, purchasing managers will be needed to oversee large consolidated purchasing networks, thus spurring some employment growth.

Employment of purchasing agents and buyers of farm products is also projected to have little or no change as overall growth in agricultural industries and retailers in the grocery-related industries consolidate. Furthermore, automation, offshoring, and the outsourcing of more services are expected to further impede employment growth.

Finally, little or no change in employment of wholesale and retail buyers, except farm products, is expected. In the retail industry, mergers and acquisitions have caused buying departments to consolidate. In addition, larger retail stores are eliminating local buying departments and creating a centralized buying department at their headquarters.

Job prospects. Persons who have a bachelor's degree in engineering, business, economics, or one of the applied sciences should have the best chance of obtaining a buyer position. Industry experience and knowledge of a technical field will be an advantage for those interested in working for a manufacturing or industrial company. Government agencies and larger companies usually require a master's degree in business or public administration for top-level purchasing positions. Most managers need experience in their respective fields.

Earnings

Median annual wages of purchasing managers were $91,440 in May 2009. The middle 50 percent earned between $69,100 and $118,740. The lowest 10 percent earned less than $52,910, and the highest 10 percent earned more than $145,960.

Median annual wages of purchasing agents and buyers of farm products were $53,150 in May 2009. The middle 50 percent earned between $40,130 and $73,630. The lowest 10 percent earned less than $30,250, and the highest 10 percent earned more than $101,480.

Median annual wages of wholesale and retail buyers, except farm products, were $48,650 in May 2009. The middle 50 percent earned between $36,800 and $65,870. The lowest 10 percent earned less than $28,870, and the highest 10 percent earned more than $88,830. Median annual wages in the industries employing the largest numbers of wholesale and retail buyers, except farm products, were the following:

Management of companies and enterprises $56,340
Wholesale electronic markets and agents and
    brokers 52,380
Grocery and related product merchant
    wholesalers 49,230
Grocery stores.. 36,600
Machinery, equipment, and supplies
    merchant wholesalers 46,420

Median annual wages of purchasing agents, except wholesale, retail, and farm products, were $54,810 in May 2009. The middle 50 percent earned between $42,350 and $72,130. The lowest 10 percent earned less than $34,160, and the highest 10 percent earned more than $89,830. Median annual wages in the industries employing the largest numbers of purchasing agents, except wholesale, retail, and farm products, were the following:

Federal executive branch $75,110
Management of companies and enterprises 59,080
Aerospace product and parts manufacturing.......... 64,290
Local government... 53,280
General medical and surgical hospitals 44,320

Purchasing managers, buyers, and purchasing agents receive the same benefits package as other workers, including vacations, sick leave, life and health insurance, and pension plans. In addition to receiving standard benefits, retail buyers often earn cash bonuses based on their performance and may receive discounts on merchandise bought from their employer.

Related Occupations

Another occupation that obtains materials and goods for businesses is procurement clerks.

Other occupations that need knowledge of marketing and the ability to assess consumer demand include advertising, marketing, promotions, public relations, and sales managers; food service managers; insurance sales agents; lodging managers; sales engineers; and sales representatives, wholesale and manufacturing.

Sources of Additional Information

Further information about education, training, employment, and certification for purchasing careers is available from

▸ American Purchasing Society, P.O. Box 256, Aurora, IL 60506.

▸ APICS, The Association for Operations Management, 8430 W. Bryn Mawr Avenue, Suite 1000, Chicago, IL 60631. Internet: www.apics.org

▸ Institute for Supply Management, P.O. Box 22160, Tempe, AZ 85285-2160. Internet: www.ism.ws

▸ National Institute of Governmental Purchasing, Inc., 151 Spring St., Suite 300, Herndon, VA 20170-5223. Internet: www.nigp.org

Radio and Telecommunications Equipment Installers and Repairers

(O*NET 49-2021.00 and 49-2022.00)

Significant Points

■ Little or no change in employment is projected.

■ Job opportunities vary by specialty; good opportunities are expected for central office installers and repairers, but station installers and repairers can expect keen competition.

■ Applicants with computer skills and postsecondary electronics training should have the best opportunities.

■ Repairers may be on call around the clock in case of emergencies; therefore, night, weekend, and holiday hours are common.

Nature of the Work

Telephones, computers, and radios depend on a variety of equipment to transmit communications signals and connect to the Internet. From electronic and optical switches that route telephone calls and packets of data to their destinations to radio transmitters and receivers that relay signals from radios in airplanes, boats, and emergency vehicles, complex equipment is needed to keep the country communicating. The workers who set up and maintain this sophisticated equipment are called radio and telecommunications equipment installers and repairers.

Telecommunications equipment installers and *repairers* have a range of skills and abilities, which vary by the type of work they do and where it is performed. Most work indoors.

Central office installers and repairers—telecommunications equipment installers and repairers who work at switching hubs called central offices—do some of the most complex work. Switching hubs contain the switches and routers that direct packets of information to their destinations. Installers and repairers set up those switches and routers, as well as cables and other equipment.

Although most telephone lines connecting houses to central offices and switching stations are still copper, the lines connecting central hubs to each other are fiber optic. Fiber-optic lines, along with newer packet switching equipment, have greatly increased the transmission capacity of each line, allowing an ever increasing amount of information to pass through the lines. Switches and routers are used to transmit, process, amplify, and direct a massive amount of information. Installing and maintaining this equipment requires a high level of technical knowledge.

Nonetheless, the increasing reliability of switches and routers has simplified maintenance as new self-monitoring telecommunications switches can now alert central office repairers to malfunctions. Some switches allow repairers to diagnose and correct problems from remote locations. When faced with a malfunction, the repairer may refer to manufacturers' manuals that provide maintenance instructions.

As cable television and telecommunications technology converge, the equipment used in both technologies is becoming more similar. The distribution centers for cable television companies, which are similar to central offices in the telecommunications sector, are called headends. *Headend technicians* perform essentially the same work as central office technicians, but they work in the cable television industry.

When problems with telecommunications equipment arise, telecommunications equipment repairers diagnose the source of the problem by testing each part of the equipment—a process that requires understanding how the software and hardware interact. To locate the problem, repairers often use spectrum analyzers, network analyzers, or both, to detect any distortion in the signal. To fix the equipment, repairers may use small hand tools, including pliers and screwdrivers, to remove and replace defective components such as circuit boards or wiring. Newer equipment is easier to repair because whole boards and parts are designed to be quickly removed and replaced. Repairers also may install updated software or programs that maintain existing software.

Another type of telecommunications installer and repairer, *PBX installers and repairers,* set up private branch exchange (PBX) switchboards, which relay incoming, outgoing, and interoffice telephone calls within a single location or organization. To install switches and switchboards, installers first connect the equipment to power lines and communications cables and install frames and supports. They test the connections to ensure that adequate power is available and that the communication links work properly. They also install equipment such as power systems, alarms, and telephone sets. New switches and switchboards are computerized and workers often need to install software or program the equipment to provide specific features. Finally, the installer performs tests to verify that the newly installed equipment functions properly. If a problem arises, PBX repairers determine whether it is located within the PBX system or whether it stems from the telephone lines maintained by the local telephone company. Newer installations may use voice-over Internet protocol (VoIP) systems—systems that operate like PBX, but they use a company's computer wiring to run Internet access, network applications, and telephone communications.

Station installers and repairers, telephone—commonly known as *home installers and repairers* or *telecommunications service technicians*—install and repair telecommunications wiring and equipment in customers' home or business premises. They install telephone, VoIP, Internet, and other communications services by installing wiring inside the home or connecting existing wiring to outside service lines. Depending on the service required, they may set up television capability or connect modems and install software on a customer's computer. To complete the connection to an outside service line, the installer may need to climb telephone poles or ladders and test the line. Later on, if a maintenance problem occurs, station repairers test the customer's lines to determine if the problem is located in the customer's premises or in the outside service lines and attempt to fix the problem if it is inside. If the problem is with the outside service lines, telecommunications line repairers usually are called to fix it.

Radio mechanics install and maintain radio transmitting and receiving equipment, excluding cellular communications systems. This includes stationary equipment mounted on transmission towers or tall buildings and mobile equipment, such as two-way radio communications systems in taxis, airplanes, ships, and emergency vehicles. Aviation and marine radio mechanics also may work on other electronic equipment, in addition to radios. Newer radio equipment is self-monitoring and may alert mechanics to potential malfunctions. When malfunctions occur, these mechanics examine equipment for damaged components and either fix them, replace the part, or make a software modification. They may use electrical measuring instruments to monitor signal strength, transmission capacity, interference, and signal delay, as well as hand tools to replace defective components and adjust equipment so that it performs within required specifications.

Work environment. Radio and telecommunications equipment installers and repairers generally work in clean, well-lighted, air-conditioned surroundings, such as a telecommunications company's central office, a customer's location, or an electronic service center. Traveling to the site of the installation or repair is common among station installers and repairers, PBX and VoIP installers and repairers, and radio mechanics. Installation may require access to rooftops, attics, ladders, and telephone poles to complete the repair. Radio mechanics may need to work on transmission towers, which may be located on top of tall buildings or mountains, as well as aboard airplanes and ships.

The work of most repairers involves lifting, reaching, stooping, crouching, and crawling. Adherence to safety precautions is important in order to guard against work hazards. These hazards include falls, minor burns, and electrical shock. Data from the U.S. Bureau of Labor Statistics show that telecommunications equipment installers and repairers, except line installers, experienced a work-related injury and illness rate that was higher than the national average.

Nearly all radio and telecommunications equipment installers and repairers work full time during regular business hours to meet the demand for repair services during the workday. Schedules are more irregular at employers that provide repair services 24 hours a day, such as for police radio communications operations or where installation and maintenance must take place after normal business hours. At these locations, mechanics work a variety of shifts, including weekend and holiday hours. Repairers may be on call around the clock, in case of emergencies, and may have to work overtime.

Training, Other Qualifications, and Advancement

Postsecondary education in electronics and computer technology is increasingly required for radio and telecommunications equipment installers and repairer jobs, and a few employers even prefer people with a bachelor's degree for some of the most complex types of work.

Education and training. As telecommunications technology becomes more complex, the education required for radio and telecommunications equipment installers and repairer jobs has increased. Most employers prefer applicants with postsecondary training in electronics and familiarity with computers. The education needed for these jobs may vary from certification to a two- or four-year degree in electronics or a related subject. Sources of training include two- and four-year college programs in electronics or communications technology, military experience in radios and electronics, trade schools, and programs offered by equipment and software manufacturers. Educational requirements are higher for central office installers and repairers and for those working in nonresidential settings.

Many in the telecommunications industry work their way up into this occupation by gaining experience at less difficult jobs. Experience as a telecommunications line installer or station installer is helpful before moving up to the job of central office installer and other more complex jobs, for example. Military experience with communications equipment is also valued by many employers in both telecommunications and radio repair.

Newly hired repairers usually receive some training from their employers. This may include formal classroom training in electronics, communications systems, or software and informal hands-on training assisting an experienced repairer. Large companies may send repairers to outside training sessions to learn about new equipment and service procedures. As networks have become more sophisticated—often including equipment from a variety of companies—the knowledge needed for installation and maintenance also has increased.

Licensure. Aviation and marine radio mechanics are required to have a license from the Federal Communications Commission before they can work on these types of radios. This requires passing several exams on radio law, electronics fundamentals, and maintenance practices.

Other qualifications. Familiarity with computers, being mechanically inclined, and being able to solve problems are traits that are highly regarded by employers. Repairers must also be able to distinguish colors, because wires are typically color-coded. For positions that require climbing poles and towers, workers must be in good physical shape and not afraid of heights. Repairers who handle assignments alone at a customer's site must be able to work without close supervision. For workers who frequently contact customers, a pleasant personality, neat appearance, and good communications skills also are important.

Certification and advancement. This is an occupation where the technology is changing rapidly. Workers must keep abreast of the latest equipment available and know how to repair it. Telecommunications equipment installers and repairers often need to be certified to perform certain tasks or to work on specific equipment. Certification usually requires taking classes. Some certifications are needed to enter the occupation; others are meant to improve one's current abilities or to advance in the occupation.

The Society of Cable and Telecommunications Engineers and the Telecommunications Industry Association offer certifications to workers in this field. Telecommunications equipment manufacturers also provide training on specific equipment.

Experienced repairers with advanced training may become specialists or troubleshooters who help other repairers diagnose difficult problems, or may work with engineers in designing equipment and developing maintenance procedures. Home installers may advance to wiring computer networks or working as a central office installer and repairer. Because of their familiarity with equipment, repairers are particularly well qualified to become manufacturers' sales workers. Workers with leadership ability also may become maintenance supervisors or service managers. Some experienced workers open their own repair service shops, or become wholesalers or retailers of electronic equipment.

Employment

Radio and telecommunications equipment installers and repairers held about 208,800 jobs in 2008. About 203,100 were telecommunications equipment installers and repairers, except line installers. The remaining 5,700 were radio mechanics.

Telecommunications equipment installers and repairers work mostly in the telecommunications industry. Increasingly, however, they can be found in the construction industry working as contractors to the telecommunications industry.

Radio mechanics work in the electronic and precision equipment repair and maintenance industry, the telecommunications industry, electronics and appliance stores, government, and other industries.

Job Outlook

Little or no change in employment of radio and telecommunications equipment installers and repairers is projected. Job opportunities vary by specialty; good opportunities are expected for central office installers and repairers, but station installers and repairers can expect keen competition. Job prospects are best for those with computer skills and postsecondary training in electronics.

Employment change. Little or no change in employment of radio and telecommunications equipment installers and repairers is expected during the 2008–2018 period. Over the next decade, telecommunications companies will provide faster Internet connections, provide video on demand, add hundreds of television stations, and many services that haven't even been invented yet. Although building the new networks required to provide these services will create jobs, these gains will be offset by a decline in maintenance work. The new equipment requires much less maintenance work because it is newer, more reliable, easier to repair, and more resistant to damage from the elements.

The increased reliability of radio equipment and the use of self-monitoring systems also will continue to lessen the need for radio mechanics. However, technological changes are also creating new wireless applications that create jobs for radio mechanics.

Job prospects. Applicants with computer skills and postsecondary training in electronics should have the best opportunities for radio and telecommunications equipment installer and repairer jobs, but opportunities will vary by specialty. Good opportunities should be available for central office and PBX installers and repairers experienced in current technology, as the growing popularity of VoIP, expanded multimedia offerings such as video on demand, and other

Projections Data from the National Employment Matrix

Occupational title	SOC Code	Employment, 2008	Projected employment, 2018	Change, 2008–2018	
				Number	Percent
Radio and telecommunications equipment installers and repairers..49-2020		208,800	208,100	−700	0
Radio mechanics..49-2021		5,700	5,500	−200	−4
Telecommunications equipment installers and repairers, except line installers...................49-2022		203,100	202,600	−500	0

NOTE: Data in this table are rounded.

telecommunications services continue to place additional demand on telecommunications networks. These new services require high data transfer rates, which can be achieved only by installing new optical switching and routing equipment. Extending high-speed communications from central offices to customers also will require telecommunications equipment installers to put in place more advanced switching and routing equipment, but opportunities for repairers will be limited by the increased reliability and automation of the new switching equipment.

Station installers and repairers can expect keen competition. Prewired buildings and the increasing reliability of telephone equipment will reduce the need for installation and maintenance of customers' telephones, as will the declining number of pay telephones in operation as use of cellular telephones grows. However, some of these losses should be offset by the need to upgrade internal lines in businesses and the wiring of new homes and businesses with fiber-optic lines.

Radio mechanics should find good opportunities if they have a strong background in electronics and an ability to work independently. Increasing competition from cellular services is limiting the growth of radio services, but employers report difficulty finding adequate numbers of qualified radio mechanics to perform repair work.

Earnings

In May 2009, median annual wages of telecommunications equipment installers and repairers, except line installers, were $55,560. The middle 50 percent earned between $42,680 and $63,960. The bottom 10 percent earned less than $31,430, whereas the top 10 percent earned more than $71,650. Median annual wages of these workers in the wired telecommunications carriers industry were $56,840 in May 2009.

Median annual wages of radio mechanics in May 2009 were $41,060. The middle 50 percent earned between $31,770 and $51,050. The bottom 10 percent earned less than $25,780, whereas the top 10 percent earned more than $61,950.

About 32 percent of radio and telecommunication equipment installers and repairers are members of unions, such as the Communications Workers of America (CWA) and the International Brotherhood of Electrical Workers (IBEW).

Telecommunications equipment installers and repairers employed by large telecommunications companies who also belong to unions often have very good benefits, including health, dental, vision, and life insurance. They also usually have good retirement and leave policies. Those working for small independent companies and contractors may get fewer benefits.

Radio mechanics tend to work for small electronics firms or government. Benefits vary widely depending upon the type of work and size of firm. Government jobs usually have good benefits.

Related Occupations

Other occupations that involve work with electronic and telecommunications equipment include broadcast and sound engineering technicians and radio operators; computer, automated teller, and office machine repairers; electrical and electronics installers and repairers; engineering technicians; and line installers and repairers.

Sources of Additional Information

For information on career and training opportunities, contact

▸ International Brotherhood of Electrical Workers, Telecommunications Department, 900 7th St. NW, Washington, DC 20001.

▸ Communications Workers of America, 501 3rd St. NW, Washington, DC 20001. Internet: www.cwa-union.org/jobs

▸ National Coalition for Telecommunications Education and Learning, CAEL, 6021 South Syracuse Way, Suite 213, Greenwood Village, CO 80111. Internet: www.nactel.org

For information on training and professional certifications in broadband telecommunications, contact

▸ Society of Cable Telecommunications Engineers, Certification Department, 140 Philips Rd., Exton, PA 19341-1318. Internet: www.scte.org

For information on training and licensing for aviation and marine radio mechanics, contact

▸ The Federal Communications Commission (FCC), 445 12th St. SW, Washington, DC 20554. Internet: http://wireless.fcc.gov/commoperators

For more information on employers, education, and training in marine electronics and radios, contact

▸ National Marine Electronics Association, 7 Riggs Ave., Severna Park, MD 21164. Internet: www.nmea.org

Radiologic Technologists and Technicians

(O*NET 29-2034.00, 29-2034.01, and 29-2034.02)

Significant Points

■ Employment is projected to grow faster than average; those with knowledge of more than one diagnostic imaging procedure will have the best employment opportunities.

- Formal training programs in radiography are offered in hospitals or colleges and universities and lead to a certificate, an associate degree, or a bachelor's degree.

- Most states require licensure, and requirements vary.

- Although hospitals will remain the primary employer, a number of new jobs will be found in physicians' offices and diagnostic imaging centers.

Nature of the Work

Radiologic technologists and technicians perform diagnostic imaging examinations. Radiologic technicians perform imaging examinations like X-rays while technologists use other imaging modalities such as computed tomography, magnetic resonance imaging, and mammography.

Radiologic technicians, sometimes referred to as *radiographers,* produce X-ray films (radiographs) of parts of the human body for use in diagnosing medical problems. They prepare patients for radiologic examinations by explaining the procedure, removing jewelry and other articles through which X-rays cannot pass, and positioning patients so that the parts of the body can be appropriately radiographed. To prevent unnecessary exposure to radiation, these workers surround the exposed area with radiation protection devices, such as lead shields, or limit the size of the X-ray beam. Radiographers position radiographic equipment at the correct angle and height over the appropriate area of a patient's body. Using instruments similar to a measuring tape, they may measure the thickness of the section to be radiographed and set controls on the X-ray machine to produce radiographs of the appropriate density, detail, and contrast.

Radiologic technologists and technicians must follow physicians' orders precisely and conform to regulations concerning the use of radiation to protect themselves, their patients, and their coworkers from unnecessary exposure.

In addition to preparing patients and operating equipment, radiologic technologists and technicians keep patient records and adjust and maintain equipment. They also may prepare work schedules, evaluate purchases of equipment, or manage a radiology department.

Radiologic technologists perform more complex imaging procedures. When performing fluoroscopies, for example, radiologic technologists prepare a solution for the patient to drink, allowing the radiologist (a physician who interprets radiographs) to see soft tissues in the body.

Some radiologic technologists specialize in computed tomography (CT), as *CT technologists*. CT scans produce a substantial amount of cross-sectional X-rays of an area of the body. From those cross-sectional X-rays, a three-dimensional image is made. The CT uses ionizing radiation; therefore, it requires the same precautionary measures that are used with X-rays.

Radiologic technologists also can specialize in Magnetic Resonance Imaging (MR) as *MR technologists*. MR, like CT, produces multiple cross-sectional images to create a three-dimensional image. Unlike CT and X-rays, MR uses non-ionizing radio frequency to generate image contrast.

Radiologic technologists might also specialize in mammography. Mammographers use low-dose X-ray systems to produce images of the breast.

In addition to radiologic technologists, others who conduct diagnostic imaging procedures include cardiovascular technologists and technicians, diagnostic medical sonographers, and nuclear medicine technologists.

Work environment. Physical stamina is important in this occupation because technologists and technicians are on their feet for long periods and may lift or turn disabled patients. Technologists and technicians work at diagnostic machines but also may perform some procedures at patients' bedsides. Some travel to patients in large vans equipped with sophisticated diagnostic equipment.

Although radiation hazards exist in this occupation, they are minimized by the use of lead aprons, gloves, and other shielding devices, and by instruments monitoring exposure to radiation. Technologists and technicians wear badges measuring radiation levels in the radiation area, and detailed records are kept on their cumulative lifetime dose.

Most full-time radiologic technologists and technicians work about 40 hours a week. They may, however, have evening, weekend, or on-call hours. Some radiologic technologists and technicians work part time for more than one employer; for those, travel to and from facilities must be considered.

Training, Other Qualifications, and Advancement

There are multiple paths to entry into this profession offered in hospitals or colleges and universities. Most states require licensure, and requirements vary.

Education and training. Formal training programs in radiography lead to a certificate, an associate degree, or a bachelor's degree. An associate degree is the most prevalent form of educational attainment among radiologic technologists and technicians. Some may receive a certificate. Certificate programs typically last around 21–24 months.

The Joint Review Committee on Education in Radiologic Technology accredits formal training programs in radiography. The committee accredited 213 programs resulting in a certificate, 397 programs resulting in an associate degree, and 35 resulting in a bachelor's degree in 2009. The programs provide both classroom and clinical instruction in anatomy and physiology, patient care procedures, radiation physics, radiation protection, principles of imaging, medical terminology, positioning of patients, medical ethics, radiobiology, and pathology.

Students interested in radiologic technology should take high school courses in mathematics, physics, chemistry, and biology.

Licensure. Federal legislation protects the public from the hazards of unnecessary exposure to medical and dental radiation by ensuring that operators of radiologic equipment are properly trained. However, it is up to each state to require licensure of radiologic technologists. Most states require licensure for practicing radiologic technologists. Licensing requirements vary by state; for specific requirements contact your state's health board.

Certification and other qualifications. The American Registry of Radiologic Technologists (ARRT) offers voluntary certification for radiologic technologists. In addition, a number of states use ARRT-administered exams for state licensing purposes. To be eligible for certification, technologists must graduate from an ARRT-approved accredited program and pass an examination. Many employers prefer to hire certified radiologic technologists. In order to maintain an ARRT certification, 24 hours of continuing education must be completed every 2 years.

Radiologic technologists should be sensitive to patients' physical and psychological needs. They must pay attention to detail, follow instructions, and work as part of a team. In addition, operating complicated equipment requires mechanical ability and manual dexterity.

Advancement. With experience and additional training, staff technologists may become specialists, performing CT scanning, MR, mammography, or bone densitometry. Technologists also may advance, with additional education and certification, to become a radiologist assistant. The ARRT offers specialty certification in many radiologic specialties as well as a credentialing for radiologist assistants.

Experienced technologists also may be promoted to supervisor, chief radiologic technologist, and, ultimately, department administrator or director. Depending on the institution, courses or a master's degree in business or health administration may be necessary for the director's position.

Some technologists progress by specializing in the occupation to become instructors or directors in radiologic technology educational programs; others take jobs as sales representatives or instructors with equipment manufacturers.

Employment

Radiologic technologists held about 214,700 jobs in 2008. About 61 percent of all jobs were in hospitals. Most other jobs were in offices of physicians; medical and diagnostic laboratories, including diagnostic imaging centers; and outpatient care centers.

Job Outlook

Employment is projected to grow faster than average. Those with knowledge of more than one diagnostic imaging procedure—such as CT, MR, and mammography—will have the best employment opportunities.

Employment change. Employment of radiologic technologists is expected to increase by about 17 percent from 2008 to 2018, faster than the average for all occupations. As the population grows and ages, there will be an increasing demand for diagnostic imaging. With age comes increased incidence of illness and injury, which often requires diagnostic imaging for diagnosis. In addition to diagnosis, diagnostic imaging is used to monitor the progress of disease treatment. With the increasing success of medical technologies in treating disease, diagnostic imaging will increasingly be needed to monitor progress of treatment.

The extent to which diagnostic imaging procedures are performed depends largely on cost and reimbursement considerations. However, accurate early disease detection allows for lower cost of treatment in the long run, which many third-party payers find favorable.

Although hospitals will remain the principal employer of radiologic technologists, a number of new jobs will be found in offices of physicians and diagnostic imaging centers. As technology advances many imaging modalities are becoming less expensive and more feasible to have in a physician's office

Job prospects. In addition to job growth, job openings also will arise from the need to replace technologists who leave the occupation. Those with knowledge of more than one diagnostic imaging procedure—such as CT, MR, and mammography—will have the best employment opportunities as employers seek to control costs by using multicredentialed employees.

Demand for radiologic technologists and technicians can tend to be regional with some areas having large demand, while other areas are saturated. Technologists and technicians willing to relocate may have better job prospects.

CT is continuing to become a frontline diagnosis tool. Instead of taking X-rays to decide whether a CT is needed, as was the practice before, it is often the first choice for imaging because of its accuracy. MR also is increasingly used. Technologists with credentialing in either of these specialties will be very marketable to employers.

Earnings

The median annual wage of radiologic technologists and technicians was $53,240 in May 2009. The middle 50 percent earned between $43,510 and $64,070. The lowest 10 percent earned less than $35,700, and the highest 10 percent earned more than $75,440. Median annual wages in the industries employing the largest numbers of radiologic technologists in 2009 were as follows:

General medical and surgical hospitals	$53,770
Offices of physicians	49,540
Medical and diagnostic laboratories	56,380
Outpatient care centers	52,550
Federal executive branch	55,600

Related Occupations

Radiologic technologists operate sophisticated equipment to help physicians, dentists, and other health practitioners diagnose and treat patients. Workers in related health-care occupations include cardiovascular technologists and technicians; diagnostic medical sonographers; nuclear medicine technologists; and radiation therapists.

Sources of Additional Information

For information on careers in radiologic technology, contact

▶ American Society of Radiologic Technologists, 15000 Central Ave. SE, Albuquerque, NM 87123. Internet: www.asrt.org

Projections Data from the National Employment Matrix

Occupational title	SOC Code	Employment, 2008	Projected employment, 2018	Change, 2008–2018	
				Number	Percent
Radiologic technologists and technicians	29-2034	214,700	251,700	37,000	17

NOTE: Data in this table are rounded.

For the current list of accredited education programs in radiography, contact

▸ Joint Review Committee on Education in Radiologic Technology, 20 N. Wacker Dr., Suite 2850, Chicago, IL 60606-3182. Internet: www.jrcert.org

For certification information, contact

▸ American Registry of Radiologic Technologists, 1255 Northland Dr., St. Paul, MN 55120-1155. Internet: www.arrt.org

Real Estate Brokers and Sales Agents

(O*NET 41-9021.00 and 41-9022.00)

Significant Points

■ A license is required in every state and the District of Columbia.

■ Residential real estate brokers and sales agents often work evenings and weekends.

■ Although gaining a job may be relatively easy, beginning workers face competition from well-established, more experienced agents and brokers.

■ Employment is sensitive to swings in the economy, as well as interest rates; during periods of declining economic activity or rising interest rates, the volume of sales and the resulting demand for sales workers fall.

Nature of the Work

One of the most complex and significant financial events in people's lives is the purchase or sale of a home or investment property. Because of the complexity and importance of this transaction, people typically seek the help of *real estate brokers* and *sales agents* when buying or selling real estate.

Real estate brokers and sales agents have a thorough knowledge of the real estate market in their communities. They know which neighborhoods will best fit clients' needs and budgets. They are familiar with local zoning and tax laws and know where to obtain financing for the purchase of property.

Brokers and agents do the same type of work, but brokers are licensed to manage their own real estate businesses. Agents must work with a broker. They usually provide their services to a licensed real estate broker on a contract basis. In return, the broker pays the agent a portion of the commission earned from the agent's sale of the property. Brokers, as independent businesspeople, often sell real estate owned by others; they also may rent or manage properties for a fee.

When selling property, brokers and agents arrange for title searches to verify ownership and for meetings between buyers and sellers during which they agree to the details of the transactions. In a final meeting, the new owners take possession of the property. Agents and brokers also act as intermediaries in price negotiations between buyers and sellers. They may help to arrange financing from a lender for the prospective buyer, which may make the difference between success and failure in closing a sale. In some cases, brokers and agents assume primary responsibility for finalizing, or closing, sales, but typically this function is done by lenders or lawyers.

Agents and brokers spend a significant amount of time looking for properties to buy or sell. They obtain listings—agreements by owners to place properties for sale with the firm. When listing a property for sale, agents and brokers compare the listed property with similar properties that recently sold, to determine a competitive market price for the property. Following the sale of the property, both the agent who sold it and the agent who obtained the listing receive a portion of the commission. Thus, agents who sell a property that they themselves have listed can increase their commission.

Before showing residential properties to potential buyers, agents meet with them to get an idea of the type of home the buyers would like and how much the buyers can afford to spend. They may also ask buyers to sign a loyalty contract, which states that the agent will be the only one to show houses to the buyer. An agent or broker then generates lists of properties for sale, their location and description, and available sources of financing. In some cases, agents and brokers use computers to give buyers a virtual tour of properties that interest them.

Agents may meet numerous times with prospective buyers to discuss and visit available properties. Agents identify and emphasize the most pertinent selling details. To a young family looking for a house, for example, they may emphasize the convenient floor plan, the area's low crime rate, and the proximity to schools and shopping. To a potential investor, they may point out the tax advantages of owning a rental property and finding a renter. If negotiation over price becomes necessary, agents must follow their client's instructions thoroughly and may present counteroffers to reach the final sales price.

Once the buyer and seller have signed a contract, the real estate broker or agent must ensure that all terms of the contract are met before the closing date. If the seller agrees to any repairs, the broker or agent ensures they are made. Increasingly, brokers and agents must deal with environmental issues as well, such as advising buyers about lead paint on the walls. In addition, the agent must make sure that any legally mandated or agreed-upon inspections, such as termite and radon inspections, take place. Loan officers, attorneys, and other people handle many details, but the agent must ensure that they are carried out.

Most real estate brokers and sales agents sell residential property. A small number—usually employed in large or specialized firms—sell commercial, industrial, agricultural, or other types of real estate. Every specialty requires knowledge of that particular type of property and clientele. Selling, buying, or leasing business property requires an understanding of leasing practices, business trends, and the location of the property. Agents who sell, buy, or lease industrial properties must know about the region's transportation, utilities, and labor supply. Whatever the type of property, the agent or broker must know how to meet the client's particular requirements.

Work environment. Real estate agents and brokers often work more than a standard 40-hour week, often working evenings and weekends for the convenience of clients. Although the hours are long and frequently irregular, most agents and brokers have the freedom to determine their own schedule.

Advances in telecommunications and the ability to retrieve data about properties over the Internet allow many real estate brokers and sales agents to work out of their homes instead of real estate offices. Even with this convenience, workers spend much of their time away from their desks—showing properties to customers, analyzing properties for sale, meeting with prospective clients, or researching the real estate market.

Training, Other Qualifications, and Advancement

In every state and the District of Columbia, real estate brokers and sales agents must be licensed. Prospective agents must be high school graduates, be at least 18 years old, and pass a written test administered by the state.

Education and training. Agents and brokers must be high school graduates. In fact, as real estate transactions have become more legally complex, many firms have turned to college graduates to fill positions. A large number of agents and brokers have some college training.

Most universities, colleges, and community colleges offer various courses in real estate. Some offer associate and bachelor's degrees in real estate, but mostly they offer certificate programs. Additionally, college courses in finance, business administration, statistics, economics, law, and English are also helpful. For those who intend to start their own company, business courses such as marketing and accounting are as important as courses in real estate or finance.

Many local real estate associations that are members of the National Association of Realtors sponsor courses covering the fundamentals and legal aspects of the field. Advanced courses in mortgage financing, property development and management, and other subjects also are available. Also, some brokerage firms offer formal training programs for both beginners and experienced agents. In addition, much of the training needed to learn the practical aspects of the trade happens on the job, under the direction of an experienced agent, who may demonstrate how to use a computer to locate or list available properties and identify sources of financing.

Licensure. In every state and the District of Columbia, real estate brokers and sales agents must be licensed. Prospective brokers and agents must pass a written examination. The examination—more comprehensive for brokers than for agents—includes questions on basic real estate transactions and the laws affecting the sale of property. Most states require candidates for the general sales license to complete between 30 and 90 hours of classroom instruction. To get a broker's license, an individual needs between 60 and 90 hours of formal training and a specific amount of experience selling real estate, usually 1 to 3 years. Some states waive the experience requirements for the broker's license for applicants who have a bachelor's degree in real estate.

State licenses typically must be renewed every 1 or 2 years; usually, no examination is needed. However, many states require continuing education for license renewals. Prospective agents and brokers should contact the real estate licensing commission of the state in which they wish to work to verify the exact licensing requirements.

Other qualifications. Personality traits are as important as academic background. Brokers look for agents who have a pleasant personality and a neat appearance. They must be at least 18 years old. Maturity, good judgment, trustworthiness, honesty, and enthusiasm for the job are required to attract prospective customers in this highly competitive field. Agents should be well organized; be detail oriented; and have a good memory for names, faces, and business particulars. A good knowledge of the local area and its neighborhoods is a clear advantage.

Advancement. As agents gain knowledge and expertise, they become more efficient in closing a greater number of transactions and increase their income. In many large firms, experienced agents can advance to sales manager or general manager. People who earn their broker's license may open their own offices. Others with experience and training in estimating property values may become real estate appraisers, and people familiar with operating and maintaining rental properties may become property managers. Experienced agents and brokers with a thorough knowledge of business conditions and property values in their localities may enter mortgage financing or real estate investment counseling.

Employment

In 2008, real estate brokers and sales agents held about 517,800 jobs; real estate sales agents held approximately 76 percent of these jobs.

Many real estate brokers and sales agents worked part time, combining their real estate activities with other careers. About 59 percent of real estate brokers and sales agents were self-employed. Real estate is sold in all areas, but employment is concentrated in large urban areas and in rapidly growing communities.

Most real estate firms are relatively small; indeed, some are one-person businesses. By contrast, some large real estate firms have several hundred agents operating out of numerous branch offices. Many brokers have franchise agreements with national or regional real estate organizations. Under this type of arrangement, the broker pays a fee in exchange for the privilege of using the more widely known name of the parent organization. Although franchised brokers often receive help in training sales staff and running their offices, they bear the ultimate responsibility for the success or failure of their firms.

Job Outlook

Employment of real estate brokers and agents is expected to grow faster than average. Beginning agents and brokers, however, will face competition from their well-established, more experienced counterparts.

Employment change. Employment of real estate brokers and sales agents is expected to grow 14 percent during the 2008–2018 decade, faster than average for all occupations. A growing population, particularly young adults who will be forming households in greater numbers, will require the services of real estate agents and brokers to buy their homes. Home sales will be sparked by the continuing desire for people to own their own homes and their perception that real estate will be a good investment over the long run. However, job growth will be somewhat limited by the increasing use of the Internet, which is improving the productivity of agents and brokers, and transforming the way they do business. For example, prospective customers often can perform their own searches for properties that meet their criteria by accessing real estate information on the Internet.

Job prospects. In addition to job growth, a large number of job openings will arise from the need to replace workers who transfer to other occupations or leave the labor force. Real estate brokers and sales agents are older, on average, than most other workers, and many are expected to leave the occupation over the next decade.

Employment of real estate brokers and sales agents is sensitive to swings in the economy, such as a recession. During periods of declining economic activity or rising interest rates, the volume of sales and the resulting demand for sales workers fall. As a result, the income of agents and brokers declines, and many work fewer hours or leave the occupation altogether. Over the coming decade,

Projections Data from the National Employment Matrix

Occupational title	SOC Code	Employment, 2008	Projected employment, 2018	Change, 2008–2018	
				Number	Percent
Real estate brokers and sales agents 41-9020		517,800	592,100	74,300	14
Real estate brokers...41-9021		123,400	134,000	10,600	9
Real estate sales agents......................................41-9022		394,400	458,200	63,700	16

NOTE: Data in this table are rounded.

the opportunity for part-time work is expected to decline. Although the occupation is relatively easy to enter, increasingly complex legal and technological requirements are raising startup costs associated with becoming an agent and making it more difficult for part-time workers to enter the occupation.

Well-trained, ambitious people who enjoy selling—particularly those with extensive social and business connections in their communities—should have the best chance for success. However, beginning agents and brokers often face competition from their well-established, more experienced counterparts in obtaining listings and in closing an adequate number of sales.

Earnings

The median annual wages, including commissions, of salaried real estate sales agents were $40,100 in May 2009. The middle 50 percent earned between $27,370 and $63,510 a year. The lowest 10 percent earned less than $20,800, and the highest 10 percent earned more than $96,410. Median annual wages in the industries employing the largest number of real estate sales agents in May 2009 were as follows:

Offices of real estate agents and brokers $42,130
Lessors of real estate 33,210
Activities related to real estate 35,990
Residential building construction......................... 47,580
Land subdivision 42,950

Median annual wages, including commissions, of salaried real estate brokers were $55,740 in May 2009. The middle 50 percent earned between $35,090 and $93,300 a year. Median annual wages in the industries employing the largest number of real estate brokers in May 2009 were as follows:

Offices of real estate agents and brokers $57,250
Activities related to real estate 51,120
Lessors of real estate 53,370
Activities related to credit intermediation 59,780
Residential building construction......................... 58,220

Commissions on sales are the main source of earnings of real estate agents and brokers. The rate of commission varies according to whatever the agent and broker agree on, the type of property, and its value. The percentage paid on the sale of farm and commercial properties or unimproved land is typically higher than the percentage paid for selling a home.

Commissions may be divided among several agents and brokers. The broker or agent who obtains a listing usually shares the commission with the broker or agent who sells the property and with the firms that employ each of them. Although an agent's share varies greatly from one firm to another, often it is about half of the total amount received by the firm. Agents who both list and sell a property maximize their commission.

Income usually increases as an agent gains experience, but individual motivation, economic conditions, and the type and location of the property also can affect income. Sales workers who are active in community organizations and in local real estate associations can broaden their contacts and increase their income. A beginner's earnings often are irregular because a few weeks or even months may go by without a sale. Although some brokers allow an agent to draw against future income from a special account, the practice is not common with new employees. The beginner, therefore, should have enough money to live for about six months or until commissions increase.

Related Occupations

Other occupations requiring knowledge of real estate include appraisers and assessors of real estate; and property, real estate, and community association managers.

Other sales workers who need these character traits include insurance sales agents; sales representatives, wholesale and manufacturing; and securities, commodities, and financial services sales agents.

Sources of Additional Information

Information on licensing requirements for real estate brokers and sales agents is available from most local real estate organizations or from the state real estate commission or board.

More information about opportunities in real estate is available on the Internet site of the following organization:

▶ National Association of Realtors. Internet: www.realtor.org

Receptionists and Information Clerks

(O*NET 43-4171.00)

Significant Points

■ Good interpersonal skills are critical.

■ A high school diploma or its equivalent is the most common educational requirement.

■ A large number of job openings are expected.

■ Opportunities should be best for persons with a wide range of clerical and technical skills, particularly those with related work experience.

Nature of the Work

Receptionists and information clerks are charged with a responsibility that may affect the success of an organization: making a good first impression. Receptionists and information clerks answer telephones, route and screen calls, greet visitors, respond to inquiries from the public, and provide information about the organization. Some are responsible for the coordination of all mail into and out of the office. In addition, they contribute to the security of an organization by helping to monitor the access of visitors—a function that has become increasingly important.

Whereas some tasks are common to most receptionists and information clerks, their specific responsibilities vary with the type of establishment in which they work. For example, receptionists and information clerks in hospitals and in doctors' offices may gather patients' personal and insurance information and direct them to the proper waiting rooms. In corporate headquarters, they may greet visitors and manage the scheduling of the board room or common conference area. In beauty or hair salons, they arrange appointments, direct customers to the hairstylist, and may serve as cashiers. In factories, large corporations, and government offices, receptionists and information clerks may provide identification cards and arrange for escorts to take visitors to the proper office. Those working for bus and train companies respond to inquiries about departures, arrivals, stops, and other related matters.

Receptionists and information clerks use the telephone, personal computers, and other electronic devices to send e-mail and fax documents, for example. Despite the widespread use of automated answering systems or voice mail, many receptionists and clerks still take messages and inform other employees of visitors' arrivals or cancellation of an appointment. When they are not busy with callers, most workers are expected to assist other administrative employees by performing a variety of office duties, including opening and sorting mail, collecting and distributing parcels, transmitting and delivering facsimiles, and performing Internet search tasks. Other duties include updating appointment calendars; preparing travel vouchers; and performing basic bookkeeping, word processing, and filing.

Companies sometimes hire off-site receptionists and information clerks called, *virtual receptionists*, to perform, or supplement, many of the duties done by the traditional receptionist. Virtual receptionists use software integrated into their phone system to instantly track their employer's location, inform them of every call, and relay vital information to their callers. Using fax mailbox services, employers can retrieve faxes from any location at any time. The service receives them for the employer in special mailboxes and then transfers them when the line is free.

Work environment. Receptionists and information clerks who greet customers and visitors usually work in areas that are highly visible and designed and furnished to make a good impression. Most work stations are clean, well lighted, and relatively quiet. Virtual receptionists work from home or at an off-site office building. The work performed by some receptionists and information clerks may be tiring, repetitive, and stressful as they may spend all day answering continuously ringing telephones and sometimes encounter difficult or irate callers. The work environment, however, may be very friendly and motivating for individuals who enjoy greeting customers face to face and making them feel comfortable. About 30 percent of receptionists and information clerks worked part time.

Training, Other Qualifications, and Advancement

A high school diploma or its equivalent is the most common educational requirement, although hiring requirements for receptionists and information clerks vary by industry and employer. Good interpersonal skills and being technologically proficient also are important to employers.

Education and training. Receptionists and information clerks generally need a high school diploma or equivalent as most of their training is received on the job. However, employers often look for applicants who already possess certain skills, such as knowledge of spreadsheet and word processing software or answering telephones. Some employers also may prefer some formal office education or training. On the job, they learn how to operate the telephone system and computers. They also learn the proper procedures for greeting visitors and for distributing mail, fax messages, and parcels. While many of these skills can be learned quickly, those who are charged with relaying information to visitors or customers may need several months to learn details about the organization.

Other qualifications. Good interpersonal and customer service skills—being courteous, professional, and helpful—are critical for this job. Being an active listener often is a key quality needed by receptionists and information clerks that requires the ability to listen patiently to the points being made, to wait to speak until others have finished, and to ask appropriate questions when necessary. In addition, the ability to relay information accurately to others is important.

The ability to operate a wide range of office technology also is helpful, as receptionists and information clerks are often asked to work on other assignments during the day.

Advancement. Advancement for receptionists generally comes about either by transferring to an occupation with more responsibility or by being promoted to a supervisory position. Receptionists with especially strong computer skills, a bachelor's degree, and several years of experience may advance to a better paying job as a secretary or an administrative assistant.

Employment

Receptionists and information clerks held about 1.1 million jobs in 2008. The health-care and social assistance industries—including offices of physicians, hospitals, nursing homes, and outpatient care facilities—employed about 36 percent of all receptionists and information clerks. Wholesale and retail trade, personal services, educational services, finance and insurance, employment services, religious organizations, and real estate industries also employed large numbers of receptionists and information clerks.

Job Outlook

Employment is projected to grow faster than the average for all occupations. Job growth, coupled with the need to replace workers who transfer to other occupations or leave the labor force, will generate a large number of job openings for receptionists and information clerks.

Employment change. Employment of receptionists and information clerks is expected to increase by 15 percent from 2008 to 2018, which is faster than the average for all occupations. Employment growth will result from growth in industries such as offices of

Projections Data from the National Employment Matrix

Occupational title	SOC Code	Employment, 2008	Projected employment, 2018	Change, 2008–2018	
				Number	Percent
Receptionists and information clerks.........................43-4171		1,139,200	1,312,100	172,900	15

NOTE: Data in this table are rounded.

physicians and in other health practitioners, legal services, personal care services, construction, and management and technical consulting.

Technology will have conflicting effects on employment growth for receptionists and information clerks. The increasing use of voice mail and other telephone automation reduces the need for receptionists by allowing one receptionist to perform work that formerly required several. At the same time, however, the increasing use of other technology has caused a consolidation of clerical responsibilities and growing demand for workers with diverse clerical and technical skills, such as virtual receptionists. Because receptionists and information clerks may perform a wide variety of clerical tasks, they should continue to be in demand. Further, they perform many tasks that are interpersonal in nature and are not easily automated, ensuring continued demand for their services in a variety of establishments.

Job prospects. In addition to job growth, numerous job opportunities will be created as receptionists and information clerks transfer to other occupations or leave the labor force altogether. Opportunities should be best for persons with a wide range of clerical and technical skills, particularly those with related work experience.

Earnings

Median hourly wages of receptionists and information clerks in May 2009 were $12.05. The middle 50 percent earned between $9.88 and $14.65. The lowest 10 percent earned less than $8.26, and the highest 10 percent earned more than $17.61. Median hourly wages in the industries employing the largest number of receptionists and information clerks in May 2009 were as follows:

Offices of physicians	$12.49
Offices of dentists	13.92
Personal care services	9.50
Offices of other health practitioners......................	11.67
Other professional, scientific, and technical services	11.35

Related Occupations

Receptionists deal with the public and often direct people to others who can assist them. Other workers who perform similar duties include customer service representatives; dispatchers, except police, fire, and ambulance; and secretaries and administrative assistants.

Sources of Additional Information

State employment offices can provide information on job openings for receptionists.

For information related to administrative occupations, including educational programs and certified designations, contact

▸ International Association of Administrative Professionals, P.O. Box 20404, Kansas City, MO 64195-0404. Internet: www.iaap-hq.org

Recreation Workers

(O*NET 39-9032.00)

Significant Points

■ The recreation field offers an unusually large number of part-time and seasonal job opportunities.

■ Opportunities for part-time, seasonal, and temporary recreation jobs will be good, but competition will remain keen for full-time career positions.

■ Many recreation workers spend most of their time outdoors and may work in a variety of weather conditions.

Nature of the Work

As participation in organized recreational activities grows, *recreation workers* will be needed to plan, organize, and direct these activities in local playgrounds and recreation areas, parks, community and senior centers, nursing homes and other senior housing, camps, and tourist attractions. These workers lead groups in activities such as arts and crafts, sports, performing arts, camping, and other special interests. They make sure that participants abide by the rules of the camps and recreational facilities and that safety practices are adhered to so that no one gets injured. Recreation workers also are found in some businesses or business groups, where they direct leisure activities for employees, such as softball or bowling, and organize sports leagues.

Recreation workers hold a variety of positions at different levels of responsibility. Those who work directly with children in residential or day camps are called *camp counselors*. These workers lead and instruct children and teenagers in a variety of outdoor recreation activities, such as swimming, hiking, horseback riding, and camping. In addition, counselors who specialize may teach campers special subjects, such as archery, boating, music, drama, gymnastics, tennis, and computers. In residential camps, counselors also provide guidance and supervise daily living and socialization. *Camp directors* typically supervise camp counselors, plan camp activities or programs, and perform the various administrative functions of a camp.

Workers who provide instruction and coaching primarily in one activity, such as art, music, drama, swimming, or tennis, are called *activity specialists*. These workers can work in camps or anywhere else where there is interest in a single activity.

Recreation leaders are responsible for a recreation program's daily operation. They primarily organize and direct participants, schedule the use of facilities, keep records of equipment use, and ensure that recreation facilities and equipment are used properly. In addition, they may lead classes and provide instruction in a recreational activity.

Recreation supervisors oversee recreation leaders and plan, organize, and manage recreational activities to meet the needs of a variety of populations. These workers often serve as liaisons between the director of the park or recreation center and the recreation leaders. Recreation supervisors with more specialized responsibilities also may direct special activities or events or oversee a major activity, such as aquatics, gymnastics, or one or more performing arts.

Directors of recreation and parks develop and manage comprehensive recreation programs in parks, playgrounds, and other settings. Directors usually serve as technical advisors to state and local recreation and park commissions and may be responsible for recreation and park budgets.

Work environment. Recreation workers work in a variety of settings—for example, a cruise ship, a nature park, a summer camp, or a playground in the center of an urban community. Many recreation workers spend most of their time outdoors and may work in a variety of weather conditions. Recreation directors and supervisors, however, typically spend most of their time in an office, planning programs and special events. Directors and supervisors generally engage in less physical activity than do lower level recreation workers. Nevertheless, recreation workers at all levels risk suffering injuries during physical activities.

Some recreation workers work about 40 hours a week. However, many people entering this field, such as camp counselors, may have some night and weekend work, irregular hours, and seasonal employment. In 2008, about 40 percent of these workers worked part time.

Training, Other Qualifications, and Advancement

The educational and training requirements for recreation workers vary widely with the type of job. Full-time career positions usually require a college degree. Many jobs, however, require demonstrated knowledge of the activity or can be learned with only a short period of on-the-job training.

Education and training. The educational needs for people entering into this occupational field vary widely depending on the job and level of responsibility. For activity specialists, it is more important to have experience and demonstrated competence in a particular activity, such as art or kayaking, than to have a degree. Camp counselors often are older teenagers or young adults who have experienced camping as a child and enjoy the camping experience. A degree is less important than the counselor's maturity level, ability to work well with children and teens, and ability to make sure that they stay safe.

Those working in administrative positions for large organizations or public recreation systems may need a bachelor's degree or higher. Full-time career professional positions usually require a college degree with a major in parks and recreation or leisure studies, but a bachelor's degree in any liberal arts field may be sufficient for some jobs in the private sector. In industrial recreation, or "employee services" as it is more commonly called, companies that offer recreational activities for their employees prefer to hire those with a bachelor's degree in recreation or leisure studies and a background in business administration.

Employers seeking candidates for some administrative positions favor those with at least a master's degree in parks and recreation,

business administration, or public administration. Most require at least an associate degree in recreation studies or a related field.

An associate or bachelor's degree in a recreation-related discipline, along with experience, is preferred for most recreation supervisor jobs and is required for most higher level administrative jobs. Graduates of associate degree programs in parks and recreation, social work, and other human services disciplines also can enter some career recreation positions. High school graduates occasionally enter career positions, but doing so is not common.

Programs leading to an associate or bachelor's degree in parks and recreation, leisure studies, or related fields are offered at several hundred colleges and universities. Many also offer master's or doctoral degrees in the field. In 2009, 89 bachelor's degree programs in parks and recreation were accredited by the National Recreation and Park Association (NRPA). Accredited programs provide broad exposure to the history, theory, and practice of park and recreation management. Courses offered include community organization; supervision and administration; recreational needs of special populations, such as the elderly or disabled; and supervised fieldwork. Students may specialize in areas such as therapeutic recreation, park management, outdoor recreation, industrial or commercial recreation, and camp management.

Specialized training or experience in a particular field, such as art, music, drama, or athletics, is an asset for many jobs. Some jobs also require certification. For example, a lifesaving certificate is a prerequisite for teaching or coaching water-related activities.

The majority of seasonal and part-time workers learn through on-the-job training.

Licensure and certification. The NRPA certifies individuals for professional and technical jobs. Certified park and recreation professionals must pass an exam. In order to qualify to take the exam, individuals need to (1) have earned a bachelor's degree in a major such as recreation, park resources, or leisure services from a program accredited by the NRPA or have at least one year of experience if the program is not accredited; (2) have earned any other bachelor's degree and have at least three years of relevant full-time work experience; or (3) have at least five years of full-time experience in the field. Continuing education is necessary to remain certified.

Many cities and localities require lifeguards to be certified. Training and certification details vary from state to state and county to county. Information on lifeguards is available from local parks and recreation departments.

Other qualifications. People planning careers in recreation should be outgoing, good at motivating people, and sensitive to the needs of others. Excellent health and physical fitness often are required, due to the physical nature of some jobs. Time management and the ability to manage others also are important.

Advancement. Recreation workers start their careers working with people. As they gain experience, they may get promoted to positions with greater responsibilities. Recreation workers with experience and managerial skills may advance to supervisory or managerial positions. Eventually, they may become the director of a recreation department.

Employment

Recreation workers held about 327,500 jobs in 2008, and many additional workers held summer jobs in the occupation. About 31 percent of recreation workers worked for local governments,

Projections Data from the National Employment Matrix

Occupational title	SOC Code	Employment, 2008	Projected employment, 2018	Change, 2008–2018	
				Number	Percent
Recreation workers..................................39-9032		327,500	375,700	48,200	15

NOTE: Data in this table are rounded.

primarily in park and recreation departments. About 16 percent of recreation workers were employed by nursing and residential care facilities, and another 10 percent were employed in civic and social organizations, such as the Boy Scouts or Girl Scouts or the YMCA and YWCA.

Job Outlook

Faster than average growth is expected. Jobs opportunities for part-time, seasonal, and temporary recreation workers will be good, but competition will remain keen for career positions as recreation workers.

Employment change. Overall employment of recreation workers is projected to increase by 15 percent between 2008 and 2018, which is faster than the average for all occupations. Although people will spend more time and money on recreation, budget restrictions in state and local government will limit the number of jobs added. Many of the new jobs will be in social assistance organizations and in nursing and residential care facilities. Civic and social organizations and fitness and sports centers will also contribute to growth.

Growth will be driven by the growing numbers of young and older Americans. The large numbers of births in recent years likely will increase the demand for recreation services for children, and retiring baby boomers are expected to have more leisure time, higher disposable incomes, and more concern for health and fitness than previous generations had. The latter factors should lead to an increasing demand for recreation services for baby boomers.

Job prospects. Applicants for part-time, seasonal, and temporary recreation jobs should have good opportunities, but competition will remain keen for career positions because the recreation field attracts many applicants and because the number of career positions is limited compared with the number of lower level seasonal jobs. Opportunities for staff positions should be best for people with formal training and experience in part-time or seasonal recreation jobs. Volunteer experience, part-time work during school, and a summer job are viewed favorably. Those with graduate degrees should have the best opportunities for supervisory or administrative positions. Job openings will stem from growth and the need to replace the large numbers of workers who leave the occupation each year.

Earnings

In May 2009, median annual wages of recreation workers who worked full time were $22,280. The middle 50 percent earned between $18,130 and $29,060. The lowest paid 10 percent earned less than $16,070, while the highest paid 10 percent earned $38,170 or more. However, earnings of recreation directors and others in supervisory or managerial positions can be substantially higher. Most public and private recreation agencies provide full-time recreation workers with typical benefits; part-time workers receive few, if any, benefits. In May 2009, median annual wages in the industries employing the largest numbers of recreation workers were as follows:

Local government...$22,150
Nursing care facilities 23,510
Civic and social organizations 20,180
Individual and family services............................. 22,400
Other amusement and recreation industries........... 19,520

The large numbers of temporary, seasonal jobs in the recreation field typically are filled by high school or college students, generally do not have formal education requirements, and are open to anyone with the desired personal qualities. Employers compete for a share of the vacationing student labor force, and although salaries in recreation often are lower than those in other fields, the nature of the work and the opportunity to work outdoors are attractive to many.

Part-time, seasonal, and volunteer jobs in recreation include summer camp counselors, craft specialists, and afterschool and weekend recreation program leaders. In addition, many teachers and college students accept jobs as recreation workers when school is not in session. The vast majority of volunteers serve as activity leaders at local day camp programs or in youth organizations, camps, nursing homes, hospitals, senior centers, and other settings.

Related Occupations

Other occupations that require leadership skills, as well as a desire to work with and help others, include the following: athletes, coaches, umpires, and related workers; counselors; fitness workers; probation officers and correctional treatment specialists; psychologists; recreational therapists; social workers; and teachers—self-enrichment education.

Sources of Additional Information

For information on jobs in recreation, contact employers such as local government departments of parks and recreation, nursing homes and other residential facilities, the Boy Scouts or Girl Scouts, and other local social or religious organizations.

For information on careers, certification, and academic programs in parks and recreation, contact

▸ National Recreation and Park Association, 22377 Belmont Ridge Rd., Ashburn, VA 20148-4501. Internet: www.nrpa.org

For information about a career as a camp counselor, contact

▸ American Camp Association, 5000 State Rd. 67 N., Martinsville, IN 46151-7902. Internet: www.acacamps.org

Registered Nurses

(O*NET 29-1111.00, 29-1111.01, 29-1111.02, and 29-1111.03)

Significant Points

■ Registered nurses (RNs) constitute the largest health-care occupation, with 2.6 million jobs.

■ About 60 percent of RN jobs are in hospitals.

■ The three typical educational paths to registered nursing are a bachelor's degree, an associate degree, and a diploma from an approved nursing program; advanced practice nurses—clinical nurse specialists, nurse anesthetists, nurse-midwives, and nurse practitioners—need a master's degree.

■ Overall job opportunities are expected to be excellent, but may vary by employment and geographic setting; some employers report difficulty in attracting and retaining an adequate number of RNs.

Nature of the Work

Registered nurses (*RNs*), regardless of specialty or work setting, treat patients, educate patients and the public about various medical conditions, and provide advice and emotional support to patients' family members. RNs record patients' medical histories and symptoms, help perform diagnostic tests and analyze results, operate medical machinery, administer treatment and medications, and help with patient follow-up and rehabilitation.

RNs teach patients and their families how to manage their illnesses or injuries, explaining post-treatment home care needs; diet, nutrition, and exercise programs; and self-administration of medication and physical therapy. Some RNs may work to promote general health by educating the public on warning signs and symptoms of disease. RNs also might run general health screening or immunization clinics, blood drives, and public seminars on various conditions.

When caring for patients, RNs establish a care plan or contribute to an existing plan. Plans may include numerous activities, such as administering medication, including careful checking of dosages and avoiding interactions; starting, maintaining, and discontinuing intravenous (IV) lines for fluid, medication, blood, and blood products; administering therapies and treatments; observing the patient and recording those observations; and consulting with physicians and other health-care clinicians. Some RNs provide direction to licensed practical nurses and nursing aides regarding patient care. (See the statements on licensed practical and licensed vocational nurses; nursing and psychiatric aides; and home health aides elsewhere in this book). RNs with advanced educational preparation and training may perform diagnostic and therapeutic procedures and may have prescriptive authority.

Specific work responsibilities will vary from one RN to the next. An RN's duties and title are often determined by their work setting or patient population served. RNs can specialize in one or more areas of patient care. There generally are four ways to specialize. RNs may work a particular setting or type of treatment, such as *perioperative nurses*, who work in operating rooms and assist surgeons. RNs may specialize in specific health conditions, as do *diabetes management nurses*, who assist patients to manage diabetes. Other RNs specialize in working with one or more organs or body system types, such as *dermatology nurses*, who work with patients who have skin disorders. RNs may also specialize with a well-defined population, such as *geriatric nurses*, who work with the elderly. Some RNs may combine specialties. For example, *pediatric oncology nurses* deal with children and adolescents who have cancer. The opportunities for specialization in registered nursing are extensive and are often determined on the job.

There are many options for RNs who specialize in a work setting or type of treatment. *Ambulatory care nurses* provide preventive care and treat patients with a variety of illnesses and injuries in physicians' offices or in clinics. Some ambulatory care nurses are involved in telehealth, providing care and advice through electronic communications media such as videoconferencing, the Internet, or by telephone. *Critical care nurses* provide care to patients with serious, complex, and acute illnesses or injuries that require very close monitoring and extensive medication protocols and therapies. Critical care nurses often work in critical or intensive care hospital units. *Emergency*, or *trauma*, nurses work in hospital or stand-alone emergency departments, providing initial assessments and care for patients with life-threatening conditions. Some emergency nurses may become qualified to serve as *transport nurses*, who provide medical care to patients who are transported by helicopter or airplane to the nearest medical facility. *Holistic nurses* provide care such as acupuncture, massage and aroma therapy, and biofeedback, which are meant to treat patients' mental and spiritual health in addition to their physical health. *Home health-care nurses* provide at-home nursing care for patients, often as follow-up care after discharge from a hospital or from a rehabilitation, long-term care, or skilled nursing facility. *Hospice and palliative care nurses* provide care, most often in home or hospice settings, focused on maintaining quality of life for terminally ill patients. *Infusion nurses* administer medications, fluids, and blood to patients through injections into patients' veins. *Long-term care nurses* provide health-care services on a recurring basis to patients with chronic physical or mental disorders, often in long-term care or skilled nursing facilities. *Medical-surgical nurses* provide health promotion and basic medical care to patients with various medical and surgical diagnoses. *Occupational health nurses* seek to prevent job-related injuries and illnesses, provide monitoring and emergency care services, and help employers implement health and safety standards. *Perianesthesia nurses* provide preoperative and postoperative care to patients undergoing anesthesia during surgery or other procedure. *Perioperative nurses* assist surgeons by selecting and handling instruments, controlling bleeding, and suturing incisions. Some of these nurses also can specialize in plastic and reconstructive surgery. *Psychiatric-mental health nurses* treat patients with personality and mood disorders. *Radiology nurses* provide care to patients undergoing diagnostic radiation procedures such as ultrasounds, magnetic resonance imaging, and radiation therapy for oncology diagnoses. *Rehabilitation nurses* care for patients with temporary and permanent disabilities. *Transplant nurses* care for both transplant recipients and living donors and monitor signs of organ rejection.

RNs specializing in a particular disease, ailment, or health-care condition are employed in virtually all work settings, including physicians' offices, outpatient treatment facilities, home health-care agencies, and hospitals. *Addictions nurses* care for patients seeking help with alcohol, drug, tobacco, and other addictions. *Intellectual and developmental disabilities nurses* provide care for patients with physical, mental, or behavioral disabilities; care may include help with feeding, controlling bodily functions, sitting or standing independently, and speaking or other communication. *Diabetes management nurses* help diabetics to manage their disease by teaching them proper nutrition and showing them how to test blood sugar levels and administer insulin injections. *Genetics nurses* provide early detection screenings, counseling, and treatment of patients with genetic disorders, including cystic fibrosis and Huntington's disease. *HIV/AIDS nurses* care for patients diagnosed with HIV and AIDS. *Oncology nurses* care for patients with various types of cancer and may assist in the administration of radiation and chemo-therapies and follow-up monitoring. *Wound, ostomy, and continence nurses* treat patients with wounds caused by traumatic injury, ulcers, or arterial disease; provide postoperative care for patients with openings that allow for alternative methods of bodily waste elimination; and treat patients with urinary and fecal incontinence.

RNs specializing in treatment of a particular organ or body system usually are employed in hospital specialty or critical care units, specialty clinics, and outpatient care facilities. *Cardiovascular nurses* treat patients with coronary heart disease and those who have had heart surgery, providing services such as postoperative rehabilitation. *Dermatology nurses* treat patients with disorders of the skin, such as skin cancer and psoriasis. *Gastroenterology nurses* treat patients with digestive and intestinal disorders, including ulcers, acid reflux disease, and abdominal bleeding. Some nurses in this field also assist in specialized procedures such as endoscopies, which look inside the gastrointestinal tract using a tube equipped with a light and a camera that can capture images of diseased tissue. *Gynecology nurses* provide care to women with disorders of the reproductive system, including endometriosis, cancer, and sexually transmitted diseases. *Nephrology nurses* care for patients with kidney disease caused by diabetes, hypertension, or substance abuse. *Neuroscience nurses* care for patients with dysfunctions of the nervous system, including brain and spinal cord injuries and seizures. *Ophthalmic nurses* provide care to patients with disorders of the eyes, including blindness and glaucoma, and to patients undergoing eye surgery. *Orthopedic nurses* care for patients with muscular and skeletal problems, including arthritis, bone fractures, and muscular dystrophy. *Otorhinolaryngology nurses* care for patients with ear, nose, and throat disorders, such as cleft palates, allergies, and sinus disorders. *Respiratory nurses* provide care to patients with respiratory disorders such as asthma, tuberculosis, and cystic fibrosis. *Urology nurses* care for patients with disorders of the kidneys, urinary tract, and male reproductive organs, including infections, kidney and bladder stones, and cancers.

RNs who specialize by population provide preventive and acute care in all health-care settings to the segment of the population in which they specialize, including newborns (neonatology), children and adolescents (pediatrics), adults, and the elderly (gerontology or geriatrics). RNs also may provide basic health care to patients outside of health-care settings in such venues as correctional facilities, schools, summer camps, and the military. Some RNs travel around the United States and throughout the world providing care to patients in areas with shortages of health-care workers.

Most RNs work as staff nurses as members of a team providing critical health care. However, some RNs choose to become advanced practice nurses, who work independently or in collaboration with physicians, and may focus on the provision of primary care services. *Clinical nurse specialists* provide direct patient care and expert consultations in one of many nursing specialties, such as psychiatric-mental health. *Nurse anesthetists* provide anesthesia and related care before and after surgical, therapeutic, diagnostic, and obstetrical procedures. They also provide pain management and emergency services, such as airway management. *Nurse-midwives* provide primary care to women, including gynecological exams, family planning advice, prenatal care, assistance in labor and delivery, and neonatal care. *Nurse practitioners* serve as primary and specialty care providers, providing a blend of nursing and health-care services to patients and families. The most common specialty areas for nurse

practitioners are family practice, adult practice, women's health, pediatrics, acute care, and geriatrics. However, there are a variety of other specialties that nurse practitioners can choose, including neonatology and mental health. Advanced practice nurses can prescribe medications in all states and in the District of Columbia.

Some nurses have jobs that require little or no direct patient care, but still require an active RN license. *Forensics nurses* participate in the scientific investigation and treatment of abuse victims, violence, criminal activity, and traumatic accident. *Infection control nurses* identify, track, and control infectious outbreaks in health-care facilities and develop programs for outbreak prevention and response to biological terrorism. *Nurse educators* plan, develop, implement, and evaluate educational programs and curricula for the professional development of student nurses and RNs. *Nurse informaticists* manage and communicate nursing data and information to improve decision making by consumers, patients, nurses, and other health-care providers. RNs also may work as health-care consultants, public policy advisors, pharmaceutical and medical supply researchers and salespersons, and medical writers and editors.

Work environment. Most RNs work in well-lit, comfortable health-care facilities. Home health and public health nurses travel to patients' homes, schools, community centers, and other sites. RNs may spend considerable time walking, bending, stretching, and standing. Patients in hospitals and nursing care facilities require 24-hour care; consequently, nurses in these institutions may work nights, weekends, and holidays. RNs also may be on call—available to work on short notice. Nurses who work in offices, schools, and other settings that do not provide 24-hour care are more likely to work regular business hours. About 20 percent of RNs worked part time in 2008.

RNs may be in close contact with individuals who have infectious diseases and with toxic, harmful, or potentially hazardous compounds, solutions, and medications. RNs must observe rigid, standardized guidelines to guard against disease and other dangers, such as those posed by radiation, accidental needle sticks, chemicals used to sterilize instruments, and anesthetics. In addition, they are vulnerable to back injury when moving patients.

Training, Other Qualifications, and Advancement

The three typical educational paths to registered nursing are a bachelor's degree, an associate degree, and a diploma from an approved nursing program. Nurses most commonly enter the occupation by completing an associate degree or bachelor's degree program. Individuals then must complete a national licensing examination in order to obtain a nursing license. Advanced practice nurses—clinical nurse specialists, nurse anesthetists, nurse-midwives, and nurse practitioners—need a master's degree.

Education and training. There are three typical educational paths to registered nursing—a bachelor's of science degree in nursing (BSN), an associate degree in nursing (ADN), and a diploma. BSN programs, offered by colleges and universities, take about 4 years to complete. ADN programs, offered by community and junior colleges, take about 2 to 3 years to complete. Diploma programs, administered in hospitals, last about 3 years. Generally, licensed graduates of any of the three types of educational programs qualify for entry-level positions as a staff nurse. There are hundreds of registered nursing programs that result in ADN or BSN; however, there are relatively few diploma programs.

Individuals considering a career in nursing should carefully weigh the advantages and disadvantages of enrolling in each type of education program. Advancement opportunities may be more limited for ADN and diploma holders compared to RNs who obtain a BSN or higher. Individuals who complete a bachelor's degree receive more training in areas such as communication, leadership, and critical thinking, all of which are becoming more important as nursing practice becomes more complex. Additionally, bachelor's degree programs offer more clinical experience in nonhospital settings. A bachelor's or higher degree is often necessary for administrative positions, research, consulting, and teaching

Many RNs with an ADN or diploma later enter bachelor's degree programs to prepare for a broader scope of nursing practice. Often, they can find an entry-level position and then take advantage of tuition reimbursement benefits to work toward a BSN by completing an RN-to-BSN program. Accelerated master's degree in nursing (MSN) programs also are available. They typically take three to four years to complete full time and result in the award of both the BSN and MSN.

There are education programs available for people interested in switching to a career in nursing as well. Individuals who already hold a bachelor's degree in another field may enroll in an accelerated BSN program. Accelerated BSN programs last 12 to 18 months and provide the fastest route to a BSN for individuals who already hold a degree. MSN programs also are available for individuals who hold a bachelor's or higher degree in another field; master's degree programs usually last 2 years.

All nursing education programs include classroom instruction and supervised clinical experience in hospitals and other health-care facilities. Students take courses in anatomy, physiology, microbiology, chemistry, nutrition, psychology and other behavioral sciences, and nursing. Coursework also includes the liberal arts for ADN and BSN students.

Supervised clinical experience is provided in hospital departments such as pediatrics, psychiatry, maternity, and surgery. A number of programs include clinical experience in nursing care facilities, public health departments, home health agencies, and ambulatory clinics.

Licensure and certification. In all states, the District of Columbia, and U.S. territories, students must graduate from an approved nursing program and pass a national licensing examination, known as the National Council Licensure Examination, or NCLEX-RN, in order to obtain a nursing license. Other eligibility requirements for licensure vary by state. Contact your state's board of nursing for details.

Other qualifications. Nurses should be caring, sympathetic, responsible, and detail oriented. They must be able to direct or supervise others, correctly assess patients' conditions, and determine when consultation is required. They need emotional stability to cope with human suffering, emergencies, and other stresses.

RNs should enjoy learning because continuing education credits are required by some states and/or employers at regular intervals. Career-long learning is a distinct reality for RNs.

Some nurses may become credentialed in specialties such as ambulatory care, gerontology, informatics, pediatrics, and many others. Credentialing for RNs is available from the American Nursing Credentialing Center, the National League for Nursing, and many

others. Although credentialing is usually voluntary, it demonstrates adherence to a higher standard and some employers may require it.

Advancement. Most RNs begin as staff nurses in hospitals and, with experience and good performance, often move to other settings or are promoted to positions with more responsibility. In management, nurses can advance from assistant unit manager or head nurse to more senior-level administrative roles of assistant director, director, vice president, or chief of nursing. Increasingly, management-level nursing positions require a graduate or an advanced degree in nursing or health services administration. Administrative positions require leadership, communication and negotiation skills, and good judgment.

Some RNs choose to become advanced practice nurses, who work independently or in collaboration with physicians, and may focus on providing primary care services. There are four types of advanced practice nurses: clinical nurse specialists, nurse anesthetists, nurse-midwives, and nurse practitioners. Clinical nurse specialists provide direct patient care and expert consultations in one of many nursing specialties, such as psychiatric-mental health. Nurse anesthetists provide anesthesia and related care before and after surgical, therapeutic, diagnostic, and obstetrical procedures. They also provide pain management and emergency services, such as airway management. Nurse-midwives provide primary care to women, including gynecological exams, family planning advice, prenatal care, assistance in labor and delivery, and neonatal care. Nurse practitioners serve as primary and specialty care providers, providing a blend of nursing and health-care services to patients and families.

All four types of advanced practice nurses require at least a master's degree. In addition, all states specifically define requirements for registered nurses in advanced practice roles. Advanced practice nurses may prescribe medicine, but the authority to prescribe varies by state. Contact your state's board of nursing for specific regulations regarding advanced practice nurses.

Some nurses move into the business side of health care. Their nursing expertise and experience on a health-care team equip them to manage ambulatory, acute, home-based, and chronic care businesses. Employers—including hospitals, insurance companies, pharmaceutical manufacturers, and managed care organizations, among others—need RNs for health planning and development, marketing, consulting, policy development, and quality assurance. Other nurses work as college and university faculty or conduct research.

Employment

As the largest health-care occupation, registered nurses held about 2.6 million jobs in 2008. Hospitals employed the majority of RNs, with 60 percent of such jobs. About 8 percent of jobs were in offices of physicians, 5 percent in home health-care services, 5 percent in nursing care facilities, and 3 percent in employment services. The remainder worked mostly in government agencies, social assistance agencies, and educational services.

Job Outlook

Overall job opportunities for registered nurses are expected to be excellent, but may vary by employment and geographic setting. Some employers report difficulty in attracting and retaining an adequate number of RNs. Employment of RNs is expected to grow much faster than the average and, because the occupation is very large, 581,500 new jobs will result, among the largest number of new jobs for any occupation. Additionally, hundreds of thousands of job openings will result from the need to replace experienced nurses who leave the occupation.

Employment change. Employment of registered nurses is expected to grow by 22 percent from 2008 to 2018, much faster than the average for all occupations. Growth will be driven by technological advances in patient care, which permit a greater number of health problems to be treated, and by an increasing emphasis on preventive care. In addition, the number of older people, who are much more likely than younger people to need nursing care, is projected to grow rapidly.

However, employment of RNs will not grow at the same rate in every industry. The projected growth rates for RNs in the industries with the highest employment of these workers are as follows:

Industry	Percent
Offices of physicians	48
Home health-care services	33
Nursing care facilities	25
Employment services	24
Hospitals, public and private	17

Employment is expected to grow more slowly in hospitals—health care's largest industry—than in most other health-care industries. While the intensity of nursing care is likely to increase, requiring more nurses per patient, the number of inpatients (those who remain in the hospital for more than 24 hours) is not likely to grow by much. Patients are being discharged earlier, and more procedures are being done on an outpatient basis, both inside and outside hospitals. Rapid growth is expected in hospital outpatient facilities, such as those providing same-day surgery, rehabilitation, and chemotherapy.

More and more sophisticated procedures, once performed only in hospitals, are being performed in physicians' offices and in outpatient care centers, such as freestanding ambulatory surgical and emergency centers. Accordingly, employment is expected to grow fast in these places as health care in general expands.

Employment in nursing care facilities is expected to grow because of increases in the number of older persons, many of whom require long-term care. Many elderly patients want to be treated at home or in residential care facilities, which will drive demand for RNs in those settings. The financial pressure on hospitals to discharge patients as soon as possible should produce more admissions to nursing and residential care facilities and referrals to home health care. Job growth also is expected in units that provide specialized long-term rehabilitation for stroke and head injury patients, as well as units that treat Alzheimer's victims.

Employment in home health care is expected to increase in response to the growing number of older persons with functional disabilities, consumer preference for care in the home, and technological advances that make it possible to bring increasingly complex treatments into the home. The type of care demanded will require nurses who are able to perform complex procedures.

Job prospects. Overall job opportunities are expected to be excellent for registered nurses. Employers in some parts of the country and in certain employment settings report difficulty in attracting and retaining an adequate number of RNs, primarily because of an aging RN workforce and a lack of younger workers to fill positions. Qualified applicants to nursing schools are being turned away because of a shortage of nursing faculty. The need for nursing faculty will only increase as many instructors near retirement. Despite the slower employment growth in hospitals, job opportunities should be excellent because of the relatively high turnover of hospital nurses. To attract and retain qualified nurses, hospitals may offer signing bonuses, family-friendly work schedules, or subsidized training. Although faster employment growth is projected in physicians' offices and outpatient care centers, RNs may face greater competition for these positions because they generally offer regular working hours and more comfortable working environments. Generally, RNs with at least a bachelor's degree will have better job prospects than those without a bachelor's. In addition, all four advanced practice specialties—clinical nurse specialists, nurse practitioners, nurse-midwives, and nurse anesthetists—will be in high demand, particularly in medically underserved areas such as inner cities and rural areas. Relative to physicians, these RNs increasingly serve as lower-cost primary care providers.

Earnings

Median annual wages of registered nurses were $63,750 in May 2009. The middle 50 percent earned between $52,520 and $77,970. The lowest 10 percent earned less than $43,970, and the highest 10 percent earned more than $93,700. Median annual wages in the industries employing the largest numbers of registered nurses in May 2009 were as follows:

General medical and surgical hospitals	$65,220
Offices of physicians	60,630
Home health-care services	60,190
Nursing care facilities	57,830
Outpatient care centers	63,150

Many employers offer flexible work schedules, child care, educational benefits, and bonuses. About 21 percent of registered nurses are union members or covered by union contract.

Related Occupations

Because of the number of specialties for registered nurses, and the variety of responsibilities and duties, many other health-care occupations are similar in some aspects of their job. Some health-care occupations with similar levels of responsibility that work under the direction of physicians or dentists are dental hygienists; diagnostic medical sonographers; emergency medical technicians and

Projections Data from the National Employment Matrix

Occupational title	SOC Code	Employment, 2008	Projected employment, 2018	Change, 2008–2018	
				Number	Percent
Registered nurses	29-1111	2,618,700	3,200,200	581,500	22

NOTE: Data in this table are rounded.

paramedics; licensed practical and licensed vocational nurses; and physician assistants.

Sources of Additional Information

For information on a career as a registered nurse and nursing education, contact

▸ National League for Nursing, 61 Broadway, 33rd Floor, New York, NY 10006. Internet: www.nln.org

For information on baccalaureate and graduate nursing education, nursing career options, and financial aid, contact

▸ American Association of Colleges of Nursing, 1 Dupont Circle NW, Suite 530, Washington, DC 20036. Internet: www.aacn.nche.edu

For additional information on registered nurses, including credentialing, contact

▸ American Nurses Association, 8515 Georgia Ave., Suite 400, Silver Spring, MD 20910. Internet: http://nursingworld.org

For information on the National Council Licensure Examination (NCLEX-RN) and a list of individual state boards of nursing, contact

▸ National Council of State Boards of Nursing, 111 E. Wacker Dr., Suite 2900, Chicago, IL 60601. Internet: www.ncsbn.org

For a list of accredited clinical nurse specialist programs, contact

▸ National Association of Clinical Nurse Specialists, 2090 Linglestown Rd., Suite 107, Harrisburg, PA 17110. Internet: www.nacns.org

For information on nurse anesthetists, including a list of accredited programs, contact

▸ American Association of Nurse Anesthetists, 222 S. Prospect Ave., Park Ridge, IL 60068. Internet: www.aana.com

For information on nurse-midwives, including a list of accredited programs, contact

▸ American College of Nurse-Midwives, 8403 Colesville Rd., Suite 1550, Silver Spring, MD 20910. Internet: www.midwife.org

For information on nurse practitioners, including a list of accredited programs, contact

▸ American Academy of Nurse Practitioners, P.O. Box 12846, Austin, TX 78711. Internet: www.aanp.org

For additional information on registered nurses in all fields and specialties, contact

▸ American Society of Registered Nurses, 1001 Bridgeway, Suite 233, Sausalito, CA 94965. Internet: www.asrn.org

Retail Salespersons

(O*NET 41-2031.00)

Significant Points

■ Good employment opportunities are expected because of the need to replace the large number of workers who leave the occupation each year.

■ Many salespersons work evenings and weekends, particularly during peak retail periods.

■ Employers look for people who enjoy working with others and who have good communication skills, an interest in sales work, a neat appearance, and a courteous demeanor.

■ Although advancement opportunities are limited, having a college degree or a great deal of experience may help retail salespersons move into management positions.

Nature of the Work

Whether selling shoes, computer equipment, or automobiles, retail salespersons assist customers in finding what they are looking for. They also try to increase sales by describing a product's features, demonstrating its uses, and promoting its value.

In addition to selling, many retail salespersons—especially those who work in department and apparel stores—conduct financial transactions with their customers. This usually involves receiving payments by cash, check, debit card, or credit card; operating cash registers; and bagging or packaging purchases. Depending on the hours they work, retail salespersons may have to open or close cash registers. This work may include counting the money in the register and separating charge slips, coupons, and exchange vouchers. Retail salespersons also may have to make deposits at a cash office. (Cashiers, who have similar duties, are discussed elsewhere in this book.) In addition, retail salespersons may help stock shelves or racks, arrange for mailing or delivery of purchases, mark price tags, take inventory, and prepare displays.

For some sales jobs, particularly those involving expensive and complex items, retail salespersons need special knowledge or skills. For example, salespersons who sell automobiles must be able to explain the features of various models, the manufacturers' specifications, the types of options and financing available, and the details of associated warranties. In addition, all retail salespersons must recognize security risks and thefts and understand their organization's procedure for handling such situations—procedures that may include notifying security guards or calling police.

Work environment. Most retail salespersons work in clean, comfortable, well-lit stores. However, they often stand for long periods and may need supervisory approval to leave the sales floor. They also may work outdoors if they sell items such as cars, plants, or lumber yard materials.

The Monday-through-Friday, 9-to-5 workweek is the exception rather than the rule for retail salespersons. Many salespersons work evenings and weekends, particularly during holidays and other peak sales periods. The end-of-year holiday season often is the busiest time, and as a result, many employers limit the use of vacation time between Thanksgiving and the beginning of January.

This occupation offers opportunities for both full-time and part-time work. About 34 percent of retail salespersons worked part time in 2008. Part-time opportunities may vary by setting, however, as many who sell big-ticket items are required to work full time.

Training, Other Qualifications, and Advancement

Retail salespersons typically learn their skills through on-the-job training. Although advancement opportunities are limited, having a college degree or a great deal of experience may help retail salespersons move into management positions.

Education and training. There usually are no formal education requirements for retail sales positions, but employers often prefer applicants with a high school diploma or its equivalent. This may be especially important for those who sell technical products or

Projections Data from the National Employment Matrix

Occupational title	SOC Code	Employment, 2008	Projected employment, 2018	Change, 2008–2018	
				Number	Percent
Retail salespersons.................................	41-2031	4,489,200	4,863,900	374,700	8

NOTE: Data in this table are rounded.

"big-ticket" items, such as electronics or automobiles. A college degree may be required for management trainee positions, especially in larger retail establishments.

Most retail salespersons receive on-the-job training, which usually lasts anywhere from a few days to a few months. In small stores, newly hired workers usually are trained by an experienced employee. In large stores, training programs are more formal and generally are conducted over several days. Topics often include customer service, security, the store's policies and procedures, and cash register operation. Depending on the type of product they are selling, employees may be given additional specialized training. For example, those working in cosmetics receive instruction on the types of products the store offers and for whom the cosmetics would be most beneficial. Likewise, those who sell computers may be instructed in the technical differences between computer products. Because providing the best possible service to customers is a high priority for many employers, employees often are given periodic training to update and refine their skills.

Other qualifications. Employers look for people who enjoy working with others and who possess good communication skills. Employers also value workers who have the tact and patience to deal with difficult customers. Among other desirable characteristics are an interest in sales work, a neat appearance, and a courteous demeanor. The ability to speak more than one language may be helpful for employment in communities where people from various cultures live and shop. Before hiring a salesperson, some employers conduct a background check, especially for a job selling high-priced items.

Advancement. Opportunities for advancement vary. In some small establishments, advancement is limited because one person—often the owner—does most of the managerial work. In others, some salespersons can be promoted to assistant manager. Large retail businesses usually prefer to hire college graduates as management trainees, making a college education increasingly important. However, motivated and capable employees without college degrees still may advance to administrative or supervisory positions in large establishments.

As salespersons gain experience and seniority, they often move into positions with greater responsibility and may be given their choice of departments in which to work. This opportunity often means moving to areas with higher potential earnings and commissions. The highest earnings potential usually lies in selling "big-ticket" items—such as cars, jewelry, furniture, and electronic equipment—although doing so often requires extensive knowledge of the product and an excellent talent for persuasion.

Previous sales experience may be an asset when one is applying for positions with larger retailers or in nonretail industries, such as financial services, wholesale trade, or manufacturing.

Employment

Retail salespersons held about 4.5 million jobs in 2008. The largest employers were clothing and clothing accessories stores, department stores, building material and supplies dealers, motor vehicle and parts dealers, and general merchandise stores such as warehouse clubs and supercenters. In addition, about 156,500 retail salespersons were self-employed.

Because retail stores are found in every city and town, employment is distributed geographically in much the same way as the population.

Job Outlook

Employment is expected to grow about as fast as average. Due to the frequency with which people leave this occupation, job opportunities are expected to be good.

Employment change. Employment is expected to grow by 8 percent over the 2008–2018 decade, about as fast as the average for all occupations. In addition, given the size of this occupation, about 374,700 new retail salesperson jobs will arise over the projections decade—more jobs than will be generated in almost any other occupation.

Employment growth among retail salespersons reflects rising retail sales stemming from a growing population. Many retail establishments will continue to expand in size and number, leading to new retail sales positions. Growth will be fastest in general merchandise stores, many of which sell a wide assortment of goods at low prices. As consumers continue to prefer these stores over other establishments with higher prices, growth in this industry will be rapid. Employment of retail salespersons is expected to decline in department stores and automobile dealers as these industries see a reduction in store locations.

Despite the growing popularity of electronic commerce, the impact of online shopping on the employment of retail salespersons is expected to be minimal. Internet sales have not decreased the need for retail salespersons. Retail stores commonly use an online presence to complement their in-store sales, and many consumers prefer to buy merchandise in person. Retail salespersons will remain important in assisting customers, providing specialized service, and increasing customer satisfaction.

Job prospects. Employment opportunities for retail salespersons are expected to be good because of the need to replace the large number of workers who transfer to other occupations or leave the labor force each year. In addition, many new jobs will be created for retail salespersons as businesses seek to expand operations and enhance customer service. A substantial number of these openings should occur in warehouse clubs and supercenters as a result of strong growth among these establishments.

Opportunities for part-time work should be abundant, and demand is expected be strong for temporary workers during peak selling periods, such as the end-of-year holiday season between Thanksgiving and the beginning of January.

During economic downturns, sales volumes and the resulting demand for sales workers usually decline. Consequently, retail sales jobs generally are more susceptible to fluctuations in the economy than are many other occupations.

Earnings

Median hourly wages of wage-and-salary retail salespersons, including commissions, were $9.74 in May 2009. The middle 50 percent earned between $8.28 and $13.11 an hour. The lowest 10 percent earned less than $7.41, and the highest 10 percent earned more than $18.49 an hour. Median hourly wages in the industries employing the largest numbers of retail salespersons in May 2009 were as follows:

Clothing stores	$8.92
Department stores	9.15
Building material and supplies dealers	11.83
Other general merchandise stores	8.93
Sporting goods, hobby, and musical instrument stores	9.09

Many beginning or inexperienced workers earn the federal minimum wage of $7.25 an hour, but many states set minimum wages higher than the federal minimum. In areas where employers have difficulty attracting and retaining workers, wages tend to be higher than the legislated minimum.

Compensation systems can vary by type of establishment and merchandise sold. Salespersons receive hourly wages, commissions, or a combination of the two. Under a commission system, salespersons receive a percentage of the sales they make. This system offers sales workers the opportunity to increase their earnings considerably, but they may find that their earnings depend strongly on their ability to sell their product and on the ups and downs of the economy.

Benefits may be limited in smaller stores, but benefits in large establishments usually are considerable. In addition, nearly all salespersons are able to buy their store's merchandise at a discount, with the savings depending on the type of merchandise. Also, to bolster revenue, employers may use incentive programs such as awards, bonuses, and profit-sharing plans to the sales staff.

Related Occupations

Other occupations that provide customer service, sell items, or operate cash registers include the following: cashiers; counter and rental clerks; customer service representatives; gaming cage workers; insurance sales agents; real estate brokers and sales agents; sales engineers; sales representatives, wholesale and manufacturing; and securities, commodities, and financial services sales agents.

Sources of Additional Information

Information on careers in retail sales may be obtained from the personnel offices of local stores or from state merchants' associations.

General information about retailing is available from

▸ National Retail Federation, 325 7th St. NW, Suite 1100, Washington, DC 20004. Internet: www.nrf.com

Information about training for a career in automobile sales is available from

▸ National Automobile Dealers Association, Public Relations Department, 8400 Westpark Dr., McLean, VA 22102-3591. Internet: www.nada.org

Roofers

(O*NET 47-2181.00)

Significant Points

■ Most roofers learn their skills on the job; some train through three-year apprenticeships.

■ Demand for roofers is less vulnerable to downturns in the economy than demand for other construction trades because most roofing work consists of repair and reroofing.

■ Most job openings will occur from the need to replace those who leave the occupation because the work can be hot, strenuous, and dirty, causing many people to switch to jobs in other construction trades.

Nature of the Work

Roofers repair and install roofs made from a combination of some of the following: tar, asphalt, gravel, rubber, thermoplastic, metal, and shingles—all of which protect buildings and their contents from water damage. A leaky roof can damage ceilings, walls, and furnishings. Repair and reroofing—replacing old roofs on existing buildings—make up the majority of work for roofers.

There are two types of roofs—low-slope and steep-slope. Low-slope roofs rise 4 inches or less per horizontal foot and are installed in layers. Steep-slope roofs rise more than 4 inches per horizontal foot and are usually covered in shingles. Most commercial, industrial, and apartment buildings contain low-slope roofs, while the majority of residential houses have steep-slope roofs. Some roofers work on both types; others specialize.

Most low-slope roofs are covered with several layers of materials. Roofers begin by installing a layer of insulation on the roof deck, followed by applying a tarlike substance called molten bitumen on top of it. Next, they install overlapping layers of roofing felt—a fabric soaked in bitumen—over the surface. Roofers use a mop to spread hot bitumen over the felt before adding another layer of felt. This seals the seams and makes the surface waterproof. Roofers repeat these steps to build up the desired number of layers, called "plies." The top layer is then glazed to make a smooth finish or has gravel embedded in the hot bitumen to create a rough surface.

An increasing number of low-slope roofs are covered with single-ply membranes of waterproof rubber or thermoplastic compounds. Roofers roll these sheets over the roof's insulation and seal the seams. Adhesive, mechanical fasteners, or stone ballast hold the sheets in place. Roofers must make sure the building is strong enough to hold the stone ballast.

A small but increasing number of buildings now have "green" roofs that incorporate landscape roofing systems. A landscape roofing system begins with a single or multiple waterproof layers. After it is proven to be leak free, roofers put a root barrier over it, and then layers of soil, in which trees and grass are planted. Roofers are responsible for making sure the roof is watertight and can endure the weight and water needs of the plants.

Most residential steep-slope roofs are covered with shingles. To apply shingles, roofers first lay, cut, and tack 3-foot strips of roofing felt over the entire roof. Starting from the bottom edge, roofers then nail overlapping rows of shingles to the roof. Roofers measure and cut the felt and shingles to fit intersecting roof surfaces and to fit around vent pipes and chimneys. Wherever two sections of the roof meet each other at an angle or where shingles reach a vent pipe or chimney, roofers cement or nail flashing strips of metal or shingle over the joints to make them watertight. Finally, roofers cover exposed nail heads with roofing cement or caulking to prevent water leakage. A similar process is used when installing tile, metal shingles, or shakes (rough wooden shingles).

Some roofers specialize in waterproofing or dampproofing masonry and concrete walls, floors, and foundations. To prepare surfaces for waterproofing, they hammer and chisel away rough spots or remove them with a rubbing brick before applying a coat of liquid waterproofing compound. They also may paint or spray surfaces with a waterproofing material or attach waterproofing membrane to surfaces. Roofers usually spray a bitumen-based coating on interior or exterior surfaces when dampproofing.

Work environment. Roofing work is strenuous. It involves heavy lifting, as well as climbing, bending, and kneeling. Roofers work outdoors in all types of weather, particularly when making repairs. However, they rarely work when it rains or in very cold weather because ice can be dangerous. In northern states, roofing work is generally not performed during winter months. During the summer, roofers may work overtime to complete jobs quickly, especially before forecasted rainfall.

Workers risk slips or falls from scaffolds, ladders, or roofs, and burns from hot bitumen, but safety precautions can prevent most accidents. In addition, roofs can become extremely hot during the summer, causing heat-related illnesses. Data from the U.S. Bureau of Labor Statistics show that full-time roofers experienced a work-related injury and illness rate that was much higher than the national average.

Training, Other Qualifications, and Advancement

Most roofers learn their skills on the job by working as helpers for experienced roofers and by taking classes, including safety training offered by their employers; some complete 3-year apprenticeships.

Education and training. A high school education, or its equivalent, is helpful and so are courses in mechanical drawing and basic mathematics. Although most workers learn roofing as helpers for experienced workers, some roofers train through 3-year apprenticeship programs administered by local union-management committees representing roofing contractors and locals of the United Union of Roofers, Waterproofers, and Allied Workers. Apprenticeship programs usually include at least 2,000 hours of paid long-term on-the-job training each year, plus a minimum of 144 hours of classroom instruction a year in tools and their use, arithmetic, safety, and other topics. On-the-job training for apprentices is similar to the training given to helpers, but an apprenticeship program is more structured and comprehensive. Apprentices, for example, also learn to damp-proof and waterproof walls.

Trainees start by carrying equipment and material and erecting scaffolds and hoists. Within 2 or 3 months, they are taught to measure, cut, and fit roofing materials and, later, to lay asphalt or fiberglass shingles. Because some roofing materials are used infrequently, such as solar tiles, it can take several years to get experience working on all types of roofing.

Other qualifications. Physical condition and strength, along with good balance, are essential for roofers. They cannot be afraid of heights. Experience with metal-working is helpful for workers who install metal roofing. Usually, apprentices must be at least 18 years old.

Advancement. Roofers may advance to become supervisors or estimators for a roofing contractor or become independent contractors themselves.

Employment

Roofers held about 148,900 jobs in 2008. About 70 percent of all salaried roofers worked for roofing contractors, while only 21 percent were self-employed. Many self-employed roofers specialized in residential work.

Job Outlook

Most job openings will occur from turnover because the work is hot, strenuous, and dirty, causing many people to switch to jobs in other construction trades. Employment is projected to grow slower than the average.

Employment change. Employment of roofers is expected to grow 4 percent between 2008 and 2018, slower than the average for all occupations. Roofs deteriorate faster than most other parts of buildings and, as a result, they need to be repaired or replaced more often. In addition to repair work, the need to install roofs on new buildings may result in some job growth. So as building construction increases, some demand for roofers can be expected.

Employment growth, nonetheless, may be impeded because a greater proportion of roofing work may be completed by other construction workers as opposed to traditional roofing contractors.

Job prospects. Job opportunities for roofers will occur primarily because of the need to replace workers who leave the occupation. The proportion of roofers who leave the occupation each year is higher than in most construction trades—roofing work is hot, strenuous, and dirty, and a considerable number of workers treat roofing as a temporary job until they find other work. Some roofers leave the occupation to go into other construction trades. Jobs should be easier to find during spring and summer.

Employment of roofers who install new roofs, like that of many other construction workers, is sensitive to fluctuations of the economy. Workers may experience periods of unemployment when the overall level of construction falls. On the other hand, shortages of these workers may occur in some areas during peak periods

Projections Data from the National Employment Matrix

Occupational title	SOC Code	Employment, 2008	Projected employment, 2018	Change, 2008–2018	
				Number	Percent
Roofers 47-2181		148,900	154,600	5,700	4

NOTE: Data in this table are rounded.

of building activity. Nevertheless, roofing work is more heavily concentrated in repair and replacement rather than new installation, making demand for roofing less vulnerable to downturns than demand for some other construction trades.

Earnings

In May 2009, median hourly wages of roofers were $16.33. The middle 50 percent earned between $13.04 and $21.91. The lowest 10 percent earned less than $10.68, and the highest 10 percent earned more than $28.35. Median hourly wages of roofers in the foundation, structure, and building exterior contractors industry were $16.44. Earnings may be less on occasions when poor weather limits the time roofers can work.

Apprentices usually begin earning about 40 percent to 50 percent of the rate paid to experienced roofers. They receive periodic raises as they master the skills of the trade.

Some roofers are members of United Union of Roofers, Waterproofers, and Allied Workers. Hourly wages and fringe benefits are generally higher for union workers.

Related Occupations

Roofers use shingles, tile, bitumen and gravel, single-ply plastic or rubber sheets, or other materials to protect and waterproof building surfaces. Workers in other occupations who cover surfaces with special materials for protection and decoration include carpenters; carpet, floor, and tile installers and finishers; cement masons, concrete finishers, segmental pavers, and terrazzo workers; drywall and ceiling tile installers, tapers, plasterers, and stucco masons; and sheet metal workers.

Sources of Additional Information

For information about apprenticeships or job opportunities in roofing, contact local roofing contractors, a local chapter of the roofers union, a local joint union-management apprenticeship committee, or the nearest office of your state employment service or apprenticeship agency. You can also find information on the registered apprenticeship system with links to state apprenticeship programs on the U.S. Department of Labor's website at www.doleta.gov/OA/eta_default. cfm. Apprenticeship information is also available from the U.S. Department of Labor's toll-free helpline: 1 (877) 872-5627.

For information about the work of roofers, contact

▸ National Roofing Contractors Association, 10255 W. Higgins Rd., Suite 600, Rosemont, IL 60018-5607. Internet: www.nrca.net

▸ United Union of Roofers, Waterproofers, and Allied Workers, 1660 L St. NW, Suite 800, Washington, DC 20036. Internet: www.unionroofers.com

For general information on apprenticeships and how to get them, see the *Occupational Outlook Quarterly* article "Apprenticeships: Career training, credentials—and a paycheck in your pocket," online at www.bls.gov/opub/ooq/2002/summer/art01.pdf and in print at many libraries and career centers.

Sales Representatives, Wholesale and Manufacturing

(O*NET 41-4011.00, 41-4011.07, and 41-4012.00)

Significant Points

■ Job prospects will be best for those with a college degree, the appropriate technical expertise, and the personal traits necessary for successful selling.

■ Earnings usually are based on a combination of salary and commission.

■ Employment opportunities and earnings may fluctuate from year to year because sales are affected by changing economic conditions.

Nature of the Work

Sales representatives are an important part of manufacturers' and wholesalers' success. Regardless of the type of products they sell, sales representatives' primary duties are to make customers interested in their merchandise and to arrange the sale of that merchandise.

The process of promoting and selling a product can be extensive, at times taking up to several months. Whether in person or over the phone, sales representatives describe their products, conduct demonstrations, explain the benefits that their products convey, and answer any questions that their customers may have.

Sales representatives—sometimes called *manufacturers' representatives* or *manufacturers' agents*—generally work for manufacturers, wholesalers, or technical companies. Some work for a single organization, while others represent several companies and sell a range of products. Rather than selling goods directly to consumers, sales representatives deal with businesses, government agencies, and other organizations. (Retail salespersons, who sell directly to consumers, are discussed elsewhere in this book.)

Some sales representatives specialize in technical and scientific products ranging from agricultural and mechanical equipment to computer and pharmaceutical goods. Other representatives deal with all other types of goods, including food, office supplies, and apparel.

Sales representatives stay abreast of new products and the changing needs of their customers in a variety of ways. They attend trade shows at which new products and technologies are showcased. They also attend conferences and conventions to meet other sales representatives and clients and discuss new product developments. In addition, the entire sales force may participate in company-sponsored meetings to review the firm's sales performance, product development, sales goals, and profitability.

Frequently, sales representatives who lack the necessary expertise about a given product may team with a technical expert. In this arrangement, the technical expert—sometimes a sales engineer—attends the sales presentation to explain the product and answer questions or concerns. The sales representative makes the preliminary contact with customers, introduces the company's product, and closes the sale. Under such an arrangement, the representative is able to spend more time maintaining and soliciting accounts and less time acquiring technical knowledge. After the sale, representatives may make follow-up visits to ensure that the equipment is functioning properly and may even help train customers' employees to operate and maintain new equipment. Those selling technical goods also may arrange for the product to be installed. Those selling consumer goods often suggest how and where merchandise should be displayed. When working with retailers, they may help arrange promotional programs, store displays, and advertising.

Sales representatives have several duties beyond selling products. They analyze sales statistics, prepare reports, and handle administrative duties such as filing expense accounts, scheduling appointments, and making travel plans. They also read about new and existing products and monitor the sales, prices, and products of their competitors.

Sales representatives generally work in either inside sales, interacting with customers over the phone from an office location, or outside "field" sales, traveling to meet clients in person.

Inside sales representatives may spend a lot of their time on the phone, selling goods, taking orders, and resolving problems or complaints about the merchandise. These sales representatives typically do not leave the office. Frequently, they are responsible for acquiring new clients by "cold calling" various organizations—calling potential customers to establish an initial contact. They also may be responsible for arranging meetings for outside sales representatives.

Outside sales representatives spend much of their time traveling to, and visiting with, current clients and prospective buyers. During a sales call, they discuss the client's needs and suggest how their merchandise or services can meet those needs. They may show samples or catalogs that describe items their company provides, and they may inform customers about prices, availability, and ways in which their products can save money and boost productivity. Because many sales representatives sell several complementary products made by different manufacturers, they may take a broad approach to their customers' business. For example, sales representatives may help install new equipment and train employees in its use.

Work environment. Some sales representatives have large territories and travel considerably. Because a sales region may cover several states, representatives may be away from home for several days or weeks at a time, often traveling by airplane. Others cover a smaller region and travel mostly by car, spending few nights away from home. Sales representatives frequently are on their feet for long periods and may carry heavy sample products, requiring some physical stamina.

In 2008, about 48 percent of sales representatives worked around 40 hours per week, but about 24 percent worked more than 50 hours per week. Since sales calls take place during regular working hours, much of the planning and paperwork involved with sales must be completed during the evening and on weekends. Although the hours are often irregular, many sales representatives have the freedom to determine their own schedules.

Workers in this occupation can encounter pressure and stress because their income and job security often depend directly on the amount of merchandise they sell and their companies usually set goals or quotas that they are expected to meet. Sales representatives also deal with many different types of people, which can be stimulating but demanding.

Training, Other Qualifications, and Advancement

There generally is no formal educational requirement for sales representative positions, but many jobs require some postsecondary education. Regardless of educational background, factors such as communication skills, the ability to sell, and familiarity with brands are essential to being a successful sales representative.

Education and training. There usually is no formal educational requirement for sales representatives. Some positions, especially those which deal with scientific and technical products, require a bachelor's degree. For other jobs, however, applicants can be fully qualified with a high school diploma or its equivalent. For these positions, previous sales experience may be desirable.

Many sales representatives attend seminars in sales techniques or take courses in marketing, economics, communication, or even a foreign language to provide the extra edge needed to make sales. Often, companies have formal training programs for beginning sales representatives that last up to two years. However, most businesses accelerate these programs to much shorter time frames in order to reduce costs and expedite the returns from training. In some programs, trainees rotate among jobs in plants and offices to learn all phases of production, installation, and distribution of the product. In others, trainees take formal classroom instruction at the plant, followed by on-the-job training under the supervision of a field sales manager.

Regardless of where they work, new employees may be trained by accompanying experienced workers on their sales calls. As they gain familiarity with the firm's products and clients, the new workers are given increasing responsibility, until they are eventually assigned their own territory. As businesses experience greater competition, representatives face more pressure to produce sales.

Other qualifications. For sales representative jobs, companies seek individuals who have excellent communication skills and the desire to sell. Those who want to become sales representatives should be goal oriented, persuasive, and able to work well both independently and as part of a team. A pleasant personality and appearance and problem-solving skills are highly valued. Patience and perseverance also are keys to completing a sale, which can take up to several months.

Manufacturers' representatives who operate a sales agency also must manage their business. Doing so requires organizational and general business skills, as well as knowledge of accounting, marketing, and administration.

Certification and advancement. Certifications are available that provide formal recognition of the skills of sales representatives. Many in this profession have either the Certified Professional Manufacturers' Representative (CPMR) certification or the Certified Sales Professional (CSP) certification, offered by the Manufacturers' Representatives Education Research Foundation. Certification typically involves completing formal training and passing an examination.

Frequently, promotion takes the form of an assignment to a larger account or territory, where commissions are likely to be greater. Those who have good sales records and leadership ability may advance to higher level positions such as sales supervisor, district manager, or vice president of sales. Others find opportunities in purchasing, advertising, or marketing research.

Projections Data from the National Employment Matrix

Occupational title	SOC Code	Employment, 2008	Projected employment, 2018	Change, 2008–2018	
				Number	Percent
Sales representatives, wholesale and manufacturing 41-4000		1,973,200	2,116,400	143,200	7
Sales representatives, wholesale and manufacturing, technical and scientific products............................ 41-4011		432,900	475,000	42,000	10
Sales representatives, wholesale and manufacturing, except technical and scientific products.................. 41-4012		1,540,300	1,641,400	101,100	7

NOTE: Data in this table are rounded.

Advancement opportunities typically depend on whether the sales representatives are working directly for a manufacturer or wholesaler or whether they are working with an independent sales agency. Experienced sales representatives working directly for a manufacturer or wholesaler may move into jobs as sales trainers and instruct new employees on selling techniques and company policies and procedures. Some leave their organization and start their own independent sales company.

Employment

Manufacturing and wholesale sales representatives held about 2 million jobs in 2008. About 432,900 of these worked with technical and scientific products. Around 61 percent of all representatives worked for wholesale companies. Others were employed in manufacturing establishments; retail organizations; and professional, technical, and scientific firms. Because of the diversity of products and services sold, employment opportunities are available throughout the country. About 73,800 sales representatives were self-employed.

Job Outlook

Job growth is expected to be about as fast as average. Job prospects will be best for those with a college degree, the appropriate technical expertise, and the personal traits necessary for successful selling.

Employment change. Employment of sales representatives, wholesale and manufacturing, is expected to grow by 7 percent between 2008 and 2018, about as fast as the average for all occupations. Given the size of this occupation, a large number of new jobs, about 143,200, will arise over the projection period. Job growth will result from the continued expansion in the variety and number of goods sold throughout the economy. Because they play an important role in the transfer of goods between organizations, sales representatives will be needed to accommodate this expansion. In addition, as technology continues to progress, sales representatives can help ensure that retailers offer the latest products to their customers and that businesses acquire the tools they need to increase their efficiency in operations.

Employment growth will be greatest in independent sales companies as manufacturers continue to outsource sales activities to independent agents rather than using in-house sales workers. Independent sales agents generally are more efficient, reducing the overhead cost to their clients. Also, by using agents who contract their services to more than one company, companies can share costs of the agents with each other.

Job prospects. Job prospects will be best for those with a college degree, the appropriate technical expertise, and the personal traits necessary for successful selling. Opportunities will be better in inde-

pendent sales companies than with manufacturers, who are expected to continue contracting out field sales duties.

Employment opportunities and earnings may fluctuate from year to year because sales are affected by changing economic conditions and businesses' preferences. In addition, many job openings will result from the need to replace workers who transfer to other occupations or leave the labor force.

Earnings

Median annual wages of sales representatives, wholesale and manufacturing, technical and scientific products, were $71,340, including commissions, in May 2009. The middle 50 percent earned between $49,690 and $100,910 a year. The lowest 10 percent earned less than $35,770, and the highest 10 percent earned more than $137,200 a year. Median annual wages in the industries employing the largest numbers of sales representatives, wholesale and manufacturing, technical and scientific products, were as follows:

Wholesale electronic markets and agents
  and brokers $77,200
Professional and commercial equipment and
  supplies merchant wholesalers 68,540
Drugs and druggists' sundries merchant
  wholesalers 77,930
Computer systems design and related services 81,300
Electrical and electronic goods merchant
  wholesalers 64,220

Median annual wages of sales representatives, wholesale and manufacturing, except technical and scientific products, were $50,920, including commission, in May 2009. The middle 50 percent earned between $35,950 and $74,310 a year. The lowest 10 percent earned less than $26,390, and the highest 10 percent earned more than $106,130 a year. Median annual wages in the industries employing the largest numbers of sales representatives, wholesale and manufacturing, except technical and scientific products, were as follows:

Wholesale electronic markets and agents
  and brokers $57,220
Machinery equipment and supplies merchant
  wholesalers 49,250
Grocery and related product merchant
  wholesalers 48,070
Professional and commercial equipment and
  supplies merchant wholesalers 50,110
Miscellaneous nondurable goods merchant
  wholesalers 43,700

Compensation methods for representatives vary significantly by the type of firm and the product sold. Most employers use a combination of salary and commissions or salary plus bonus. Commissions usually are based on the value of sales, whereas bonuses may depend on individual performance, on the performance of all sales workers in the group or district, or on the company's performance. Unlike those working directly for a manufacturer or wholesaler, sales representatives working for an independent sales company usually are not reimbursed for expenses. Depending on the type of product or products they are selling, their experience in the field, and the number of clients they have, they can earn significantly more or less than those working in direct sales for a manufacturer or wholesaler.

In addition to receiving their earnings, sales representatives working directly for a manufacturer or wholesaler usually are reimbursed for expenses such as the costs of transportation, meals, hotels, and entertaining customers. They often receive benefits, including personal use of a company car and frequent flyer mileage. Some companies offer incentives such as free vacation trips or gifts for achieving an outstanding sales performance.

Related Occupations

Sales representatives, wholesale and manufacturing, must have sales ability and knowledge of the products they sell. Other occupations that require similar skills include the following advertising sales agents; insurance sales agents; purchasing managers, buyers, and purchasing agents; real estate brokers and sales agents; retail salespersons; sales engineers; sales worker supervisors; and securities, commodities, and financial services sales agents.

Sources of Additional Information

Information on careers for manufacturers' representatives and sales agents is available from

▸ Manufacturers' Agents National Association, 16 A Journey, Suite 200, Aliso Viejo, CA 92656-3317. Internet: www.manaonline.org

▸ Manufacturers' Representatives Educational Research Foundation, 8329 Cole St., Arvada, CO 80005. Internet: www.mrerf.org

Sales Worker Supervisors

(O*NET 41-1011.00 and 41-1012.00)

Significant Points

■ Employment is projected to increase more slowly than the average for all occupations.

■ Competition is expected for jobs; applicants with a college degree or sales experience should have the best opportunities.

■ Long, irregular hours, including evenings and weekends, are common.

Nature of the Work

Sales worker supervisors oversee the work of sales and related workers, such as retail salespersons, cashiers, customer service representatives, stock clerks and order fillers, sales engineers, and wholesale sales representatives. Sales worker supervisors are responsible for interviewing, hiring, and training employees. They also may prepare work schedules and assign workers to specific duties. Many of these supervisors hold job titles such as *sales manager, department manager*, or *shift supervisor*.

In retail establishments, sales worker supervisors ensure that customers receive satisfactory service and quality goods. They also answer customers' inquiries, deal with complaints, and sometimes handle purchasing, budgeting, and accounting.

Responsibilities vary with the size and type of establishment. As the size of retail stores grows and the variety of goods and services increases, supervisors tend to specialize in one department or one aspect of merchandising. Sales worker supervisors in large retail establishments are often referred to as department supervisors or managers. They provide day-to-day oversight of individual departments, such as shoes, cosmetics, or housewares in department stores; produce or meat in grocery stores; and car sales in automotive dealerships. Department supervisors establish and implement policies, goals, and procedures for their specific departments; coordinate activities with other department heads; and strive for smooth operations within their departments. They supervise employees whose responsibilities may include pricing and ticketing goods and placing them on display; cleaning and organizing shelves, displays, and inventories in stockrooms; and inspecting merchandise to ensure that nothing is outdated. Sales worker supervisors review inventory and sales records, develop merchandising techniques, and coordinate sales promotions. In addition, they may greet and assist customers and promote sales and good public relations.

Sales worker supervisors in nonretail establishments oversee and coordinate the activities of sales workers who sell industrial products, insurance policies, or services such as advertising, financial, or Internet services. Sales worker supervisors may prepare budgets, make personnel decisions, devise sales-incentive programs, and approve sales contracts.

In small or independent companies and retail stores, sales worker supervisors not only directly supervise sales associates, but they also are responsible for the operation of the entire company or store. Some are self-employed business or store owners.

Work environment. Most sales worker supervisors have offices. In retail trade, their offices are within the stores, usually close to the areas they oversee. Although they spend some time in the office completing merchandise orders or arranging work schedules, a large portion of their workday is spent on the sales floor, supervising employees or selling merchandise.

Work hours of supervisors vary greatly among establishments because work schedules usually depend on the needs of the customer. Supervisors generally work at least 40 hours a week. Long, irregular hours are common, particularly during sales, holidays, busy shopping seasons, and at times when inventory is recorded. Supervisors are expected to work some evenings and weekends but usually are given a day off during the week. Hours can change weekly, and supervisors sometimes must report to work on short notice, especially when employees are absent. Independent owners often can set their own schedules, but hours must be convenient to customers.

Training, Other Qualifications, and Advancement

Sales worker supervisors usually gain knowledge of management principles and practices through work experience. Many supervisors begin their careers as salespersons, cashiers, or customer service representatives. These workers should be patient, decisive, and sales-oriented.

Education and training. There is no standard educational requirement for sales worker supervisors, and the educational backgrounds of these workers vary widely. For some jobs, a college degree is required. Supervisors who have college degrees often hold associate or bachelor's degrees in liberal arts, social sciences, business, or management. College graduates usually can enter directly into management training programs sponsored by their company, without much experience. Many supervisors, however, are hired without postsecondary education. For these workers, previous experience in a sales occupation is essential. Most sales worker supervisors have retail sales experience or experience as a customer service representative. In these positions, they learn merchandising, customer service, and the basic policies and procedures of the company.

Regardless of education level or major area of study, recommended high school or college courses include those related to business, such as accounting, marketing, management, and sales, as well as those related to social science, such as psychology, sociology, and communication. To gain experience, many college students participate in internship programs that usually are developed jointly by schools and businesses.

The type and amount of training available to supervisors varies by company. Many national retail chains and companies have formal training programs for management trainees that include both classroom and on-site training. Training time may be as brief as 1 week or may last more than 1 year, giving trainees experience during all sales seasons.

Ordinarily, classroom training includes topics such as interviewing, customer service skills, inventory management, employee relations, and scheduling. Training programs for retail franchises are generally extensive, covering all functions of the company's operation, including budgeting, marketing, management, finance, purchasing, product preparation, human resource management, and compensation.

Other qualifications. Sales worker supervisors must possess good communication skills and get along with all types of people. They need initiative, self-discipline, good judgment, and decisiveness. Patience and a conciliatory temperament are necessary when dealing with demanding customers. Supervisors also must be able to motivate, organize, and direct the work of their employees. Supervisors who own their own establishment need good business skills and strong customer service and public relations skills.

Advancement. Supervisors who display leadership and team-building skills, motivation, and decisiveness may become candidates for promotion to assistant manager or manager. A postsecondary degree may speed their advancement into management. In many retail establishments, managers are promoted from within the company. In small retail establishments, where the number of positions is limited, advancement to a higher management position also may be limited. Large establishments often have extensive career ladder programs and may offer supervisors the opportunity to transfer to another store in the chain or to the central office. Although promotions may occur more rapidly in large establishments, some managers may need to relocate every several years to be able to advance.

Supervisors also can become advertising, marketing, promotions, public relations, and sales managers—workers who coordinate marketing plans, monitor sales, and propose advertisements and promotions. They may also become purchasing managers, buyers,

or purchasing agents—workers who purchase goods and supplies for their organization or for resale.

Some supervisors who have worked in their industry for a long time open their own stores or sales firms. However, retail trade and sales occupations are highly competitive, and although many independent owners succeed, some fail to cover expenses and eventually go out of business.

Employment

Sales worker supervisors held about 2.2 million jobs in 2008. Approximately 34 percent were self-employed, many of whom were store owners. About 48 percent of sales worker supervisors were wage and salary workers employed in the retail sector. Some of the largest employers were grocery stores, department stores, clothing and clothing accessory stores, and general merchandise stores such as warehouse clubs and supercenters. The remaining sales worker supervisors worked in nonretail establishments.

Job Outlook

Employment is projected to grow more slowly than average. Competition for jobs is expected; applicants with a college degree or sales experience should have the best opportunities.

Employment change. Employment of sales worker supervisors is expected to grow by 5 percent between 2008 and 2018, more slowly than the average for all occupations. Job growth will be limited as retail companies increase the responsibilities of retail salespersons and existing sales worker supervisors, and as the retail industry, overall, grows at a slow rate.

Projected employment growth of sales worker supervisors will mirror, in part, the patterns of employment growth in the industries in which they work. For example, faster growth is expected in the professional, scientific, and technical services industry, as a result of strong demand for the services that this industry provides. Conversely, growth of sales worker supervisors will increase more slowly in the retail sector, in-line with overall industry growth.

Job prospects. Similar to other supervisor positions, competition is expected for sales worker supervisor jobs over the 2008–2018 period. Candidates who have a college degree, and those with experience—as a sales representative, cashier, or customer service representative, for example—will have the best opportunities.

Some job openings over the next decade will occur as experienced supervisors move into higher levels of management, transfer to other occupations, or leave the labor force. However, these job openings will not be great in number since movement into upper management is also competitive.

Earnings

Wages of sales worker supervisors vary substantially, depending on a worker's level of responsibility; length of service; and the type, size, and location of the firm.

Median annual wages of supervisors of retail sales workers were $34,900, including commissions, in May 2009. The middle 50 percent earned between $27,030 and $45,650. The lowest 10 percent earned less than $21,690, and the highest 10 percent earned more than $60,400. Median annual wages in the industries employing the largest numbers of wage and salary supervisors of retail sales workers were as follows:

Projections Data from the National Employment Matrix

Occupational title	SOC Code	Employment, 2008	Projected employment, 2018	Change, 2008–2018	
				Number	Percent
Supervisors, sales workers.........................41-1000		2,192,300	2,305,100	112,800	5
First-line supervisors/managers of retail sales workers...41-1011		1,685,500	1,773,900	88,400	5
First-line supervisors/managers of nonretail sales workers..41-1012		506,800	531,200	24,400	5

NOTE: Data in this table are rounded.

Other general merchandise stores $29,760	
Grocery stores.. 35,700	
Clothing stores.. 34,550	
Department stores 29,860	
Building material and supplies dealers................. 36,920	

Median annual wages of supervisors of nonretail sales workers were $67,470, including commissions, in May 2009. The middle 50 percent earned between $50,570 and $96,580. The lowest 10 percent earned less than $36,510, and the highest 10 percent earned more than $135,890. Median annual wages in the industries employing the largest numbers of wage and salary supervisors of nonretail sales workers were as follows:

Wholesale electronic markets and agents and brokers $80,260	
Machinery equipment and supplies merchant wholesalers 67,890	
Postal service 63,150	
Grocery and related product merchant wholesalers 67,050	
Professional and commercial equipment and supplies merchant wholesalers 82,650	

Compensation systems vary by type of establishment and by merchandise sold. Many supervisors receive a commission or a combination of salary and commission. Under a commission system, supervisors receive a percentage of department or store sales. Thus, these supervisors' earnings depend on their ability to sell their product and the condition of the economy. Those who sell large amounts of merchandise or exceed sales goals often receive bonuses or other awards.

Related Occupations

Sales worker supervisors serve customers, supervise workers, and direct and coordinate the operations of an establishment. Workers with similar responsibilities include administrative services managers; advertising, marketing, promotions, public relations, and sales managers; food service managers; lodging managers; and office and administrative support worker supervisors and managers.

Sources of Additional Information

Information on employment opportunities for sales worker supervisors may be obtained from the employment offices of various retail establishments or from state employment service offices.

General information on management careers in retail establishments is available from

▸ National Retail Federation, 325 7th St. NW, Suite 1100, Washington, DC 20004. Internet: www.nrf.com

Information about management careers and training programs in the motor vehicle dealers industry is available from

▸ National Automobile Dealers Association, Public Relations Dept., 8400 Westpark Dr., McLean, VA 22102-3591. Internet: www.nada.org

Science Technicians

(O*NET 19-4011.00, 19-4011.01, 19-4011.02, 19-4021.00, 19-4031.00, 19-4041.00, 19-4041.01, 19-4041.02, 19-4051.00, 19-4051.01, 19-4051.02, 19-4091.00, 19-4092.00, and 19-4093.00)

Significant Points

■ Many science technicians work indoors in laboratory settings, but certain technicians work outdoors, sometimes in remote locations.

■ Most science technicians need some postsecondary training, such as an associate degree or a certificate in applied science or science-related technology; biological and forensic science technicians usually need a bachelor's degree.

■ Overall growth is expected to be about as fast as average, although growth will vary by specialty.

■ Job opportunities are expected to be best for graduates of applied science technology programs who are well trained on equipment used in laboratories or production facilities.

Nature of the Work

Science technicians use the principles and theories of science and mathematics to assist in research and development and to help invent and improve products and processes. However, their jobs are more practically oriented than those of scientists. Technicians set up, operate, and maintain laboratory instruments, monitor experiments, make observations, calculate and record results, and often develop conclusions. They must keep detailed logs of all of their work. Those who perform production work monitor manufacturing processes and may ensure quality by testing products for proper proportions of ingredients, for purity, or for strength and durability.

As laboratory instrumentation and procedures have become more complex, the role of science technicians in research and development has expanded. In addition to performing routine tasks, many technicians, under the direction of scientists, now develop and adapt laboratory procedures to achieve the best results, interpret data, and devise solutions to problems. Technicians must develop expert knowledge of laboratory equipment so that they can adjust settings when necessary and recognize when equipment is malfunctioning.

Most science technicians specialize, learning their skills and working in the same disciplines in which scientists work. Occupational titles, therefore, tend to follow the same structure as those for scientists.

Agricultural and food science technicians work with related scientists to conduct research, development, and testing on food and other agricultural products. Agricultural technicians are involved in food, fiber, and animal research; production; and processing. Some conduct tests and experiments to improve the yield and quality of crops or to increase the resistance of plants and animals to disease, insects, or other hazards. Other agricultural technicians breed animals for the purpose of investigating nutrition. Food science technicians assist food scientists and technologists in research and development, production technology, and quality control. For example, food science technicians may conduct tests on food additives and preservatives to ensure compliance with Food and Drug Administration regulations regarding color, texture, and nutrients. These technicians analyze, record, and compile test results; order supplies to maintain laboratory inventory; and clean and sterilize laboratory equipment.

Biological technicians work with biologists studying living organisms. Many assist scientists who conduct medical research—helping to find a cure for cancer or AIDS, for example. Those who work in pharmaceutical companies help develop and manufacture medicines. Those working in the field of microbiology generally work as laboratory assistants, studying living organisms and infectious agents. Biological technicians also analyze organic substances, such as blood, food, and drugs. Biological technicians working in biotechnology apply knowledge and techniques gained from basic research, including gene splicing and recombinant DNA, and apply them to product development.

Chemical technicians work with chemists and chemical engineers, developing and using chemicals and related products and equipment. Generally, there are two types of chemical technicians: research technicians who work in experimental laboratories and process control technicians who work in manufacturing or other industrial plants. Many chemical technicians working in research and development conduct a variety of laboratory procedures, from routine process control to complex research projects. For example, they may collect and analyze samples of air and water to monitor pollution levels, or they may produce compounds through complex organic synthesis. Most process technicians work in manufacturing, testing packaging for design, integrity of materials, and environmental acceptability. Often, process technicians who work in plants focus on quality assurance, monitoring product quality or production processes and developing new production techniques. A few work in shipping to provide technical support and expertise.

Environmental science and protection technicians perform laboratory and field tests to monitor environmental resources and determine the contaminants and sources of pollution in the environment. They may collect samples for testing or be involved in abating and controlling sources of environmental pollution. Some are responsible for waste management operations, control and management of hazardous materials inventory, or general activities involving regulatory compliance. Many environmental science technicians employed at private consulting firms work directly under the supervision of an environmental scientist.

Forensic science technicians investigate crimes by collecting and analyzing physical evidence. Often, they specialize in areas such as DNA analysis or firearm examination, performing tests on weapons or on substances such as fiber, glass, hair, tissue, and body fluids to determine their significance to the investigation. Proper collection and storage methods are important to protect the evidence. Forensic science technicians also prepare reports to document their findings and the laboratory techniques used, and they may provide information and expert opinions to investigators. When criminal cases come to trial, forensic science technicians often give testimony as expert witnesses on laboratory findings by identifying and classifying substances, materials, and other evidence collected at the scene of a crime. Some forensic science technicians work closely with other experts or technicians. For example, a forensic science technician may consult either a medical expert about the exact time and cause of a death or another technician who specializes in DNA typing in hopes of matching a DNA type to a suspect.

Forest and conservation technicians compile data on the size, content, and condition of natural lands, such as rangeland and forests. These workers usually work under the supervision of a conservation scientist or forester, doing specific tasks such as measuring timber, tracking wildlife movement, assisting in road building operations, and locating property lines and features. They may gather basic information, such as data on water and soil quality, disease and insect damage to trees and other plants, and conditions that may pose a fire hazard. In addition, forest and conservation technicians train and lead forest and conservation workers in seasonal activities, such as planting tree seedlings and maintaining recreational facilities. Increasing numbers of forest and conservation technicians work in urban forestry—the study of individual trees in cities—and other nontraditional specialties, rather than in forests or rural areas.

Geological and petroleum technicians assist in oil and gas exploration operations, collecting and examining geological data or testing geological samples to determine their petroleum content and their mineral and element composition. Some petroleum technicians, called scouts, collect information about oil well and gas well drilling operations, geological and geophysical prospecting, and land or lease contracts.

Nuclear technicians operate nuclear test and research equipment, monitor radiation, and assist nuclear engineers and physicists in research. Some also operate remote-controlled equipment to manipulate radioactive materials or materials exposed to radioactivity. Workers who control nuclear reactors are classified as *nuclear power reactor operators*, and are not included in this statement.

Other science technicians perform a wide range of activities. Some collect weather information or assist oceanographers; others work as laser technicians or radiographers.

Work environment. Science technicians work under a wide variety of conditions. Most work indoors, usually in laboratories, and have regular hours. Some occasionally work irregular hours to monitor experiments that cannot be completed during regular working hours. Production technicians often work in 8-hour shifts around the clock. Others, such as agricultural, forest and conservation, geological and petroleum, and environmental science and protection technicians, perform much of their work outdoors, sometimes in remote locations.

Advances in automation and information technology require technicians to operate more sophisticated laboratory equipment. Science technicians make extensive use of computers, electronic measuring equipment, and traditional experimental apparatus.

Some science technicians may be exposed to hazards from equipment, chemicals, or toxic materials. Chemical technicians sometimes work with toxic chemicals or radioactive isotopes; nuclear technicians may be exposed to radiation, and biological technicians sometimes work with disease-causing organisms or radioactive agents. Forensic science technicians often are exposed to human body fluids and firearms. However, these working conditions pose little risk if proper safety procedures are followed. For forensic science technicians, collecting evidence from crime scenes can be distressing and unpleasant.

Training, Other Qualifications, and Advancement

Most science technicians need some formal postsecondary training, such as an associate degree or a certificate in applied science or science-related technology. Biological and forensic science technicians usually need a bachelor's degree. Science technicians with a high school diploma and no college degree typically begin work as trainees under the direct supervision of a more experienced technician, and they eventually earn a two-year degree in science technology.

Education and training. There are many ways to qualify for a job as a science technician. Most employers prefer applicants who have at least two years of specialized postsecondary training or an associate degree in applied science or science-related technology. Some science technicians have a bachelor's degree in the natural sciences, while others have no formal postsecondary education and learn their skills on the job.

Some science technician specialties have higher education requirements. For example, biological technicians often need a bachelor's degree in biology or a closely related field. Forensic science positions also typically require a bachelor's degree, either in forensic science or another natural science. Knowledge and understanding of legal procedures also can be helpful. Chemical technician positions in research and development also often require a bachelor's degree, but most chemical process technicians have a two-year degree instead, usually an associate degree in process technology.

Many technical and community colleges offer programs in a specific technology or more general education in science and mathematics. A number of associate degree programs are designed to provide easy transfer to bachelor's degree programs at colleges or universities. Technical institutes usually offer technician training, but they provide less theory and general education than community colleges. The length of programs at technical institutes varies, although one-year certificate programs and two-year associate degree programs are common. Some schools offer cooperative-education or internship programs, allowing students the opportunity to work at a local company or some other workplace while attending classes during alternate terms. Participation in such programs can significantly enhance a student's employment prospects.

Whatever their formal education, science technicians usually need hands-on training, which they can receive either in school or on the job. Job candidates with extensive hands-on experience using a variety of laboratory equipment, including computers and related equipment, usually require only a short period of on-the-job training. Those with a high school diploma and no college degree typically have a more extensive training program where they work as trainees under the direct supervision of a more experienced technician.

People interested in careers as science technicians should take as many high school science and math courses as possible. Science courses taken beyond high school, in an associate or bachelor's degree program, should be laboratory oriented, with an emphasis on bench skills. A solid background in applied chemistry, physics, and math is vital.

Other qualifications. Communication skills are important because technicians are often required to report their findings both orally and in writing. In addition, technicians should be able to work well with others. Because computers often are used in research and development laboratories, technicians should also have strong computer skills, especially in computer modeling. Organizational ability and skill in interpreting scientific results are important as well, as are high mechanical aptitude, attention to detail, and analytical thinking.

Advancement. Technicians usually begin work as trainees in routine positions under the direct supervision of a scientist or a more experienced technician. As they gain experience, technicians take on more responsibility and carry out assignments under only general supervision, and some eventually become supervisors. Technicians who have a bachelor's degree often are able to advance to scientist positions in their field after a few years of experience working as a technician or after earning a graduate degree.

Employment

Science technicians held about 270,800 jobs in 2008. As indicated by the following tabulation, chemical and biological technicians accounted for 54 percent of all jobs:

Biological technicians	79,500
Chemical technicians	66,100
Environmental science and protection technicians, including health	35,000
Forest and conservation technicians	34,000
Agricultural and food science technicians	21,900
Geological and petroleum technicians	15,200
Forensic science technicians	12,800
Nuclear technicians	6,400

About 30 percent of biological technicians worked in professional, scientific, or technical services firms; most other biological technicians worked in educational services, government, or pharmaceutical and medicine manufacturing. Chemical technicians primarily worked in chemical manufacturing and professional, scientific, or technical services firms. Most environmental science and protection technicians worked for professional, scientific, and technical services firms and for state and local governments. About 75 percent of forest and conservation technicians held jobs in the federal government, mostly in the Forest Service. Around 34 percent of agricultural and food science technicians worked in educational institutions and 25 percent worked for food manufacturing companies. Forensic science technicians worked primarily for state and local governments. Approximately 56 percent of all geological and petroleum technicians worked in the mining and oil and gas industries, while 51 percent of nuclear technicians worked for utilities.

Job Outlook

Employment of science technicians is projected to grow about as fast as the average for all occupations, although employment change will vary by specialty. Job opportunities are expected to be best for graduates of applied science technology programs who are well trained on equipment used in laboratories or production facilities.

Projections Data from the National Employment Matrix

Occupational title	SOC Code	Employment, 2008	Projected employment, 2018	Change, 2008–2018	
				Number	Percent
Science technicians.......................................—		270,800	302,600	31,800	12
Agricultural and food science technicians..........19-4011		21,900	23,800	1,900	9
Biological technicians......................................19-4021		79,500	93,500	14,000	18
Chemical technicians 19-4031		66,100	65,500	–500	–1
Geological and petroleum technicians 19-4041		15,200	15,400	200	2
Nuclear technicians 19-4051		6,400	7,000	600	9
Environmental science and protection technicians, including health..........................19-4091		35,000	45,200	10,100	29
Forensic science technicians 19-4092		12,800	15,300	2,500	20
Forest and conservation technicians 19-4093		34,000	36,900	2,900	9

NOTE: Data in this table are rounded.

Employment change. Overall employment of science technicians is expected to grow by 12 percent during the 2008–2018 decade, about as fast as the average for all occupations. The continued growth of scientific and medical research—particularly research related to biotechnology—will be the primary driver of employment growth, but the development and production of technical products should also stimulate demand for science technicians in many industries.

Employment of biological technicians should increase by 18 percent, faster than average, as the growing number of agricultural and medicinal products developed from the results of biotechnology research boosts demand for these workers. Also, an aging population and continued competition among pharmaceutical companies are expected to contribute to the need for innovative and improved drugs, further spurring demand. Most growth in employment will be in professional, scientific, and technical services and in educational services.

Job growth for chemical technicians is projected to decline by 1 percent, signifying little or no change. The chemical manufacturing industry, except pharmaceutical and medicine manufacturing, is anticipated to experience a decline in overall employment as companies downsize and turn to outside contractors and overseas production. However, there will still be a need for chemical technicians, particularly in pharmaceutical research.

Employment of environmental science and protection technicians is expected to grow much faster than average, at a rate of 29 percent; these workers will be needed to help regulate waste products; to collect air, water, and soil samples for measuring levels of pollutants; to monitor compliance with environmental regulations; and to clean up contaminated sites. Most of this growth is expected to be in firms that assist other companies in environmental monitoring, management, and regulatory compliance.

Employment of forest and conservation technicians is expected to grow by 9 percent, about as fast as average. Opportunities at state and local governments within specialties such as urban forestry may provide some new jobs. In addition, an increased emphasis on specific conservation issues, such as environmental protection, preservation of water resources, and control of exotic and invasive pests, will spur demand.

Employment of agricultural and food science technicians is projected to grow by 9 percent, about as fast as average. Research in biotechnology and other areas of agricultural science will increase as it becomes more important to balance greater agricultural output with protection and preservation of soil, water, and the ecosystem. In addition, there will be increased research into the use of agricultural products as energy sources, also known as biofuels.

Jobs for forensic science technicians are expected to increase by 20 percent, which is much faster than average. Employment growth in state and local government should be driven by the increasing application of forensic science techniques, such as DNA analysis, to examine, solve, and prevent crime.

Employment growth of about 2 percent, representing little or no change, is expected for geological and petroleum technicians as oil companies continue to search for new resource deposits to meet world demand for petroleum products and natural gas. The outlook for these workers is strongly tied to the price of oil; historically, when prices are low, companies limit exploration and curtail hiring of technicians, but when prices are high, they expand exploration activities. In the long run, continued high oil prices will maintain demand for these workers.

Nuclear technicians should grow by 9 percent, about as fast as average, as more are needed to monitor the nation's aging fleet of nuclear reactors and research future advances in nuclear power. Although no new nuclear power plants have been built for decades in the United States, energy demand has recently renewed interest in this form of electricity generation and may lead to future construction. Technicians also will be needed to work in defense-related areas, to develop nuclear medical technology, and to improve and enforce waste management and safety standards.

Job prospects. In addition to job openings created by growth, many openings should arise from the need to replace technicians who retire or leave the labor force for other reasons. Job opportunities are expected to be best for graduates of applied science technology programs who are well trained on equipment used in laboratories or production facilities. As the instrumentation and techniques used in industrial research, development, and production become increasingly more complex, employers will seek individuals with highly developed technical skills.

Earnings

Median hourly wages of science technicians in May 2009 were as follows:

Nuclear technicians $32.37
Geological and petroleum technicians 25.60

Forensic science technicians 24.75

Chemical technicians 20.23

Environmental science and protection technicians,
    including health 19.61

Biological technicians 18.61

Agricultural and food science technicians 16.54

Forest and conservation technicians...................... 15.80

In March 2009, the average annual salary in the federal government was $39,538 for biological science technicians, $55,527 for physical science technicians, and $42,733 for forestry technicians.

Related Occupations

Other technicians who apply scientific principles and who usually have some postsecondary education include broadcast and sound engineering technicians and radio operators; clinical laboratory technologists and technicians; diagnostic medical sonographers; drafters; engineering technicians; and radiologic technologists and technicians.

Sources of Additional Information

General information on a variety of technology fields is available from the Pathways to Technology website: www.pathwaystotechnology.org

For information about a career as a biological technician, contact

▶ Bio-Link, 1855 Folsom St., Suite 643, San Francisco, CA 94103. Internet: www.bio-link.org

For information about a career as a chemical technician, contact

▶ American Chemical Society, Education Division, Career Publications, 1155 16th St. NW, Washington, DC 20036. Internet: www.acs.org

For career information and a list of undergraduate, graduate, and doctoral programs in forensic sciences, contact

▶ American Academy of Forensic Sciences, 410 N. 21st St., Colorado Springs, CO, 80904. Internet: www.aafs.org

For general information on forestry technicians and a list of schools offering education in forestry, contact

▶ Society of American Foresters, 5400 Grosvenor Ln., Bethesda, MD 20814. Internet: www.safnet.org

Secretaries and Administrative Assistants

(O*NET 43-6011.00, 43-6012.00, 43-6013.00, and 43-6014.00)

Significant Points

■ This occupation ranks among those with the largest number of job openings.

■ Opportunities should be best for applicants with extensive knowledge of computer software applications.

■ Secretaries and administrative assistants are increasingly assuming responsibilities once reserved for managerial and professional staff.

Nature of the Work

As the reliance on technology continues to expand in offices, the role of the office professional has greatly evolved. Office automation and organizational restructuring have led *secretaries and administrative assistants* to increasingly assume responsibilities once reserved for managerial and professional staff. In spite of these changes, however, the core responsibilities for secretaries and administrative assistants have remained much the same: performing and coordinating an office's administrative activities and storing, retrieving, and integrating information for dissemination to staff and clients.

Secretaries and administrative assistants perform a variety of administrative and clerical duties necessary to run an organization efficiently. They serve as information and communication managers for an office; plan and schedule meetings and appointments; organize and maintain paper and electronic files; manage projects; conduct research; and disseminate information by using the telephone, mail services, websites, and e-mail. They may also handle travel and guest arrangements.

Secretaries and administrative assistants use a variety of office equipment, such as fax machines, photocopiers, scanners, and videoconferencing and telephone systems. In addition, secretaries and administrative assistants often use computers to do tasks previously handled by managers and professionals; they create spreadsheets, compose correspondence, manage databases, and create presentations, reports, and documents using desktop publishing software and digital graphics. They may also negotiate with vendors, maintain and examine leased equipment, purchase supplies, manage areas such as stockrooms or corporate libraries, and retrieve data from various sources. At the same time, managers and professionals have assumed many tasks traditionally assigned to secretaries and administrative assistants, such as keyboarding and answering the telephone. Because secretaries and administrative assistants do less dictation and word processing, they now have time to support more members of the executive staff. In a number of organizations, secretaries and administrative assistants work in teams to work flexibly and share their expertise.

Many secretaries and administrative assistants provide training and orientation for new staff, conduct research on the Internet, and operate and troubleshoot new office technologies.

Specific job duties vary with experience and titles. *Executive secretaries and administrative assistants* provide high-level administrative support for an office and for top executives of an organization. Generally, they perform fewer clerical tasks than do secretaries and more information management. In addition to arranging conference calls and supervising other clerical staff, they may handle more complex responsibilities such as reviewing incoming memos, submissions, and reports in order to determine their significance and to plan for their distribution. They also prepare agendas and make arrangements for meetings of committees and executive boards. They may also conduct research and prepare statistical reports.

Some secretaries and administrative assistants, such as *legal* and *medical secretaries*, perform highly specialized work requiring knowledge of technical terminology and procedures. For instance, legal secretaries prepare correspondence and legal papers such as summonses, complaints, motions, responses, and subpoenas under the supervision of an attorney or a paralegal. They may also review legal journals and assist with legal research—for example, by verifying quotes and citations in legal briefs. Additionally, legal secretaries often teach newly minted lawyers how to prepare documents for submission to the courts. Medical secretaries transcribe dictation, prepare correspondence, and assist physicians or medical scientists with reports, speeches, articles, and conference proceedings. They also record simple medical histories, arrange for patients to be hospitalized, and order supplies. Most medical secretaries need to be familiar with insurance rules, billing practices, and hospital or laboratory procedures. Other technical secretaries who assist engineers or scientists may prepare correspondence, maintain their organization's technical library, and gather and edit materials for scientific papers.

Secretaries employed in elementary schools and high schools perform important administrative functions for the school. They are responsible for handling most of the communications between parents, the community, and teachers and administrators who work at the school. As such, they are required to know details about registering students, immunizations, and bus schedules, for example. They schedule appointments, keep track of students' academic records, and make room assignments for classes. Those who work directly for principals screen inquiries from parents and handle those matters not needing a principal's attention. They may also set a principal's calendar to help set her or his priorities for the day.

Some secretaries and administrative assistants, also known as *virtual assistants*, are freelancers who work at a home office. They use the Internet, e-mail, fax, and the phone to communicate with clients. Other duties include medical or legal transcription, writing and editing reports and business correspondence, answering e-mail, data entry, setting appointments, making travel arrangements, bookkeeping, and desktop publishing.

Work environment. Secretaries and administrative assistants usually work in schools, hospitals, corporate settings, government agencies, or legal and medical offices. Virtual assistants work from a home office. Their jobs often involve sitting for long periods. If they spend a lot of time keyboarding, particularly at a computer monitor, they may encounter problems of eyestrain, stress, and repetitive motion ailments such as carpal tunnel syndrome.

The majority of secretaries and administrative assistants are full-time employees who work a standard 40-hour week. About 18 percent of secretaries work part time and many others work in temporary positions. A few are self-employed, freelance (such as virtual assistants), or participate in job-sharing arrangements, in which two people divide responsibility for a single job.

Training, Other Qualifications, and Advancement

Word processing, writing, and communication skills are essential for all secretaries and administrative assistants. Employers increasingly require extensive knowledge of computer software applications, such as desktop publishing, project management, spreadsheets, and database management.

Education and training. High school graduates who have basic office skills may qualify for entry-level secretarial positions. They can acquire these skills in various ways. Training ranges from high school vocational education programs that teach office skills and typing to 1-year and 2-year programs in office administration offered by business and vocational-technical schools, and community colleges. Many temporary placement agencies also provide formal training in computer and office skills. Most medical and legal secretaries must go through specialized training programs that

teach them the language of the industry. Virtual assistant training programs are available at many community colleges in transcription, bookkeeping, website design, project management, and computer technology. There are also online training and coaching programs.

Employers of executive secretaries increasingly are seeking candidates with a college degree, as these secretaries work closely with top executives. A degree related to the business or industry in which a person is seeking employment may provide the job seeker with an advantage in the application process.

Most secretaries and administrative assistants, once hired, tend to acquire more advanced skills through on-the-job instruction by other employees or by equipment and software vendors. Others may attend classes or participate in online education to learn how to operate new office technologies, such as information storage systems, scanners, or new updated software packages. As office automation continues to evolve, retraining and continuing education will remain integral parts of secretarial jobs.

Other qualifications. Secretaries and administrative assistants should be proficient in typing and good at spelling, punctuation, grammar, and oral communication. Employers also look for good customer service and interpersonal skills because secretaries and administrative assistants must be tactful in their dealings with people. Discretion, good judgment, organizational or management ability, initiative, and the ability to work independently are especially important for higher-level administrative positions. Changes in the office environment have increased the demand for secretaries and administrative assistants who are adaptable and versatile.

Certification and advancement. Testing and certification for proficiency in office skills are available through organizations such as the International Association of Administrative Professionals; National Association of Legal Secretaries (NALS), Inc.; Legal Secretaries International, Inc; and International Virtual Assistants Association (IVAA). As secretaries and administrative assistants gain experience, they can earn several different designations. Prominent designations include the Certified Professional Secretary (CPS) and the Certified Administrative Professional (CAP), which can be earned by meeting certain experience or educational requirements and passing an examination. Similarly, those with 1 year of experience in the legal field, or who have concluded an approved training course and who want to be certified as a legal support professional, can acquire the Accredited Legal Secretary (ALS) designation through a testing process administered by NALS. NALS offers two additional designations: Professional Legal Secretary (PLS), considered an advanced certification for legal support professionals, and a designation for proficiency as a paralegal. Legal Secretaries International confers the Certified Legal Secretary Specialist (CLSS) designation in areas such as intellectual property, criminal law, civil litigation, probate, and business law to those who have 5 years of legal experience and pass an examination. In some instances, certain requirements may be waived. There is currently no set standard of certification for virtual assistants. A number of certifications exist which involve passing a written test covering areas of core competencies and business ethics. The IVAA has three certifications available: Certified Virtual Assistant, Ethics Checked Virtual Assistant; and the Real Estate Virtual Assistant.

Secretaries and administrative assistants generally advance by being promoted to other administrative positions with more responsibilities. Qualified administrative assistants who broaden their knowledge of a company's operations and enhance their skills may be promoted to senior or executive secretary or administrative assistant, clerical supervisor, or office manager. Secretaries with word processing or data entry experience can advance to jobs as word processing or data entry trainers, supervisors, or managers within their own firms or in a secretarial, word processing, or data entry service bureau. Secretarial and administrative support experience also can lead to jobs such as instructor or sales representative with manufacturers of software or computer equipment. With additional training, many legal secretaries become paralegals.

Employment

Secretaries and administrative assistants held about 4.3 million jobs in 2008, ranking it among the largest occupations in the U.S. economy. The following tabulation shows the distribution of employment by secretarial specialty:

Secretaries, except legal, medical, and
    executive 2,020,000
Executive secretaries and administrative
    assistants... 1,594,400
Medical secretaries 471,100
Legal secretaries 262,600

Secretaries and administrative assistants are employed in organizations of every type. Around 90 percent are employed in service-providing industries, ranging from education and health care to government and retail trade. Most of the rest work for firms engaged in manufacturing or construction.

Job Outlook

Employment is projected to grow about as fast as the average. Secretaries and administrative assistants will have among the largest number of job openings due to growth and the need to replace workers who transfer to other occupations or leave this occupation. Opportunities should be best for applicants with extensive knowledge of computer software applications.

Employment change. Employment of secretaries and administrative assistants is expected to increase by 11 percent, which is about as fast as the average for all occupations, between 2008 and 2018. Projected employment varies by occupational specialty. Above average employment growth in the health-care and social assistance industry should lead to much-faster-than-average growth for medical secretaries, while moderate growth in legal services is projected to lead to faster than average growth in employment of legal secretaries. Employment of executive secretaries and administrative assistants is projected to grow as fast as the average for all occupations. Growing industries—such as construction; educational services; health

care and social assistance; and professional, scientific, and technical services—will continue to generate the most new jobs. Slower than average growth is expected for secretaries, except legal, medical, or executive, who account for about 46 percent of all secretaries and administrative assistants.

Increasing office automation and organizational restructuring will continue to make secretaries and administrative assistants more productive in coming years. Computers, e-mail, scanners, and voice message systems will allow secretaries and administrative assistants to accomplish more in the same amount of time. The use of automated equipment is also changing the distribution of work in many offices. In some cases, traditional secretarial duties such as typing, filing, photocopying, and bookkeeping are being done by clerks in other departments or by the professionals themselves. For example, professionals and managers increasingly do their own word processing and data entry, and handle much of their own correspondence. In some law and medical offices, paralegals and medical assistants are assuming some tasks formerly done by secretaries. Also, many small and medium-sized organizations are outsourcing key administrative functions, such as data entry, bookkeeping, and Internet research, to virtual assistants.

Developments in office technology are certain to continue. However, many secretarial and administrative duties are of a personal, interactive nature and, therefore, are not easily automated. Responsibilities such as planning conferences, working with clients, and instructing staff require tact and communication skills. Because technology cannot substitute for these personal skills, secretaries and administrative assistants will continue to play a key role in most organizations.

As paralegals and medical assistants assume more of the duties traditionally assigned to secretaries, offices will continue to replace the traditional arrangement of one secretary per manager with secretaries and administrative assistants who support the work of systems, departments, or units. This approach means that secretaries and administrative assistants will assume added responsibilities and will be seen as valuable members of a team.

Job prospects. In addition to jobs created from growth, numerous job opportunities will arise from the need to replace secretaries and administrative assistants who transfer to other occupations, including exceptionally skilled executive secretaries and administrative assistants who often move into professional occupations. Job opportunities should be best for applicants with extensive knowledge of computer software applications, with experience as a secretary or administrative assistant, or with advanced communication and computer skills. Applicants with a bachelor's degree will be in great

Projections Data from the National Employment Matrix

Occupational title	SOC Code	Employment, 2008	Projected employment, 2018	Change, 2008–2018	
				Number	Percent
Secretaries and administrative assistants 43-6000		4,348,100	4,819,700	471,600	11
Executive secretaries and administrative assistants 43-6011		1,594,400	1,798,800	204,400	13
Legal secretaries 43-6012		262,600	311,000	48,400	18
Medical secretaries 43-6013		471,100	596,600	125,500	27
Secretaries, except legal, medical, and executive...43-6014		2,020,000	2,113,300	93,300	5

NOTE: Data in this table are rounded.

demand to act more as managerial assistants and to perform more complex tasks.

Earnings

Median annual wages of secretaries, except legal, medical, and executive, were $29,980 in May 2009. The middle 50 percent earned between $24,000 and $37,290. The lowest 10 percent earned less than $19,190, and the highest 10 percent earned more than $45,170. Median annual wages in the industries employing the largest numbers of secretaries, except legal, medical, and executive, in May 2009 were as follows:

Elementary and secondary schools	$31,180
Local government	33,300
Colleges, universities, and professional schools	32,380
General medical and surgical hospitals	31,980
Offices of physicians	29,440

Median annual wages of executive secretaries and administrative assistants were $41,650 in May 2009. The middle 50 percent earned between $33,700 and $52,240. The lowest 10 percent earned less than $27,780, and the highest 10 percent earned more than $64,330. Median annual wages in the industries employing the largest numbers of executive secretaries and administrative assistants in May 2009 were as follows:

Colleges, universities, and professional schools	$40,850
Local government	43,880
State government	36,780
Management of companies and enterprises	46,610
Elementary and secondary schools	41,380

Median annual wages of legal secretaries were $41,080 in May 2009. The middle 50 percent earned between $31,930 and $52,340. The lowest 10 percent earned less than $26,330, and the highest 10 percent earned more than $63,980. Medical secretaries earned median annual wages of $30,190 in May 2009. The middle 50 percent earned between $24,950 and $36,830. The lowest 10 percent earned less than $21,080, and the highest 10 percent earned more than $44,060.

Virtual assistants set their own rate structure and billing terms based on the type of work, skill level, cost of living in their area, experience, and personal financial needs. Those who bill using an hourly rate can range anywhere from $25 to $100 per hour. Some also bill on a per page or project rate.

Related Occupations

Workers in a number of other occupations also type, record information, and process paperwork. Among them are bookkeeping, accounting, and auditing clerks; communications equipment operators; computer operators; court reporters; data entry and information processing workers; human resources assistants, except payroll and timekeeping; medical assistants; medical records and health information technicians; paralegals and legal assistants; and receptionists and information clerks.

A growing number of secretaries and administrative assistants share in managerial and human resource responsibilities. Occupations requiring these skills include administrative services managers; computer and information systems managers; human resources, training, and labor relations managers and specialists; and office and administrative support worker supervisors and managers.

Sources of Additional Information

State employment offices provide information about job openings for secretaries and administrative assistants.

For information on the latest trends in the profession, career development advice, and the CPS or CAP designations, contact

▸ International Association of Administrative Professionals, P.O. Box 20404, Kansas City, MO 64195-0404. Internet: www.iaap-hq.org

▸ Association of Executive and Administrative Professionals, 900 S. Washington St., Suite G-13, Falls Church, VA 22046. Internet: www.theaeap.com

Information on the CLSS designation can be obtained from

▸ Legal Secretaries International Inc., 2302 Fannin St., Suite 500, Houston, TX 77002-9136. Internet: www.legalsecretaries.org

Information on the ALS, PLS, and paralegal certifications is available from

▸ National Association of Legal Secretaries, Inc., 8159 E. 41st. St., Tulsa, OK 74145. Internet: www.nals.org

Information on virtual assistant certification can be obtained from

▸ International Virtual Assistants Association, 561 Keystone Ave., Suite 309, Reno, NV 89503. Internet: www.ivaa.org

Security Guards and Gaming Surveillance Officers

(O*NET 33-9031.00 and 33-9032.00)

Significant Points

■ Job opportunities should be favorable, but competition is expected for some higher-paying jobs.

■ Because of limited formal training requirements and flexible hours, this occupation attracts many individuals seeking a second or part-time job.

■ These jobs can be hazardous.

Nature of the Work

Security guards, also called *security officers*, patrol and inspect property to protect against fire, theft, vandalism, terrorism, and illegal activity. They protect their employer's property, enforce laws on the property, deter criminal activity, and other problems. These workers may be armed. They use various forms of telecommunications to call for assistance from police, fire, or emergency medical services. Security guards write comprehensive reports outlining their observations and activities during their assigned shift. They also may interview witnesses or victims, prepare case reports, and testify in court.

Although all security guards perform essentially the same function, their specific tasks depend on whether they work in a "static," or stationary, security position or on a mobile patrol. Guards assigned to static security positions usually stay at one location for a specified length of time. These guards must become closely acquainted with the property and people associated with their station and must often monitor alarms and closed-circuit TV cameras. In contrast, guards assigned to mobile patrol drive or walk from one location to another and conduct security checks within an assigned area. They may detain or arrest criminal violators, answer service calls concerning criminal activity or other safety concerns, and issue traffic violation warnings.

The security guard's job responsibilities also vary from one employer to another. In department stores, guards protect people, records, merchandise, money, and equipment. They often work with undercover store detectives to prevent theft by customers or employees, and help apprehend shoplifting suspects prior to the arrival of the police. Some shopping centers and theaters have officers who patrol their parking lots to deter assaults, car thefts, and robberies. In office buildings, banks, and hospitals, guards maintain order and protect the institution's customers, staff, and property. At air, sea, and rail terminals and other transportation facilities, guards and *screeners* protect people, freight, property, and equipment. Using metal detectors and other identification equipment, they may screen passengers and visitors for weapons and explosives, ensure that nothing is stolen while a vehicle is being loaded or unloaded, and watch for fires and criminals.

Guards who work in public buildings such as museums or art galleries protect paintings and exhibits by watching people and inspecting packages entering and leaving the building. In factories, laboratories, government buildings, data processing centers, and military bases, security officers protect information, products, computer codes, and defense secrets and check the credentials of people and vehicles entering and leaving the premises. Guards working at universities, parks, and sports stadiums perform crowd control, supervise parking and seating, and direct traffic. Security guards stationed at the entrance to bars and nightclubs prevent access by minors, collect cover charges at the door, maintain order among customers, and protect patrons and property.

Armored car guards protect money and valuables during transit. They also protect individuals responsible for making commercial bank deposits from theft or injury. They pick up money or other valuables from businesses and transport them to another location. Carrying money between the truck and the business can be extremely hazardous. As a result, armored car guards usually wear bulletproof vests and often carry firearms.

Gaming surveillance officers, also known as *surveillance agents*, and *gaming investigators* act as security agents for casino employees, managers, and patrons. Using primarily audio and video equipment in an observation room, they observe casino operations for irregular activities, such as cheating or theft, and monitor compliance with rules, regulations and laws. They maintain and organize recordings from security cameras, since these are sometimes used as evidence in police investigations. Some casinos use a catwalk over one-way mirrors located above the casino floor to augment electronic surveillance equipment. Surveillance agents occasionally leave the surveillance room and walk the casino floor.

All security officers must show good judgment and common sense, follow directions, testify accurately in court, and follow company policy and guidelines. In an emergency, they must be able to take charge and direct others to safety. In larger organizations, a security manager might oversee a group of security officers. In smaller organizations, however, a single worker may be responsible for all security.

Work environment. Most security guards and gaming surveillance officers spend considerable time on their feet, either assigned to a specific post or patrolling buildings and grounds. Guards may be stationed at a guard desk inside a building to monitor electronic security and surveillance devices or to check the credentials of people entering or leaving the premises. They also may be stationed at a guardhouse outside the entrance to a gated facility or community and may use a portable radio or cellular telephone to be in constant contact with a central station. Guards who work during the day may have a great deal of contact with other employees and the public. Gaming surveillance officers often work behind a bank of monitors controlling numerous cameras in a casino and thus can develop eyestrain.

Guards usually work shifts of 8 hours or longer and are often on call in case of an emergency. When employers need 24-hour coverage 7 days a week, guards may rotate work schedules for total coverage. In 2008, about 16 percent of security guards and gaming surveillance officers worked part time, and some held a second job as a guard to supplement their primary earnings.

The work usually is routine, but these jobs can be hazardous. Guards must be constantly alert for threats to themselves and the property they are protecting. In 2008, gaming surveillance workers had one of the highest rates of nonfatal on-the-job injuries.

Training, Other Qualifications, and Advancement

Generally, there are no specific education requirements for security guards, but employers usually prefer to fill armed guard positions with people who have at least a high school diploma. Gaming surveillance officers often need some education beyond high school. In most states, guards must be licensed.

Education and training. Many employers of unarmed guards do not have any specific educational requirements. For armed guards, employers usually prefer individuals who are high school graduates or who hold an equivalent certification.

Many employers give newly hired guards instruction before they start the job and provide on-the-job training. The amount of training guards receive varies. Training is more rigorous for armed guards because their employers are legally responsible for any use of force. Armed guards receive formal training in areas such as weapons retention and laws covering the use of force. They may be periodically tested in the use of firearms.

An increasing number of states are making ongoing training a legal requirement for retention of licensure. Guards may receive training in protection, public relations, report writing, crisis deterrence, first aid, and specialized training relevant to their particular assignment.

ASIS International has written voluntary training guidelines that are intended to provide regulating bodies consistent minimum standards for the quality of security services. These guidelines recommend that security guards receive at least 48 hours of training within the first 100 days of employment. The guidelines also suggest that security guards be required to pass a written or performance examination covering topics such as sharing information with law enforcement, crime prevention, handling evidence, the use of force, court testimony, report writing, interpersonal and communication skills, and emergency response procedures. In addition, they recommend annual retraining and additional firearms training for armed officers.

Some employers prefer to hire security guards with some higher education, such as a police science or criminal justice degree. In addition, there are other programs and courses available at some postsecondary schools that focus specifically on security guards.

Guards who are employed at establishments that place a heavy emphasis on security usually receive extensive formal training. For example, guards at nuclear power plants undergo several months of training before going on duty—and even then, they perform their tasks under close supervision for a significant period of time. They are taught to use firearms, administer first aid, operate alarm systems and electronic security equipment, and spot and deal with security problems.

Gaming surveillance officers and investigators usually need some training beyond high school but not usually a bachelor's degree. Several educational institutes offer certification programs. Classroom training usually is conducted in a casino-like atmosphere and includes the use of surveillance camera equipment. Previous security experience is a plus. Employers prefer either individuals with casino experience and significant knowledge of casino operations or those with law enforcement and investigation experience.

Licensure and certification. Most states require that guards be licensed. To be licensed as a guard, individuals must usually be at least 18 years old, pass a background check, and complete classroom training in such subjects as property rights, emergency procedures, and detention of suspected criminals. Drug testing often is required and may be ongoing and random. Guards who carry weapons must be licensed by the appropriate government authority, and some receive further certification as special police officers, allowing them to make limited types of arrests while on duty. Armed guard positions also have more stringent background checks and entry requirements than those of unarmed guards.

In addition to being licensed, some security guards can become certified. Certifications are not mandatory. ASIS International offers the Certified Protection Professional for security people who want a transferrable validation of their knowledge and skills.

Other qualifications. Most jobs require a driver's license. For positions as armed guards, employers often seek people who have had responsible experience in other occupations or former law enforcement officers.

Rigorous hiring and screening programs consisting of background, criminal record, and fingerprint checks are becoming the norm in the occupation. Applicants are expected to have good character references, no serious police record, and good health. They should be mentally alert, emotionally stable, and physically fit to cope with emergencies. Guards who have frequent contact with the public should have good communication skills.

Like security guards, gaming surveillance officers and gaming investigators must have keen observation skills and excellent verbal and writing abilities to document violations or suspicious behavior. They also need to be physically fit and have quick reflexes because they sometimes must detain individuals until local law enforcement officials arrive.

Advancement. Compared with unarmed security guards, armed guards and special police usually enjoy higher earnings and benefits, greater job security, and more potential for advancement. Because many people do not stay long in this occupation, opportunities for advancement are good for those who make a career in security. Most large organizations use a military type of ranking that offers the possibility of advancement in both position and salary. Some guards may advance to supervisor or security manager positions. Guards with postsecondary education often have an advantage in securing supervisory positions. Guards with management skills may open their own contract security guard agencies. Guards can also move

to an organization that needs higher levels of security, which may result in more prestige or higher pay.

Employment

Security guards and gaming surveillance officers held 1.1 million jobs in 2008. About 55 percent of all jobs for security guards were in investigation and security services, including guard and armored car services. These organizations provide security on a contract basis, assigning their guards to buildings and other sites as needed. Most other security officers were employed directly by a wide variety of businesses and governments. Guard jobs are found throughout the country, most commonly in metropolitan areas.

Gaming surveillance officers work primarily in gambling industries; traveler accommodation, which includes casino hotels; and local government. They are employed only in those states and on those Indian reservations where gambling is legal.

A significant number of law enforcement officers work as security guards when they are off duty, in order to supplement their incomes. Often working in uniform and with the official cars assigned to them, they add a high-profile security presence to the establishment with which they have contracted. At construction sites and apartment complexes, for example, their presence often deters crime. (Police and detectives are discussed elsewhere in this book.)

Job Outlook

Opportunities for security guards and gaming surveillance officers should be favorable, although competition is expected for some higher paying jobs. Numerous job openings will stem from faster than average employment growth—driven by the demand for increased security—and from the need to replace those who leave this large occupation each year.

Employment change. Employment of security guards is expected to grow by 14 percent between 2008 and 2018, which is faster than the average for all occupations. This occupation will have a very large number of new jobs arise, about 152,500 over the projections decade. Concern about crime, vandalism, and terrorism continues to increase the need for security. Demand for guards also will grow as private security firms increasingly perform duties—such as providing security at public events and in residential neighborhoods—that were formerly handled by police officers. Additionally, private security firms are expected to provide more protection to facilities, such as hospitals and nursing homes.

Employment of gaming surveillance officers and gaming investigators is expected to grow by 12 percent between 2008 and 2018, as fast as the average for all occupations. Casinos will hire more surveillance officers if more states legalize gambling or if the number of casinos increases in states where gambling is already legal. In addition, casino security forces will employ more technically trained personnel as technology becomes increasingly important in thwarting casino cheating and theft.

Job prospects. Job opportunities for security guards should be favorable because of growing demand for these workers and the need to replace experienced workers who leave the occupation. In addition to full-time job opportunities, the limited training requirements and flexible hours attract many people seeking part-time or second jobs. However, competition is expected for higher-paying positions that require longer periods of training; these positions usually are found at facilities that require a high level of security,

Projections Data from the National Employment Matrix

Occupational title	SOC Code	Employment, 2008	Projected employment, 2018	Change, 2008–2018	
				Number	Percent
Security guards and gaming surveillance officers........ 33-9030		1,086,000	1,239,500	153,600	14
Gaming surveillance officers and gaming investigators... 33-9031		9,300	10,400	1,100	12
Security guards... 33-9032		1,076,600	1,229,100	152,500	14

NOTE: Data in this table are rounded.

such as nuclear power plants or weapons installations. Applicants with prior experience in the gaming industry should enjoy the best prospects for jobs as gaming surveillance officers.

Earnings

Median annual wages of security guards were $23,820 in May 2009. The middle 50 percent earned between $19,460 and $30,580. The lowest 10 percent earned less than $16,840, and the highest 10 percent earned more than $40,230. Median annual wages in the industries employing the largest numbers of security guards were as follows:

Investigation and security services	$22,490
Local government...	29,470
General medical and surgical hospitals	29,350
Elementary and secondary schools	28,690
Traveler accommodation	26,320

Gaming surveillance officers and gaming investigators had median annual wages of $30,220 in May 2009. The middle 50 percent earned between $24,050 and $39,060. The lowest 10 percent earned less than $20,320, and the highest 10 percent earned more than $48,760.

Related Occupations

Other security and protective service occupations include correctional officers; gaming services occupations; police and detectives; and private detectives and investigators.

Sources of Additional Information

Further information about work opportunities for guards is available from local security and guard firms and state employment service offices. Information about licensing requirements for guards may be obtained from the state licensing commission or the state police department. In states where local jurisdictions establish licensing requirements, contact a local government authority such as the sheriff, county executive, or city manager.

For more information about security careers, about the Certified Protection Professional, and for a list of colleges and universities offering security-related courses and majors, contact

▸ ASIS International, 1625 Prince St., Alexandria, VA 22314-2818. Internet: www.asisonline.org

For more information related to jobs with the Transportation Security Administration, call the TSA Recruitment Center at (800) 887-1895 or (800) 887-5506 (TTY), or visit their website. Internet: www.tsa.gov/join/careers/careers_security_jobs.shtm

Sheet Metal Workers

(O*NET 47-2211.00)

Significant Points

■ Sheet metal workers are primarily employed in construction and manufacturing industries.

■ Workers learn through informal on-the-job training or formal apprenticeship programs.

■ Job opportunities in construction should be good, particularly for individuals who have apprenticeship training or who are certified welders; applicants for jobs in manufacturing will experience competition.

Nature of the Work

Sheet metal workers make, install, and maintain heating, ventilation, and air-conditioning duct systems; roofs; siding; rain gutters; downspouts; skylights; restaurant equipment; outdoor signs; railroad cars; tailgates; customized precision equipment; and many other products made from metal sheets. They also may work with fiberglass and plastic materials. Although some workers specialize in fabrication, installation, or maintenance, most do all three jobs. Sheet metal workers do both construction-related work and mass production of sheet metal products in manufacturing.

Sheet metal workers first study plans and specifications to determine the kind and quantity of materials they will need. They measure, cut, bend, shape, and fasten pieces of sheet metal to make ductwork, countertops, and other custom products. Sheet metal workers program and operate computerized metalworking equipment. They cut, drill, and form parts with computer-controlled saws, lasers, shears, and presses.

In shops without computerized equipment, and for products that cannot be made with such equipment, sheet metal workers make the required calculations and use tapes, rulers, and other measuring devices for layout work. They then cut or stamp the parts with machine tools.

Before assembling pieces, sheet metal workers use measuring instruments such as tape measures, calipers, and micrometers to check each part for accuracy. If necessary, they use hand, rotary, or squaring shears and hacksaws to finish pieces. After inspecting the pieces, workers fasten seams and joints together with welds, bolts, cement, rivets, solder, or other connecting devices. They then take the parts constructed in the shop and assemble the pieces further as they install them. These workers install ducts, pipes, and tubes by joining them end to end and hanging them with metal hangers secured to a ceiling or a wall. They also use shears, hammers, punches, and drills to make parts at the work site or to alter parts made in the shop.

Some jobs are done completely at the job site. When installing a metal roof, for example, sheet metal workers usually measure and cut the roofing panels onsite. They secure the first panel in place and interlock and fasten the grooved edge of the next panel into the grooved edge of the first. Then they nail or weld the free edge of the panel to the structure. This two-step process is repeated for each additional panel. Finally, the workers fasten machine-made molding at joints, along corners, and around windows and doors, for a neat, finished effect.

In addition to installation, some sheet metal workers specialize in testing, balancing, adjusting, and servicing existing air-conditioning and ventilation systems to make sure they are functioning properly and to improve their energy efficiency. Properly installed duct systems are a key component of heating, ventilation, and air-conditioning (HVAC) systems; sometimes duct installers are called HVAC technicians. A growing activity for sheet metal workers is the commissioning of a building—a complete mechanical inspection of the building's HVAC, water, and lighting systems.

Sheet metal workers in manufacturing plants make sheet metal parts for products such as aircraft or industrial equipment. Although some of the fabrication techniques used in large-scale manufacturing are similar to those used in smaller shops, the work may be highly automated and repetitive. Sheet metal workers doing such work may be responsible for reprogramming the computer control systems of the equipment they operate.

Work environment. Sheet metal workers usually work a 40-hour week. Those who fabricate sheet metal products work in small shops and manufacturing plants that are usually well lighted and well ventilated. However, they stand for long periods and lift heavy materials and finished pieces. Those performing installation at construction sites or inside buildings do considerable bending, lifting, standing, climbing, and squatting, sometimes in close quarters or awkward positions. Working outdoors exposes sheet metal workers to various kinds of weather.

Sheet metal workers must follow safety practices, because this occupation has a relatively high rate of nonfatal injuries. Some sheet metal workers work around high-speed machines, which can be dangerous. Others are subject to cuts from sharp metal, burns from soldering or welding, and falls from ladders or scaffolds. They often are required to wear safety glasses and must not wear jewelry or loose-fitting clothing that could easily be caught in a machine. To avoid repetitive-type injuries, they may work at a variety of different production stations.

Training, Other Qualifications, and Advancement

Sheet metal workers learn their trade through both formal apprenticeships and informal on-the-job training programs. Formal apprenticeships are more likely to be found in construction.

Education and training. To become a skilled sheet metal construction worker usually takes between four and five years of both classroom and on-the-job training. Although there are a number of different ways to obtain this training, generally the more formalized the training received by an individual, the more thoroughly skilled the person becomes and the more likely he or she is to be in demand by employers. For some, this training begins in a high school, where

classes in English, algebra, geometry, physics, mechanical drawing and blueprint reading, and general shop are recommended.

After high school, there are a number of different ways to train. One way is to get a job with a contractor who will provide training on the job. Entry-level workers generally start as helpers, assisting more experienced workers. Most begin by carrying metal and cleaning up debris in a metal shop, learning about materials, tools, and their uses as they go about their tasks. Later, they learn to operate machines that bend or cut metal. In time, helpers go to the job site to learn installation. Employers may send their employees to a trade or vocational school to take courses or to a community college to receive further formal training. Helpers may be promoted to the journeyman level if they show the requisite knowledge and skills. Most sheet metal workers in large-scale manufacturing receive on-the-job training, with additional classwork or in-house training as necessary. The training needed to become proficient in manufacturing takes less time than the training for proficiency in construction.

Apprenticeship programs combine paid on-the-job training with related classroom instruction. Usually, apprenticeship applicants must be at least 18 years old and meet local requirements. The length of the program, typically four to five years, varies with the apprentice's skill. Apprenticeship programs provide comprehensive instruction in both sheet metal fabrication and sheet metal installation. They may be administered by local joint committees composed of the Sheet Metal Workers' International Association and local chapters of the Sheet Metal and Air-Conditioning Contractors National Association.

Sheet metal workers can choose one of many specialties. Workers can specialize in commercial and residential HVAC installation and maintenance, industrial welding and fabrication, exterior or architectural sheet metal installation, sign fabrication, service and refrigeration, and testing and balancing of building systems.

On the job, apprentices receive first safety training and then training in tasks that allow them to begin work immediately. They use materials such as fiberglass, plastics, and other nonmetallic materials. Workers focus on a particular sheet metal career path. In the classroom, apprentices learn computer-aided drafting; reading of plans and specifications; trigonometry and geometry applicable to layout work; welding; the use of computerized equipment; the principles of heating, air-conditioning, and ventilation systems. In addition, apprentices learn the relationship between sheet metal work and other construction work.

Other qualifications. Sheet metal workers need to be in good physical condition and have mechanical and mathematical aptitude and good reading skills. Good eye-hand coordination, accurate perception of spaces and forms, and manual dexterity also are important. Courses in algebra, trigonometry, geometry, mechanical drawing, and shop provide a helpful background for learning the trade, as does related work experience obtained in the U.S. Armed Services.

Certification and advancement. It is important for experienced sheet metal workers to keep abreast of new technological developments, such as the use of computerized layout and laser-cutting machines. In addition, new software, called B.I.M., which stands for "building information modeling," allows contractors, architects, and engineers to coordinate their efforts and increase efficiency at work sites.

Certifications in one of the specialties also can be beneficial to workers. Certifications related to sheet metal specialties are offered by a wide variety of associations, several of which are listed in the sources of additional information at the end of this statement.

Sheet metal workers in construction may advance to supervisory jobs. Some of these workers take additional training in welding and do more specialized work. Workers who perform building and system testing are able to move into construction and building inspection. Others go into the contracting business for themselves. Because a sheet metal contractor must have a shop with equipment to fabricate products, this type of contracting business is more expensive to start than other types of construction contracting.

Sheet metal workers in manufacturing may advance to positions as supervisors or quality inspectors. Some of these workers may move into other management positions.

Employment

Sheet metal workers held about 170,700 jobs in 2008. About 63 percent of all sheet metal workers were in the construction industry, including 46 percent who worked for plumbing, heating, and air-conditioning contractors; most of the rest in construction worked for roofing contractors and for building finishing contractors. Some worked for general contractors engaged in residential and commercial building and for other special trade contractors.

About 23 percent of all sheet metal workers were in manufacturing industries, such as the fabricated metal products, machinery, and aerospace products and parts industries. Some sheet metal workers work for the federal government.

Compared with workers in most construction craft occupations, relatively few sheet metal workers are self-employed.

Job Outlook

Slower than average employment growth is projected. Job opportunities should be best for individuals who have apprenticeship training or who are certified welders. Applicants for jobs in manufacturing will experience competition.

Employment change. Employment of sheet metal workers is expected to increase by 6 percent between 2008 and 2018, slower than the average for all occupations. This change reflects anticipated growth in the number of industrial, commercial, and residential structures to be built over the decade. In addition, it reflects the need to install energy-efficient air-conditioning, heating, and ventilation systems in older buildings and to perform other types of renovation and maintenance work on these systems. Also, the popularity of decorative sheet metal products and increased architectural restoration are expected to add to the demand for sheet metal workers.

Sheet metal workers in manufacturing, however, are expected to experience a moderate decline in employment as the industry becomes more automated and some of the work is done in other countries.

Job prospects. Job opportunities are expected to be good for sheet metal workers in the construction industry, reflecting both employment growth and openings arising each year as experienced sheet metal workers leave the occupation. Opportunities should be particularly good for individuals who have apprenticeship training or who are certified welders. Applicants for jobs in manufacturing will experience competition.

Sheet metal workers in construction may experience periods of unemployment, particularly when construction projects end and economic conditions dampen construction activity. However, because maintenance of existing equipment makes up a large part of the work done by sheet metal workers, they are less affected by construction downturns than are some other construction occupations. Installation of new air-conditioning and heating systems in existing buildings is expected to continue as individuals and businesses adopt more energy-efficient equipment to cut utility bills. In addition, a large proportion of sheet metal installation and maintenance is done indoors, so sheet metal workers usually lose less work time because of bad weather than do other construction workers.

Earnings

In May 2009, median hourly wages of sheet metal workers were $19.54. The middle 50 percent earned between $14.64 and $27.19. The lowest 10 percent of all sheet metal workers earned less than $11.78, and the highest 10 percent earned more than $35.46. The median hourly wages of the largest industries employing sheet metal workers were as follows:

```
Building equipment contractors........................... $20.30
Foundation, structure, and building exterior
    contractors.................................................... 17.42
Architectural and structural metals manufacturing ... 17.45
Federal government ............................................ 24.47
Ventilation, heating, air-conditioning, and
    commercial refrigeration equipment
    manufacturing ................................................. 15.11
```

Apprentices normally start at about 40 to 50 percent of the rate paid to experienced workers. As apprentices acquire more skills, they receive periodic pay increases, until their pay approaches that of experienced workers.

About 32 percent of all sheet metal workers belong to a union. Union workers in some areas receive supplemental wages from the union when they are laid off or experience shortened workweeks.

Related Occupations

To fabricate and install sheet metal products, sheet metal workers combine metalworking skills and knowledge of construction materials and techniques. Other occupations in which workers lay out and fabricate metal products include the following: assemblers and fabricators; machine setters, operators, and tenders—metal and plastic; machinists; and tool and die makers.

Projections Data from the National Employment Matrix

Occupational title	SOC Code	Employment, 2008	Projected employment, 2018	Change, 2008–2018	
				Number	Percent
Sheet metal workers..47-2211		170,700	181,800	11,100	6

NOTE: Data in this table are rounded.

Construction occupations requiring similar skills and knowledge include the following: glaziers; and heating, air-conditioning, and refrigeration mechanics and installers.

Sources of Additional Information

For more information about apprenticeships or other work opportunities, contact local sheet metal contractors or heating, refrigeration, and air-conditioning contractors; a local of the Sheet Metal Workers International Association; a local of the Sheet Metal and Air-Conditioning Contractors National Association; a local joint union-management apprenticeship committee; or the nearest office of your state employment service or apprenticeship agency. You also can find information on the registered apprenticeship system with links to state apprenticeship programs on the U.S. Department of Labor's website: www.doleta.gov/OA/eta_default.cfm. Apprenticeship information is available as well from the U.S. Department of Labor's toll-free help line: (877) 872-5627.

For general and training information about sheet metal workers, contact

▸ Fabricators and Manufacturers Association, International, 833 Featherstone Rd., Rockford, IL 61107-6301. Internet: www.fmanet.org

▸ International Training Institute for the Sheet Metal and Air-Conditioning Industry, 601 N. Fairfax St., Suite 240, Alexandria, VA 22314-2083. Internet: www.sheetmetal-iti.org

▸ National Center for Construction Education and Research, 3600 NW 43rd St., Bldg. G, Gainesville, FL 32606-8134. Internet: www.nccer.org

▸ Sheet Metal and Air-Conditioning Contractors' National Association, 4201 Lafayette Center Dr., Chantilly, VA 20151-1209. Internet: www.smacna.org

▸ Sheet Metal Workers International Association, 1750 New York Ave. NW, 6th Floor, Washington, DC 20006-5301. Internet: www.smwia.org

For general information on apprenticeships and how to get them, see the *Occupational Outlook Quarterly* article "Apprenticeships: Career training, credentials—and a paycheck in your pocket," online at www.bls.gov/opub/ooq/2002/summer/art01.pdf and in print at many libraries and career centers.

Shipping, Receiving, and Traffic Clerks

(O*NET 43-5071.00)

Significant Points

■ Shipping, receiving, and traffic clerks generally are entry-level workers who need no more than a high school diploma.

■ Employers prefer to hire those familiar with computers and other electronic office and business equipment.

■ Employment is expected to decline moderately as a result of increasing automation; however, job openings will result from the need to replace workers who leave the occupation.

Nature of the Work

Shipping, receiving, and traffic clerks keep records of all goods shipped and received. Their duties depend on the size of the establishment they work for and the level of automation used. Larger companies typically are more able to finance the purchase of computers, scanners, and other equipment to handle some or all of a clerk's responsibilities. In smaller companies, a clerk maintains records, prepares shipments, sorts packages, and accepts deliveries.

Shipping clerks keep records of all outgoing shipments. They prepare shipping documents and mailing labels and make sure that orders have been filled correctly. Also, they record items taken from inventory and note when orders were filled. Sometimes they fill the order themselves, taking merchandise from the stockroom, noting when inventories run low, and wrapping or packing the goods in shipping containers. They also address and label packages, look up and compute freight or postal rates, and record the weight and cost of each shipment. In addition, shipping clerks may prepare invoices and furnish information about shipments to other parts of the company, such as the accounting department. In modern warehouses, the recording of this shipping information and the printing of mailing labels can be automated with the use of a computer and barcode scanner. Once a shipment is checked and ready to go, shipping clerks may sort and move the goods from the warehouse to the shipping dock or truck terminal and direct their loading.

Receiving clerks perform tasks similar to those of shipping clerks. They determine whether orders have been filled correctly by verifying incoming shipments against the original order and the accompanying bill of lading or invoice. They make a record of the shipment and the condition of its contents. In many firms, receiving clerks either use handheld scanners to record barcodes on incoming products or manually enter the information into a computer. These data then can be transferred to the appropriate departments. An increasing number of clerks at larger, more modern companies are using radio-frequency identification (RFID) scanners, which store and remotely retrieve data by using tags or transponders. Clerks then check the shipment for any discrepancies in quantity, price, and discounts. Receiving clerks may route or move shipments to the proper department, warehouse section, or stockroom. They also may arrange for adjustments with shippers if merchandise is lost or damaged. Receiving clerks in small businesses may perform some duties similar to those of stock clerks. In larger establishments, receiving clerks may control all receiving platform operations, such as the scheduling of trucks, recording of shipments, and handling of damaged goods.

Traffic clerks maintain records on the destination, weight, and charges for all incoming and outgoing freight. They verify rate charges by comparing the classification of materials with rate charts. In many companies, this work may be automated. Information either is scanned or is entered by hand into a computer for use by the accounting department or other departments within the company. Traffic clerks also keep a file of claims for overcharges and for damage to goods in transit.

It is common, especially in smaller companies, for workers to perform the functions of all three positions. These workers are responsible for incoming and outgoing packages, as well as the logistical details of shipping them. Some shipping, receiving, and traffic clerks share responsibilities with material moving workers (see statement found elsewhere in this book) and must sort, load, unload,

Projections Data from the National Employment Matrix

Occupational title	SOC Code	Employment, 2008	Projected employment, 2018	Change, 2008–2018	
				Number	Percent
Shipping, receiving, and traffic clerks......................43-5071		750,500	701,200	–49,300	–7

NOTE: Data in this table are rounded.

or store items. Clerks with these additional responsibilities may use machinery, such as forklifts, to transport items in a warehouse.

Work environment. Shipping, receiving, and traffic clerks often work in offices inside manufacturing plants or warehouses. Most jobs involve frequent standing, bending, walking, and stretching. Lifting and carrying smaller items also may be involved, especially at small companies with less automation. Although automated devices have lessened the physical demands of this occupation, their use remains somewhat limited. The work still can be strenuous, even though mechanical material handling equipment, such as computerized conveyor systems, may be used to move heavy items.

The typical workweek is Monday through Friday; however, evening and weekend hours are common in some jobs and may be required when large shipments are involved or during major holiday periods.

Training, Other Qualifications, and Advancement

Shipping, receiving, and traffic clerks generally are entry-level workers who need no more than a high school diploma. Because of increasing automation, however, employers prefer to hire those familiar with computers and other electronic office and business equipment.

Education and training. Shipping, receiving, and traffic clerks typically learn the job by doing routine tasks under close supervision. They first learn how to count and mark stock, and then start keeping records and taking inventory.

Training in the use of automated equipment usually is done informally on the job. As these occupations become more automated, however, workers may need longer periods of training to master the use of the equipment and technology. Many employers prefer to hire workers experienced with computers and other electronic equipment.

Other qualifications. Strength, stamina, communication skills, attention to detail, and an ability to work at repetitive tasks, sometimes under pressure, are important characteristics.

Advancement. Shipping, receiving, and traffic clerks may be promoted to supervisory roles, and those with an understanding of other tasks in their firm can move into other positions, such as purchasing managers or logisticians.

Employment

Shipping, receiving, and traffic clerks held about 750,500 jobs in 2008. About 71 percent were employed in manufacturing or by wholesale and retail establishments. Although jobs for shipping, receiving, and traffic clerks are found throughout the country, many clerks work in urban areas, where shipping depots in factories and wholesale establishments usually are located.

Job Outlook

Employment is expected to decline moderately as a result of increasing automation. However, job openings will result from the need to replace shipping, receiving, and traffic clerks who leave the occupation.

Employment change. Employment of shipping, receiving, and traffic clerks is expected to decline moderately by 7 percent between 2008 and 2018. As companies increasingly use computers and high-technology scanners to store and retrieve shipping and receiving records, fewer clerks will be needed to oversee these activities.

Methods of handling materials have changed significantly in recent years. Large warehouses increasingly are becoming automated, with equipment such as automatic sorting systems, robots, computer-directed trucks, and automated identification and data collection (AIDC) systems. This automation, coupled with the growing use of handheld barcode and RFID scanners in shipping and receiving departments, should increase the productivity of shipping, receiving, and traffic clerks.

Job prospects. Despite the projected employment decline, many job openings will occur because of the need to replace shipping, receiving, and traffic clerks who leave the occupation. This is a large entry-level occupation, and many vacancies are created as workers leave as part of their normal career progression. Because smaller warehouses, distribution centers, and trucking terminals will continue to rely on sorting and moving goods by hand, job opportunities at those facilities may be better than at larger, more automated centers.

Earnings

Median annual wages of shipping, receiving, and traffic clerks in May 2009 were $28,250. The middle 50 percent earned between $22,530 and $35,530. The lowest 10 percent earned less than $18,680, and the highest 10 percent earned more than $43,980.

These workers usually receive the same benefits as most other workers. If uniforms are required, employers generally provide them or offer an allowance to purchase them.

Related Occupations

Shipping, receiving, and traffic clerks record, check, and often store materials that a company receives. They also process and pack goods for shipment. Other workers who perform similar duties are cargo and freight agents; material moving occupations; postal service clerks; production, planning, and expediting clerks; and stock clerks and order fillers.

Sources of Additional Information

Additional information about job opportunities may be obtained from local employers and local offices of the state employment service.

Social and Human Service Assistants

(O*NET 21-1093.00)

Significant Points

■ A high school diploma is the minimum educational requirement, but employers often seek individuals with relevant work experience or education beyond high school.

■ Employment is projected to grow much faster than the average for all occupations.

■ Job opportunities should be excellent, particularly for applicants with appropriate postsecondary education, but wages remain low.

Nature of the Work

Social and human service assistants help social workers, health-care workers, and other professionals to provide services to people. Social and human service assistant is a generic term for workers with a wide array of job titles, including *human service worker, case management aide, social work assistant, community support worker, mental health aide, community outreach worker, life skills counselor, social services aide, youth worker, psychological aide, client advocate,* or *gerontology aide.* They usually work under the direction of workers from a variety of fields, such as nursing, psychiatry, psychology, or social work. The amount of responsibility and supervision they are given varies a great deal. Some have little direct supervision. For example, they may run a group home. Others work under close direction.

Social and human service assistants provide services to clients to help them improve their quality of life. They assess clients' needs, investigate their eligibility for benefits and services such as food stamps, Medicaid and welfare, and help clients obtain them. They also arrange for transportation, if necessary, and provide emotional support. They monitor and keep case records on clients and report progress to supervisors and case managers.

Social and human service assistants play a variety of roles in the community. For example, they may organize and lead group activities, assist clients in need of counseling or crisis intervention, or administer food banks or emergency fuel programs. In halfway houses, group homes, and government-supported housing programs, they assist adults who need supervision with personal hygiene and daily living tasks. They review clients' records, ensure that they take prescribed medication, talk with family members, and confer with medical personnel and other caregivers to provide insight into clients' needs. Assistants also give emotional support and help clients become involved in community recreation programs and other activities.

In psychiatric hospitals, rehabilitation programs, and outpatient clinics, social and human service assistants work with psychiatrists, psychologists, social workers, and others to help clients master everyday living skills, communicate more effectively, and live well with others. They support the client's participation in a treatment plan, such as individual or group counseling or occupational therapy.

The work, while satisfying, can be emotionally draining. Understaffing and relatively low pay can add to the pressure.

Work environment. Working conditions of social and human service assistants vary. Some work in offices, clinics, and hospitals, while others work in group homes, shelters, and day programs. Traveling to see clients is required for some jobs. Sometimes working with clients can be dangerous, even though most agencies do everything they can to ensure their workers' safety. Some work in the evening and on weekends.

Training, Other Qualifications, and Advancement

A high school diploma is the minimum education requirement, but employers often seek individuals with relevant work experience or education beyond high school.

Education and training. Many employers prefer to hire people with some education beyond high school. Certificates or associate degrees in subjects such as human services, gerontology or one of the social or behavioral sciences meet many employers' requirements. Some jobs may require a bachelor's or master's degree in human services or a related field, such as counseling, rehabilitation, or social work.

Human services degree programs have a core curriculum that trains students to observe patients and record information, conduct patient interviews, implement treatment plans, employ problem-solving techniques, handle crisis intervention matters, and use proper case management and referral procedures. Many programs utilize field work to give students hands-on experience. General education courses in liberal arts, sciences, and the humanities also are part of most curriculums. Most programs also offer specialized courses related to addictions, gerontology, child protection, and other areas. Many degree programs require completion of a supervised internship.

Workers level of education often determines the kind of work they are assigned and the degree of responsibility that is given to them. For example, workers with no more than a high school education are likely to work in direct-care services and help clients to fill out paperwork. They may receive extensive on-the-job training on how to perform these tasks. Workers with a college degree, however, might do supportive counseling, coordinate program activities, or manage a group home. Social and human service assistants with proven leadership ability, especially acquired from paid or volunteer experience in social services, often have greater autonomy in their work. Regardless of the academic or work background of employees, most employers provide some form of in-service training, such as seminars and workshops, to their employees.

Other qualifications. These workers should have a strong desire to help others, effective communication skills, a sense of responsibility, and the ability to manage time effectively. Many human services jobs involve direct contact with people who are vulnerable to exploitation or mistreatment; so patience and understanding are also highly valued characteristics.

It is becoming more common for employers to require a criminal background check, and in some settings, workers may be required to have a valid driver's license.

Advancement. Formal education is almost always necessary for advancement. In general, advancement to case management or social work jobs requires a bachelor's or master's degree in human services, counseling, rehabilitation, social work, or a related field.

Projections Data from the National Employment Matrix

Occupational title	SOC Code	Employment, 2008	Projected employment, 2018	Change, 2008–2018	
				Number	Percent
Social and human service assistants 21-1093		352,000	431,500	79,400	23

NOTE: Data in this table are rounded.

Employment

Social and human service assistants held about 352,000 jobs in 2008. More than 65 percent were employed in the health-care and social assistance industries, and almost 24 percent were employed by state and local governments.

Job Outlook

Employment of social and human service assistants is expected to grow much faster than the average for all occupations. Job prospects are expected to be excellent, particularly for applicants with relevant postsecondary education.

Employment change. The number of social and human service assistants is expected to grow by nearly 23 percent between 2008 and 2018, which is much faster than the average for all occupations. This is due in large part to the aging population and increased demand for mental health and substance abuse treatment.

As the elderly population continues to grow, the demand for social and human service assistants will expand. This is due in large part to the increased need for social services demanded by this population, such as adult day care, meal delivery programs, and support during medical crises. Social and human service assistants, who assist in locating and providing these services, will be needed to meet this increased demand.

Opportunities are expected to be good in private social service agencies. Employment in private agencies will grow, as state and local governments continue to contract out services to the private sector in an effort to cut costs.

The number of jobs for social and human service assistants in state and local governments will grow, but not as fast as employment for social and human service assistants in other industries. Employment in the public sector may fluctuate with the level of funding provided by state and local governments and with the number of services contracted out to private organizations.

Job prospects. Job prospects for social and human service assistants are expected to be excellent, particularly for individuals with appropriate education after high school. Job openings will come from job growth, but also from the need to replace workers who advance into new positions, retire, or leave the workforce for other reasons. There will be more competition for jobs in urban areas than in rural ones, but qualified applicants should have little difficulty finding employment.

Earnings

Median annual wages of social and human service assistants were $27,940 in May 2009. The middle 50 percent earned between $23,230 and $35,620. The top 10 percent earned more than $44,760, while the lowest 10 percent earned less than $18,300.

Median annual wages in the industries employing the largest numbers of social and human service assistants in May 2009 were the following:

Individual and family services	$26,960
Local government	32,580
State government	34,450
Residential mental retardation, mental health and substance abuse facilities	23,770
Vocational rehabilitation services	24,620

Related Occupations

Workers in other occupations that require skills similar to those of social and human service assistants include child care workers; correctional officers; counselors; eligibility interviewers, government programs; health educators; home health aides and personal and home care aides; occupational therapist assistants and aides; probation officers and correctional treatment specialists; psychologists; recreational therapists; and social workers.

Sources of Additional Information

For information on programs and careers in human services, contact

▶ Council for Standards in Human Services Education, 1935 S. Plum Grove Rd., PMB 297, Palatine, IL 60067. Internet: www.cshse.org

▶ National Organization for Human Services, 5341 Old Highway 5, Suite 206, #214, Woodstock, GA 30188. Internet: www.nationalhumanservices.org

Information on job openings may be available from state employment service offices or directly from city, county, or state departments of health, mental health and mental retardation, and human resources.

Surveyors, Cartographers, Photogrammetrists, and Surveying and Mapping Technicians

(O*NET 17-1021.00, 17-1022.00, 17-1022.01, 17-3031.00, 17-3031.01, and 17-3031.02)

Significant Points

■ About 7 out of 10 jobs are in architectural, engineering, and related services.

■ Employment is expected to grow faster than the average for all occupations.

■ Surveyors, cartographers, and photogrammetrists who have a bachelor's degree and strong technical skills should have favorable job prospects.

Nature of the Work

Surveyors, cartographers, photogrammetrists, and surveying and mapping technicians are responsible for measuring and mapping the earth's surface. *Surveyors* establish official land, airspace, and water boundaries. They write descriptions of land for deeds, leases, and other legal documents; define airspace for airports; and take measurements of construction and mineral sites. Other surveyors provide data about the shape, contour, location, elevation, or dimension of land or land features. *Cartographers and photogrammetrists* collect, analyze, interpret, and map geographic information using data from surveys and photographs. *Surveying and mapping technicians* assist these professionals by collecting data in the field, making calculations, and helping with computer-aided drafting. Collectively, these occupations play key roles in the field of geospatial information.

Surveyors measure distances, directions, and angles between points on, above, and below the earth's surface. In the field, they select known survey reference points and determine the precise location of important features in the survey area using specialized equipment. Surveyors also research legal records, look for evidence of previous boundaries, and analyze data to determine the location of boundary lines. They are sometimes called to provide expert testimony in court regarding their work or the work of other surveyors. Surveyors also record their results; verify the accuracy of data; and prepare plots, maps, and reports.

Some surveyors perform specialized functions that support the work of other surveyors, cartographers, and photogrammetrists. For example, *geodetic surveyors* use high-accuracy techniques, including satellite observations, to measure large areas of the earth's surface. *Geophysical prospecting surveyors* mark sites for subsurface exploration, usually to look for petroleum. *Marine or hydrographic surveyors* survey harbors, rivers, and other bodies of water to determine shorelines, the topography of the bottom, water depth, and other features.

Surveyors use the Global Positioning System (GPS) to locate reference points with a high degree of precision. To use this system, a surveyor places a satellite signal receiver—a small instrument mounted on a tripod—on a desired point, and another receiver on a point for which the geographic position is known. The receiver simultaneously collects information from several satellites and the known reference point to establish a precise position. The receiver also can be placed in a vehicle for tracing out road systems. Because receivers now come in different sizes and shapes, and because the cost of receivers has fallen, much more surveying work can be done with GPS. Surveyors then interpret and check the results produced by GPS.

Field measurements are often taken by a survey party that gathers the information needed by the surveyor. A typical survey party consists of a *party chief* and one or more surveying technicians and helpers. The party chief, who may be either a surveyor or a senior surveying technician, leads day-to-day work activities. Surveying technicians assist the party chief by adjusting and operating surveying instruments, such as the total station, which measures and records angles and distances simultaneously. Surveying technicians

compile notes, make sketches, and enter the data obtained from surveying instruments into computers either in the field or at the office.

Photogrammetrists and cartographers measure, map, and chart the earth's surface. Their work involves everything from performing geographical research and compiling data to producing maps. They collect, analyze, and interpret both spatial data—such as latitude, longitude, elevation, and distance—and nonspatial data—such as population density, land-use patterns, annual precipitation levels, and demographic characteristics. Their maps may give both physical and social characteristics of the land. They prepare maps in either digital or graphic form, using information provided by geodetic surveys and remote sensing systems including aerial cameras, satellites, light-imaging detection and ranging (LIDAR), or other technologies.

LIDAR uses lasers attached to planes and other equipment to digitally map the topography of the earth. It is often more accurate than traditional surveying methods and also can be used to collect other forms of data, such as the location and density of forests. Data developed by LIDAR can be used by surveyors, cartographers, and photogrammetrists to provide spatial information to specialists in geology, seismology, forestry, construction, and other fields.

Geographic Information Systems (GIS) have become an integral tool for surveyors, cartographers, photogrammetrists, and surveying and mapping technicians. Workers use GIS to assemble, integrate, analyze, and display data about location in a digital format. They also use GIS to compile information from a variety of sources. GIS typically are used to make maps which combine information useful for environmental studies, geology, engineering, planning, business marketing, and other disciplines. As more of these systems are developed, many mapping specialists are being called *geographic information specialists*.

Work environment. Surveyors and surveying technicians usually work an 8-hour day, 5 days a week and may spend a lot of time outdoors. Sometimes, they work longer hours during the summer, when weather and light conditions are most suitable for field work. Construction-related work may be limited during times of inclement weather.

Surveyors and technicians engage in active, sometimes strenuous, work. They often stand for long periods, walk considerable distances, and climb hills with heavy packs of instruments and other equipment. They also can be exposed to all types of weather. Traveling is sometimes part of the job, and surveyors and technicians may commute long distances, stay away from home overnight, or temporarily relocate near a survey site. Surveyors also work indoors while planning surveys, searching court records for deed information, analyzing data, and preparing reports and maps.

Cartographers and photogrammetrists spend most of their time in offices using computers. However, certain jobs may require extensive field work to verify results and acquire data.

Training, Other Qualifications, and Advancement

Most surveyors, cartographers, and photogrammetrists have a bachelor's degree in surveying or a related field. Every state requires that surveyors be licensed.

Education and training. In the past, many people with little formal training started as members of survey crews and worked their way up to become licensed surveyors, but this has become increasingly difficult. Now, most surveyors need a bachelor's degree. A number of universities offer bachelor's degree programs in surveying, and many community colleges, technical institutes, and vocational schools offer one-year, two-year, and three-year programs in surveying or surveying technology.

Cartographers and photogrammetrists usually have a bachelor's degree in cartography, geography, surveying, engineering, forestry, computer science, or a physical science, although a few enter these positions after working as technicians. With the development of GIS, cartographers and photogrammetrists need more education and stronger technical skills—including more experience with computers—than in the past.

Most cartographic and photogrammetric technicians also have specialized postsecondary education. High school students interested in surveying and cartography should take courses in algebra, geometry, trigonometry, drafting, mechanical drawing, and computer science.

Licensure. All 50 states and all U.S. territories license surveyors. For licensure, most state licensing boards require that individuals pass a series of written examinations given by the National Council of Examiners for Engineering and Surveying (NCEES). After passing a first exam, the Fundamentals of Surveying, most candidates work under the supervision of an experienced surveyor for four years before taking a second exam, the Principles and Practice of Surveying. Additionally, most states also require surveyors to pass a written examination prepared by the state licensing board.

Specific requirements for training and education vary among the states. An increasing number of states require a bachelor's degree in surveying or in a closely related field, such as civil engineering or forestry, regardless of the number of years of experience. Some states require the degree to be from a school accredited by the Accreditation Board for Engineering and Technology (ABET). Most states also have a continuing education requirement.

Additionally, a number of states require cartographers and photogrammetrists to be licensed as surveyors, and some states have specific licenses for photogrammetrists.

Other qualifications. Surveyors, cartographers, and photogrammetrists should be able to visualize objects, distances, sizes, and abstract forms. They must work with precision and accuracy because mistakes can be costly. Surveying and mapping are cooperative operations, so good interpersonal skills and the ability to work as part of a team are important.

Certification and advancement. High school graduates with no formal training in surveying usually start as apprentices. Beginners with postsecondary school training in surveying usually can start as technicians or assistants. With on-the-job experience and formal training in surveying—either in an institutional program or from a correspondence school—workers may advance to senior survey technician, then to party chief. Depending on state licensing requirements, they may advance to licensed surveyor in some cases.

The National Society of Professional Surveyors, a member organization of the American Congress on Surveying and Mapping, has a voluntary certification program for surveying technicians. Technicians are certified at four levels requiring progressive amounts of experience and the passing of written examinations. Although it is not required for state licensure, many employers require certification for promotion to positions with greater responsibilities.

The American Society for Photogrammetry and Remote Sensing (ASPRS) has voluntary certification programs for technicians and professionals in photogrammetry, remote sensing, and GIS. To qualify for these professional distinctions, individuals must meet work experience and training standards and pass a written examination. The professional recognition these certifications bestow can help workers gain promotions.

Employment

Surveyors, cartographers, photogrammetrists, and surveying technicians held about 147,000 jobs in 2008. Employment was distributed by occupational specialty as follows:

Surveying and mapping technicians 77,000
Surveyors 57,600
Cartographers and photogrammetrists................... 12,300

The architectural, engineering, and related services industry—including firms that provided surveying and mapping services to other industries on a contract basis—provided 7 out of 10 jobs for these workers. Federal, state, and local governmental agencies provided about 15 percent of these jobs. Major federal government employers are the U.S. Geological Survey (USGS), the Bureau of Land Management (BLM), the National Oceanic and Atmospheric Administration, the U.S. Forest Service, and the Army Corps of Engineers. Most surveyors in state and local government work for highway departments or urban planning and redevelopment agencies. Utility companies also employ surveyors, cartographers, photogrammetrists, and surveying technicians.

Job Outlook

These occupations should experience faster than average employment growth. Surveyors, cartographers, and photogrammetrists who have a bachelor's degree and strong technical skills should have favorable job prospects.

Employment change. Employment of surveyors, cartographers, photogrammetrists, and surveying and mapping technicians is expected to grow 19 percent from 2008 to 2018, which is faster than the average for all occupations. Increasing demand for fast, accurate, and complete geographic information will be the main source of job growth.

An increasing number of firms are interested in geographic information and its applications. For example, GIS can be used to create maps and information used in emergency planning, security, marketing, urban planning, natural resource exploration, construction, and other applications. Also, the increased popularity of online interactive mapping systems and GPS devices has created a higher demand for and awareness of current and accurate digital geographic information among consumers.

Growth in construction stemming from increases in the population and the related need to upgrade the nation's infrastructure will cause growth for surveyors and surveying technicians who ensure that projects are completed with precision and in line with original plans. These workers are usually the first on the job for any major construction project, and they provide information and recommendations to engineers, architects, contractors, and other professionals during all phases of a construction project.

Job prospects. In addition to openings from growth, job openings will continue to arise from the need to replace workers who transfer to other occupations or who leave the labor force altogether. Many cartographers and surveyors are approaching retirement

Projections Data from the National Employment Matrix

Occupational title	SOC Code	Employment, 2008	Projected employment, 2018	Change, 2008–2018	
				Number	Percent
Surveyors, cartographers, photogrammetrists, and surveying and mapping technicians .... —		147,000	174,500	27,600	19
Surveyors, cartographers, and photogrammetrists 17-1020		70,000	81,800	11,900	17
Cartographers and photogrammetrists 17-1021		12,300	15,600	3,300	27
Surveyors 17-1022		57,600	66,200	8,600	15
Surveying and mapping technicians 17-3031		77,000	92,700	15,700	20

NOTE: Data in this table are rounded.

age. Surveyors, cartographers, and photogrammetrists who have a bachelor's degree and strong technical skills should have favorable job prospects.

Opportunities for surveyors, cartographers, photogrammetrists, and technicians should remain concentrated in engineering, surveying, mapping, building inspection, and drafting services firms. Increasing demand for geographic data, as opposed to traditional surveying services, will mean better opportunities for mapping technicians and professionals who are involved in the development and use of GIS and digital mapmaking.

The demand for traditional surveying services is strongly tied to construction activity, and opportunities will vary by year and geographic region, depending on local economic conditions. During a recession, when real estate sales and construction slow down, surveyors and surveying technicians may face greater competition for jobs and sometimes layoffs. However, because these workers can work on many different types of projects, they may have steadier work than other workers when construction slows.

Earnings

Median annual wages of cartographers and photogrammetrists were $54,050 in May 2009. The middle 50 percent earned between $41,050 and $71,030. The lowest 10 percent earned less than $32,520 and the highest 10 percent earned more than $90,410.

Median annual wages of surveyors were $54,180 in May 2009. The middle 50 percent earned between $39,400 and $72,140. The lowest 10 percent earned less than $30,130 and the highest 10 percent earned more than $89,120. Median annual earnings of surveyors employed in architectural, engineering, and related services were $52,790 in May 2009.

Median annual wages of surveying and mapping technicians were $37,190 in May 2009. The middle 50 percent earned between $28,730 and $48,700. The lowest 10 percent earned less than $22,680, and the highest 10 percent earned more than $59,780. Median annual wages of surveying and mapping technicians employed in architectural, engineering, and related services were $34,720 in May 2009, while those employed by local governments had median annual wages of $41,990.

Related Occupations

Workers who use surveying data in land development and construction include architects, except landscape and naval; engineers; and landscape architects.

Cartography is related to the work of environmental scientists and specialists; social scientists, other; and urban and regional planners.

Sources of Additional Information

For career information on surveyors, cartographers, photogrammetrists, and surveying technicians, contact

▶ American Congress on Surveying and Mapping, 6 Montgomery Village Ave., Suite 403, Gaithersburg, MD 20879. Internet: www.acsm.net

Information about career opportunities, licensure requirements, and the surveying technician certification program is available from

▶ National Society of Professional Surveyors, 6 Montgomery Village Ave., Suite 403, Gaithersburg, MD 20879. Internet: www.nspsmo.org

For information on a career as a geodetic surveyor, contact

▶ American Association of Geodetic Surveying (AAGS), 6 Montgomery Village Ave., Suite 403, Gaithersburg, MD 20879. Internet: www.aagsmo.org

For career information on photogrammetrists, photogrammetric technicians, remote sensing scientists, and image-based cartographers or geographic information system specialists, contact

▶ ASPRS: Imaging and Geospatial Information Society, 5410 Grosvenor Lane, Suite 210, Bethesda, MD 20814-2160. Internet: www.asprs.org

Information about careers in remote sensing, photogrammetry, surveying, GIS, and other geography-related disciplines also is available from the Spring 2005 *Occupational Outlook Quarterly* article "Geography Jobs," available online at www.bls.gov/opub/ooq/2005/spring/art01.pdf.

Teacher Assistants

(O*NET 25-9041.00)

Significant Points

■ Almost 40 percent of teacher assistants work part time.

■ Educational requirements range from a high school diploma to some college training.

■ Favorable job prospects are expected.

■ Opportunities should be best for those with at least two years of formal postsecondary education, those with experience in helping special education students, or those who can speak a foreign language.

Nature of the Work

Teacher assistants provide instructional and clerical support for classroom teachers, allowing teachers more time for lesson planning and teaching. They support and assist children in learning class material using the teacher's lesson plans, providing students with individualized attention. Teacher assistants also supervise students in the cafeteria, schoolyard, and hallways, or on field trips; they record grades, set up equipment, and help prepare materials for instruction. Teacher assistants also are called *teacher aides* or *instructional aides*. Some assistants refer to themselves as *paraprofessionals* or *paraeducators*.

Some teacher assistants perform exclusively noninstructional or clerical tasks, such as monitoring nonacademic settings. Playground and lunchroom attendants are examples of such assistants. Most teacher assistants, however, perform a combination of instructional and clerical duties. They generally provide instructional reinforcement to children, under the direction and guidance of teachers. They work with students individually or in small groups—listening while students read, reviewing or reinforcing class lessons, or helping them find information for reports. At the secondary school level, teacher assistants often specialize in a certain subject, such as math or science. Teacher assistants often take charge of special projects and prepare equipment or exhibits, such as for a science demonstration. Some assistants work in computer laboratories, helping students to use computers and educational software programs.

In addition to instructing, assisting, and supervising students, teacher assistants may grade tests and papers, check homework, keep health and attendance records, do typing and filing, and duplicate materials. They also stock supplies, operate audiovisual equipment, and keep classroom equipment in order.

Many teacher assistants work extensively with special education students. As schools become more inclusive and integrate special education students into general education classrooms, teacher assistants in both general education and special education classrooms increasingly assist students with disabilities. They attend to the physical needs of students with disabilities, including feeding, teaching grooming habits, and assisting students riding the school bus. They also provide personal attention to students with other special needs, such as those who speak English as a second language and those who need remedial education. Some work with young adults to help them obtain a job or to help them apply for community services that will support them after their schooling ends. Teacher assistants help assess a student's progress by observing the student's performance and recording relevant data.

Although the majority of teacher assistants work in primary and secondary educational settings, others work in preschools and other child care centers. Often, one or two assistants will work with a lead teacher in order to better provide the individual attention that young children require. In addition to assisting in educational instruction, teacher assistants supervise the children at play and assist in feeding and other basic care activities.

Teacher assistants also work with infants and toddlers who have developmental delays or other disabilities. Under the guidance of a teacher or therapist, teacher assistants perform exercises or play games to help the child develop physically and behaviorally.

Work environment. Teacher assistants work in a variety of settings—including preschools, child care centers, and religious and community centers, where they work with young adults—but most work in classrooms in elementary, middle, and secondary schools.

They also may work outdoors, supervising recess when weather allows, and they may spend time standing, walking, or kneeling. However, many spend much of the day sitting while working with students.

Approximately 40 percent of teacher assistants work part time. Most assistants who provide educational instruction work the traditional 9-month to 10-month school year.

Seeing students develop and learn can be very rewarding. However, working closely with students can be both physically and emotionally tiring. Teacher assistants who work with special education students often perform more strenuous tasks, including lifting, as they help students with their daily routine. Those who perform clerical work may tire of administrative duties, such as copying materials or entering data.

Training, Other Qualifications, and Advancement

Training requirements for teacher assistants vary by state or school district and range from a high school diploma to some college training. Increasingly, employers are preferring applicants with some related college coursework.

Education and training. Many teacher assistants need only a high school diploma and on-the-job training. However, a college degree or related coursework in child development improves job opportunities. In fact, teacher assistants who work in Title 1 schools—those with a large proportion of students from low-income households—must have college training or proven academic skills. They face federal mandates that require assistants to hold a two-year or higher degree, have a minimum of two years of college, or pass a rigorous state or local assessment.

A number of colleges offer associate degrees or certificate programs that either prepare graduates to work as teacher assistants or provide additional training for current teacher assistants.

All teacher assistants receive some on-the-job training. Teacher assistants need to become familiar with the school system and with the operation and rules of the school they work in. Those who tutor and review lessons must learn and understand the class materials and instructional methods used by the teacher. Teacher assistants also must know how to operate audiovisual equipment, keep records, and prepare instructional materials, as well as have adequate computer skills.

Other qualifications. Many schools require previous experience in working with children and a valid driver's license. Most require the applicant to pass a background check. Teacher assistants should enjoy working with children from a wide range of cultural backgrounds and be able to handle classroom situations with fairness and patience. Teacher assistants also must demonstrate initiative and a willingness to follow a teacher's directions. They must have good writing skills and be able to communicate effectively with students and teachers. Teacher assistants who speak a second language, especially Spanish, are in great demand for communicating with growing numbers of students and parents whose primary language is not English.

Advancement. Advancement for teacher assistants—usually in the form of higher earnings or increased responsibility—comes primarily with experience or additional education. Some school districts provide time away from the job or tuition reimbursement so that teacher assistants can earn their bachelor's degrees and pursue

Projections Data from the National Employment Matrix

Occupational title	SOC Code	Employment, 2008	Projected employment, 2018	Change, 2008–2018	
				Number	Percent
Teacher assistants....................................	25-9041	1,312,700	1,447,600	134,900	10

NOTE: Data in this table are rounded.

licensed teaching positions. In return for tuition reimbursement, assistants are often required to teach for a certain length of time in the school district.

Employment

Teacher assistants held about 1.3 million jobs in 2008. Many worked for public and private educational institutions. Child care centers and religious organizations employed most of the rest.

Job Outlook

Many job openings are expected for teacher assistants due to turnover and about as fast as the average employment growth in this large occupation, resulting in favorable job prospects.

Employment change. Employment of teacher assistants is expected to grow by 10 percent between 2008 and 2018, which is about as fast as the average for all occupations. School enrollments are projected to increase slowly over the next decade, but faster growth is expected among special education students and students for whom English is a second language, and those students will increase as a share of the total school-age population. Teacher assistants often are necessary to provide these students with the attention they require.

Legislation that requires both students with disabilities and nonnative English speakers to receive an education equal to that of other students will continue to generate jobs for teacher assistants, who help to accommodate these students' special needs. Children with special needs require more personal attention, and teachers rely heavily on teacher assistants to provide much of that attention. An increasing number of afterschool programs and summer programs also will create new opportunities for teacher assistants.

The greater focus on school quality and accountability that has prevailed in recent years is likely to lead to an increased demand for teacher assistants as well. Growing numbers of teacher assistants may be needed to help teachers prepare students for standardized testing and to provide extra assistance to students who perform poorly on the tests. Job growth of assistants may be moderated, however, if schools are encouraged to hire more teachers for instructional purposes.

Job prospects. Favorable job prospects are expected. Opportunities for teacher assistant jobs should be best for those with at least two years of formal postsecondary education, those with experience in helping special education students, and those who can speak a foreign language. Demand is expected to vary by region of the country. Regions in which the population and school enrollments are expected to grow faster, such as many communities in the South and West, should have rapid growth in the demand for teacher assistants.

In addition to job openings stemming from employment growth, numerous openings will arise as assistants leave their jobs and must be replaced. Many assistant jobs require limited formal education and offer relatively low pay, so many workers transfer to other occupations or leave the labor force to assume family responsibilities, return to school, or for other reasons.

Although opportunities will be favorable, there may be a limited number of full-time positions because many school districts prefer to hire these workers part time.

Earnings

Median annual wages of teacher assistants in May 2009 were $22,820. The middle 50 percent earned between $18,260 and $28,820. The lowest 10 percent earned less than $15,870, and the highest 10 percent earned more than $35,350.

Full-time workers usually receive health coverage and other benefits. Teacher assistants who work part time ordinarily do not receive benefits. In 2008, about 37 percent of teacher assistants belonged to unions or were covered by a union contract—mainly the American Federation of Teachers and the National Education Association—which bargain with school systems over wages, hours, and the terms and conditions of employment.

Related Occupations

Teacher assistants who instruct children have duties similar to those of child care workers; library technicians and library assistants; occupational therapist assistants and aides; teachers—kindergarten, elementary, middle and secondary; teachers—preschool, except special education; teachers—special education; and teachers—vocational.

Sources of Additional Information

For information on teacher assistants, including training and certification, contact

▶ American Federation of Teachers, Paraprofessional and School Related Personnel Division, 555 New Jersey Ave. NW, Washington, DC 20001. Internet: www.aft.org/psrp/index.html

▶ National Education Association, Educational Support Personnel Division, 1201 16th St. NW, Washington, DC 20036. Internet: www.nea.org/esphome

▶ National Resource Center for Paraprofessionals, 6526 Old Main Hill, Utah State University, Logan, UT 84322. Internet: www.nrcpara.org

Human resource departments in school systems, school administrators, and state departments of education also can provide details about employment opportunities and required qualifications for teacher assistant jobs.

Teachers—Preschool, Except Special Education

(O*NET 25-2011.00)

Significant Points

- Training requirements are set by each state and range from a high school diploma to a college degree, although a high school diploma and a little experience are adequate for many preschool teaching jobs.

- Employment of preschool teachers is projected to grow faster than the average through 2018. Job prospects are expected to be excellent due to high turnover.

Nature of the Work

Preschool teachers nurture, teach, and care for children who have not yet entered kindergarten. They provide early childhood care and education through a variety of teaching strategies. They teach children, usually aged 3 to 5, both in groups and one on one. They do so by planning and implementing a curriculum that covers various areas of a child's development, such as motor skills, social and emotional development, and language development.

Preschool teachers play a vital role in the development of children. They introduce children to reading and writing, expanded vocabulary, creative arts, science, and social studies. They use games, music, artwork, films, books, computers, and other tools to teach concepts and skills.

Preschool children learn mainly through investigation, play, and formal teaching. Preschool teachers capitalize on children's play to further language and vocabulary development (using storytelling, rhyming games, and acting games), improve social skills (having the children work together to build a neighborhood in a sandbox), and introduce scientific and mathematical concepts (showing the children how to balance and count blocks when building a bridge or how to mix colors when painting). Thus, an approach that includes small and large group activities, one-on-one instruction, and learning through creative activities such as art, dance, and music, is adopted to teach preschool children. Letter recognition, phonics, numbers, and awareness of nature and science are introduced at the preschool level to prepare students for kindergarten.

Preschool teachers often work with students from varied ethnic, racial, and religious backgrounds. With growing minority populations in most parts of the country, it is important for teachers to be able to work effectively with a diverse student population. Accordingly, some schools offer training to help teachers enhance their awareness and understanding of different cultures. Teachers may also include multicultural programming in their lesson plans, to address the needs of all students, regardless of their cultural background.

Work environment. Seeing students develop new skills and gain an appreciation of knowledge and learning can be very rewarding. Preschool teachers in private programs and schools generally enjoy smaller class sizes and more control over establishing the curriculum and setting standards for performance and discipline.

Part-time schedules are common among preschool teachers. Many teachers work the traditional 10-month school year with a 2-month vacation during the summer. During the vacation break, those on the 10-month schedule may teach in summer sessions, take other jobs, travel, or pursue personal interests. Many enroll in college courses or workshops to continue their education. Teachers in districts with a year-round schedule typically work 8 weeks, are on vacation for 1 week, and have a 5-week midwinter break. Preschool teachers working in day care settings often work year round.

Training, Other Qualifications, and Advancement

Education requirements vary greatly from state to state and range from a high school diploma to a college degree. The requirements also vary based on employer requirements and the source of the funding of the preschool program.

Education and training. The training and qualifications required of preschool teachers vary widely. Each state has its own licensing requirements that regulate caregiver training. These requirements range from a high school diploma and a national Child Development Associate (CDA) credential to community college courses or a college degree in child development or early childhood education.

Different public funding streams may set other education and professional development requirements. For example, many states have separate funding for prekindergarten programs for 4-year-old children and typically set higher education degree requirements for those teachers, including those providing prekindergarten in a child care center. Head Start programs must meet federal standards for teacher requirements. For example, by 2011 all Head Start teachers must have at least an associate degree.

Some employers may prefer workers who have taken secondary or postsecondary courses in child development and early childhood education or who have work experience in a child care setting. Other employers require their own specialized training. An increasing number of employers require at least an associate degree in early childhood education

Other qualifications. In addition to being knowledgeable about the subjects they teach, preschool teachers must have the ability to communicate, inspire trust and confidence, and motivate students, as well as an understanding of the students' educational and emotional needs. Preschool teachers must be able to recognize and respond to individual and cultural differences in students and employ different teaching methods that will result in higher student achievement. They should be organized, dependable, patient, and creative. Teachers also must be able to work cooperatively and communicate effectively with other teachers, support staff, parents, and members of the community. Private schools associated with religious institutions also desire candidates who share the values that are important to the institution.

Advancement. Preschool teachers usually work their way up from assistant teacher, to teacher, to lead teacher—who may be responsible for the instruction of several classes—and, finally, to director of the center. Those with a bachelor's degree frequently are qualified to teach kindergarten through grade 3 as well. Teaching at these higher grades often results in higher pay.

Employment

Preschool teachers, except special education, held 457,200 jobs in 2008. They are most often employed in child day care services (65 percent), and public and private educational services (15 percent).

Projections Data from the National Employment Matrix

Occupational title	SOC Code	Employment, 2008	Projected employment, 2018	Change, 2008–2018	
				Number	Percent
Preschool teachers, except special education............25-2011		457,200	543,900	86,700	19

NOTE: Data in this table are rounded.

Employment of teachers is geographically distributed much the same as the population.

Job Outlook

Employment of preschool teachers is projected to grow faster than the average through 2018. Job prospects are expected to be excellent due to high turnover.

Employment change. Employment of preschool teachers is expected to grow by 19 percent from 2008 to 2018, which is faster than the average for all occupations. Continued emphasis on early childhood education is increasing the demand for preschool teachers. Some states are instituting programs to improve early childhood education, such as offering full-day and universal preschool. These programs, along with projected higher enrollment growth for preschool age children, will create new jobs for preschool teachers.

However, this growth will be moderated by slower growth in the number of children aged 3 to 5, the age group most often enrolled in preschool programs. In addition, these workers are often assisted by child care workers and teacher assistants and higher demand for these workers may temper growth for preschool teachers.

Job prospects. High replacement needs should create good job opportunities for preschool teachers. Qualified persons who are interested in this work should have little trouble finding and keeping a job. Many preschool teachers must be replaced each year as they leave the occupation to fulfill family responsibilities, to study, or for other reasons. Others leave because they are interested in pursuing other occupations or because of low wages.

Earnings

Median annual wages of preschool teachers were $24,540 in May 2009; the middle 50 percent earned $19,280 to $32,240; the bottom 10 percent earned less than $16,420 and the top 10 percent earned more than $43,570.

Related Occupations

Preschool teaching requires a talent for working with young children; related occupations include the following: child care workers; teachers assistants; teachers—kindergarten, elementary, middle, secondary; and teachers—special education.

Sources of Additional Information

Information on licensure or certification requirements and approved teacher training institutions is available from local school systems and state departments of education.

For information on careers in educating children and issues affecting preschool teachers, contact either of the following organizations:

▸ National Association for the Education of Young Children, 1313 L St. NW, Suite 500, Washington, DC 20005. Internet: www.naeyc.org

▸ Council for Professional Recognition, 2460 16th St. NW, Washington, DC 20009-3575. Internet: www.cdacouncil.org

Teachers—Self-Enrichment Education

(O*NET 25-3021.00)

Significant Points

■ Many self-enrichment teachers are self-employed or work part time.

■ Teachers should have knowledge and enthusiasm for their subject, but little formal training is required.

■ Employment is projected to grow much faster than the average for all occupations and job prospects should be favorable; opportunities may vary by subject taught.

Nature of the Work

Self-enrichment teachers provide instruction on a wide variety of subjects that students take for fun or self-improvement. Some teach classes that provide students with useful life skills, such as cooking, personal finance, and time management. Others provide group instruction intended solely for recreation, such as photography, pottery, and painting. Many others provide one-on-one instruction in a variety of subjects, including singing, or playing a musical instrument. Some teachers conduct courses on academic subjects, such as literature, foreign languages, and history, in a nonacademic setting. The classes taught by self-enrichment teachers seldom lead to a degree, and attendance is voluntary. At the same time, these courses can provide students with useful skills, such as knowledge of computers or foreign languages, which make them more attractive to employers.

Among self-enrichment teachers, their styles and methods of instruction can differ greatly. Most self-enrichment classes are relatively informal. Some classes, such as pottery or sewing, may be largely hands-on, with the instructor demonstrating methods or techniques for the class, observing students as they attempt to do it themselves, and pointing out mistakes to students and offering suggestions for improving their techniques. Other classes, such as those involving financial planning or religion and spirituality, might center on lectures or rely more heavily on group discussions. Self-enrichment teachers may also teach classes offered through religious institutions, such as marriage preparation or classes in religion for children.

Many of the classes that self-enrichment educators teach are shorter in duration than classes taken for academic credit; some finish in 1 or 2 days or several weeks. These brief classes tend to be introductory in nature and generally focus on only one topic—for example, a cooking class that teaches students how to make bread. Some self-enrichment classes introduce children and youth to activities such as piano or drama, and they may be designed to last from 1 week to several months.

Many self-enrichment teachers provide one-on-one lessons to students. The instructor might only work with the student for 1 or 2 hours per week and then provide the student with instructions on what to practice in the interim until the next lesson. Many instructors work with the same students on a weekly basis for years and derive satisfaction from observing them mature and gain expertise.

All self-enrichment teachers must prepare lessons beforehand and stay current in their fields. The amount of time required for preparation can vary greatly, depending on the subject being taught and the length of the course. Many self-enrichment teachers are self-employed and provide instruction as part of a personal business. As such, they must collect any fees or tuition and keep records of their students' accounts. Although doing so is not a requirement for most self-enrichment classes, teachers often use computers and other modern technologies in their instruction or to maintain their business records.

Work environment. Few self-enrichment education teachers are full-time salaried workers. Most either work part time or are self-employed. Some have several part-time teaching assignments, but it is most common for teachers to have a full-time job in another occupation, often related to the subject that they teach. Although jobs in this occupation are primarily part time and pay is relatively low, most teachers enjoy their work because it gives them the opportunity to share with others a subject that they enjoy.

Many classes for adults are held in the evenings and on weekends to accommodate students who have a job or family responsibilities. Similarly, self-enrichment classes for children are usually held after school, on weekends, or during school vacations.

Because students in self-enrichment programs attend classes by choice, they tend to be highly motivated and eager to learn. Students bring their own unique experiences to class, and many teachers find this aspect of the work especially rewarding and satisfying. Self-enrichment teachers must have a great deal of patience, however, particularly when working with young children.

Training, Other Qualifications, and Advancement

The main qualification for self-enrichment teachers is expertise in their subject area, but requirements vary greatly with the type of class taught and the place of employment.

Education and training. In general, there are few educational or training requirements for a job as a self-enrichment teacher beyond being an expert in the subject taught. To demonstrate expertise, however, self-enrichment teachers may be required to have formal training in disciplines such as art or music, where specific teacher training programs are available. Prospective dance teachers, for

example, may complete programs that prepare them to teach many types of dance—from ballroom to ballet. Other employers may require a portfolio of a teacher's work. For example, to secure a job teaching a photography course, an applicant often needs to show examples of previous work. Some self-enrichment teachers are trained educators or other professionals who teach enrichment classes in their spare time. In many self-enrichment fields, however, instructors are simply experienced in the field, and want to share that experience with others.

Other qualifications. Self-enrichment teachers should have good speaking skills and a talent for making the subject interesting. Patience and the ability to explain and instruct students at a basic level are important as well, particularly for teachers who work with children.

Advancement. Opportunities for advancement in this profession are limited. Some part-time teachers are able to move into full-time teaching positions or program administrator positions, such as coordinator or director. Experienced teachers may mentor new instructors.

Employment

Teachers of self-enrichment education held about 253,600 jobs in 2008. The largest numbers of teachers were employed by public and private educational institutions and providers of social assistance.

Job Outlook

Employment of self-enrichment education teachers is expected to grow much faster than the average for all occupations, and job prospects should be favorable. New opportunities arise constantly because many of these kinds of jobs are short term and they are often held as a second job.

Employment change. Employment of self-enrichment education teachers is expected to increase over the 2008–2018 period by 32 percent, which is much faster than the average for all occupations. The need for self-enrichment teachers is expected to grow as more people embrace lifelong learning and course offerings expand. Demand for self-enrichment education will also increase, as more people seek to gain or improve skills that will make them more attractive to prospective employers. Some self-enrichment teachers offer instruction in foreign languages, computer programming or applications, public speaking, and many other subjects that help students gain marketable skills. People increasingly take courses to improve their job skills, which creates more demand for self-enrichment teachers.

Job prospects. Job prospects should be generally favorable in the coming decade, as increasing demand and high turnover create many opportunities. These opportunities may vary, however, because some fields have more prospective teachers than others. Opportunities should be best for teachers of subjects that are not easily researched on the Internet and those that benefit from hands-on

Projections Data from the National Employment Matrix

Occupational title	SOC Code	Employment, 2008	Projected employment, 2018	Change, 2008–2018	
				Number	Percent
Self-enrichment education teachers..........................25-3021		253,600	334,900	81,300	32

NOTE: Data in this table are rounded.

experiences, such as cooking, crafts, and the arts. Classes on self-improvement, personal finance, and computer and Internet-related subjects are also expected to be popular.

Earnings

Median hourly wages of self-enrichment teachers were $17.52 in May 2009. The middle 50 percent earned between $12.82 and $25.17. The lowest 10 percent earned less than $9.43, and the highest 10 percent earned more than $33.15. Self-enrichment teachers are generally paid by the hour or for each class that they teach. Earnings may also be tied to the number of students enrolled in the class.

Part-time instructors are usually paid for each class that they teach, and receive few benefits. Full-time teachers are generally paid a salary and may receive health insurance and other benefits.

Related Occupations

The work of self-enrichment teachers is closely related to artists and related workers; athletes, coaches, umpires, and related workers; dancers and choreographers; musicians, singers, and related workers; recreation workers; teachers—kindergarten, elementary, middle, and secondary; and teachers—preschool, except special education.

Sources of Additional Information

For information on employment of self-enrichment teachers, contact local schools, colleges, or companies that offer self-enrichment programs.

Welding, Soldering, and Brazing Workers

(O*NET 51-4121.00, 51-4121.06, 51-4121.07, and 51-4122.00)

Significant Points

- About two out of three jobs in this occupation are in manufacturing industries.

- Training ranges from a few weeks to several years of school and on-the-job training.

- Employment is projected to experience little or no change.

- Job prospects should be good for skilled welders because employers are reporting difficulty finding enough qualified people.

Nature of the Work

Welding is the most common way of permanently joining metal parts. In this process, heat is applied to metal pieces, melting and fusing them to form a permanent bond. Because of its strength, welding is used in shipbuilding, automobile manufacturing and repair, aerospace applications, and thousands of other manufacturing activities. Welding also is used to join beams in the construction of buildings, bridges, and other structures and to join pipes in pipelines, powerplants, and refineries.

Welders may work in a wide variety of industries, from car racing to manufacturing. The work done in the different industries and the equipment used may vary greatly. The most common and simplest type of welding today is arc welding, which uses electrical currents to create heat and bond metals together, but there are over 100 different processes that a welder can employ. The type of weld used is normally determined by the types of metals being joined and the conditions under which the welding is to take place. Steel, for instance, can be welded more easily than titanium. Some of these processes involve manually using a rod and heat to join metals, while others are semiautomatic, with a welding machine feeding wire to bond materials. Automated welding, done completely by robots, is increasingly being used in the manufacturing industry.

Like welders, *soldering and brazing workers* use molten metal to join two pieces of metal. However, the metal added during the soldering and brazing process has a melting point lower than that of the piece, so only the added metal is melted, not the piece. Soldering uses metals with a melting point below 840 degrees Fahrenheit; brazing uses metals with a higher melting point. Because soldering and brazing do not melt the pieces being joined, these processes normally do not create the distortions or weaknesses in the pieces that can occur with welding. Soldering commonly is used to make electrical and electronic circuit boards, such as computer chips. Soldering workers tend to work with small pieces that must be precisely positioned. Brazing often is used to connect copper plumbing pipes and thinner metals that the higher temperatures of welding would warp. Brazing also can be used to apply coatings to parts to reduce wear and protect against corrosion.

Skilled welding, soldering, and brazing workers generally plan work from drawings, called blueprints, or specifications and use their knowledge of welding processes and base metals to determine how best to join the parts. The difficulty of the weld is determined by its position—horizontal, vertical, overhead, or 6G (circular, as in large pipes)—and by the type of metals to be fused. Highly skilled welders often are trained to work with a wide variety of materials, such as titanium, aluminum, or plastics, in addition to steel. Welders then select and set up welding equipment, execute the planned welds, and examine the welds to ensure that they meet standards or specifications.

Automated welding is being used in an increasing number of production processes. In these instances, a machine or robot performs the welding tasks while being monitored by a welding machine operator. *Welding, soldering, and brazing machine setters, operators, and tenders* follow specified layouts, work orders, or blueprints. Operators must load parts correctly and monitor the machine constantly to ensure that it produces the desired bond. About 12 percent of all welding, soldering, and brazing workers operate automated machinery.

The work of *arc, plasma, and oxy-gas cutters* is closely related to that of welders. However, instead of joining metals, cutters use the heat from an electric arc, a stream of ionized gas called plasma, or burning gases to cut and trim metal objects to specific dimensions. Cutters also dismantle large objects, such as ships, railroad cars, automobiles, buildings, or aircraft. Some operate and monitor cutting machines similar to those used by welding machine operators.

Work environment. Welding, soldering, and brazing workers often are exposed to a number of hazards, including very hot materials and the intense light created by the arc. They wear safety shoes, goggles, masks with protective lenses, and other devices designed to prevent burns and eye injuries and to protect them from falling objects. The Occupational Safety and Health Administration (OSHA) requires that welders work in safely ventilated areas to avoid the danger from inhalation of gases and particulates that can result from welding processes. Because of these hazards, welding, soldering, and brazing workers suffer more work-related injuries than do workers in most occupations, but injuries can be minimized if proper safety procedures are followed. Automated welding, soldering, and brazing machine operators are not exposed to as many dangers, and a face shield or goggles usually provide adequate protection for these workers.

Welders and cutters may work outdoors, often in inclement weather, or indoors, sometimes in a confined area designed to contain sparks and glare. Outdoors, they may work on a scaffold or platform high off the ground. In addition, they may be required to lift heavy objects and work in a variety of awkward positions while bending, stooping, or standing to perform work overhead.

Although about 50 percent of welders, solderers, and brazers work a 40-hour week, overtime is common, and about 1 out of 5 welders works 50 hours per week or more. Many manufacturing firms offer two or three shifts, ranging from 8 to 12 hours, which allows them to continue production around the clock if needed.

Training, Other Qualifications, and Advancement

Training for welding, soldering, and brazing workers can range from a few weeks of school or on-the-job training for low-skilled positions to several years of combined school and on-the-job training for highly skilled jobs.

Education and training. Formal training is available in high schools and postsecondary institutions, such as vocational-technical institutes, community colleges, and private welding, soldering, and brazing schools. The U.S. Armed Forces operate welding and soldering schools as well. Some employers are willing to hire inexperienced entry-level workers and train them on the job, but many prefer to hire workers who have been through formal training programs. Courses in blueprint reading, shop mathematics, mechanical drawing, physics, chemistry, and metallurgy are helpful. An understanding of electricity also is very helpful, and knowledge of computers is gaining importance, especially for welding, soldering, and brazing machine operators, who are becoming more responsible for programming robots and other computer-controlled machines. Because understanding the welding process and inspecting welds are important for both welders and welding machine operators, companies hiring machine operators prefer workers with a background in welding.

Certification and other qualifications. Some welding positions require general certifications in welding or certifications in specific skills such as inspection or robotic welding. The American Welding Society certification courses are offered at many welding schools. Some employers have developed their own internal certification tests. Some employers are willing to pay training and testing costs for employees, while others require workers to pay for classes and certification themselves.

The Institute for Printed Circuits offers certifications and training in soldering. In industries such as aerospace and defense, where highly accurate and skilled work is required, many employers require these certifications. In addition, the increasing use of lead-free soldering techniques, which require more skill than traditional lead-based soldering techniques, has increased the importance of certification to employers.

Welding, soldering, and brazing workers need good eyesight, hand-eye coordination, and manual dexterity, along with good math, problem-solving, and communication skills. They should be able to concentrate on detailed work for long periods and be able to bend, stoop, and work in awkward positions. In addition, welders increasingly must be willing to receive training and perform tasks required in other production jobs.

Advancement. Welders can advance to more skilled welding jobs with additional training and experience. For example, they may become welding technicians, supervisors, inspectors, or instructors. Some experienced welders open their own repair shops. Other welders, especially those who obtain a bachelor's degree or have many years of experience, may become welding engineers.

Employment

In 2008, welders, cutters, solderers, and brazers held about 412,300 jobs and welding, soldering, and brazing machine setters, operators, and tenders held about 54,100 jobs. About 65 percent of welding jobs were found in manufacturing. Jobs were concentrated in fabricated metal product manufacturing, transportation equipment manufacturing, machinery manufacturing, architectural and structural metals manufacturing, and construction.

Job Outlook

Employment is projected to experience little or no change over the next decade. Good job opportunities are expected for skilled welders because some employers are reporting difficulty finding qualified workers.

Employment change. Employment of welders, cutters, solderers, and brazers is expected to experience little or no change, declining by about 2 percent over the 2008–2018 decade, while employment of welding, soldering, and brazing machine setters, operators, and tenders is expected to decline moderately by about 7 percent over the same decade. Continued enhancements in productivity and increased automation will reduce the need for welders, although the outlook for welders in manufacturing is stronger than that for other occupations in this industry because of the importance and versatility of welding as a manufacturing process. The basic skills of welding are the same across industries, so welders can easily shift from one industry to another, depending on where they are needed most. For example, welders laid off in the automotive manufacturing industry may be able to find work in the oil and gas industry, although the shift may require relocating.

Automation will affect welders and welding machine operators differently than other manufacturing occupations. Semiautomated and automated welding machines can be used for many types of welds, but welders still are needed to operate the machines and to inspect the weld and make adjustments. In addition, much of the work in custom applications is difficult or impossible to automate. This type of work includes manufacturing small batches of items, construction work, and making repairs in factories.

Job prospects. Job prospects for welders will vary with the welder's skill level. Prospects should be good for welders trained in the latest technologies. Welding schools report that graduates have little difficulty finding work, and many welding employers report difficulty finding properly skilled welders. However, welders without up-to-date training may face competition for job openings. For all welders, prospects will be better for workers who are willing to relocate to different parts of the country.

Projections Data from the National Employment Matrix

Occupational title	SOC Code	Employment, 2008	Projected employment, 2018	Change, 2008–2018	
				Number	Percent
Welding, soldering, and brazing workers 51-4120		466,400	455,900	−10,500	−2
Welders, cutters, solderers, and brazers 51-4121		412,300	405,600	−6,700	−2
Welding, soldering, and brazing machine setters, operators, and tenders 51-4122		54,100	50,300	−3,800	−7

NOTE: Data in this table are rounded.

Earnings

Median wages of welders, cutters, solderers, and brazers were $16.71 an hour in May 2009. The middle 50 percent earned between $13.60 and $20.39. The lowest 10 percent earned less than $11.26, and the top 10 percent earned more than $25.20. The range of wages of welders reflects the wide range of skill levels in the occupation. Median hourly wages of welders, cutters, solderers, and brazers in the industries employing the largest numbers of them were as follows:

Architectural and structural metals manufacturing ... 15.45
Agriculture, construction, and mining machinery
   manufacturing 16.85
Commercial and industrial machinery and
   equipment (except automotive and electronic)
   repair and maintenance 16.41
Other general-purpose machinery manufacturing.... $16.79
Motor vehicle body and trailer manufacturing.......... 15.38

Median wages of welding, soldering, and brazing machine setters, operators, and tenders were $15.74 an hour in May 2009. The middle 50 percent earned between $13.04 and $18.99. The lowest 10 percent earned less than $10.72, and the top 10 percent earned more than $22.93. Median wages in motor vehicle parts manufacturing, the industry employing these workers in the largest numbers, were $15.31 an hour in May 2009.

About 20 percent of welders belong to labor unions; the particular unions that welders belong to depend on the industry and company in which the welder is employed.

Related Occupations

Other skilled metal workers include the following: assemblers and fabricators; boilermakers; computer control programmers and operators; jewelers and precious stone and metal workers; machine setters, operators, and tenders—metal and plastic; machinists; plumbers, pipelayers, pipefitters, and steamfitters; sheet metal workers; and tool and die makers.

Sources of Additional Information

For information on training opportunities and jobs for welding, soldering, and brazing workers, contact local employers, the local office of the state employment service, or schools providing welding, soldering, or brazing training.

Information on careers, certifications, and educational opportunities in welding is available from

▶ American Welding Society, 550 N.W. LeJeune Rd., Miami, FL 33126. Internet: www.aws.org

▶ Fabricators and Manufacturers Association, 833 Featherstone Rd., Rockford, IL 61107 Internet: www.fmanet.org

Woodworkers

(O*NET 51-7011.00, 51-7021.00, 51-7031.00, 51-7032.00, 51-7041.00, 51-7042.00, and 51-7099.00)

Significant Points

■ Most woodworkers are trained on the job; becoming a skilled woodworker often requires several years of experience.

■ Job prospects should be excellent for highly skilled woodworkers who are proficient users of computerized numerical control machines.

■ Employment is highly sensitive to economic cycles; during economic downturns, workers are subject to layoffs or reductions in hours.

Nature of the Work

Despite the abundance of plastics, metals, and other materials, wood products continue to be an important part of our daily lives. Many of these products are mass produced, including most furniture, kitchen cabinets, and musical instruments. Other products are custom-crafted in shops using specialized tools. The people who design, produce, and test these products are called *woodworkers*.

Although the term woodworker may evoke the image of a craftsman who builds ornate furniture using hand tools, the modern woodworking trade is highly technical and relies on advanced equipment and highly skilled operators. Workers use automated machinery, such as computerized numerical control (CNC) machines, to do much of the work. Even specialized artisans generally use a variety of power tools in their work. Much of the work is often done in a high production assembly line facility, but there is also some work that is customized and does not lend itself to assembly line fabrication. Woodworkers are employed in every part of the secondary wood products industry—from sawmill to finished product—and their activities vary greatly.

Woodworkers set up, operate and tend all types of machines, such as drill presses, lathes, shapers, routers, sanders, planers, and wood-nailing machines. Operators set up the equipment; cut and shape wooden parts; and verify dimensions using a template, caliper, or rule. After wood parts are made, woodworkers add fasteners and adhesives and connect the pieces to form a complete unit. Products are then sanded, stained, and, if necessary, coated with a sealer, such as a lacquer or varnish.

In some cases, these tasks are managed by different workers with specialized training. For instance, *woodworking machine setters, operators, and tenders* may specialize in operating specific pieces of woodworking machinery. *Furniture finishers* stain and seal wood products; they often work with antiques and must make judgments about how to best preserve and repair them.

On the other hand, some woodworkers are less specialized, and must know how to complete many stages of the process. *Cabinetmakers* and *bench carpenters* often design and create sets of cabinets that are customized for particular spaces. In some cases, their duties could begin with designing a set of cabinets to particular specifications and end with installing them. *Architectural woodworkers* design and create customized wooden furniture and accents that are part of a building. This might include a desk that is built into a hotel lobby, a bar in a pub, or booths in a restaurant. Other woodworkers, such as *model makers*, create scale models of products or buildings that are used in construction; *patternmakers* construct dies that are used for castings.

Work environment. Working conditions vary greatly, depending on specific job duties. Workers may have to handle heavy, bulky materials and often encounter excessive noise and dust. Workers must often wear earplugs, gloves, and goggles to protect themselves. These occupations tend to have relatively high nonfatal injury rates, since woodworkers spend much of their time using power tools, which can be dangerous. Data from the U.S. Bureau of Labor Statistics show that sawing machine operators experienced a work-related injury and illness rate that was much higher than the national average.

Training, Other Qualifications, and Advancement

Becoming a fully trained woodworker requires many skills, and generally takes several years of on-the-job training. Skill with computers and computer-controlled machinery is increasingly important.

Education and training. Many employers seek applicants with a high school diploma or the equivalent because of the growing sophistication of machinery and the constant need for retraining. People seeking woodworking jobs can enhance their employment and advancement prospects by completing high school and receiving training in mathematics and computer applications.

Some woodworkers acquire skills through technical schools or community college courses. Others may attend universities that offer training in wood technology, furniture manufacturing, wood engineering, and production management. These programs prepare students for positions in production, supervision, engineering, and management and are increasingly important as woodworking technology advances.

While education is helpful, woodworkers are primarily trained on the job, where they learn skills from experienced workers. Beginning workers are assigned basic tasks, such as putting a piece of wood through a machine or catching the wood at the end of the process. As they gain experience, they perform more complex jobs with less supervision. They can learn basic machine operations and job tasks in about a year. Skilled workers learn to read blueprints, set up machines, and plan work sequences. Becoming a skilled woodworker often requires 3 or more years.

Other qualifications. In addition to training, woodworkers need mechanical ability, manual dexterity, and the ability to pay attention to detail and safety. They should be comfortable working with geometric concepts; for example, they must be able to visualize how shapes will fit together in three dimensions. Skill with computers and computer-controlled machinery is increasingly important in this high-tech occupation.

Advancement. Advancement opportunities depend on education and training, seniority, and a worker's skills and initiative. Experienced woodworkers often become supervisors responsible for the work of a group of woodworkers. Others may become full-time CNC operators, designing woodwork using computer-aided design software. Still others become inspectors, making sure that products are built to proper specifications. Production workers can advance into these positions by assuming additional responsibilities and attending workshops, seminars, or college programs. Those who are highly skilled may set up their own woodworking shops.

Employment

Woodworkers held about 323,300 jobs in 2008. Self-employed woodworkers accounted for 12 percent of these jobs. About 76 percent of woodworkers were employed in manufacturing. About 39 percent worked in establishments manufacturing furniture and related products, and 32 percent worked in wood product manufacturing, producing a variety of raw, intermediate, and finished woodstock. Wholesale and retail lumber dealers, furniture stores, reupholstery and furniture repair shops, and construction firms also employ woodworkers.

Woodworking jobs are found throughout the country. However, lumber and wood products-related production jobs are concentrated in the Southeast, Midwest, and Northwest, close to the supply of wood. Furniture-making jobs are more prevalent in the Southeast. Custom shops can be found everywhere, but generally are concentrated in or near highly populated areas.

Job Outlook

Employment of woodworkers is expected to grow more slowly than the average for all occupations. Job prospects will be excellent for highly qualified workers.

Employment change. Employment of woodworkers is expected to grow by 6 percent during the 2008–2018 decade, which is slower than the average for all occupations. Increased automation in the wood products manufacturing industry has led to slow job growth for some time, but this has been tempered in recent years by increased demand for domestic wood products. Technology has become very important to this industry, and automation has greatly reduced the number of people required to produce a finished product. While this has slowed employment growth somewhat, improved efficiency has made domestic wood products more competitive with imports.

Demand for these workers will stem from increases in population, personal income, and business expenditures and from the continuing need for repair and renovation of residential and commercial properties. Therefore, opportunities should be available for workers who specialize in items such as moldings, cabinets, stairs, and windows. Firms that focus on custom woodwork will be best able to compete against imports without transferring jobs offshore.

Projections Data from the National Employment Matrix

Occupational title	SOC Code	Employment, 2008	Projected employment, 2018	Change, 2008–2018	
				Number	Percent
Woodworkers...51-7000		323,300	344,000	20,600	6
Cabinetmakers and bench carpenters....................51-7011		131,700	143,700	11,900	9
Furniture finishers...51-7021		26,500	27,700	1,200	4
Model makers and patternmakers, wood...............51-7030		3,500	3,500	0	−1
Model makers, wood.......................................51-7031		1,700	1,700	0	2
Patternmakers, wood......................................51-7032		1,900	1,800	−100	−3
Woodworking machine setters, operators, and tenders...51-7040		138,400	145,100	6,700	5
Sawing machine setters, operators, and tenders, wood...51-7041		52,600	53,400	800	1
Woodworking machine setters, operators, and tenders, except sawing.............................51-7042		85,700	91,700	6,000	7
All other woodworkers......................................51-7099		23,300	24,000	800	3

NOTE: Data in this table are rounded.

Employment in all woodworking specialties is highly sensitive to economic cycles. During economic downturns, workers are subject to layoffs or reductions in hours.

Job prospects. Prospects should be excellent for highly qualified workers. In general, opportunities for more highly skilled woodworkers will be better than for woodworkers in specialties susceptible to automation and competition from imported wood products. The need for woodworkers with technical skills to operate their increasingly advanced computerized machinery will be especially great. Workers who know how to create and execute custom designs on a computer will be in strong demand. These jobs require an understanding of wood and a strong understanding of computers—a combination that can be somewhat difficult to find.

The number of new workers entering these occupations has declined greatly in recent years, as training programs become less available or popular. Opportunities should be best for woodworkers who, through vocational education or experience, develop highly specialized woodworking skills or knowledge of CNC machine tool operation.

Earnings

Median hourly wages of cabinetmakers and bench carpenters were $14.22 in May 2009. The middle 50 percent earned between $11.35 and $17.79. The lowest 10 percent earned less than $9.36, and the highest 10 percent earned more than $21.95.

Median hourly wages of sawing machine setters, operators, and tenders, wood were $12.51. The middle 50 percent earned between $9.95 and $15.43. The lowest 10 percent earned less than $8.40, and the highest 10 percent earned more than $19.05.

Median hourly wages of woodworking machine setters, operators, and tenders, except sawing were $12.25. The middle 50 percent earned between $9.98 and $15.07. The lowest 10 percent earned less than $8.46, and the highest 10 percent earned more than $18.18.

Median hourly wages were $13.26 for furniture finishers and $11.43 for all other woodworkers.

Related Occupations

Occupations that require similar skills include carpenters; computer control programmers and operators; machinists; sheet metal workers; and structural and reinforcing iron and metal workers.

Sources of Additional Information

For information about careers and education and training programs in woodworking, contact

▶ Architectural Woodwork Institute, 46179 Westlake Dr., Suite 120, Potomac Falls, VA 20165. Internet: www.awinet.org

▶ WoodIndustryEd.org, c/o AWFS, 500 Citadel Dr., Suite 200, Commerce, CA 90040. Internet: www.woodindustryed.org

▶ WoodLINKS USA, P.O. Box 445, Tuscola, IL 61953. Internet: www.woodlinksusa.org

QUICK
JOB SEARCH

Seven Steps to Getting a Good Job in Less Time

The Complete Text of a Results-Oriented Book by Michael Farr

Millions of job seekers have found better jobs faster using the techniques in the *Quick Job Search*. So can you! The *Quick Job Search* covers the essential steps proven to cut job search time in half and is used widely by job search programs throughout North America. Topics include how to identify your key skills, define your ideal job, write a great resume quickly, use the most effective job search methods, get more interviews, and much more.

If you completed "Using the Job-Match Grid to Choose a Career" earlier in this book, the activities in this section will complement those efforts by helping you to define other skills you possess, focus your resume, and get a job quickly.

While it is a section in this book, the *Quick Job Search* is available from JIST Publishing as a separate booklet.

Quick Job Search Is Short, But It May Be All You Need

While *Quick Job Search* is short, it covers the basics on how to explore career options and conduct an effective job search. While these topics can seem complex, I have found some simple truths about looking for a job:

- If you are going to work, you might as well look for what you really want to do and are good at.

- If you are looking for a job, you might as well use techniques that will reduce the time it takes to find one—and that help you get a better job than you might otherwise.

That's what I emphasize in *Quick Job Search*.

Trust Me—Do the Worksheets. I know you will resist completing the worksheets. But trust me. They are worth your time. Doing them will give you a better sense of what you are good at, what you want to do, and how to go about getting it. You will also most likely get more interviews and present yourself better. Is this worth giving up a night of TV? Yes, I think so.

Once you finish this book and its activities, you will have spent more time planning your career than most people do. And you will know more than the average job seeker about finding a job.

Why Such a Short Book? I've taught job-seeking skills for many years, and I've written longer and more-detailed books than this one. Yet I have often been asked to tell people, in a few minutes or hours, the most important things they should do in their career planning or job search. Instructors and counselors also ask the same question, because they have only a short time to spend with folks they're trying to help. I've given this a lot of thought, and the seven topics in this book are the ones I think are most important to know.

This book is short enough to scan in a morning and conduct a more effective job search that afternoon. Granted, doing all the activities would take more time, but they will prepare you far better than scanning the book. Of course, you can learn more about all the topics it covers, but this book, *Quick Job Search,* may be all you need.

I wish you well.

You can't just read about getting a job. The best way to get a job is to go out and get interviews! And the best way to get interviews is to make a job out of getting a job.

After many years of experience, I have identified just seven basic things you need to do that make a big difference in your job search. Each will be covered and expanded on in this book.

1. Identify your key skills and develop a "skills language" to describe yourself.

2. Define your ideal job.

3. Use the most effective methods to find a job in less time.

4. Write a simple resume now and a better one later.

5. Organize your time to get two interviews a day.

6. Dramatically improve your interviewing skills.

7. Follow up on all job leads.

So, without further delay, let's get started!

STEP 1: Identify Your Key Skills and Develop a "Skills Language" to Describe Yourself

One survey of employers found that about 90 percent of the people they interviewed might have the required job skills, but they could not describe those skills and thereby prove that they could do the job they sought. They could not answer the basic question "Why should I hire you?"

Knowing and describing your skills is essential to doing well in interviews. This same knowledge is important to help you decide what type of job you will enjoy and do well. For these reasons, I consider identifying your skills a necessary part of a successful career plan or job search.

The Three Types of Skills

Most people think of their skills as job-related skills, such as using a computer. But we all have other types of skills that are important for success on a job—and that are important to employers. The following triangle arranges skills in three groups, and I think that this is a very useful way to consider skills as you use this book, *Quick Job Search.*

Let's look at these three types of skills—self-management, transferable, and job-related—and identify those that are most important to you.

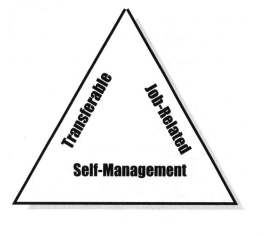

Self-Management Skills

Self-management skills (also known as adaptive skills or personality traits) are the things that make you a good worker. They describe your basic personality and your ability to adapt to new environments, as well as provide the foundation for other skills. They are some of the most important skills to emphasize in interviews, yet most job seekers don't realize their importance—and don't mention them.

Review the Self-Management Skills Checklist that follows and put a check mark beside any skills you have. The key self-management skills listed first cover abilities that employers find particularly important. If one or more of the key self-management skills apply to you, mentioning them in interviews can help you greatly.

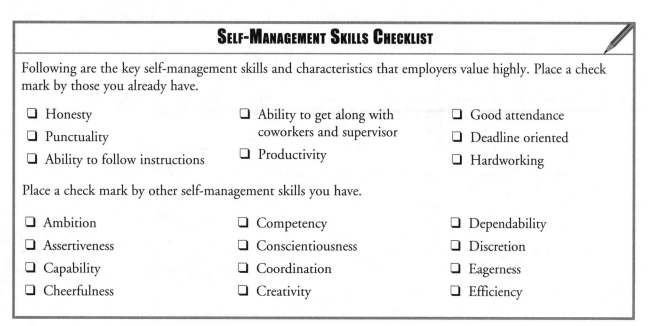

SELF-MANAGEMENT SKILLS CHECKLIST

Following are the key self-management skills and characteristics that employers value highly. Place a check mark by those you already have.

- ❏ Honesty
- ❏ Punctuality
- ❏ Ability to follow instructions

- ❏ Ability to get along with coworkers and supervisor
- ❏ Productivity

- ❏ Good attendance
- ❏ Deadline oriented
- ❏ Hardworking

Place a check mark by other self-management skills you have.

- ❏ Ambition
- ❏ Assertiveness
- ❏ Capability
- ❏ Cheerfulness

- ❏ Competency
- ❏ Conscientiousness
- ❏ Coordination
- ❏ Creativity

- ❏ Dependability
- ❏ Discretion
- ❏ Eagerness
- ❏ Efficiency

(continued)

(continued)

- ❑ Energy
- ❑ Enthusiasm
- ❑ Expression
- ❑ Flexibility
- ❑ Formality
- ❑ Friendliness
- ❑ Good nature
- ❑ Helpfulness
- ❑ Humbleness
- ❑ Imagination
- ❑ Independence
- ❑ Industriousness
- ❑ Informality
- ❑ Inquisitiveness
- ❑ Intelligence
- ❑ Intuition
- ❑ Leadership

- ❑ Learning ability
- ❑ Learning oriented
- ❑ Loyalty
- ❑ Maturity
- ❑ Methodicalness
- ❑ Modesty
- ❑ Motivation
- ❑ Open-mindedness
- ❑ Optimism
- ❑ Organization
- ❑ Originality
- ❑ Patience
- ❑ Persistence
- ❑ Physical strength
- ❑ Practice
- ❑ Pride
- ❑ Problem solving

- ❑ Reliability
- ❑ Responsibility
- ❑ Results orientation
- ❑ Self-confidence
- ❑ Self-motivation
- ❑ Sense of humor
- ❑ Sincerity
- ❑ Spontaneity
- ❑ Steadiness
- ❑ Tact
- ❑ Tenacity
- ❑ Thoroughness
- ❑ Thrift
- ❑ Trustworthiness
- ❑ Versatility

List the other self-management skills you have that are not on the list but you think are important to include.

_____

_____

_____

After you finish checking the list, circle the five skills you feel are most important for the job you want and write them in the box that follows.

YOUR TOP FIVE SELF-MANAGEMENT SKILLS

1. _____

2. _____

3. _____

4. _____

5. _____

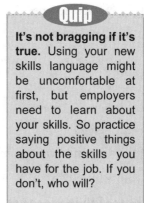

N o t e *When thinking about their skills, some people find it helpful to complete the Essential Job Search Data Worksheet that starts on page 341. It organizes skills and accomplishments from previous jobs and other life experiences. Take a look at it and decide whether to complete it now or later.*

Transferable Skills

Transferable skills are skills that can be used on more than one job. Often these skills are things that you naturally do well or that are an essential part of your personality, and are the foundations for other skills. We all have skills that can transfer from one job or career to another. For example, the ability to organize events could be used in a variety of jobs and may be essential for success in certain occupations.

Your mission is to find a job that requires the skills you have and enjoy using. But first, you need to identify your top transferable skills.

> **Quip**
>
> **It's not bragging if it's true.** Using your new skills language might be uncomfortable at first, but employers need to learn about your skills. So practice saying positive things about the skills you have for the job. If you don't, who will?

TRANSFERABLE SKILLS CHECKLIST

Following are the key transferable skills that employers value highly. Place a check mark by those you already have. You may have used them in a previous job or in some nonwork setting.

- ❑ Managing money/budgets
- ❑ Speaking in public
- ❑ Managing people
- ❑ Organizing/managing projects

- ❑ Meeting deadlines
- ❑ Solving problems
- ❑ Meeting the public
- ❑ Writing well

- ❑ Negotiating
- ❑ Increasing sales or efficiency

Place a check mark by the skills you have for **working with data.**

- ❑ Analyzing data
- ❑ Auditing/checking for accuracy
- ❑ Budgeting
- ❑ Calculating/computing
- ❑ Classifying data

- ❑ Comparing/evaluating
- ❑ Compiling/recording facts
- ❑ Counting/taking inventory
- ❑ Investigating
- ❑ Keeping financial records

- ❑ Observing/inspecting
- ❑ Paying attention to details
- ❑ Researching/locating information
- ❑ Synthesizing

Place a check mark by the skills you have for **working with people.**

- ❑ Administering
- ❑ Being diplomatic and tactful

- ❑ Being kind
- ❑ Being outgoing

- ❑ Being patient
- ❑ Being sensitive and empathetic

(continued)

(continued)

❑ Being sociable
❑ Caring for others
❑ Coaching
❑ Confronting others
❑ Counseling people
❑ Demonstrating

❑ Handling criticism
❑ Having insight
❑ Helping others
❑ Instructing/teaching others
❑ Interviewing people
❑ Listening

❑ Persuading
❑ Supervising
❑ Tolerating
❑ Trusting
❑ Understanding

Place a check mark by your skills in **working with words and ideas.**

❑ Being articulate
❑ Being inventive
❑ Being logical
❑ Communicating verbally
❑ Corresponding with others
❑ Creating new ideas
❑ Designing

❑ Editing
❑ Reasoning
❑ Remembering information
❑ Researching information
❑ Speaking publicly
❑ Writing clearly

Place a check mark by the **leadership skills** you have.

❑ Being competitive
❑ Delegating
❑ Directing others
❑ Explaining concepts
❑ Getting results
❑ Having self-confidence
❑ Influencing others
❑ Making decisions

❑ Mediating problems
❑ Motivating people
❑ Motivating yourself
❑ Negotiating agreements
❑ Planning
❑ Running meetings
❑ Solving problems
❑ Taking risks

Place a check mark by your **creative or artistic skills.**

❑ Appreciating music
❑ Creating, inventing
❑ Dancing
❑ Drawing, painting
❑ Expressing yourself artistically

❑ Performing/acting
❑ Playing instruments
❑ Presenting artistic ideas
❑ Writing creatively

Place a check mark by your skills for **working with things.**

❑ Assembling or making things
❑ Building, observing, and inspecting things
❑ Constructing or repairing things

❑ Driving or operating vehicles
❑ Operating tools/machines
❑ Using your hands

Add the other transferable skills you have that have not been mentioned but you think are important to include.

_____

_____

_____

When you are finished, circle the five transferable skills you feel are most important for you to use in your next job and list them below.

YOUR TOP FIVE TRANSFERABLE SKILLS

1. _____

2. _____

3. _____

4. _____

5. _____

Job-Related Skills

Job-content or job-related skills are those you need to do a particular occupation. A carpenter, for example, needs to know how to use various tools. Before you select job-related skills to emphasize, you must first have a clear idea of the jobs you want. So let's put off developing your job-related skills list until you have defined the job you want—the topic that is covered next.

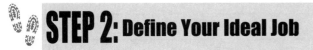

STEP 2: Define Your Ideal Job

Too many people look for a job without clearly knowing what they are looking for. Before you go out seeking a job, I suggest that you first define exactly what you want—not just _a job_ but _the job_.

Most people think that a job objective is the same as a job title, but it isn't. You need to consider other elements of what makes a job satisfying for you. Then, later, you can decide what that job is called and what industry it might be in. You can compromise on what you consider your ideal job later if you need to.

EIGHT FACTORS TO CONSIDER IN DEFINING YOUR IDEAL JOB

As you try to define your ideal job, consider the following eight important questions. When you know what you want, your task then becomes finding a position that is as close to your ideal job as possible.

1. **What skills do you want to use?** From the skills lists in Step 1, select the top five skills that you enjoy using and most want to use in your next job.

    a.＿＿＿＿＿＿＿＿＿＿＿＿＿＿＿＿＿＿＿＿＿＿＿＿＿＿＿＿＿＿＿

    b.＿＿＿＿＿＿＿＿＿＿＿＿＿＿＿＿＿＿＿＿＿＿＿＿＿＿＿＿＿＿＿

    c.＿＿＿＿＿＿＿＿＿＿＿＿＿＿＿＿＿＿＿＿＿＿＿＿＿＿＿＿＿＿＿

    d.＿＿＿＿＿＿＿＿＿＿＿＿＿＿＿＿＿＿＿＿＿＿＿＿＿＿＿＿＿＿＿

    e.＿＿＿＿＿＿＿＿＿＿＿＿＿＿＿＿＿＿＿＿＿＿＿＿＿＿＿＿＿＿＿

2. **What type of special knowledge do you have?** Perhaps you know how to fix radios, keep accounting records, or cook food. Write down the things you know from schooling, training, hobbies, family experiences, and other sources. One or more of these knowledge areas could make you a very desirable applicant in the right setting.

    ＿＿＿＿＿＿＿＿＿＿＿＿＿＿＿＿＿＿＿＿＿＿＿＿＿＿＿＿＿＿＿＿

    ＿＿＿＿＿＿＿＿＿＿＿＿＿＿＿＿＿＿＿＿＿＿＿＿＿＿＿＿＿＿＿＿

3. **With what types of people do you prefer to work?** Do you like to work with competitive people, or do you prefer hardworking folks, creative personalities, relaxed people, or some other types?

    ＿＿＿＿＿＿＿＿＿＿＿＿＿＿＿＿＿＿＿＿＿＿＿＿＿＿＿＿＿＿＿＿

    ＿＿＿＿＿＿＿＿＿＿＿＿＿＿＿＿＿＿＿＿＿＿＿＿＿＿＿＿＿＿＿＿

4. **What type of work environment do you prefer?** Do you want to work inside, outside, in a quiet place, in a busy place, or in a clean or messy place; or do you want to have a window with a nice view? List the types of environments you prefer.

    ＿＿＿＿＿＿＿＿＿＿＿＿＿＿＿＿＿＿＿＿＿＿＿＿＿＿＿＿＿＿＿＿

    ＿＿＿＿＿＿＿＿＿＿＿＿＿＿＿＿＿＿＿＿＿＿＿＿＿＿＿＿＿＿＿＿

5. **Where do you want your next job to be located—in what city or region?** If you are open to living and working anywhere, what would your ideal community be like? Near a bus line? Close to a child care center?

    ＿＿＿＿＿＿＿＿＿＿＿＿＿＿＿＿＿＿＿＿＿＿＿＿＿＿＿＿＿＿＿＿

    ＿＿＿＿＿＿＿＿＿＿＿＿＿＿＿＿＿＿＿＿＿＿＿＿＿＿＿＿＿＿＿＿

6. **What benefits or income do you hope to have in your next job?** Many people will take less money or fewer benefits if they like a job in other ways—or if they need a job quickly to survive. Think about the minimum you would take as well as what you would eventually like to earn. Your next job will probably pay somewhere in between.

   _____

   _____

7. **How much and what types of responsibility are you willing to accept?** Usually, the more money you want to make, the more responsibility you must accept. Do you want to work by yourself, be part of a group, or be in charge? If you want to be in charge, how many people are you willing to supervise?

   _____

   _____

8. **What values are important or have meaning to you?** Do you have important values you would prefer to include in considering the work you do? For example, some people want to work to help others, clean up the environment, build structures, make machines work, gain power or prestige, or care for animals or plants. Think about what is important to you and how you might include this in your next job.

   _____

   _____

   _____

Is It Possible to Find Your Ideal Job?

Can you find a job that meets all the criteria you just defined? Perhaps. Some people do. The harder you look, the more likely you are to find it. But you will likely need to compromise, so it is useful to know what is *most* important to include in your next job. Go back over your responses to the eight factors and mark a few of those that you would most like to have in your ideal job.

FACTORS I WANT IN MY IDEAL JOB

Write a brief description of your ideal job. Don't worry about a job title, whether you have the necessary experience, or other practical matters yet.

_____

_____

_____

How Can You Explore Specific Job Titles and Industries?

You might find your ideal job in an occupation you haven't considered yet. And, even if you are sure of the occupation you want, it may be in an industry that is unfamiliar to you. This combination of occupation and industry forms the basis for your job search, and you should consider a variety of options.

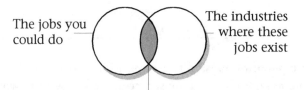

The jobs you could do — The industries where these jobs exist

Your ideal job exists in the overlap of those jobs that interest you most *and* in those industries that best meet your needs and interests!

REVIEW THE TOP JOBS IN THE WORKFORCE

The list of job titles that follows was based on a list developed by the U.S. Department of Labor. It contains 289 major jobs that employ about 90 percent of the U.S. workforce.

The job titles are organized within 16 major groupings called interest areas, presented in bold type. These groupings will help you quickly identify fields most likely to interest you. Job titles are presented in regular type within these groupings.

Begin with the interest areas that appeal to you most, and underline any job title that interests you. (Don't worry for now about whether you have the experience or credentials to do these jobs.) Then quickly review the remaining interest areas, underlining any job titles there that interest you. Note that some job titles are listed more than once because they fit into more than one interest area. When you have gone through all 16 interest areas, go back and circle the 5 to 10 job titles that interest you most. These are the ones you will want to research in more detail.

1. **Agriculture, Food, and Natural Resources:** Agricultural and Food Scientists; Agricultural Inspectors; Agricultural Workers, Other; Animal Care and Service Workers; Biological Scientists; Computer Support Specialists; Conservation Scientists and Foresters; Economists; Engineering Technicians; Environmental Scientists and Specialists; Farmers, Ranchers, and Agricultural Managers; Fishers and Fishing Vessel Operators; Floral Designers; Food Processing Occupations; Forest and Conservation Workers; Graders and Sorters, Agricultural Products; Graphic Designers; Grounds Maintenance Workers; Hazardous Materials Removal Workers; Heavy Vehicle and Mobile Equipment Service Technicians and Mechanics; Logging Workers; News Analysts, Reporters, and Correspondents; Office and Administrative Support Supervisors and Managers; Pest Control Workers; Retail Salespersons; Sales Worker Supervisors; Science Technicians; Veterinarians; Water and Liquid Waste Treatment Plant and System Operators.

2. **Architecture and Construction:** Architects, Except Landscape and Naval; Boilermakers; Brickmasons, Blockmasons, and Stonemasons; Carpenters; Carpet, Floor, and Tile Installers and Finishers; Cement Masons, Concrete Finishers, Segmental Pavers, and Terrazzo Workers; Coin, Vending, and Amusement Machine Servicers and Repairers; Construction and Building Inspectors; Construction Equipment Operators; Construction Laborers; Construction Managers; Cost Estimators; Drafters; Drywall and Ceiling Tile Installers, Tapers, Plasterers, and Stucco Masons; Electricians; Engineering and Natural Sciences Managers; Engineering Technicians; Engineers; Glaziers; Heating, Air-Conditioning, and

Refrigeration Mechanics and Installers; Home Appliance Repairers; Insulation Workers; Interior Designers; Landscape Architects; Line Installers and Repairers; Maintenance and Repair Workers, General; Painters and Paperhangers; Plumbers, Pipelayers, Pipefitters, and Steamfitters; Roofers; Structural and Reinforcing Iron and Metal Workers; Surveyors, Cartographers, Photogrammetrists, and Surveying and Mapping Technicians.

3. **Arts, Audio/Video Technology, and Communications:** Actors, Producers, and Directors; Announcers; Archivists, Curators, and Museum Technicians; Artists and Related Workers; Authors, Writers, and Editors; Bookbinders and Bindery Workers; Broadcast and Sound Engineering Technicians and Radio Operators; Commercial and Industrial Designers; Communications Equipment Operators; Dancers and Choreographers; Data Entry and Information Processing Workers; Desktop Publishers; Electronic Home Entertainment Equipment Installers and Repairers; Fashion Designers; Graphic Designers; Interior Designers; Musicians, Singers, and Related Workers; News Analysts, Reporters, and Correspondents; Painting and Coating Workers, Except Construction and Maintenance; Photographers; Photographic Process Workers and Processing Machine Operators; Prepress Technicians and Workers; Printing Machine Operators; Public Relations Specialists; Radio and Telecommunications Equipment Installers and Repairers; Social Scientists, Other; Technical Writers; Television, Video, and Motion Picture Camera Operators and Editors; Theatrical and Performance Makeup Artists.

4. **Business, Management, and Administration:** Accountants and Auditors; Administrative Services Managers; Advertising Sales Agents; Advertising, Marketing, Promotions, Public Relations, and Sales Managers; Billing and Posting Clerks and Machine Operators; Bookkeeping, Accounting, and Auditing Clerks; Brokerage Clerks; Budget Analysts; Cargo and Freight Agents; Communications Equipment Operators; Computer and Information Systems Managers; Computer Network, Systems, and Database Administrators; Construction Managers; Cost Estimators; Couriers and Messengers; Customer Service Representatives; Data Entry and Information Processing Workers; Dispatchers, Except Police, Fire, and Ambulance; Economists; File Clerks; Financial Analysts; Financial Managers; Gaming Cage Workers; Gaming Services Occupations; Human Resources Assistants, Except Payroll and Timekeeping; Human Resources, Training, and Labor Relations Managers and Specialists; Industrial Production Managers; Interviewers, Except Eligibility and Loan; Management Analysts; Market and Survey Researchers; Meter Readers, Utilities; Office and Administrative Support Supervisors and Managers; Office Clerks, General; Operations Research Analysts; Order Clerks; Payroll and Timekeeping Clerks; Postal Service Clerks; Postal Service Mail Carriers; Postal Service Mail Sorters, Processors, and Processing Machine Operators; Procurement Clerks; Public Relations Specialists; Purchasing Managers, Buyers, and Purchasing Agents; Receptionists and Information Clerks; Secretaries and Administrative Assistants; Shipping, Receiving, and Traffic Clerks; Statisticians; Technical Writers; Top Executives; Weighers, Measurers, Checkers, and Samplers, Recordkeeping.

5. **Education and Training:** Athletes, Coaches, Umpires, and Related Workers; Counselors; Dietitians and Nutritionists; Education Administrators; Fitness Workers; Instructional Coordinators; Interpreters and Translators; Librarians; Library Technicians and Library Assistants; Recreation Workers; Social Scientists, Other; Teacher Assistants; Teachers—Adult Literacy and Remedial Education; Teachers—Kindergarten, Elementary, Middle, and Secondary; Teachers—Postsecondary; Teachers—Preschool, Except Special Education; Teachers—Self-Enrichment Education; Teachers—Special Education; Teachers—Vocational.

6. **Finance:** Actuaries; Bill and Account Collectors; Budget Analysts; Claims Adjusters, Appraisers, Examiners, and Investigators; Credit Authorizers, Checkers, and Clerks; Financial Analysts; Financial Managers; Insurance Sales Agents; Insurance Underwriters; Loan Interviewers and Clerks; Loan

(continued)

(continued)

Officers; Personal Financial Advisors; Securities, Commodities, and Financial Services Sales Agents; Tellers.

7. **Government and Public Administration:** Accountants and Auditors; Administrative Services Managers; News Analysts, Reporters, and Correspondents; Sociologists and Political Scientists; Surveyors, Cartographers, Photogrammetrists, and Surveying and Mapping Technicians; Tax Examiners, Collectors, and Revenue Agents; Top Executives; Urban and Regional Planners.

8. **Health Science:** Athletic Trainers; Audiologists; Biological Scientists; Cardiovascular Technologists and Technicians; Chefs, Head Cooks, and Food Preparation and Serving Supervisors; Chiropractors; Clinical Laboratory Technologists and Technicians; Computer Scientists; Computer Support Specialists; Computer Systems Analysts; Cooks and Food Preparation Workers; Counselors; Dental Assistants; Dental Hygienists; Dentists; Diagnostic Medical Sonographers; Dietitians and Nutritionists; Emergency Medical Technicians and Paramedics; Engineers; Food Processing Occupations; Health Educators; Home Health Aides and Personal and Home Care Aides; Licensed Practical and Licensed Vocational Nurses; Massage Therapists; Medical and Health Services Managers; Medical Assistants; Medical Records and Health Information Technicians; Medical Scientists; Medical Transcriptionists; Medical, Dental, and Ophthalmic Laboratory Technicians; Nuclear Medicine Technologists; Nursing and Psychiatric Aides; Occupational Health and Safety Specialists; Occupational Health and Safety Technicians; Occupational Therapist Assistants and Aides; Occupational Therapists; Office and Administrative Support Supervisors and Managers; Opticians, Dispensing; Optometrists; Pharmacists; Pharmacy Technicians and Aides; Physical Therapist Assistants and Aides; Physical Therapists; Physician Assistants; Physicians and Surgeons; Podiatrists; Psychologists; Radiation Therapists; Radiologic Technologists and Technicians; Receptionists and Information Clerks; Recreational Therapists; Registered Nurses; Respiratory Therapists; Respiratory Therapy Technicians; Secretaries and Administrative Assistants; Social and Human Service Assistants; Speech-Language Pathologists; Surgical Technologists; Veterinarians; Veterinary Technologists and Technicians.

9. **Hospitality and Tourism:** Building Cleaning Workers; Chefs, Head Cooks, and Food Preparation and Serving Supervisors; Cooks and Food Preparation Workers; Food and Beverage Serving and Related Workers; Food Processing Occupations; Food Service Managers; Gaming Services Occupations; Lodging Managers; Reservation and Transportation Ticket Agents and Travel Clerks; Travel Agents.

10. **Human Services:** Barbers, Cosmetologists, and Other Personal Appearance Workers; Child Care Workers; Counselors; Eligibility Interviewers, Government Programs; Epidemiologists; Funeral Directors; Health Educators; Home Health Aides and Personal and Home Care Aides; Interpreters and Translators; Makeup Artists, Theatrical and Performance; Probation Officers and Correctional Treatment Specialists; Psychologists; Recreation Workers; Sales Worker Supervisors; Social Workers; Sociologists and Political Scientists; Teachers—Preschool, Except Special Education; Textile, Apparel, and Furnishings Occupations.

11. **Information Technology:** Artists and Related Workers; Computer and Information Systems Managers; Computer Network, Systems, and Database Administrators; Computer Operators; Computer Scientists; Computer Software Engineers and Computer Programmers; Computer Support Specialists; Computer Systems Analysts; Engineering and Natural Sciences Managers; Engineers; Graphic Designers.

12. **Law, Public Safety, Corrections, and Security:** Correctional Officers; Court Reporters; Fire Fighters; Fire Inspectors and Investigators; Judges, Magistrates, and Other Judicial Workers; Lawyers; Paralegals and Legal Assistants; Police and Detectives; Police, Fire, and Ambulance Dispatchers; Private Detectives

and Investigators; Science Technicians; Security Guards and Gaming Surveillance Officers; Social Workers.

13. **Manufacturing:** Aircraft and Avionics Equipment Mechanics and Service Technicians; Assemblers and Fabricators; Automotive Service Technicians and Mechanics; Bookbinders and Bindery Workers; Camera and Photographic Equipment Repairers; Computer Control Programmers and Operators; Computer Support Specialists; Computer, Automated Teller, and Office Machine Repairers; Cost Estimators; Electrical and Electronics Installers and Repairers; Elevator Installers and Repairers; Engineering Technicians; Fashion Designers; Hazardous Materials Removal Workers; Heavy Vehicle and Mobile Equipment Service Technicians and Mechanics; Industrial Machinery Mechanics and Millwrights; Inspectors, Testers, Sorters, Samplers, and Weighers; Interior Designers; Jewelers and Precious Stone and Metal Workers; Line Installers and Repairers; Machine Setters, Operators, and Tenders—Metal and Plastic; Machinists; Material Moving Occupations; Medical Equipment Repairers; Musical Instrument Repairers and Tuners; Occupational Health and Safety Specialists; Painting and Coating Workers, Except Construction and Maintenance; Power Plant Operators, Distributors, and Dispatchers; Science Technicians; Semiconductor Processors; Sheet Metal Workers; Stationary Engineers and Boiler Operators; Surveyors, Cartographers, Photogrammetrists, and Surveying and Mapping Technicians; Textile, Apparel, and Furnishings Occupations; Tool and Die Makers; Watch Repairers; Welding, Soldering, and Brazing Workers; Woodworkers.

14. **Marketing, Sales, and Service:** Advertising, Marketing, Promotions, Public Relations, and Sales Managers; Appraisers and Assessors of Real Estate; Cashiers; Counter and Rental Clerks; Demonstrators and Product Promoters; Gaming Cage Workers; Hotel, Motel, and Resort Desk Clerks; Interior Designers; Lodging Managers; Market and Survey Researchers; Meeting and Convention Planners; Models; Property, Real Estate, and Community Association Managers; Purchasing Managers, Buyers, and Purchasing Agents; Real Estate Brokers and Sales Agents; Reservation and Transportation Ticket Agents and Travel Clerks; Retail Salespersons; Sales Engineers; Sales Representatives, Wholesale and Manufacturing; Sales Worker Supervisors; Stock Clerks and Order Fillers; Travel Agents; Truck Drivers and Driver/Sales Workers.

15. **Science, Technology, Engineering, and Mathematics:** Archivists, Curators, and Museum Technicians; Atmospheric Scientists; Biological Scientists; Chemists and Materials Scientists; Computer Network, Systems, and Database Administrators; Computer Software Engineers and Computer Programmers; Computer Support Specialists; Cost Estimators; Dietitians and Nutritionists; Drafters; Economists; Engineering and Natural Sciences Managers; Engineering Technicians; Engineers; Epidemiologists; Geoscientists and Hydrologists; Market and Survey Researchers; Mathematicians; Medical Scientists; Operations Research Analysts; Physicists and Astronomers; Psychologists; Science Technicians; Social Scientists, Other; Sociologists and Political Scientists; Statisticians; Surveyors, Cartographers, Photogrammetrists, and Surveying and Mapping Technicians.

16. **Transportation, Distribution, and Logistics:** Air Traffic Controllers; Aircraft and Avionics Equipment Mechanics and Service Technicians; Aircraft Pilots and Flight Engineers; Automotive Body and Related Repairers; Automotive Service Technicians and Mechanics; Bus Drivers; Construction Equipment Operators; Diesel Service Technicians and Mechanics; Electrical and Electronics Installers and Repairers; Flight Attendants; Material Moving Occupations; Painting and Coating Workers, Except Construction and Maintenance; Production, Planning, and Expediting Clerks; Rail Transportation Occupations; Shipping, Receiving, and Traffic Clerks; Small Engine Mechanics; Taxi Drivers and Chauffeurs; Truck Drivers and Driver/Sales Workers; Water Transportation Occupations; Woodworkers.

N o t e

You can find thorough descriptions for the job titles in the preceding list in the Occupational Outlook Handbook, *published by the U.S. Department of Labor. Its descriptions include information on earnings training and education needed to hold specific jobs, working conditions, advancement opportunities, projected growth, and sources for additional information. Most libraries have this book.*

You also can find descriptions of these jobs on the Internet. Go to www.bls.gov/oco/.

CONSIDER MAJOR INDUSTRIES

What industry you work in is often as important as the occupation. For example, some industries pay much better than others, and others may simply be more interesting to you. The *Career Guide to Industries,* a Web-only publication of the U.S. Department of Labor (at www.bls.gov/oco/cg), contains very helpful profiles of the major industries mentioned in the following list.

Underline industries that interest you, and then learn more about the opportunities they present. Jobs in most careers are available in a variety of industries, so consider what industries fit you best and focus your job search in these.

Agriculture and natural resources: Agriculture, forestry, and fishing; mining; oil and gas extraction.

Manufacturing, construction, and utilities: Aerospace product and parts manufacturing; chemical manufacturing, except drugs; computer and electronic product manufacturing; food manufacturing; machinery manufacturing; motor vehicle and parts manufacturing; pharmaceutical and medicine manufacturing; printing; steel manufacturing; textile, textile products, and apparel manufacturing; utilities.

Trade: Automobile dealers; clothing, accessories, and general merchandise stores; grocery stores; wholesale trade.

Transportation: Air transportation; truck transportation and warehousing.

Information: Broadcasting; Internet service providers, Web search portals, and data-processing services; motion picture and video industries; publishing, except software; software publishing; telecommunications.

Financial activities: Banking; insurance; securities, commodities, and other investments.

Professional and business services: Advertising and public relations; computer systems design and related services; employment services; management, scientific, and technical consulting services; scientific research and development services.

Education, health care, and social services: Child day care services; educational services; health care; social assistance, except child care.

Leisure and Hospitality: Art, entertainment, and recreation; food services and drinking places; hotels and other accommodations.

Government and advocacy, grantmaking, and civic organizations: Advocacy, grantmaking, and civic organizations; federal government; state and local government, except education and health care.

THE TOP JOBS AND INDUSTRIES THAT INTEREST YOU

Go back over the lists of job titles and industries. For numbers 1 and 2 below, list the jobs that interest you most. Then select the industries that interest you most, and list them below in number 3. These are the jobs and industries you should research most carefully. Your ideal job is likely to be found in some combination of these jobs and industries, or in more specialized but related jobs and industries. Put a star next to the one you like best.

1. The five job titles that interest you most

   a. _____

   b. _____

   c. _____

   d. _____

   e. _____

2. The five next-most-interesting job titles

   a. _____

   b. _____

   c. _____

   d. _____

   e. _____

3. The industries that interest you most

   a. _____

   b. _____

   c. _____

   d. _____

   e. _____

Is Self-Employment or Starting a Business an Option?

More than one in 10 workers are self-employed or own their own businesses. If these options interest you, consider them as well. Talk to people in similar roles to gather information, and look for books and websites that provide information on options that are similar to those that interest you. Examples of jobs with high percentages of self-employed workers include

❑ Farmers and ranchers

❑ Multimedia artists and animators

❑ Copywriters

❑ Poets, lyricists, and creative writers

❑ Massage therapists

❑ Real estate brokers

The Small Business Administration's website at www.sba.gov is a good source of basic information on starting your own business.

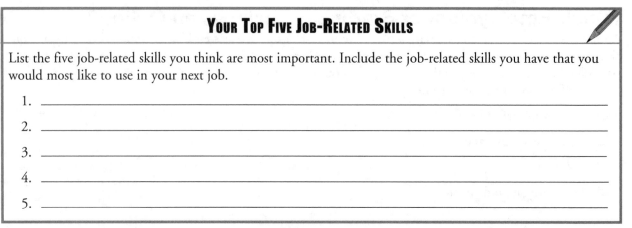

SELF-EMPLOYMENT AREAS OF INTEREST

In the following space, write your current interest in self-employment or starting a business in an area related to your general job objective.

Are you interested in working for yourself? _____

What types of businesses are related to the jobs that interest you most?

_____

_____

Who can you talk with to get more information about what it's like to be self-employed in this field?

_____

_____

Identify Your Job-Related Skills for Your Ideal Job

Back on page 301, I suggested that you should first define the job you want and then identify key job-related skills you have that support your ability to do that job. These are the job-related skills to emphasize in interviews.

So, now that you have determined your ideal job (the one you put a star next to on page 309), you can pinpoint the job-related skills it requires. If you haven't done so, complete the Essential Job Search Data Worksheet on pages 341–346. Completing it will give you specific skills and accomplishments to highlight. Look up your ideal job at http://online.onetcenter.org/. See which skills are required for this job. Then see how many of those overlap with the skills you have.

Yes, completing that worksheet requires time, but doing so will help you clearly define key skills to emphasize in interviews—when what you say matters so much. People who complete that worksheet will do better in their interviews than those who don't. After you complete the Essential Job Search Data Worksheet, you are ready to list your top five job-related skills.

YOUR TOP FIVE JOB-RELATED SKILLS

List the five job-related skills you think are most important. Include the job-related skills you have that you would most like to use in your next job.

1. _____

2. _____

3. _____

4. _____

5. _____

STEP 3: Use the Most Effective Methods to Find a Job in Less Time

Employer surveys have found that most employers don't advertise their job openings. They most often hire people they already know, people who find out about the jobs through word of mouth, or people who happen to be in the right place at the right time. Although luck plays a part in finding job openings, you can use the tips in this step to increase your luck.

Most job seekers don't know how ineffective some traditional job hunting techniques tend to be. For example, the chart below shows that fewer than 15 percent of all job seekers get jobs from the newspaper want ads, most of which also appear online. Other traditional techniques include using public and private employment agencies, filling out paper and electronic applications, and mailing or e-mailing unsolicited resumes.

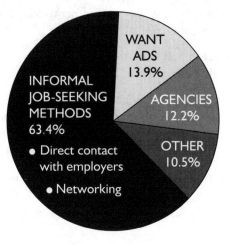

How people find jobs.

Informal, nontraditional job-seeking methods have a much larger success rate. These methods are active rather than passive and include making direct contact with employers and networking.

The truth is that every job search method works for someone. But experience and research show that some methods are more effective than others are. Your task in the job search is to spend more of your time using more effective methods—and increase the effectiveness of all the methods you use. Let's start by looking at the most effective job search methods.

Use the Two Job Search Methods That Work Best

The fact is that most jobs are not advertised, so how do *you* find them? The same way that about two-thirds of all job seekers do: networking with people you know (which I call making warm contacts) and directly contacting employers (which I call making cold contacts). Both of these methods are based on the job search rule you should know above all:

The Most Important Job Search Rule: Don't wait until the job opens before contacting the employer!

Employers fill most jobs with people they meet before a job is formally open. The trick is to meet people who can hire you before a job is formally available. Instead of asking whether the employer has any jobs open, I suggest that you say, *"I realize you may not have any openings now, but I would still like to talk to you about the possibility of future openings."*

Most Effective Job Search Method 1: Develop a Network of Contacts in Five Easy Stages

Studies find that 40 percent of all people located their jobs through a lead provided by a friend, a relative, or an acquaintance. That makes the people you know your number one source of job leads—more effective than all the traditional methods combined! Developing and using your contacts is called *networking,* and here's how it works:

1. **Make lists of people you know.** Make a thorough list of anyone you are friendly with. Then make a separate list of all your relatives. These two lists alone often add up to 25 to 100 people or more. Next, think of other groups of people that you have something in common with, such as former coworkers or classmates, members of your social or sports groups, members of your professional association, former employers, neighbors, and other groups. You might not know many of these people personally or well, but most will help you if you ask them. An easy way to find networking contacts is to join an online networking site such as LinkedIn (www.linkedin.com).

2. **Contact each person in your list in a systematic way.** Obviously, some people will be more helpful than others, but any one of them might help you find a job lead.

3. **Present yourself well.** Begin with your friends and relatives. Call and tell them you are looking for a job and need their help. Be as clear as possible about the type of employment you want and the skills and qualifications you have. Look at the sample JIST Card and phone script later in this step for good presentation ideas.

4. **Ask your contacts for leads.** It is possible that your contacts will know of a job opening that interests you. If so, get the details and get right on it! More likely, however, they will not, so you should ask each person the Three Magic Networking Questions.

The Three Magic Networking Questions

- **Do you know of any openings for a person with my skills?**

  If the answer is "No" (which it usually is), then ask…

- **Do you know of someone else who might know of such an opening?**

  If your contact does, get that name and ask for another one. If he or she doesn't, ask…

- **Do you know of anyone who might know of someone else who might know of a job opening?**

  Another good way to ask this is "Do you know someone who knows lots of people?" If all else fails, this will usually get you a name.

5. **Contact these referrals and ask them the same questions.** From each person you contact, try to get two names of other people you might contact. Doing this consistently can extend your network of acquaintances by hundreds of people. Eventually, one of these people will hire you or refer you to someone who will!

If you are persistent in following these five steps, networking might be the only job search method you need. It works.

Most Effective Job Search Method 2: Contact Employers Directly

It takes more courage, but making direct contact with employers is a very effective job search technique. I call these "cold contacts" because people you don't know in advance will need to warm up to your inquiries. Two basic techniques for making cold contacts follow.

Use the yellow pages to find potential employers. Begin by looking at the index in the front of your phone book's yellow pages. For each entry, ask yourself, "Would an organization of this kind need a person with my skills?" If you answer "Yes," then that organization or business type is a possible target. You can also rate "Yes" entries based on your interest, writing a "1" next to those that seem very interesting, a "2" next to those that you are not sure of, and a "3" next to those that aren't interesting at all.

Next, select a type of organization that got a "Yes" response and turn to that section of the yellow pages. Call each organization listed there and ask to speak to the person who is most likely to hire or supervise you—typically the manager of the business or a department head—not the personnel or human resources manager. A sample telephone script is included later in this section to give you ideas about what to say.

You can easily adapt this approach for use on the Internet by using sites such as www.yellowpages.com to get contacts anywhere in the world, or you can find phone and e-mail contacts on an employer's own website.

Drop in without an appointment. Another effective cold contact method is to just walk into a business or organization that interests you and ask to speak to the person in charge. Although dropping in is particularly effective in small businesses, it also works surprisingly well in larger ones. Remember to ask for an interview even if there are no openings now. If your timing is inconvenient, ask for a better time to come back for an interview.

Most Jobs Are with Small Employers

Businesses and organizations with fewer than 250 employees employ half of all workers and create more than 75 percent of all new jobs each year. They are simply too important to overlook in your job search! Many of them don't have personnel departments, which makes direct contacts even easier and more effective.

Create a Powerful Job Search Tool: The JIST Card®

Look at the sample cards that follow. They are JIST Cards, and they get results. They can be computer printed or even neatly written on a 3-by-5–inch card. JIST Cards include the essential information employers want to know.

A JIST Card Is a Mini Resume

JIST Cards have been used by thousands of job search programs and millions of people. Employers like their direct and timesaving format, and they have been proven as an effective tool to get job leads. Attach one to your resume. Give them to friends, relatives, and other contacts and ask them to pass them along to others who might know of an opening. Enclose them in thank-you notes after interviews. Leave one with employers as a business card. However you get them in circulation, you may be surprised at how well they work.

You can easily create JIST Cards on a computer and print them on card stock you can buy at any office-supply store. Or you can have a few hundred printed cheaply by a local quick-print shop. Although they are often done as 3-by-5 cards, they can be printed in any size or format, including standard business card size.

Sandy Nolan

Position: General Office/Clerical

Cell phone: (512) 232-9213

Email: snolan@aol.com

More than two years of work experience plus one year of training in office practices. Type 55 wpm, trained in word processing, post general ledger, have good interpersonal skills, and get along with most people. Can meet deadlines and handle pressure well.

Willing to work any hours.

Organized, honest, reliable, and hardworking.

Richard Straightarrow   Home: (602) 253-9678
                                             Cell: (602) 257-6643
                                             E-mail: RSS@email.com

Objective: **Electronics installation, maintenance, and sales**

Four years of work experience plus a two-year A.S. degree in Electronics Engineering Technology. Managed a $360K annual business while attending school full time, with grades in the top 25%. Familiar with all major electronic diagnostic and repair equipment. Hands-on experience with medical, consumer, communication, and industrial electronics equipment and applications. Good problem-solving and communication skills. Customer service oriented.

Willing to do what it takes to get the job done.

A JIST Card Can Lead to an Effective Phone Script

The phone is an essential job search tool that can get you more interviews per hour than any other method. But the technique won't work unless you use it actively throughout your search. After you have created your JIST Card, you can use it as the basis for a phone script to make warm or cold calls. Revise your JIST Card content so that it sounds natural when spoken, and then edit it until you can read it out loud in about 30 seconds. The sample phone script that follows is based on the content of a JIST Card. Use it to help you modify your own JIST Card into a phone script.

> "Hello. My name is Pam Nykanen. I am interested in a position in hotel management. I have four years of experience in sales, catering, and accounting with a 300-room hotel. I also have an associate degree in hotel management, plus one year of experience with the Brady Culinary Institute. During my employment, I helped double revenues from meetings and conferences and increased bar revenues by 46 percent. I have good problem-solving skills and am good with people. I am also well organized, hardworking, and detail oriented. When may I come in to talk with you about opportunities in your organization?"

With your script in hand, make some practice calls to warm or cold contacts. If making cold calls, contact the person most likely to supervise you. Then present your script just as you practiced it—without stopping.

Although the sample script assumes that you are calling someone you don't know, you can change it to address warm contacts and referrals. Making cold calls takes courage but works very well for many who are willing to do it.

Use the Internet in Your Job Search

The Internet has limitations as a job search tool. While many have used it to get job leads, it has not worked well for far more. Too many assume they can simply add their resume to resume databases and employers will line up to hire them. Just like the older approach of sending out lots of resumes, good things sometimes happen, but not often.

I recommend two points that apply to all job search methods, including using the Internet:

- It is unwise to rely on just one or two methods in conducting your job search.

- It is essential that you use an active rather than a passive approach in your job search.

Use More Than One Job Search Method

I encourage you to use the Internet in your job search, but I suggest that you use it along with other techniques. Use the same sorts of job search techniques online as you do offline, including contacting employers directly and building up a network of personal contacts that can help you with your search.

Tips to Increase Your Effectiveness in Internet Job Searches

The following tips can increase the effectiveness of using the Internet in your job search:

- **Be as specific as possible in the job you seek.** This is important in using any job search method, and it's even more important in using the Internet in your job search. The Internet is enormous, so it is essential to be as focused as possible in your search. Narrow your job title or titles to be as specific as possible. Limit your search to specific industries or areas of specialization. Locate and use specialized job banks in your area of interest.

- **Have reasonable expectations.** Success on the Internet is more likely if you understand its limitations and strengths. For example, employers trying to find someone with skills in high demand, such as nurses, are more likely to use the Internet to recruit job candidates.

- **Limit your geographic options.** If you don't want to move or would move only to certain areas, state this preference on your resume and restrict your search to those areas. Many Internet sites allow you to view or search for only those jobs that meet your location criteria.

- **Create an electronic resume.** With few exceptions, resumes submitted to Internet resume databases end up as simple text files with no graphic elements. Employers search these databases for resumes that include keywords or meet other searchable criteria. So create a simple text resume for Internet use and include words that are likely to be used by employers searching for someone with your abilities. (See Step 4 for more on creating an electronic resume or online portfolio.)

- **Get your resume into the major resume databases.** Most Internet employment sites let you add your resume for free and then charge employers to advertise openings or to search for candidates. Although adding your resume to these databases is not likely to result in job offers, doing so allows you to use your stored resume to easily apply for positions that are posted at these sites. These easy-to-use sites often provide all sorts of useful information for job seekers.

- **Make direct contacts.** Visit the websites of organizations that interest you and learn more about them. Many post openings, allow you to apply online, offer information on benefits and work environment, or even provide access to staff who can answer your questions. Even if they don't, you can always search the site or e-mail a request for the name of the person in charge of the work that interests you and then communicate with that person directly.

- **Network.** You can network online, too, finding names and e-mail addresses of potential employer contacts or of other people who might know someone with job openings. The best place to start your online networking is LinkedIn (www.linkedin.com). Twitter (www.twitter.com) is also a powerful online networking tool, and you can even find some good leads among your Facebook friends. In addition, look at and participate in interest groups, professional association sites, alumni sites, chat rooms, e-mail discussion lists, and employer sites—these are just some of the many creative ways to network and interact with people via the Internet.

Check Out Career-Specific Sites First

Thousands of Internet sites provide lists of job openings and information on careers or education. The best-known general job boards are CareerBuilder (www.careerbuilder.com), Monster (www.monster.com), and Yahoo! Hotjobs (http://hotjobs.yahoo.com/). Perhaps even more helpful are job aggregator sites, which pull jobs from all over the Web into one place. Two of the best-known aggregators are Indeed (www.indeed.com) and Simply Hired (www.simplyhired.com).

Get the Most Out of Less Effective Job Search Methods

Now let's look at some traditional job search methods and how you can increase their effectiveness. Only about one-third of all job seekers get their jobs using one of these methods, but you should still consider using them to some extent in your search.

Newspaper and Internet Help-Wanted Ads

Most jobs are never advertised, and fewer than 15 percent of all people get their jobs through the want ads. Everyone who reads the paper knows about these openings, so competition is fierce for the few advertised jobs.

The Internet also lists many job openings. But, as happens with newspaper ads, enormous numbers of people view these postings. Many job seekers make direct contact with employers via a company's website. Some people do get jobs through the bigger sites, so go ahead and apply. Just be sure to spend most of your time using more effective methods.

Filling Out Applications

Most employers require job seekers to complete a paper application form, a kiosk application on a computer at the front of the store, or an online application on the company's website. Applications are designed to collect negative information, and employers use applications to screen people out. If, for example, your training or work history is not the best, you will often never get an interview, even if you can do the job.

Completing applications is a more effective approach for young and entry-level job seekers. The reason is that there is usually greater need for workers for the relatively low-paying jobs typically sought by less-experienced job seekers. As a result, when employers try to fill those positions, they are more willing to accept a lack of experience or fewer job skills. Even so, you will get better results by filling out the application, if asked to do so, and then requesting an interview with the person in charge.

When you complete an application, make it neat and error free, and do not include anything that could get you screened out. If necessary, leave a problem section blank. You can always explain situations in an interview.

Public and Private Employment Agencies and Services

There are three types of employment agencies. One is operated by the government and is free. The others, private employment agencies and temp agencies, are run as for-profit businesses and charge a fee to either you or an employer. Following are the advantages and disadvantages to using each.

The government employment service and One-Stop centers. Each state and province has a network of local offices to pay unemployment compensation, provide job leads, and offer other services—at no charge to you or to employers. The service's name varies by region. It may be called Job Service, Department of Labor, Unemployment Office, Workforce Development, WorkOne, or another name. All of these offices are now online. You can find your local office at www.careeronestop.org.

The Employment and Training Administration website at www.doleta.gov gives you information on the programs provided by the government employment service, plus links to other useful sites.

Visit your local office early in your job search. Find out whether you qualify for unemployment compensation and learn more about its services. Look into it—the price is right.

Private employment agencies. Private employment agencies are businesses that charge a fee either to you or to the employer that hires you. Fees can be from less than one month's pay to 15 percent or more of your annual salary. You will often see these agencies' ads in the help-wanted section of the newspaper. Most have websites.

Be careful about using fee-based employment agencies. Recent research indicates that more people use and benefit from fee-based agencies than in the past. However, relatively few people who register with private agencies get a job through them.

If you use a private employment agency, ask for interviews with the employers who agree to pay the agency's fee. Do not sign an exclusive agreement or be pressured into accepting a job. Also, continue to actively look for your own leads. You can find these agencies in the phone book's yellow pages, and many state- or province-government websites offer lists of the private employment agencies in their states.

Temporary agencies. Temporary agencies offer jobs that last from several days to many months. They charge the employer an hourly fee, and then pay you a bit less and keep the difference. You pay no direct fee to the agency. Many private employment agencies now provide temporary jobs as well.

Temp agencies have grown rapidly for good reason. They provide employers with short-term help, and employers often use them to find people they might want to hire later. If the employers are dissatisfied, they can just ask the agency for different temp workers.

Temp agencies can help you survive between jobs and get experience in different work settings. Temp jobs provide a very good option while you look for long-term work, and you might get a job offer while working in a temp job. Holding a temporary job might even lead to a regular job with the same or a similar employer.

School and Other Employment Services

Only a small percentage of job seekers use school and other special employment services, probably because few job seekers have the service available to them. If you are a student or graduate, find out about any employment services at your school. Some schools provide free career counseling, resume writing help, referrals to job openings, career interest tests, reference materials, websites listing job openings, and other services. Special career programs work with veterans, people with disabilities, welfare recipients, union members, professional groups, and many others. So check out these services and consider using them.

Mailing Out Lots of Resumes Blindly

Many job search experts used to suggest that sending out lots of resumes was a great technique. That advice probably helped sell their resume books, but mailing resumes to people you do not know was never an effective approach. It very rarely works. A recent survey of 1,500 successful job seekers showed that only 2 percent found their positions through sending an unsolicited resume. The same is true for the Internet.

Although mailing your resume to strangers doesn't make much sense, posting it on the Internet might because

- It doesn't take much time.

- Many employers have the potential to find your resume.

- You can post your resume on niche sites that attract only employers in your field.

- Your Internet resume is easily updated, allowing you to post your current accomplishments.

- You can easily link your resume to projects and websites that highlight your accomplishments.

Job searching on the Internet has its limitations, just like other methods. I'll cover resumes in more detail later and provide tips on using the Internet throughout this book.

STEP 4: Write a Simple Resume Now and a Better One Later

Sending out resumes and waiting for responses is not an effective job seeking technique. But many employers *will* ask you for a resume, and it can be a useful tool in your job search. I suggest that you begin with a simple resume you can complete quickly. I've seen too many people spend weeks working on a resume when they could have been out getting interviews instead. If you want a better resume, you can work on it on weekends and evenings. So let's begin with the basics.

The following tips make sense for any resume format:

- **Write it yourself.** It's okay to look at other resumes for ideas, but write yours yourself. Doing so will force you to organize your thoughts and background.

- **Make it error free.** One spelling or grammar error will create a negative impression. Get someone else to review your final draft for any errors. Then review it again because these rascals have a way of slipping in.

- **Make it look good.** Poor copy quality, cheap paper, bad type quality, or anything else that creates a poor appearance will turn off employers to even the best resume content. Get professional help with design and printing if necessary. Many professional resume writers and even print shops offer writing and desktop design services if you need help.

- **Be brief, be relevant.** Many good resumes fit on one page, and few justify more than two. Include only the most important points. Use short sentences and action words. If it doesn't relate to and support the job objective, cut it!

- **Be honest.** Don't overstate your qualifications. If you end up getting a job you can't handle, who does it help? And a lie can result in your being fired later.

- **Be positive.** Emphasize your accomplishments and results. A resume is no place to be too humble or to display your faults.

- **Be specific.** Instead of saying, "I am good with people," say, "I supervised four people in the warehouse and increased productivity by 30 percent." Use numbers whenever possible, such as the number of people served, percentage of sales increase, or amount of dollars saved.

Get Your Resume Online

Employers may ask you to send them your resume online. Pay attention to their instructions, because they will probably specify whether they want you to send your Word file as an attachment, send a PDF, or transmit a plain-text resume via e-mail or their website. Louise Kursmark, coauthor of *15-Minute Cover Letter,* provides these steps for converting your resume to plain text:

1. Save your resume with a different name and select "text only," "ASCII," or "Plain Text (*.txt)" in the "Save As Type" option box.

2. Reopen the file. Your word processor has automatically reformatted your resume into Courier font, removed all formatting, and left-justified the text.

3. Reset the margins to 2 inches left and right, so that you have a narrow column of text rather than a full-page width. Adjust line lengths to fit within the narrow margins by adding hard returns.

4. Fix any glitches such as odd characters that may have been inserted to take the place of "curly" quotes, dashes, accents, or other nonstandard symbols.

5. Remove any tabs and adjust spacing as necessary. You might add a few extra blank spaces, move text down to the next line, or add extra blank lines for readability.

6. Consider adding horizontal dividers to break the resume into sections. You can use a row of any standard typewriter symbols, such as *, -, (,), =, +, ^, or #.

When you close the file, it will be saved with the .txt file extension. When you are ready to use it, just open the file, select and copy the text, and paste it into the online application or e-mail message.

Never delay or slow down your job search because your resume is not good enough. The best approach is to create a simple and acceptable resume as quickly as possible and then use it. As time permits, create a better one if you feel you must.

Writing Chronological Resumes

Most resumes use a chronological format where the most recent experience is listed first, followed by each preceding job. Most employers prefer this format. It works fine for someone with work experience in several similar jobs, but not as well for those with limited experience or for career changers.

Look at the two resumes for Judith Jones that follow. Both use the chronological approach.

The first resume would work fine for most job search needs. It could be completed in about an hour. Notice that the second one includes some improvements. The first resume is good, but most employers would like the additional positive information in the improved resume.

Basic Chronological Resume Example

Everything in this resume supports the candidate's job objective. The emphasis on all related education is important because it helps overcome her lack of extensive work experience.

Judith J. Jones

115 South Hawthorne Avenue
Chicago, Illinois 66204
tel: (312) 653-9217
email: jj@earthlink.com

JOB OBJECTIVE

A position in the office management, accounting, or administrative assistant area that enables me to grow professionally.

EDUCATION AND TRAINING

Acme Business College, Lincoln, IL
Graduate of a one-year business program.

John Adams High School, South Bend, IN
Diploma, business education.

U.S. Army
Financial procedures, accounting functions.

Other: Continuing-education classes and workshops in business communication, spreadsheet and database applications, scheduling systems, and customer relations.

EXPERIENCE

2006–present—Claims Processor, Blue Spear Insurance Co., Wilmette, IL. Process customer medical claims, develop management reports based on created spreadsheets and develop management reports based on those forms, exceed productivity goals.

2005–2006—Returned to school to upgrade business and computer skills. Completed courses in advanced accounting, spreadsheet and database programs, office management, human relations, and new office techniques.

2002–2005—E4, U.S. Army. Assigned to various stations as a specialist in finance operations. Promoted prior to honorable discharge.

2001–2002—Sandy's Boutique, Wilmette, IL. Responsible for counter sales, display design, cash register, and other tasks.

1999–2001—Held part-time and summer jobs throughout high school.

STRENGTHS AND SKILLS

Reliable, hardworking, and good with people. General ledger, accounts payable, and accounts receivable. Proficient in Microsoft Word, WordPerfect, Excel, and Outlook.

Improved Chronological Resume Example

This improved version of the basic resume adds lots of details and specific numbers throughout to reinforce skills.

Judith J. Jones

115 South Hawthorne Avenue
Chicago, IL 66204

jj@earthlink.com
(312) 653-9217 (cell)

JOB OBJECTIVE

A position requiring excellent business management expertise in an office environment. Position should require a variety of skills, including office management, word processing, and spreadsheet and database application use.

EDUCATION AND TRAINING

Acme Business College, Lincoln, IL
Completed one-year program in **Professional Office Management.** Achieved GPA in top 30% of class. Courses included word processing, accounting theory and systems, advanced spreadsheet and database applications, graphics design, time management, and supervision.

John Adams High School, South Bend, IN
Graduated with emphasis on **business courses.** Earned excellent grades in all business topics and won top award for word-processing speed and accuracy.

Other: Continuing-education programs at own expense, including business communications, customer relations, computer applications, and sales techniques.

EXPERIENCE

2006–present—**Claims Processor, Blue Spear Insurance Company,** Wilmette, IL. Process 50 complex medical insurance claims per day, almost 20% above department average. Created a spreadsheet report process that decreased department labor costs by more than $30,000 a year. Received two merit raises for performance.

2005–2006—**Returned to business school to gain advanced office skills.**

2002–2005—**Finance Specialist (E4), U.S. Army.** Systematically processed more than 200 invoices per day from commercial vendors. Trained and supervised eight employees. Devised internal system allowing 15% increase in invoices processed with a decrease in personnel. Managed department with a budget equivalent of more than $350,000 a year. Honorable discharge.

2001–2002—**Sales Associate promoted to Assistant Manager, Sandy's Boutique,** Wilmette, IL. Made direct sales and supervised four employees. Managed daily cash balances and deposits, made purchasing and inventory decisions, and handled all management functions during owner's absence. Sales increased 26% and profits doubled during tenure.

1999–2001—**Held various part-time and summer jobs through high school while maintaining GPA 3.0/4.0.** Earned enough to pay all personal expenses, including car insurance. Learned to deal with customers, meet deadlines, work hard, and handle multiple priorities.

STRENGTHS AND SKILLS

Reliable, with strong work ethic. Excellent interpersonal, written, and oral communication and math skills. Accept supervision well, effectively supervise others, and work well as a team member. General ledger, accounts payable, and accounts receivable expertise. Proficient in Microsoft Word, Excel, PowerPoint, and Outlook; WordPerfect.

Tips for Writing a Simple Chronological Resume

Follow these tips as you write a basic chronological resume:

- **Name:** Use your formal name (not a nickname).

- **Address and contact information:** Avoid abbreviations in your address and include your ZIP code. If you might move, use a friend's address or include a forwarding address. Most employers will not write to you, so provide reliable phone numbers, e-mail addresses, and other contact options. Always include your area code in your phone number because you never know where your resume might travel. Make sure that you have an answering machine or voice mail, and record a professional-sounding message.

- **Job objective/professional summary statement:** You should almost always have one, even if it is general. Notice how Judith Jones keeps her options open with her broad job objective in her basic resume on page 320. Writing "secretary" or "clerical" might limit her from being considered for other jobs. Professional applicants might consider using an impressive summary statement instead, with a heading that states the desired job target.

- **Education and training:** Include any training or education you've had that supports your job objective. If you did not finish a formal degree or program, list what you did complete and emphasize accomplishments. If your experience is not strong, add details here such as related courses and extracurricular activities. In the two examples, Judith Jones puts her business schooling in both the education and experience sections. Doing this fills a job gap and allows her to present her training as equal to work experience.

- **Previous experience:** Include the basics such as employer name, job title, dates employed, and responsibilities—but emphasize specific skills, results, accomplishments, superior performance, and so on.

- **Personal data:** Do not include irrelevant details such as height, weight, and marital status or a photo. Current laws do not allow an employer to base hiring decisions on these points. Providing this information can cause some employers to toss your resume. You can include information about hobbies or leisure activities that directly support your job objective in a special section. The first sample includes a Personal section in which Judith lists some of her strengths, which are often not included in a resume.

- **References:** Make sure that each reference will make nice comments about you and ask each to write a letter of recommendation that you can give to employers. You do not need to list your references on your resume. List them on a separate page and give it to employers who ask.

When you have a simple, errorless, and eye-pleasing resume, get on with your job search. There is no reason to delay! If you want to create a better resume, you can work on improving it in your spare time (evenings or weekends).

Tips for an Improved Chronological Resume

Use these tips to improve your simple resume:

- **Job objective:** A poorly written job objective or summary statement can limit the jobs an employer might consider you for. Think of the skills you have and the types of jobs you want to do; describe them in general terms. Instead of using a narrow job title such as "restaurant manager," you might write "manage a small to mid-sized business."

- **Education and training:** New graduates should emphasize their recent training and education more than those with a few years of related work experience would. A more detailed education and training section might include specific courses you took, and activities or accomplishments that support your job objective or reinforce your key skills. Include other details that reflect how hard you work, such as working your way through school.

- **Skills and accomplishments:** Include those that support your ability to do well in the job you seek now. Even small details count. Maybe your attendance was perfect, you met a tight deadline, or you did the work of others during vacations. Be specific and include numbers—even if you have to estimate them. Judith's improved chronological resume example features a detailed strengths and skills section and more accomplishments and skills. Notice the impact of the numbers to reinforce results.

- **Job titles:** Past job titles might not accurately reflect what you did. For example, your job title may have been "cashier," but you also opened the store, trained new staff, and covered for the boss on vacations. Perhaps "head cashier and assistant manager" would be more accurate. Check with your previous employer if you are not sure.

- **Promotions:** If you were promoted or got good evaluations, say so—"cashier, promoted to assistant manager," for example. You can list a promotion to a more responsible job as a separate job if doing so results in a stronger resume.

- **Gaps in employment and other problem areas:** Employee turnover is expensive, so few employers want to hire people who won't stay or who won't work out. Gaps in employment, jobs held for short periods, or a lack of direction in the jobs you've held are all concerns for employers. So consider your situation and try to give an explanation of a problem area. Here are a few examples:

> **Quip**
> A resume is not the most effective tool for getting interviews. A better approach is to make direct contact with those who hire or supervise people with your skills and ask them for an interview, even if no openings exist now. Then send a resume.

2009—Continued my education at…

2010—Traveled extensively throughout…

2008 to present—Self-employed as barn painter and…

2008—Took year off to have first child

Use entire years to avoid displaying employment gaps you can't explain easily. If you had a few months of unemployment at the beginning of 2008 and then began a job in mid-2008, for example, you can list the job as "2008 to present."

Writing Skills and Combination Resumes

The skills resume emphasizes your most important skills, supported by specific examples of how you have used them. This type of resume allows you to use any part of your life history to support your ability to do the job you want.

While skills resumes can be very effective, creating them requires more work. And some employers don't like them because they can hide a job seeker's faults (such as job gaps, lack of formal education, or little related work experience) better than a chronological resume can. Still, a skills resume may make sense for you.

Look over the sample resumes that follow for ideas. Notice that one resume includes elements of a skills *and* a chronological resume. This so-called combination resume makes sense if your previous job history or education and training are positive.

Put Your Credentials on the Web

These days there are countless options for getting your resume online. If employers or networking contacts ask for your resume, you can give them a URL and let them look at your credentials instantly. One option for an online resume/portfolio with all the bells and whistles is VisualCV (www.visualCV.com). You can include work samples, audio, video, and photos to support your resume details. Another option is to sign up for the business networking site LinkedIn (www.linkedin.com) and fill in the details on your profile. You can then share the profile URL with people who want to know more about your work history.

More Resume Examples

Find resume layout and presentation ideas in the four examples that follow.

Use the information from your completed Essential Job Search Data Worksheet to write your resume. You can find an online version of this worksheet at www.jist.com/pdf/EJSDW.pdf.

The Chronological Resume to Emphasize Results

This resume focuses on accomplishments through the use of numbers. While Jon's resume does not say so, it is obvious that he works hard and that he gets results.

Jon Feder

2140 Beach Road	Phone: (222) 333-4444
Pompano Beach, Florida 20000	E-mail: jfeder@email.com

Objective

Management position in a major hotel

Summary of Experience

Three years of experience in sales, catering banquet services, and guest relations in a 75-room hotel. Doubled sales revenues from conferences and meetings. Increased dining room and bar revenues by 40%. Won prestigious national and local awards for increased productivity and services.

Experience

Beachcomber Hotel, Pompano Beach, Florida
Assistant Manager
20XX to Present
- Oversee a staff of 24, including dining room and bar, housekeeping, and public relations operations.
- Introduced new menus and increased dining room revenues by 40%. Awarded *Saveur* magazine's prestigious first place Hotel Cuisine award as a result of my selection of chefs.
- Attracted 58% more bar patrons by implementing Friday Night Jazz at the Beach.

Tidewater Suites, Hollywood Beach, Florida
Sales and Public Relations
20XX to 20XX
- Doubled revenues per month from weddings, conferences, and meetings.
- Chosen Chamber of Commerce Newcomer of the Year 20XX for the increase in business within the community.

Education

Associate degree in Hotel Management, Sullivan Technical Institute
Certificate in Travel Management, Phoenix University

The Skills Resume for Those with Limited Work Experience

This resume is for a recent high school graduate whose only work experience was at a school office.

Catalina A. Garcia

2340 N. Delaware Street
Denver, Colorado 81613
Cell phone: (413) 123-4567
E-mail: cagarcia@net.net

Position Desired

Office assistant in a fast-paced business

Skills and Abilities

Communication	Excellent written and verbal presentation skills. Use proper grammar and have a good speaking voice.
Interpersonal	Get along well with all types of people. Accept supervision. Helped up to 50 students, visitors, and callers a day in the school office.
Flexible	Willing to try new tasks and am interested in improving efficiency of assigned work.
Attention to Detail	Maintained confidential student records accurately and efficiently.
Hard Working	Worked in the school office during my junior and senior years and maintained above-average grades.
Dependable	Never absent or late in four years.
Award	English Department Student of the Year, May XXXX.

Education

Denver North High School. Graduated in the top 30% of my class. Took advanced English and communication classes. Member of the student newspaper staff for three years.

Girls' basketball team for four years. This activity taught me discipline, teamwork, how to follow instructions, and hard work.

© JIST Works

The Combination Resume for Those Changing Careers

This resume emphasizes Grant's relevant education and transferable skills because he has little work experience in the field.

Grant Thomas

717 Carlin Court • Mundelein, IL 60000 • (555) 555-5555 • E-mail: gthomas@aol.com

Profile

- Outstanding student and tutor
- Winner of international computer software design competition three years
- Self-directed and independent, but also a team player
- Effective oral and written communicator
- Creative problem solver

Education and Training

M.S. in Software Engineering, Massachusetts Institute of Technology, Cambridge, MA
B.S. in Computer Engineering, California State University, Fullerton, CA
A rigorous education focusing on topics such as

- Structure and interpretation of computer programs
- Circuits and electronics
- Signals and systems
- Computation structures
- Microelectronic devices and circuits
- Computer system engineering
- Computer language engineering
- Mathematics for computer science
- Analog electronics laboratory
- Digital systems laboratory

Highlights of Experience and Abilities

- Develop, create, and modify general computer applications.
- Analyze user needs and develop software solutions.
- Confer with systems analysts, computer programmers, and others.
- Modify existing software system installation and monitor equipment functioning to ensure specifications are met.
- Supervise work of programmers and technicians.
- Train customers and employees to use new and modified software.

Employment History

Software Specialist, First Rate Computers, Mundelein, IL 20XX to present

- Technician and Customer and Employee Trainer throughout high school
- Promoted to software specialist and worked as a full-time telecommuting employee while completing B.S. and M.S. degrees.

© JIST Works

The Electronic Resume

This resume is appropriate for scanning or e-mail submission. It has a plain format that is easily read by scanners. It also has lots of keywords that increase its chances of being selected when an employer searches a database.

```
SAMUEL FEINMAN
489 Smithfield Road
Salem, OR 97301
503.491.3033
samfine@earthlink.net

= = = = = = = = = = = = = = = = = = = = =

SALES PROFESSIONAL

Dynamic, motivated, award-winning sales professional with extensive
experience. Troubleshooter and problem-solver. Team player who can
motivate self and others. Excellent management and training skills.

= = = = = = = = = = = = = = = = = = = = =

RELATED EXPERIENCE

Jackson Chevrolet, Springfield, OR
GENERAL MANAGER, XXXX-Present
* Consistently achieve top-ten volume dealer in the Northwest.
* Manage all dealership operations including computer systems, sales,
parts, service, and administration.
* Profitably operate dealership through difficult economic times.
* Meet or exceed customer service, parts, sales, and car service
objectives.
* Maintain high-profile used-car operation.

Afford-A-Ford, Albany, OR
ASSISTANT GENERAL MANAGER, XXXX-XXXX
* Consistently in top five for sales in district; met or exceeded sales
objectives.
* Supervised and trained staff of 90.
* Helped to convert a consistently money-losing store into a profitable
operation by end of first year.
* Focused on customer satisfaction through employee satisfaction and
training.
* Built strong parts and service business, managing excellent
interaction among parts, service, and sales.
* Instituted fleet-sales department and became top fleet-sales dealer
three years running.
* Built lease portfolio from virtually none to 31% of retail.

WetWater Pool Products, Salem, OR
SALES/CUSTOMER SERVICE, XXXX-XXXX
* Advised customers to purchase products that best met their needs while
focusing attention on products more profitable to company.
* Troubleshot and solved customer problems, identifying rapid solutions
and emphasizing customer satisfaction and retention.
* Oversaw shipping and receiving staff.

= = = = = = = = = = = = = = = = = = = = =

ADDITIONAL EXPERIENCE

State of Oregon, Salem, OR
COMPUTER TECHNICIAN INTERN, XXXX-XXXX
* Built customized computers for state offices.
* Worked with team on installation of computer systems.

= = = = = = = = = = = = = = = = = = = = =

EDUCATION

AS, Oregon Community College, Troy, OR
Major: Business studies

= = = = = = = = = = = = = = = = = = = = =

REFERENCES AVAILABLE ON REQUEST
```

Quick Tips for Writing a Cover Letter in 15 Minutes

Whether you're mailing, faxing, or e-mailing your resume, it is important to provide a letter along with your resume that explains why you are sending it—a cover letter (or cover message, in the case of e-mailing). Even when you post your resume in an online database (also known as a resume bank), the website where you're posting often has a place where you can upload or paste a cover letter. A cover letter highlights your key qualifications, explains your situation, and asks the recipient for some specific action, consideration, or response.

No matter to whom you are writing, virtually every good cover letter should follow these guidelines.

1. Write to Someone in Particular

Avoid sending a cover letter "To whom it may concern" or using some other impersonal opening. We all get enough junk mail, and if you don't send your letter to someone by name, it will be treated like junk mail.

2. Make Absolutely No Errors

One way to offend people right away is to misspell their names or use incorrect titles. If you are not 100 percent certain, call and verify the correct spelling of the name and other details before you send the letter. Also, review your letters carefully to be sure that they contain no typographical, grammatical, or other errors.

3. Personalize Your Content

No one is impressed by form letters, and you should not use them. Those computer-generated letters that automatically insert a name (known as merge mailings) never fool anyone, and cover letters done in this way are offensive. Small, targeted mailings to a carefully selected group of prospective employers can be effective if you tailor your cover letter to each recipient, but large mass mailings are a waste of time. If you can't customize your letter in some way, don't send it.

4. Present a Good Appearance

Your contacts with prospective employers should always be professional, so buy good-quality stationery and matching envelopes for times when you'll be mailing or hand-delivering a letter and resume. Use papers and envelopes that match or complement your resume paper. The standard 8½ × 11–inch paper size is typically used, but you can also use the smaller Monarch-size paper with matching envelopes. For colors, use white, ivory, or light beige—whatever matches your resume paper. Employers expect cover letters to be word processed and produced with excellent print quality.

Use a standard letter format that complements your resume type and format. You might find it easier to use your word-processing software's template functions than to create a format from scratch. Your letters don't have to be fancy; they do have to look professional. And don't forget the envelope! It should be typed and printed carefully, without errors.

You will send many of your cover letters as e-mail messages. All the rules for traditional cover letters apply equally to e-mail cover letters. Just because e-mail is a less formal means of communicating doesn't mean you can be careless with writing, spelling, grammar, punctuation, or presentation. But e-mail letters should be shorter and crisper than traditional paper letters.

5. Begin with a Friendly Opening

Start your letter by sharing the reason you are writing and, if appropriate, a reminder of any prior contacts or the name of the person who referred you. See the examples on pages 331 and 332 for ideas for beginning your letters.

6. Target Your Skills and Experiences

To effectively target your skills and experiences, you must know something about the organization, the job opportunity, or the person with whom you are dealing. Present any relevant background that may be of particular interest to the person to whom you are writing.

7. Close with an Action Statement

Don't close your letter without clearly identifying what you will do next. Don't leave it up to the employer to contact you, because that doesn't guarantee a response. Close on a positive note and let the employer know how and when you will be following up.

Sample Printed Cover Letter

Allan P. Raymond, CPA

29 Brookside Drive, Mystic, CT 06433
860.239.7671 • allanraymond@verizon.net

March 15, 20XX

Carol P. Graves, CPA
President, Graves & Andrews
254 Court Street
New London, CT 06320

Dear Carol:

I enjoyed our conversation at the recent CPA Society meeting and, as you suggested, I am forwarding my resume with this letter of interest in joining your firm.

You and I agreed that your clients deserve the best: the best accountants, the best strategies, and the greatest dedication to customer service. I am confident I can bring "the best" in both attitude and execution to your firm.

With more than ten years of accounting experience—the last five as a CPA and owner of an accounting firm specializing in tax—I have strong and well-proven professional skills. I thrive on the challenges and intricacies of tax accounting and stay up-to-date with tax code changes through both in-person and online training programs.

What satisfies me most in my professional life is the opportunity to help clients better manage, control, and benefit from their money. One of the keys to the good advice I give my clients is my deep understanding of the consequences of investment decisions on their tax situation. I have worked with businesses of all sizes—from one person to complex multimillion-dollar organizations—in diverse industries and have contributed strategies and planning recommendations as well as tax-related accounting services.

Having just concluded the sale of my business, I am eager for new professional challenges. I would like to explore my value as a tax accountant with your firm, and in pursuit of that objective I will call you next week to schedule a meeting. Thank you.

Best regards,

Allan P. Raymond

enclosure: resume

Written by Louise Kursmark

Sample E-mail Cover Letter

Dear Ms. Gold:

My sister, Tracy Oswald, tells me that you are looking for a systems administrator for your growing San Francisco operation.

I am experienced, reliable, loyal, and customer focused and would like to talk with you about joining your team.

The enclosed resume describes nearly 15 years of experience with Anthem Blue Cross/Blue Shield, during which I advanced to increasingly responsible technical positions. Whether independently or with a team, I worked hard to provide the best possible service and support to my "customers." I was recognized for my strong technical skills, ability to guide less experienced support people, and 100% reliability.

A recent downsizing at Anthem caused my position to be eliminated, and I am looking for a new opportunity with a company like yours, where my technical abilities, positive attitude, and dedication will be valued.

I will call you next week in hopes of getting together soon.

Yours truly,

Kevin Oswald

****
Attachment: resume

Written by Louise Kursmark

STEP 5: Organize Your Time to Get Two Interviews a Day

The average job seeker gets about five interviews a month—fewer than two a week. Yet many job seekers use the methods in this *Quick Job Search* to get two interviews a day. Getting two interviews a day equals 10 a week and 40 a month. That's 800 percent more interviews than the average job seeker gets. Who do you think will get a job offer quicker?

You might think that getting two interviews a day sounds impossible. However, getting two interviews a day is quite possible if you redefine what counts as an interview and use the networking techniques from step 3.

> **The New Definition of an Interview:** Any face-to-face contact with someone who has the authority to hire or supervise a person with your skills—even if no opening exists at the time you talk with them.

If you use this new definition, it becomes *much* easier to get interviews. You can now interview with all sorts of potential employers, not just those who have job openings now. While most other job seekers look for advertised or actual openings, you can get interviews before a job opens up or before it is advertised and widely known. You will be considered for jobs that may soon be created but that others will not know about. And, of course, you can also interview for existing openings just as everyone else does.

Spending as much time as possible on your job search and setting a job search schedule are important parts of this step. Researchers at the University of Missouri found in a 2009 study that developing and following a job search plan from the start, as well as having a positive attitude about your search, had a significant impact on job search success (*U.S. News & World Report*, September 24, 2009).

Make Your Search a Full-Time Job

Job seekers average fewer than 15 hours a week looking for work. On average, unemployment lasts three or more months, with some people out of work far longer (for example, older workers and higher earners). My many years of experience researching job seeking indicate that the more time you spend on your job search each week, the less time you will likely remain unemployed.

Of course, using the more effective job search methods presented in this book also helps. Many job search programs that teach job seekers my basic approach of using more effective methods and spending more time looking have proven that these seekers often find a job in half the average time. More importantly, many job seekers also find better jobs using these methods.

So, if you are unemployed and looking for a full-time job, you should plan to look on a full-time basis. It just makes sense to do so, although many do not, or they start out well but quickly get discouraged. Most job seekers simply don't have a structured plan—they have no idea what they are going to do next Thursday. The plan that follows will show you how to structure your job search like a job.

Decide How Much Time You Will Spend Looking for Work Each Week and Day

First and most importantly, decide how many hours you are willing to spend each week on your job search. You should spend a minimum of 25 hours a week on hardcore job search activities with no goofing around. The following worksheet walks you through a simple but effective process to set a job search schedule for each week.

PLAN YOUR JOB SEARCH WEEK

1. How many hours are you willing to spend each week looking for a job?

   _____

   _____

2. Which days of the week will you spend looking for a job?

   _____

   _____

3. How many hours will you look each day?_____

   _____

4. At what times will you begin and end your job search on each of these days?

   _____

   _____

Create a Specific Daily Job Search Schedule

Having a specific daily schedule is essential because most job seekers find it hard to stay productive each day. The sample daily schedule that follows is the result of years of research into what schedule gets the best results. I tested many schedules in job search programs I ran, and this particular schedule worked best.

Consider using a schedule like this sample daily schedule. Why? Because it works.

A Sample Daily Schedule That Works

Time	Activity
7–8 a.m.	Get up, shower, dress, eat breakfast.
8–8:15 a.m.	Organize workspace, review schedule for today's interviews and promised follow-ups, check e-mail, and update schedule as needed.
8:15–9 a.m.	Review old leads for follow-up needed today; develop new leads from want ads, yellow pages, the Internet, warm contact lists, and other sources; complete daily contact list.
9–10 a.m.	Make phone calls and set up interviews.
10–10:15 a.m.	Take a break.
10:15–11 a.m.	Make more phone calls; set up more interviews.
11 a.m.–Noon	Send follow-up notes and do other office activities as needed.
Noon–1 p.m.	Lunch break, relax.
1–3 p.m.	Go on interviews; make cold contacts in the field.
Evening	Read job search books, make calls to warm contacts not reachable during the day, work on a better resume, spend time with friends and family, exercise, relax.

If you are not accustomed to using a daily schedule book or electronic planner, promise yourself to get a good one today. Choose one that allows for each day's plan on an hourly basis, plus daily to-do lists. Record your daily schedule in advance, and then add interviews as they come. Get used to carrying your planner with you and use it!

You can find a variety of computer programs and smartphone apps to help organize your job search. An example of a website that offers a free job search planning system online is JibberJobber (www.jibberjobber.com).

STEP 6: Dramatically Improve Your Interviewing Skills

Interviews are where the job search action is. You have to get them; then you have to do well in them. According to surveys of employers, most job seekers do not effectively present the skills they have to do the job. Even worse, most job seekers can't answer one or more problem questions.

This lack of performance in interviews is one reason why employers will often hire a job seeker who does well in the interview over someone with better credentials. The good news is that you can do simple things to dramatically improve your interviewing skills. This section emphasizes interviewing tips and techniques that make the most difference.

Your First Impression May Be the Only One You Make

Some research suggests that if the interviewer forms a negative impression in the first five minutes of an interview, your chances of getting a job offer approach zero. I know from experience that many job seekers can create a lasting negative impression within seconds.

Tips for Interviewing

Because a positive first impression is so important, I share these suggestions to help you get off to a good start:

- **Make a good impression before you arrive.** Your resume, e-mails, applications, and other written correspondence create an impression before the interview, so make them professional and error free.

- **Do some homework on the organization before you go.** You can often get information on a business and on industry trends from the Internet or a library.

- **Dress and groom the same way the interviewer is likely to be dressed—but better!** Employer surveys find that almost half of all people's dress or grooming creates an initial negative impression. So this is a big problem. If necessary, get advice on your interviewing outfits from someone who dresses well. Pay close attention to your grooming, too—little things do count.

- **Be early.** Leave in plenty of time to be a few minutes early to an interview.

- **Be friendly and respectful with the receptionist.** Doing otherwise will often get back to the interviewer and result in a quick rejection.

- **Follow the interviewer's lead in the first few minutes.** The interview often begins with informal small talk, but the interviewer uses this time to see how you interact. This is a good time to make a positive comment on the organization or even something you see in the office.

- **Understand that a traditional interview is not a friendly exchange.** In a traditional interview situation, there is a job opening, and you will be one of several applicants for it. In this setting, the employer's task is to eliminate all applicants but one. The interviewer's questions are designed to elicit information that can be used to screen you out. And your objective is to avoid getting screened out. It's hardly an open and honest interaction, is it?

   Setting up interviews before an opening exists eliminates the stress of a traditional interview. In pre-interviews, employers are not trying to screen you out, and you are not trying to keep them from finding out stuff about

(continued)

(continued)

you. Having said that, knowing how to answer questions that might be asked in a traditional interview is good preparation for any interview you face.

● **Be prepared to answer the tough interview questions.** Your answers to a few key problem questions may determine whether you get a job offer. There are simply too many possible interview questions to cover one by one. Instead, 10 basic questions cover variations of most other interview questions. So, if you can learn to answer the Top 10 Problem Interview Questions well, you will know how to answer most others.

● **Be prepared for the most important interview question of all.** "Why should I hire you?" is the most important question of all to answer well. Do you have a convincing argument why someone should hire you over someone else? If you don't, you probably won't get that job you really want. So think carefully about why someone should hire you and practice your response. Then make sure you communicate this in the interview, even if the interviewer never asks the question in a clear way.

Top 10 Problem Interview Questions

1. Why should I hire you?
2. Why don't you tell me about yourself?
3. What are your major strengths?
4. What are your major weaknesses?
5. What sort of pay do you expect to receive?
6. How does your previous experience relate to the jobs we have here?
7. What are your plans for the future?
8. What will your former employer (or references) say about you?
9. Why are you looking for this type of position, and why here?
10. Why don't you tell me about your personal situation?

Follow the Three-Step Process for Answering Interview Questions

I've developed a three-step process for answering interview questions. I know this might seem too simple, but the three-step process is easy to remember and can help you create a good answer to most interview questions. The technique has worked for thousands of people, so consider trying it.

1. **Understand what is really being asked.** Most questions are designed to find out about your self-management skills and personality, but interviewers are rarely this blunt. The employer's *real* question is often one or more of the following:

    ● Can I depend on you?

    ● Are you easy to get along with?

    ● Are you a good worker?

    ● Do you have the experience and training to do the job if we hire you?

    ● Are you likely to stay on the job for a reasonable period of time and be productive?

    Ultimately, if you don't convince the employer that you will stay and be a good worker, it won't matter if you have the best credentials—he or she won't hire you.

2. **Answer the question briefly in a nondamaging way.** Present the facts of your particular work experience as advantages, not disadvantages. Many interview questions encourage you to provide negative information. One classic question in the list of Top 10 Problem Interview Questions is "What are your major weaknesses?" This is obviously a trick question, and many people are just not prepared for it.

   A good response is to mention something that is not very damaging, such as "I have been told that I am a perfectionist, sometimes not delegating as effectively as I might." But your answer is not complete until you continue with the next step.

3. **Answer the real question by presenting your related skills.** Base your answer on the key skills you have that support the job, and give examples to support these skills. For example, an employer might say to a recent graduate, "We were looking for someone with more experience in this field. Why should we consider you?" Here is one possible answer:

   "I'm sure there are people who have more experience, but I do have more than six years of work experience, including three years of advanced training and hands-on experience using the latest methods and techniques. Because my training is recent, I am open to new ideas and am used to working hard and learning quickly."

   In the previous example (about your need to delegate), a good skills statement might be

   "I've been working on this problem and have learned to let my staff do more, making sure that they have good training and supervision. I've found that their performance improves, and it frees me up to do other things."

Whatever your situation, learn to answer questions in ways that present you well. It's essential to communicate your skills during an interview, and the three-step process can help you answer problem questions and dramatically improve your responses. It works!

How to Earn a Thousand Dollars a Minute

What do you do when the employer asks, "How much money would it take to get you to join our company?"

Tips on Negotiating Pay

Remember these few essential tips when it comes time to negotiate your pay:

● **The #1 Salary Negotiation Rule: The person who names a specific amount first loses.**

● **The only time to negotiate is after you have been offered the job.** Employers want to know how much you want to be paid so that they can eliminate you from consideration. They figure if you want too much, you won't be happy with the job and won't stay. And if you will take too little, they may think you don't have enough experience. So never discuss your salary expectations until an employer offers you the job.

● **If pressed, speak in terms of wide pay ranges.** If you are pushed to reveal your pay expectations early in an interview, ask the interviewer what the normal pay range is for this job. Interviewers will often tell you, and you can say that you would consider offers in this range.

   If you are forced to be more specific, speak in terms of a wide pay range. If you figure that the company will likely pay from $25,000 to $29,000 a year, for example, say that you would consider "any fair offer in the mid-twenties to low thirties." This statement covers the employer's range and goes a bit higher. If all else fails, tell the interviewer that you would consider any reasonable offer.

   For this tip to work, you must know in advance what the job is likely to pay. You can get this information by asking people who do similar work, or from a variety of books and Internet sources of career information, such as the *Occupational Outlook Handbook* (www.bls.gov/oco) or Salary.com.

● **If you want the job, you should say so.** This is no time to be playing games.

(continued)

(continued)

- **Don't say "no" too quickly.** Never, ever turn down a job offer during an interview! Instead, thank the interviewer for the offer and ask to consider the offer overnight. You can turn it down tomorrow, saying how much you appreciate the offer and asking to be considered for other jobs that pay better. And it is okay to ask for additional pay or other concessions. But if you simply can't accept the offer, say why and ask the interviewer to keep you in mind for future opportunities. You just never know.

STEP 7: Follow Up on All Job Leads

It's a fact: People who follow up with potential employers and with others in their network get jobs more quickly than those who do not.

Rules for Effective Follow-Up

Here are four rules to guide you in following up in your job search:

- **Send a thank-you note or e-mail to every person who helps you in your job search.**
- **Send the note within 24 hours after speaking with the person.**
- **Enclose JIST Cards with thank-you notes and all other correspondence.**
- **Develop a system to keep following up with good contacts.**

Thank-You Notes Make a Difference

Although thank-you notes can be e-mailed, most people appreciate and are more impressed by a mailed note. Here are some tips about mailed thank-you notes that you can easily adapt to e-mail use:

- You can handwrite or type thank-you notes on quality paper and matching envelopes.

- Keep the notes simple, neat, and error free.

- Make sure to include a few copies of your JIST Card in the envelope.

Following is an example of a simple thank-you note.

April 5, XXXX

M. Kijek,

Thanks so much for your willingness to see me next Wednesday at 9 a.m. I know that I am one of many who are interested in working with your organization. I appreciate the opportunity to meet you and learn more about the position.

I've enclosed a JIST Card that presents the basics of my skills for this job and will bring my resume to the interview. Please call me if you have any questions at all.

Sincerely,

Bruce Vernon

Use Job Lead Cards to Follow Up

If you use contact management software or an app on your phone, use it to schedule follow-up activities. But the simple paper system I describe here can work very well or can be adapted for setting up your contact management software.

- Use a simple 3-by-5–inch card to record essential information about each person in your network.
- Buy a 3-by-5–inch card file box and tabs for each day of the month.
- File the cards under the date you want to contact the person.
- Follow through by contacting the person on that date.

I've found that staying in touch with a good contact every other week can pay off big. Here's a sample card to give you ideas about creating your own.

ORGANIZATION: _Mutual Health Insurance_

CONTACT PERSON: _Anna Tomey_   PHONE: _317-355-0216_

SOURCE OF LEAD: _Aunt Ruth_

NOTES: _4/10 Called. Anna on vacation. Call back 4/15. 4/15 Interview set 4/20 at 1:30. 4/20 Anna showed me around. They use the same computers we used in school! (Friendly people.) Sent thank-you note and JIST Card, call back 5/1. 5/1 Second interview 5/8 at 9 a.m.!_

In Closing

This is a short section, but it may be all you need to get a better job in less time. I hope this will be true for you, and I wish you well in your search. Remember this: You won't get a job offer because someone knocks on your door and offers one. Job seeking does involve luck, but you are more likely to have good luck if you are out getting interviews.

I'll close this section with a few final tips:

- **Approach your job search as if it were a job itself.** Create and stick to a daily schedule, and spend at least 25 hours a week looking.

- **Follow up on each lead you generate and ask each contact for referrals.**

- **Set out each day to schedule at least two interviews.** Remember the new definition of an interview—an interview can just be talking to a potential employer that doesn't have an opening now but might in the future.

- **Send out lots of thank-you notes and JIST Cards.**

- **When you want the job, tell the employer that you want it and why you should be hired over everyone else.**

Don't get discouraged. There are lots of jobs out there, and someone needs an employee with your skills—your job is to find that someone.

I wish you luck in your job search and in your life.

ESSENTIAL JOB SEARCH DATA WORKSHEET

Take some time to complete this worksheet carefully. It will help you write your resume and answer interview questions. You can also photocopy it and take it with you to help complete applications and as a reference throughout your job search. Use an erasable pen or pencil to allow for corrections. Whenever possible, emphasize skills and accomplishments that support your ability to do the job you want. Use extra sheets as needed. You can also find this worksheet online at www.jist.com/pdf/EJSDW.pdf.

Your name_____

Date completed_____

Job objective_____

Key Accomplishments

List three accomplishments that best prove your ability to do the kind of job you want.

1. _____
2. _____
3. _____

Education and Training

Name of high school(s) and specific years attended_____

_____

Subjects related to job objective_____

_____

_____

Related extracurricular activities/hobbies/leisure activities_____

_____

_____

Accomplishments/things you did well_____

_____

_____

Specific things you can do as a result_____

_____

_____

(continued)

(continued)

Schools you attended after high school, specific years attended, and degrees/certificates earned

_____

_____

_____

Courses related to job objective_____

_____

_____

Related extracurricular activities/hobbies/leisure activities_____

_____

_____

Accomplishments/things you did well_____

_____

_____

Specific things you can do as a result_____

_____

_____

Other Training

Include formal or informal learning, workshops, military training, skills you learned on the job or from hobbies—anything that will help support your job objective. Include specific dates, certificates earned, or other details as needed._____

_____

_____

Work and Volunteer History

List your most recent job first, followed by each previous job. Military experience, unpaid or volunteer work, and work in a family business should be included here, too. If needed, use additional sheets to cover *all* significant paid or unpaid work experiences. Emphasize details that will help support your new job objective. Include numbers to support what you did: the number of people served over one or more years, number of transactions processed, percentage of sales increased, total inventory value you were responsible for, payroll of the staff you supervised, total budget responsible for, and so on. Emphasize results you achieved, using numbers to support them whenever possible. Mentioning these things on your resume and in an interview will help you get the job you want.

Job 1

Dates employed _____

Name of organization _____

Supervisor's name and job title _____

Address _____

_____

Phone number/e-mail address/website _____

_____

What did you accomplish and do well? _____

_____

_____

Things you learned; skills you developed or used _____

_____

_____

Raises, promotions, positive evaluations, awards _____

_____

_____

Computer software, hardware, and other equipment you used _____

_____

_____

Other details that might support your job objective _____

_____

_____

(continued)

(continued)

Job 2

Dates employed _____

Name of organization _____

Supervisor's name and job title _____

Address _____

_____

Phone number/e-mail address/website _____

_____

What did you accomplish and do well? _____

_____

_____

Things you learned; skills you developed or used _____

_____

_____

Raises, promotions, positive evaluations, awards _____

_____

_____

Computer software, hardware, and other equipment you used _____

_____

_____

Other details that might support your job objective _____

_____

_____

Job 3

Dates employed _____

Name of organization _____

Supervisor's name and job title _____

Address _____

_____

Phone number/e-mail address/website _____

_____

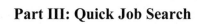

What did you accomplish and do well? _____

_____

_____

Things you learned; skills you developed or used _____

_____

_____

Raises, promotions, positive evaluations, awards _____

_____

_____

Computer software, hardware, and other equipment you used _____

_____

_____

Other details that might support your job objective _____

_____

_____

References

Think of people who know your work well and will be positive about your work and character. Past supervisors are best. Contact them and tell them what type of job you want and your qualifications, and ask what they will say about you if contacted by a potential employer. Some employers will not provide references by phone, so ask them for a letter of reference in advance. If a past employer may say negative things, negotiate what he or she will say or get written references from others you worked with there.

Reference name _____

Position or title _____

Relationship to you _____

Contact information (complete address, phone number, e-mail address)

_____

_____

Reference name _____

Position or title _____

Relationship to you _____

Contact information (complete address, phone number, e-mail address)

_____

_____

(continued)

(continued)

Reference name_____

Position or title_____

Relationship to you_____

Contact information (complete address, phone number, e-mail address)

_____

_____

Additional Resources

Thousands of books and countless Internet sites provide information on career subjects. Space limitations do not permit me to describe the many good resources available, so I list here some of the most useful ones. Because this is my list, I've included books I've written or that JIST publishes. You should be able to find these and many other resources at libraries, bookstores, and Web bookselling sites such as Amazon.com.

Resume and Cover Letter Books

My books: *The Quick Resume & Cover Letter Book* is one of the top-selling resume books. It is very simple to follow and has good sample resumes written by professional resume writers. For more in-depth but still quick help, check out my two books in the *Help in a Hurry* series: *Same-Day Resume* (with advice on creating a simple resume in an hour and a better one later) and *15-Minute Cover Letter,* co-authored with Louise Kursmark (offering sample cover letters and tips for writing them fast and effectively).

Other books published by JIST: The following titles include many sample resumes written by professional resume writers, as well as good advice: *Amazing Resumes* by Jim Bright and Joanne Earl; *Cover Letter Magic* by Wendy S. Enelow and Louise M. Kursmark; the entire *Expert Resumes* series by Enelow and Kursmark; *Federal Resume Guidebook* by Kathryn Kraemer Troutman; *Gallery of Best Resumes, Gallery of Best Cover Letters,* and other books by David F. Noble; *Résumé Magic* by Susan Britton Whitcomb; *30-Minute Resume Makeover* by Louise Kursmark; and *Step-by-Step Resumes* by Evelyn Salvador.

Job Search and Interviewing Books

My books: You may want to check out my book in the *Help in a Hurry* series *Next-Day Job Interview* (quick tips for preparing for a job interview at the last minute). *The Very Quick Job Search* is a thorough book with detailed advice and a "quick" section of key tips you can finish in a few hours. *Getting the Job You Really Want* includes many in-the-book activities and good career decision-making and job search advice.

Other books published by JIST: *Job Search Magic, Interview Magic,* and *The Christian's Career Journey* by Susan Britton Whitcomb; *Make Job Loss Work for You* by Richard and Terri Deems; *Military-to-Civilian Career Transition Guide* by Janet Farley; *Your Dream Job Game Plan* by Molly Fletcher; *Ultimate Job Search* by Richard H. Beatty; *The Career Coward's Guide* series by Katy Piotrowski; and *The Twitter Job Search Guide* by Susan Britton Whitcomb, Chandlee Bryan, and Deb Dib.

Books with Information on Jobs

JIST's primary reference books: The *Occupational Outlook Handbook* is the source of job titles listed in this book. Published by the U.S. Department of Labor and updated every other year, the *OOH* covers about 90 percent of the workforce. The *O*NET Dictionary of Occupational Titles* book has descriptions for 950 jobs based on the O*NET (Occupational Information Network) database developed by the Department of Labor. The *Enhanced Occupational Outlook Handbook* includes the *OOH* descriptions plus more than 5,600 additional descriptions of related jobs from the O*NET and other sources.

Other books published by JIST: Here are a few good books that include job descriptions and helpful details on career options: *Best Jobs for the 21st Century, 50 Best Jobs for Your Personality, 40 Best Fields for Your Career, 200 Best Jobs for College Graduates,* and *300 Best Jobs Without a Four-Year Degree.* These books include selected jobs from the *OOH* and other information: The *Top Careers* series and *Overnight Career Choice.*

Internet Resources

There are too many websites to list, but here are a few places you can start. A book by Anne Wolfinger titled *Best Career and Education Web Sites* gives unbiased reviews of the most helpful sites and ideas on how to use them. *Job Seeker's Online Goldmine,* by Janet Wall, lists the extensive free online job search tools from government and other sources. The *Occupational Outlook Handbook*'s job descriptions also include Internet addresses for related organizations. Be aware that some websites provide poor advice, so ask your librarian, instructor, or counselor for suggestions on those best for your needs.

Other Resources

Libraries: Most libraries have the books mentioned here, as well as many other resources. Many also provide Internet access so that you can research online information. Ask the librarian for help with finding what you need.

People: People who hold the jobs that interest you are among the best career information sources. Ask them what they like and don't like about their work, how they got started, and the education or training needed. Most people are helpful and will give advice you can't get any other way.

Career counseling: A good vocational counselor can help you explore career options. Take advantage of this service if it is available to you! Also consider a career-planning course or program, which will encourage you to be more thorough in your thinking.

Use a Career Portfolio to Support Your Resume

Your resume is impressive, but there is another way that you can show prospective employers evidence of who you are and what you can do: a career portfolio.

What Is a Career Portfolio?

Unlike a resume, a career portfolio is a collection of documents that can include a variety of items. Here are some items you may want to place in your portfolio:

- Resume.

- School transcripts.

- Summary of skills.

- Credentials, such as diplomas and certificates of recognition.

- Reference letters from school officials and instructors, former employers, or coworkers.

- List of accomplishments: Describe hobbies and interests that are not directly related to your job objective and are not included on your resume.

- Examples of your work: Depending on your situation, you can include samples of your art, photographs of a project, audio, video, images of Web pages you developed, and other media that can provide examples of your work.

Place each item on a separate page when you assemble your career portfolio.

Create a Digital Portfolio

A digital portfolio, also known as an electronic portfolio, contains all the information from your career portfolio in an electronic format. This material is then copied onto a CD-ROM or published on a website. With a digital portfolio, you can present your skills to a greater number of people than you can your paper career portfolio. VisualCV (www.visualcv.com) is one site that helps you build a digital portfolio and post it online.

YOUR CAREER PORTFOLIO

On the following lines, list the items you want to include in your career portfolio. Think specifically of those items that show your skills, education, and personal accomplishments.

_____

_____

_____

_____

_____

_____

_____

_____

_____

_____

_____

_____

_____

_____

_____

_____

_____

_____

_____

_____

_____

_____

_____

_____

_____

_____

_____

_____

_____

_____

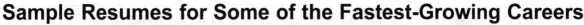

Sample Resumes for Some of the Fastest-Growing Careers

If you read the previous information, you know that I believe you should not depend on a resume alone in your job search. Even so, you will most likely need one, and you should have a good one.

Unlike some career authors, I do not preach that there is only one right way to do a resume. I encourage you to be an individual and to do what you think will work well for you. But I also know that some resumes are clearly better than others. The following pages contain some resumes that you can use as examples when preparing your own resume.

Each resume was written by a professional resume writer who is a member of one or more professional associations. These writers are highly qualified and hold various credentials. Most will provide help (for a fee) and welcome your contacting them (although this is not a personal endorsement).

The resumes appear in books published by JIST Publishing, including the following:

- *Expert Resumes for Health Care Careers,* Second Edition, by Wendy S. Enelow and Louise M. Kursmark

- *Expert Resumes for People Returning to Work,* Second Edition, by Wendy S. Enelow and Louise M. Kursmark

Contact Information for Resume Contributors

The following professional resume writers contributed resumes to this section. Their names are listed in alphabetical order. Each entry indicates which resume(s) that person contributed.

Arnold G. Boldt, CPRW, JCTC
Arnold-Smith Associates
625 Panorama Trail
Bldg. One, Suite 120
Rochester, NY 14625
Phone: (585) 383-0350
E-mail: Arnie@ResumeSOS.com
www.ResumeSOS.com
Resume on pages 363–364

Carolyn Braden, CPRW
Hendersonville, TN
Resume on page 356

Alice P. Braxton, CPRW, CEIP
President, Accutype Resumes &
  Secretarial Services
2634 Trail Five
Burlington, NC 27215
Phone: (336) 227-9091
E-mail: accutype@triad.rr.com
Resume on page 355

Norine T. Dagliano, BA, CPRW
Principal, ekm Inspirations
Hagerstown, MD 21740
Phone: (301) 766-2032 or
  (240) 217-5075
Fax: (301) 745-5700
E-mail: norine@ekminspirations.com
www.ekminspirations.com
Resume on pages 357–358

Denise Lupardo
Lake Forest, CA
Resume on page 362

Linda Matias, JCTC, CIC, NCRW
Executive Director, CareerStrides
182 Merrill St.
Brentwood, NY 11717
Phone: (631) 382-2425
E-mail: linda@careerstrides.com
www.careerstrides.com
Resume on page 352

Ellen Mulqueen, M.A., CERW, CECC
In memoriam
Resume on page 359

Makini Siwatu, CPRW, IJCTC, CEIP,
  CJST
Seattle, WA
Resume on pages 360–361

Ann Stewart, CPRW
President, Advantage Services
P.O. Box 525
Roanoke, TX 76262
Phone: (817) 424-1448
Fax: (817) 329-7165
E-mail: ASresume@charter.net
Resume on pages 353–354

Pearl White, JCTC, CPRW, CEIP
Principal, A 1st Impression Resume &
  Career Coaching Services
41 Tangerine
Irvine, CA 92618
Phone: (949) 651-1068
Fax: (949) 651-9415
E-mail: pearlwhite1@cox.net
www.a1stimpression.com
Resume on page 365

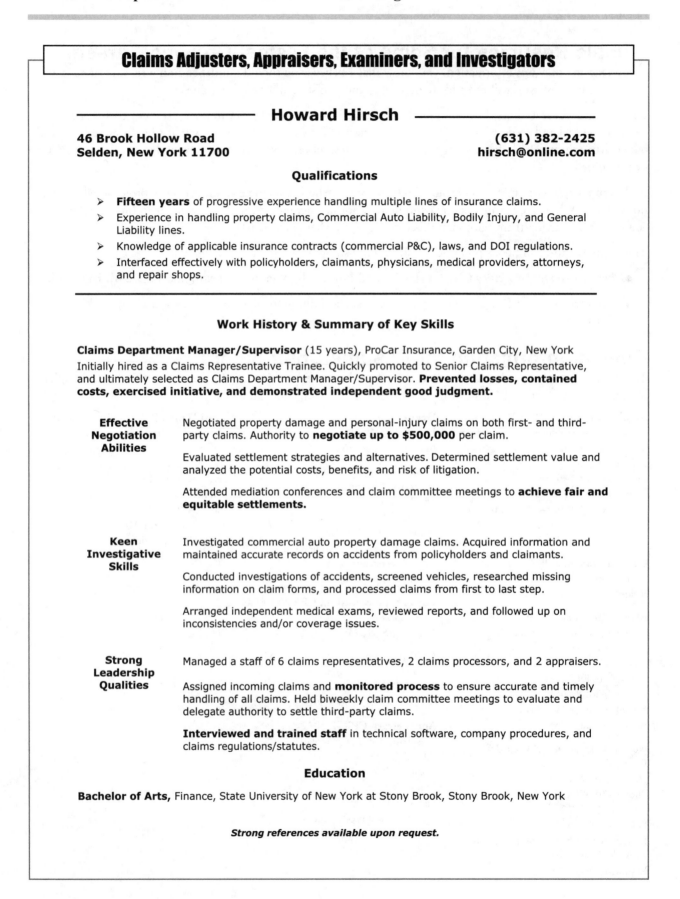

Claims Adjusters, Appraisers, Examiners, and Investigators

Howard Hirsch

46 Brook Hollow Road
Selden, New York 11700

(631) 382-2425
hirsch@online.com

Qualifications

➢ **Fifteen years** of progressive experience handling multiple lines of insurance claims.

➢ Experience in handling property claims, Commercial Auto Liability, Bodily Injury, and General Liability lines.

➢ Knowledge of applicable insurance contracts (commercial P&C), laws, and DOI regulations.

➢ Interfaced effectively with policyholders, claimants, physicians, medical providers, attorneys, and repair shops.

Work History & Summary of Key Skills

Claims Department Manager/Supervisor (15 years), ProCar Insurance, Garden City, New York

Initially hired as a Claims Representative Trainee. Quickly promoted to Senior Claims Representative, and ultimately selected as Claims Department Manager/Supervisor. **Prevented losses, contained costs, exercised initiative, and demonstrated independent good judgment.**

Effective Negotiation Abilities	Negotiated property damage and personal-injury claims on both first- and third-party claims. Authority to **negotiate up to $500,000** per claim.
	Evaluated settlement strategies and alternatives. Determined settlement value and analyzed the potential costs, benefits, and risk of litigation.
	Attended mediation conferences and claim committee meetings to **achieve fair and equitable settlements.**
Keen Investigative Skills	Investigated commercial auto property damage claims. Acquired information and maintained accurate records on accidents from policyholders and claimants.
	Conducted investigations of accidents, screened vehicles, researched missing information on claim forms, and processed claims from first to last step.
	Arranged independent medical exams, reviewed reports, and followed up on inconsistencies and/or coverage issues.
Strong Leadership Qualities	Managed a staff of 6 claims representatives, 2 claims processors, and 2 appraisers.
	Assigned incoming claims and **monitored process** to ensure accurate and timely handling of all claims. Held biweekly claim committee meetings to evaluate and delegate authority to settle third-party claims.
	Interviewed and trained staff in technical software, company procedures, and claims regulations/statutes.

Education

Bachelor of Arts, Finance, State University of New York at Stony Brook, Stony Brook, New York

Strong references available upon request.

Computer Network, Systems, and Database Administrators

PAUL M. CLARK
500 Park Avenue   (972) 280-7240
Dallas, TX 75234   mclark@msn.com

Information Technology Professional

**Offering a broad range of technical experience and skills and
a strong desire to return to an IT support role.**

Hardware	Server:	Compaq and Hewlett-Packard
	Desktop:	Hewlett-Packard, Compaq, Dell, and IBM
	Midrange:	IBM AS/400
Software		Novell NetWare, Microsoft Windows NT, Windows Vista and XP, OS/400, SNADS, TCP/IP, and RPG400.
Certifications		Novell 200, Networking Technologies, Microsoft M803, Administering Microsoft Windows NT 4.0, Microsoft 770, Install/Configure Windows NT 4.0.

PROFESSIONAL EXPERIENCE

2004–Present   **Clark Software Distribution • Dallas, Texas, owner**
Metroplex Technology Systems • Fort Worth, Texas, partner
Entrepreneur

Plan and manage all aspects of the business, including goal setting, marketing and sales, financial planning, operations, and reporting.

2002–2004   **Security Technology Southwest Division • Dallas, Texas**
Regional Support Services Manager

Managed IT support services in the Dallas region: server administration, desktop/server training, LAN technical support, regional vendor management, and product evaluation; deployment of desktop hardware, operating system software, office applications software, anti-virus utilities, server operating system software, backup utilities, and server anti-virus utilities.

- Under the direction of the vice president of regional support services, established organizational goals based on business needs; defined project priorities; played leadership role in planning, strategy, and status sessions with vice president and functional managers. Managed up to $5 million annual IT budget.
- Managed 24/7 operation in client/server environment; supported more than 30 servers in a corporate network of more than 500.
- Provided IT services to more than 2,800 users in the Dallas region.
- Set corporate standard for servers and desktop hardware and software configuration (30,000 desktops).
- Led development of first Building Server Administration Operations Manual, implemented company-wide.

(continued)

(continued)

PAUL M. CLARK, page 2

1997–2002   **Security Technology Retirement Services Company • Dallas, Texas**
Systems Manager, 1999–2002
Project Manager, 1997–1998
Project Leader, 1997

Supported the Institutional Retirement (401k) record-keeping business. Resolved diverse problems and developed, enhanced, and implemented client/server applications, client/server hardware, mainframe business applications, AS/400 business applications and hardware, network communications, and the corresponding operating systems software.

- Promoted from project leader, managing small to medium-sized projects, to project manager, and then to systems manager, responsible for establishing organizational goals, defining project priorities, and participating in planning, strategy, and status sessions with vice president and functional managers.
- Automated Microfiche Data Routing process, saving $200,000 and reducing turnaround time from 5–7 days to 2–3 days.
- Implemented desktop PCs at Cincinnati, Ohio, site; removed mainframe terminals.
- Designed, developed, and implemented new AS/400 computer room and its infrastructure.
- Recognized with Outstanding Service Award for managing successful move of 1,000+ users to two new buildings (500+ each).
- Led Client Service Operation Forum, a traveling road show designed to communicate technology direction to upper management of Security Technology's business community.

EDUCATION

DeVry Institute • Irving, Texas
Computer Science
Certificate of Completion, 1988

Brookhaven College • Dallas, Texas
Business Administration course work, 1982–1985

Significant corporate continuing education:

       Technical Skill-Building
       Project Management
       Strategic Coaching
       Performance Management

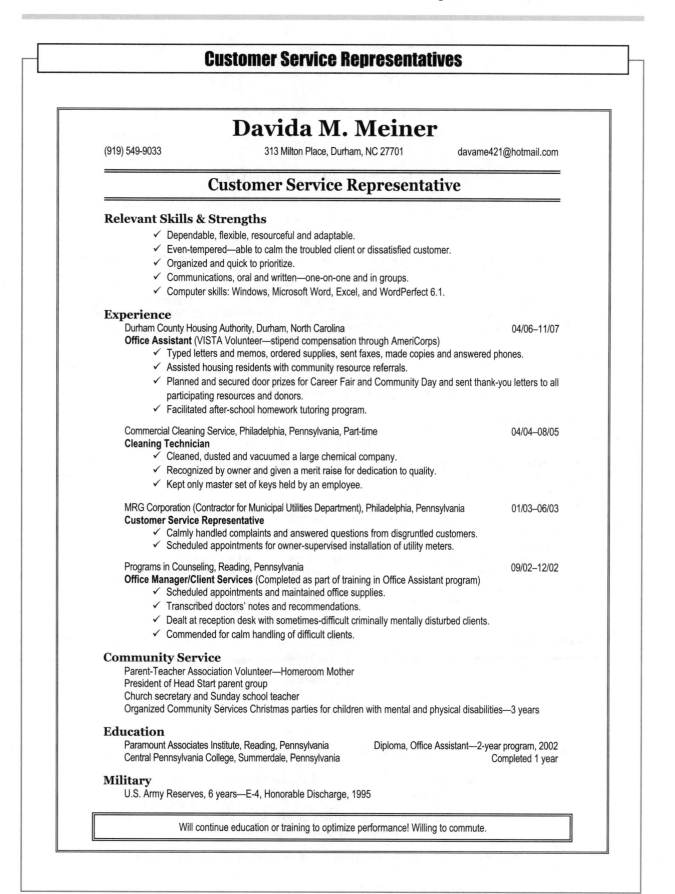

Customer Service Representatives

Davida M. Meiner

(919) 549-9033   313 Milton Place, Durham, NC 27701   davame421@hotmail.com

Customer Service Representative

Relevant Skills & Strengths
- ✓ Dependable, flexible, resourceful and adaptable.
- ✓ Even-tempered—able to calm the troubled client or dissatisfied customer.
- ✓ Organized and quick to prioritize.
- ✓ Communications, oral and written—one-on-one and in groups.
- ✓ Computer skills: Windows, Microsoft Word, Excel, and WordPerfect 6.1.

Experience
Durham County Housing Authority, Durham, North Carolina   04/06–11/07
Office Assistant (VISTA Volunteer—stipend compensation through AmeriCorps)
- ✓ Typed letters and memos, ordered supplies, sent faxes, made copies and answered phones.
- ✓ Assisted housing residents with community resource referrals.
- ✓ Planned and secured door prizes for Career Fair and Community Day and sent thank-you letters to all participating resources and donors.
- ✓ Facilitated after-school homework tutoring program.

Commercial Cleaning Service, Philadelphia, Pennsylvania, Part-time   04/04–08/05
Cleaning Technician
- ✓ Cleaned, dusted and vacuumed a large chemical company.
- ✓ Recognized by owner and given a merit raise for dedication to quality.
- ✓ Kept only master set of keys held by an employee.

MRG Corporation (Contractor for Municipal Utilities Department), Philadelphia, Pennsylvania   01/03–06/03
Customer Service Representative
- ✓ Calmly handled complaints and answered questions from disgruntled customers.
- ✓ Scheduled appointments for owner-supervised installation of utility meters.

Programs in Counseling, Reading, Pennsylvania   09/02–12/02
Office Manager/Client Services (Completed as part of training in Office Assistant program)
- ✓ Scheduled appointments and maintained office supplies.
- ✓ Transcribed doctors' notes and recommendations.
- ✓ Dealt at reception desk with sometimes-difficult criminally mentally disturbed clients.
- ✓ Commended for calm handling of difficult clients.

Community Service
Parent-Teacher Association Volunteer—Homeroom Mother
President of Head Start parent group
Church secretary and Sunday school teacher
Organized Community Services Christmas parties for children with mental and physical disabilities—3 years

Education
Paramount Associates Institute, Reading, Pennsylvania   Diploma, Office Assistant—2-year program, 2002
Central Pennsylvania College, Summerdale, Pennsylvania   Completed 1 year

Military
U.S. Army Reserves, 6 years—E-4, Honorable Discharge, 1995

Will continue education or training to optimize performance! Willing to commute.

Dental Assistants

DENISE A. WOLFE

7102 Dalewood Court — Nashville, Tennessee 37207 — (615) 860-2922 — dwolfe@email.com

SUMMARY OF QUALIFICATIONS

- **REGISTERED DENTAL ASSISTANT** with ten years of experience assisting with direct patient care. Special interest in pediatric patient care, with the desire and willingness to learn other areas of dentistry.

- Graduate of Dental Assistant program at Volunteer State Community College. Continuing Dental Education in Coronal Polishing. CPR certified.

- Special expertise in patient management and making patients of all ages feel as relaxed and comfortable as possible, relieving any anxiety or tension they might have. Skilled working with handicapped and other special-needs patients.

- Sound knowledge of clinical procedures and dental/medical terminology.

DENTAL HEALTHCARE EXPERIENCE

DENTAL ASSISTANT .... 2004 to 2010
David A. Lambert, D.D.S. — Montgomery, Alabama

- Performed general chairside duties (four-handed dentistry) and assisted with all types of procedures, including extraction, crowns, pulpotomy, and composites. Monitored nitrous oxide and applied topical anesthetics.
- Prepared patients (children, adolescents, young adults, handicapped, special needs) for treatment, making them as comfortable and at ease as possible. Assisted with in-hospital visits and procedures.
- Performed coronal polishing, oral examinations, and charting.
- Sterilized instruments and equipment. Prepared tray setups for procedures.
- Mixed amalgams, cements, and other dental materials. Took and poured impressions.
- Took, processed, and mounted X-rays. Used intraoral camera equipment.
- Scheduled and confirmed appointments. Ordered dental supplies and maintained inventory levels.

DENTAL ASSISTANT .... 2000 to 2004
Timothy J. Koeppel, D.M.D. — Hendersonville, Tennessee

- Took impressions, poured and trimmed models, and made night guards.
- Took and processed panorex and cephalometric X-rays.
- Instructed and encouraged patients to develop good oral-hygiene habits.

EDUCATION AND TRAINING

Coronal Polishing — Continuing Dental Education — 2004
University of Tennessee, Memphis College of Dentistry

Dental Assistant Certificate of Proficiency — 2000
Volunteer State Community College — Gallatin, Tennessee

Certified in CPR through American Heart Association — 2000 to Present

Licensed Practical and Licensed Vocational Nurses

Sarah K. Markell, LPN
11539 Sunset Drive, # 8 ♦ Hyattstown, MD 20871   (301) 420-8693 ♦ skm20871@aol.com

Professional Overview

- Dedicated and well-qualified healthcare professional with **hospital, nursing home, home healthcare,** and **doctor's office** experience.
- Excel in working independently, professionally managing caseloads, and setting priorities.
- A dependable and knowledgeable professional whose attention to detail in documentation and chart maintenance led to an award for *Outstanding Contributions to Patient Education.*
- Highly adaptive, flexible style; efficiently and competently work with diverse patient populations.
- Demonstrate a solid understanding of regulatory compliance and an ability to skillfully navigate the Medicare and Medicaid systems.
- Skill strengths include:

Diabetic education	Child psychiatric outpatient
Geriatric care & administration	Pediatric care
Post surgical & wound care	Phlebotomy

Credentials: Maryland # LP34047; Commonwealth of Virginia LP # 0002042663
Certifications: IV Therapy, Intensive Coronary Care, CPR

Highlights of Professional Experience

Hospital ICU, ER, and Med-Surgical Unit
- Secured a position as a Nurse Tech at an 80-bed facility while completing nursing school.
- Acquired cross-functional training in acute care, orthopedics, and surgery.
- Assisted with direct delivery of patient care and self-management education in a pre/post-op environment.
- Instrumental in setting the standards for 12-hour shift scheduling, initiating the program in cooperation with another LPN.
- Selected to complete Intensive Coronary Care certification to support two ICUs.

Private Physician's Office
- Instrumental in helping a doctor of internal medicine build a private practice from 10 to more than 3,000 patients in the first two years of practice.
- Demonstrated outstanding organization and time-management skills in tending more than 40 patients daily.
- Independently completed all initial assessments; charted medical stats, symptoms, and medications; instructed patients in health self-management; called in prescription orders.
- Administered a compassionate level of patient care, directly contributing to ongoing patient referrals and sustained growth of the practice.

Nursing Home and Rehabilitation Facilities
- Delivered comprehensive geriatric nursing care to patients at a 240-bed residential facility. Began employment as a full-time GNA; transitioned to part-time while pursuing LPN certification.
- Supervised a team of four to six GNAs assigned to a unit of a 180-bed geriatric facility; coordinated daily schedule; managed orientation and staff assignments.
- Mastered, through on-the-job training, the care of comatose/near-comatose ventilator-dependent patients in a 100-bed rehabilitation facility.

(continued)

(continued)

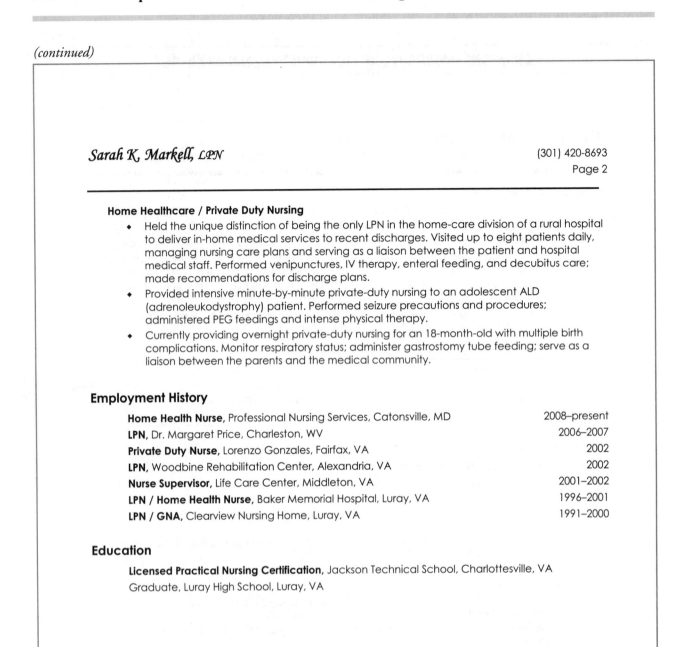

Sarah K. Markell, LPN

(301) 420-8693

Page 2

Home Healthcare / Private Duty Nursing

- Held the unique distinction of being the only LPN in the home-care division of a rural hospital to deliver in-home medical services to recent discharges. Visited up to eight patients daily, managing nursing care plans and serving as a liaison between the patient and hospital medical staff. Performed venipunctures, IV therapy, enteral feeding, and decubitus care; made recommendations for discharge plans.
- Provided intensive minute-by-minute private-duty nursing to an adolescent ALD (adrenoleukodystrophy) patient. Performed seizure precautions and procedures; administered PEG feedings and intense physical therapy.
- Currently providing overnight private-duty nursing for an 18-month-old with multiple birth complications. Monitor respiratory status; administer gastrostomy tube feeding; serve as a liaison between the parents and the medical community.

Employment History

Home Health Nurse, Professional Nursing Services, Catonsville, MD	2008–present
LPN, Dr. Margaret Price, Charleston, WV	2006–2007
Private Duty Nurse, Lorenzo Gonzales, Fairfax, VA	2002
LPN, Woodbine Rehabilitation Center, Alexandria, VA	2002
Nurse Supervisor, Life Care Center, Middleton, VA	2001–2002
LPN / Home Health Nurse, Baker Memorial Hospital, Luray, VA	1996–2001
LPN / GNA, Clearview Nursing Home, Luray, VA	1991–2000

Education

Licensed Practical Nursing Certification, Jackson Technical School, Charlottesville, VA

Graduate, Luray High School, Luray, VA

Machine Setters, Operators, and Tenders—Metal and Plastic

OLIVER ORTIZ

oliver278@aol.com   3083 43rd SW   206.948.8088
                                 Seattle, WA 98136

PROFILE

Experienced in machine operations, customer relations, and organizing materials. Willing worker, able to work independently or as part of a team. Bilingual in English and Spanish.

EXPERIENCE

Packager, Signature Packaging Solutions, Monroe, WA   2005–2007
- Packaged items for Starbucks using a variety of packaging machines.

Machine Operator/Molding, ABC Company, Seattle, WA   1996–1999
- Molded plastics on injection and compression machines.
- Mixed ingredients for plastics.

Delivery Driver, Rent-A-Center, Seattle, WA   1994–1996
- Delivered and picked up merchandise for customers.
- Assisted customers with concerns.
- Completed sales forms.
- Handled currency.
- Serviced damaged equipment.

Casual Mail Handler, United States Parcel Service, Hartford, CT   1992–1994
- Sorted and distributed mail to various departments.
- Weighed airmail and dispatched it to the appropriate airlines.
- Operated and maintained postage machines.

Returned-Goods Clerk, Electrical Wholesalers, Hartford, CT   1991–1992
- Received goods.
- Stocked shelves.
- Picked and checked orders.
- Coordinated with purchasing departments.
- Kept records and inventory.

EDUCATION

Center for Professional Advancement, Capital Community College, Hartford, CT
Studied basic computers and job skills.

Medical Records and Health Information Technicians

RUBY F. HALLIDAY, A.R.T.

347 Cotter Avenue, San Mateo, California 94040   rubyf@gmail.com ◆ (650) 594-2214

MEDICAL RECORDS MANAGER

Proven combination of management and organizational abilities in Health Information Services.
Strong problem-solving, communication, analytical, negotiation, and development skills.
Computer literate: Excel, Word, WordPerfect, Windows; Internet proficient.

◆ Energetic   ◆ Enthusiastic   ◆ Dependable   ◆ Optimistic   ◆ Dedicated   ◆ Conscientious

QUALIFICATIONS SUMMARY

Management/Supervision
- Successfully managed technical and clerical operations at two hospitals and maintained primary work load.
- Assisted in planning staff reduction without reduction in service or patient care.
- Addressed problems quickly; followed through until issues were resolved.
- Demonstrated exemplary interviewing techniques; excelled at evaluating prospective employees.
- Maintained excellent rapport with staff, coworkers, patients, and physicians.
- Assisted in budget planning and kept supplies well within budget.

Training/Development
- Assisted in revising employee tasks prior to layoff and trained staff in new functions.
- Collaborated with I.S. analyst to prepare chart-tracking training and implementation.
- Planned, implemented, and trained staff on new Phamis chart tracking system.

Organization/Planning
- Initiated and managed implementation of standardized medical records procedures resulting in multiple system-wide benefits, including
  - increased productivity and quality, especially in records transfer and billing
  - smoother work flow, less time to prepare
  - consistency and uniformity of process
- Successfully revised clerical-related patient care process. Widely accepted by patients and implemented system-wide.
- Participated in smooth transition to "in-house" outpatient coding.
- Facilitated effective transition of birth certificate function to Perinatal Department.

PROFESSIONAL EXPERIENCE

HILLVIEW SONOMA HEALTH SYSTEM, Burlingame, CA   1997–Present
Assistant Director, Medical Records (2003–Present)
Manage technical and clerical operations of Medical Records Department for both Hillview and Sonoma Hospitals.
- Prioritize, schedule, and assign workload.
- Liaise between Medical Records Department and Information Systems.
- Develop departmental policies and procedures, revising and updating as needed.
- Assist in budget preparations.

RUBY F. HALLIDAY, A.R.T. ◆ rubyf@gmail.com   Page Two

Medical Record Specialist (1997–2003)
Provided supervision to the Medical Records Department; liaison with Business Services.
- Ensured accurate submission of all medical data necessary to properly bill patient accounts.
- Performed technical backup to department positions; managed work flow.
- Monitored systems to ensure accuracy and adequacy of department functions.
- Trained, supervised, and developed staff.

CODING UNLIMITED, Palm Springs, CA   1993–1997
Consultant
Participated in specialized health information projects throughout the Bay Area, including:

Interim Manager (1995–1997)
Stanford Health Services, Palo Alto, CA
Managed successful implementation of Clinical Data Abstraction Program.
- Hired and trained staff, coordinated activities, and formulated procedures. Liaison with software provider and Santa Clara County Office of Vital Records.
- Reviewed and made recommendations for improvement of Health Information Management Services process, including chart completion, physician suspension, and customer service.
- Provided comparative analysis of data associated with medical transcription (i.e., turnaround time and employee productivity).

Medical Records Analyst (1993–1995)
Sequoia Hospital, Redwood City, CA
Analyzed medical records for quality of content. Maintained daily hospital inpatient census. Interfaced with physicians and other departments.

RECOVERY INN OF LOS GATOS, Los Gatos, CA   1992
RECOVERY INN OF MENLO PARK, Menlo Park, CA
Consultant
Established policies and procedures for two new outpatient surgical facilities, following Title 22 requirements and JCAHO guidelines. Assisted with selection of filing and record-management systems.

PROFESSIONAL AFFILIATIONS
California Health Information Association
- Delegate, Annual Meeting, 2003, 2006
- Annual Symposium Committee, 1999
- President, Local Chapter, 2001–2002
- Education Chairman, 1998–1999

EDUCATION
Zenger-Miller Frontline Leadership; 2005
A.S., Accredited Record Technician, Chabot College, Hayward, CA; 1996
Medical Record Technology courses, Bellevue Area College, Bellevue, WA; 1995
Business Administration courses, University of Puget Sound, Tacoma, WA; 1993–1995

Paralegals and Legal Assistants

8945 Town Court
Naperville, IL 60566
(630) 555-0945
rmax@gmail.com

R A C H E L   M A X

LEGAL ASSISTANT / PARALEGAL

OVERVIEW

Highly motivated legal assistant dedicated to professionalism and quality.
A proven record of providing dependable assistance as a team member in a law environment.

SKILLS

- Effectively interface with supervisors, professional staff, and clientele.
- Effective problem solver; prioritize and manage heavy work flow without direct supervision.
- Strong communication and interpersonal skills.
- Knowledge of Corel WordPerfect, Microsoft Word, TimeSlips, and various software and office equipment.

EDUCATION

PARALEGAL CERTIFICATION (1996)
Focus: Litigation
University of California, Irvine, CA

GENERAL COURSE WORK
Focus: Business / Social Sciences
Irvine Valley College, Irvine, CA

EXPERIENCE

LEGAL ASSISTANT (2004–2006)
Smith & Jones, San Diego, CA
- Aided litigation partner in coordinating real estate transactions and corporate documents.
- Expedited preparation and editing of correspondence, discovery, and pleadings.
- Assisted counsel in preparing for court hearings, depositions, and trials.
- Responsible for maintaining court calendar, attorney's personal calendar, billing documents, and files.

PARALEGAL (2000–2004)
San Diego Management Company, San Diego, CA
- Responsible for daily review and organization of litigation files and calendar.
- Prepared corporate minutes and assisted with administrative support.
- Appointed to correspond with outside counsel regarding ongoing litigation.
- Reviewed and supervised monthly billing statements of outside counsel.

LEGAL ASSISTANT / PARALEGAL (1998–2000)
Little, Marcus, & Preston, San Diego, CA
- Drafted discovery motions and correspondence, prepared court forms for filing and service, and maintained court calendar.
- Prepared deposition summaries and maintained files.

PARALEGAL (1996–1998)
Gold Coast Management Company, San Diego, CA
- Assisted with the preparation, filing, and service of litigation documents.
- Prepared unlawful-detainer pleadings, court forms, and motions for Bankruptcy Court.
- Monitored court calendar and prepared miscellaneous office correspondence.

PAST/PRESENT
AFFILIATIONS

California Association of Independent Paralegals California Real
Estate Licensure

Radiologic Technologists and Technicians

LISA A. MILLS, RT-M, LRT
414 St. John Place
Rochester, New York 14623
585-765-4321
millsla@earthlink.com

RADIOLOGIC TECHNOLOGIST / MAMMOGRAPHY TECHNOLOGIST
Healthcare ◆ Teaching ◆ Consulting / Private Industry

Accomplished healthcare professional with track record of acquiring and applying leading-edge technologies and procedures in clinical settings. Outstanding patient rapport and exceptional patient satisfaction. Superb teamwork skills, plus strong organizational/administrative capabilities. Excellent project management skills, encompassing sourcing and purchasing capital equipment and supplies, collaborating with engineers on facilities-construction issues, and developing written procedures for new clinical techniques.

PROFESSIONAL EXPERIENCE

ROCHESTER GENERAL HOSPITAL; Rochester, New York (1992–Present)
Mammography / Radiologic Technician—Women's Health Center   2005–Present
- See up to 30 mammogram patients daily.
- Assist physicians with various procedures, including stereotactic procedures and breast biopsies.
- Educate patients about procedures and train coworkers in new protocols.
- Ensure that quality standards, including Mammography Quality Standards Act (MQSA) inspection requirements, are maintained.

Key Accomplishments:

Chosen to serve on team that pioneered Women's Health Center at Rochester General Hospital, with specific accountability for setup and launch of Mammography Department.
- Conferred with clinical engineers and medical physicists on the physical layout of the department.
- Ensured that facilities met federal and state regulations for quality standards and environmental issues.
- Sourced and evaluated equipment and supplies; made purchase recommendations to decision-makers.
- Wrote manuals and policies for mammography, breast biopsies, and other related procedures.

Played a key role in introducing stereotactic breast biopsy procedures to the department.
- Evaluated equipment and reviewed facilities needs for this new technology.
- Established sterile processes and set up surgical procedures.
- Collaborated with other hospital departments to ensure that all clinical requirements were met.
- Coordinated administrative procedures with outpatient registration and nursing staff to facilitate processing of patients and proper charting/documentation.

Radiologic Technologist   1992–2005
Performed general radiography tests and procedures.
- Utilized portable radiography equipment and performed operating-room procedures.
- Conducted gastro-intestinal (GI) tract and vascular tests.
- Performed mammography tests until joining Women's Health Center in 2005.
- Maintained positive and productive rapport with emergency, nursing, and OR departments.

Key Accomplishment:

Pioneered introduction of mammography to RGH in 1993. Acquired specialized training, instructed colleagues in newly learned techniques, and ensured that strict quality standards were maintained. Functioned as in-house mammography specialist, leading to participation in setup of Women's Health Center.

(continued)

(continued)

Lisa A. Mills • millsla@earthlink.com   Résumé—Page Two

ADDITIONAL EXPERIENCE

FINGER LAKES COMMUNITY COLLEGE; Canandaigua, New York
Adjunct Instructor   **1993–Present**
Train and mentor college students majoring in Radiologic Technology.
- Follow three to four students during extensive clinical rotations.
- Provide hands-on training on various equipment and procedures.
- Conduct competency tests to establish students' speed and accuracy in performing tests.

EAST ROCHESTER UNION FREE SCHOOL DISTRICT; Rochester, New York
Mentor   **1996–1997**
Introduced middle school students to radiography as a potential career choice. Allowed students to observe day-to-day activities and responded to questions about radiography.

EDUCATION

FINGER LAKES COMMUNITY COLLEGE; Canandaigua, New York
Associate of Applied Science, Radiologic Technology   **1991**
GPA: 3.75; Honors Graduate

Associate of Applied Science, Secretarial Science (Medical)   **1989**
GPA: 3.5

PROFESSIONAL DEVELOPMENT

SLOAN-KETTERING CANCER INSTITUTE; New York, New York
—Breast Radiology, Chemotherapy & Radiation Therapy, Stereotactic Positioning (one-day program)

Numerous additional continuing education programs and professional conferences.

TECHNICAL PROFICIENCIES

Fisher Stereotactic Table; LoRad Mammography techniques; GE and Phillips radiology equipment. Windows, Microsoft Office, online patient information systems.

LICENSURE

American Registry of Radiologic Technologists (1991–Present).
American Registry of Radiologic Technologists—Mammography (1998–Present).
NYS Department of Health—Diagnostic Radiology (1991–Present).

Security Guards and Gaming Surveillance Officers

Charles Malcolm

5839 Wood Lane
Yorba Linda, CA 92714

Email: cmalcolm@cox.net

Home: 714/849-0907
Cell: 714/604-6485

SECURITY / LOSS PREVENTION

Professional security advisor with proven leadership skills and comprehensive knowledge of security whose effective management of people and resources minimizes criminal activity and maximizes the safety and protection of the public and employees. Provide optimal productivity and efficiency by training clients' personnel to effectively utilize crime and loss prevention techniques. Excellent communication skills with the ability to teach individually and make presentations to groups. Set the highest standards of excellence for myself and team members. Acquired substantial intuitive wisdom and completed extensive courses on law enforcement, safety, and security as an Officer during 14 years with the Los Angeles County Sheriff's Department.

AREAS OF EXPERTISE

Personal and Corporate Background Checks
Countersurveillance
Retail / Industrial Theft
Personal Injury
Highly Publicized Event Security
Labor-Related Investigations
Missing Persons

PERSONAL QUALITIES

Professional, Dedicated, and Ethical
Motivated, Energetic, and Enthusiastic
Resourceful, Diligent, Decisive, and Results-Oriented
Work Independently and as a Team Member
Quickly Identify, Assess, and Resolve Problems
Work Well Under Pressure
Adaptable and Flexible

PROFESSIONAL EXPERIENCE

Law Enforcement Officer, <u>Los Angeles County Sheriff's Department</u>, Los Angeles, CA   1992–2006

- Made arrests and restored order at the Rodney King riots during my first assignment.
- Subsequently assigned to the men's central jail in downtown Los Angeles. Duties included writing criminal reports and supervising and escorting high-security inmates.
- Assigned to an emergency response team in 1994. Duties included responding to countywide emergencies, county jail riots, and major disturbances.
- Promoted to training officer duties (2000–2006). Trained new deputies in laws of arrest, report writing, officer safety, and all necessary duties to be a qualified law enforcement officer.

EDUCATION / TRAINING

Suicide Prevention, Legal Update, Advanced Officer, First Aid/CPR Courses   2000
- Rio Hondo College, Los Angeles, CA
Certificate of Completion, Los Angeles County Sheriff's Department, Los Angeles, CA   1996
- Finished in the Top Ten (of 126 Cadets) in Academics and Physical Fitness
Criminal Investigations Course, Irvine Valley College, Irvine, CA   1992
Graduate, Pacifica High School, Garden Grove, CA   1990

COMMENDATIONS

- **Personal courage and ethics** in subduing a volatile inmate that resulted in a colleague being cared for and deploying the absolute minimum amount of force necessary to resolve the situation. These actions personified the L.A. Sheriff Department's core values and brought credit to the law enforcement profession (2001).
- **Willingness to step forward and help with a task,** put forth the effort, and go the extra mile to recover lost property that belonged to an inmate. The teamwork attitude and concern displayed were an example of service-oriented policing (2000).
- **Quick response to a potentially violent situation** of racial tension in the Central Jail that was subdued with minimal altercations. Recognized for professionalism, tactics, cooperation, teamwork, and solid police work (2000).
- **Helped subdue a mini-riot** and reinstate order in the Central Jail. Acknowledged for self-discipline, clear thinking, professionalism, and custody expertise (1999).

Important Trends in Jobs and Industries

In putting this section together, our objective was to give you a quick review of major labor market trends. To accomplish this, we included three excellent articles that originally appeared in U.S. Department of Labor publications.

The first article is "Overview of the 2008–2018 Projections." It provides a superb—and short—review of the major trends that will affect your career in the years to come. Read it for ideas on selecting a career path for the long term.

The second article is "Employment Trends in Major Industries." While you may not have thought much about it, the industry you work in is just as important as your occupational choice. This great article will help you learn about major trends affecting various industries.

The third article, "Job Outlook for People Who Don't Have a Bachelor's Degree," discusses the large number of job openings for people without a four-year degree. It also covers high-paying jobs that do not require a four-year degree. The article can help you focus on promising careers in many industries.

Overview of the 2008–2018 Projections

Job openings result from the relationship between the population, the labor force, and demand for goods and services. The population restricts the size of the labor force, which consists of working individuals and those looking for work. The size and productivity of the labor force limits the quantity of goods and services that can be produced. In addition, changes in the demand for goods and services influence which industries expand or contract. Industries respond by hiring the workers necessary to produce

The analysis underlying BLS employment projections uses currently available information to focus on long-term structural changes in the economy. The 2008–2018 projections assume a full-employment economy in 2018. The impact of the recent recession, which began in December of 2007, on long-term structural changes in the economy will not be fully known until some point during or after the recovery. Because the 2008 starting point is a recession year, the projected growth to an assumed full-employment economy in 2018 will generally be stronger than if the starting point were not a recession year.

goods and provide services. However, improvements to technology and productivity, changes in which occupations perform certain tasks, and changes to the supply of workers all affect which occupations will be employed by those industries. Examining past and present changes to these relationships in order to project future shifts is the foundation of the Employment Projections Program. This article presents highlights of population, labor force, and occupational and industry employment projections for 2008–2018. For more information, see the additional information about the projections.

Population

Shifts in the size and composition of the population can create a number of changes to the U.S. economy. Most importantly, population trends produce corresponding changes in the size and composition of the labor force. The U.S. civilian noninstitutional population, including individuals aged 16 and older, is expected to increase by 25.1 million from 2008 to 2018 (Chart 1). The projected 2008–2018 growth rate of 10.7 percent is less than the 11.2 percent growth rate for the 1988–1998 period and the 13.9 percent rate for the 1998–2008 period. As in the past few decades, population growth will vary by age group, race, and ethnicity.

As the baby boomers continue to age, the 55-and-older age group is projected to increase by 29.7 percent, more than any other age group. Meanwhile, the 45-to-54 age group is expected to decrease by 4.4 percent, reflecting the slower birth rate following the

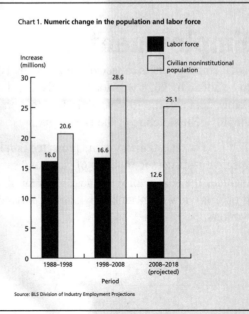

Chart 1. **Numeric change in the population and labor force**

Source: BLS Division of Industry Employment Projections

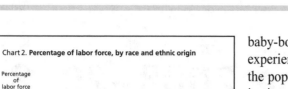

Chart 2. **Percentage of labor force, by race and ethnic origin**

Percentage of labor force

- 2008
- 2018 (projected)

White: 81.4, 79.4
Black: 11.5, 12.1
Asian: 4.7, 5.6
All other race groups: 2.4, 2.9
Other than Hispanic origin: 85.7, 82.4
Hispanic origin: 14.3, 17.6

Race and ethnic origin

Note: The four race groups add to the total labor force. The two ethnic origin groups also add to the total labor force. Hispanics may be of any race.

Source: BLS Division of Industry Employment Projections

baby-boom generation. The 35-to-44 age group is anticipated to experience little change, with a growth rate of 0.2 percent, while the population aged 16 to 24 will grow 3.4 percent over the projection period. Minorities and immigrants are expected to constitute a larger share of the U.S. population in 2018. The numbers of Asians and people of Hispanic origin are projected to continue to grow much faster than those of other racial and ethnic groups.

Labor Force

Population is the single most important factor in determining the size and composition of the labor force. The civilian labor force is projected to reach 166.9 million by 2018, which is an increase of 8.2 percent.

The U.S. workforce is expected to become more diverse by 2018. Among racial groups, Whites are expected to make up a decreasing share of the labor force, while Blacks, Asians, and all other groups will increase their share (Chart 2). Among ethnic groups, persons of Hispanic origin are projected to increase their share of the labor force from 14.3 percent to 17.6 percent, reflecting 33.1 percent growth.

The number of women in the labor force will grow at a slightly faster rate than the number of men. The male labor force is projected to grow by 7.5 percent from 2008 to 2018, compared with 9.0 percent for the female labor force.

The share of the youth labor force, workers aged 16 to 24, is expected to decrease from 14.3 percent in 2008 to 12.7 percent by 2018. The primary working-age group, those between 25 and 54 years old, is projected to decline from 67.6 percent of the labor force in 2008 to 63.5 percent by 2018. Workers aged 55 years and older, by contrast, are anticipated to leap from 18.1 percent to 23.9 percent of the labor force during the same period (Chart 3).

Employment

Total employment is expected to increase by 10 percent from 2008 to 2018. However, the 15.3 million jobs expected to be added by 2018 will not be evenly distributed across major industry and occupational groups. Changes in consumer demand, improvements in technology, and many other factors will contribute to the continually changing employment structure of the U.S. economy.

The next two sections examine projected employment change within industries and occupations. The industry perspective is discussed in terms of wage and salary employment. The exception is employment in agriculture, which includes the self-employed and unpaid family workers in addition to wage and salary workers. The occupational profile is viewed in terms of total employment—including wage and salary, self-employed, and unpaid family workers.

Employment Change by Industry

Goods-producing industries. Employment in goods-producing industries has declined since the 1990s. Although overall employment is expected to change little, projected growth among goods-producing industries varies considerably (Chart 4).

Mining, quarrying, and oil and gas extraction. Employment in mining, quarrying, and oil and gas extraction is expected to decrease by 14 percent by 2018. Employment in support activities for mining will be responsible for most of the job loss in this industry with a decline of 23 percent. Other mining industries, such as nonmetallic mineral mining and quarrying and coal mining, are expected to see little or no change or a small increase in employment. Employment stagnation in these industries is attributable mainly to strict environmental regulations and technology gains that boost worker productivity.

Construction. Employment in construction is expected to rise 19 percent. Demand for commercial construction and an increase in road, bridge, and tunnel construction will account for the bulk of job growth.

Manufacturing. Overall employment in this sector will decline by 9 percent as productivity gains, automation, and international competition adversely affect employment in most manufacturing industries. Employment in household appliance manufacturing is expected to decline by 24 percent over the decade. Similarly, employment in machinery manufacturing, apparel manufacturing, and computer and electronic product manufacturing will decline as well. However, employment in a few manufacturing industries will increase. For example, employment in pharmaceutical and medicine manufacturing is expected to grow by 6 percent by 2018; however, this increase is expected to add only 17,600 new jobs.

Agriculture, forestry, fishing, and hunting. Overall employment in agriculture, forestry, fishing, and hunting is expected to decrease by 1 percent. Employment is projected to continue to decline because of rising costs of production, increasing consolidation, and more imports of food and lumber. Within this sector, the only industry that is expected to add jobs is support activities for agriculture and forestry, which includes farm labor contractors and farm management services. This industry is anticipated to grow by 13 percent, but this corresponds to an increase of only 13,800 new jobs.

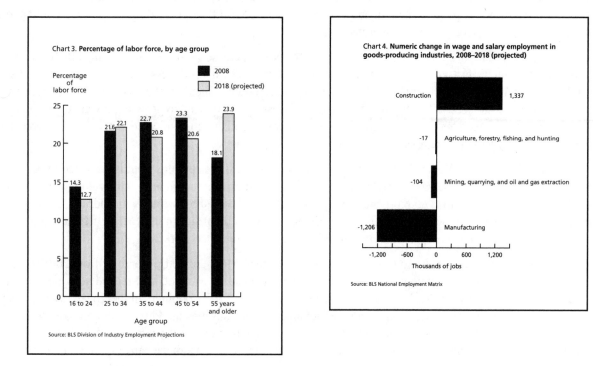

Chart 3. Percentage of labor force, by age group

Percentage of labor force

■ 2008
□ 2018 (projected)

16 to 24: 14.3, 12.7
25 to 34: 21.6, 22.1
35 to 44: 22.7, 20.8
45 to 54: 23.3, 20.6
55 years and older: 18.1, 23.9

Age group

Source: BLS Division of Industry Employment Projections

Chart 4. Numeric change in wage and salary employment in goods-producing industries, 2008–2018 (projected)

Construction: 1,337
Agriculture, forestry, fishing, and hunting: -17
Mining, quarrying, and oil and gas extraction: -104
Manufacturing: -1,206

Thousands of jobs

Source: BLS National Employment Matrix

Service-providing industries. The shift in the U.S. economy away from goods-producing in favor of service-providing is expected to continue. Service-providing industries are anticipated to generate approximately 14.5 million new wage and salary jobs. As with goods-producing industries, growth among service-providing industries will vary (Chart 5).

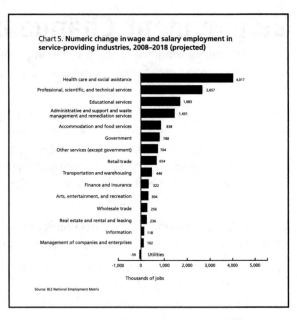

Chart 5. Numeric change in wage and salary employment in service-providing industries, 2008–2018 (projected)

Industry	Thousands of jobs
Health care and social assistance	4,017
Professional, scientific, and technical services	2,657
Educational services	1,683
Administrative and support and waste management and remediation services	1,431
Accommodation and food services	838
Government	788
Other services (except government)	704
Retail trade	654
Transportation and warehousing	446
Finance and insurance	322
Arts, entertainment, and recreation	304
Wholesale trade	256
Real estate and rental and leasing	236
Information	118
Management of companies and enterprises	102
Utilities	-59

Source: BLS National Employment Matrix

Utilities. Employment in utilities is projected to decrease by 11 percent through 2018. Despite increased output, employment in electric power generation, transmission, and distribution and in natural gas distribution is expected to decline because of improved technology that will increase worker productivity. However, employment in the water, sewage, and other systems industry is anticipated to increase 13 percent by 2018. As the population continues to grow, more water treatment facilities are being built. Further, changing federal and state government water quality regulations may require more workers to ensure that water is safe to drink and to release into the environment.

Wholesale trade. The number of workers in wholesale trade is expected to increase by 4 percent, adding about 255,900 jobs. The consolidation of wholesale trade firms into fewer and larger companies will contribute to slower-than-average employment growth in the industry.

Retail trade. Employment in retail trade is expected to increase by 4 percent. Despite slower-than-average growth, this industry is projected to add about 654,000 new jobs over the 2008–2018 period. Slower job growth reflects both continued consolidation and slower growth in personal consumption than in the previous decade.

Transportation and warehousing. Employment in transportation and warehousing is expected to increase by 10 percent, adding about 445,500 jobs to the industry total. Truck transportation is anticipated to grow by 10 percent, and the warehousing and storage sector is projected to grow by 12 percent. Demand for truck transportation and warehousing services will expand as many manufacturers concentrate on their core competencies and contract out their product transportation and storage functions.

Information. Employment in the information sector is expected to increase by 4 percent, adding 118,100 jobs by 2018. The sector contains fast-growing computer-related industries. The data-processing, hosting, and related services industry, which is expected to grow by 53 percent, includes establishments that provide Web and application hosting and streaming services. Internet publishing and broadcasting is expected to grow rapidly as it gains market share from newspapers and other more traditional media. Software publishing is projected to grow by 30 percent as organizations of all types continue to adopt the newest software products.

The information sector also includes the telecommunications industry, whose employment is projected to decline 9 percent. Despite an increase in demand for telecommunications services, more reliable networks along with consolidation among organizations will lead to productivity gains, reducing the need for workers. In addition, employment in the publishing industry is expected to decline by 5 percent, which is the result of increased efficiency in production, declining newspaper revenues, and a trend towards using more freelance workers.

Finance and insurance. The finance and insurance industry is expected to increase by 5 percent from 2008 to 2018. Employment in the securities, commodity contracts, and other financial investments and related activities industry is projected to expand 12 percent by 2018, which reflects the number of baby boomers in their peak savings years, the growth of tax-favorable retirement plans, and the globalization of securities markets. Employment in the credit intermediation and related activities industry, which includes banks, will grow by about 5 percent, adding 42 percent of all new jobs within the finance and insurance sector. Employment in the insurance carriers and related activities industry is expected to grow by 3 percent, translating into 67,600 new jobs by 2018. The number of jobs in the agencies, brokerages, and other insurance-related activities industry is expected to grow by 14 percent. Growth will stem from both the needs of an increasing population and new insurance products on the market.

Real estate and rental and leasing. The real estate and rental and leasing industry is expected to grow by 11 percent through 2018. Growth will be due, in part, to increased demand for housing as the population expands. The fastest-growing industry in the real estate and rental and leasing services sector will be lessors of nonfinancial intangible assets (except copyrighted works), which will increase by 34 percent over the projection period.

Professional, scientific, and technical services. Employment in professional, scientific, and technical services is projected to grow by 34 percent, adding about 2.7 million new jobs by 2018. Employment in computer systems design and related services is expected to increase by 45 percent, accounting for nearly one-fourth of all new jobs in this industry sector. Employment growth will be driven by growing demand for the design and integration of sophisticated networks and Internet and intranet sites. Employment in management, scientific, and technical consulting services is anticipated to expand a staggering 83 percent, making up about 31 percent of job growth in this sector. Demand for these services will be spurred by businesses' continued need for advice on planning and logistics; the implementation of new technologies; and compliance with workplace safety, environmental, and employment regulations.

Management of companies and enterprises. Management of companies and enterprises is projected to grow relatively slowly, by 5 percent, as companies focus on reorganization to increase efficiency.

Administrative and support and waste management and remediation services. Employment in this sector is expected to grow by 18 percent by 2018. The largest growth will occur in employment services, an industry that is anticipated to account for 42 percent of all new jobs in the administrative and support and waste management and remediation services sector. The employment services industry ranks fifth among industries with the most new employment opportunities in the nation over the 2008–2018 period and is expected to grow faster than the average for all industries. Projected growth stems from the strong need for seasonal and temporary workers and for specialized human resources services.

Educational services. Employment in public and private educational services is anticipated to grow by 12 percent, adding about 1.7 million new jobs through 2018. Rising student enrollments at all levels of education will create demand for educational services.

Health care and social assistance. About 26 percent of all new jobs created in the U.S. economy will be in the health-care and social assistance industry. This industry—which includes public and private hospitals, nursing and residential care facilities, and individual and family services—is expected to grow by 24 percent, or 4 million new jobs. Employment growth will be driven by an aging population and longer life expectancies.

Arts, entertainment, and recreation. The arts, entertainment, and recreation industry is expected to grow by 15 percent by 2018. Most of the growth will be in the amusement, gambling, and recreation sector. Job growth will stem from public participation in arts, entertainment, and recreation activities, reflecting increasing incomes, leisure time, and awareness of the health benefits of physical fitness.

Accommodation and food services. Employment in accommodation and food services is expected to grow by 7 percent, adding about 838,200 new jobs through 2018. Job growth will be concentrated in food services and drinking places, reflecting an increase in the population and the convenience of many new food establishments.

Other services (except government and private households). Employment is expected to grow by 13 percent in other services. Personal care services comprise the fastest-growing industry in this sector at 32 percent. This industry includes barbers, salons, and spas, which have experienced growing demand as individuals increasingly are seeking to improve their personal appearance.

Government. Between 2008 and 2018, government employment, excluding employment in public education and hospitals, is expected to increase by 7 percent. Growth in government employment will be fueled by expanding demand for public safety services and assistance provided to the elderly, but dampened by budgetary constraints and the outsourcing of government jobs to the private sector. State and local governments, excluding education and hospitals, are anticipated to grow by 8 percent as a result of the continued shift of responsibilities from the federal government to state and local governments. Federal government employment, including the postal service, is expected to increase by 3 percent.

Employment Change by Occupation

Industry growth or decline will affect demand for occupations. However, job growth is projected to vary among major occupational groups (Chart 6).

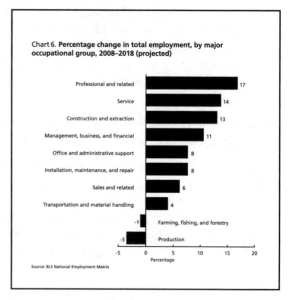

Chart 6. **Percentage change in total employment, by major occupational group, 2008–2018 (projected)**

Management, business, and financial occupations. Workers in management, business, and financial occupations plan and direct the activities of business, government, and other organizations. Their employment is expected to increase by 11 percent by 2018. These workers will be needed to help organizations navigate the increasingly complex and competitive business environment. A large portion of these jobs will arise in the management, scientific, and technical consulting industry sector. A substantial number, in addition, are expected in several other large or rapidly growing industries, including government, health care and social assistance, finance and insurance, and construction.

Employment in management occupations is projected to grow slowly over the projection period, increasing by 5 percent, an addition of 454,300 new jobs. Growth is being affected by declines in several occupations, including farmers and ranchers. Employment of farmers and ranchers is projected to decline as the agricultural industry produces more output with fewer workers.

Employment in business and financial operations occupations is projected to grow by 18 percent, resulting in 1.2 million new jobs. Increasing financial regulations and the need for greater accountability will drive demand for accountants and auditors, adding roughly 279,400 jobs to this occupation from 2008 to 2018. Further, an increasingly competitive business environment will grow demand for management analysts, an occupation that is expected to add 178,300 jobs. Together, these two occupations are anticipated to account for 38 percent of new business and financial operations jobs.

Professional and related occupations. This occupational group, which includes a wide variety of skilled professions, is expected to be the fastest-growing major occupational group, at 17 percent, and is projected to add the most new jobs—about 5.2 million.

Employment among health-care practitioners and technical occupations, a subgroup of the professional and related category, is expected to increase by 21 percent. This growth, resulting in a projected 1.6 million new jobs, will be driven by increasing demand for health-care services. As the number of older people continues to grow, and as new developments allow for the treatment of more medical conditions, more health-care professionals will be needed.

Education, training, and library occupations are anticipated to add more than 1.3 million jobs, representing a growth rate of more than 14 percent. As the U.S. population increases, and as a larger share of adults seeks educational services, demand for these workers will increase.

Computer and mathematical science occupations are projected to add almost 785,700 new jobs from 2008 to 2018. As a group, these occupations are expected to grow more than twice as fast as the average for all occupations in the economy. Demand for workers in computer and mathematical occupations will be driven by the continuing need for businesses, government agencies, and other organizations to adopt and utilize the latest technologies.

Employment in community and social services occupations is projected to increase by 16 percent, growing by roughly 448,400 jobs. As health insurance providers increasingly cover mental and behavioral health treatment and as a growing number of elderly individuals seek social services, demand for these workers will increase.

Employment in arts, design, entertainment, sports, and media occupations is expected to grow by 12 percent from 2008 to 2018, resulting in almost 332,600 new jobs. Growth will be spread broadly across different occupations within the group. Media and communications occupations will add a substantial number of jobs, led by rapid growth among public relations specialists, who will be needed in greater numbers as firms place a greater emphasis on managing their public image. Employment among entertainers and performers and those in sports and related occupations also will increase, partly as a result of increasing demand for coaches and scouts. Furthermore, art and design occupations will see substantial growth, with demand increasing for graphic and interior designers. As more advertising is conducted over the Internet, a medium that generally includes many graphics, and as businesses and households increasingly seek professional design services, a greater number of these workers will be needed.

Employment in life, physical, and social science occupations is projected to increase by nearly 277,200 jobs over the 2008–2018 projection period. This increase represents a growth rate of 19 percent, almost twice the average for all occupations across the economy. About 116,700 of these jobs are expected to be created among social science and related occupations, led by strong growth among market and survey researchers, as businesses increase their marketing efforts in order to remain competitive and as public policy firms and government agencies utilize more public opinion research. Employment in life science occupations, in addition, will increase rapidly as developments from biotechnology research continue to be used to create new medical technologies, treatments, and pharmaceuticals.

Architecture and engineering occupations are projected to add roughly 270,600 jobs, representing a growth rate of 10 percent. Much of this growth will occur among engineering occupations, especially civil engineers. As greater emphasis is placed on improving the nation's infrastructure, these specialists will be needed to design, implement, or upgrade municipal transportation, water supply, and pollution control systems.

Legal occupations will add the fewest new jobs among all professional and related subgroups, increasing by about 188,400. However, with a growth rate of 15 percent, this group will grow faster than the average for all occupations in the economy. Of the new jobs created, lawyers will account for 98,500 while paralegals and legal assistants will account for 74,100. Paralegals and legal assistants are expected to grow by 28 percent as legal establishments begin to expand the role of these workers and assign them more tasks once performed by lawyers.

Service occupations. The duties of service workers range from fighting fires to cooking meals. Employment in service occupations is projected to increase by 4.1 million, or 14 percent, which is both the second-largest numerical gain and the second-largest growth rate among the major occupational groups.

Among service occupation subgroups, the largest number of new jobs will occur in health-care support occupations. With more than 1.1 million new jobs, employment in this subgroup is expected to increase by 29 percent. Much of the growth will be the result of increased demand for health-care services as the expanding elderly population requires more care.

Employment in personal care and service occupations is anticipated to grow by 20 percent over the projection period, adding more than 1 million jobs. As consumers become more concerned with health, beauty, and fitness, the number of cosmetic and health spas will increase, causing an increase in demand for workers in this group. However, the personal care and service group contains a wide variety of occupations, and two of them—personal and home care aides and child care workers—will account for most of this group's new jobs. Personal and home care aides will experience increased demand as a growing number of elderly individuals require assistance with daily tasks. Child care workers, in addition, will add jobs as formal preschool programs, which employ child care workers alongside preschool teachers, become more prevalent.

Employment in food preparation and serving and related occupations is projected to increase by roughly 1 million jobs from 2008 to 2018, representing a growth rate of 9 percent. Growth will stem from time-conscious consumers patronizing fast-food establishments and full-service restaurants.

Employment in building and grounds cleaning and maintenance occupations is expected to grow by almost 483,900 jobs over the projection period, representing a growth rate of 8 percent. As businesses place a larger emphasis on grounds aesthetics and as households increasingly rely on contract workers to maintain their yards, grounds maintenance workers will see rapid growth. In addition, more building cleaning workers will be needed to maintain an increasing number of residential and commercial structures.

Protective service occupations are expected to gain the fewest new jobs among all service subgroups: about 400,100, or 12 percent growth. These workers protect businesses and other organizations from crime and vandalism. In addition, there will be increased demand for law enforcement officers to support the growing U.S. population.

Sales and related occupations. Sales and related workers solicit goods and services for businesses and consumers. Sales and related occupations are expected to add 980,400 new jobs by 2018, growing by 6 percent. As organizations offer a wider array of products and devote an increasing share of their resources to customer service, many new retail salesworkers will be needed. Job growth in this group will be spread across a wide variety of industries, but almost half will occur in retail sales establishments.

Office and administrative support occupations. Office and administrative support workers perform the day-to-day activities of the office, such as preparing and filing documents, dealing with the public, and distributing information. Employment in these occupations is expected to grow by 8 percent, adding 1.8 million new jobs by 2018. Customer service representatives are anticipated to add the most new jobs, 399,500, as businesses put an increased emphasis on building customer relationships. Other office and administrative support occupations will experience declines as advanced technology improves productivity, decreasing the number of workers necessary to perform some duties.

Farming, fishing, and forestry occupations. Farming, fishing, and forestry workers cultivate plants, breed and raise livestock, and catch animals. These occupations are projected to decline by about 1 percent, losing 9,100 jobs, by 2018. Productivity increases in agriculture will lead to declining employment among agricultural workers, offsetting small gains among forest, conservation, and logging workers.

Construction and extraction occupations. Construction and extraction workers build new residential and commercial buildings and also work in mines, quarries, and oil and gas fields. Employment of these workers is expected to grow 13 percent, adding about 1 million new jobs. Construction trades and related workers will account for about 808,400 of these jobs. Growth will result from increased construction of homes, office buildings, and infrastructure projects. Declines in extraction occupations will reflect overall employment stagnation in the mining and oil and gas extraction industries.

Installation, maintenance, and repair occupations. Workers in installation, maintenance, and repair occupations install new equipment and maintain and repair older equipment. These occupations are projected to add 440,200 jobs by 2018, growing by 8 percent. More than 1 in 3 new jobs in this group will occur in the construction industry because these workers are integral to the development of buildings, communication structures, transportation systems, and other types of infrastructure. As construction on these types of projects increases over the projection period, installation, maintenance, and repair workers will be needed in greater numbers.

Production occupations. Production workers are employed mainly in manufacturing, where they assemble goods and operate plants. Production occupations are expected to decline by 3 percent, losing 349,200 jobs by 2018. As productivity improvements reduce the need for workers and as a growing number of these jobs are offshored, demand for production workers will decline. Some jobs will be created in production occupations, mostly in food processing and woodworking.

Transportation and material moving occupations. Transportation and material moving workers transport people and materials by land, sea, or air. Employment of these workers is anticipated to increase by 4 percent, accounting for 391,100 new jobs. As the economy grows over the projection period and the demand for goods increases, truck drivers will be needed to transport those goods to businesses, consumers, and other entities. In addition, a substantial number of jobs will arise among bus drivers, as well as taxi drivers and chauffeurs, as a growing number of people utilize public transportation.

Employment Change by Detailed Occupation

Occupational growth can be considered in two ways: by the rate of growth and by the number of new jobs created by growth. Some occupations both have a fast growth rate and create a large number of new jobs. However, an occupation that employs few workers may experience rapid growth, although the resulting number of new jobs may be small. For example, a small occupation that employs just 1,000 workers and is projected to grow 50 percent over a 10-year period will add only 500 jobs. By contrast, a large occupation that employs 1.5 million workers may experience only 10 percent growth, but will add 150,000 jobs. As a result, in order to get a complete picture of employment growth, both measures must be considered.

Occupations with the fastest growth. Of the 20 fastest-growing occupations in the economy (Table 1), half are related to health care. Health care is experiencing rapid growth, due in large part to the aging of the baby-boom generation, which will require more medical care. In addition, some health-care occupations will be in greater demand for other reasons. As health-care costs continue to rise, work is increasingly being delegated to lower-paid workers in order to cut costs. For example, tasks that were previously performed by doctors, nurses, dentists, or other health-care professionals increasingly are being performed by physician assistants, medical assistants, dental hygienists, and physical therapist aides. In addition, patients increasingly are seeking home care as an alternative to costly stays in hospitals or residential care facilities, causing a significant increase in demand for home health aides. Although not classified as health-care workers, personal and home care aides are being affected by this demand for home care as well.

Two of the fastest-growing detailed occupations are in the computer specialist occupational group. Network systems and data communications analysts are projected to be the second-fastest-growing occupation in the economy. Demand for these workers will increase as organizations continue to upgrade their information technology capacity and incorporate the newest technologies. The growing reliance on wireless networks will result in a need for more network systems and data communications analysts as well. Computer applications software engineers also are expected to grow rapidly from 2008 to 2018. Expanding Internet technologies have spurred demand for these workers, who can develop Internet, intranet, and Web applications.

Developments from biotechnology research will continue to be used to create new medical technologies, treatments, and pharmaceuticals. As a result, demand for medical scientists and for biochemists and biophysicists will increase. However, although employment of biochemists and biophysicists is projected to grow rapidly, this corresponds to only 8,700 new jobs over the projection period. Increased medical research and demand for new medical technologies also will affect biomedical engineers. The aging of the population and a growing focus on health issues will drive demand for better medical devices and equipment designed by these workers. In fact, biomedical engineers are projected to be the fastest-growing occupation in the economy. However, because of its small size, the occupation is projected to add only about 11,600 jobs.

Increasing financial regulations will spur employment growth both of financial examiners and of compliance officers, except agriculture, construction, health and safety, and transportation.

Self-enrichment teachers and skin care specialists will experience growth as consumers become more concerned with self-improvement. Self-enrichment teachers are growing rapidly as more individuals seek additional training to

Table 1. Occupations with the fastest growth

Occupation	Percent change	Number of new jobs (in thousands)	Wages (May 2008 median)	Education/ training category
Biomedical engineers	72	11.6	$77,400	Bachelor's degree
Network systems and data communications analysts	53	155.8	71,100	Bachelor's degree
Home health aides	50	460.9	20,460	Short-term on-the-job training
Personal and home care aides	46	375.8	19,180	Short-term on-the-job training
Financial examiners	41	11.1	70,930	Bachelor's degree
Medical scientists, except epidemiologists	40	44.2	72,590	Doctoral degree
Physician assistants	39	29.2	81,230	Master's degree
Skin care specialists	38	14.7	28,730	Postsecondary vocational award
Biochemists and biophysicists	37	8.7	82,840	Doctoral degree
Athletic trainers	37	6.0	39,640	Bachelor's degree
Physical therapist aides	36	16.7	23,760	Short-term on-the-job training
Dental hygienists	36	62.9	66,570	Associate degree
Veterinary technologists and technicians	36	28.5	28,900	Associate degree
Dental assistants	36	105.6	32,380	Moderate-term on-the-job training
Computer software engineers, applications	34	175.1	85,430	Bachelor's degree
Medical assistants	34	163.9	28,300	Moderate-term on-the-job training
Physical therapist assistants	33	21.2	46,140	Associate degree
Veterinarians	33	19.7	79,050	First professional degree
Self-enrichment education teachers	32	81.3	35,720	Work experience in a related occupation
Compliance officers, except agriculture, construction, health and safety, and transportation	31	80.8	48,890	Long-term on-the-job training

SOURCE: BLS Occupational Employment Statistics and Division of Occupational Outlook

make themselves more appealing to prospective employers. Skin care specialists will experience growth as consumers increasingly care about their personal appearance.

Of the 20 fastest-growing occupations, 12 are in the associate degree or higher category. Of the remaining 8, 6 are in an on-the-job training category, 1 is in the work experience in a related occupation category, and 1 is in the postsecondary vocational degree category. Eleven of these occupations earn at least $10,000 more than the national annual median wage, which was $32,390 as of May 2008. In fact, 9 of the occupations earned at least twice the national median in May 2008.

Occupations with the largest numerical growth. The 20 occupations listed in Table 2 are projected to account for more than one-third of all new jobs—5.8 million combined—over the 2008–2018 period. The occupations with the largest numerical increases cover a wider range of occupational categories than do those occupations with the fastest growth rates. Health occupations will account for some of these increases in employment, as will occupations in education, sales, and food service. Office and administrative support services occupations are expected to grow by 1.3 million jobs, accounting for about one-fifth of the job growth among the 20 occupations with the largest growth. Many of the occupations listed in the table are very large and will create more new jobs than occupations with high growth rates. Only 3 out of the 20 fastest-growing occupations—home health aides, personal and home care aides, and computer software application engineers—also are projected to be among the 20 occupations with the largest numerical increases in employment.

Table 2. Occupations with the largest numerical growth

Occupation	Number of new jobs (in thousands)	Percent change	Wages (May 2008 median)	Education/ training category
Registered nurses 581.5	22	$62,450	Associate degree
Home health aides..460.9	50	20,460	Short-term on-the-job training
Customer service representatives...................................399.5	18	29,860	Moderate-term on-the-job training
Combined food preparation and serving workers, including fast food..394.3	15	16,430	Short-term on-the-job training
Personal and home care aides 375.8	46	19,180	Short-term on-the-job training
Retail salespersons...374.7	8	20,510	Short-term on-the-job training
Office clerks, general...358.7	12	25,320	Short-term on-the-job training
Accountants and auditors 279.4	22	59,430	Bachelor's degree
Nursing aides, orderlies, and attendants 276.0	19	23,850	Postsecondary vocational award
Postsecondary teachers...256.9	15	58,830	Doctoral degree
Construction laborers 255.9	20	28,520	Moderate-term on-the-job training
Elementary school teachers, except special education.....244.2	16	49,330	Bachelor's degree
Truck drivers, heavy and tractor-trailer 232.9	13	37,270	Short-term on-the-job training
Landscaping and groundskeeping workers 217.1	18	23,150	Short-term on-the-job training
Bookkeeping, accounting, and auditing clerks 212.4	10	32,510	Moderate-term on-the-job training
Executive secretaries and administrative assistants 204.4	13	40,030	Work experience in a related occupation
Management analysts..178.3	24	73,570	Bachelor's or higher degree, plus work experience
Computer software engineers, applications....................175.1	34	85,430	Bachelor's degree
Receptionists and information clerks 172.9	15	24,550	Short-term on-the-job training
Carpenters 165.4	13	38,940	Long-term on-the-job training

SOURCE: BLS Occupational Employment Statistics and Division of Occupational Outlook

The education or training categories and wages of the occupations with the largest numbers of new jobs are significantly different than those of the fastest-growing occupations. Twelve of these occupations are in an on-the-job training category, and just 7 are in a category that indicates any postsecondary education. Ten of the 20 occupations with the largest numbers of new jobs earned less than the national median wage in May 2008.

Occupations with the fastest decline. Declining occupational employment stems from falling industry employment, technological advances, changes in business practices, and other factors. For example, technological developments and the continued movement of textile production abroad are expected to contribute to a decline of 71,500 sewing machine operators over the projection period (Table 3). Fifteen of the 20 occupations with the largest numerical decreases are either production occupations or office and administrative support occupations, both of which are adversely affected by increasing plant and factory automation or the implementation of office technology, reducing the need for workers in those occupations. The difference between the office and administrative support occupations that are expected to experience the largest declines and those that are expected to see the largest increases is the extent to which job functions can be easily automated or performed by other workers. For instance, the duties of executive secretaries and administrative assistants involve a great deal of personal interaction that cannot be automated, whereas the duties of file clerks—adding, locating, and removing business records—can be automated or performed by other workers.

Only two of the occupations with the fastest percent decline are in a category that indicates workers have any postsecondary education, while the rest are in an on-the-job training category. Eleven of these occupations earned less than $30,000 in May 2008, below the national median wage of $32,390.

Table 3. Occupations with the fastest decline

Occupation	Number of new jobs (in thousands)	Percent change	Wages (May 2008 median)	Education/ training category
Textile bleaching and dyeing machine operators and tenders	−45	−7.2	$23,680	Moderate-term on-the-job training
Textile winding, twisting, and drawing out machine setters, operators, and tenders	−41	−14.2	23,970	Moderate-term on-the-job training
Textile knitting and weaving machine setters, operators, and tenders	−39	−11.5	25,400	Long-term on-the-job training
Shoe machine operators and tenders	−35	−1.7	25,090	Moderate-term on-the-job training
Extruding and forming machine setters, operators, and tenders, synthetic and glass fibers	−34	−4.8	31,160	Moderate-term on-the-job training
Sewing machine operators	−34	−71.5	19,870	Moderate-term on-the-job training
Semiconductor processors	−32	−10.0	32,230	Postsecondary vocational award
Textile cutting machine setters, operators, and tenders	−31	−6.0	22,620	Moderate-term on-the-job training
Postal Service mail sorters, processors, and processing machine operators	−30	−54.5	50,020	Short-term on-the-job training
Fabric menders, except garment	−30	−0.3	28,470	Moderate-term on-the-job training
Wellhead pumpers	−28	−5.3	37,860	Moderate-term on-the-job training
Fabric and apparel patternmakers	−27	−2.2	37,760	Long-term on-the-job training
Drilling and boring machine tool setters, operators, and tenders, metal and plastic	−27	−8.9	30,850	Moderate-term on-the-job training
Lathe and turning machine tool setters, operators, and tenders, metal and plastic	−27	−14.9	32,940	Moderate-term on-the-job training
Order clerks	−26	−64.2	27,990	Short-term on-the-job training
Coil winders, tapers, and finishers	−25	−5.6	27,730	Short-term on-the-job training
Photographic processing machine operators	−24	−12.5	20,360	Short-term on-the-job training
File clerks	−23	−49.6	23,800	Short-term on-the-job training
Derrick operators, oil and gas	−23	−5.8	41,920	Moderate-term on-the-job training
Desktop publishers	−23	−5.9	36,600	Postsecondary vocational award

SOURCE: BLS Occupational Employment Statistics and Division of Occupational Outlook

Employment Change by Education and Training Category

Education and training categories for each occupation are determined by the most significant source of education and training obtained by workers in that occupation. Growth for each education and training category is calculated by adding the growth across all occupations in the category. As a result, there is some variation in the growth rates between categories.

In general, occupations in a category with some postsecondary education are expected to experience higher rates of growth than those in an on-the-job training category. Occupations in the associate degree category are projected to grow the fastest, at about 19 percent. In addition, occupations in the master's and first professional degree categories are anticipated to grow by about 18 percent each, and occupations in the bachelor's and doctoral degree categories are expected to grow by about 17 percent each. However, occupations in the on-the-job training categories are expected to grow by 8 percent each (Chart 7).

Total Job Openings

Job openings stem from both employment growth and replacement needs (Chart 8). Replacement needs arise as workers leave occupations. Some transfer to other occupations, while others retire, return to school, or quit to assume household responsibilities. Replacement needs are projected to account for 67 percent of the approximately 50.9 million job openings between 2008 and 2018. Thus, even occupations that are projected to experience slower-than-average growth or to decline in employment still may offer many job openings.

Professional and related occupations are projected to have the largest number of total job openings, 11.9 million, and 56 percent of those will be due to replacement needs. Replacement needs generally are greatest in the largest occupations and in those with relatively low pay or limited training requirements. As a result, service occupations are projected to have the greatest number of job openings due to replacements, about 7.6 million.

Office automation will significantly affect many individual office and administrative support occupations. Although these occupations are projected to grow about as fast as average, some are projected to decline rapidly. Office and administrative support occupations are expected to create 7.3 million total job openings from 2008 to 2018, ranking third behind professional and related occupations and service occupations.

Farming, fishing, and forestry occupations and production occupations should offer job opportunities despite overall declines in employment. These occupations will lose 9,100 and 349,200 jobs, respectively, but are expected to provide more than 2.4 million total job openings. Job openings will be due solely to the replacement needs of a workforce characterized by high levels of retirement and job turnover.

Additional Information About the 2008–2018 Projections

Readers interested in more information about the projections; about the methods and assumptions that underlie them; or about details on economic growth, the labor force, or industry and occupational employment should consult the November 2009 *Monthly Labor Review* or the Winter 2009–2010 *Occupational Outlook Quarterly* (both of which are available online).

More information about employment change, job openings, earnings, and training requirements by occupation is available on the Bureau's Employment Projections home page at www.bls.gov/emp. The *Career Guide to Industries*, which presents occupational information from an industry perspective, is also accessible.

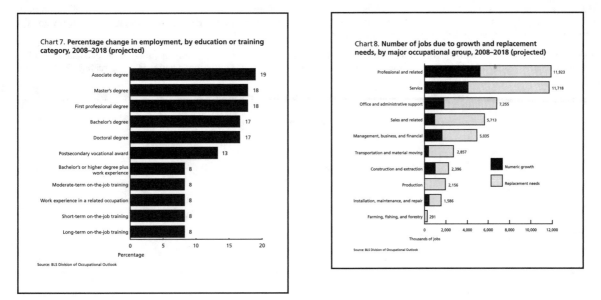

Chart 7. Percentage change in employment, by education or training category, 2008–2018 (projected)

Category	Percentage
Associate degree	19
Master's degree	18
First professional degree	18
Bachelor's degree	17
Doctoral degree	17
Postsecondary vocational award	13
Bachelor's or higher degree plus work experience	8
Moderate-term on-the-job training	8
Work experience in a related occupation	8
Short-term on-the-job training	8
Long-term on-the-job training	8

Source: BLS Division of Occupational Outlook

Chart 8. Number of jobs due to growth and replacement needs, by major occupational group, 2008–2018 (projected)

Occupational group	Thousands of jobs
Professional and related	11,923
Service	11,718
Office and administrative support	7,255
Sales and related	5,713
Management, business, and financial	5,035
Transportation and material moving	2,857
Construction and extraction	2,396
Production	2,156
Installation, maintenance, and repair	1,586
Farming, fishing, and forestry	291

Numeric growth / Replacement needs

Source: BLS Division of Occupational Outlook

Classification of occupations by most significant source of education or training

Postsecondary awards

First professional degree. Completion of the degree usually requires at least three years of full-time academic study beyond a bachelor's degree. Examples are lawyers and physicians and surgeons.

Doctoral degree. Completion of a Ph.D. or other doctoral degree usually requires at least three years of full-time academic study beyond a bachelor's degree. Examples are postsecondary teachers and medical scientists, except epidemiologists.

Master's degree. Completion of the degree usually requires one or two years of full-time academic study beyond a bachelor's degree. Examples are educational, vocational, and school counselors and clergy.

Bachelor's or higher degree plus work experience. Most occupations in this category are management occupations. All require experience in a related nonmanagement position for which a bachelor's or higher degree is usually required. Examples are general and operations managers and judges, magistrate judges, and magistrates.

Bachelor's degree. Completion of the degree generally requires at least four years, but not more than five years, of full-time academic study. Examples are accountants and auditors and elementary school teachers, except special education.

Associate degree. Completion of the degree usually requires at least two years of full-time academic study. Examples are paralegals and legal assistants and medical records and health information technicians.

Postsecondary vocational award. Some programs last only a few weeks, others more than a year. Programs lead to a certificate or other award, but not a degree. Examples are nursing aides, orderlies, and attendants and hairdressers, hairstylists, and cosmetologists.

Work-related training

Work experience in a related occupation. Most of the occupations in this category are first-line supervisors or managers of service, sales and related, production, or other occupations or are management occupations.

Long-term on-the-job training. Occupations in this category generally require more than 12 months of on-the-job training or combined work experience and formal classroom instruction for workers to develop the skills necessary to be fully qualified in the occupation. These occupations include formal and informal apprenticeships that may last up to five years. Long-term on-the-job training also includes intensive occupation-specific, employer-sponsored programs that workers must complete. Among such programs are those conducted by fire and police academies and by schools for air traffic controllers and flight attendants. In other occupations—insurance sales and securities sales, for example—trainees take formal courses, often provided on the jobsite, to prepare for the required licensing exams. Individuals undergoing training generally are considered to be employed in the occupation. Also included in this category is the development of a natural ability—such as that possessed by musicians, athletes, actors, and other entertainers—that must be cultivated over several years, frequently in a nonwork setting.

Moderate-term on-the-job training. In this category of occupations, the skills needed to be fully qualified in the occupation can be acquired during 1 to 12 months of combined on-the-job experience and informal training. Examples are truck drivers, heavy and tractor-trailer, and secretaries, except legal, medical, and executive.

Short-term on-the-job training. In occupations in this category, the skills needed to be fully qualified in the occupation can be acquired during a short demonstration of job duties or during one month or less of on-the-job experience or instruction. Examples of these occupations are retail salespersons and waiters and waitresses.

Employment Trends in Major Industries

The U.S. economy can be broken down into numerous industries, each with its own set of characteristics. The Department of Labor has identified 45 industries that account for three-quarters of all workers. This section provides an overview of the outlook for the various industries and for the economy as a whole.

Nature of the Industry

Industries are defined by the processes they use to produce goods and services. Workers in the United States produce and provide a wide variety of products and services, and as a result, the types of industries in the U.S. economy range widely—from agriculture, forestry, and fishing to aerospace manufacturing. Each industry has a unique combination of occupations, production techniques, inputs and outputs, and business characteristics. Understanding the nature of industries that interest you is important because it is this combination that determines working conditions, educational requirements, and the job outlook.

Industries consist of many different places of work, called *establishments*. Establishments are physical locations at which people work, such as the branch office of a bank, a gasoline service station, a school, a department store, or a plant that manufactures machinery. Establishments range from large factories and corporate office complexes employing thousands of workers to small community stores, restaurants, professional offices, and service businesses employing only a few workers. Establishments should not be confused with companies or corporations, which are legal entities. Thus, a company or corporation may have a single establishment or more than one establishment. Establishments that use the same or similar processes to produce goods or services are organized together into *industries*. Industries, in turn, are organized together into *industry groups*, which are further organized into *industry subsectors* and then, ultimately, into *industry sectors*. For the purposes of labor market analysis, the Bureau of Labor Statistics organized industry sectors into *industry supersectors*. A company or corporation could own establishments classified in more than one industry, industry sector, or even industry supersector.

Each industry subsector is made up of a number of industry groups, which are, as mentioned, determined by differences in production processes. An easily recognized example of these distinctions is in the food manufacturing subsector, which is made up of industry groups that produce meat products, preserved fruits and vegetables, bakery items, and dairy products, among others. Each of these industry groups requires workers with varying skills and employs unique production techniques. Another example of these distinctions is found in utilities, which employ workers in establishments that provide electricity, natural gas, and water.

There were about 8.8 million private business establishments in the United States in 2008, predominantly small establishments: About 61.6 percent of all establishments employed fewer than 5 workers in March 2008. However, the medium-to-large establishments employ a greater proportion of all workers. For example, establishments that employed 50 or more workers accounted for only 4.5 percent of all establishments, yet employed 56.2 percent of all workers. The large establishments—those with more than 500 workers—accounted for only 0.2 percent of all establishments, but employed 16.7 percent of all workers. Table 1 presents the percent distribution of employment according to establishment size.

Table 1. Percent distribution of establishments and employment in all private industries by establishment size, March 2008

Establishment size (number of workers)	Percent of Establishments	Percent of Employment
Total	100.0	100.0
1 to 4	61.6	6.9
5 to 9	15.9	8.3
10 to 19	10.6	11.3
20 to 49	7.4	17.4
50 to 99	2.5	13.5
100 to 249	1.4	16.7
250 to 499	0.3	9.3
500 to 999	0.1	6.5
1,000 or more	0.1	10.2

SOURCE: BLS Quarterly Census of Employment and Wages

The average size of these establishments varies widely across industries. Most establishments in the construction; wholesale trade; retail trade; finance and insurance; real estate and rental and leasing; and professional, scientific, and technical services industries are small, averaging fewer than 20 employees per establishment. However, wide differences within industries can exist. Hospitals, for example, employ an average of 576.8 workers, while physicians' offices employ an average of 10.5. Similarly, although there is an average of 14.5 employees per establishment for all of retail trade, department stores employ an average of 119.7 people and jewelry stores employ an average of only 5.6.

Establishment size can play a role in the characteristics of each job. Large establishments generally offer workers greater occupational mobility and advancement, whereas small establishments may provide their employees with broader experience by requiring them to assume a wider range of responsibilities. Also, small establishments are distributed throughout the nation: every locality has a few small businesses. Large establishments, in contrast, employ more workers and are less common, but they play a much more prominent role in the economies of the areas in which they are located.

Working Conditions

Just as the goods and services produced in each industry are different, working conditions vary significantly among industries. In some industries, the work setting is quiet, temperature controlled, and virtually hazard free, whereas other industries are characterized by noisy, uncomfortable, and sometimes dangerous work environments. Some industries require long workweeks and shift work, but standard 40-hour workweeks are common in many other industries. In still other industries, a lot of the jobs can be seasonal, requiring long hours during busy periods and abbreviated schedules during slower months. Production processes, establishment size, and the physical location of the work usually determine these varying conditions.

Work schedules are another important reflection of working conditions, and the operational requirements of each industry lead to large differences in hours worked and in part-time versus full-time status. In food services and drinking places, for example, fully 37.9 percent of employees worked part time in 2008, compared with only 2.0

percent in aerospace product and parts manufacturing. Table 2 presents industries having relatively high and low percentages of part-time workers.

Table 2. Part-time workers as a percent of total employment, selected industries, 2008

Industry	Percent part-time
All industries	15.9
Many part-time workers	
Food services and drinking places	37.9
Clothing, accessories, and general merchandise stores	30.6
Grocery stores	30.4
Arts, entertainment, and recreation	29.4
Child day care services	29.4
Motion picture and video industries	21.7
Social assistance, except child day care	23.3
Few part-time workers	
Mining	2.6
Computer and electronic product manufacturing	3.1
Pharmaceutical and medicine manufacturing	2.2
Steel manufacturing	2.2
Motor vehicle and parts manufacturing	2.1
Utilities	2.1
Aerospace product and parts manufacturing	2.0

SOURCE: BLS Current Population Survey, 2008

The low proportion of part-time workers in some manufacturing industries often reflects the continuous nature of the production processes, which makes it difficult to adapt the volume of production to short-term fluctuations in product demand. Once these processes are begun, it is costly to halt them: Machinery must be tended and materials must be moved continuously. For example, the chemical-manufacturing industry produces many different chemical products through controlled chemical reactions. These reactions require chemical operators to monitor and adjust the flow of materials into and out of the line of production. Because production may continue 24 hours a day, 7 days a week under the watchful eyes of chemical operators who work in shifts, full-time workers are more likely to be employed. Retail trade and service industries, by contrast, have seasonal cycles marked by various events, such as school openings or important holidays, that affect the hours worked. During busy times of the year, longer hours are common, whereas slack periods lead to cutbacks in work hours and shorter workweeks. Jobs in these industries are generally appealing to students and others who desire flexible, part-time schedules.

Employment

The total number of jobs in the United States in 2008 was 150.9 million, comprising 11.6 million self-employed workers, 121,500 unpaid workers in family businesses, and 139.2 million wage and salary jobs. The total number of jobs is projected to increase to 166.2 million by 2018, and wage and salary jobs are projected to account for almost 153.8 million of them.

As shown in Table 3, wage and salary jobs are the vast majority of all jobs, but they are not evenly divided among the various industries. Education, health, and social services had the largest number of jobs in 2008, almost 30.3 million. The trade supersector was the second largest, with about 21.3 million jobs, followed by professional and business services, with 17.6 million jobs in 2008. Manufacturing accounted for roughly 13.4 million jobs in the United States in 2008. Wage and salary employment ranged from just 159,000 in steel manufacturing to more than 14.3

million in health care, among the industries covered in Table 3. The three largest industries—education services, health care, and food services and drinking places—together accounted for 37.4 million jobs, more than one-quarter of the nation's wage and salary employment.

Table 3. Wage and salary employment in industries covered in the *Career Guide*, 2008, and projected change, 2008–2018 (Employment in thousands)

Industry	2008		2018		2008–2018	
	Employment	Percent distribution	Employment	Percent distribution	Percent change	Employment change
All industries	139,206	100.0	153,842	100.0	10.5	14,635
Natural resources, construction, and utilities	9,796	7.0	10,966	7.1	11.9	1,170
Agriculture, forestry, and fishing	1,305	0.9	1,300	0.8	-0.4	-5
Construction	7,215	5.2	8,552	5.6	18.5	1,337
Mining	717	0.5	613	0.4	-14.5	-104
Utilities	560	0.4	501	0.3	-10.6	-59
Manufacturing	13,431	9.6	12,225	7.9	-9.0	-1,206
Aerospace product and parts manufacturing	504	0.4	502	0.3	-0.3	-2
Chemical manufacturing, except drugs	560	0.4	486	0.3	-13.3	-74
Computer and electronic product manufacturing	1,248	0.9	1,007	0.7	-19.3	-241
Food manufacturing	1,485	1.1	1,483	1.0	-0.1	-2
Machinery manufacturing	1,186	0.9	1,095	0.7	-7.6	-90
Motor vehicle and parts manufacturing	877	0.6	734	0.5	-18.3	-143
Pharmaceutical and medicine manufacturing	290	0.2	307	0.2	6.1	18
Printing	594	0.4	499	0.3	-18.0	-95
Steel manufacturing	159	0.1	139	0.1	-12.7	-20
Textile, textile product, and apparel manufacturing	497	0.4	259	0.2	-47.9	-238
Trade	21,320	15.3	22,230	14.5	4.3	910
Automobile dealers	1,186	0.9	1,118	0.7	-5.7	-68
Clothing, accessory, and general merchandise stores	4,531	3.3	5,034	1.3	11.1	503
Grocery stores	2,497	1.8	2,509	1.6	0.5	12
Wholesale trade	5,964	4.3	6,220	4.0	4.3	256
Transportation and warehousing	4,505	3.2	4,950	3.2	9.9	446
Air transportation	493	0.4	529	0.3	7.5	37
Truck transportation and warehousing	2,064	1.5	2,290	1.5	11.0	226
Information	2,997	2.2	3,115	2.0	3.9	118
Broadcasting	316	0.2	340	0.2	7.4	24
Motion picture and video industries	362	0.3	413	0.3	14.1	51
Publishing, except software	619	0.4	499	0.3	-19.3	-120
Software publishers	264	0.2	343	0.2	30.0	79
Telecommunications	1,022	0.7	932	0.6	-8.8	-90
Financial activities	8,146	5.9	8,703	5.7	6.8	557
Banking	1,842	1.3	1,987	1.3	7.9	145
Insurance	2,309	1.7	2,376	1.5	2.9	68
Securities, commodities, and other investments	858	0.6	959	0.6	11.8	101

Industry	2008		2018		2008–2018	
	Employment	Percent distribution	Employment	Percent distribution	Percent change	Employment change
Professional and business services	17,552	12.6	21,644	14.1	23.3	4,092
Advertising and public relations services	462	0.3	499	0.3	8.0	37
Computer systems design and related services	1,450	1.0	2,107	1.4	45.3	656
Employment services	3,144	2.3	3,744	2.4	19.1	600
Management, scientific, and technical consulting services	1,009	0.7	1,844	1.2	82.8	835
Scientific research and development services	622	0.4	779	0.5	25.3	157
Education, health, and social services	30,316	21.8	36,016	23.4	18.8	5,700
Child day-care services	859	0.6	992	0.6	15.5	133
Educational services	13,471	9.7	15,154	9.9	12.5	1,683
Health care	14,336	10.3	17,559	11.4	22.5	3,223
Social assistance, except child day care	1,650	1.2	2,311	1.5	40.1	661
Leisure and hospitality	13,459	10	14,601	9	8.5	1,142
Arts, entertainment, and recreation	1,970	1.4	2,274	1.5	15.5	304
Food services and drinking places	9,632	6.9	10,371	6.7	7.7	739
Hotels and other accommodations	1,857	1.3	1,957	1.3	5.4	99
Government and advocacy, grantmaking, and civic organizations	11,581	8.3	12,648	8.2	9.2	1,067
Advocacy, grantmaking, and civic organizations	1,289	0.9	1,471	1.0	14.1	182
Federal government	2,017	1.4	2,209	1.4	9.5	192
State and local government, except education and health	8,275	5.9	8,968	5.8	8.4	694

NOTE: May not add to totals due to omission of industries not covered in the *Career Guide to Industries.*
SOURCE: BLS National Employment Matrix, 2008–2018

Although workers of all ages are employed in each industry, certain industries tend to hire workers of distinct age groups. Thus, for the reasons mentioned previously, retail trade employs a relatively high proportion of younger workers to fill part-time and temporary positions. The manufacturing sector, in contrast, has a relatively high median age, because many jobs in the sector require a number of years to learn and perfect specialized skills that do not easily transfer to other industries. Also, manufacturing employment has been declining, providing fewer opportunities for younger workers to get jobs. As a result, nearly one-fourth of the workers in retail trade were 24 years of age or younger in 2008, compared with only 7.8 percent of workers in manufacturing. Table 4 contrasts the age distribution of workers in all industries with the distributions in five very different industries.

Table 4. Percent distribution of wage and salary workers by age group, selected industries, 2008

Industry	Age group			
	16 to 24	25 to 44	45 to 64	65 and older
All industries	13	45	38	4
Computer systems design and related services	6	58	34	2
Educational services	9	42	44	4
Food services and drinking places	42	39	17	2
Telecommunications	9	52	38	1
Utilities	5	42	51	2

SOURCE: BLS Current Population Survey, 2008

Employment in some industries is concentrated in a few regions of the country. Such industries often are located near a source of raw or unfinished materials upon which the industry relies. For example, oil and gas extraction jobs are concentrated in Texas, Louisiana, and Oklahoma; many textile mills and manufacturing jobs are found in North Carolina, South Carolina, and Georgia; and a significant proportion of motor vehicle manufacturing jobs are located in Michigan and Ohio. In contrast, some industries—such as grocery stores and educational services—have jobs distributed throughout the nation, reflecting the general population density.

Occupations in the Industry

The occupations found in each industry depend on the types of services provided or goods produced. For example, because construction companies require skilled tradesworkers to build and renovate buildings, these companies employ large numbers of carpenters, electricians, plumbers, painters, and sheet metal workers. Other occupations common to construction include construction equipment operators and mechanics, installers, and repairers. Retail trade, in contrast, displays and sells manufactured goods to consumers. As a result, retail trade employs numerous retail salespersons and other workers, including more than three-fourths of all cashiers. Table 5 shows the industry sectors and the occupational groups that predominate in each.

Table 5. Industry sectors and their largest occupational group, 2008

Industry sector	Largest occupational group	Percentage of industry wage and salary jobs
Agriculture, forestry, fishing, and hunting	Farming, fishing, and forestry occupations	60.0
Mining	Construction and extraction occupations	41.8
Construction	Construction and extraction occupations	65.7
Manufacturing	Production occupations	52.3
Wholesale trade	Sales and related occupations	26.8
Retail trade	Sales and related occupations	54.5
Transportation and warehousing	Transportation and material moving occupations	59.7
Utilities	Installation, maintenance, and repair occupations	26.1
Information	Professional and related occupations	34.0
Finance and insurance	Office and administrative support occupations	48.4
Real estate and rental and leasing	Sales and related occupations	24.9
Professional, scientific, and technical services	Professional and related occupations	45.6
Management of companies and enterprises	Management, business, and financial occupations	35.6
Administrative and support and waste management and remediation services	Service occupations	32.5
Educational services, public and private	Professional and related occupations	67.4
Health care and social assistance	Professional and related occupations	43.5
Arts, entertainment, and recreation	Service occupations	59.0
Accommodation and food services	Service occupations	86.9
Government	Service occupations	25.4

SOURCE: BLS National Employment Matrix

The nation's occupational distribution clearly is influenced by its industrial structure, yet there are many occupations, such as general managers or secretaries, that are found in all industries. In fact, some of the largest occupations in the U.S. economy are dispersed across many industries. For example, professional and related occupations make up the largest major group of occupations in the nation while also experiencing the fastest growth rate. (See Table 6.) Other large major occupational groups include service occupations; office and administrative support occupations; sales and related occupations; and management, business, and financial occupations.

Table 6. Total employment and projected change by broad occupational group, 2008–2018 (Employment in thousands)

Occupational group	Employment, 2008	Percent change, 2008–2018
Total, all occupations	150,932	10.1
Professional and related occupations	31,054	16.8
Service occupations	29,576	13.8
Office and administrative support occupations	24,101	7.7
Sales and related occupations	15,903	6.2
Management, business, and financial occupations	15,747	10.6
Production occupations	10,083	-3.5
Transportation and material moving occupations	9,826	4.0
Construction and extraction occupations	7,810	13.0
Installation, maintenance, and repair occupations	5,798	7.5
Farming, fishing, and forestry occupations	1,035	-0.9

SOURCE: BLS National Employment Matrix, 2008–2018

Training and Advancement

Workers prepare for employment in many ways, but the most fundamental form of job training in the United States is a high school education. About 90 percent of the nation's workforce possessed a high school diploma or its equivalent. However, many occupations require more training, so growing numbers of workers pursue additional training or education after high school. For example, 29 percent of the nation's workforce reported having completed some college or an associate degree as their highest level of education, while an additional 32 percent continued in their studies and attained a bachelor's or higher degree. In addition to these types of formal education, other sources of qualifying training include formal company-provided training, apprenticeships, informal on-the-job training, correspondence courses, Armed Forces vocational training, and non-work-related training.

The unique combination of training required to succeed in each industry is determined largely by the industry's production process and the mix of occupations it requires. For example, manufacturing employs many machine operators, who generally need little formal education after high school, but sometimes complete considerable on-the-job training. In contrast, educational services employs many types of teachers, most of whom require a bachelor's or higher degree. Training requirements by industry sector are shown in Table 7.

Table 7. Percent distribution of workers by highest grade completed or degree received, by industry sector, 2008

Industry sector	High school diploma or less	Some college or associate degree	Bachelor's degree or higher
All industries	39.1	29.1	31.8
Agriculture, forestry, fishing, and hunting	62.5	22.2	15.2
Mining	56.9	26.4	16.8
Construction	62.5	25.5	12.0
Manufacturing	48.5	26.2	25.3
Wholesale trade	41.8	29.2	29.0
Retail trade	49.0	33.4	17.7
Transportation and warehousing	50.9	32.5	16.6
Utilities	38.3	34.9	26.8
Information	24.3	31.9	43.8
Finance and insurance	20.5	31.6	47.9
Real estate and rental and leasing	32.0	33.5	34.5

(continued)

(continued)

Industry sector	High school diploma or less	Some college or associate degree	Bachelor's degree or higher
Professional, scientific, and technical services	12.6	23.5	63.9
Administrative and support and waste management services	53.7	27.7	18.6
Educational services	16.3	19.2	64.5
Health care and social assistance	28.5	34.8	36.7
Arts, entertainment, and recreation	37.3	31.9	30.9
Accommodation and food services	58.6	29.5	11.9

SOURCE: BLS Current Population Survey

On the one hand, persons with no more than a high school diploma accounted for about 62.5 percent of all workers in agriculture, forestry, fishing, and hunting; 62.5 percent in construction; 58.6 percent in accommodation and food services; 56.9 percent in mining; 53.7 percent in administrative and support and waste management services; and 50.9 in transportation and warehousing. On the other hand, those who had acquired a bachelor's or higher degree accounted for 64.5 percent of workers in private educational services; 63.9 percent in professional, scientific, and technical services; 47.9 percent in finance and insurance; and 43.8 percent in information.

Education and training also are important factors in the variety of paths to advancement that are found in different industries. Each industry has some unique paths, but workers who complete additional on-the-job training or education generally help their chances of being promoted. In much of the manufacturing sector, for example, production workers who receive training in management and computer skills increase their likelihood of being promoted to supervisory positions. Other factors that affect advancement and that may figure prominently in industries include the size of the establishments, institutionalized career tracks, and the mix of occupations in the industry. As a result, persons who seek jobs in particular industries should be aware of how the paths to advancement and other factors in those industries may shape their careers.

Outlook

Total wage and salary employment in the United States is projected to increase by about 11 percent over the 2008–2018 period. Employment growth, however, is only one source of job openings; the total number of openings in any industry also depends on the industry's current employment level and its need to replace workers who leave their jobs. Throughout the economy, replacement needs will create more job openings than will employment growth. Employment size is a major determinant of job openings: Larger industries generally have larger numbers of workers who must be replaced; hence, these industries provide more openings. The occupational composition of an industry is another factor. On the one hand, industries with high concentrations of professional, technical, and other jobs that require more formal education—jobs that workers tend to leave less frequently—generally have fewer openings resulting from replacement needs. On the other hand, more replacement openings generally occur in industries with high concentrations of service, laborer, and other jobs that require little formal education and have lower wages, because workers in these jobs are more likely to leave their occupations.

Employment growth is determined largely by changes in three factors: demand for the goods and services provided by an industry, worker productivity, and foreign competition. Each industry is affected by a different set of variables that determines the number and composition of jobs that will be available. Even within an industry, employment may grow at different rates in different occupations. For example, changes in technology, production methods, and business practices in an industry might eliminate some jobs while creating others. Some industries may be growing rapidly overall, yet opportunities for workers in occupations could be stagnant or even declining because the workers are adversely affected by technological change. Conversely, employment in some occupations may be declining in the economy as a whole, yet may be increasing in a rapidly growing industry.

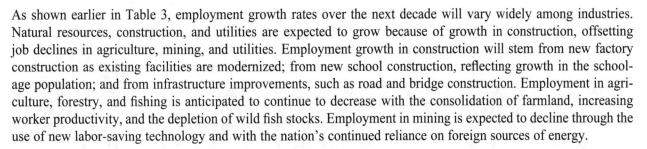
As shown earlier in Table 3, employment growth rates over the next decade will vary widely among industries. Natural resources, construction, and utilities are expected to grow because of growth in construction, offsetting job declines in agriculture, mining, and utilities. Employment growth in construction will stem from new factory construction as existing facilities are modernized; from new school construction, reflecting growth in the school-age population; and from infrastructure improvements, such as road and bridge construction. Employment in agriculture, forestry, and fishing is anticipated to continue to decrease with the consolidation of farmland, increasing worker productivity, and the depletion of wild fish stocks. Employment in mining is expected to decline through the use of new labor-saving technology and with the nation's continued reliance on foreign sources of energy.

Employment in manufacturing is projected to decline overall, though with some growth in selected manufacturing industries. Employment declines are expected in chemical manufacturing, except drugs; computer and electronic product manufacturing; machinery manufacturing; motor vehicle and parts manufacturing; printing; steel manufacturing; and textile, textile product, and apparel manufacturing. Textile, textile product, and apparel manufacturing is projected to lose about 238,200 jobs over the 2008–2018 period—more than any other manufacturing industry—primarily because increasing imports are replacing domestic products.

Employment gains are expected in some manufacturing industries. Employment growth in pharmaceutical and medicine manufacturing is expected as sales of pharmaceuticals increase with the growth of the population—particularly the elderly—and with the introduction of new medicines into the market. Pharmaceutical and medicine manufacturing also have growing export markets. Agricultural equipment manufacturing is the only machinery manufacturing industry expected to grow as the diverse range of products it produces is supplied to both domestic and foreign consumers.

Growth in overall employment will result primarily from growth in service-providing industries over the 2008–2018 period. Almost all of those industries are expected to have increasing employment. Job growth is expected to be led by health care and educational services—the two largest industries in the U.S. economy. Large numbers of new jobs also are expected in food services and drinking places; social assistance, except child day care; management, scientific, and technical consulting services; employment services; state and local government, except education and health care; arts, entertainment, and recreation; computer systems design and related services; and wholesale trade. Together, these sectors will account for nearly two-thirds of all new wage and salary jobs across the nation. Employment growth is expected in many other service-providing industries, but such growth will result in far fewer numbers of new jobs.

Health care will account for the most new wage and salary jobs, almost 3.2 million over the 2008–2018 period. Population growth, advances in medical technologies that increase the number of treatable diseases, and the older age groups' growing share of the population will drive employment growth. Hospitals, public and private—the largest health-care industry group—are expected to account for about 571,000 of these new jobs.

Educational services are expected to grow by 12 percent over the 2008–2018 period, adding about 1.7 million new jobs. A growing emphasis on improving education and making it available to more children and young adults will be the primary factors contributing to this industry's employment growth. Growth is expected at all levels of education, particularly the postsecondary level, as children of the baby boomers continue to reach college age and as more adults pursue continuing education to enhance or update their skills.

Employment in the nation's fastest-growing industry—management, scientific, and technical consulting services—is expected to increase by 83 percent, adding 835,200 jobs over the 2008–2018 period. The industry's projected job growth can be attributed primarily to economic growth and to the increasing complexity of business. A growing number of businesses will result in increased demand for advice in all areas of business operations and planning.

The food services and drinking places industry is expected to add 738,800 new jobs over the 2008–2018 projection period. Population growth, a rise in the number of dual-income families, and increasing dining sophistication will contribute to job growth. In addition, the increasing diversity of the population will contribute to job growth in food services and drinking places, many of which will offer a wider variety of ethnic foods and drinks.

State and local government, except education and health care, is expected to add 693,500 jobs. The industry's growth of 8 percent over the 2008–2018 period will result primarily from increases in the population and its demand for public services. Additional job growth will ensue as state and local governments continue to assume greater responsibility from the federal government for administering federally funded programs.

Wholesale trade is expected to add more than 255,900 new jobs over the coming decade, reflecting growth both in trade and in the overall economy. Most new jobs will be for sales representatives at the wholesale and manufacturing levels. However, industry consolidation and the growth of electronic commerce using the Internet are expected to limit job growth to 4 percent over the 2008–2018 period, less than the 11 percent projected for wage and salary jobs in all industries.

Earnings

Like other characteristics, earnings differ by industry as a result of a highly complicated process that reflects a number of factors. For example, earnings may vary with the nature of the occupations in the industry, the average hours worked, the geographical location, workers' average age, educational requirements, industry profits, and the degree of union representation of the workforce. In general, wages are highest in metropolitan areas, to compensate for the higher cost of living there. Also, as would be expected, industries that employ a large proportion of unskilled minimum-wage or part-time workers tend to have lower earnings.

The difference in earnings between the software publishing and food services and drinking places industries illustrates how various characteristics of industries can result in great differences in earnings. In software publishing, earnings of nonsupervisory wage and salary workers averaged $1,458 a week in 2009, while in food services and drinking places, earnings averaged $351 weekly. The difference is large primarily because software publishing establishments employ more highly skilled, full-time workers, while food services and drinking places employ many lower-skilled workers on a part-time basis. In addition, most workers in software publishing are paid an annual salary, whereas many workers in food services and drinking places are paid an hourly wage, although they are able to supplement their low hourly wage rate with money they receive as tips. Table 8 highlights the industries with the highest and lowest average weekly earnings.

Table 8. Average weekly earnings of production or nonsupervisory workers on private nonfarm payrolls, selected industries, 2009

Industry	Earnings
All industries	$704
Industries with high earnings	
Software publishers	1,407
Computer systems design and related services	1,333
Scientific research and development services	1,276
Aerospace product and parts manufacturing	1,142
Securities, commodities, and other investments	1,202
Utilities	1,103
Industries with low earnings	
Employment services	563
Arts, entertainment, and recreation	469
Hotels and other accommodations	421
Child day care services	405
Grocery stores	398
Food services and drinking places	351

SOURCE: BLS Occupational Employment Statistics, May 2009

Employee benefits, once a minor addition to wages and salaries, continue to grow in diversity and cost. In addition to providing traditional benefits—paid vacations, life and health insurance, and pensions—many employers now offer various benefits to accommodate the needs of a changing labor force. Such benefits include child care; employee assistance programs that provide counseling for personal problems; and wellness programs that encourage exercise, stress management, and self-improvement. Benefits vary among occupational groups, full- and part-time workers, public- and private-sector workers, regions, unionized and nonunionized workers, and small and large establishments. Data indicate that full-time workers and workers in medium-sized and large establishments—those with 100 or more workers—usually receive better benefits than do part-time workers and workers in smaller establishments.

Union representation of the workforce varies widely by industry and also may play a role in determining earnings and benefits. In 2008, about 14 percent of workers throughout the nation were union members or were covered by union contracts. As Table 9 demonstrates, union affiliation of workers varies widely by industry. The highest rate of union membership was 46 percent, in air transportation, followed by 38 percent in educational services and 36 percent in public administration. Industries with the lowest unionization rates were software publishing, 2 percent; food services and drinking places, 1.9 percent; computer systems design and related services, 1.7 percent; and management, scientific, and technical consulting services, 1.4 percent.

Table 9. Union members and other workers covered by union contracts as a percentage of total employment, selected industries, 2008

Industry	Percent union members or covered by union contract
All industries	13.7
Industries with high unionization rates	
Air transportation	46.4
Educational services	38.4
Public administration	36.0
Utilities	30.2
Industries with low unionization rates	
Software publishing	2.0
Food services and drinking places	1.9
Computer systems design and related services	1.7
Management, scientific, and technical consulting services	1.4

SOURCE: BLS Current Population Survey, 2008

Continual changes in the economy have far-reaching and complex effects on employment in every industry. Job seekers should be aware of these changes, keeping alert for developments that can affect both job opportunities in industries and the variety of occupations that are found in each industry.

Editor's Note: The preceding article was adapted from the Career Guide to Industries. *This publication of the U.S. Department of Labor is available only on the Web, at www.bls.gov/oco/cg.*

Job Outlook for People Who Don't Have a Bachelor's Degree

Good news for those not planning to earn a four-year degree: Millions of job openings are projected for high school graduates over the 2008–2018 decade, according to the U.S. Bureau of Labor Statistics (BLS). But job seekers will probably need training beyond a high school diploma, particularly if they want a job with high pay.

Most jobs are filled by workers who do not have a bachelor's degree, and BLS expects that to continue in the future. Between 2008 and 2018, job openings for workers who are entering their occupation for the first time and who don't have a bachelor's degree are expected to total roughly 40 million. That's more than twice the number of job openings for four-year college graduates.

But many of these job openings will be in occupations that require some training after high school. In fact, high-paying occupations almost always require training. That training could include taking a few college courses, getting an associate degree, training on the job in an apprenticeship program, or taking vocational classes at a technical school.

Which occupations should people prepare for? Which are expected to have the best prospects? Read on to discover the occupations that are projected to have the most openings over the 2008–2018 decade for people who do not have a bachelor's degree and which occupations tend to pay well. Next, learn more about career fields—including construction, maintenance and repair, health care, and computers—that are expected to provide many opportunities for new workers. A later section of this article describes in detail the methods used to develop this information.

All of the numbers in this article are estimates. They are based on projections of future job growth and decline and on estimates of how many workers will leave their occupations and, thus, make room for new workers. The results shown here also rely on survey data that describe the education levels of current workers. And the results assume that future workers will have education levels similar to those of current workers.

Job Openings and Occupations

Between 2008 and 2018, BLS expects about 50 million job openings to be filled by workers who are new to their occupation. Of this total, more than 39 million openings are projected to be filled by workers who do not have a bachelor's degree and who are entering their occupation for the first time. About 34 million of these openings are expected to be held by workers who have a high school diploma or less education. Another 5 million openings are expected for workers who have some college education or an associate degree but do not have a bachelor's degree.

Job openings are expected in every type of occupation. But some occupations and career fields are projected to have more job openings and better earnings than others.

Occupations with Potential

Two main factors determine whether an occupation will have many job openings. One factor is how many workers will leave the occupation permanently. Large occupations—that is, occupations in which many jobs exist nationwide—have more workers and, thus, also have more workers who leave the occupation and create openings. Occupations that have few training requirements or low earnings also have more workers who leave. And occupations that have many older workers usually provide more openings because of retirements.

The second factor affecting job openings is job growth. Some occupations gain new jobs faster than others, providing more openings.

The occupations that are expected to need the most new workers between 2008 and 2018 employ workers who have widely varying levels of education. People in some occupations can start work after high school. In other occupations, especially higher-paying ones, workers often have more education or training. Sometimes, people can enter these occupations if they don't have training after high school, but they often earn less while they train on the job.

Occupations with the most openings. Most of the occupations projected to have the most job openings between 2008 and 2018 for people who have less education than a bachelor's degree involve working with the public.

Median earnings are the point at which half of the workers in the occupation make more than that amount and half make less. All but four of the occupations with the most openings had median earnings below $28,580—the median for all workers in 2009.

But median earnings don't show the wide variation in pay that exists in some occupations. For example, earnings for some customer service representatives, such as those who provide help for complex computer problems, are sometimes significantly higher than the median. These workers are usually highly skilled and have several months of on-the-job training; some also have a bachelor's degree.

You can enter most of the occupations if you have a high school diploma or less education. Workers often qualify for jobs after less than one month of on-the-job training. But six of the occupations—customer service representatives; truck drivers; bookkeeping, accounting, and auditing clerks; registered nurses; executive secretaries and administrative assistants; and general maintenance workers—require more training. These are also the highest-paying occupations.

Customer service representatives, who often receive one month to one year of training, usually start their jobs by observing experienced workers. Truck drivers usually need one month to one year of training on the job; some attend vocational schools to learn the basics of commercial driving. Bookkeeping, accounting, and auditing clerks also require one month to one year of training, and many have an associate degree in business.

Registered nurses, unlike the other occupations, almost always have some college training. In fact, among registered nurses in 2008, more than 35 percent had an associate degree and more than 55 percent had a bachelor's or higher degree. Executive secretaries and administrative assistants usually need one month to one year of on-the-job training, and more than 45 percent of these workers have completed some college coursework. Most general maintenance workers learn on the job or in vocational classes they take during or after high school.

Occupations with high earnings and lots of openings. According to BLS data, about 360 of the occupations expected to provide openings for high school graduates also had higher-than-average median earnings in 2009. Of the high-paying occupations that are expected to have the most openings, all require technical skills or supervisory responsibilities. And all usually require moderate or long-term on-the-job training, college courses, or vocational classes.

Nearly half of the occupations relate to construction or maintenance and repair. Some of these occupations require physical strength, but many, such as painters, do not. Completing a formal apprenticeship increases your chances of getting a job in these occupations. Taking algebra classes and vocational classes in high school also helps people qualify. Seven of these occupations have very high median earnings—above $43,600.

Another way to a high-paying career is to work toward becoming a supervisor. Many high school graduates transfer to managerial occupations as they gain experience. According to some studies, having formal training or taking college courses can increase the chances of becoming a supervisor.

Competing with college workers. Some of the occupations are expected to provide jobs for workers who have a bachelor's degree, as well as for workers who don't. When an occupation includes workers who have different levels of education, workers with more education are often better able to compete for jobs. This is particularly true if the occupations require academic skills, such as mathematics or science.

If you do not have a bachelor's degree, you can increase your competitiveness in a number of ways. For example, you can gain work or volunteer experience, take high school or college courses that relate to an occupation, or complete a certification.

Additionally, consider contacting your state's labor market information office to learn about work, volunteer, education, and training opportunities. You can also find out which training programs have high placement rates and which occupations are most in demand in your area.

Career Fields with Prospects

Good opportunities exist in almost every career field. The tables in this section show the expected job openings and common educational requirements for occupations in eight different fields. Career fields that are projected to have the most openings are discussed first.

The tables show occupations expected to have many openings over the 2008–2018 decade. The tables also show 2009 earnings and the education levels of current workers aged 25 to 44. Also listed is the specific type of training—such as on-the-job training, a vocational certificate, or an associate degree—that BLS analysts deemed most significant in the occupation.

Table 1
Selected office and administrative support occupations

Occupation	Net job openings for workers without a bachelor's degree, projected 2008–2018 (thousands)	Median annual earnings, 2009	Most significant source of postsecondary education or training	Percent of workers aged 25 to 44 with…		
				High school diploma or less	Some college or associate degree	Bachelor's or higher degree
Customer service representatives	699	$30,290	Moderate-term on-the-job training	35%	43%	22%
Office clerks, general	518	26,140	Short-term on-the-job training	39	44	18
Stock clerks, and order fillers	392	20,960	Short-term on-the-job training	62	30	8
Receptionists and information clerks	348	25,070	Short-term on-the-job training	44	43	13
Bookkeeping, accounting, and auditing clerks	332	33,450	Moderate-term on-the-job training	36	49	15
Executive secretaries and administrative assistants	284	41,650	Work experience in a related occupation	36	48	17
First-line supervisors/ managers of office and administrative support workers	275	46,910	Work experience in a related occupation	29	42	29
Secretaries, except legal, medical, and executive	247	29,980	Moderate-term on-the-job training	36	48	17
Tellers	209	23,980	Short-term on-the-job training	43	43	14
Shipping, receiving, and traffic clerks	133	28,250	Short-term on-the-job training	64	29	7

Office and administrative support. People who have good organizational skills can expect many opportunities in office and administrative support occupations. Between 2008 and 2018, these occupations are expected to provide about 4.8 million openings for workers who do not have a bachelor's degree. You can qualify for many of these openings, such as those for receptionists and information clerks, right after high school without much additional training. (See Table 1.) Summer jobs or high school classes in English, typing, and computer-related subjects can pave the way.

Other occupations, such as customer service representatives or executive secretaries and administrative assistants, often require months of on-the-job training. Many office workers also take some college courses to hone their skills, earn certificates, and increase their chances for advancement.

Table 2
Selected maintenance, repair, and production occupations

Occupation	Net job openings for workers without a bachelor's degree, projected 2008–2018 (thousands)	Median annual earnings, 2009	Most significant source of postsecondary education or training	Percent of workers aged 25 to 44 with…		
				High school diploma or less	Some college or associate degree	Bachelor's or higher degree
Maintenance and repair workers, general	246	$34,620	Moderate-term on-the-job training	57%	36%	7%
Team assemblers	176	26,820	Moderate-term on-the-job training	70	25	5
Automotive service technicians and mechanics	121	35,420	Postsecondary vocational award	65	31	4
Heating, air conditioning, and refrigeration mechanics and installers	95	41,100	Postsecondary vocational award	56	39	5
Welders, cutters, solderers, and brazers	93	34,750	Postsecondary vocational award	74	24	2
First-line supervisors/ managers of mechanics, installers, and repairers	92	58,610	Work experience in a related occupation	46	41	12
Helpers—installation, maintenance, and repair workers	66	24,150	Short-term on-the-job training	78	18	4
Helpers—production workers	64	22,370	Short-term on-the-job training	76	18	6
First-line supervisors/ managers of production and operating workers	61	52,060	Work experience in a related occupation	52	33	15
Assemblers and fabricators, all other	53	27,860	Moderate-term on-the-job training	70	25	5

Maintenance, repair, and production. People who have mechanical skills can expect many opportunities; about 2.7 million openings are projected in maintenance, repair, and production between 2008 and 2018.

As Table 2 shows, education varies widely in this group. General maintenance and repair workers, who are projected to find the most openings, usually train on the job in a few months. Some workers also take vocational classes. Welders, who are among the highest paid workers shown on the table, often train in apprenticeship programs for a year or more, earning wages as they go. Automotive service technicians and mechanics also sometimes complete apprenticeship programs, but more often, they earn certificates at vocational schools.

Table 3
Selected health-care occupations

Occupation	Net job openings for workers without a bachelor's degree, projected 2008–2018 (thousands)	Median annual earnings, 2009	Most significant source of postsecondary education or training	Percent of workers aged 25 to 44 with…		
				High school diploma or less	Some college or associate degree	Bachelor's or higher degree
Registered nurses	388	$63,750	Associate degree	1%	43%	56%
Home health aides	381	20,480	Short-term on-the-job training	57	35	8
Licensed practical and licensed vocational nurses	294	39,820	Postsecondary vocational award	22	71	7
Nursing aides, oderlies, and attendants	291	24,040	Postsecondary vocational award	57	35	8
Medical assistants	146	28,650	Moderate-term on-the-job training	34	54	12
Dental assistants	114	33,230	Moderate-term on-the-job training	36	54	10
Pharmacy technicians	113	28,070	Moderate-term on-the-job training	30	53	17
Dental hygienists	55	67,340	Associate degree	3	62	35
Medical records and health information technicians	46	31,290	Associate degree	38	48	14
Radiologic technologists and technicians	45	53,240	Associate degree	9	67	24

Health care. For workers who like helping people and who have an interest in science, health-care occupations are expected to provide some of the most plentiful and highest-paying career opportunities in the economy. Overall, health-care occupations are projected to provide about 2.2 million job openings between 2008 and 2018 for workers who don't have a bachelor's degree. Many of these openings are expected to come from fast job growth in the occupations.

As Table 3 shows, training varies widely in the health-care field. For example, the most significant source of preparation for home health aides is one month or less of on-the-job training. Nursing aides usually need vocational training, but a large number of aides have also taken college courses—either to earn certifications, qualify for specific jobs, or prepare for other, higher-paying health-care occupations. Some aides may have completed college coursework unrelated to their job.

Having a job in one occupation while training for another is a common advancement strategy for health-care workers. Emergency medical technicians and paramedics, for example, need certification and some formal training before they start working. With additional training and experience, these workers can progress to higher levels of certification and new job duties. To receive the highest level of certification, most paramedics must earn an associate degree.

In part because the skills they need are becoming more complex, health-care workers are getting more training. Often, this extra education pays off. Although many dental assistants train on the job, for example, about 54 percent of workers aged 25 and older have some college or an associate degree. And median earnings of dental assistants who have an associate degree are about 20 percent higher than earnings of those who have a high school diploma or less education.

Table 4
Selected construction occupations

Occupation	Net job openings for workers without a bachelor's degree, projected 2008–2018 (thousands)	Median annual earnings, 2009	Most significant source of postsecondary education or training	Percent of workers aged 25 to 44 with…		
				High school diploma or less	Some college or associate degree	Bachelor's or higher degree
Construction laborers	258	$29,150	Moderate-term on-the-job training	76%	18%	6%
Carpenters	222	39,470	Long-term on-the-job training	68	24	7
Electricians	177	47,180	Long-term on-the-job training	49	43	8
First-line supervisors/ managers of construction trades and extraction workers	163	58,330	Work experience in a related occupation	58	31	11
Plumbers, pipefitters, and steamfitters	123	46,320	Long-term on-the-job training	66	29	4
Operating engineers and other construction equipment operators	90	39,770	Moderate-term on-the-job training	76	21	3
Painters, construction and maintenance	77	33,720	Moderate-term on-the-job training	73	19	8
Cement masons and concrete finishers	64	35,440	Moderate-term on-the-job training	84	14	2
Brickmasons and blockmasons	40	46,740	Long-term on-the-job training	80	16	3
Sheet metal workers	38	40,640	Long-term on-the-job training	65	30	4

Construction. An interest in building can lead to a career with prospects. About 1.7 million job openings are projected for workers entering construction occupations between 2008 and 2018. And most of these occupations pay more than the median for all occupations.

There are many types of construction occupations. Some require outdoor work, others don't; some involve a high level of mathematics, others require math skills that are more basic. Many workers in construction occupations start in apprenticeships, taking vocational classes and getting paid for on-the-job training. Some workers receive college credit for the vocational classes that they take.

Table 4 shows the construction occupations that are expected to have the most job openings over the 2008–2018 decade. In 2009, median earnings for all but construction laborers were above the median for all occupations. Electricians, plumbers, pipefitters, and steamfitters are licensed occupations that should have a favorable outlook due to projected job growth.

Table 5
Selected protective service occupations

Occupation	Net job openings for workers without a bachelor's degree, projected 2008–2018 (thousands)	Median annual earnings, 2009	Most significant source of postsecondary education or training	Percent of workers aged 25 to 44 with…		
				High school diploma or less	Some college or associate degree	Bachelor's or higher degree
Security guards	245	$23,820	Short-term on-the-job training	46%	39%	15%
Correctional officers and jailers	105	39,050	Moderate-term on-the-job training	38	49	12
Fire fighters	94	45,050	Long-term on-the-job training	21	60	18
Police and sheriff's patrol officers	77	53,210	Long-term on-the-job training	17	51	32
Lifeguards, ski patrol, and other recreational protective service workers	51	18,700	Short-term on-the-job training	45	30	25
Protective service workers, all other	40	29,420	Short-term on-the-job training	45	30	25
First-line supervisors/managers of fire fighting and prevention workers	19	68,250	Work experience in a related occupation	19	59	22
Crossing guards	18	23,390	Short-term on-the-job training	69	26	5
First-line supervisors/managers of police and detectives	15	76,500	Work experience in a related occupation	15	46	38
First-line supervisors/managers, protective service workers, all other	14	44,480	Work experience in a related occupation	25	43	31

Police and other protective service. Workers who keep the public safe from crime, disasters, and fire are projected to be in high demand. Between 2008 and 2018, protective service occupations are expected to provide about 700,000 job openings for workers who don't have a bachelor's degree. As Table 5 shows, most of those openings are projected to be in three occupations: security guards, correctional officers and jailers, and fire fighters.

Security guards can usually qualify for their jobs with a high school diploma or less education. Once employed, security guards often receive some on-the-job training. Guards who carry weapons must have training and licensure. Guards working in specialized fields, such as nuclear power plant security, receive extensive formal training after being hired and usually earn more than other guards.

Most police train on the job at service academies; many also have degrees. Fire fighters usually also have degrees and train at fire department training centers and academies. And almost all fire departments require fire fighters to be certified as emergency medical technicians.

Table 6
Selected science and engineering occupations

| Occupation | Net job openings for workers without a bachelor's degree, projected 2008–2018 (thousands) | Median annual earnings, 2009 | Most significant source of postsecondary education or training | Percent of workers aged 25 to 44 with… | | |
				High school diploma or less	Some college or associate degree	Bachelor's or higher degree
Civil engineering technicians	26	$45,970	Associate degree	27%	56%	17%
Electrical and electronic engineering technicians	25	54,820	Associate degree	27	56	17
Architectural and civil drafters	22	45,600	Postsecondary vocational award	14	61	25
Surveying and mapping technicians	20	37,190	Moderate-term on-the-job training	37	55	7
Engineering technicians, except drafters, all other	15	57,530	Associate degree	27	56	17
Industrial engineering technicians	15	46,760	Associate degree	27	56	17
Mechanical drafters	10	47,790	Postsecondary vocational award	14	61	25
Life, physical, and social science technicans, all other	9	42,110	Associate degree	20	37	43
Environmental engineering technicians	8	42,350	Associate degree	27	56	17
Chemical technicians	7	42,070	Associate degree	32	36	32

Science and engineering. Occupations related to science and engineering are expected to provide many high-paying opportunities, especially for those who have the right kind of training. About 200,000 openings in science-related occupations are expected between 2008 and 2018 for workers who don't have a bachelor's degree.

Engineering technicians, several types of which are shown in Table 6, often have an associate degree. Most take college algebra and trigonometry. Some technicians earn a vocational certificate instead of a degree.

Survey technicians, also in the table, sometimes begin work right after high school. But many complete additional training, such as an associate degree or apprenticeship.

Table 7
Selected computer occupations

Occupation	Net job openings for workers without a bachelor's degree, projected 2008–2018 (thousands)	Median annual earnings, 2009	Most significant source of postsecondary education or training	Percent of workers aged 25 to 44 with…		
				High school diploma or less	Some college or associate degree	Bachelor's or higher degree
Computer support specialists	69	$44,300	Associate degree	14%	45%	41%
Network systems and data communication analysts	45	73,250	Bachelor's degree	9	35	56
Network and computer systems administrators	34	67,710	Bachelor's degree	9	41	50
Computer operators	7	36,110	Moderate-term on-the-job training	31	44	25
Computer systems analysts	<1	77,080	Bachelor's degree	7	28	65
Computer and information systems managers	<1	113,720	Bachelor's or higher degree, plus work experience	5	25	70
Computer programmers	<1	70,940	Bachelor's degree	6	24	70
Computer specialists, all other	<1	77,010	Associate degree	7	28	65
Database administrators	<1	71,550	Bachelor's degree	5	26	69

Computer. Rapid growth in information technology is expected to create many openings for people who like working with computers. Openings in computer-related occupations for workers who don't have a bachelor's degree are expected to total about 150,000 between 2008 and 2018.

In this field, credentials, such as industry certifications or an associate degree in a computer-related field, are especially important, in part because many college graduates compete for these jobs.

Some occupations are easier to enter than others for people who have skills but not a degree. According to industry experts, computer-savvy people who don't have a bachelor's degree may find it easiest to enter the occupations of computer support specialist, network and computer systems administrator, or network systems and data communication analyst.

The computer support specialist occupation is projected to provide the most openings for those who don't have a bachelor's or higher degree. (See Table 7.) Specialists who don't have a four-year degree increase their marketability by earning certifications or getting computer experience in other jobs.

Networking and computer systems administrators are also expected to have opportunities, whatever their level of education. Workers who don't have a bachelor's degree often begin their careers as computer support specialists, switching into the more highly paid administrator occupation after they gain experience.

Web masters, computer security professionals, and local area network (LAN) support staff are also expected to be in high demand. All of these workers are part of the occupation of network systems and data communications analysts. Many have a bachelor's degree, but others substitute coursework, experience, or certifications.

Each of these occupations had earnings that were above the median for all workers in 2009. But the earnings of workers who have a bachelor's degree are included in those figures; earnings might be lower for workers who have less education.

Table 8
Selected education and personal service occupations

Occupation	Net job openings for workers without a bachelor's degree, projected 2008–2018 (thousands)	Median annual earnings, 2009	Most significant source of postsecondary education or training	Percent of workers aged 25 to 44 with…		
				High school diploma or less	Some college or associate degree	Bachelor's or higher degree
Personal and home care aides	393	$19,680	Short-term on-the-job training	59%	31%	11%
Child care workers	324	19,240	Short-term on-the-job training	53	34	13
Teacher assistants	263	22,820	Short-term on-the-job training	36	45	19
Hairdressers, hairstylists, and cosmetologists	169	23,330	Postsecondary vocational award	56	38	7
Amusement and recreation attendants	99	18,120	Short-term on-the-job training	42	33	25
Fitness trainers and aerobics instructors	56	30,670	Postsecondary vocational award	24	35	42
First-line supervisors/ managers of personal service workers	55	35,330	Work experience in a related occupation	39	38	23
Ushers, lobby attendants, and ticket takers	54	18,050	Short-term on-the-job training	47	34	19
Recreation workers	48	22,280	Short-term on-the-job training	24	35	42
Nonfarm animal caretakers	48	19,550	Short-term on-the-job training	48	35	16

Education and personal service. Career opportunities will continue to be plentiful for people interested in working with children or providing personal services to the public. About 1.8 million openings are expected in these fields between 2008 and 2018 for workers who don't have a bachelor's degree.

Personal and home care aides, who are expected to have the most openings for high school graduates among occupations in this group, often qualify after a short period of training. But some earn an associate degree and certification to increase their opportunities. (See Table 8.)

Teacher assistants are often required to have an associate degree or to pass an exam, but many others train on the job.

Working in education and personal service does not usually bring above-average earnings, however. Among the occupations in the table, only a management occupation had median earnings higher than $33,190, the median for all workers in 2009.

How These Numbers Were Developed

Measuring job outlook by education is complicated, and there are many ways to do it. This analysis used job openings as a way to measure outlook because the number of job openings helps to determine how easy it will be for workers to enter an occupation. First, the number of future job openings in each occupation was estimated. Then, survey data were used as an objective way to estimate how many job openings would be filled by workers with various levels of education.

Like any analysis based on projections and estimates, however, this one has limitations. Understanding these limitations will help you to better use the results. The methods and limitations are described in detail in this section.

Methods Used

To determine job prospects, BLS analysts started by projecting the total number of job openings available between 2008 and 2018 for workers entering an occupation for the first time. Next, analysts estimated how many of those openings would be filled by workers who do not have a bachelor's degree (that is, would be for occupations that normally do not require a bachelor's) and how many openings would be in high-paying occupations.

Job openings. Job openings come from two sources: the need to fill newly created positions and the need to replace workers who leave an occupation permanently. To estimate the number of openings that will come from newly created positions, analysts projected how much each occupation would grow or decline between 2008 and 2018.

There are many reasons why the number of jobs in an occupation might change. Sometimes, the demand for a certain type of good or service increases—for example, an aging population creates the need for more health-care services and, as a result, more health-care technicians. The way a good is produced or a service is provided also can create more jobs in a particular occupation, such as when library technicians gain jobs faster than librarians do because employment of technicians is considered a more cost-effective way to provide library services.

Many occupations that employ people who do not have a bachelor's degree are projected to gain jobs rapidly. In fact, for 3 of the 10 fastest-growing occupations, the most significant source of training is less than a bachelor's degree. The occupation projected to be the third fastest-growing of all occupations over the 2008–2018 decade is home health aide. It usually employs people who train on the job.

The need to replace workers who leave an occupation permanently is expected to provide even more openings than job growth will. To estimate how many workers will need to be replaced during the 2008–2018 decade, analysts studied both past trends in each occupation and the ages of current workers. In some occupations, workers usually stay for many years. In other occupations, people tend to leave more quickly. These considerations affect replacement needs.

Openings by education. After analysts projected the total number of job openings in each occupation, they estimated how many of those openings would be filled by workers who had one of three different education levels: a high school diploma or less, some college or an associate degree, or a bachelor's or higher degree. Analysts determined which levels of education were significant in each occupation by looking at the education levels of current workers as reported in data from the Current Population Surveys. If at least 20 percent of workers had a particular level of education, that level was deemed significant.

Expected job openings were divided among each of the significant education levels, according to how common that education level was for workers in the occupation. For example, fire fighters include workers who have each of the three levels of education: About 21 percent have a high school diploma or less, about 60 percent have completed some college or an associate degree, and about 18 percent have a bachelor's or higher degree. Therefore, the expected openings for fire fighters were divided among these categories using the corresponding percentages. The openings for workers who had less education than a bachelor's degree were added to the totals used in this article.

In addition to describing the three educational attainment categories, this article discusses specific education and training requirements for some occupations. These discussions are based on occupational analyses conducted for the *Occupational Outlook Handbook.*

Openings by earnings. The earnings data in this article are from the BLS Occupational Employment Statistics survey. The survey reflects the May 2009 earnings of *all* workers, without regard to education level or experience. Also, the survey does not include self-employed workers. In this analysis, occupations were considered high paying if their median earnings were above the median for all workers in 2009.

Limitations of the Data

To measure total job openings and openings by education level, BLS analysts needed to make some assumptions about the future. First, analysts assumed that the education levels in each occupation would remain roughly the same over the 2008–2018 decade. In reality, the educational characteristics of some occupations change over time. Many occupations—such as registered nurses and police officers—have shown a gradual increase in the education levels of their workers.

Analysts also ignored education levels that were uncommon in an occupation; as stated previously, if less than 20 percent of workers in an occupation had a given level of education, that level of education was ignored. So, for example, even though 16 percent of today's massage therapists have a high school diploma or less, none of that occupation's future openings were slated for workers with that level of education.

Another limitation of this study is that it focuses on the number of job openings expected in an occupation. Job openings give only a partial view of the prospects that workers can expect. The number of people who will compete for those openings is also important. For most occupations, BLS analysts do not have enough information about the future supply of workers to analyze the competition for jobs in specific occupations.

Finally, the accuracy of this study is limited by its use of survey data. Surveys always have some error because not every worker is counted and because the information gathered is sometimes incorrect. The education levels of many of the occupations studied here, including some in the tables, could not be counted with enough statistical accuracy because the number of workers surveyed was too small. In those cases, analysts substituted the education levels of similar occupations or groups of occupations that had larger numbers of workers.

Despite the assumptions and limitations of this analysis, however, there is evidence that the methods used produce accurate results. When existing jobs are separated into educational categories using this method, the results closely match current numbers.

For More Information

To learn more about the occupations described here and about the hundreds of other occupations expected to provide openings for workers who don't have a bachelor's degree, see the most recent edition of the *Occupational Outlook Handbook,* available from JIST Publishing, in many libraries and career centers, and online at www.bls.gov/oco. The *Handbook* describes the job outlook, education and training requirements, job duties, and more for nearly 290 occupations.

Another BLS publication, the 2010–2011 *Occupational Projections and Training Data* bulletin, explains in greater detail the methods used in this study and lists the projected job openings and worker education levels for every occupation studied by the BLS Office of Occupational Statistics and Employment Projections. The bulletin is available only online at www.bls.gov/emp/optd.

The *Occupational Outlook Quarterly* also has articles that describe occupations that don't usually require a bachelor's degree. For example, the fall 2009 issue (www.bls.gov/opub/ooq/2009/fall/home.htm) contains articles about careers in auto racing. In other issues, the *Quarterly* describes training and education for workers who don't have a bachelor's degree; these include "Apprenticeship: Career training, credentials—and a paycheck in your pocket," in the summer 2002 issue (available online at www.bls.gov/opub/ooq/2002/summer/art01.pdf), and "Military training for civilian careers (Or: How to gain practical experience while serving your country)," in the spring 2007 issue (online at www.bls.gov/opub/ooq/2007/spring/art02.pdf).

And to help workers prepare for a career, the U.S. Department of Education offers information about financial aid for people attending two-year colleges, four-year colleges, and vocational schools. Call the financial aid hotline toll-free at 1 (800) 4FED-AID (433-3243); write the Federal Student Aid Information Center, P.O. Box 84, Washington, D.C. 20044-0084; or visit online at www.studentaid.ed.gov.

Studying potential job openings is only a starting point when deciding on a career. Many other considerations are important, including individual skills and interests, personal circumstances, and the needs of local employers. To explore these and other factors in making your career decision, visit state labor market information offices and career centers. Information is available online at www.servicelocator.org or by calling the U.S. Department of Labor's toll-free helpline, 1 (877) US2-JOBS (872-5627).

Opportunities are as varied as the workers who seek them. And when it comes to training, finding what is best for you is one of the surest routes to reward.

Editor's Note: The preceding article was adapted from one written by Olivia Crosby and Roger Moncarz, originally published in the Fall 2006 issue of the Occupational Outlook Quarterly, *a publication of the U.S. Department of Labor. The information about earnings, job outlook, and education and training has been updated with more recent facts from the Bureau of Labor Statistics, in keeping with the methodology of the original article.*

Index